WINDOWS 2000

Security Handbook

ABOUT THE AUTHORS

Philip Cox

Philip Cox is a consultant with SystemExperts Corporation, a consulting firm that specializes in system security and management. He is a well-known authority on system security and in particular, securing Windows and mixed Windows-Unix environments. Phil's day-to-day responsibilities include performing overall security and architecture reviews, penetration testing, and designing enterprise-scale intrusion detection systems for many of the largest e-commerce companies in the world.

In addition to being the lead author of this book and a featured columnist for the USENIX Association Magazine ";login:", he also serves on the editorial board of the *SANS NT Digest*. Phil is also one of the highest-rated and most well-regarded speakers on issues dealing with Unix and Windows security at major conferences around the world, such as USENIX, SANS, NetWorld-Interop, and The Information Security Conference.

Phil has a B.S. in Computer Science and is currently a Microsoft Certified Systems Engineer (MCSE). He can be reached at **Phil.Cox@SystemExperts.com**.

Tom Sheldon

Tom Sheldon is no stranger to the computer industry. Since the late 1970s, he has worked as a computer programmer, consultant, and network administrator. He has been designing and building networks since the invention of Ethernet. Tom has written 30 books and his articles have appeared in *PC World Magazine, PC Magazine, Byte Magazines, Windows NT Magazine,* and *Windows Pro Magazine*. His latest book is the *McGraw-Hill Encyclopedia of Networking*, now in its third edition.

Tom runs a computer- and software-testing laboratory where he does research for Microsoft, Novell, and other companies. He has been instrumental in many major network installations, including sites such as Lockheed Space Operations and various government and educational institutions on the West Coast.

Tom is familiar to thousands of computer users who have learned about computers and Windows by watching his best-selling educational videotapes.

He lives on the Big Sur coast of California and enjoys mountain biking, ocean kayak fishing, and golfing.

About the Contributing Authors

Dallas Bishoff

Dallas Bishoff is an information security consultant with over 10 years of experience in the federal sector, as well as in private industry. He is a Certified Information Systems Security Professional (CISSP), Microsoft Certified Systems Engineer + Internet Specialist (MCSE+I), Microsoft Certified Trainer (MCT), Citrix Certified Administrator (CCA), Internet Security Systems Certified Engineer (ICE), Certified Check Point Security Engineer (CSSE), Nokia Security Administrator (NSA) and Instructor, and an RSA Certified Instructor and SecurID Support Engineer. He has also completed the National Security Agency course on the INFOSEC Assessment Methodology (IAM), which is used to audit federal information systems. He can be reached at **Dallas_Bishoff@Hotmail.com**.

David Bork

David Bork is a consultant with SystemExperts Corporation. He is an exceptional security professional with experience in intrusion detection, cryptography, and security code development on Sun Solaris, IBM's AIX, Cisco Routers, and Windows NT. David worked in network security for IBM and AT&T designing the architecture of, programming, maintaining, and supporting the intrusion detection systems in use today.

Among many other projects, David assisted in the writing of AT&T's CP and CPS for AT&T's current PKI solution and designed the layered security infrastructure protecting the CA. David provided security analysis and support for both the Sydney and the Nagano Olympics. After the merger of IBM's and AT&T's networking businesses, David worked on the design, integration, and implementation of their respective customer networks using Cisco PIX firewalls. David has participated in Microsoft beta tests of Windows and Windows NT. Prior to his work in intrusion detection, David led numerous database-related projects and developed real-time interfaces to network management systems to store network status as well as automate network recovery.

Paul B. Hill

Paul B. Hill, Senior Programmer Analyst and Co-Team Lead of the Kerberos Development Team at MIT, has not only been involved in Kerberos development since 1992, but is also working on MIT's Windows 2000 deployment project. Paul also consults on system security.

David Mackey

David Mackey is working as a project manager for a Fortune 500 company in Boulder, Colorado. In his free time, he is a systems consultant, webmaster, and writer. His latest works include a contribution to *Special Edition Using Windows 2000 Server* (Que) and co-authorship of *1001 Windows 2000 Professional Tips* (Jamsa Press). David also co-created the popular Windows Troubleshooting site, **http://www.FixWindows.com**, to offer free troubleshooting information and help for weary Windows users. His educational pursuits have earned him a B.A. in Russian Studies from the University of Colorado at Boulder, Microsoft Certified Systems Engineer certification, and a Certified Novell Administrator certificate. In his spare time (what he has left), David likes to play guitar and spend time with his wife, Andrea, and son, Nathan.

Ken Sandlin

Ken Sandlin is chairman and co-founder of the computer security firm Bluekey.net, Inc. He is a Microsoft Certified System Engineer (MCSE), Microsoft Certified Trainer (MCT), Check Point Certified Security Engineer (CCSE), RSA Certified SecurID Support Engineer (CSSE), Internet Security Systems Certified in RealSecure, SAFESuite Decisions, Internet Scanner, System Scanner, and Database Scanner, Citrix Certified Administrator (CCA), Citrix Certified Instructor (CCI), New York City chapter member of the FBI InfraGard computer security program, and a Professional Member of the National Speakers Association (**www.nsaspeaker.com**). He was a federal government contractor in Washington D.C. at both the Department of State and Federal Aviation Administration Headquarters where his project team was awarded the FAA's Team Excellence Award. He is currently securing the Win2K Public Key Infrastructure (PKI) for one of the Internet's 126 Public Class A networks. He can be reached at **ksandlin@bluekey.net**.

About the Technical Reviewer

Eric Schultze

Eric Schultze has been involved with information technology and security for the past nine years, with a majority of his time focused on assessing and securing Microsoft technologies and platforms. He is a frequent speaker at security conferences, including NetWorld Interop, USENIX, BlackHat, SANS, and MIS, and is a faculty instructor for the Computer Security Institute. Mr. Schultze has also appeared on TV and in many publications, including NBC, CNBC, *TIME*, *ComputerWorld*, and *The Standard*. Mr. Schultz's prior employers include Foundstone, Inc., SecurityFocus.com, Ernst & Young, Price Waterhouse, Bealls Inc., and Salomon Brothers. A contributing author to the first edition of *Hacking Exposed*, he is currently a Security Program Manager for Microsoft.

WINDOWS 2000

Security Handbook

PHILIP **COX**
TOM **SHELDON**

Tata McGraw-Hill Publishing Company Limited

NEW DELHI

McGraw-Hill Offices

New Delhi New York St Louis San Francisco Auckland Bogotá
Caracas Kuala Lumpur Lisbon London Madrid Mexico City Milan
Montreal San Juan Santiago Singapore Sydney Tokyo Toronto

Tata McGraw-Hill

*A Division of The **McGraw·Hill** Companies*

Windows 2000 Security Handbook

Tata McGraw-Hill Edition 2001

Reprinted in India by arrangement with the The McGraw-Hill Companies, Inc., New York

Sales territories: India, Nepal, Bangladesh, Sri Lanka and Bhutan

ISBN 0-07-043618-5

Published by Tata McGraw-Hill Publishing Company Limited, 7 West Patel Nagar, New Delhi 110 008, and printed at S P Printers, Noida 201 301

This book is dedicated to Jesus Christ, my Lord, for the gifts and abilities that He has given me (1 Corinthians 10:31). Vickie, my soul mate and wife, for all of her encouragement. To Christopher, Steven, and Holly for their patience during the lost hours with dad while he was writing.

—*Phil*

CONTENTS

Part I

Security 101

Part II

Windows 2000 Security

Part III

Securing Windows 2000

Part IV

Securing Windows 2000 Networks

Part V

Other Issues

Part VI

Appendixes

ACKNOWLEDGMENTS

Thanks to Jon Gossels of SystemExperts for giving me the time and encouragement to push this over the finish line, and Brad Johnson for pushing for excellence. To the other SystemExperts: Dick Mackey, Mark Mellis, Cheng Tang, and Jason Reed, for taking up the slack I left while writing. A heartfelt thanks to Jane Brownlow, who tried her best to keep me on track, and to Tara Davis, LeeAnn Pickrell, Ross Doll, and the whole hard-working Production staff, and everybody else at Osborne. To Eric Schultze for his technical expertise and invaluable help in making things relevant.

—*Phil*

Thanks Phil! Your expertise, hard work, and time have made this second edition a reality.

—*Tom*

INTRODUCTION

This book is about security for Microsoft Windows 2000 computers, both as standalone desktop systems or as network-connected workstations and servers. The information presented here will scare you into taking action to protect your systems, and it will show you how to put together a defensive strategy.

Paranoia is good thing. The more paranoid you are, the more likely you are to protect your systems from attack. Reading this book and just concentrating on security is a good start. In fact, you need to start planning and managing your network with security as the number one goal. Many network administrators get so wrapped up in attaining performance or some other objective that they leave their systems wide open for attack. What good is the fastest server or network if some unknown user can bring your system down at any time and thus deny access to legitimate users?

As the network becomes the computer (i.e. Microsoft's new .NET initiative), the need for security will increase significantly. Over the past few years security has become more of a concern primarily because businesses feel the need to be "on the Internet." Because of this increase in the use of networks in general, and the Internet specifically, you need to be diligent in your security efforts.

Everyone knows that security threats come from both the Internet and internal sources. It has always been a widely understood fact that insiders pose a significant threat. First, internal users know more about your systems and where valuable data is located. Internal users are also more likely to hijack some other user's account or access some system because improper security measures are in place. You probably trust many of your coworkers, but in an open internetworked environment, you need to reevaluate how much trust you want to extend. Plus, with the rapid expansion and "collaboration" between many networks, this insider/outsider line is beginning to blur. The lines may not be as clear as they were in the past.

About the Book

This book is about tightening the security on your Windows 2000 (Win2K) systems and networks to prevent malicious users from attacking your systems and valuable data. There are six main sections, as described here:

▼ **Part I: Security 101** Provides a general description of security problems on networks in general and networks that are connected to the Internet in particular. You'll learn the scary truth about hacker and cracker attacks and ways to mitigate them. You'll also learn the importance of managing security policies.

■ **Part II: Windows 2000 Security** Provides more detailed information about Win2K security. You'll learn about the security features in Win2K, as well as the networking services that Win2K has to offer. We'll cover specific Win2K risks and their solutions.

■ **Part III: Securing Windows 2000** Covers security features in the Active Directory, using Group Policy and user and group management. The last chapters in this section cover logon authentication, file systems, resource sharing, and auditing.

■ **Part IV: Securing Windows 2000 Networks** Covers Intranet-, Internet-, and TCP/IP -specific security threats and countermeasures. You'll also learn about how to build firewalls between your networks and the Internet (or your own internal networks), how to do business on the Internet in a safe and secure way, and how to use the Microsoft Proxy server to protect your network. We'll discuss Virtual Private Networks (VPNs) and remote access issues. We'll also cover security in an enterprise environment as well as special considerations for securing clients.

■ **Part V: Other Issues** Covers properly setting up and securing the Microsoft Internet Information Server (IIS) 5.0, along with the tools and techniques that Win2K provides for fault tolerance and data protection and a specific chapter devoted to hardening Win2K.

▲ **Part VI: Appendixes** If you want to learn about management, monitoring, and auditing, the Microsoft Internet Security and Acceleration (ISA) Server, or Intrusion Detection, refer to the appendixes. You'll also find a discussion of valuable tools and techniques that can help you protect your system.

NOTE: Keep in mind that this book points out known security problems and makes recommendations that can help you secure your systems and networks; however, every environment is different, and some of the suggestions provided here might not be appropriate in your case. Always test any changes or security recommendations mentioned in this book on a non-production test platform before you implement those changes on an actual system.

About the Companion Web Site

There are a number of additional chapters and appendices that will be published only on the Web. Topics covered include

▼   Web Chapter 1: Certificate Server

■   Web Appendix A: Win2K Services

▲   Web Appendix B: Ports and Protocols in TCP/IP

All of this and more can be found at **www.osborne.com**.

PART I

Security 101

CHAPTER 1

TCP Is King

In the past few decades, information systems have gone from large, centralized computers running over proprietary networks and protocols to decentralized desktop systems and departmental networks running over open and standard protocols. Information may no longer be stored in a safe location at a single site, but may potentially be everywhere in the organization. Also because of the support of open standards and the desire to interconnect everything, the number and type of systems that can access the data has increased exponentially. This change has profoundly affected how people view computer systems and information technology.

Once upon a time, a long time ago in Internet time, a company used the marketing catch phrase, "The network is the computer." They don't use this as their marketing tagline anymore, probably because everyone has internalized the concept to such a degree that it doesn't distinguish any particular brand or vendor in the mind of the typical consumer. Almost everyone dealing with business information systems and information technology today thinks in terms of interconnected systems. This trend of connectivity to everyone, using open standards like TCP/IP, is accelerating and expanding to include not just our traditional computers but also our cell phones, pagers, PDAs, and even our cars.

Ultimately, the goal of all of this connectivity is effective communication. By this we mean that people, and systems, want accurate information delivered to them in a timely manner and in a form that they can readily understand. Frequently, an additional requirement is that the information only be delivered to a limited set of people or systems.

Microsoft's Windows 2000 (Win2K) operating system provides a large number of tools and features based on these open standards to interconnect various systems and deliver information to people and systems in a timely, accurate, and secure manner.

This book is designed to help you deploy Win2K in the environment securely. But before we delve too deeply into the services that Win2K offers, we will take the time to look at one of the (if not *the*) key underlying standards Microsoft has built Win2K around: TCP/IP.

THE TCP/IP PROTOCOL

When researchers and businesses first started working on interconnecting computer systems, a number of disjointed, parallel efforts were made. People tended to first concentrate on interconnecting similar systems from a single vendor. Over time efforts were expanded to include dissimilar computers from different vendors. During this time, there were lots of competing protocols, including LAT, XNS, IPX, NetBEUI, SNA, AppleTalk, and TCP/IP. Eventually, TCP/IP emerged as the clear winner.

TCP/IP stands for *Transmission Control Protocol/Internet Protocol*. When we talk about TCP/IP, or specifically IP, we are normally referring to version 4 of the Internet Protocol, which is what Win2K supports natively.

Where It Started

The development of TCP/IP was funded by the Defense Advanced Research Projects Agency (DARPA). One of the goals was to make the protocol suitable for use by the military. It was designed to ensure continuous communications connections with the expectation that the network would sustain damage. TCP/IP has been designed to be robust and automatically recover from any node or transmission line failure even in the face of natural disasters or in the event of a nuclear war. Testaments to its reliability include the use of the Internet for communications in the San Francisco area immediately after the 1989 earthquake and the UN forces' inability to knock out Iraq's TCP/IP communications system during the Persian Gulf War.

It turns out that the design of the protocol allows the construction of very large networks with very little central management. In addition, some of the DARPA funding was used to make the protocol widely available in source form. That availability in turn led to TCP/IP being available on many different operating systems.

A Design Criteria Flaw

Surprisingly, although funded by the military, the TCP/IP protocol was not designed to be highly secure. It was instead expected to provide a base layer of communication infrastructure with security to be designed at a higher layer. Furthermore, although the protocol is robust against failures of nodes and transmission lines it is not robust against active attacks against the protocol designed to render the network resources nonfunctional.

A quick perusal of any major Internet search engine reveals many papers that talk about security issues related to the TCP/IP protocol, such as

▼ *Security Problems in the TCP/IP Protocol Suite* by Steven M. Bellovin, 1989. A broad overview of problems within TCP/IP itself, as well as many common application layer protocols that rely on TCP/IP.

■ *Sequence Number Attacks* by Rik Farrow, December 1994. A brief article that gives an overview of TCP sequence number attacks. (Includes RFC 1948, which shows how to protect against TCP sequence number attacks.)

▲ *A Simple Active Attack Against TCP* by Laurent Joncheray, 1995. This paper describes an active attack against TCP that allows re-direction (hijacking) of the TCP stream.

Over the past few years the Internet community has seen a number of attacks and programs against implementations of the TCP/IP protocol. These have names like SYN, Smurf, Teardrop, and Land. Some implementations of the TCP/IP protocol are better than others. At one time Microsoft's implementation for Windows NT (WinNT) did not have a very good reputation. It seemed like a new exploit was found every few weeks that could be used to knock a WinNT machine off the Internet. Microsoft recognized this problem and took the time and resources to perform a full audit of their stack and rewrite the sections where they found problems. Their commitment has paid off. There have been fewer exploits that are specific to the Windows protocol stack, and the stability of WinNT was much improved.

TCP/IP and Win2K

In order to deliver the features for Win2K, Microsoft's TCP/IP developers had to rewrite portions of the stack once again. The WinNT stack was not designed to support plug-and-play devices; it didn't support Quality of Service (QoS), nor secure IP (IPSec). Microsoft spent a lot of time developing a new architecture for their stack implementation, with a goal of making it extensible and robust. To a large extent this effort has been very beneficial to users of Win2K.

However, not all is perfect in the world. While writing this book, we have seen the emergence of some new attacks, and it appears that the Win2K TCP/IP stack is vulnerable. The latest exploit going around as this book is being written is a UDP fragmentation attack. Initial reports say that this attack can cause a Win2K machine to lock up, using 100 percent of its CPU cycles to process the UDP fragments. You can be sure that Microsoft will issue a patch to address this particular attack. It's also a safe bet to assume that this form of attack will affect many other TCP/IP implementations running on different operating systems. Luckily, it appears from an initial analysis of the attack that the implementation is pretty simplistic and the attack is not really very sophisticated.

The Evolution

Over time the TCP/IP protocol has evolved, although most of the evolution has involved recommendations to implementers and not a redesign of the protocol. The standards body responsible for change of the TCP/IP protocol is the Internet Engineering Task Force (IETF). The IETF is a volunteer organization that is responsible for most of the protocols on which the Internet runs. It issues standards documents in the form of Requests for Comments (RFCs). The RFCs define not only TCP/IP but also SMTP, SNMP, POP, IMAP, HTTP, FTP, and just about any other protocol that is used on the Internet. Throughout this book, we make frequent references to specific RFCs where appropriate. The Web site of the IETF can be found at **http://www.ietf.org**.

New features directly related to TCP/IP have been introduced in the past few years. These include QoS and IPSec. As mentioned previously, Win2K does offer support of these features. The IETF has also created an evolutionary form of IP called IP version 6 (IPv6). Microsoft does not offer support for IPv6 at this time. However, a version for research, educational, and testing purposes is available for download from Microsoft Research.

Routers

If you have been playing close attention you may have noticed that we mentioned that routers communicate with each other, and you may be wondering if they do this using TCP/IP. The answer is yes, but they actually use a variety of router protocols that are layered on top of TCP/IP. The router protocols include GGP, EGP, RIP, and OSPF. Like the TCP/IP protocol itself, the IETF issues and maintains the standards that define these protocols.

Although Win2K does include some support for routing functions, most companies and virtually all Internet Service Providers (ISPs) use special-purpose hardware for routing. Cisco dominates this market, and some estimates state that 90 percent of all Internet traffic passes through Cisco equipment somewhere along the delivery path. This book does not discuss the security aspects of routing or routing protocols; however, we do briefly talk about the Microsoft support of these functions in Chapters 14 and 15.

TCP/IP NETWORKS

We've looked at a tiny bit of the history and information about the TCP/IP protocol but we haven't talked at all about how it is used to form computer networks. In this section we will address that.

TCP/IP and the OSI Seven-Layer Model

Networking protocols like TCP/IP are built in a highly structured way. They have protocol hierarchies and definite layers in terms of what they accomplish. The base reference model for networking has become the OSI Reference Model, better known as the Seven-Layer Model. It specifies what each layer should do, and not exactly how it is supposed to be done. The seven layers and their corresponding TCP/IP counterpart are shown in the next illustration.

OSI	TCP/IP
Application layer Specifies how application programs interface to the network and provides services to them	**Application layer** Handles everything else; TCP/IP network daemons and applications have to perform the jobs of the OSI presentation layer and part of its session layer themselves (many protocols and services)
Presentation layer Specifies data representation to applications	
Session layer Creates, manages, and terminates network connections.	**Transport layer** Manages all aspects of data routing and delivery, including session initiation, error control, and sequence checking (TCP and UDP protocols)
Transport layer Handles error control and sequence checking for data moving over the network	
Network layer Responsible for data addressing and routing and communications flow control	**Internet layer** Responsible for data addressing, transmission, and packet fragmentation and reassembly (IP protocol)
Data link layer Defines access methods for the physical medium	**Network access layer** Specifies procedures for transmitting data across the network, including how to access the physical medium (many protocols including Ethernet and FDDI)
Physical layer Specifies the physical medium's physical and procedural operating characteristics	

How It Works

TCP/IP networks are shared communication systems, meaning that many different communications sessions can take place at the same time. The data transferred in each session is divided up and placed into individual packets. These packets are addressed to a destination computer and sent out over the network. The network may be a small *local area network (LAN)* that only interconnects a few computers. The network may also be a *wide area network (WAN)* that connects the computers that belong to a single organization that are dispersed over a metropolitan area. Or the network may even be connected to the global Internet.

Large networks, including the Internet, are a mesh of connections with many possible paths that the packets can take through the network. Devices called *routers* interconnect transmission channels. When a packet reaches a router, the router forwards the packet along the best available path to its destination. The routers communicate with one another to determine what the best available path should be. These work at the network layer in the TCP/IP stack.

Freeway systems provide a good analogy for the way the Internet works. People get into cars and drive to their destination. Each car (packet) is an independent delivery system. At intersections (routers), cars can switch paths to get on a more direct route to a destination. An appropriate exit is taken for the final leg of the trip. Of course, if everybody is starting from the same point and going to the same point it might make sense to put them all on a bus. The TCP/IP protocol does have the ability to adjust packet sizes (within a certain range) to make transmission efficient.

A typical communication session might involve hundreds or thousands of individual packets of information traveling along cables and routers on the network (shown next). Information is divided up into packets by the sending computer and reassembled by the receiving computer. One advantage of using packets is that a small glitch on the network may affect only a few of the packets. When this happens, only the lost packets are retransmitted, not the entire message. The packet nature of the network makes it easy to avoid problem areas. If a transmission line is down, a router simply sends packets along another path.

Packets

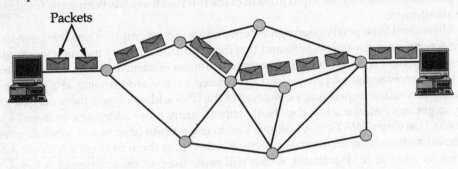

THE INTERNET ARCHITECTURE

In December of 1991, the IETF issued Request for Comment (RFC) 1287, "Towards the Future Internet Architecture." The RFC pointed out that there were four basic assumptions that needed to be addressed regarding the networking world of the next five to ten years:

▼   The TCP/IP and OSI suites will coexist for a long time.

■   The Internet will continue to include diverse networks and services and will never be comprised of a single network technology.

■   Commercial and private networks will be incorporated, but we cannot expect the common carriers to provide the entire service. There will be a mix of public and private networks, common carriers, and private lines.

▲   The Internet architecture needs to be able to scale to 10^9 networks.

It turns out that the first assumption has pretty much gone away but the other three assumptions are still valid today. For several years following the release of RFC 1287, there wasn't a lot of discussion within the IETF about "The Internet Architecture." People pretty much focused on their tasks at hand and were busy getting the work done. Everybody expected that the architecture was understood and there were few problems. At the last couple of IETF meetings there has been a lot of discussion about "The Internet Architecture" once again.

Things Are Changing

During the 1980s and even the early 1990s, few sites used firewalls. Running out of address space wasn't a top priority for most companies and even good security wasn't a top concern of very many people. Times have changed, and as people have rushed to solve the problems caused by the rapid growth of the Internet there has been some fracturing of the architecture.

There used to be pretty good agreement that a valid assumption was that peer-to-peer connections were always possible and that the IP address of every machine was routable. This is no longer true. With the increasing awareness of security needs, firewalls are everywhere and the use of proxies and distributed caches are growing at a phenomenal rate. Also, with the impending exhaustion of the IPv4 address space, there needed to be a way to get more machines on the "Net" without using more addresses. In steps *Network Address Translation (NAT)*. NAT allows you to use private (that is, not routable over the Internet) addresses on an internal system, but then pass them through a *Network Address Translator* (that is, *NAT gateway*), which will route the packets to Internet systems. Network Address Translators have appeared, and their use has become widespread. The pessimistic view is that the Internet has become balkanized. But all is not lost. The last time we checked it was still working pretty well.

The downside is that some technologies that are created for market expediency, such as NAT, are conflicting with solutions that have been created to address major security concerns, such as IPSec. For example, if you are using NAT, you will not be able to use end-to-end IPSec across the Internet to secure your connections, because the way the technologies work conflict with one another. Other security protocols also run into problems with NAT. Nevertheless, because of the IPv4 address problems, NAT will probably be with us for a long time to come.

One thing you can expect from the IETF in the future is another RFC that further clarifies "the Internet Architecture" and talks about important issues that will need to be resolved.

TCP/IP-BASED INFORMATION SERVICES

We mentioned a couple of facts about TCP/IP, a little bit about networks and routers, and we've even mentioned a little bit about the Internet architecture—so what's left? The short answer is: all the rest. TCP/IP and the Internet are just a communications foundation. What makes them important is the variety of work that can be done using these as a foundation. The following illustration shows the use of that foundation for many of the more commonly used protocols.

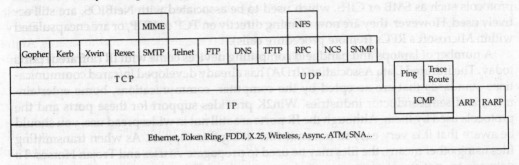

The Internet has made system and network administrators rethink the way they provide information to users. In particular, the *World Wide Web* has provided a whole new model for client-server computing during the past seven years. The Web is built onto the Internet and uses TCP/IP protocols to transport information from place to place. When the Web appeared, people almost immediately realized that it would be a significant tool for delivering information.

During the few short years that the Web has been around, there has been a great deal of change. People aren't just delivering static displays of information. They have developed powerful interactive applications that provide rich authentication and authorization models. Multitier systems are being created that tie into databases, financial systems, reservation systems, and more. They are delivering new features to new customers.

One of the most interesting, and disconcerting trends for some, is that while a traditional security perspective has called for keeping people out of sensitive stores of information or communications networks, we are now involved with activities that increasingly involve the exact opposite. Businesses are increasingly inviting people from around the world to come into their systems—with varying degrees of recognition of the implications. We do this when we create systems that enable customers to view sales and product information. We do this when we create systems that enable customers to place orders with us via the Web. We do this when we create systems that tie our business processes into the systems of our suppliers and partners. Doing all of this well without jeopardizing our businesses is difficult. As you will see from the rest of the book, Win2K offers many features and services that enable it to be part of the solution.

NETBIOS, WAP, AND IrDA

While this chapter has focused on the fact that TCP/IP is the king of communications protocols in that it *is* the foundation of today's computer networks, you should be aware that other low-level protocols may be involved.

Historically, a lot of Microsoft networking has been built on top of NetBIOS. NetBIOS defines a software interface, not a protocol. Many sites using NetBIOS on WinNT have actually been using TCP as the transport mechanism. Microsoft has supported this for many years. With the advent of Win2K, NetBIOS is being deprecated. Other Microsoft protocols such as SMB or CIFS, which used to be associated with NetBIOS, are still actively used. However, they are now running directly on TCP or UDP, or are encapsulated within Microsoft's RPCs (remote procedure calls).

A number of laptops and handheld computing devices come with IR (infrared) ports today. The Infrared Data Association (IrDA) has already developed infrared communications standards that are accepted by the computer, communications, home entertainment, and semiconductor industries. Win2K provides support for these ports and the protocols used by them. Although the IR ports are still not in widespread use, you should be aware that it is very easy to transmit files using this support. As when transmitting files using other means, the files may be used to propagate viruses and Trojan Horses. To date, we are not aware of any reported worms using IrDA ports as transmission vector. This book does not cover the authentication, authorization, or auditing issues raised by the use of IrDA ports.

We started this chapter talking about how the trend of extending connectivity is expanding to include our cell phones, pagers, PDAs, and even our cars. One of the protocols that you will probably encounter in the future is *Wireless Application Protocol (WAP)*. The WAP specification was initially released on April 30, 1998. Since then, most cellular vendors have been active in the development of network components and terminals for WAP.

Although Win2K does not provide any native support for WAP at this time, some of you will probably be involved in the creation of gateways between your existing network and WAP at some point in the next few years. It will be interesting to see how the authentication and authorization issues are handled.

RECAP

It was not so many years ago that it was thought that TCP/IP would be a protocol of the past, but with its wide acceptance and implementation, it is here to stay, albeit in an ever-growing and changing manner. If you are to understand Win2K, its services, and how to secure them, then you will have to understand TCP/IP. A few of the more notable thoughts from this chapter:

▼ TCP/IP is the communications protocol used to interconnect most computers and form most computer networks in the world today.

■ The IPv4 (and TCP/IP in general) protocol is robust but not secure.

■ IPv4 is the most prevalent protocol on the Internet today, but IPv6 is coming.

▲ IPv6 is attempting to correct some of those security issues, but it will take a long time to be widely deployed.

Security for existing TCP/IP networks is handled at higher layers in the stack, and Win2K provides many security features.

CHAPTER 2

Security Threats

"Just because you're paranoid doesn't mean they're not out to get you!"

—Unknown

The three primary attributes of traditional security are confidentiality, integrity, and availability (a.k.a. CIA). When we talk about threats, what we are really talking about are things that could adversely affect any or all of those three attributes. Threats come in a wide range, from those we readily think of, such as a burglar or earthquake, to those that are not so readily assumed, like an untrained operator making an error and deleting a critical file.

Although there is almost an infinite number of specific threats that pose risks to our systems, we can classify those threats pretty easily. In order to classify them, we must really understand them and look at how they affect our data. Using the CIA attributes, we will classify attacks in one or more of the following categories: data disclosure, data modification, and data availability.

This chapter will outline some of the more common threats to the security of your computer systems and networks, as well as discuss a bit about the attackers that are after your systems. Keep in mind that some of these threats have been perpetrated in the Unix environment, but not yet in the Windows environment, or vice versa. Specific Win2K security threats are covered in more detail in Chapter 7, as well as other chapters when appropriate. This chapter is meant to introduce you to "hacking," "cracking," "spoofing," and "sniffing"—activities performed by the underground community of pranksters, hardened criminals, industrial spies, and international terrorists who want to break into your systems for profit and pleasure.

TIP: If you're not the paranoid type, then hire a security manager who is. There must be someone who can lay down the law and enforce the essential security you need to protect your business.

CURRENT STATE OF AFFAIRS

It is a well-known fact that computer attacks are increasing in frequency, type, sophistication, and tenacity. Statistics show that in 1999 alone, CERT (Computer Emergency Response Team, based out of the Carnegie Melon University Software Engineering Institute) handled more than 8,200 incidents. This was over a two-fold increase compared to their 1998 caseload. CIAC (Computer Incident Advisory Capability for the U.S. Department of Energy) and other incident response teams have indicated the same startling trends. The Computer Security Institute (CSI) reported that their annual survey showed approximately $263 million in losses from security breaches in 1998-1999.

We can just look at the recent Distributed Denial of Service attacks that occurred in March of 2000 to note that the current "security" state in computers is far from adequate. It is worthy of note that not only are attacks increasing, but malicious attacks are increasing as well: Electronic sabotage is on the increase, as clearly indicated by the proliferation of security software products and their race to keep up with the latest attacks and holes. The Internet as well as some corporate networks are hostile computing environments, so you need to look at it in that light.

ATTACKERS: WHO ARE THEY AND WHY ARE THEY HERE?

You may not know any attackers personally. On the other hand, an attacker might be your next-door neighbor's son—someone who has a computer and DSL connection (maybe a modem), who is familiar with what you do, and who might guess your logon password because you use some derivative of your children's names. The people who do it see hacking as an electronic sport. They will spend all of their free time breaking into systems just for the thrill of having done so. Don't try to understand why, just know that they are out there. Here is a description of one attacker's idea of an exciting Friday night (from a conversation we had with him):

"...We gather our tools: my laptop with extra batteries and a spool of phone wire. My friend is good with phones, so we drive around until we find a building that we can get to the phone box on. He will connect the spool to their phone system, so we can dial-out on their bill, and then run the wire back to some bushes that we can sit in. I have some dial-up usernames and passwords that I got off the attacker's lists, so I use them to get access. We just hack around until the batteries run dry, then we'll pack up and maybe come back tomorrow."

Dangerous attackers are very knowledgeable about computers and security techniques, and they use sophisticated techniques to break into computer systems. Your competitor may hire such an attacker. If attackers cover their tracks, or you are not watching, you might never know that they have stolen your customer mailing list or trade secrets. The information that your competitors, foreign governments, and other attackers are after may include the following:

▼ Research information

■ Product information

■ Customer lists and proprietary customer information

■ Information about your organization, such as employee records, financial data, or legal information

■ CPU cycles

■ Disk storage

■ Bandwidth

▲ Almost anything else of value

Attackers learn about hacking by sharing information with their fellow attackers. The sociology of the cracking community is unlike the sociology of many other malicious subcultures. As an example, car thieves don't share new techniques with hundreds or thousands of other car thieves, while the cracking community readily shares their discoveries with others. There is an incredible amount of information available. Literally thousands of Web sites, bulletin boards, and electronic newsletters exist for the purpose of spreading this information around.

Attackers like to get online to brag about their techniques and exploits. It is kind of like an electronic "King of the Hill" game that is played by having the biggest or most prestigious list of compromised systems.

Attackers often intend to make a profit or want to obtain free services. A phone attacker is intent on obtaining logon information to online services or on making long-distance phone calls through your phone system so that you pick up the charges (as described earlier). Attackers often use information obtained during one break-in to access and break into another computer system. They might sell information obtained during a break-in, such as credit card numbers and access codes, to foreigners or competitors.

A trend is code cracking by so-called *cypherpunks*, a loosely organized group of attackers who often work together to break encryption schemes. The idea is to pool resources and computing power in order to crack encryption keys that would normally take many years to break. Cypherpunks use the Internet as a communication platform to consolidate their efforts.

E.B. White said that "the most time-consuming thing is to have an enemy." Your company is on the right track if it has hired a security officer and provided funds for security. If your company is broken into, learn from the experience and tighten up your security. If the attackers didn't do any damage, try to track the path of their break-in and, in your mind, thank them for helping you discover a security weakness.

ATTACKS: THE PROCESSES

One of the more overlooked issues when dealing with attacks is the process that is used in actually performing the attack. There are three common processes used by attackers today:

▼ **Hodgepodge** This is a very unorganized attack and is typically very easy to spot because it is electronically "noisy." You can classify it as the "throw everything at them and I don't care if they see me" attack. This is the most typical attack process that is discovered because it is not hard to spot. The attack is either by someone who does not care if you spot them, or a script kiddie.

■ **Methodical** This is a purposeful step-by-step attack. It has a specific "flow of attack" in the sense that there is a "method" being used. Typically, this uses a number of attacks that depend on each other, such as a DoS attack on a trusted machine followed by IP spoofing of the trusted host, then data interjection to that host. The attack is typical of a skilled attacker and is usually not detected unless you are doing more than the average "looking" for it.

▲ **Low and Slow**   This is a refinement on the methodical process, in that it is purposeful and uses a specific "flow of attack." The main difference is that the attack is coordinated. It uses a number of different source machines to initiate the attack and is done over a long period of time. The entire purpose of this type of attack is to gather the information but in a way that puts the attacker just under the radar screen of the site he is attacking. This attack is typical of a group of skilled attackers working in coordination.

WHAT ARE THE TARGETS?

Before we can look at threats, we need to have an idea of what is being threatened. This may seem obvious, but sometimes it isn't. The major targets of attack will be your data, resources, and your reputation. Thus anything that will affect any of these areas will be a target that you need to worry about.

DATA   Attackers that are after data are after your business! You need to realize this and understand that any machine that has valuable data is a prime target. As stated earlier, "valuable" may mean different things to different people. If you are in the midst of a legal battle, for example, internal memos may be the target to the opposing legal team.

RESOURCES   As stated earlier, the majority of all the intrusion attacks on systems are focused on getting resources. If you have a machine that has a resource that is accessible, then it is a target.

REPUTATION DAMAGE   Attackers will pick targets that will either damage your reputation or give them bragging rights (as described earlier). The social aspects of an attack should not be underestimated, and should be considered a main issue when identifying potential targets on your network.

Business Viewpoint

There are some questions that need to be asked from a business standpoint when identifying targets. You need to think both in terms of how data, resources, and reputation affect your business.

▼   What are you protecting?

■   How important is it to protect it?

■   How likely is someone to try to attack/steal/corrupt it?

- How hard will they try and how likely are they to succeed?
▲ How much will it hurt you if an attacker succeeds?

What About Windows?

Historically, Microsoft operating systems have tended to be targets for gathering data or reputation type of attacks. There have been few "compromise then install the server" type attacks, when compared with attacks on Unix-based systems. With the advent of Windows 2000, the power of the platform has made it more desirable to attackers that are interested in installing their own services on other people's hardware. You need to ensure you have a realistic view of the potential targets on your network. If you don't ask these things, then chances are you might be protecting the wrong things or not protecting enough of the important things. See Chapter 4 for more information on identifying risks.

WHAT ARE THE THREATS?

Threats are anything that cause unwanted or unauthorized modification, disclosure of data, or the unavailability of that data.

Some threats are easy to understand and the techniques for protecting against them are well known. But threats perpetrated by malicious users, disgruntled employees, and unknown attackers are a true nightmare. It is important to understand that the threats that have existed for years are the same as the ones we are dealing with today. It is not the threats that have changed, but the sheer number and types of methods used to implement them that is the real issue. Every day thousands of new computers are added to corporate networks, and some new technique for attacking systems (or a modified technique of an existing attack) is developed to exploit them.

You may not know you are being attacked or have been attacked, especially if you are not looking for it. No site is an exception. Even small businesses like corner food stores are targets for local attackers who notice an online computer system while in the store. They break in using their computer and modem just for the fun or challenge. Often these systems are the least secure because the owners think that no one would care about their system or even know it exists. One noted firewall security expert has said that within 60 seconds of placing a new server on the Internet, you are being scanned.We will now look at some of the more common threat sources.

The Internal Threat

It has been documented by numerous surveys that most security experts believe that internal employees are the biggest threat to their information systems. Employees are familiar with the network, know which systems hold valuable information, and may have easy access to those systems through their own account or the account of another user. The American Society for Industrial Security estimates that insiders perpetrate 77 percent of information theft.

Revenge is a common theme: workers against co-workers, employees against personnel staff, subordinates against managers, and so on. Downsizing may put people in jobs where they are overworked and underpaid. They may break into company employee records or, to cover a trail of theft, alter inventory and asset records. An employee who is being laid off may plant a virus.

Janitors have become dangerous in the information age. They steal information that can be used to break into computer systems from the outside, such as user accounts and even passwords that users paste on their walls. Mailing lists used by the cracking community have been used to share information about how to get a job as a janitor!

Contractual partners are also a threat. Organizations involved in *electronic data interchange* (EDI) set up communication links with other companies for the purpose of exchanging business information. Attackers take advantage of these links. The attacker may be an employee of the other company, or an external attacker who has found a way into one company and uses the link to gain access to the other company. Any data-exchange agreement with other companies should be considered a potential threat in which your company's trade secrets and other vital information are at risk.

Trusted users are a constant security threat as well. They spread viruses from one system to another. They can inadvertently leak sensitive information or reveal their password to unauthorized users. They can even be duped by a caller into giving out a password or some other vital information. These last two points describe what is often called "social engineering."

The Changing Landscape

Although most of the current statistics show that internal employees are the biggest threat to a company's information systems it is clear that business changes that have occurred in the past several years are changing the threat model as well. Traditionally companies concentrated on keeping people out of sensitive stores of information. Businesses used leased lines to interconnect offices instead of using the public Internet. Today's business environment is the exact opposite. The goal is to invite people from around the world to come to the business's systems. This is done for marketing, sales, support, and even business-to-business relationships. Such a change in expectations and perspective is changing the dynamics of the threats faced by businesses.

Mobile and Remote Users

Providing network logon services to mobile and remote users is another problem. The number of mobile users has greatly increased, causing heightened management problems. A typical mobile user travels with a portable computer and connects to a company's network, usually with full client rights and permissions. The mobile user exposes your system to potential security problems in a number of ways:

▼　Someone sitting next to a user in an airport or other public area can monitor the user's logon, either visually or by using devices that eavesdrop on devices in close proximity.

- Logons take place over public lines that can be monitored by attackers who are looking for ways to break into systems.

- Portable computers are often stolen. Any valuable company information on the system will be available to the thief, including user account names from e-mail address books, passwords that the user has stored on disk, and sensitive company information that the user has downloaded to his or her own computer.

▲ A remote system may be at a location where an attacker can physically sit at the computer and hack away at the system for hours without being disturbed by a user or a security officer.

There are a number of ways to protect portable systems, including encryption of data and using two-way authentication devices in which a user enters the password produced by the card and the memorized password to gain access to a network.

The Internet and TCP/IP

When you decide to use the Internet protocols and TCP/IP networking, you open your system to a variety of potential attacks that are well known in the attacker community. Ethernet networks are vulnerable to attackers who utilize sniffer devices to monitor traffic (transmitted packets) on networks and use the information they obtain to mount an attack. If a single cable connects two systems, then it is fairly easy to read all the packets sent between those systems. If two systems communicate across the Internet and a sniffer is connected to the Internet, the sniffer might be able to capture some of the packets of the communication session, but it would be difficult to capture all of them. That is because the Internet is a mesh of many different paths that packets can travel between systems. However, the sniffer can be connected to the "last leg" of a route through which all the packets must travel to get to a destination system, or the sniffer can be attached to an internal network.

Any attacker who obtains only some of the packets transmitted between two computers might be able to discern enough information to launch an attack. Packets contain information such as addresses, IDs, and even non-encrypted passwords in some cases. Once the attacker has found a communication session of interest, he can use filtering options on the sniffer to display only packets for that session. The attacker might monitor a network connection for a long time to collect millions of bits of data that might hold just one vital piece of information. A sorting and searching routine makes it fairly easy to isolate useful information.

An attacker can also masquerade as another user/system by generating packets that appear to come from that system. The attacker "wedges" packets into the transmission that replace the original systems packets, and the original system is bumped. This type of attack is difficult because the timing must be just right. However, it has been done.

Physical

The threat to systems from a physical standpoint should not be underestimated. If you have done a good job of securing a system electronically, but allow an attacker physical access, then all of your work may potentially be in vain—potentially because there are some electronic mechanisms that will protect a system even if physical access is not secured, such as an encryption. But there are other things that are easily defeated if you have physical access, such as a boot password or file system permissions.

Needless to say, the simple fact is that if a system is not physically secure, then almost any other steps you have taken can be bypassed.

Phone Attacks

A chapter on threats would not be complete without a discussion of phone system attacks. A *phreaker* is a person who takes advantage of the telecommunications system to make free long-distance telephone calls, listen to private conversations, access internal systems, or hack into other systems via the system broken into. Phreakers are familiar with telephone switches, networks, and other equipment, and often have manuals from the manufacturers of telecom equipment that describe exactly how to operate and repair that equipment. Experienced phreakers can manipulate telephone billing, access codes, and call routing.

Phreakers can make free long-distance phone calls by gaining "dial-in/dial-out" capabilities. For example, a phreaker calls a number in your organization, then asks to be transferred back to the operator. He then poses as an important person within the company and asks for an outside line. His call is now looped through your company, and you pay the bill. Attacks on other systems may be perpetrated in this way. Worse, the targets of the attack may think your company is responsible.

Attackers and phreakers even pose as service technicians to gain access to phone closets and PBX systems, where they reprogram the systems, install bugs, or set up circuits that can be accessed later and used to attack your company or other companies.

Other Systems

Other systems may be used as conduits into your systems. In the current wave of things, everything is going on the network cable, or even wireless. Now many other systems are run over your physical backbone. This lends itself to a very useful topology, but also brings with it many unknown security threats. Now if someone hacks your alarm company's network and there is no separation between it and your data network, they may be able to get to your IP network. Just imagine an attacker breaking into your alarm system company and then going back into your network that way. Or an attacker using your phone system to compromise your database server. You may think "no way," but trust us, the time is coming when it will happen.

TIP: You need to treat any and all physical connections to your network as potential threat sources.

Natural Threats

Obviously, not all threats to the integrity of your network come from people. Power surges, failing components, and other problems may bring down systems and cost your organization thousands or millions of dollars in downtime. In some cases, continuous access to information is critical to the operation of the entire business. The following list covers most major natural threats:

▼ Electrical power may be lost during storms or for other reasons. Backup power supplies are essential.

■ Hardware failures can cause loss of data availability. Redundant systems and backup are imperative.

▲ Fires, floods, earthquakes, and other disasters require backup systems, alternate data centers, and disaster recovery plans.

Bypassing Intrusion Detection Systems (IDS)

Another threat that is not given much thought is the eluding of ID systems. The fact that people are using intrusion detection (ID) systems may not be adequate if they can be easily eluded. There have been a few tests that show that it is entirely possible to elude most current ID systems, given enough time and technical skill. It is important that you understand this, more for the sake of not thinking "I've got an IDS, so I don't have to worry anymore."

Current commercial ID systems can be bypassed or may miss things that really matter. There are two major ID systems on the market today: host-based and network-based. While they both provide a needed function, they can be bypassed. A host-based IDS will not alert on things that it does not know about, or that appear normal. Network ID systems can be tricked with a bit of packet manipulation or encryption.

It is important that you recognize the threat posed by an attacker's ability to bypass the ID system you have in place. It is a real threat, and you should take that into consideration.

In any of these situations, communication lines that are essential to the operation of your company may be cut. You need to establish alternate lines or backup methods to keep systems online in emergencies. These techniques are discussed in Chapter 11.

Social Engineering

Social engineering is when a potential attacker uses social means rather than technical methods to get information. This typically involves personal interaction either over the phone or in person. Social engineering over the phone is the most common, but do not doubt that a potential computer attacker, industrial spy, or other unauthorized person will one day walk into your building looking for useful information to steal.

ATTACK METHODS

Now that we have discussed the potential targets and source of threats to our systems, we will look at some of the actual methods that are used to perform the attacks. We will look at attacks from two perspectives: classes and specifics. We will discuss the basic class that attack falls into, which is kind of an "architectural" view. Then, for each class, we will discuss some of the specific threats that are a reality today. The recommended countermeasures are addressed in the next chapter.

Authentication Compromises

This method of attack focuses on acquiring an account and password or some other reusable authentication token. This is a primary target for attackers, and there are many ways in which they may obtain this information. It is not uncommon for attackers to run network sniffers, plant bugs, tap into wires, set up hidden cameras, or dive into dumpsters to get the information they need. Once the information is obtained, your systems and possibly those of your business partners, customers, and employees are at risk.

Once intruders have access to an account, they will attempt to elevate their privilege level. The process is often like a journey for attackers: getting deeper and deeper into a system, with each level bringing greater excitement. Attackers may return every night as if playing some sort of video game. Primary targets are system files, which the attackers use to execute management programs and gain greater privilege, and log files, which they use to cover their tracks. Covering tracks allows the attacker to return again and again. Attackers may also create a "backdoor" into the system to use at another time in case their current entry point is no longer available.

One of the worst things that can happen to your system is for an attacker to gain access to administrative accounts or directories that contain administrator-only programs and files. An attacker may gain this access through a weak security scheme or by obtaining a password in an unscrupulous way. Once in, the attacker can change passwords for other accounts in order to access them later or do some other nasty things, such as mess around with the Win2K Registry.

Hacking User Accounts and Passwords

The two main ways that usernames and passwords are compromised are with sniffers and easily guessed passwords. As mentioned earlier, an attacker's first priority is to obtain user account names and passwords since this provides easy access to a system. Once inside, the attacker will find a way to elevate his privileges. The attacker can often obtain a list of user account names from a number of likely sources. For example, the company e-mail system might provide such lists. In high-security environments, make sure these lists are not readily available. Internal users will usually have easy access to account names.

Once an attacker obtains a legitimate user account name, cracking the password is the next step. Attackers take advantage of common passwords: If they know the user of an account, they may try various combinations of the user's kids' and pets' names. Many people use the same password to log on to other systems, such as ATM machines. A co-worker/attacker could obtain this password by watching you at the bank machine with a pair of binoculars (yes, it's done). A good reason to choose an obscure password is to make it difficult for people with good eyes to follow your keystrokes as you type it.

If an attacker obtains a user account name, but not a password, he can try brute force methods of breaking into the account. A program is set up to try thousands or millions of different passwords until the account opens. This method is ineffective if logon restrictions are set to limit the number of attempted logons. Win2K can lock out an account, but by default it is not enabled. However, the Administrator account never gets locked out at the console. This prevents a denial of service attack on this account but introduces other problems.

Exhaustion attacks and dictionary attacks are methods for cracking password files and other encrypted information. In an *exhaustion attack*, thousands of password combinations are used until a password is guessed. In a *dictionary attack*, a complete dictionary of common passwords in multiple languages is tried until a password is guessed. Attackers often know the manufacturer's default passwords to equipment such as routers and depend on the fact that the passwords are not changed.

Default Configurations

Default configurations are a major cause of all successful intrusions. Systems have been, and will continue to be, shipped for ease of use, not security. It is that simple. Anytime you take a system right out of the box, you should assume that it can be compromised with little effort. Remember "connect and get hit in 60 seconds?"

The well-known IIS 4.0 and RDS/MDAC vulnerability allowed remote execution of commands under the context of the LocalSystem account. This vulnerability was found on a large percentage of Win2K servers running IIS, yet the functionality was used on very few. It was installed as part of the default configuration and never removed.

> *CAUTION:*   This is by far one of the greatest threats, second only to poorly selected (that is, easily guessed) passwords.

SNMP

Most systems come with some sort of SNMP agent on them, but many are not enabled. The problem with SNMP is that it gives copious amounts of information about a system and usually has default passwords for accessing it. By default, most systems have a default read community string (that is, password) of *public* and write community string of *private*. This allows anyone with one of the common SNMP client utilities to gain *valuable* information such as system name, OS level, and even usernames in Win2K.

Files and Directories

File systems in general are vulnerable due to the fact that the default permissions are usually inadequate from a strong security standpoint, as well as the actual format. Win2K provides two file systems: the traditional File Allocation Table (FAT) file system and the NT File System (NTFS). FAT does not provide the file system security that NTFS does. With FAT, someone can boot a computer with DOS and access files in any directory. NTFS directories and files can be accessed only by properly authenticated users, which means that you must first boot a system and log on with a password.

A program called NTFSDOS allows full read/write access to an NTFS volume to a user who boots a system with DOS or Windows. While this sounds like the end of Win2K security, appropriate security measures can protect data. Basically, you must lock up servers and prevent booting from floppy drives. We'll discuss this more in the "Exploiting Physical Access" section.

Default Service Installations

Many operating systems will install and start unneeded services if set up by an inexperienced user. If you attempt to install all the Win2K services, you are opening a security *can-o-worms*. There are more compromises because of default configurations than almost any other attack point.

Improper Input Validation

Improper input validation or no validation is an exploit mechanism for two major classes of attacks: buffer overflows and HTTP form variables. Programmers who do not validate the input that is passed through variables into their programs or Web page forms are allowing a user to potentially send input that can cause the program to crash or cause the program to perform an operation that the programmer did not intend.

Buffer Overflows

Buffer overflows have been around for a long time but they tend to be difficult to initially detect and properly exploit. As other areas of system security have improved, the cracker community has refocused on buffer overflows on all type of platforms. Some weeks it feels like these are the "attack du jour." They work, because programmers do not "bounds check" the values that are passed to their programs. The basic premise is to overwrite the return stack pointer to point to another area in memory that has some code that the attacker wants to be executed. This is a common problem with frequently used system calls that do not have length arguments (that is, SPRINTF, STRCPY, and GETs).

HTTP Form Variables

Web servers that use forms and accept client variable inputs via the GET or POST mechanism are regularly exploited. The attacker will modify the variable to have the data that he wants. This data is usually in the form of a long string to cause a buffer overflow or a modified command to have the Web server do something that was not intended. One example of the command modification is to modify a SQL statement that is passed as a parameter, which adds a statement to have the SQL server execute a local command, such as adding a user. This is a purely remote attack.

Compromised Trusted Systems

Network computer systems maintain *trust relationships* with each other so that users on one system can access another, or so that a program on one computer can access information stored on another computer. Data is often replicated (copied) to trusted systems. Attackers use these trust relationships to their advantage. In fact, an attacker will often have less interest in the computer he is currently attacking than in the computers it has trust relationships with. He may be able to obtain access to a legitimate account that has access to another system. In addition, it may be possible to attack the trust relationship, which often acts like a secure user account and allows two systems to exchange information or to run processes on one another.

Trust relationships in Win2K are usually transitive (see Chapter 8). If System A extends its trust to System B, and System B extends its trust to System C, then a trust relationship is established between Systems A and C through System B. This may be good in some cases, but it also opens up many unknowns and potential security holes. The old adage that "you are only as strong as your weakest link" is very applicable in these architectures. This is discussed further in Chapter 7.

IP Spoofing

There are two primary IP spoofing techniques: *blind* using TCP sequence number prediction and *inline* using sniffed data to set TCP sequence numbers. This type of attack is used primarily to exploit TCP applications that use trusted host-based authentication (that is, programs that rely on IP addresses for authentication, like most versions of RSH) and is typically used against Unix-based systems. That is because Win2K and Windows NT do not use IP address in trust relationships. Note that spoofing UDP packets is ultimately trivial since it is connectionless—you just put in the IP address you want, and let it fly.

Session Hijacking

When an attacker attempts to commandeer an existing TCP session, this is called session hijacking. The attacker will use a coordinated DoS attack to take the legitimate host "out of sync" or "off-line," then synchronize their system with the victim. This attack is used against clear text interactive sessions for the most part, for instance, Telnet, Rlogin, and FTP. With the introduction of Telnet as a default service, session hijacking is quite likely.

Man-in-the-Middle

This attack tricks the victim host into establishing a session with the attacker, then the attacker establishes a session with the real destination and pass packets back and forth, taking whatever data they desire. To do this, the attacker must have a way to get the victim to initiate a session or be waiting to perform the attack when the victim initiates a session.

This is a remote attack, but could be initiated by a local program. It would be easier to just grab the data before it left the machine if it were going to be a local attack.

DNS Cache Poison

DNS is vital to all Internet-based systems and all Win2K systems. The consequences of compromise in the data that is provided by the DNS server is severe. *DNS cache poisoning* is a method by which an attacker will inject invalid data into the cache of a DNS server. Then when the DNS server is queried for the data, it will return the cached values, which are compromised. For example, if an attacker asks the victim for DNS information about host.attacker.net, the victim's DNS server will query the attacker's DNS server for the information on that host, and the attacker's DNS server sends back the answer (host.attacker.net = 127.0.0.1) *plus* some *poison* information (pop.example.com = someTrojanedMailServerIP). The victim's DNS server then caches the bad data and will return it to any future client that asks for it.

War Dialing

War dialing is another technique that attackers use to gain access to systems that are potentially trusted. Internal systems are usually more trusted than external systems, so if attackers can get access to an internal system, they have a more trusted machine than they started with. Basically, they are betting that somewhere in the company, someone has placed a modem on a system and left it unsecured. This is a *very* good bet. They may not know the exact number to call, but they do know the prefix that you use, so they will try them all! The war dialer discovers phone numbers of modem-connected computer systems by dialing one number after another until a modem answers. When a modem is found, the phone number is put into a log and the system continues to search. This may go on all day or all night. Once the list is complete, the attacker calls each of the systems on the list and attempts to break in. There are numerous auto-dialing programs that are commonly available on Web sites and bulletin boards.

Sniffers

A *packet sniffer* is a device or software that can read transmitted packets. Packet sniffing is a passive eavesdropping technique that is hard to detect. The packet-sniffing devices may be installed on internal or external networks. Although packet sniffing an Internet transmission line is not necessarily informative, sniffing a cable that runs into your facilities is. Overall, the biggest threat is from people inside or near your facilities who are armed with packet sniffers or from attackers who have penetrated your building and planted listening devices.

Networks were designed to make sharing information easy. The most common LAN protocol is Ethernet, and by design, any computer on an Ethernet LAN broadcasts information on the open wire that all other computers can hear—much as a radio station broadcasts within a specific area. Most LAN adapters can be switched into what is called "promiscuous" mode, a setting that allows the adapter to receive all packets on the network. These packets can then be captured and saved for analysis. A *packet-sniffing* program makes this task a lot easier. It has all the controls an administrator (or attacker) needs to filter and sort through the transmissions to find and evaluate specific network traffic.

NOTE: A sniffer is located on one LAN segment, and can monitor the traffic only on that segment. Cable modems for several homes normally share a segment. Internet services that are provided in some hotels usually consist of one LAN segment.

Communication Systems

Communication systems such as microwave and satellite links between your sites are vulnerable to monitoring and tapping. A microwave system may emit a signal the diameter of a nickel. That same signal will have a diameter of one mile when it reaches a receiving dish approximately 20 miles away. Anyone with the right equipment can monitor the signal if they are within the beam path. A communication satellite has a footprint that is as big as North America. Once again, the signal is easy to monitor. All of your sensitive transmissions must be protected with encryption.

Wireless 802.11

The 802.11 wireless standard is gaining popularity very quickly. This is a radio broadcast although with a weak signal. Businesses considering the deployment of this type of infrastructure should be very concerned with the potential for abuse. Prior to deploying this you should determine what type of information might be exposed and determine which applications you can easily protect with adequate encryption.

Applications and Services

Applications and services are the reason that we have computers and networks in the first place; we can't live without them, but they provide many avenues for exploitation. There exist a number of vulnerable services and applications, just by the nature of *what* or *how* they do what they do.

The following three categories are some of the more egregious areas of attack.

Highly Vulnerable Services

The following protocols and utilities have been available on Unix systems and TCP/IP networks for some time and now are standard on Win2K. They tend to be targets in all attack attempts and are highly exploited. Because these utilities may be present in your own Win2K network environment, this section discusses some of the more significant security problems.

TELNET   This is a terminal program. A logon procedure is used to provide access. One problem is that you cannot normally trust any system that initiates a Telnet session since packets may be spoofed. Telnet is often used as a means of attack. When used for legitimate reasons, other problems exist. For example, all information is sent as clear text, including usernames and passwords, so that anyone monitoring or sniffing the session can see it. For security reasons, do not run Telnet services on any Win2K Server. There are some secure versions of Telnet, but these are not widely deployed.

FILE SHARING   The two major file-sharing protocols that are exploited heavily are Network File System (NFS) and Server Message Block (SMB). NFS has been around for many years as a system for accessing files on network-connected computers. It was originally developed by Sun Microsystems and used in the Unix environment, although versions of it have appeared in almost every operating system environment. But NFS comes with a history of security problems. For more information about NFS, see Chapter 18.

SMB has also been around for quite a bit, but almost exclusively in the Microsoft realm. It was developed by IBM using the NetBIOS protocol over the NetBEUI and IPX/SPX network and transport layer protocols. Note that NetBEUI is a LAN protocol, which is not routable. Microsoft helped in extending the NetBIOS API to run over IP, and thus the ability to run SMB over IP. This has brought much attention to looking for and compromising servers that run both the older and newer protocols. For more information about the risks of SMB and CIFS (Common Internet File System), see Chapter 7.

ELECTRONIC MAIL PROTOCOLS   Simple Mail Transport Protocol (SMTP) is an electronic mail protocol and Sendmail is an e-mail program that uses SMTP. Sendmail has been a notorious security breach. Older versions of e-mail allow all sorts of unscrupulous activity, such as access to the root-level of a system. It is also hard to verify the authenticity and sender of a message. In addition, the e-mail server and gateway may contain the e-mail addresses of everyone in an organization. Also, a mail gateway is susceptible to e-mail attacks in which large numbers of useless messages are sent in an attempt to overwhelm it. Microsoft Exchange provides a relatively safe SMTP implementation.

The identification of a sender can be forged, and users may receive bogus mail from what appears to be someone they trust. Users should trust only mail that they know is in transit, and then it is probably wise to verify messages with the sender. Encryption and digital signature methods are available to validate messages, as discussed in Appendix B. The ability to deny having sent a message is another problem, especially when it comes to business transactions. For example, someone who purchases stocks using e-mail might attempt to deny having placed the order if the stock goes down in price. Digital signatures can prove the source, time, and authenticity of messages.

Spamming is another problem. In a spamming attack, the perpetrator sends hundreds or thousands of phony or useless e-mail messages to your site in an attempt to overload your systems and stop all communications.

MIME (MULTIPURPOSE INTERNET MAIL EXTENSIONS)   MIME provides a way to insert a variety of different media formats into messages. It is a potential problem since messages may contain executables that carry viruses or Trojan Horse programs. Messages that appear legitimate may actually be sent by someone who has altered message header information. MIME messages can also carry Postscript files that may cause problems.

FTP (FILE TRANSFER PROTOCOL)   This utility allows file transfers on TCP/IP networks and the Internet. There is an anonymous FTP logon facility that lets anyone access files in a specific directory or subdirectories. The directories should implement Read Only rights; otherwise, attackers might copy viruses or Trojan Horse programs into the directory. Since logon is often to an anonymous account, you will not know who is accessing the system. In Win2K, you can create drop boxes, which might better be called "black hole" directories. Files can go in, but the user cannot see or do anything with files in the directory once they have been put in. Only authorized users can get at the files.

DNS (DOMAIN NAME SYSTEM)   Your DNS servers contain information about your site, such as computer names and IP addresses, from which an intruder can glean details about the structure of your organization. An attacker can use this information to spoof packets and attack specific systems. You may have noted that many of these utilities are not considered secure because they send passwords in the clear that could be vulnerable to sniffing. However, you might be better off setting up services like FTP and HTTP with anonymous user access. That way, users don't even need to enter a password to access the system and risk the possibility of exposing some password that they use to access more sensitive systems. Obviously, this is useful only on public servers that do not have sensitive information, but at least users don't need to use passwords that might be the same password they used to access more secure systems.

Data-Driven Attacks

Data-driven, or content-driven, attacks deal primarily with Java, ActiveX, JavaScript, and VBScript being executed on the client machine. This is a server-to-client attack, which is just the opposite of what we normally think of as the attack direction. These attacks tend to be implementation bugs or may be exploited as a result of poor system administration. The attacks tend to do one or more of the following:

▼ Read local files.

■ Gather private information.

■ Start service.

■ Install Trojan Horses or viruses.

▲ Execute commands.

Port Stealing and Covert Channels

Port stealing and protocol misuse are becoming much more popular. Port stealing is when a malicious program *listens* on a port that is typically used by a legitimate service. For example, an attacker could set up a program that listens on port 23 waiting for someone to connect. When someone does, the program acts as the regular service, but captures data or modifies it as it desires.

A covert channel is described as "any communication channel that can be exploited by a process to transfer information in a manner that violates the systems security policy" (U. S. Department of Defense, 1985, *Trusted Computer System Evaluation Criteria*). This basically means that the communication channel is not being used for the purpose for which it was intended. In an IP-based network, there are many different methods to set up covert channels.

For example, a ICMP covert channel tool called Loki was described in November of 1996. The purpose of Loki was to provide an "interactive" shell by tunneling commands in the data portion of ICMP_ECHO and ICMP_ECHOREPLY packets. Loki exploits the fact that most network devices do not look at the contents of ICMP_ECHO and ICMP_ECHOREPLY traffic. If ICMP is checked at all, it is normally to make a decision to pass, drop, or return them. The covert channel looks like common ICMP_ECHO traffic, with the exception that there is data in the packets that the server will now use as command input. This covert channel assumes that the client and server are already set up to communicate, and that ICMP_ECHO and ICMP_ECHOREPLY packets can flow between the two hosts.

Denial of Service (DoS)

DoS is focused on removing a system or resource from the network. Its specific purpose is to remove the "availability" attribute from whatever system/resource that is the target. Focal points typically are Web servers, firewalls, routers, and trusted hosts. They are also often used as part of larger attacks, such as IP spoofing and DNS cache poison. This is by far the most common type of attack.

DoS can be categorized into three groups: feature- or protocol-driven, inappropriate configurations, or programming flaws. The feature-driven DoS uses "features" in the service or protocol specifications to accomplish its purpose. They are basically unpreventable, unless you change the protocol/feature. The configuration-based DoS uses improper configurations to perform the DoS. The programming flaw DoS exploits is a software bug to cause the system/resource to stop providing the service.

Distributed Denial of Service

Distributed Denial of Service (DDoS) is just a different way of doing DoS. It uses agents that are controlled by the command program. The agents are placed on hacked machines in as many locations as possible on the Internet, and the command program is usually on another hacked machine or the attacker's personal machine. The attacker then issues commands to the agents, such as "run a SYN flood against example.com." The agent will then start the attack. As you can probably tell, this is *very* effective, and there is little defense against it.

Viruses, Worms, and Trojan Horses

Computer worms are programs that propagate themselves over a computer network, reproducing themselves as they go. A true worm does not need any user interaction to perform the propagation except the initial invocation.

Computer viruses are programs that are so named because they search out other programs and "infect" them, turning the infected file into a Trojan Horse. In the worst cases, their spread throughout computer systems resembles the epidemic spread of biological viruses. They get into computer systems by being copied from contaminated disks or downloaded from online services by unsuspecting users. Once a system is contaminated, the virus executes some immediate action, or waits until a specified time or for a specific command executed by the user. Viruses may display harmless messages or destroy the information stored on entire hard disks. Unlike a worm, a virus cannot infect other systems without assistance.

Viruses are especially dangerous on networks because once they contaminate one system, they may spread to systems throughout the entire network. The biggest threat is that unsuspecting employees will pick up viruses through normal business transactions and spread them throughout an organization.

Virus contamination comes from a number of sources:

▼ Library computers or company kiosk computers that many different people use

■ Service technicians who use disk-based utilities to check computers

■ Computers infected by malicious users or by disgruntled employees who want to get even with the company or another employee

▲ Yes, even packages of off-the-shelf software

In fact, viruses were available for sale in a recent magazine advertisement for the purpose of testing your anti-virus software! Anyone not sure how to get a virus can now just buy one in order to infect someone else's system.

Viruses are created by authors who are fascinated by how quickly their virus may spread through computer systems. Terrorists and industrial spies create viruses that cause damage in order to seek revenge on an opponent or to damage the operations of a competitor. Some viruses are intended for a specific target, but get out of control and spread to unintended targets.

Fortunately, you can protect yourself against viruses by implementing appropriate security measures, training users, and using virus-protection programs. Some new strains of viruses are especially dangerous because they have the ability to change themselves in order to avoid detection by popular virus-protection programs. It is important to choose such programs from reputable vendors that provide continuous updates to their programs.

A *Trojan Horse* is any program that purports to do one task but upon execution performs a furtive task. The program may contain a virus, or it may perform any other task, such as installing a keyboard or network sniffer. A simple Trojan Horse would be one that displays the login dialog box and gathers the passwords that unsuspecting users enter. This is why you should always press CTRL-ALT-DEL when logging into NT or Windows 2000.

Backdoors and Program Bugs

A *backdoor* is a hole into a program, left there purposely by the original programmer or designer. I once attended a training session in which a Novell instructor described a backdoor method for getting into a version of the NetWare operating system. The instructions were meant to be used by certified NetWare representatives who needed to help their customer gain access to a system after losing a password; however, I'm sure that a number of attackers managed to attend the classes or get the information from other sources.

A backdoor (or *trapdoor*) is often put into a program by a developer as a way to bypass a particular system or process until the program is complete. Backdoors can simplify the program-testing process by bypassing certain steps or control procedures that might require a lot of time to complete and are not necessary when testing. However, programmers often forget to remove backdoors or are not aware of other holes that the backdoor might have created. A person who discovers a backdoor may find a way to use it to exploit a system.

When a backdoor is discovered, it usually doesn't take long for the attacker community to spread information about it onto bulletin boards and e-mail lists. This hole becomes a prime target for attackers who may already have access into your network. By using the newly discovered security hole, they may elevate their privileges to gain further access to your systems or find some technique for doing damage.

Exploiting Physical Access

As described earlier, exploiting physical access is a very effective way to compromise the security of a system. It is easy to see that with no physical access restrictions, there isn't anything to keep you from stealing any or all of the system that you are attempting to penetrate. Other options are to remove the battery so as to reset/remove the boot password, or even replace the BIOS.

Probably one of the most devastating forms of physical exploitation is the ability to boot an operating system from removable media that will provide access to the resources on the system. The most likely target of this type of physical attack is the data that resides on the hard disk.

Dual-Boot OS

Most people don't think about physical security, but the ability to dual-boot a system to bypass access controls inherent in the "other" operating system is on the rise. There are programs, such as NTFSDOS, that allow you to read (and potentially write) files off NTFS partition while booted under Win 9*x*. There is also a Linux boot disk that will allow you to change a non-syskeyed user password in the SAM file. It accomplishes this by booting a small Linux OS and using a limited write Linux NTFS driver to mount the NTFS partition and make the change. By default, Win2K uses syskey, so it is not vulnerable to this attack.

RECAP

Attackers want access to something you have: resources, data, reputation, whatever. To do this they must get some type of access, which is typically done by compromising a user account, or getting a service to do something for you to get you access (that is, a buffer overflow). It is really quite simple, but the technical solution is elusive. If you realize what the threats are, where they are likely to come from, and what they are going after, then you can plan accordingly. This chapter has introduced you to some of these concepts and hopefully gotten you thinking about security.

CHAPTER 3

Countermeasures

"Talk does not cook rice."

—Unknown

In the last chapter, we discussed many of the threats to your computing systems. In this chapter, we will look at the countermeasures to those threats. Although the term "countermeasures" conjures up images of high-tech sophisticated electronics to some, the reality is much more prosaic. Planning and implementing your countermeasures is a lot like sitting down with your auditor. There are a number of protective measures that help you "harden" your defenses, put up walls, and lessen the chances that someone is going to physically or electronically attack your systems. A few obvious steps are

▼ Create security policies, plans, and job positions as appropriate.

■ Set up a security-response team—experts who handle security problems. The team can provide a place for users to report security breaches or contacts by suspicious people who may be industrial spies.

■ Factor in your human resources as appropriate. This may include performing background checks on personnel and keeping tabs on employees who are disgruntled, who are working closely with other companies, and who are in the process of leaving the company.

■ Develop your access control or authorization model as appropriate. This may include classifying your employees much the way the military classifies its personnel, giving some people higher clearance than others for access to sensitive information. Make sure to differentiate between part-time and temporary employees.

▲ Simulate attacks against your own company to check its vulnerability. This may be done by current employees if they have the necessary skills, or you may wish to outsource this function.

IDENTIFYING YOUR LIKELY TARGETS

To protect systems, you have to identify them. In the last chapter, we discussed what systems and networks were likely to be targets for attackers. To make it personal, you will need to ask questions about your systems and networks, such as

▼ What data is important to the ongoing operation of our company?

■ What data and/or resources could cause damage to the reputation of the company? Identify anything that, if disrupted, will damage your reputation and affect business.

■ Where does the data reside? Servers only? Workstations? Both?

▲ What resources are accessible from the Internet? Internal network? Physically?

It is very important that you identify all resources that are potential targets to ensure that the countermeasure you decide upon will be adequate or if you will need to take additional steps. It is also a good idea to group the resources according to their connectivity (that is, reachable externally and/or internally).

Make sure you get this information not only from the technical people, but also from the business people as well. Ask the CEO (or his or her proxy) the following questions:

▼ What are we trying to protect?

■ How important is it to protect it?

▲ How much will it hurt you if an attacker succeeds?

With the answer to those three questions, you should have a good view of what matters from the business viability perspective.

ATTACK COUNTERMEASURES

Since we know attacks are going to occur, and we have discussed some of the more likely classes that those attacks will come in, we need to cover how we can defend against them. This section will deal with the countermeasures for each of them.

Countermeasures to Authentication Compromises

There are three basic ways to protect against authentication-based compromises: Use strong authentication, protection of the authentication data, and proper file permissions for authentication-related files. By using these countermeasures in conjunction with one another, you will thwart almost any authentication-based attack.

Before we delve into the specifics of any particular authentication system, we should introduce a couple of concepts. First, remember that when we talk about authentication what we're really talking about is how a system knows that we are who we claim to be. There are typically three factors that can be used in authentication schemes:

▼ Something you have, such as a smartcard

■ Something you know, such as a PIN or password

▲ Something you are, such as your thumb print

Two-factor authentication uses at least two of these factors, and most of the time those factors will be *something you have* and *something you know*.

Using Strong Authentication

A number of people having been using the phrase "strong authentication" for the past few years, but it is not clear that all of the people using the phrase know what it is intended to imply. The phrase is intended to describe authentication systems that are not subject to man-in-the-middle attacks, replay attacks, and cryptanalysis attacks that are successful within a useful period of time.

Historically, too many authentication systems have been implemented that do not meet these criteria. The commonly deployed versions of Telnet and FTP send passwords over the network as clear text. Any person using a sniffer is then able to use the same username and password combination at a later time to perform similar operations. Many other systems have used simple schemes for obscuring the password, but attackers can easily exploit these as well. In some cases, the attacker never needs to know the username/password combination; all they are required to do is simply replay part of successful authentication to gain subsequent illicit entry.

When good cryptography is employed in an authentication system, the attacker resorts to other techniques. Today, even the authentication systems that use good cryptography require the user to simply know their account name and a password. Hence, the attacker will try to attack the password instead of the complete authentication system. The most common form of attack is a dictionary attack. In a dictionary attack, the attacker attempts to log in repeatedly to the same account using a large number of passwords. Fortunately, Win2K provides system administrators with tools to combat this form of attack.

Accounts can be locked out if too many unsuccessful attempts to log in occur. Password policies can be implemented and enforced using either simple rules or sophisticated filters. These options are discussed in more detail in Chapters 10 and 11.

In addition to basic username/password authentication, Win2K provides support for other technologies. These are also further discussed in Chapter 11, but you should be aware that Win2K does include support for Digital Certificates and smartcards.

Many vendors are providing a number of alternative methods for authenticating users, including such things as

▼ Dial-back systems

■ Remote Authentication Dial-In User Service (RADIUS)

■ Global Positioning Systems

■ Token devices

▲ Biometric devices

Making Strong Reusable Passwords

Although the use of two-factor authentication methods are very attractive to people concerned about security, the reality is that these devices are not widely deployed and add cost to a system. It is expected that the majority of logons will continue to use passwords at some point during the process for many years to come. Although fewer protocols will expose the password to eavesdroppers on the network, you still need to be concerned about the possible attacks that exist. These include

▼ An insecure host that has a keyboard monitor

■ Configuring the machine not to require the CTRL-ALT-DEL key sequence before logging into a Win2K system

- Someone watching you type in the password
- Programs or Web pages that prompt the user to enter their password
- Using applications that perform clear text authentication (FTP, Telnet, and so on)
- ▲ The use of NTLMv1 in mixed-mode domains without the user's knowledge

Obviously, anyone who obtains a password for an account can access a computer system with all the rights and privileges of that account. It can be especially disastrous if someone obtains the password for the Administrator account. Two-way authentication schemes that use cards and passwords are recommended for maintaining secure environments. Win2K also provides logon policies and auditing help in securing the passwords as well. Chapters 10 and 11 cover logon authentication and managing user accounts and passwords in more detail.

PASSWORD QUALITY One important principle when using reusable passwords is to make them hard to guess. This means that they should not be made up of easy-to-guess word combinations but a mixture of characters, numbers, and special symbols. A password such as "Qp&yTxT8e3" has adequate complexity, in that it is extremely difficult to guess or even crack, but there is one major problem: it is also easy to forget. A potentially more effective method is to create a phrase and use the first letter of each word as the password. For example, the password "Mbiot4oJ" is derived from "My birthday is on the 4th of July." You can use Win2K account policies (detailed in Chapter 10) to require a definable password quality when setting, resetting, or changing a user's password. Chapter 11 also discusses password quality and some options that Win2K provides.

Change the password often, and don't use the same password that you use to access any other secure system, such as your bank machine. (By the way, don't use the passwords detailed here; now that they've been published someone might add them to the dictionary of a password-cracking program.)

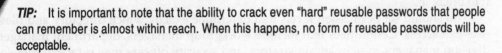

TIP: It is important to note that the ability to crack even "hard" reusable passwords that people can remember is almost within reach. When this happens, no form of reusable passwords will be acceptable.

Protection of Authentication Data

As stated earlier, reusable passwords make up a large percentage of all authentications. As described earlier, this data is easily sniffed from the network, and thus must be protected (that is, encrypted). You can accomplish this in one of two ways: Encrypt the password, or send something that proves you know the password but is not the password. The digest authentication in IIS is an example of encrypting the password data using a function that is theoretically impossible to reverse (that is, crack). Kerberos is an example of the second method. Kerberos is the default network-based authentication protocol in Win2K and is detailed in Chapter 11.

Both of these options prevent a sniffer from easily grabbing the password, but any technique that sends the password on the Internet, in any form, is subject to a

To Write or Not to Write?

We are going out on a limb here to go against almost every good security book you have ever read. Most security experts will say "Never write a password down!" Well, sometimes it is *better* to write it down than forget it, because the threat is electronic and the risk is acceptable. It all has to do with where the threat lies and the risk in doing so. If you have evaluated the threat, and believe it only to be from external sources, that is, not someone with physical access, then it is perfectly acceptable to write down a strong password like "Qp&yTxT8e3." But remember, most threats are from inside, and there are very few sites that you cannot get access to physically if you try hard enough. Do you hire janitors?

password-guessing attack. The second method is usually the safer method, but both rely on the protocol and algorithm for their strength. Sniffer countermeasures are covered later in this chapter.

There are a number of security protocols that can provide secure connections between servers and clients. For example, you can use security protocols such as SSL (Secure Sockets Layer) and S-HTTP (Secure Hypertext Transfer Protocol) to strengthen the security of client-server Web connections. SSL can be used with any networking protocol, while S-HTTP is designed for HTTP use only. You should use these protocols when you are authenticating to specific services as well.

Access Controls on Authentication Files

Another way to prevent authentication compromise is by preventing attackers from having free access to your files that contain authentication information. This may seem simplistic, but it happens all too often. Many authentication compromises began by an attacker having the ability to get a password file or a portion of the accounts database as a "guest" or "anonymous" account. Once hackers have the information, then they can use it to break in.

You should set permission levels that determine exactly which directory and files a user can access. Committees that include workgroup managers, department managers, division managers, system administrators, and security officers may establish these access controls. Once the control policies are set, network administrators who grant access to individual user accounts or to groups of user accounts put them into place. While access controls may restrict the activities of users, they also help protect a user's personal files from the prying eyes of other users.

Default Configuration Countermeasures

I remember a conversation that I once had with one of my favorite engineers. It went something like this:

"I visited my son this weekend. I can't believe how foolish he is. I rode with him in his car and let him drive. He drove over a hundred miles an hour."

"But Bruce, you drive the same way."

"But he doesn't set up his own suspension. He just drives it as it came from the dealer."

If you are using a computer for business and it is connected to a network, you probably don't want to be using the default configuration supplied by the vendor. Default configurations are there to show off some functionality and to let the customer initially start up the system without any hassles. Historically, a large number of compromises have occurred because a customer was running the default configuration and had not performed any steps to provide additional security.

The default configuration of Win2K is more secure than the default configuration for WinNT but it is unlikely to meet your needs. Systems you place on the network need to accomplish a specific function or set of functions for you; there should never be a need for the out-of-the-box configurations. Given that it is easy to fix, there is no excuse for being vulnerable in this area. Here are a few straightforward things that can be done to eliminate all of these exposures.

▼ *Always validate and tighten default security settings.*   Don't just use default settings. If you need some of the default configuration, then take time to validate what is there, and remove the portions that you don't need. If what you need is known to be a target for attack (for example, RDS/MDAC on IIS), then set up an Intrusion Detection system (described later) to watch for attacks of that nature.

■ *Use proper configuration management and testing when installing systems and applications.*   This is pretty self-explanatory, but you should have a configuration management system that ensures a machine is "as tight as possible or desired" before it is placed on the network. Once you have a process in place, then the chances of a rogue machine appearing that is not properly configured is significantly reduced.

▲ *Perform "spot" checks to see how the process is working.*   There should be periodic testing to ensure the configuration that is being applied is adequate, and that the systems are secured from new attacks. See the section on defensive penetration analysis later in this chapter.

Improper Input Validation Countermeasures

This is another "it should never happen" category because the fix is simple (at least theoretically): Validate the input! While it seems simple, the reality is that it takes time to do that, and companies are trying to crank code out as fast as possible—thus we have the problem. This is really a developer/programmer issue, and cannot be fixed (on a large scale) anywhere else. Although it is a big problem, there are some steps that you can take:

▼ *Validate the input.* This means that for *any and all* input you get, you don't assume it's correct—you validate it. For example, if you expect that a FORM variable in your Web page will contain a hidden value that you put in, then validate that it is *that* value and not something the user changed.

■ *Use system and API functions that will do bounds checking on variables.* Buffer overflows are the result of strings that overflow variables. When you write code or do security review of code, ensure that the developers are checking the length of the variables they are passing to API/system calls. For example, use vsnprintf versus sprintf, because the former allows a length argument and the latter does not.

■ *Use architectures that only allow minimal variable manipulation by the client.* This goes with the preceding recommendation, in that you want to control as much of the variable format as possible. The less you can give a client to manipulate, the better chances you have to secure it. Something like a Web-based SQL query would be a good example. You would probably want the statement created on the Web server from variables passed in by the client (and validated by the server), instead of having the client pass the whole SQL statement in as a variable.

▲ *Install system patches and hotfixes.* It is very important to patch systems as soon as possible. The chances of your being attacked with an exploit that there is a patch for is high. This topic is revisited in Chapters 9 and 17.

Trusted Systems Countermeasures

Remember that "trusted systems" are traditionally talking about using IP-based trust (that is, granting trust based on IP address or DNS name). The best thing to do to protect against trusted systems is to not trust them. If this is not an option, then there are a few things that can be done to reduce the risk, although at this stage in the game you can't completely prevent it.

▼ *Secure your DNS structure.* Since a majority of trust will use information from the DNS structure, you need to ensure that the DNS information your systems are getting is valid. You can accomplish this in a couple of ways. One way is using a "closed loop" DNS structure for your trusted machines, in which the information they get is not subject to external input. Along with that, or completely separate, is using a secure mechanism to update the DNS server information. Chapter 8 deals with securing DNS in a Win2K environment.

■ *Use router filters to prevent IP spoofing.* Packets that leave your network should have source IP addresses of a system on your internal network and destination addresses somewhere else (since it is going from you to them). Conversely, packets entering your network should have source addresses from somewhere else and destination addresses on your network (since this packet is coming from them to you).

▲   *Use strong host-based authentication with IPSec when possible.* IPSec uses strong cryptographic protocols to do the authentication versus relying on IP addresses. Unfortunately this is not widely deployed or available today. But this service is very applicable to homogeneous Win2K environments. This is covered in more detail in Chapter 16.

Sniffing Countermeasures

Cable and wireless forms of data transmission are subject to monitoring by people with network sniffers or receiving devices. You can protect internal network cables from tampering by posting guards and securing the wiring closets as appropriate. Check the credentials and closely monitor the activities of all computer service technicians, telephone repair technicians, and other service personnel, including air-conditioning and heating technicians.

If you have long runs of outside cable between sites, consider using fiber-optic cable, which does not emanate a signal outside the cable and cannot be monitored with devices that read cable signals (like the way your radio receiver reads radio signals). In addition, it is relatively easy to detect taps into the cable with optical-cable analysis equipment.

Data encryption is your best bet to preventing eavesdroppers from easily viewing any transmitted data. There are a number of bridging and routing devices for building long-distance networks between your corporate site, branch offices, and other facilities. Encryption is available with some devices. Each packet is encrypted and put into a new packet with a new header for transmission over the lines. The only information that eavesdroppers can glean from these packets is the addresses of the sending and receiving devices.

NOTE: Virtual Private Networks are covered further in Chapter 16.

Denial of Service (DoS) Countermeasures

As described in Chapter 2, there are three types of DoS attacks: feature, configuration, and programming problems. It is very hard to protect against a feature-based DoS, because they are just that—"features." You can put measures in place to limit the effect of a feature driven DoS, such as timers and limits, but if the protocol allows certain functionality, then it can be exploited to some extent. To really make a change, you have to change the protocol or feature. For the configuration-based DoS, the fix is simple: Understand what functionality your systems have, and use only that which you need and understand. If you don't understand what a feature is for, then don't implement it until you do. The best way to defend against a programming flaw is to not run the program. Barring that, defend against a programming flaw-based DoS by patching the systems (preferably) or by using a firewall to block the packets that form the attack.

A word about the distributed DoS (DDoS) is in order. This is not some new DoS, but a different method of performing a DoS. The countermeasures are the same as previously described, because the attacks are the same.

Worms, Virus, and Trojan Horse Countermeasures

The previous chapter defined worms, viruses, and Trojan Horses as well as discussed how they are spread. You will need to determine which countermeasures are appropriate for your computers and users.

The most popular form of defense is a virus-checking program that runs on each and every one of your computers. These have been around for a long time. You may have noticed that their existence hasn't stopped the proliferation of these attacks. The problem is there are always new programs that the virus-checking software needs to be aware of. This means that users need to install updates to the virus-checking software or updates to the data files used by the software. Unfortunately most users consider this a low priority and not a valuable use of their time.

In response to this, many of the companies that have developed these programs have incorporated features that make updating them easier, for example, using a network connection to perform a regularly scheduled update to the software. This has helped, but it is not a universal panacea. Your firewall will need to be properly configured to allow this. Your users will have to leave their computers turned on and connected. And you must account for the fact that some of your users may inadvertently disable the update feature. Finally, this model doesn't work very well for people who travel frequently or use a laptop that is only intermittently connected to the network.

Some companies use virus-checking software that resides on a central file or application server. The idea is that all files on the server will be checked, usually before they can be spread to other systems. It is also assumed that these machines are always running and always connected, so the software can always be updated when a new version becomes available. One of the assumptions built into this model is that the server system administrators consider the maintenance of the virus-checking software part of their job functionality and not a waste of their time; unfortunately, for servers run by individual departments within an organization this is not always a valid assumption.

Larger organizations that consider the presence of a worm, virus, or Trojan Horse to be a significant financial risk are trying to apply their countermeasures at the border. They have created systems that check e-mail attachments before they are ever delivered to an end user. They are also using systems that examine the content on their Web caches and proxy servers to ensure that any active content delivered to their internal users is not harmful. Sites that are using such systems usually have a team dedicated to the maintenance of the virus defense system.

You should be aware that countermeasures may fail. In the event of a successful attack, you are probably going to need to restore uninfected versions of your operating system, application programs, and data files. Chapter 20 talks more about redundant systems including backup strategies.

It is also important to know that a virus is often hard to detect. It may lie dormant on your system for some period of time before it executes. You can monitor your system for telltale signs of virus activity, such as increased file sizes, changes in file timestamps, unusual disk activity, or an abrupt decrease in disk space. The auditing capabilities of Win2K are discussed in Chapter 13.

Physical Access Countermeasures

You need to have appropriate physical security measures to protect your systems and data from theft, corruption, and natural disasters. To some extent the function of a particular machine helps to dictate what type of physical security is appropriate. Most people would agree that it is probably more important to ensure the physical security of a robot that manages all of your tape backups than a machine that sits on the desk of your receptionist.

Security guards, key-card access systems, and surveillance equipment may be critical if you share facilities or if your information is extremely sensitive. In other cases, there may be existing policies or regulations prohibiting the use of surveillance equipment.

Thieves who steal a computer or a hard disk from a computer can take their time cracking encrypted files at their own site. The obvious way to prevent theft is to lock down systems. You can put a locked protective cover over a computer case, place computers in a sealed office, or use the locks that are installed in most desktop computers.

Some other points related to physical security are outlined here and relate to both desktop computers and servers:

▼ If you configure a computer's startup settings in CMOS memory to ask for passwords or set special system configurations, lock the cover so no one can erase the CMOS by removing the battery.

■ Enable boot passwords and other security features on desktop PCs.

■ Disable or remove floppy drives to prevent files from being copied to disk and to prevent users from uploading files that might contain viruses.

■ If users must have access to a floppy drive, set the CMOS so the system always boots from drive C. This prevents intruders from starting a system with their own operating system disk.

▲ Secure your network equipment and cable to prevent wire taps. Always monitor the activities of service personnel. Don't trust anyone who wants access to this equipment.

Record all serial numbers on systems and mark them to indicate your company's ownership. If systems are stolen and recovered, these records and markings can be used as evidence, improving your chances of getting your systems back after the case is closed.

In addition, a thief might sell your system to a "good citizen," who may in turn report the equipment as possibly stolen.

Social Engineering Countermeasures

Social engineering is a very tough thing to defend against, because it has the most variable and misunderstood factor: people. It is very hard to determine how different people will react to different situations. One simple rule to keep in mind is that simple clear policies and procedures are easier to remember and therefore more likely to be followed. Again, you must think about what is appropriate for your organization. A policy that may be appropriate for a small company of 20 people that occupy a single building may not work well for a multinational company. It may not even work well for a company of 20 people that are spread over a large geographic area and travel constantly. There are a few things that can be done to attempt to mitigate the people factor:

▼ **Policies and procedures**   It is important that people have policies that state what is and is not acceptable. For example, you should have a policy that users never deal with password-related issues over the phone, no matter who they are talking to. Of course, this doesn't scale well in many organizations. You may want to create a system that allows people to have their password reset over the phone. But this means that you probably want to maintain some sort of shared secrets, such as a date of birth, mother's maiden name, and employee ID number. On the other hand, do you want to maintain that specific data? What happens if your database is compromised? Do you become liable if a thief then uses that data to impersonate an employee when talking to a credit card company?

■ **Practices and procedures**   You need procedures and practices for things that are likely to be targeted by attackers. Let's continue the preceding example and say that the person on the other line was a user who forgot his or her password and needed it changed. You would then have a practice or procedure that would be followed to accomplish that. This ensures that things are handled in the most secure and consistent manner.

▲ **Training**   User education on security matters is a must. If you do not train them on these issues, and make them aware that it happens, the chances of an attacker successfully gaining critical information via social means is high.

Have good policies, procedures, and practices (the three Ps). One such practice is that users should always log off of a computer when leaving a system. A password-protected screen saver can be used to lock out the keyboard and screen and to protect programs that run while the user is away. These screen savers can also be set to engage if there is no keyboard activity for a period of time. It's a good idea to set these options just in case a user of a system walks away from the system unexpectedly without logging off. Chapter 4 goes into many of these concepts in more detail.

Natural Threats

Power surges, failing components, and other problems may bring down systems and cost your organization thousands or millions of dollars in downtime. In some cases, continuous access to information is critical to the operation of the entire business. In any of these situations, communication lines that are essential to the operation of your company may be cut You need to establish alternate lines or backup methods to keep systems online in emergencies. These techniques are discussed in Chapter 20.

GENERAL SECURITY CONTROLS

There are a group of items which fit into a general category insofar as countermeasures go. For the most part, they could even be classified as "prudent" from a purely operational standpoint, but they do have value from a security standpoint so we'll discuss them here.

Firewalls

The words "secure" and "Internet" are rarely used together. The Internet used to be like a small town where everybody knew their neighbors and few people even bothered to lock their front doors. Today the Internet is more like a busy metropolitan center; you might not know your next door neighbors and everybody locks their doors. Firewalls are a lot like the locks on a door. They keep a lot of people out but they're unlikely to withstand a determined attack. An insurance company is unlikely to want to do business with a company that doesn't even have a lock on its front door. It's unclear what the legal implications are for a business that doesn't install a firewall. A *firewall* is a system that puts up a defensive wall to keep intruders out of your internal network when properly managed. A firewall is often called a *choke point* because it restricts traffic flow to a well-defined, easily monitored channel. At the firewall, you can implement various filters and services to allow and deny packets, and you can monitor traffic to look for intruders. In order to have an effective firewall someone has to decide how the filters should behave, what services should be allowed, and what should be denied. Firewalls are covered in detail in Chapter 14.

Access Controls

Access controls are the restraints that prevent authorized users and attackers from having free access to your information systems and data. As discussed briefly in the authentication section, this is an important step, as the attacker does not always have a highly privileged account.

Protecting Directories and Files

Security for directories and file systems is your best tool for controlling post-logon access to a system. With it, you can control access on a granular level to directories and files, and put up restrictions that prevent intruders from gaining access to various systems and data areas. You can grant some users the ability to only read files while allowing others to both read and change files. You can also grant access to entire directories or just to specific files within directories. The NTFS file system in Win2K is required to achieve this level of security. You can choose this disk-format option during setup, or upgrade an existing FAT drive at any time. See Chapter 12 for details on file systems and resource sharing.

Another safety measure is to keep files that are available to the public on a disk or disk partition that is separate from your operating system, application, or personal files. The public directories and the files in them should be marked as Read-Only so the files can't be changed or corrupted. If Internet users need to put files or other information on your server, create a "drop box" directory that has Write-Only permissions. This action allows users to put files in the directory but not to view, change, or execute any files in the directory. Be sure to check these files for virus contamination before using them.

Fault Tolerance and Redundant Systems

Fault-tolerant systems are designed to withstand hardware failures and software errors. A fault-tolerant feature called *disk mirroring* writes data to two disks at the same time. If one disk in the pair fails, the other remains accessible to users. Win2K supports disk mirroring options as well as RAID (redundant arrays of inexpensive disks) systems.

For some companies, it is not unreasonable to create redundant data centers located far from any disaster that might destroy the primary data center. The military uses this strategy. You can build a complete secondary site or a scaled-down site that can be brought into service at a moment's notice. At this site, you can also store backups that can be restored quickly.

Win2K also supports *uninterruptible power supplies* (UPSs). A UPS can provide battery power to a server in the event of a power failure. The UPS automatically begins supplying power as soon as normal power is lost. While Win2K is running on battery power, it automatically begins an orderly shutdown procedure that closes files and writes information to disk should the battery power run out as well. More details about the fault tolerance features of Win2K are described in Chapter 20.

Backups

Backups are essential. You already know that. If your systems are stolen, destroyed by fire, or corrupted by hackers, you'll need to go back to the last uncorrupted backup. The procedures you use to restore backups are especially critical in the case of virus attacks. Your backups may be corrupted, in which case you'll need to go back in the archive until you find a non-corrupted backup set. Back up as frequently as possible and place backup media into permanent archives as often as possible. Virus contamination can destroy a whole series of backups, and you may need to go into permanent archives for the last good set of data.

A user who backs up files must have Read privileges in the directories that require backup and Write privileges to restore files. You must give these rights to trustworthy people because they could use them for unauthorized activities. Anyone restoring files must be knowledgeable about virus-contamination issues to prevent viruses from being written to disk. In the Win2K environment, a backup operator with special rights is charged with handling backup and restoring operations.

If you need to rebuild systems from backup, carefully scan the backups to detect viruses. Start with the most recent set of backups and remove any viruses found, if possible. Otherwise, go back through the archives until you find an uncontaminated set. If you do need to rebuild a system, back up the most recent data files only. Executable files may contain unknown viruses. You can restore program files from your original program disks, assuming they are uncontaminated.

Securing Remote Connections and Mobile Users

As an increasing number of companies move from a local economy to full participation in the global economy, distributed computing and the security concerns it entails play an ever increasing role. A recurring theme is that companies want their employees to be fully functional from their homes, branch offices, customer's sites, or hotel rooms. However, remote and mobile systems present many challenges when considering the security implications. Can the remote host be trusted? Is there a network sniffer in the communication path? Is there a man in the middle? It's also important to remember that remote and mobile systems are subject to theft or to intruders who manage to access your enterprise network through the accounts of authorized users at remote sites. You can't be sure who is on the other end of a remote connection.

Lax security at remote sites gives intruders a chance to break in and plant bugs, viruses, and monitoring devices on computers. There is little choice but to tighten up security policies and practices. Much of the information in this book is applicable to effectively securing your computers when they are accessed from remote systems or mobile users.

Once you've improved the security on the side of the remote user also consider changing some of your current business processes. For example, your sales staff needs access to price sheets and inventory reports, but do they really need direct access to the database to obtain this information? A multitier system that makes the information available via a Web server might be just as effective. The Microsoft Internet Information Server (included with Win2K) supports strong authentication over network connections. This means that you could limit this information to just the individual to whom you wish to grant access.

Creating this type of system limits what a remote user, or an attacker, can do, but it can still provide the functionality that the employees need. See Chapter 19 for more details about using IIS securely.

Some other ideas include

▼ Requiring your staff use hard-to-guess passwords, or using hardware assisted authentication such as smartcards.

■ Enabling passwords on laptops to prevent thieves from easily accessing information on the systems. You enable passwords by setting options in the setup program for the system.

▲ Requiring that all remote users encrypt sensitive information stored on their portable computers. Then if the system is stolen, all but the most determined hackers will be unable to view the information. Win2K comes with the Encrypting File System (EFS) to accomplish this. See Chapter 12 for more information.

AUDITING SYSTEMS

Accounting and auditing systems are designed to track the activities of users. When an auditing system is enabled, processes and activities are logged to files for later review. Users who access the system leave a trail that auditing administrators can follow to determine if the user is engaged in unauthorized activity.

Auditing a system tends to reduce that system's performance. Each event is written to disk, which can fill quickly with auditing information. In addition, sorting through auditing logs can be a chore. The Win2K auditing system lets you audit specific events to help keep the auditing load minimized. For example, you can audit only the systems that are most vulnerable to hackers or only those that unauthorized employees might attempt to access. You should always audit failed logon attempts, attempts to access sensitive data, and changes to security settings. Monitor the audit logs on a regular basis to locate intrusions.

If you know that your system is under attack, you should enable appropriate auditing options to monitor the attacker. Keep in mind that an attacker who has gained access to administrative accounts may be able to change the audit logs and hide his activities. You'll need to monitor your system in real time if you suspect this type of activity. Be careful in this case. If a hacker knows he has been detected, he may lock you out or destroy information on the system before you manage to lock him out.

It's a good idea to select an auditor who can watch over the audit and system logs and maintain a somewhat neutral position with regard to your other system administrators. In addition to managing the auditing system, an auditor might also use various security diagnostics tools to evaluate the security settings of systems on your network and make necessary corrections.

The auditing system can also be used to detect virus outbreaks. You can monitor unexpected attempts to access executable files (.EXE) and program libraries (.DLL), or attempts to modify these files or create new executable files. However, auditing these events may generate a lot of information, so do this only when actively monitoring a system. You'll find more information about auditing in Chapter 13.

INTRUSION DETECTION SYSTEMS (IDS)

The timely detection of security problems is an issue of significant concern. You cannot rely on your security controls to safeguard a computer system against all threats. System vulnerabilities cannot be totally eliminated in most circumstances, and thus detection of security incidents play an important role in computer security. Most ID systems use some part of the auditing functionality described previously and in Chapter 13. You should become very familiar with the auditing capabilities of Win2K as well as *if* and *how* your ID system uses them.

Intrusion Detection (ID) systems are not a new concept; however, it is only recently that the topic has gotten a lot of attention. The products and the market for them is changing rapidly. Much like firewalls a few years ago, the ID systems of today are rather primitive and not terribly robust. There is much research and development currently happening in this area though, and you should expect significant functional improvements over the next few years. Win2K does not include an IDS, but its auditing capabilities provide a valuable hook for third-party tools to build on top of.

What We "Know"

It's hard to do "forensics" if there isn't a trail. We also know that it is practically impossible to re-create the trail if we need to find out what has happened. This means that we need to proactively create trails as the events are occurring. This can make all the difference. You need to know what you want to log, then for that data, you want to watch in many ways and LOG, LOG, LOG. Traditionally, security officers reviewed audit logs to detect suspicious activity or break-in attempts. Maybe it's more accurate to say that traditionally security officers collected audit logs and occasionally had the resources to review them for suspicious activity. Unfortunately, much of the logged data was (and is) irrelevant to intrusion detection or security-related events. The volume of information can often overwhelm our resources to evaluate. We need a way to separate the wheat from the chaff; this is where we can use computers to help computers. Computers can review audit trails to identify and record security-relevant activity. This allows the IDS to provide a focused view of the data that a human can feasibly review.

Needless to say, a fully functional IDS is not needed by everybody, but many companies do need some form of IDS. Appendix C has more details on the specifics of ID systems.

Detecting and Dealing with Attacks

Before you ever notice suspicious activity on your systems or your audit logs show signs of attackers, you should know how you are going to respond. Are you going to take immediate action to block these activities? Or are you going to secretly monitor their activities and attempt to find out who they are and what they are doing?

The first option is dangerous because the hacker may take some immediate action if he knows he has been discovered, such as taking whatever information he needs before you are able to deny him access. For all you know the attacker may have additional points of entry into your systems. The second option is dangerous because you allow him to continue breaking into your system, but that might be essential if you are interested in apprehending him.

While monitoring the hacker, keep your activities hidden. If the hacker finds out that he has been discovered, he may access your system through other unknown routes to lose you. He may also damage some part of the system or steal information in a last-ditch effort. You may prefer just to cover up the holes in your security and block out the intruder as soon as possible.

In addition to the auditing system, backups can provide a sort of "log" that helps you locate files that the hacker may have altered or changed. For example, you can check file sizes and dates; if they have been changed, try to determine unauthorized access.

If you suspect that the hacker is an inside operator, use the audit logs to determine which system is perpetrating the attacks, then set up hidden cameras or equipment to monitor keystrokes and catch the hacker red-handed, so to speak. To track a hacker outside your organization, get the help of local and/or long-distance telephone carriers, Internet service providers (ISPs), local police, and possibly the FBI. Keep in mind that computer-related crimes are still misunderstood by the law-enforcement community. Officials in most areas are not familiar with techniques for investigating these crimes and may not have the proper equipment or staff to do so. They may also have little experience in prosecuting a hacker they apprehend.

DEFENSIVE PENETRATION ANALYSIS

Defensive penetration analysis is a process by which you systematically attempt to compromise one or more of the security countermeasures that you have in place. This allows

---

Counterattack!

"And if you wrong us shall we not revenge?"

—William Shakespeare

To some people, revenge is a viable option. (Whatever makes you feel better.) If your system is under attack and you know the attackers, why not attack their system? Cyberwarfare! Some have even proposed that such attacks are justified. Some hackers think themselves so smart that they fail to put up defenses of their own. In that case, you might be able to knock out the hacker's ability to attack your system, at least for a while.

In reality, counterattacks are probably not a good idea. First, your attacker might not be causing any real harm but might attempt to damage your system if you counterattack. Second, the attacker might be doing a good job of masquerading as someone else and lead you to launch your counterattack against an innocent third party. Third, your attacker might be able to hide all of his activities on your system but record yours, then press charges claiming that you are the attacker. You'd better know what you're doing before you annoy an attacker!

you to test your site the way others would and helps you keep current with the "latest" attacks. It also helps you think like the "bad guys," so you can potentially guess their next step and prevent it. It points you to potential vulnerabilities that you may have overlooked at some other point. It can be used as a spot-check to see if systems are being set up in accordance with your configuration management plan and can provide an "action item" list for you to act on to better secure existing systems.

The Hows of Penetration Analysis

There are really two different levels of penetration analysis: shallow (tools only) and in-depth (human element). The shallow level just uses automated scanning tools. The tools are legitimate programs that were designed to help network administrators find security holes and other problems in their networks. These can be commercial or public domain, but if you decide to use public domain, make sure you can review the source code; otherwise, you may be installing backdoors on your systems.

The in-depth analysis uses not only tools, but also a highly skilled professional. This person, or more likely a company, should have a solid background in security architecture and implementation, as well as an understanding that security is a business enabler, not vice versa. The reason they should know how to build it, and not just break into it, is that they will need to make recommendations on how to fix it. This, by definition, means not just a simple patch, but further recommendations as to changes in architecture or process.

RECAP

This chapter has been a brief foray into the world of threat prevention and countermeasures. Although we have covered the majority of things that should be done, complete coverage is another book in and of itself. You can gain great strides in your security if you start to look at security and countermeasures as part of the overall design and the ongoing maintenance as a cost that must be borne. Here is a summary list of the countermeasures we have discussed:

- ▼ Policies, procedures, and practices
- ■ System patches
- ■ Defensive configuration
- ■ Routers and hardening hosts
- ■ Security-aware programming
- ■ Encryption/authentication
- ■ Architecture and design
- ■ Firewalls

- Switched networks
- Intrusion Detection systems
- ▲ Integrity checkers

One of the most important things to do is to stay up to date on the trends in the security field. The best bet is to have at least one person on staff dedicated to making sure that you are aware of all the options, and what is coming down the road.

"Go to the ant, you sluggard; consider its ways and be wise!"

—Proverbs 6:6

CHAPTER 4

Security Policies
and Management

"If you fail to plan, you plan to fail"

—Unknown

First, let's start with what this chapter is not about. It's not about Group Policies, the Microsoft Management Console, or any other technical implementation. It is about policies and managing them in the most general sense. Despite all the counter measures you can take to protect your systems, perhaps the most practical way to provide security is through a consistent set of policies and procedures. Policies must be implemented company-wide and adhered to by everyone. You can hire a security manager or create a security committee or task force to locate security weaknesses, develop policies, and enforce the rules. Good security also depends on a well-defined hierarchy of administrators, system operators, and users as well as a policy clearly defining user access to resources. Some of the other things you need to implement as part of your security plan are discussed in this chapter.

TIP: The single best resource for policy information is the *IETF Site Security Handbook*. You are *highly* encouraged to get a copy. It goes far beyond the information covered here.

THE FOUNDATION

Before you can press on into policies and the like, you need to set a foundation around which you will develop all policies and procedures for the organization you are securing.

Security Is a Means Not an End

The first thing to remember is that policy must be born out of business requirements. It is hard for some security people to grasp (we are some of them) that being secure is not an end unto itself. If your business is secure but can't do its business, then you won't be in business for long. The same goes for no security: If you have something of value and you don't protect it, it will be gone, then you are also out of business. So both ends of the extreme are not viable. The key thought here is to "use security to *enable* business, not *disable* it."

Security Attributes

Historically, it is the case that a technology's security is evaluated in accordance with three standard attributes that the technology provides (or does not provide, as the case may be). Those three attributes are confidentiality, integrity, and availability. These are better known as CIA (not to be confused with the United States Central Intelligence Agency).

▼ **Confidentiality** is the concept that information is unavailable to those who are unauthorized to access it. It is usually associated with the authentication and authorization services of a technology.

■ **Integrity** ensures that information cannot be modified in unexpected ways. It is usually associated with the accuracy and data modification services of a technology.

▲ **Availability** prevents resources from being deleted or becoming inaccessible. It is usually associated with the reliability and timeliness services of a technology.

Although these are the big three, we will be adding another attribute for our discussion, and it will become more and more relevant as digital documents become more mainstream. The term is *non-repudiation.*

▼ **Non-repudiation** provides unforgettable evidence that a specific action occurred. It is usually associated with the origin, submission, and delivery services of a technology and is highly linked to the signing of documents and e-mail.

Together we will refer to them as CIA-NR.

Supervising by Risk

It is important to evaluate all of your security decisions in terms of risk to the company. Notice that you are not evaluating in terms of risk to the service/technology, but to the company. In order to do this you will need to know the value that the company puts on the data/service. For some things this will be easy. For example, if you are an e-commerce shop, and your servers go away, this cost is whatever business you have lost while the servers are down. Using that simplistic method, we come up with a basic formula to put a value to risk:

Risk to company = (Value of data) (Probability of exploitation)

As the probability of exploitation increases, so does the risk.

You should evaluate the risk for each security attribute for each service/technology you are planning on using. This is a *very* arduous task in the beginning, but will pay huge dividends in the long run. This should be part of the architecture design anyway. This little formula can be used with both high-level technologies (that is, authentication in general) or specific instances (that is, using reusable passwords for authentication).

VIP: Take the time to understand your risks, and architect for them. Remember that security is risk reduction not risk elimination.

What Is Your Stance?

A security stance is basically how you look at new technologies. It determines whether you will implement, then evaluate, or evaluate, then implement. As the opening quote alludes, without a plan you have planned not to have a plan. In the same manner, if you do not have an explicit stance, you will get the stance of whoever is looking at a particular technology.

You need a security stance, and there are two to choose from:

▼ **Inclusive**　That which is not expressly prohibited is allowed. This is what we refer to as the "Russian roulette" stance.

▲ **Exclusive**　That which is not expressly allowed is denied. This is what we refer to as the "only real security" stance.

Which model you choose is dependent on the goals of your business. If your business is to provide an open research environment where people are expected to try new and exciting things with your network then the inclusive model is probably your only choice. If you are a financial institution, then the exclusive model is the prudent choice.

For the most part, people who are not responsible for security or, for that matter, who do not understand it, like the *inclusive* stance because it makes their life easier. They can pick and choose the things they don't want to allow, and the things they do not understand won't break. In most cases, this model is doomed to failure because it assumes that they know and have secured all of the services that they are allowing through. This is a very large assumption!

The *exclusive* stance is really the only one that works in the long run, but it is much tougher because it takes work to maintain. You have to actually evaluate services before you just let them through. This model enforces the idea that computer security is part of everyone's responsibility.

Using Zones of Risk

When you are evaluating your risk, remember that there are different zones of risk. It would be foolish to consider the risks associated with Internet attackers the same as those coming from an internal user. This is not always the case. If you run a public library, an Internet café, or an application hosting service, your internal users may be hostile users. Within the educational market sector, system administrators frequently encounter a blurring of distinctions between internal and external users. For instance, is a student an internal or external user? The more useful distinction to make is that a zone changes where the business rules change. There are two different zones that we consider:

▼ **Inter-zone**　This deals with the risks that exist because of, or between, different levels of trust.

▲ **Intra-zone**　This deals with the risks within the same level of trust.

Some people like to refer to these as *perimeters* or *boundaries*. However you look at it, the issue of trust and risk go hand in hand, and must be evaluated together and delineated by the business rules.

Security Concepts

The last fundamental that we will look at is a set of concepts that should govern the way you look at and apply security.

▼ **Least privileged**   Give a user or process the least amount of privileges it needs to accomplish the task. You could say this is the "give them what they need and no more" philosophy.

■ **Defense in depth**   Architect security so that there is no single point of failure. This deals with applying security at the host, network, and physical layers. This is just the opposite of the "hard crunchy shell, soft chewy center" security design.

■ **Weakest link**   Remember that your security is only as strong as the weakest link. This is especially prudent when dealing with partner networks.

■ **Fail-safe stance**   If it breaks, what does it do? Does it allow or block traffic? It should fail to a safe position. For computers and security that usually means it fails shut or closed.

■ **Universal participation**   Security is not an optional component of the company. Everyone is involved, and understands their roles.

▲ **Simplicity**   The old adage "Keep it simple, stupid" (KISS) is the rule here. It is significantly easier to secure a simple structure than a complex one. If you have two solutions that will work, and one is simpler, go with the simpler one.

PLANNING FOR SECURITY

To create a security policy, first identify the problems with the existing systems and get some idea of your objectives. Look at your current systems and assess your needs:

▼ What are the current problems? Interview managers, users, technicians, and anyone else who can provide information about security problems and requirements.

■ Gather information about people, data, and resources, and how they are managed. Flow charts, personnel profiles, job descriptions, and other information should be available from personnel departments, division managers, and department managers.

■ Based on job descriptions, determine who needs to access what and grant users the lowest level of access possible for the resources they need to access.

■ What types of protection do you need? Look at your physical security requirements and the requirements of systems and software.

- Evaluate each component and grade its importance so you know which systems require the most immediate attention.

- Determine the cost of the system and work it into your budget without spending too much money on a technology so difficult to use that users circumvent it.

▲ Consider your liabilities. If private information about employees or customers gets into public hands, you or your organization may end up in court. The United States has 6 percent of the world's population and 70 percent of its lawyers.

Each one of these areas may require the attention of a separate person on your security management team, or the attention of department, workgroup, or division managers, depending on the size of your organization. Specific items to develop in your security policy and plans include

▼ Physical protection measures to prevent theft and guard against natural disasters

- Security measures for desktop systems that prevent theft of equipment or data

- Password policies that specify long, hard-to-guess (but easy-to-remember) passwords or coding schemes that create hard-to-guess passwords from phrases and other information

- Security for local area network and wide area network communication to prevent line monitoring or transmissions by unauthorized areas

- Virus and Trojan Horse controls for the entire network

- Internet security such as firewalls, Web server access, and secure business transactions

- Electronic mail and business-transaction safeguards, including the use of digital signatures to validate messages

- Encryption techniques to protect stored files, backups, electronic mail, and data transmissions across private or public networks

- Encryption techniques to protect proprietary information on laptops and other portable computers

- Management structures that define administrators, local managers, users, information security officers (ISOs), and information security auditors (ISAs)

- Active monitoring to detect break-ins, hacker activities, or unauthorized access to resources by employees

- Data protection plans that define backup procedures, off-site storage, and data recovery methods

- Methods for securely distributing programs and information throughout the organization

- ■ Intrusion detection/reporting and lockout policies that protect the company and its officers from accusations of cover-ups, misappropriations, and theft

- ▲ Employee training programs designed to reduce security exposures and to define your security policies for legal purposes

The controls you put in place should be consistent throughout the organization and enforced equally in all areas. A breakdown in one area will create security holes that may put the rest of the system in jeopardy.

Your objective is to discover and define all the threats that may exist for your organization. Constantly re-evaluate your systems and your operating procedures to find new holes or problems that could lead to security exposure. If you have formed a security committee or security team, schedule regular meetings where everyone can discuss issues.

Implement the plan at an appropriate speed. You'll need to make a smooth transition to a security system that implements many new controls. Implement the plan in stages, tightening controls further at each stage.

Getting Help

There are a number of organizations that will help you build security into your information systems, and of course, there are appropriate responses for dealing with hacker attacks. *Computer Emergency Response Team* (*CERT*) is a group that watches over security threats on the Internet. It provides advisories, security tips, and information about recovering from and preventing intrusions. You can contact CERT at **www.cert.org**.

Another organization that can provide you with information about security is the Computer Security Institute (CSI). CSI is an international organization that trains security professionals and provides a wide variety of information to members and nonmembers. It publishes several newsletters and holds conferences and exhibitions. You can connect with CSI's Web page at **www.gocsi.com**.

The Information Systems Security Association (ISSA) is an international organization of information security professionals that provides educational materials, publications, and general knowledge about security issues. ISSA's goal is to promote management practices that ensure the availability, integrity, and confidentiality of resources on computers and networks. ISSA's Web site is at **www.uhsa.uh.edu/issa/**.

The National Computer Security Association provides information and material about security in general and can be contacted at **www.ncsa.com**.

INFORMATION MANAGEMENT AND CONTROL ISSUES

Your organization no doubt owns the information it generates, but who controls this information and access rights to it? Where do you store information? Who handles backups and archives? Usually, individual departments, workgroups, or divisions claim ownership and control over the information they create. That makes it difficult to implement company-wide security plans and procedures. You need to work closely with these groups, but getting too many people involved can be chaotic. Upper-level management may need to dictate a centralized security plan to meet the information protection needs of the company. Information owners need to be made aware of their role and responsibilities in regards to information protection.

In client-server environments, these issues get complicated. Users have powerful desktop computers generating information that is stored on local drives. Can you keep this information secure from hackers, theft, or corruption? Managing information that is spread out all over the network can be a nightmare, but centralizing the data on servers at a data center may be a monumental task that creates other requirements, such as the need to protect against local disasters or to improve network response times due to increased traffic.

There are, of course, advantages to centralized operations: servers and other equipment can be kept in very secure rooms where a trained staff can manage systems under tight supervision. Backup systems are then easier to implement, and expenses are lower in most cases.

Access Issues

How do you decide who gets access to information and at what level? This process is simplified if users are assigned to groups such as "temporary employees," "clerks," "engineers," or "department managers." Workgroups are groups of people who work together on projects but may not work in the same department. For example, a workgroup that designs a new product may consist of people from engineering, marketing, sales, and administration. A hierarchy of managers who set security policies can decide how access is assigned to these groups.

Generally, a Windows network consists of the management and user-level groups outlined here. You should create a hierarchical structure on paper that defines access for these groups:

▼ **Top-level administrator**   The person who controls the Administrator account for Win2K servers in local groups or domains.

■ **Administrators**   Managers from different departments, workgroups, or divisions who control and manage information resources for specific areas of the company.

■ **Trusted users**   Employees who have access to sensitive information.

■ **Risky users**   Employees who should have limited access to network resources. They are either temporary employees, new users, or users with limited job responsibilities.

■ **Public users**   As organizations connect to the Internet, users on the Internet may access resources on FTP servers and Web servers. These users have very limited access to information on specific servers. You may require system logon with a password so you can track who is accessing a system.

■ **Anonymous users and guests**   Public users or internal users who sign onto the network without a name or password. They use the generic anonymous or guest account to access limited resources.

▲ **Intruders**   Anyone attempting non-authorized access to any resources on a network.

Administrators

The administrator on a Win2K server or network holds an incredible amount of power. He or she controls access to all system resources and information. This is no mindless position! It's a full-time job that requires a competent person. For security reasons, you need to run a thorough background check on any person hired for the job. Some organizations may choose to establish a committee of managers who execute the highest-level administrative tasks. As mentioned in the previous chapter, each person on the committee has a piece of a password that must be entered with the other members' pieces to gain access to the system.

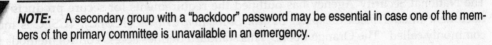

NOTE: A secondary group with a "backdoor" password may be essential in case one of the members of the primary committee is unavailable in an emergency.

The Win2K environment is organized around domains, which are hierarchical groups of computers that belong to companies, individual departments, divisions, workgroups, or other structures. Trust relationships are set up between domains so that a user in one domain can access resources in other domains. Each domain may have its own administrator who either sets policies or answers to a higher-level administrator who sets policies for the entire organization.

Large organizations will have organizational administrators who manage either various resources on the network or systems at branch offices. These administrators are not always familiar with the inner workings of the systems they manage; they may need detailed policies and procedures to help them perform more effectively. Make sure that all system managers are properly trained.

If the organization has a diversity of systems, security policies will be difficult to implement because mainframes and network servers have different security implementations. The administrative staff should include people who are familiar with the security and management requirements of each system.

Information Security Officers

An information security officer (ISO) specializes in planning, implementing, and monitoring the security policies of the organization. The ISO must have a technical background to outwit wily hackers and attackers. He or she must know about the inner workings of operating systems, network communication, monitoring equipment (sniffers), software analysis tools, and techniques for detecting problems and catching intruders. At the same time, the ISO should have a good business sense and the ability to work with the rest of the organization.

ISOs are security police who look for and track potential security problems. They must ensure uniform levels of security to prevent weak spots. The ISO also collects information from employees about security incidents and contacts by suspicious people. Simply having a security officer helps improve security because that means someone is concentrating solely on the problems of security.

Security Auditor

The security officer may also be the security auditor, but in large organizations separate auditors are used to spot suspicious activities, policy deviations, and other security problems. The auditor watches the activities of all employees, including administrators and managers. The auditor must operate in a somewhat detached way from the rest of the organization.

SECURITY STANDARDS

The National Security Agency has outlined the requirements for secure products in a document titled *Trusted Computer System Evaluation Criteria (TCSEC)*. TCSEC is more commonly called "The Orange Book." This standard defines access-control methods for computer systems that computer vendors can follow to comply with Department of Defense security standards. Secure networking is defined in the "Red Book," or "Trusted Network Interpretation." The C2 rating refers to a set of security policies that define how a secure system operates and is the most overused term in the security industry.

The security policy defined in C2 is called *Discretionary Access Control (DAC)*. It is implemented in Win2K as a system in which users own objects. Objects such as files are easy to understand, while the Clipboard and a window are a little more esoteric. Users control protections over the objects they own and are accountable for all their actions related to object access. This system differs from the NSA's B-level security, which defines classified objects and a Mandatory Access Control (MAC) system in which objects have a security level defined independently from the owner's discretion. A user who receives a file marked "secret" cannot give other users permission to view the file unless they have a "secret" clearance.

NOTE: No operating system is ever C2 certified. Certification applies only to a complete installation that includes not only the operating system, but also hardware, software, and the environment in which a system is installed.

EDUCATING USERS

Education is the key to ensuring that employees take your security plan seriously. In large organizations, it is critical that everyone in the organization comply with security policies in a consistent way.

If your users are not aware of security risks or security policies, you will end up with security breaches, accidents, lost data, or other problems. Educating users will increase your confidence that your network is secure. It helps to make users aware of the following:

▼   The security policies of your organization

- The sensitivity of personal and corporate data
- The need to keep an organization's data private
- ▲ The need to keep logon information private

After educating users, it's a good idea to have them sign a statement to verify their understanding and agreement to the policies and procedures for your network. The document can be used for legal purposes in cases where employees are caught deliberately hacking your network.

Tell users what level of access they have to resources on the network so they don't attempt to access files or devices that they don't have access to. You can also tell them how the auditing system tracks user activities!

You can educate users with training sessions, a newsletter (printed or sent over e-mail), brochures, and other techniques. You can even stage security intrusions and drills.

For more information about making people aware of the importance of security, get your hands on a copy of CSI's "Manager's Guide to Computer Security Awareness." It describes how to get a security-awareness program started and how to use various tools, such as presentations, slides, posters, pamphlets, and newsletters, to keep in touch with computer users. You can get the brochure by visiting CSI's Web page at **www.gocsi.com**.

RECOVERING FROM DISASTERS

An essential part of your security policy is recovery from disasters. Consider how much of your business relies on your information systems. Loss from downtime could cost hundreds of thousands to millions of dollars, as well as your job once the smoke clears. Do people know how to do their job manually if systems are down for extended periods of time?

Identify the most critical applications and services in your organization, then identify the hardware systems these applications require and any dependencies on other systems. Also watch for shifts in what qualifies as the most critical system in your organization.

You may need to keep backup equipment nearby or build an alternate data center, depending on your budget and the critical nature of the information. Spare equipment can become a lifesaver in a disaster. All those old PCs that your company moved out during an upgrade can be stored in a warehouse away from the main site. Set up a small network with servers in the warehouse that can be quickly expanded in case of emergency. In an emergency, your most critical business functions can be handled from this site, if necessary.

Your backups are your most important recovery tools. Test your backups and the procedures you use to restore them. Store backups as permanent archives in off-site locations. You might need to go back through several sets of archived backups if malicious users or a virus corrupted information. Keep records of changes made to system settings, user accounts, and data files. You might need to redo these changes after you restore data.

Replication servers can protect against local disasters by copying information on a real-time basis to servers at other locations. Also consider creating multiple connections between sites to protect against failed links. Ideally, those links should follow different paths and connect with different service providers.

Finally, create an emergency response team and train the members to handle problems as they occur, such as virus incidents or failed equipment. Assign a team leader who will coordinate plans and activities in preparation for disasters as well as during disaster drills and actual disasters. A rehearsal can involve the following:

▼ The immediate response once a problem is discovered. For example, if a virus is discovered on a server, you might want to abort a planned backup or disable replication of information to other servers.

■ Contacting the appropriate people to rebuild systems, re-enter critical information that was lost, or manage the restoration of sensitive information.

■ Steps for getting systems back online or moving the operations to a backup site.

■ Rebuilding systems as appropriate.

▲ Recovering backups from off-site storage and restoring them.

You get the idea. There are many steps involved in this process, and your safest approach is to develop a well-conceived plan that can be tested and proven effective in an emergency situation.

SECURITY POLICIES

A security policy is an organization's statement about how it will provide security, handle intrusions, and recover from damage caused by security breaches. It sets policies for employees and for how security is managed. Write security policies into employment contracts and include some level of "user accountability" to ensure that users comply with policies. Use auditing and other techniques to monitor policy compliance and track users who might be compromising the system. Post notices on bulletin boards and on computer logon screens that describe the policies of the organization.

Once a policy is in place, compliance is important to maintaining the same level of security throughout the organization. However, that does not mean that deviation is not allowed. In fact, the policy must be flexible enough to allow for changes in policy. But changes must be handled appropriately. Managers and users should not change policy on their own. Any changes must be authorized by management and written as an amendment to the policy.

Policies conjure up images of large unreadable documents and difficult rules that are sometimes ignored. Strive for a policy that is easy for you to implement and for users to understand and follow. In fact, the process of developing a policy is probably more important than the policy itself, because it forces you to look at all the things you must do to attain a level of security that is appropriate for your organization. You must also consider what actions you will take in the event of an intrusion or disaster before these events occur. A policy is a tool that prepares you for the worst.

Policy and Procedure Statements

This section discusses policy highlights for Win2K networks. If you need to know more about the policy-writing process, including appropriate structure and wording, refer to books on the subject, or contact organizations such as CSI (**www.gocsi.com**) and NCSA (**www.ncsa.com**).

Logon Policies and Procedures

The logon process is a potential security risk. Attackers will try to get logon credentials using any means possible. The following points should be included in logon policies and procedures:

▼   Warn users to protect their passwords and use caution when entering passwords during logon. Someone could be looking over their shoulder.

■   Implement a password policy. Change passwords frequently and avoid using passwords that are easy to guess. Never write passwords down.

■   Log off when leaving a computer, or use a password-protected screen saver.

■   To avoid accidents, managers should avoid logging on as the Administrator.

■   Do not log on to any administrative account from workstations in unfamiliar environments. Viruses could attack critical system files. Logons could be monitored with hidden cameras or other devices.

▲   Display information to users about the last time they logged on so they can detect if anyone else has been using their account.

User Accounts and Groups Policies and Procedures

Users and Groups are fundamental to the security of Win2K. Include these points in the policies and procedures for Users and Groups:

▼   Administrative users need two accounts: one with extended privileges that is only used to manage the system, the other with limited privileges to use for all other activities.

■   Rename the Administrator account with an obscure, hard-to-guess name.

■   As an option, implement a fail-safe Administrator account logon in which two or more people have a piece of the logon username and password and must be present to sign on.

■   Set logon-failure lockouts for user accounts to prevent security intrusions.

■   Disable or delete user accounts when employees leave the company.

■   All users should use an account with only the privileges necessary to perform their assigned tasks. Assign as few privileges to an account as possible.

- Disable the Guest account, or if you need to keep it, carefully review where it has privileges.

- Keep no unnecessary accounts on any system.

▲ Set up separate system-management roles for backup operators and printing-system operators.

Directory and File System Policies and Procedures

Attackers are primarily after files. The following points should be included for directories and file systems:

▼ Use NTFS (NT File System). It provides advanced security to protect files and directories from being accessed by those without explicit permission to access them.

- Make users aware of the permissions attached to files, and inform them that the permissions may be lost when files are copied.

- Do not grant mistrusted users the ability to execute programs in a directory where they can copy files.

- Never copy sensitive files to directories that do not have adequate security settings.

- Create directory structures on servers to help you protect files.

▲ If you provide information to the public, restrict access to isolated directories on isolated systems if possible.

Data-Protection Policies and Procedures

Protecting data is key to overall information security. The following points should be included in the policies and procedures for data-protection:

▼ Don't leave the backup media in the backup device where they can be stolen.

- Encrypt backups if the information is sensitive.

- Use tape-rotation methods and store permanent backups in safe off-site locations.

- Ensure the protection of backups during delivery to off-site locations.

- Document and catalog all backups to provide evidence of theft.

- Perform periodic data-recovery drills to test the integrity of backups as well as backup and restore procedures.

▲ Back up files on workstations as appropriate.

Secure Transmissions Policies and Procedures

Like protecting data on the physical disk, protecting it while in transmission is another key to information security. Include these points in the policies and procedures for secure transmissions:

▼ Take active measures to protect against eavesdroppers, wire-tapping, and hijacked sessions.

■ Physically secure all areas where cables run or terminate.

■ Monitor the activities of outside service technicians and consultants who might put a tap on an internal network.

■ Use fiber-optic cable for all cable runs that cross public areas, such as between buildings in campus settings.

■ Require encryption to transmit sensitive information and to prevent packets captured by sniffers from being replayed on your network.

▲ If you use the Internet to connect to remote sites, use link-encryption devices that automatically maintain links between sites and encrypt all transmitted information.

Remote and Mobile Users Policies and Procedures

Remote connectivity tends to be loosely administered and is often an exposure point. Include these points in your policies and procedures for remote and mobile users:

▼ Establish strict policies for anyone who travels with company information on portable computers or who connects to the company's network from a remote site.

■ Require and implement additional identification procedures for remote users, such as one-time logon devices.

■ Use difficult-to-guess logon names, passwords, and key card systems.

■ Don't let users save their passwords on disk for the next logon. A hacker who steals a computer could break the passwords and log on to a network.

■ Encrypt sensitive company files on portable computers to make it difficult, if not impossible, for hackers to view them.

■ Use callback systems in which a computer calls a remote user back at a known and trusted telephone number.

▲ Change logon names and passwords often, as well as the phone numbers that users dial into. If you use callback options, change remote phone numbers often, if possible.

Virus-Control Policies and Procedures

Viruses are prevalent, and steps must be taken to mitigate their impact. Following are the points to include in your policies and procedures:

▼ Control how software is shared to prevent the spread of viruses.

■ Control the use of public-domain software, such as shareware and freeware.

■ Run anti-virus software on systems throughout the organization and get the latest updates.

- Check files from unknown sources with anti-virus software.

- Control how disks and mobile systems move in and out of the company.

- Make users aware of virus problems through training, education programs, and regular postings on company bulletin boards or e-mail.

- Lock down computers to prevent malicious people from directly copying viruses to them.

- Keep up with the latest virus information by reading weekly computer journals or joining organizations like the National Computer Security Association (**www.ncsa.com**).

▲ Set up a quarantine computer to test disks, programs, and other possible virus-carrying media until they can be cleared as virus-free.

Electronic Mail Policies

Electronic mail is a staple in the networking world; it is important to define both technical and social restrictions for users. Include these points in your policies and procedures:

▼ Write a strong, enforceable policy that outlines appropriate uses for e-mail and penalties for abuse.

- Reserve the right to monitor e-mail.

- Implement security controls and virus protections.

- Consider the use of encryption and digital signatures.

- Ensure the physical security of the post office server.

- Promote security awareness for users.

- Establish procedures for destruction and/or retention of archives.

▲ Have users read and sign e-mail policies, as outlined in the preceding chapter.

Post and Display Legal Notices

Your policies must specify the posting of legal notices. You can post these notices on bulletin boards throughout the company and on the logon screens of users' computers. A legal message should notify users that they could be held legally responsible for any ac-

Authorized Users Only

The information on this computer and network is the property of (company) and is protected by intellectual property rights. You must be assigned an account on this computer to access information and are only allowed to access information as defined by the system administrators. Your activities may be monitored.

tivities on the computer that are outside their normal activities or that undermine the security of the information systems.

If legal notices do not exist, users may feel they can freely browse the network and access directories and files without restriction. Win2K provides a way to display a legal notice upon logon. The following is an example of a legal notice that may appear on a user's screen at logon.

Elements of a Good Policy

The components of a good security policy include the following:

▼ Computer Technology Purchasing Guidelines, which specify required, or preferred, security features. These should supplement existing purchasing policies and guidelines.

■ A Privacy Policy, which defines reasonable expectations of privacy regarding such issues as monitoring of electronic mail, logging of keystrokes, and access to users' files.

■ An Access Policy, which defines access rights and privileges to protect assets from loss or disclosure by specifying acceptable use guidelines for users, operations staff, and management.

■ An Accountability Policy, which defines the responsibilities of users, operations staff, and management. It should specify an audit capability and provide incident handling guidelines.

■ An Authentication Policy, which establishes trust through an effective password policy and by setting guidelines for remote location authentication and the use of authentication devices.

■ An Availability Statement, which sets users' expectations for the availability of resources.

■ An Information Technology System and Network Maintenance Policy, which describes how both internal and external maintenance people are allowed to handle and access technology.

■ A Violations Reporting Policy, which indicates which types of violations (such as privacy and security, internal and external) must be reported and to whom the reports are made.

■ Supporting Information, which provides users, staff, and management with contact information for each type of policy violation; guidelines on how to handle outside queries about a security incident; or information which may be considered confidential or proprietary, and so on.

▲ Any regulatory requirements that affect some aspects of your security policy (such as line monitoring). The creators of the security policy should consider seeking legal assistance in the creation of the policy. At a minimum, the policy should be reviewed by legal counsel.

NOTE: The gist of this section was taken from the *Site Security Handbook* (IETF RFC 2196, September 1997, Editor B. Fraser, **http://www.ietf.org/rfc/rfc2196.txt?number=2196**).

AN ALTERNATIVE WAY OF DOING THINGS: THE SECURITY LIFECYCLE

What we have discussed up to now is a pretty standard method for developing policy. This next bit is a slightly different method, and may be useful in some situations.

The first thing to understand is that security is not a single task, it is a process, or what we will call a *lifecycle*. You don't just say, "I've secured it, so now it's done and I can move on." You need to look at the process of securing your resources as a lifecycle, which contains multiple components: business requirements; architecture design; risk analysis/security assessment; policy development; security procedures (plan); testing and implementation; and auditing, maintenance, and support. In general, those steps can be represented in the "Security Lifecycle" flow diagram illustrated here:

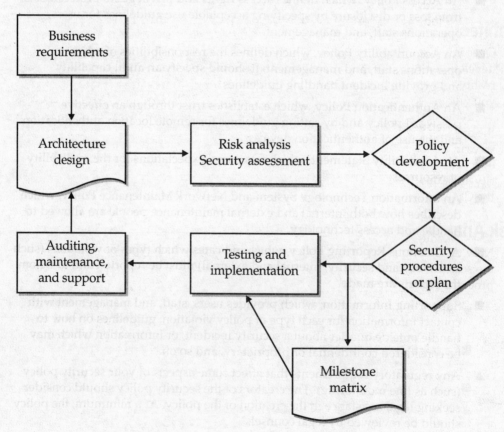

Each of these steps are critical in designing a proper security "fit" for your company. We will look at each one in a bit more depth.

Business Requirements

Since we talked about security being an enabler of business, and not vice versa, it is only logical to start with business requirements. In this section you would consider the following:

▼ What does your company do?

■ What are your legal requirements for CIA-NR?

■ What are your internal requirements for CIA-NR?

■ What are the major business processes and their requirements?

▲ What services do you need to provide?

This is also the time that you attempt to put the "cost" value on a particular service so that it can be used in the risk assessment portion. You will have to do it sometime, and now is as good a time as any.

Architecture Design

Once you have a good understanding of the business requirements, then you can look at developing an architecture if you are starting from scratch. However, most of us aren't; in reality, you are looking at trying to retrofit security into an already existing structure, and you will have your work cut out for you.

In the design phase, you will be doing a lot that has nothing to do with security, but the one step that will need to be done is prioritizing security attributes for proposed services in certain zones of risk. What this really means is that for every proposed service (or every running service if this is a retrofit) you will determine a priority for each of the security attributes (CIA-NR). This assumes that you have defined the zones and understand the CIA-NR of the services that you are offering. This is not a trivial task.

Risk Analysis/Security Assessment

Now that you have the architecture done and you know the services and the priority of the security attributes, you can do a proper risk analysis and security assessment. The process involves

▼ Identifying critical resources (consider the importance of the information to the institution *rather than* the size of the installation).

■ Identifying the potential vulnerabilities (see Chapter 7) of those services in each of the CIA-NR areas.

■ Assigning a business risk value to each critical resource/security attribute pair.

▲ Performing a cost/benefit analysis on the business risks.

Using our formula, and an example of unsecured e-mail as the service, you will see how this is done. We have determined that confidentiality is the highest priority, and the result of critical information leaking out could be catastrophic in the sense that 5 percent of our customers would leave because of such a breach. We also know that, by default, all e-mail is in the clear and the only thing that prevents an inadvertent release of critical information is proper user operation. We make a subjective rating that there is a 50 percent probability that a user will inadvertently release critical information, and since everything is in the clear, there is a 100 percent probability that whoever gets it can read it. Our current income is $10M, so 5 percent would be $500K. Given this, our first pass at calculating the risk is

$$Risk = (\$500K)(50\%) = \$250K$$

So now we need to find a solution that will reduce the probability of a likely exposure to less than $250K. If we can, then we can show a cost/benefit. If our solution costs $500K, then it's not worth it. Remember, you will need to factor in cost over a period of years to get a proper *return on investment (ROI)*. I know it's simplistic, but it drives the point home.

Policy Development

This section is where you try to develop policies that will reduce the probability of a successful exposure. You will also deal with such things as "acceptable use" and other areas that may or may not be technical. This policy usually does the following:

▼ Addresses issues uncovered in analysis

■ *Must* be supported by upper management

■ Sets high-level policy *only*

■ Is consistent in overall corporate policy

■ Deals with *all* issues regarding information security

▲ Should only change when business requirements change

Security Procedures (Plan)

Once you have a policy, you can develop security procedures or a security plan to implement the policies. The procedures and plan do the following:

▼ Deal with the technical implementation of the security policy goals and objectives.

■ Map the policy requirements to current technology.

■ Set out information from which operations manuals may be derived.

▲ Do not address *all* of the plan (such as the human resources policy), only that which deals with the data system technology.

For our earlier example, we might determine that all mail must be encrypted. Thus an inadvertent release would still go out, but no one would be able to read it, so the probability goes to almost zero.

Milestone Matrix

A tangent is in order. Now that you've gotten this far, you usually will have a tendency to push on through to testing and implementation. This is usually not prudent. There is an old construction rule: Measure twice and cut once. This is what we are going to do. With the milestone matrix, you will go back and validate (measure, if you will) the implementation details you are about to test/implement. You will ensure that the proposed solution actually accomplishes what you want.

In our example, we would evaluate "Will encrypting all e-mail prevent loss of confidentiality of any e-mail message?" The answer would be "Yes," so we have measured twice before we cut. We would also take a look to make sure the cost of the proposed solution was still within bounds.

You can skip this step if you want, but chances are you will wish you hadn't.

VIP: A large number of organizations combine the policy and the procedures/plan together. This is acceptable, but it is important to keep high-level requirements such as "data must be secure" separate from technical details such as "encrypt data with triple DES."

Testing and Implementation

Don't be too quick to jump to the implementation part of this step; testing of a proposed solution is critical to its ultimate success. In this step we would perform the actual testing of the proposed security plan solutions following these steps:

1. Set up an isolated test and configuration area.

2. Connect hardware to isolated test net.

3. Configure hardware and software (don't attach it to any production network).

4. Download, compile, configure, and install any required software (if applicable). Use CDs, tapes, or floppies, not the Internet.

5. Perform test plan and correct deficiencies.

After the test plan passes, certify the system as available and perform the following steps:

1. Train operators and administrators on the system.

2. Ensure integrity of the security systems while implementing the plan.

3. Make the implementation process on a "need-to-know" basis.

4. Impact normal operations as little as possible.

Auditing, Maintenance, and Support

As stated earlier, security is a process, not a project. Here are some guidelines to follow:

▼ Audit regularly; modify infrequently.

■ Audit and re-analyze annually or after changes.

■ Perform backup and recovery testing to ensure they work.

▲ Flow all of this information back into the design.

RECAP

Policies are the things that are always left out, because they are boring to design and not fun to implement. Nobody likes you when you are writing one, and everyone complains that you are making his or her job impossible to do. In spite of all that, they are necessary! If you have a policy and a plan, then chances are you will not be a statistic, and you are making decent use of the resources that you are spending. If you do not have a policy and plan, then you are probably wasting valuable resources and biding your time until the "big one" hits.

It is also important to realize that not everyone needs to behave as if they are designing an e-commerce site. There are many alternative strategies that can be used to secure a site that has less stringent requirements. This chapter has focused on the more secure side of things, as it is always easier to loosen things up, in this case, disregard the draconian security tactics, than it is to lock things down. As far as how to create and implement a policy, we have touched on a couple of issues, and a couple of methods. There are other methods of accomplishing what we just went through, but this method gets you thinking about all the parts and just how complex the task is.

PART II

Windows 2000 Security

PART II

Windows 2000 Security

CHAPTER 5

An Overview of Windows 2000 Security

"Are you driving in circles, or are you taking us someplace?"

—*Rudy Costa*

Let us start by saying that this chapter is not about all of the features in Windows 2000 (Win2K). It is about a subset of them—those that relate to security. Win2K provides a suite of security services that can be used to tighten the security of your Win2K systems and networks. Win2K security is based heavily on its predecessor, Windows NT (WinNT), and all of the significant security features of WinNT have been carried over to Win2K. Most of the core features of the architecture and object-oriented design of Win2K came from WinNT. You should think of Win2K as a *very significant* upgrade, (that is, it is tuned, tweaked, and extended), but it is *not* new.

In general, Win2K had some specific goals of improving the scalability, reliability, and security of WinNT, as well as integrating many of the add-on features into the OS. This was done to address the major shortcomings of WinNT, reduce development costs, use more industry standards, and make Win2K the e-commerce platform of choice. Here are some of the enhancements in each category:

▼ **Scalability** Better memory management, job object management, kernel tuning, Windows Driver Model, Microsoft Installer (MSI), Change and Configuration Management (CCM)

■ **Reliability** Write-protected driver and kernel code segments, driver verification, Repair Console, and Safe Boot

■ **New and Integrated Features** Terminal services, Plug and Play, and Power management

▲ **Security** Active Directory, Group Policies, Encrypting File System, Kerberos, CryptoAPI, IP Security, Public Key Infrastructure, and Kernel security enhancements

NOTE: When we talk about "industry standards" in the Microsoft world, you have to remember that Microsoft will "embrace and extend" those standards. Sometimes this has the undesired effect of making them inoperable with others who have used the same standard, but not "extended" it.

WIN2K SYSTEM ARCHITECTURE

Win2K comes in four distributions: Professional (a.k.a. workstation), Server, Advanced Server, and Datacenter. The basics of the operating systems are the same, but their use and administration can be significantly different. For the sake of practicality, this book will cover two roles: server and workstation.

Win2K is made up of components, and Figure 5-1 shows how the components fit together into the Win2K architecture. Like most other models, it is layered with the computer hardware at the bottom and high-level applications at the top. Users interact with the highest-level components. All the layers in between provide services to upper layers and interact with lower layers.

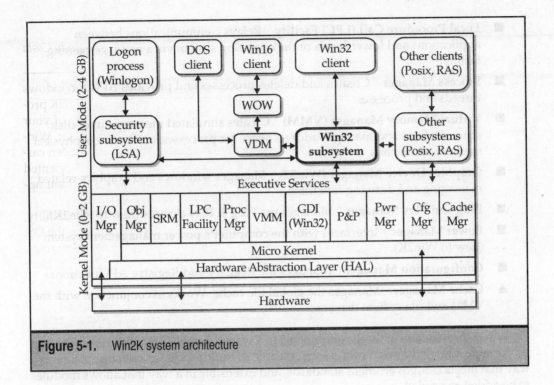

Figure 5-1. Win2K system architecture

The Kernel schedules activities for the processor to run. These processes are called *threads*, and the Kernel is in charge of keeping the processor busy running threads. It makes sure that higher-priority threads are pushed ahead of lower-priority threads. The Kernel is like the guy who shovels coal into a speeding locomotive: He shovels and shovels to keep the engine running hot.

The Kernel provides what is known as *executive services*, which are provided by different components of the kernel. All of these components reside in the `ntoskrnl.exe`, except the GDI, which is in `win32k.sys`. The executive services consist of

▼   **I/O Manager**   Manages communication between the operating system and the outside world. It handles *device drivers*, which are software modules that help the operating system access physical devices such as network interface cards, disk drives, and cache memory.

■   **Object Manager**   Manages objects, including files, folders, ports, processes, and threads. The Object Manager is in charge of naming, maintaining security, allocating, and disposing of objects.

■   **Security Reference Monitor (SRM)**   Validates access rights. This component compares a process' access token with an object's ACL and determines whether the process should be granted the requested access right(s). The Object Manager calls this.

- **Local Procedure Call (LPC) Facility**   Relays communications between applications and lower levels of the operating system via a message-passing facility.

- **Process Manager**   Creates and deletes processes and provides APIs for threads and processes.

- **Virtual Memory Manager (VMM)**   Creates simulated memory out of disk space. Defines and manages address space for processes, and controls physical memory allocations.

- **Graphics Device Manager (Win32)**   Manages windows and graphics-related messaging and drawing functions.

- **Plug and Play Manager**   Manages the Plug & Play devices (new to Win2K).

- **Power Manager**   Interfaces with the computer's power management system (new to Win2K).

- **Configuration Manager**   Manages the Registry and Registry API functions.

- ▲ **Cache Manager**   Manages the global file cache. Works in conjunction with the VMM and file system drivers.

Win2K provides all of these components in a system designed from the ground up to be portable among different processors, scalable to multiprocessor systems, secure in a way that meets U.S. government standards, and extensible in a way that allows modules to be added as needed.

Object-Oriented Design

Almost everything in the Win2K operating system is represented as an *object:* files, memory, devices, system processes, threads, and even windows that appear on the desktop. Objects are the key to providing a high level of security in the Win2K operating system:

- ▼ An object is a self-contained entity that contains its own data and the functions needed to manipulate that data.

- There are many types of objects; what they can do is defined by the *object type*.

- All objects in Win2K can be accessed only by the operating system itself through strict controls.

- ▲ The security system checks all access to objects, and the auditing system can log these events.

The concept of a self-contained object with its own data and functions seems a little odd at first. Think of an object as a box that contains information and functions for manipulating that information. Perhaps the object contains information about your bank account. On the outside of the box are functions (think of buttons) for retrieving information such as your current balance. Any process outside the object must use the functions to get information from the object.

A typical application may be built from hundreds or thousands of objects. A good analogy is a car, which is built by assembling many small objects. For example, the steering wheel object controls the steering objects. It connects to those objects through a standard interface. The driver who is at the upper level of all this simply turns the wheel and doesn't need to be concerned about the underlying objects that make it work.

What does this have to do with security? First, objects hide their data from the outside and provide information only in certain ways, as defined by the functions of the objects. This prevents external processes from accessing internal data directly. That makes sense when you consider that a data file is an object that you restrict access to by controlling who gets to look inside. Just keep in mind that everything in the Win2K operating system is an object.

Win2K achieves high levels of security by never letting programs access objects directly. Any action on an object is authorized and performed by the operating system. It is relatively easy for Win2K to perform these checks on objects since individual objects hold much of the information that is needed to do a security validation.

WIN2K SECURITY

Win2K security is quite complex, especially when you look at how it works deep down in the operating system, so a solid understanding of the basics is required. Win2K security attempts to accomplish the following goals:

▼ Single sign-on in the enterprise

■ Integrated security services

■ Delegation and scalability of administration

■ Strong authentication

■ Standards-based protocols for interoperability

▲ Auditing services

The ability to provide a majority of this functionality is based on policies and the Active Directory (AD). Policies are used to group security features (that apply to groups of computers) together, and the AD is the mechanism by which most of the security functionality in Win2K is distributed out. Without the AD, a Win2K network is not much different than a WinNT 4.0 network. As a matter of fact, Win2K machines can exist quite happily, albeit with less enterprise-level security features, as members of a WinNT domain. As a matter of fact, isolated systems (i.e. workgroups) are often the configuration used for bastion hosts. See Chapter 21 for hardening Win2K.

> **NOTE:** We will discuss policies and the Active Directory later in this chapter, as well as in Chapters 8 and 9.

To accomplish some of the goals listed at the beginning of this section, Win2K uses the concept of a security model. This model defines the way the different parts of the Win2K operating system work together. Some of the underlying principles in this architecture are

▼ Servers provide access to objects.

■ Clients can only access objects through servers (a.k.a. services).

■ The Object Manager and Security Reference Monitor (SRM) determine who has what rights to an object.

■ There are multiple protocols that can be used to authenticate a user.

▲ You can manage security policies globally or locally.

The Win2K Security Subsystem

The Win2K security subsystem affects the entire Win2K operating system. It provides a single system through which all access to objects, including files on disk, processes in memory, or ports to external devices, are checked so that no application or user gets access without proper authorization. The security subsystem components described here are pictured in Figure 5-2.

ACTIVE DIRECTORY SERVICE   Provides Win2K directory services and replication. It supports the Lightweight Directory Access Protocol (LDAP) and manages sections of the data.

KERBEROS (VERSION 5)   The default authentication protocol in Win2K. This is used for all authentication between Win2K machines as well as clients that support Kerberos authentication. This also provides the Kerberos Key Distribution Center (KDC) service, which provides authentication services as well as ticket-granting services to the clients.

LOCAL SECURITY AUTHORITY (LSA)   The central component of the security subsystem that generates access tokens, manages security policies on the local computer, and provides authentication for user logons.

MSV1_0   The authentication package for WinNT authentication. This is used for compatibility support of Windows clients that do not support Kerberos authentication.

MULTIPLE AUTHENTICATION PROVIDER (MAP)   Provides the glue, which integrates the other pieces of the security subsystem. IT makes the decision as to which authentication provider to use. These can be the default Kerberos or NTLM, or a third-party authentication package.

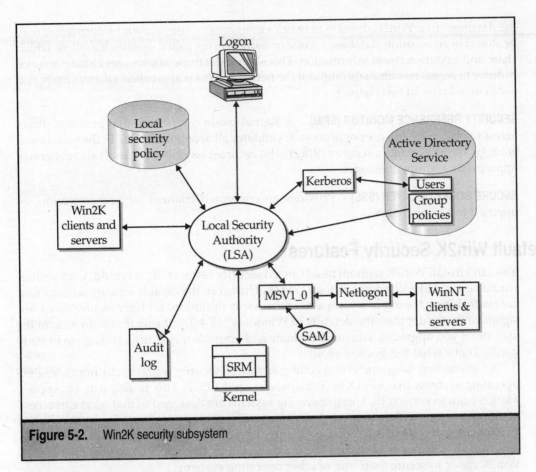

Figure 5-2. Win2K security subsystem

NETLOGON SERVICE   Used to pass user credentials to the domain controller and return the domain security identifiers for the user. It is supported for backward compatibility with older Windows clients and NTLM.

NTLM   The default Win2K authentication protocol used for workgroups and logons to a local user account. It is also still supported in domain logons for backward compatibility with older Windows-based machines. Win2K supports both NTLMv1 and NTLMv2.

SECURITY ACCOUNTS MANAGER (SAM)   The Security Accounts Manager is a database of local users and groups (a.k.a. the accounts database). This database is used for login authentication of local users and setting of User Rights for all logins. The accounts database is stored locally on all non-domain controller Win2K computers and can be used to log in with a local account or when no domain controller is available.

In a network environment the accounts database may exist on a number of machines. When a user logs on to a local machine, the SAM on that machine retrieves user IDs from the database. In a Win2K domain network environment, user account information may be stored in an accounts database on one or more servers called *domain controllers*, which share and update account information. This shared database allows users to log on once in order to access resources throughout the network. This is also called a *domain logon* and is discussed later in this chapter.

SECURITY REFERENCE MONITOR (SRM)   A Kernel mode component that prevents direct access to objects by any user or process. It validates all access to objects. In the warehouse analogy, the SRM is like a security officer who enforces security policies. It also generates appropriate auditing messages.

SECURE SOCKETS LAYER (SSL)   Provides an encrypted channel for authentication, as opposed to a clear channel.

Default Win2K Security Features

You can't install Win2K without its advanced security features. If you could, your system would be more like Windows 98 than Win2K. However, the default security settings that are made during the initial setup are not necessarily optimized for tight security (they are significantly tighter than the defaults in Windows NT 4.0, but *only* if you do a clean install, not if you upgrade). You must evaluate and upgrade the security settings to fit your needs. That's what this book is about.

An interesting side point is that getting advanced security is practically impossible on operating systems like MS-DOS, Windows 9*x*, and OS/2. This is also true of Apple's MacOS prior to version 10. These operating systems are designed so that users can access system resources with few, if any, restrictions. The underlying operating system is too weak to allow the addition of strong security. Win2K is an object-oriented operating system, and its security is built into the lowest levels of the object structure. That makes Win2K easier to secure than a lot of other operating systems.

Win2K takes advantage of features in the Intel Pentium (and later) processors to implement some of its security features. Protected-memory features prevent any program from accessing the code or data used by another program or by the operating system itself. Every program runs in its own protected memory. Unauthorized attempts by one program or process to access the memory of another program or process is denied by the operating system.

This chapter will explain the underlying security controls and the elaborate security systems that have been built on top of those controls in Win2K. First, we'll discuss the basic access controls as they apply to a Win2K computer, whether it is Server or Professional (previously known as "workstation" in Windows NT). Then, under the section "Win2K Network Models," we'll discuss how Microsoft uses Win2K to extend security to network users.

NOTE: As you read through this chapter, keep in mind that operating systems don't make security problems go away. No operating system can provide you with a complete security solution. You must define a level of security that fits your needs and integrate Win2K and its security features into your scheme. Your security plans must include both physical and logical security measures. Your objective is to build the best defense you can against intruders and accidents.

USER ACCOUNTS AND GROUPS

Any user who wants to access a Win2K system must have a user account on that system. A username identifies the user and a password validates the user. Groups are collections of users. It is far easier for an administrator to assign rights and permissions to groups of users than to individual users one at a time. Groups can also be the focus of electronic mail lists and scheduling activities.

Users and groups are discussed in greater depth in Chapter 10.

User Accounts

User accounts contain information about users, such as their full name, their username, a password, the location of their home directory, information about when and how users can log on, and personal desktop settings if they are using Windows 9x, NT, or 2000.

When a new user account is created, Win2K assigns it a unique security identifier (SID). All internal processes use the SID—rather than the username for the account—to identify a user account. This SID is unique for each account. If you create an account, delete it, then create a new account with the same name, the new account will have a different SID.

When you first install a Win2K server or Win2K professional computer, two accounts are created: Administrator and Guest.

Administrator

An Administrator account is the highest-level account that provides full access to a system or domain. It is used to set up domains and alternate administrative accounts. The account cannot be deleted or disabled, but should be renamed and assigned a password to hide it from attacks.

A system administrator is responsible for managing network and server equipment, system planning, user accounts, data storage, and a variety of other things. If other people will be managing a system by using the Administrator account, you should create alternate Administrator accounts (that is, separate accounts that are members of the Administrators group) for a very good reason: Each account can be tracked individually in the audit log to detect malicious activities. If only one Administrator account were in use by several people, you would not be able to tell which user was doing what.

Guest

This account allows very restricted access to a system for people who do not have an account. It is generally used for accessing information on public systems; it should not have the ability to write or delete information in most cases. By default, it is disabled.

If the Guest account is enabled, unknown users can access any resource on a computer to which Guests and the Everyone group have access. The account is disabled by default. Carefully review the status of this account on all of your Win2K computers. Keep in mind that users who log on as Guest don't need to specify a username, so you have no idea who is using the Guest account and you cannot audit a specific user's activities.

TIP: Keep the Guest account deactivated!

On Win2K domain controllers an additional account is created: Krbtgt.

Krbtgt

This account is used for the Kerberos authentication. The existence and name of this account is specified in RFC 1510. This account can't be deleted or renamed. The password is automatically managed and should not be changed manually.

Groups

Groups are collections of user accounts. It is far easier to grant rights and permissions to groups of users rather than to individual users, although you can still do the latter in special cases. After you create a group, you add user accounts to it and assign rights and permissions as appropriate.

Win2K has a number of predefined groups. They fall into four categories: local, domain local, domain global, and universal groups.

Local Groups

This type of group defines permissions and rights for users and groups on the local machines within a domain, but you can add User and Group accounts from other domains to this group. Built-in groups fall into this category.

Domain Local Groups

Domain local groups contain members from any domain in the forest, but can only be used in the local domain. Members in this group are valid only in the domain where they are defined and are not replicated to the global catalog. This group is used only to contain other types of groups in your domain. It provides a mechanism for local domain control. These groups may contain individual users, global groups, and universal groups.

Domain Global Groups

Global groups contain members from the same domain, but can be seen in any domain in the forest. They are similar to the WinNT global groups, but have the ability to be nested when running the Win2K in "native" mode. You would use nesting to keep group size to a minimum for replication performance reasons. You can put users and other global groups into global groups. They can't contain universal or domain local groups. These groups are replicated throughout the domain, but *not* the entire domain tree or AD. They are also included in the Global Catalog. Members of this group are not listed in the GC.

Universal Groups

Universal groups can contain any user or global group within the AD forest, and can be used in any ACL in the forest. This combines the functions of the local domain and global domain groups in that they contain members from any domain in the forest, but they can be used in an ACL on any object in the forest. These groups are only available in "native" mode. All members are listed in the GC.

The following illustration shows the inclusion rules for groups in Win2K native-mode.

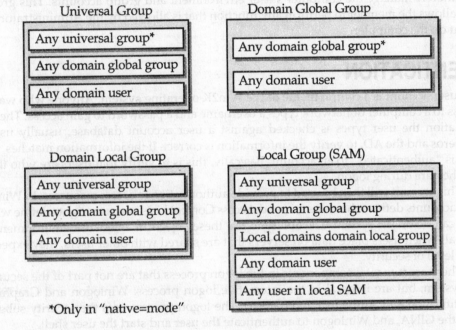

*Only in "native=mode"

The following is a list of predefined groups for a domain. Note that except for Users and Guests, these groups are designed for management tasks; they have specific rights to administer devices or settings in the domain. Users added to these groups obtain the rights of the group:

▼ **Administrators**   Users with rights to manage the system

■ **Account Operators**   Users with rights to manage user accounts

■ **Server Operators**   Users with rights to manage servers

■ **Backup Operators**   Users with rights to back up and restore files

■ **Replicators**   Users with rights to manage replication between servers

- ■ **Print Operators** Users with rights to manage printers
- ■ **Users** Normal users with accounts
- ▲ **Guests** Users without accounts who have very restricted rights

Predefined groups on Win2K professional computers and Win2K server computers that are not domain controllers include Administrators, Power Users, Backup Operators, Users, Guests, and Everyone. The Account Operators group is missing because these computers do not contain a copy of the directory database, nor do they participate in user and group management. Note that on standalone Win2K computers that are not connected to a domain, only predefined local groups are created.

For management purposes, a global group called Domain Admins is added to the local Administrators group on any Win2K computer that becomes part of a domain. This group allows anyone in the Domain Admin group working at Win2K server computers to remotely manage the computer's user environment and group accounts. This group also allows the member to perform any function that is allowed by the Administrator account on the computer.

AUTHENTICATION

The user account is a central theme of the Win2K operating system. Anyone who wants access to a computer or network types a username and a password to gain access. The information the user types is checked against a user account database, usually using Kerberos and the AD, to verify the information is correct. If the information matches, the user is "authenticated" to an account. Basically, this is to verify that users are who they say they are during logon.

This account will then be used to provide authorization to access resources. In Win2K user accounts define who users are, and Access Control Lists and user rights define what they can do on the system. The ability to use these objects in a network environment is critical. When users place data on servers that are shared with other users, they expect a high level of security.

There are two vital components in the logon process that are not part of the security subsystem, but are integral in the interactive logon process: Winlogon and Graphical Identification and Authentication (GINA). The logon process uses the security subsystem, the GINA, and Winlogon to authenticate the user and start the user shell.

NOTE: See Chapter 11 for details on the logon and authentication process.

Winlogon

Winlogon is the process that manages the logon and logoff of interactive users. Some of the functions are

▼ Recognizing the Secure Attention Sequence (SAS), and calling the appropriate GINA processing routine

■ Assigning an access token to a user shell

■ Loading a user profile

■ Protecting the machine and desktop

■ Controlling the screen saver

▲ Handling remote Performance Monitor requests

Graphical Identification and Authentication (GINA)

The GINA is a component loaded in Winlogon's process. It is responsible for gathering the logon data from the user and passing it to the LSA for validation. You can develop replacement GINAs to implement other authentication mechanisms. For instance, there is a GINA for authenticating against a Unix NIS server, as well as a GINA that has a smartcard interface. The GINA is responsible for catching the SAS and initiating a logon. By default, Win2K uses the MSGINA, which is invoked with the well-known Windows NT Secure Attention Sequence of CTRL-ALT-DEL.

Interactive Logon

The GINA interface determines the process of gaining access to a Win2K system. By default, it is msgina.dll and will start the logon process when the SAS is pressed. The SAS protects against logon Trojan Horse-type programs that masquerade as the operating system to trick users into typing their logon name and password. The SAS assures you that a valid Win2K logon sequence will initiate. This key sequence should always be pressed when logging on to a machine that is already running. Win2K can use two services to perform domain logons: Kerberos and Netlogon.

TIP: Win2K Professional has an option during installation that will preset an account to automatically log on the computer on startup. This is used to emulate the start up process of Win 9x and should never be used when security is an issue.

NOTE: Win2K and Windows NT are the only Microsoft operating systems that offer this mandatory logon protection, but the AutoAdminLogon registry key, when set, will automatically log the user on. This appears to bypass this mandatory logon, but logon has happened.

The logon process also allows users at desktop systems to have their own personal desktop configurations. When users log on, the settings they had in a previous session are fetched from a profile and restored.

Security ID (SID)

A *SID* is a globally unique value that identifies a user, group, or computer account. It is guaranteed to be globally unique within an Active Directory, and for all practical purposes, it is globally unique across all Windows environments. Each user, group, and computer is assigned a unique SID when the account is first created, and the SID is used for all authorization decisions. Since they must remain unique, they cannot be re-created; if you create an account, then delete it and re-create it with the same username, you will not be able to get the original SID back. Any rights or permissions previously granted to the old SID (that is, account) are not available to similarly named user accounts with different SIDs. (Administrators, however, may always "take ownership" of these resources and re-ACL for other users.)

When using Active Directory a user may actually have multiple SIDs by using the SID history mechanism. SID histories are usually created when using a migration tool to facilitate migration from an existing NT domain to a Win2K domain. During the migration, users will get new SIDs; however, for access control, their old files will still have the previous SID associated with them. If the migration tool creates a SID history for the user, then you can use this information to preserve the previous file access control behavior. A user is limited to 127 historical SIDs.

More About the Logon Process

Users can either log on to a local computer using an account on that computer or log on by being validated by another computer. In domain networks, a domain controller that holds a copy of the accounts database validates the user (this is the Active Directory for Win2K). The outcome depends on what the user types into the Domain field of the Logon dialog box:

▼ If the user types the local computer name in the Domain field, the local computer will log the user on to the local system.

▲ If the user types a domain name in the Domain field, an interactive logon takes place in which the logon request is sent to the domain controller for verification. In Win2K, this means that the client initiates a Kerberos Authentication Session (AS) that will follow the "trust" path to the proper domain. This occurs because the AS must follow the "transitive" trust path to the domain controller. Unlike NT 4.0, which has non-transitive "trust" (that is, all "trusted" domains are just one hop away), the "transitive" trust model of Kerberos will follow the path until it reaches the domain the account is in. Actually, the user object would be in the global catalog, and thus the machine would know if it was a legitimate user before the session actually started. Thus, it is very possible (actually highly likely) that multiple domains will be traversed when using a remote domain account in Win2K.

By default, domain controllers authenticate users with the Kerberos authentication protocol. Also note that if a normal logon fails, the user will be logged in to the Guest account, but only if the Guest account is enabled and passwords are not required.

Network Logon

When you access a remote Windows-based resource from the computer you have logged on to, you are not required to provide information in a dialog box as you are required to do when you log on at a keyboard (unless when you connect for the first time to a resource, your username and password do not match and guest access is not enabled, in which case you will be prompted for another set of credentials). Instead, the LSA on your workstation requests a Kerberos session ticket for the desired server from a domain controller in the server's domain (this will walk the tree just like the Authentication Session). Once the LSA gets the session ticket, it will establish a session with the server.

Secondary Logon

The secondary logon capability allows you to start applications in different security contexts without having to log off. This, in effect, allows you to log on to a different user account. This feature is primarily intended for administration purposes, but can be used by any user. This service is provided with the Secondary Logon Service and started with the runas command line.

Restricted Access Tokens

Win2K provides a restricted access token for use with the Job object. This allows you to create a new access token, with reduced privileges or groups, from an existing one. This allows a service to not only impersonate a client, but also remove any privileges or groups that that client may have in a full access token. This means that even if a client has a privilege, you can make a token without it. See MSDN documentation on the CreateRestrictedToken API call for detailed information.

Authentication Protocols

Win2K supports several protocols for verifying the identities of users who claim to have accounts on the system. These include protocols for authenticating dial-up connections and protocols for authenticating external users who are trying to connect to the network over the Internet.

Kerberos v5

Kerberos v5 authentication is the default protocol for domain authentication in Win2K. It is also available on Windows 95 or Windows 98 with the Distributed Systems Client upgrade installed.

Smartcards

The smartcard stores a private/public key pair, which Kerberos uses instead of the shared secret key derived from the user's password. The insertion of the card signals the SAS (like CTRL-ALT-DEL in MSV1_0). Winlogon then calls the MSGINA, and the user types in a Personal Identification Number (PIN).

Certificate Mapping

Win2K can use public key certificates stored in the AD to map to users. The users can then authenticate by means of the public key instead of a password. There is the ability to map multiple public keys to an individual user.

NTLM

The NTLM protocol was the default protocol for domain authentication in WinNT 4.0. It is retained for workgroup and local logons, as well as compatibility reasons in Win2K. It allows communication with clients and servers that are running earlier versions of the Windows operating system.

AUTHORIZATION

As mentioned previously, objects in Win2K include everything from files to communication ports to threads of execution. Authorization to access these objects is done via two methods: User Rights and Discretionary Access Control Lists (DACLs). Every object can be secured individually or as a group. Also, the groups of objects can have different types of rights and permissions that are used to grant or deny access to them. For example, file objects can have Read, Write, and Execute permissions while print queues have permissions such as Manage Documents and Print. Keep in mind that access controls and user-account rights are two different aspects of the Win2K security system. User-account rights deal with general types of actions such as "Debug a process," while access controls restrict what access a user has to an object.

All objects have a security descriptor that describes their security attributes. The security descriptor includes

▼ The security ID of the user who owns the object, usually the one who created the object

■ The DACL, which holds information about which users and groups can access the object

- ■ A System Access Control List (SACL), which defines the auditing on an object
- ▲ A group security ID that is used by the POSIX subsystem, a Unix-like environment

Discretionary Access Control Lists (DACLs)

An Access Control List (ACL) is the part of an object that will determine if a specific SID has authorization to access the object in the manner requested. A Discretionary ACL is an ACL that is set by the user. This is different than a mandatory ACL, which would be set by the system itself, and over which the user would have no control.

The DACL is a list of Access Control Entries (ACE). Each ACE has a SID (signifying a user or group) and what permissions that SID has to that object. ACLs are not shared; either an object has its own ACL or it does not have one at all (that is, file objects that reside on FAT partitions do not have an ACL associated with them). Owners of objects can make entries in the ACL using tools like Explorer or by setting properties for files and folders with Group Policies. One method for setting permissions on a large number of systems is using the Group Policy Editor (see Chapter 9 for more details).

Users might have multiple entries in an object's ACL that provide them different levels of access. For example, a user might have Read permission to a file based on his or her user account and Read/Write permission based on a group membership. Each of these permissions is a separate ACE in the ACL.

When a user attempts to access an object, he or she usually has a certain *desired access* such as Read or Read/Write. To grant (or deny) access, the Security Reference Monitor compares information in the user's access token with entries in the ACL. Remember that the access token contains SIDs and the list of groups that the user belongs to. The SRM will compare this information with one or more entries in the ACL until it finds sufficient permissions to grant the desired access. If it doesn't find sufficient permissions, access is denied.

If the SRM finds several entries for the user, it will look at each entry to see if that entry or a combination of the entries can grant the user the desired permission to use the object. Only the requested permissions are given, no more. For example, in Figure 5-3, user AColgan has requested Read/Write access to a file object. The Security Reference Monitor compares AColgan's access token to the file's ACL. Entry 1 is checked first, and this is not associated with the user or groups in the access token, so it is ignored. Entry 2 is next, and the SRM finds that the Users group has Read permission and AColgan is a member of the Users group. However, AColgan has requested Read/Write access, so the SRM checks the next entry with similar results. Entry 4 provides a correct match because AColgan belongs to the Managers group and has requested Read/Write privileges.

Entry 5 is not needed because Entry 4 has satisfied the security requirements. Because the request was only for Read/Write, that is all that is granted, even though Entry 5 gives Full Control. Note that some entries in an ACL may deny access rather than allow access to an object. For example, if AColgan were in the Sales group, the first ACE would have denied Write access, and thus the entire request. Even though he has Full Control in Entry 5, denies take precedence. Thus a Deny Full Control would revoke all access to an object even though a user might have access permissions through other entries in the ACL. The

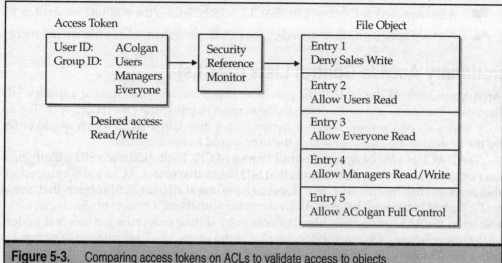

Figure 5-3. Comparing access tokens on ACLs to validate access to objects

SRM checks all entries, even if the requested access is granted in the first few. This is to ensure that any No Access ACE will be applied. Deny ACEs are supposed to be listed first in the ACL, so this should not be the case.

TIP: Permissions are cumulative, but No Access overrides.

Inheritance

Inheritance allows an ACE to propagate from the container where it is applied to the container's children. Inheritance allows us to set a DACL and/or SACL (explained next) on a directory, and have that propagate down its directory structure. There is a specific bit in the attribute field on an object that will tell the SRM to look at the parent DACL/SACL for additional ACL information. This will continue up the object tree until the bit is not set or the root node is reached.

NOTE: This is different than the WinNT version of inheritance. In WinNT, inheritance just meant that the object was re-permissioned with the DACL/SACL of the directory where it was placed.

By default, permissions on child objects are automatically inherited from their parent. Those permissions

▼ Are automatically applied to the child object.

- ■ Cannot be changed at the child object.
- ▲ Are limited by the Apply Onto field of the dialog box permissions. Child directory must have the Allow Inheritable Permissions from Parent to Propagate to This Object option set (see the "Inherit" section).

Permission Types

There are three types of permissions in Win2K: inherit, explicit, and protected.

INHERIT Inherit means that the permissions flow down the tree. These set of permissions are applied to an object if the Allow Inheritable Permissions from Parent to Propagate to This Object option is selected for the object (which it is by default, as shown in Figure 5-4). The scope of the permissions are limited by the Apply Onto field, which

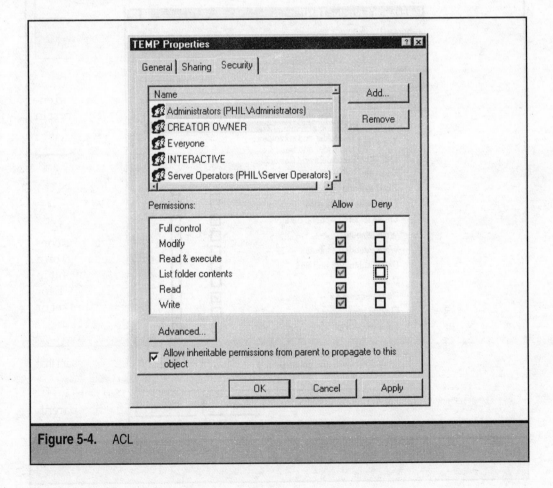

Figure 5-4. ACL

allows you to select combinations of folder, subfolders, and files, as shown in Figure 5-5. When inherited permissions are set, permission can only be changed on the Parent object that has the DACL/SACL attached to it.

EXPLICIT   Explicit permissions are to allow for additional permissions to be set on a child object. They are added to inherited permissions and can be modified on the child object itself at any time.

PROTECTED   Protected permissions do not allow the child to inherit—in other words, only Explicit permissions exist. The ACL editor will ask what to do with currently inherited permissions. Any child objects with permissions not consistent with inheritable permissions defined on the parent are automatically protected under the ACL inheritance.

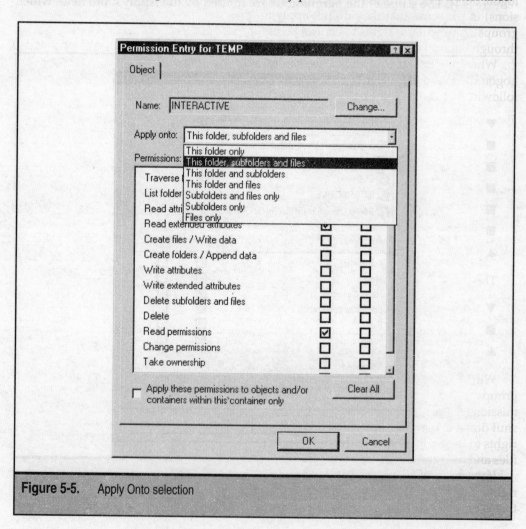

Figure 5-5.   Apply Onto selection

Per Property Object ACL

Win2K also extended the granularity of the ACL to not only the object, but to each property on that object. This allows a security descriptor to have a DACL or SACL that refers to different properties of an object. For example, one ACE of a file's DACL could allow changes to the document text, and another ACE could deny changes to the document's title.

User Rights

User rights are used to authorize users and groups (actually, the SID associated with the users and groups) to perform specific actions. These actions are things like interactive logon, debugging a process, or backing up a directory. Rights differ from ACLs (permissions) in the sense that they do not apply to specific objects, but to accounts (users or groups). You will use rights to control access at the local level. Although they can be set through Group Policies, they are applied at the individual system level.

When we look at user rights, we can group them into logon rights and privileges. Logon rights are those rights that are specific to logons, and privileges are the rest. The following list shows some of the privileges that can be assigned to a user:

▼ Back up files and directories

■ Change the system time

■ Debug programs

■ Force shutdown from a remote system

■ Manage auditing and security log

■ Shut down the system

▲ Take ownership of files or other objects

The following list shows some of the logon rights that can be assigned to a user:

▼ Access this computer from network

■ Log on locally

▲ Deny access to this computer from the network

Win2K has some predefined groups that have specific sets of rights. You use these groups to make management easier. Users added to groups obtain all the rights and permissions of the group. For example, a Print Operators group has rights to log on locally, shut down the system, and share/stop sharing printers. A Backup Operators group has rights to log on locally, shut down the system, back up files and directories, and restore files and directories.

If the predefined groups don't fit your needs, you can create new groups with special rights. You can also grant a right to an individual user on a case-by-case basis, although this is not practical if you have a lot of users. Groups and rights are a critical aspect of maintaining a secure Win2K environment. Remember that if you assign rights to a group, all members of that group get the right, and users that are members of multiple groups may be assigned conflicting rights. This is discussed more in Chapter 10.

CAUTION: Some privileges override object permissions. The Backup right is one example. If a user has this right, it will take precedence over all file and directory permissions. The Debug Programs right is very powerful. With this right, a user can attach to any other process on the system and examine or modify its state. A holder of this right may use it to obtain administrator privileges.

Group Policies

Group Policies are used to define configurations for users and computers. Much like System Policies in WinNT, the Group Policy allows you to create a granular configuration for users and groups. You can configure things such as desktop settings, registry-based policies, security settings, software installation, scripts, and folder redirection. The group policy (a.k.a. Security Group Policy) has the following general categories:

- ▼ **Accounts** Includes Kerberos policy, password policy, and account lockout policy.
- ■ **Local Computer** Includes audit policy, user rights policy, and security options (registry settings).
- ■ **Event Log** Sets log size, rotation methods, and length of time logs are kept.
- ■ **Restricted Groups** Tracks and manages membership of groups.
- ■ **Systems Services** Specifies startup options, service rights and permissions, and service auditing.
- ■ **Registry** Sets access options and auditing.
- ■ **File System** Sets access options and auditing.
- ▲ **Active Directory Objects** Sets access options and auditing.

Account Policies

Of special relevance to user accounts are the account policies. The account policies that should be looked at are those that control password restrictions and account lockouts. You set account policies for all user accounts at the same time on individual computers or in domains. The account policies are set in the Group Policy Editor (MMC snap-in) and is shown here:

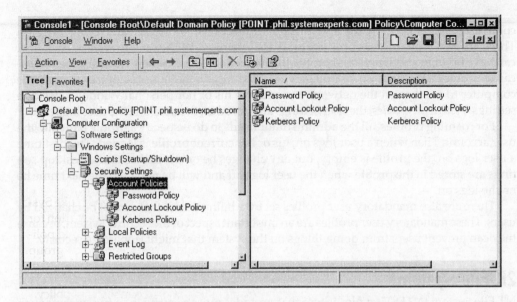

All of the settings on the Account Policy dialog box are critical if you want to enable strong security. They ensure that passwords are not implemented carelessly by users and are hard to guess. You can set the following options:

▼ Have passwords expire after a certain number of days.

■ Force users to create passwords that have a minimum number of characters.

▲ Ensure that users don't reuse passwords that were recently used.

In addition, you can control intruder break-ins by setting the Account Lockout options. If an intruder is attempting to break into a user account by guessing passwords, you can lock that account out after a certain number of unsuccessful logon attempts.

NOTE: These policies are discussed in depth in Chapter 9.

Jser Profiles

When a user logs on to a client computer running Windows, he or she can have various work environment settings loaded by the system. These settings include desktop layouts, color arrangements, network and printer connections, shortcuts, and other settings. There are two types of user profiles: local and roaming. With *roaming profiles*, each user can have his or her own personal profile that is used no matter where he or she logs on because profiles are stored on central servers. That means that a user can travel from one computer to another on the network and retrieve his or her personal Windows desktop settings. With *local profiles*, the user settings are stored on the machine the user logs onto.

For roaming profiles, all the administrator needs to do is specify a profile path into the user account. Then when a user logs on, his or her current profile is loaded. The first time a user logs on, the profile is empty, but any changes he or she makes to the desktop settings are stored in the profile when the user logs off and will be reloaded the next time he or she logs on.

There are also mandatory user profiles set by administrators that cannot be changed by users. These mandatory user profiles are an important aspect of the security system, because they can prevent users from doing things on the system that might jeopardize security.

Win2K File Systems

NT File System (NTFS) is a file system that provides more security than file systems such as the FAT system used in DOS. During Win2K installation, you're given a choice of file systems, but if you're interested in security, you should always choose NTFS. NTFS provides a number of protections for files and directories that let you specify which users and groups get access to what information and exactly how they can access it.

There are some important distinctions between Win2K and the NTFS file system as compared to other operating systems such as DOS. These features provide better security and higher performance:

▼ Win2K does not rely upon DOS system services in any way. It boots on its own and uses its own services.

■ Win2K-specific software drivers, not the disk drivers that are embedded in a computer's ROM BIOS, perform all low-level disk access functions.

▲ If you run a DOS program from within Win2K, the operating system does not allow the program to directly write to hard drives.

While NTFS provides a high level of security, it is important to understand that this security is available only when the Win2K operating system is up and running unless you use the Encrypting File System. Someone who steals your system or hard drive could use a low-level byte editor to scan the drive and read or change its contents. NTFS provides a way to control access to files and directories with permissions, but those permissions do no good if the operating system is not available to control access. Your security must include physical security measures, and you might want to install encryption utilities to protect stored data.

Assuming that your physical security is in place, you can use the NTFS file system's special security features to restrict local and network user access to the drives. Keep in mind that permissions are the "other side" of security in Win2K; they control access to all sorts of objects, not just file system objects. The other parts of security are user logon, account management, and access rights.

Permissions determine the level of access that users and groups have to directories or files. You can set permissions on directories that are inherited by any files or subdirectories. You can also set individual permissions on files within directories.

Encrypting File System

The Encrypting File System (EFS) is a notable "add on" package that has been integrated as a feature in Win2K NTFS (NTFSv5). It provides an integrated method of encrypting NTFS data on disk. It uses public key technology and is an integrated service in Win2K. One of its best features is that it is almost transparent to the user—almost in that encryption always has a performance price, and depending on your computer, this may be very noticeable. File systems are discussed in detail in Chapter 12.

Sharing Resources

There are two aspects to file system security. The first is restricting access to information on a local computer to people who log on to that computer. The second is restricting access to information that is shared over the network. When a directory is shared, users can access it from workstations attached to the network based on permissions.

To make information on a Windows system available to other users on a network, you share a folder. When you share a folder, all the files and all the subfolders in it are shared as well. You can then change the access permissions on any file or folder in the shared folder if you need to block access.

The name of a shared directory appears in the Network Neighborhood window for Windows 9x, NT, and Win2K computers. MS-DOS users must use the Net View commands to see shared directories and files while Windows for Workgroups users can open shared folders in the File Manager.

Setting Permissions

Access to folders and files is controlled by permissions, and permissions are set by administrators or the owners of a resource. There are standard permissions and individual permissions. The individual permissions are used in combination to make up standard permissions.

The standard permissions are designed to provide a set of permissions appropriate for the most common user requirements. Of course, you can create your own "special access permissions" at any time to fit a custom need.

The illustration shown here reveals how permissions can be individually allowed or denied. This is unlike WinNT, where No Access was the only deny option.

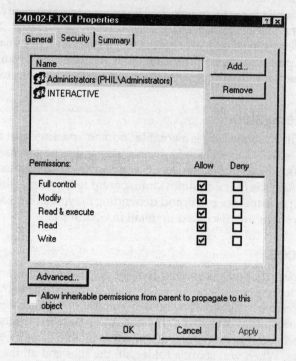

Users may get permission to access folders or files from a number of sources. For example, they might have Read permissions through their user account and Change permissions because they are members of a group. The highest-level permission applies and the permissions are cumulative, so that permission assignments from different sources are combined. However, a No Access permission from any source denies access to the file or directory, no matter what other permissions are granted.

NOTE: Chapter 12 provides a more thorough explanation of permissions and the NTFS file system.

AUDITING

The Win2K security system does two primary things: It restricts access to objects (which we have discussed) and provides an auditing service that keeps track of operations on objects. The auditing system collects information about how objects are used, stores the information in log files, and lets you review those events to identify security breaches or performance problems. If a security breach is discovered, the audit logs help you determine the extent of damage so you can restore your system and lock out future intrusions.

You control the extent to which the auditing system tracks events on your systems. Too much auditing can slow a system down and use tremendous amounts of disk space. You'll need to carefully evaluate how much auditing you need. When you suspect unauthorized activities, probably the best approach is to audit these types of events:

▼ Failed logon attempts

■ Attempts to access sensitive data

▲ Changes to security settings

You can use the Event Viewer snap-in to view the following security events:

▼ User and group management events, such as creating a new user or changing the membership of a group

■ Subject tracking, which tracks the activities of users, such as when they start a program or access objects

■ Logon and logoff events on the local system or for the network

■ Object access, both successful and unsuccessful

■ Changes to security policies, such as changes to privileges and logon capabilities

- Attempts to use privileges
- System events that affect the security of the entire system or audit log

Here is the security log in the Event Viewer:

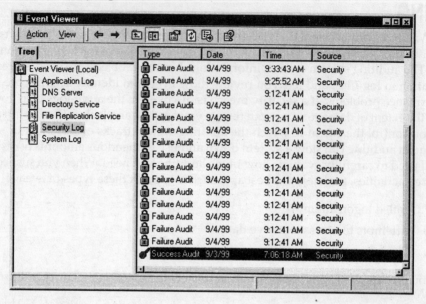

By double-clicking any event in the log, you can get detailed information about that event. In this example, a file was successfully opened and closed. Tracking these types of events will require quite of bit of the system's time and disk space if many files are opened and closed on your system.

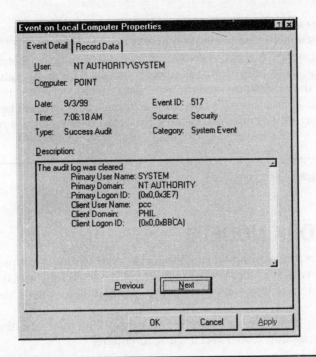

Event on Local Computer Properties

Event Detail | Record Data

User: NT AUTHORITY\SYSTEM

Computer: POINT

Date: 9/3/99   Event ID: 517
Time: 7:06:18 AM   Source: Security
Type: Success Audit   Category: System Event

Description:

The audit log was cleared
    Primary User Name: SYSTEM
    Primary Domain: NT AUTHORITY
    Primary Logon ID: (0x0,0x3E7)
    Client User Name: pcc
    Client Domain: PHIL
    Client Logon ID: (0x0,0xBBCA)

    Previous   Next

        OK   Cancel   Apply

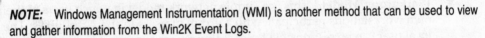

NOTE: Windows Management Instrumentation (WMI) is another method that can be used to view and gather information from the Win2K Event Logs.

The auditing system tracks security events by two IDs: the user ID and the impersonation ID. This is to help identify users who might otherwise be impersonated by certain processes in the system. A process-tracking mechanism is also used to track new processes as they are created and provide information about both the user account that is performing an action and the program that was used to perform the action.

The auditing system has one drawback that is true of auditing systems on almost any operating system: It can tell you which account was used for an operation, but it can't be sure that it was the original owner who was using the account. It is not that difficult to construct another access token if you are the administrator, so don't be quick to blame a user for unauthorized activities just because his or her user account is recorded for those activities.

NOTE: Chapter 13 provides details on auditing in Win2K.

WIN2K NETWORK MODELS

While this book is primarily about Win2K and its security model, a typical Windows network consists of Windows for Workgroups, Windows 9*x*, Windows 4.0, and Win2K professional computers. These computers can implement their own schemes for sharing resources.

First, consider that there are basically two networking models in the Windows environment: the workgroup model and the domain model.

▼ **Workgroup Model**   This is a simple network model in which users at their own workstations participate with a group of users to share resources. The local user can be responsible for granting access to resources on his or her computer to other users in the workgroup. All current versions of Windows support workgroup networking out of the box. The names of computers are important in this model, as this is how resources are located.

▲ **Domain Model**   In the domain model, the user accounts database and computer policies are stored in a shared fashion. Thus any computer in the domain has access to the domain-wide policy settings as well as the user account information. Win2K provides a much more granular and scalable way to distribute the security policy settings to users and computers and manage user accounts than Windows NT. The domain model is really a very advanced form of the workgroup model. The collection of workgroup computers simply becomes a domain in which user account security and system policies are handled by the domain controller. However, even when the domain model is in use, any client can still choose to share a resource on her computer with another computer on the network. Win2K domains are provided through the Active Directory service.

The Workgroup Model

Workgroups are ideal for small department networks in which a few people need to share resources. Figure 5-6 illustrates a network that consists of three workstations that share the

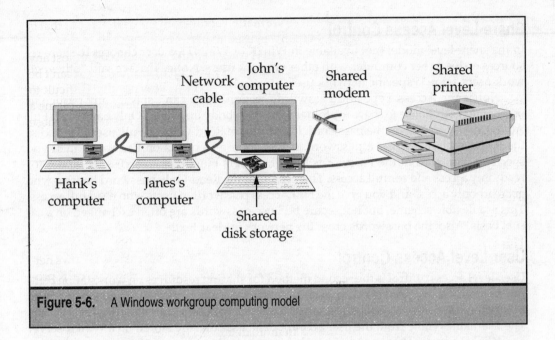

Figure 5-6.   A Windows workgroup computing model

resources on one of the workstations. Larger networks might consist of linked workgroups in different departments, such as accounting, sales, manufacturing, and design.

The workgroup concept does not imply any sort of security. Its main benefit is to make it easy for a user to locate a computer when browsing the network. For example, if only one workgroup were used for a network of 100 or more computers, users would need to browse a long list of over 100 computers to find a system they want to access. If the computers are divided into workgroups, the user chooses a specific workgroup to open a window on a much smaller list of computers in that workgroup.

On Windows-based clients, you can choose between two access control methods: *share-level* access control and *user-level* access control. The first is available on any down-level (that is, all Windows clients except Windows NT and Win2K) Windows clients, while the latter requires that an authentication server be attached to the network to handle user accounts. This can be a Win2K or WinNT server or any number of Unix-based servers that provide account services for Windows clients, such as Samba and Advanced File Services for Unix. Incidentally, if you want to set up an Active Directory domain, you need a Win2K server computer. As of this writing, there are no non-Microsoft compatible AD servers as there are for Windows NT.

To specify either share-level or user-level access control, you go to each workstation on the network and enable the option of choice in the Network utility. Use the Access Control tab and choose one of the options. If you choose User-Level Access Control, you must specify the name of a Win2K (or WinNT) computer that holds a list of user accounts.

Share-Level Access Control

In the share-level model (not available in Win2K or WinNT), a user chooses to share resources on his or her computer with other network users. Notice that we said "other network users," not "a specific network user."

Notice the Access Type and Passwords sections. You can't specify any particular username. You choose to share the folder with everybody on a Read-Only basis, with Full Access, or depending on the password. If you choose Read-Only or Full, users can access the folder without typing a password. If you choose Depends on Password, then you specify a password in the Passwords field that users must type to access the folder for read-only access and for full access. Then you give the Read-Only password to users who get read-only access and you give the Full Access password to users who need full access. This is a flexible scheme, but not secure because passwords are often exchanged on a casual basis. Also, the passwords cross the network in clear text!

User-Level Access Control

User-level access control is the second method for sharing resources on workstation computers attached to a network. Once again, settings are made at client workstations. With this method, access to resources is granted to individual users rather than just everybody. The usernames come from the user account databases that are stored on a Win2K server or a WinNT server. These are discussed in more detail in Chapter 12.

The Domain Model

As mentioned earlier, domains provide for the sharing of security information. This mostly deals with user accounts and security policies. Win2K supports two domain models: Win2K domains and WinNT domains. The WinNT domains are there for backwards compatibility and are limited in scalability of security and management. Win2K domains are much more robust and scalable. Domains are discussed in more detail in "Domain Architectures," a bit later in this chapter.

Security Limitations

Share-level and user-level access controls restrict users on a network from freely accessing files on another network computer. But this only works over the network. Security on client computers running Windows 9*x*, Windows 3.1, and DOS is basically non-existent because anyone can walk up to the computers and copy files to a diskette. There is no logon process or file permission system that prevents users from accessing files. Win2K and WinNT computers are secure in this respect because they have strong logon requirements and implement the security system discussed previously that includes Access Control Lists, user IDs, and permissions.

With user-level security, users are already validated by typing their own personal password when logging on to the network. You don't need to share a password with the people who will access the shared resources on the workstation, so there's no proliferation of passwords throughout the workgroups. User-level access controls give administrators more centralized control of security on networks where individual users are sharing resources on their own computers.

Another option for small networks is to designate a single Win2K computer as a shared computer that everybody on the network accesses. In this setup, no other computers share resources. Only ten users can access Win2K Professional at a time, while a Win2K server can be accessed by an unlimited number of users, depending on the licenses purchased. In this arrangement, an administrator needs to manage only user accounts on the servers.

DOMAIN ARCHITECTURES

Domains are collections of computers and computer users that are managed by a central authority. Domains may span departments, divisions, and/or workgroups, as well as other types of computer groups. You use them to make groups of computers more manageable and to apply a security policy to specific areas of your network.

Because domains are groups of computers, they share some of the features of workgroups. For example, you can use domains to logically split up large networks into groups of resources that make it easy for users to find those resources. Also, users can still share the resources on their own computers when a domain is established using the user-level model. What Win2K domain networking provides is a way to

▼ Create a highly secure network

■ Apply strict access controls based on user accounts

■ Delegate administrative control

▲ Provide scalability

A *distributed network* is one in which networks in different divisions, departments, or workgroups, all with different data sources, have been linked together to provide an enterprise-wide information system, as pictured in Figure 5-7. Domains provide a way to maintain a hierarchy of users in large distributed-network environments. Because a domain is an administrative entity that encompasses a collection of computers, those computers might be next to each other or separated by some distance.

Domains can provide

▼ A single user account for any user, even though the network may consist of many different interconnected networks

■ One-time logon for access to resources anywhere on the network

▲ Flexible network administration of users, groups, and resources

In a Win2K domain environment, network users have user accounts that are maintained on a Win2K server *domain controller* in an *accounts database* (a portion of the domain) in the *Active Directory*. Each domain has at least one domain controller and may have more. The Active Directory holds all the accounts and security information for a

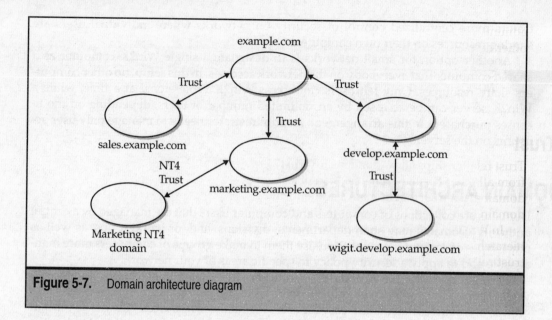

Figure 5-7. Domain architecture diagram

domain. It is replicated (updated) between domain controllers in the domain for reliability reasons and to make it more readily available to people in different geographic locations. Replication is automatic among domain controllers. Unlike WinNT domains, which had one writeable copy of the database on the Primary Domain Controller (PDC) and readable copies on the Backup Domain Controller (BDC), Win2K domain controllers all maintain writeable copies.

Active Directory

Win2K stores domain information in the Active Directory (AD). Each domain defines an administrative and security boundary, and there can be multiple domains in an AD (see Chapter 8 for details on the Active Directory). Domains are considered administrative and security boundaries because administrative privileges do not have to be extended to other domains, and each domain (potentially) has its own security policy. Policies flow down a domain much the same way that inheritance flows down a file system tree.

The AD can store domains in a hierarchical manner. This is different from the flat domain structure of WinNT. This hierarchy allows for a more robust directory search and storage capability in Win2K. The AD provides a Global Catalog, which gives you the ability to search the entire domain for an object in a single query.

Of course, domains are an important part of security in the Win2K environment. If a company has two separate divisions, each may have its own domain, and the domains can provide an administrative barrier between the divisions that can be closely monitored and managed. Each domain may have its own administrator, and together those administrators determine how resources in one domain will be accessed by users in the other domain. Trust relationships make this work, as will be discussed next.

NOTE: WinNT domains are supported by Win2K for backward compatibility.

Trust

Trust relationships allow domains to "trust" the authentication and security information from all other trusted domains. If an object is authenticated by a domain, then all other domains that trust that domain's authentication will trust that object. Objects in a trusted domain have access to resources in the trusting domain.

In Win2K, domains can be part of a domain tree, which can be part of a forest. In this hierarchical design, each child and parent will have a two-way trust relationship. These trust relationships are transitive by default and are applied to all members of a forest. *Transitive trust* means that if you trust one domain, you also trust all the domains that that domain trusts. This means that in Win2K there is complete trust between all domains in the AD. Win2K trust is based on Kerberos trust.

TIP: You can explicitly set up a non-transitive trust relationship in Win2K.

For example, in Figure 5-7 the parent domain (example.com) has a child domain (develop.example.com) and a grandchild domain (wigit.develop.example.com). If a user is authenticated in wigit.develop.example.com, the user can access resources in any of the example.com-related domains (that is, any child or grandchild of the root). In the same way, a user authenticated in example.com would have access to any resource in the child or grandchild domains. This is transitive trust, where trust is extended through domains.

NOTE: Trust deals with authentication and not authorization. Although the user can authenticate to a resource, local ACLs or policies may limit the actual use.

WinNT Domains

As a refresher, remember that WinNT trust relationships are one way, not transitive. Thus if you want a two-way trust relationship, you have to explicitly create two one-way trust relationships. Also, the domains, although connected by trust relationships for sharing of authentication information, are not related in any other way (that is, for administration or delegation).

Win2K and NT4 Domains

Trust relationships between Win2K domains and WinNT domains are always non-transitive and one-directional. Win2K domains can run in a "mixed-mode" mode, which allows them to serve requests for both Win2K domains and WinNT domains.

OTHER WIN2K SECURITY FEATURES

There are other features which directly affect the ability of Win2K to implement its security model. This section describes those Win2K security features.

CryptoAPI

The Cryptographic Application Programming Interface (CryptoAPI) provides an abstraction between the cryptographic services and the application. This allows application developers to use generic cryptographic functions without knowing, or having to write, the underlying implementation. The default Cryptographic Service Providers (CSP) that come with Win2K are

▼ **Microsoft Base Cryptographic Provider**   A general-purpose provider that supports digital signatures and data encryption. RSA public-key is used for all public-key operations.

■ **Microsoft Strong Cryptographic Provider**   An extension of the Base Cryptographic Provider, it is currently available only within the United States and Canada. It supports all of the algorithms of the Enhanced CSP and all of the same key lengths. To support backwards compatibility, it uses the same default key lengths as the Base CSP.

■ **Microsoft Enhanced Cryptographic Provider**   Base CSP with longer keys and additional algorithms (see Table 5-1), it is currently available only within the United States and Canada.

Algorithm	Base Provider Key Length	Strong Provider Key Length	Enhanced Provider Key Length
RSA public-key	512 bits	512 bits	1,024 bits
RC2	40 bits	40 bits	128 bits Salt length: settable
RC4	40 bits	40 bits	128 bits Salt length: settable
DES	Not supported	56 bits	56 bits
Triple DES (2 key)	Not supported	112 bits	112 bits
Triple DES (3 key)	Not supported	168 bits	168 bits

Table 5-1.   Microsoft Cryptographic Service Provider Defaults

- ■ **Microsoft DSS Cryptographic Provider**   Supports hashing, data signing, and signature verification. Uses the Secure Hash Algorithm (SHA) and Digital Signature Standard (DSS).

- ■ **Microsoft Base DSS and Diffie-Hellman Cryptographic Provider**   The DSS Cryptographic Provider with added support for Diffie-Hellman key exchange (40-bit DES).

- ■ **Microsoft DSS and Diffie-Hellman/Schannel Cryptographic Provider**   Same as preceding, with the additions of generating Diffie-Hellman (D-H) keys and exporting a D-H key. Also supports key derivation for the SSL3 and TLS1 protocols.

- ▲ **Microsoft RSA/Schannel Cryptographic Provider**   Supports hashing, data signing, and signature verification. The hash consists of a concatenation of an MD5 hash, a SHA hash, and signed with a RSA private key.

See the platform SDK and MSDN for more detailed information.

VIP: On January 14, 2000, the U.S. Government issued new export regulations that will allow Microsoft to ship strong encryption products to its customers worldwide, except to U.S. embargoed destinations (**http://www.microsoft.com/exporting/TermsMx.htm**).

Data Protection with VPNs

A Virtual Private Network (VPN) is an extension of a private network across untrusted or public networks (that is, the Internet). A VPN will securely transmit your data across untrusted networks and give you a virtual point-to-point private link. The VPN will encrypt the data, then encapsulate that encrypted blob into a packet suitable for routing over the untrusted network.

   IPSec is a method of doing VPNs. It is an industry standard and will likely be supported on almost any IP-capable host. IPSec is based on an end-to-end security model. This means that any host in the middle of an IPSec path does not need to know anything about the packet. The way IPSec works, the data is encapsulated, and then IP headers are placed on the packet. Any interim stop on the path to the final destination only sees that the packet is destined for the other end of the VPN. No one can determine what is in the packet or where it is going after it reaches the other end of the VPN. With this model, you can use IPSec on LANs, WANs, and dial-ups. Win2K also supports L2TP and PPTP as protocols to implement VPNs. See Chapter 16 for more detailed information on IPSec and VPNs for Win2K.

Public Key Infrastructure

Win2K supports many components that can be used to build a comprehensive Public Key Infrastructure (PKI). Win2K attempts to provide an integrated set of services, as well as administrative tools for developing, administrating, and deploying public key-based applications.

The PKI in Win2K is designed to work in conjunction with the Win2K domain architecture and to assist in dealing with the security needs of the Internet and extranets. Win2K PKI is made up of the Microsoft Certificate Services, Active Directory, and Certificate Authority policies. See Web Chapter 1 for more details on the Certificate Services in Win2K (**www.osborne.com**).

There are many parts of the PKI support in Win2K. They exist in three primary groups: client services, server services, and enterprise services. The core functions are implemented in the CryptoAPI.

▼ **Client**   Authenticode, Certificate and Key management, Secure Channel, EFS, smartcards, cryptography

■ **Server**   Certificate and Key management, Secure Channel, cryptography, and Certificate Services for standalone servers

▲ **Enterprise**   Certificate Services, Certificate policies, and Active Directory integration

Device Driver Signing

Win2K has the concept of signed device drivers. If you try to install a device driver that Microsoft has not signed, then you will be prompted with a dialog box that asks you if you are sure. This is more of a reliability issue, but it is definitely a security plus, especially considering that device drivers run in kernel mode.

Windows File Protection

Win2K provides a service that will detect any change of critical system files from the original (or patched) system using a hash mechanism. If it detects the file to be changed, it will prompt you for confirmation to restore the file to the original version. This again was designed for reliability, but is a nice security feature as well.

TOOLS

There are two primary tools that are used extensively in the day-to-day security-related operations of a Win2K environment: the Microsoft Management Console (MMC) and the Security Configuration Tool Set. Both of these are described in this section. Note that there are a vast number of new programs, but you will find yourself using these two more than any others.

Microsoft Management Console

The Microsoft Management Console (MMC) is an extensible framework for management applications. It allows you to design modules called *snap-ins*, which perform some type of management function. The purpose of the MMC is to provide a single location from which all management occurs. It does not provide any functionality itself, but relies on the snap-ins. The idea behind it is that vendors will provide snap-ins for the MMC to manage their applications. An early example of using the MMC was the Internet Service Manager in the Windows NT 4.0 Option Pack.

Win2K uses the MMC extensively. All of the administration-related tools are just snap-ins for the MMC. The MMC can be used to manage hardware, software, and network components on the Win2K systems.

Operation Modes

There are two general ways that you can use the MMC:

▼ **User Mode**   This mode allows you varying levels of access to the MMC snap-in functionality and is primarily for administering a system.

▲ **Author Mode**   This mode allows you all user mode functionality, plus the ability to add and remove MMC functionality (that is, snap-ins) and change MMC properties.

Snap-Ins

A snap-in is just a module that the MMC uses to provide functionality. The added functionality can be part of the console tree, menu items, toolbars, property pages, or wizards to a snap-in already installed in the console. They must run in the MMC and cannot run by themselves. All snap-ins on the system are available to users that have author access to the MMC, unless access is restricted by an ACL or Group Policy.

Snap-ins come in two flavors: standalone and extensions. The standalone snap-in can be added to the MMC without the need of any other snap-in already existing in the MMC. The extension snap-in, on the other hand, adds functionality to an already existing snap-in (standalone or extension).

ADDING A SNAP-IN   Since this is such a critical tool to understand, we will go through adding the Event Viewer snap-in as an exercise, just to ensure you know how.

1. First start the MMC. Do this by running `mmc.exe` from a command prompt or the Run menu. This will bring up a blank MMC.

2. Then to add a snap-in, select Console | Add/Remove Snap-In to get the dialog box shown in Figure 5-8.

3. Select the standalone snap-in type (the default) and click Add to get to the dialog box shown in Figure 5-9.

4. Scroll down to find the Event Viewer snap-in, and select it.

5. This will take you to the screen shown in Figure 5-10, which will prompt you for the machine you want this Event Viewer to monitor; select Local.

6. Click Finish, Close, and OK to get back to the MMC, as shown in Figure 5-11. Now you can use the Event Viewer to look at events on the local system.

You should note that we added a standalone snap-in, and if it were an extension snap-in, we would have used the Extensions tab shown in Figure 5-8. If any extension snap-ins are present on the system, you will be able to add them. By default there are none.

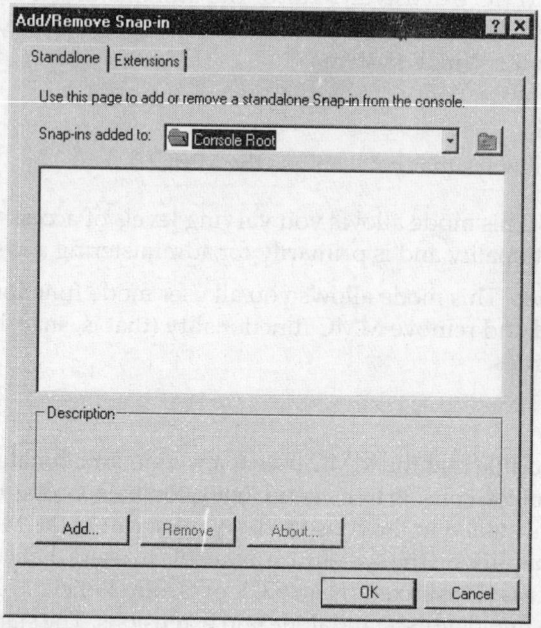

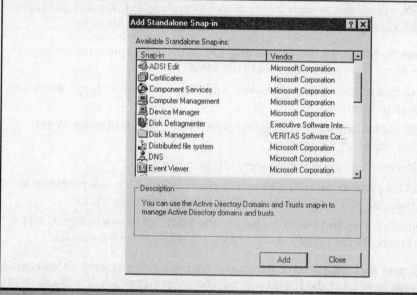

Figure 5-8. Add/Remove Snap-In screen

Figure 5-9. Snap-in list

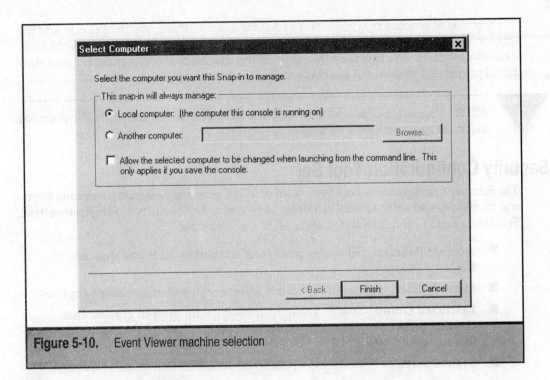

Figure 5-10.   Event Viewer machine selection

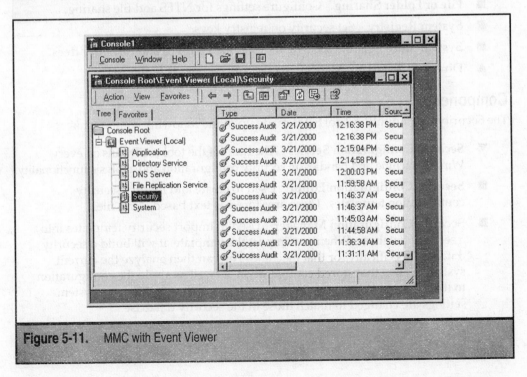

Figure 5-11.   MMC with Event Viewer

You may also notice that when you added the snap-in, there was an option to add the snap-in to another portion of the MMC console, as opposed to the default Console Root. This allows you to structure the MMC console tree in a hierarchical manner for organizational purposes and does not affect functionality of the snap-in.

> **NOTE:** You can add other items to the MMC such as ActiveX controls and links to Web pages and folders, but the primary item is the snap-in.

Security Configuration Tool Set

The Security Configuration Tool Set is a set of MMC snap-ins designed to provide a central location for security-related administrative tasks. The Security Configuration Tool Set allows you to configure and analyze all of the following:

▼ **Account Policies**   Set access, password, account lockout, and domain Kerberos policy.

■ **Local Policies**   Set audit, user rights assignment, and other security options.

■ **Restricted Group**   Assign group memberships for built-in groups. This should be used to validate/control membership of groups that have elevated privileges.

■ **System Services**   Set startup options and access control on these services.

■ **File or Folder Sharing**   Configure settings for NTFS and file sharing.

■ **System Registry**   Set security on registry keys.

■ **System Store**   Set the security for local file volumes and directory trees.

▲ **Directory Security**   Manage the security on objects in the AD.

Components

The Security Configuration Tool Set is made up of the following components:

▼ **Security Configuration Service**   The heart of the tool set. It runs on every Win2K machine and handles all security configuration and analysis functionality.

■ **Security Configuration Editor**   Used to create and modify security configuration templates. These are stored as text based .inf files.

■ **Security Configuration Manager**   Used to import security templates into a security database. When you import the template, it will build a security database specifically for that machine. You can then analyze the current system against that stored configuration, as well as apply the configuration to the machine. When you apply (or configure) the machine, the system settings are changed to match those in the security database.

- ■ **Group Policy Editor Security Settings** ˙Allows you to define a security configuration as an integral part of your group policy.
- ▲ **Secedit.exe**   The command-line interface to the tool set.

NOTE   Chapters 9, 10, and 17 describe the use of these tools in more detail.

RECAP

We have covered a lot of information and some very fundamental Win2K security features. The security services that Win2K provides are daunting and very thorough. It appears that Microsoft decided, "You want security options? Well here they are!" The major problem, though, is actually figuring out what to use and when to use it. That is what the rest of the book is about. All of the information that we have covered in this chapter will be covered in detail throughout the rest of the book.

In summary, here are some of the old features enhanced, new features added, and external services incorporated:

- ▼ **Old Features Enhanced**   Majority of the kernel, the entire security paradigm, NTLM, SAM, SRM, Netlogon, MSV1_0, SSL, DACL and SACL, CryptoAPI
- ■ **New Features Added**   Active Directory, Kerberos, inheritance, smartcards, Certificate mapping, IPSec, Plug and Play, Power Management, object property-specific ACLs, universal groups, MMC, EFS, device driver signing, windows file protection, Group Policies, PKI, CCM
- ▲ **External Services Incorporated**   Terminal Services, Certificate Services, DFS

Remember, Win2K is not new—it's Windows NT *embraced and extended.*

CHAPTER 6

Network Protocols and Services in Win2K

"The price of greatness is responsibility."

—Sir Winston Churchill

As you learned in Chapter 2, IT security threats come from a variety of sources. Your phone systems, your physical location, and your employees may all open windows of opportunity for the waiting data assailant. It is the responsibility of every employee and manager to close these windows. All areas of operation must be assessed, addressed, and strengthened.

For you, the IT professional, areas of operation usually include computer systems, network devices, network connections, electronic data, and possibly the phone system. In terms of security, your responsibility can be stated more generally as keeping your network systems and devices secure, securing the transfer of data over your network, and protecting the data stored on your networked systems. This book helps you accomplish each of these three tasks; however, this chapter strives to provide you with enough information to tackle securing the transfer of data over your network. Specifically, this chapter gives you an overview of the various protocols and services involved in the transfer of electronic data and Win2K's implementation of each, building on the general introduction to TCP/IP in Chapter 1.

NETWORK PROTOCOLS

A *protocol* is simply an agreed-upon standard that ensures that data sent from one location is received and interpreted properly at the receiving location. In terms of network communications, protocols form the fundamental building blocks for the proper transfer of data. And while most of us think of security vulnerabilities within our software applications and services, security is just as big a concern at the lower levels of network communication.

To help with the discussion of network communication, it may be helpful to review the Open System Interconnection (OSI) data communications model. The International Organization for Standardization (ISO) developed the OSI model to describe a network framework for implementing network protocols in a layered approach. In this way, network communications could move to a more modular model so that network administrators could replace individual components of the network *stack* without disrupting communications. Previous network stacks included one protocol that encompassed end-to-end communications from the network adapter to the network application.

Using this model, data then, in theory, is passed from one layer to the next. In reality, many network protocols do not fit nicely into one layer and may encompass several layers or skip layers during the communication process. Figure 6-1 shows the OSI model, the TCP/IP model, and where various protocols discussed in this chapter fit.

In the OSI model, the physical layer deals with the interface cards, cables, connections, and signals associated with data communication. Within the data link layer, data communication is organized into *frames* for link establishment. A frame contains a header

OSI	TCP/IP
Application layer Specifies how application programs interface to the network and provides services to them	**Application layer** Handles everything else; TCP/IP network daemons and applications have to perform the jobs of the OSI presentation layer and part of its session layer themselves (many protocols and services)
Presentation layer Specifies data representation to applications	
Session layer Creates, manages, and terminates network connections.	**Transport layer** Manages all aspects of data routing and delivery, including session initiation, error control, and sequence checking (TCP and UDP protocols)
Transport layer Handles error control and sequence checking for data moving over the network	
Network layer Responsible for data addressing and routing and communications flow control	**Internet layer** Responsible for data addressing, transmission, and packet fragmentation and reassembly (IP protocol)
Data link layer Defines access methods for the physical medium	**Network access layer** Specifies procedures for transmitting data across the network, including how to access the physical medium (many protocols including Ethernet and FDDI)
Physical layer Specifies the physical medium's physical and procedural operating characteristics	

Figure 6-1.   OSI as compared to TCP/IP and where various protocols fit

with address information to identify the source and destination of the transmitted information, the actual information being transmitted, and a trailer for error correction. At the network layer, data communication is organized into *datagrams*, which contain the necessary information to route the information to the proper destination. Protocols within the transport layer are responsible for error checking and flow control. The session layer deals with establishing a link between two devices or computers. The presentation layer is gaining more of the spotlight in today's networks because its primary purposes of compression and encryption have become integral components of network communications. And finally, the application layer is the interface between the other OSI model layers and your networked application.

Once you understand the theoretical structure of the OSI model, it is important to see where Win2K's popular protocols fit. The next sections will give you an overview of TCP/IP, IPX/SPX, and NetBEUI; discuss each protocol's vulnerabilities; and outline steps you can take to secure your Win2K environment at the most fundamental communication level.

The TCP/IP Protocol Suite

As you learned in Chapter 1, the Internet that we know today has its roots in the Department of Defense. DOD's Advanced Research Projects Agency (ARPA) partnered with universities and other scientific research organizations to explore new data communication technologies. Through the combined efforts of all of the involved institutions, the ARPA Network, or ARPANET, was created.

Though a data communication success, the protocols used for ARPANET were slow and prone to data loss. In 1974, Vinton Cerf and Robert Kahn proposed a new set of protocols to improve data communication that subsequently became the *Internet Protocol (IP)* and *Transmission Control Protocol (TCP)*. The biggest advantages to these new protocols were and still are

▼ **Universality** TCP/IP is supported by almost every operating system in the market today. This universality allows computer users to communicate with Windows, Unix, Macintosh, and other popular systems. In addition, any computer that connects to the Internet must employ TCP/IP.

■ **Interoperability** Since data can be routed between different networks, TCP/IP can travel across many different network devices and computer systems to reach its final destination. Other protocols, such as NetBEUI, were never designed to send data outside their own network.

▲ **Scalability** Since TCP/IP employs an addressing scheme that can scale to a network of two systems up to a network of hundreds of thousands, TCP/IP can be used on the smallest of home networks or scale to the largest corporate networks. Because of this scalability, the largest network in the world—the Internet—uses the TCP/IP protocol for data communications.

For these reasons, TCP/IP is fast becoming the de facto protocol in data communication. And while most people refer to TCP/IP as being one protocol, it is, in fact, a *protocol suite*. This protocol suite is comprised of a number of protocols that encompass a wide range of functionality. Here is a brief overview of some of the TCP/IP protocol suite's components, additional protocols that rely on TCP/IP, and how they all relate to Win2K.

IP

The *Internet Protocol (IP)* is a *connection-less* protocol that lies within the Network layer of the OSI model. The term "connection-less" refers to the fact that IP depends on another protocol located within the transport layer to actually establish and maintain a connection among the various data senders and receivers. IP, however, does have a little communication intelligence in that it uses basic message sequencing to reassemble messages and a checksum to provide error checking. For more information on IP, refer to RFC 791 for version 4 specifications and RFC 2460 for IP version 6 specifications.

INSTALLATION AND CONFIGURATION Normally, the TCP/IP protocol suite is installed by default during the Win2K installation process or when adding a network interface. If, however, you need to install IP manually on a particular Win2K system, do the following:

1. Right-click the Network Places desktop icon and choose the Properties menu option.
2. Select the network connection where you would like to install IP, and then right-click and select Properties.
3. Click the Install button, select Protocol, and click the Add button.
4. Select Internet Protocol (TCP/IP), and then click OK.

After the IP installation is complete, you will see it installed within the Properties dialog box. From there you can further modify the properties of IP, such as the IP address, default gateway, DNS servers, WINS servers, DHCP settings, and other TCP/IP-related settings.

TCP

Transmission Control Protocol (TCP) lies within the transport layer and provides IP's necessary *connection-oriented* functionality protocol. Its primary purpose is to ensure the proper reception and delivery of IP traffic. Since TCP must provide a stable and reliable connection, the associated data activity when establishing and maintaining these connections does add overhead to the data communication process. When using TCP, the client first sends a request for a connection using a unique *sequence number* to describe the connection. The server then acknowledges the request and submits a request back with its own unique sequence number to the client to establish a connection. The client then acknowledges the request and establishes a connection for data transfer.

In addition, TCP provides error correction and data integrity by organizing data into numbered *segments* that allow the receiver to piece together data packets regardless of the order in which they are received. For more information about TCP, refer to RFC 793.

TCP is installed whenever the Internet Protocol (TCP/IP) Windows component is installed.

UDP

The *User Datagram Protocol (UDP)* is a close sibling to TCP. Like TCP, it operates within the transport layer; however, it is a connection-less protocol that is optimized for faster data communication. Instead of reliable delivery and reception of data, UDP sends data using a best-effort delivery. If using TCP is equivalent to using a phone to dial your friend and conversing, UDP is the equivalent to sending your friend a letter and hoping that it is received. For more information on UDP, refer to RFC 768.

UDP is installed whenever the Internet Protocol (TCP/IP) Windows component is installed.

ICMP

The *Internet Control Message Protocol (ICMP)* lies within the network layer and is another protocol that sits atop IP for communication. Its purpose, however, is to report error and status information between network hosts and devices. One of the most popular uses of ICMP is *PINGing* a network device or system to ensure its availability. Win2K's PING utility sends a request to the designated host and records the responses it receives, as well as the time it takes to receive the response. For more information about ICMP, refer to RFC 792.

ICMP is installed whenever the Internet Protocol (TCP/IP) Windows component is installed.

ICMP ROUTER DISCOVERY Win2K Server also includes an ICMP Router Discovery Service. This service will allow your Win2K Server to assign the default gateway to workstations on your network. This can be extremely useful whenever a router is unavailable or removed from the network; the Win2K Server will dynamically assign a different default gateway to the workstations on the network.

To install the ICMP Discovery Advertisements (which offer the service piece of ICMP Router Discovery), you must have a server with Routing and Remote Access already enabled. Once you have the server installed, perform these steps:

1. Launch the Routing and Remote Access tool from the Administrative Tools window.

2. With the RRAS tool, select IP Routing | General.

3. Within the right pane, right-click the interface on which you would like to enable ICMP Discovery Advertisement and select Properties.

4. Within the General sheet, select the Enable Router Discovery Advertisements option, as shown here.

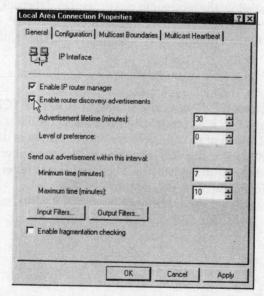

NOTE: Unfortunately, only Windows 98, Windows ME, and Win2K currently support ICMP Router Discovery at the workstation level.

IGMP

Like ICMP, the *Internet Group Management Protocol (IGMP)* lies within the network layer. Its purpose, however, is similar to that of your e-mail distribution list. With IGMP, a host or network device can send a message to multiple hosts by only addressing it to a single address. This process is also known as *multicasting*. Like UDP, IGMP uses a best-effort attempt to send information and does not guarantee data transmission. For more information about IGMP, refer to RFC 1112.

INSTALLATION AND CONFIGURATION   IGMP is typically not necessary on a Win2K Server since its native routing protocols allow multicasting. If, however, a direct connection between an IGMP host and IGMP server is not possible, you can install the IGMP router or IGMP proxy to route multicast packets between networks. To install the IGMP components, you must use the Routing and Remote Access Services (RRAS) snap-in.

ARP and RARP

The *Address Resolution Protocol (ARP)* resolves an IP address to the Media Access Control (MAC) address of your physical network device. For example, you can determine which network interface in which network device or system is using a particular IP address. Conversely, the *Reverse Address Resolution Protocol (RARP)* resolves a MAC address to an IP address. Both ARP and RARP operate within the network layer. For more information on ARP and RARP, refer to RFCs 826 and 903, respectively. Win2K offers the ARP utility to view the translation between IP addresses and MAC addresses. From a command prompt, type **arp –a**.

ARP and RARP are installed whenever the Internet Protocol (TCP/IP) Windows component is installed.

FTP

Most of you are familiar with the File Transfer Protocol (FTP). This protocol is used to transfer files between hosts and lies higher up the data communication food chain within the application layer. For more information, refer to RFC 959. The FTP protocol runs over TCP/IP, so the client or server can run whenever the Internet Protocol (TCP/IP) Windows component is installed. By default, the IIS sever is installed, and it includes an FTP server. To disable or manage this, use the Internet Services Manager (as described in Chapter 19). Win2K comes with an FTP client by default.

Telnet

Telnet is another important application layer protocol that allows you to connect to a remote computer, run programs remotely, view files, and perform a variety of other operations. Fortunately for functionality and unfortunately for security, any Win2K product can run a Telnet server to allow remote logins from other network systems.

For this reason, you must pay particular attention to this protocol and service to help you close unnecessary security holes. For more information on Telnet, refer to RFC 854.

Like FTP, Telnet protocol runs over TCP/IP, so the client or server can run whenever the Internet Protocol (TCP/IP) Windows component is installed. By default there is both a Telnet server and client installed on all Win2K systems. To use the Telnet client to remotely log in to another host, type **telnet** at a command prompt.

TELNET SERVER   The Win2K Telnet server is disabled by default. To allow remote hosts to log in to your Win2K system, double-click the Telnet Server Administration icon within the Administrative Tools folder. Once the Telnet Server starts, type **4** at a command prompt to start the Telnet service, as shown here.

```
Telnet Server Administration
Select one of the following options:

0) Quit this application
1) List the current users
2) Terminate a user session ...
3) Display / change registry settings ...
4) Start the service
5) Stop the service

Type an option number [0 - 5] to select that option: 4
Starting Microsoft Telnet Service ...
Microsoft Telnet Service started successfully

Select one of the following options:

0) Quit this application
1) List the current users
2) Terminate a user session ...
3) Display / change registry settings ...
4) Start the service
5) Stop the service

Type an option number [0 - 5] to select that option:
```

NOTE: You can exit the Telnet Server Administration tool by typing **0** at the command prompt. This only closes the Telnet Server Administration tool; it does not stop the Telnet service. You must type **5** to stop the Telnet service.

SNMP

The *Simple Network Management Protocol (SNMP)*, as its name implies, is a management protocol that is used to monitor network devices and systems. An SNMP management system works by installing an SNMP *agent* on a desired host or network device. The SNMP agent then monitors and collects information according to the instructions and format of a particular *Management Information Base (MIB)*. This information can then be communicated to a central management system via SNMP messages. SNMP lies within the application layer of the OSI model. For more information on SNMP, refer to RFC 1157.

INSTALLATION AND CONFIGURATION   To install the SNMP service on a Win2K system, double-click the Add/Remove program icon within the Control Panel. Select Add/Remove Windows Components, and then select the Management and Monitoring Tools and the Simple Network Management Protocol options. You may then be prompted for the Win2K installation media.

After the installation is complete, you can (and should) modify SNMP's properties. Within the Computer Management tool, select Services and Applications | Services. Right-click the SNMP Service and select Properties. The Agent, Traps, and Security sheets display the common SNMP configuration options. Refer to the "SNMP Attacks" section later in this chapter for tips on securing SNMP communications.

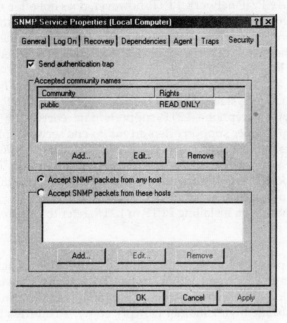

SMTP and POP

The *Simple Mail Transfer Protocol (SMTP)* is used to send Internet mail while the *Post Office Protocol (POP)* is used to receive Internet mail. Both protocols lie within the application layer. For more information on SMTP and POP, refer to RFCs 821 and 1725, respectively. For more information on the security vulnerabilities and solutions for SMTP and POP, refer to Chapter 19.

SMTP and POP are normally not installed unless you are running a mail server like Microsoft Exchange. There is also an SMTP server that gets installed by default with IIS; see Chapter 19 for more information. You will, however, use an SMTP and POP client (such as Outlook Express, Outlook, and so on) to access Internet mail from your Win2K machine.

L2TP and PPTP

A *Virtual Private Network (VPN)* allows you to create a secure connection over a public medium. For example, many companies today establish VPNs using the Internet. This type of connectivity allows companies to save a great deal of money by avoiding direct frame-relay connections between small offices and by avoiding dial-in banks of modems for dial-up access. For more information on VPNs, refer to Chapter 16.

To establish a VPN, you must use a new breed of protocols. *Point-to-Point Tunneling Protocol (PPTP)* is a modification of the older *Point-to-Point Protocol (PPP)* established for remote connections. PPTP allows the encapsulation of PPP frames into IP datagrams for transmission over a TCP/IP network. PPTP, however, does not offer an end-to-end security solution since this protocol offers only encryption methods for the data transmitted between the client and VPN server. If data is sent from the client to the VPN server and is then routed to another network server or device, the data sent is not encrypted. For more information on PPTP, refer to RFC 2637.

Luckily, Win2K also includes the *Layer 2 Tunneling Protocol (L2TP)*. L2TP is a combination of PPTP and Cisco Systems' Layer 2 Forwarding Protocol (L2F). L2TP is similar to PPTP with one major exception—L2TP supports data encryption using IP Security (IPSec). The addition of IPSec support offers an end-to-end security solution that protects your data even if it is routed beyond the VPN server. According to RFC 2661, L2TP can be implemented over a variety of networks; however, in Microsoft's implementation of L2TP, it is only supported over IP networks, which is perfect for creating tunnels over the Internet. For more information about L2TP, refer to RFC 2661.

For more information on installing PPTP or L2TP, refer to Chapter 16.

LDAP

In increasingly complex networks, the need to store and find information becomes critical to network communication and administration. For instance, network users may need to look up information like employees' names, locations, e-mail addresses, and other attributes that are associated with another network entity. To address this growing need, the international community developed the *X.500 standard* (see RFC 1274) to store these types of attributes within a central *directory*. A directory, in turn, is simply a hierarchical database that acts as an information repository.

The X.500 standard originally called for the use of the *Directory Access Protocol (DAP)* to allow clients to access directory information. However, this protocol was too resource-intensive for most PCs to handle, which significantly slowed the adoption of the X.500 standard. To remedy the situation, a smaller version of DAP, named *LDAP* or *Lightweight Directory Access Protocol*, was proposed.

LDAP was designed to run over TCP, making it universally accessible to TCP/IP networks and Internet-connected users and companies. (The protocol itself resides within the application layer of the OSI model.) Sacrificing the immense functionality of DAP, LDAP strives to provide necessary functionality but with less network traffic. LDAP reduces network traffic by allowing a client to submit a request for information or a request for action with the directory. The directory server is then responsible for performing the necessary actions within the directory and returning the information to the client. This arrangement minimizes the amount of information that is actually passed over the wire.

In relation to Win2K, LDAP allows network users to gather information from Active Directory and administrators to perform administrative tasks within AD. Specifically,

Win2K supports LDAP versions 2 and 3 to access Active Directory. For more information about LDAP, refer to RFC 2251.

LDAP is installed with Windows 2000 to natively access AD. If you have Windows 9*x* clients, you can install the Active Directory client contained on the Win2K Server installation medium under the folder \Clients\Win9x. The Active Directory client for Windows NT 4.0 is included with SP7.

Protocol Vulnerabilities

The TCP/IP suite of protocols is, by far, the most widely exploited. The benefits mentioned earlier—universality, interoperability, and scalability—are also liabilities that cause TCP/IP networks to fall victim to electronic attacks or information theft. Now that you have an understanding of the protocol suite and its components, we will review some of the more relevant TCP/IP security vulnerabilities (see Chapter 2 for more details).

IP SPOOFING, SESSION HIJACKING, MAN-IN-THE-MIDDLE, AND SNIFFERS   As mentioned in Chapter 2, IP spoofing, session hijacking, man-in-the-middle attacks, and sniffers are all used to exploit applications that rely on IP addresses for authentication.

In an IP spoof attack, the attacker either tries to predict or steal a sequence number for a TCP connection. With a sequence number in hand, the attacking system can then impersonate a real client or server on the network. This ability allows the attacker to receive stolen data or even transmit bad data to another system on the network. Since WinNT and Win2K do not use IP addresses in establishing authentication between systems, this attack is not as much of a threat. However, if you plan on integrating your Windows server into a network containing Unix, VMS, or other types of servers, the possibility of an IP spoofing attack exists.

Session hijacking is much like jamming radio signals. The intent is to broadcast with more "wattage" and overcome real data communication. This disruption in service allows a doppelganger system to impersonate another host or device on the network. With this impersonating system in place, your data is stolen or disrupted. This type of attack should be especially disconcerting considering Win2K Server now comes with the Telnet server enabled by default.

In a man-in-the-middle attack, the attacker sits between the client and the requested server. The attacking system then must trick the client into initiating a session. Once the session is initiated, the attacker passes data between the client and server. The primary purpose of this attack is to steal electronic data.

Sniffers "listen" on either the data sender or receiver's network segment and steal data. This type of data attack is also a low threat since the sniffer must have physical connectivity to either the source or destination segment. Most sniffer attacks are perpetrated by data thieves who physically break into a segment on your network or by employees within your organization who already have access to the network segments.

SOURCE ROUTING   In a source-routing attack, the malicious computer user steals a client's request for a TCP connection. In turn, the attacking system uses the source path of the request to obtain the client's IP address. Once the IP address and subnet mask are obtained, the attacking system can deduce an IP address of a trusted system on the network and gain the trust of the client system. Again, this is less likely within a Windows network since WinNT/2000 does not use IP addresses to trust other systems. This can be a concern, however, in heterogeneous environments where Windows integrates with Unix, VMS, and other systems.

SNMP ATTACKS   Many network administrators install SNMP on their servers and network devices to gain information about their network and monitor the status of their devices. However, the use of SNMP also exposes your network systems and devices to intelligence gathering from malicious users. Most SNMP agents are installed allowing anyone with SNMP installed read-only access to system monitoring information. This may sound benign, but by using a monitoring tool, a malicious user could gain access to the data collected by the SNMP agent to obtain your OS version, IP address, MAC address, and a host of other sensitive information about your system and network.

If you install the SNMP agent on your Win2K system, secure the agent by performing, at minimum, the following tasks:

▼ Remove PUBLIC from the accepted community names. Create a unique community name for your SNMP agents to use.

■ Only allow read-only access to your agent's SNMP traps. Never allow read-write or read-create unless absolutely necessary.

▲ Specifically designate from which hosts your Win2K system can accept SNMP packets. Do not enable the Accept SNMP Packets from Any Host option.

ANONYMOUS FTP   When configuring an FTP server using Win2K's IIS 5.0, you have the ability to set up anonymous FTP access. This allows anyone with a connection to your FTP server and an FTP client to access your FTP server and the files served. The best security practice is not to enable an FTP server. The second-best security option is to only enable users with the proper login and password to gain access to your FTP server. The third and less than optimal security option is to enable anonymous FTP access. In this situation, it is imperative that you apply and maintain the latest patches for Win2K and IIS and ensure that all available files served via FTP are not of a sensitive or confidential nature. Remember, because the FTP connection is anonymous, anyone has access and worse yet, you will not have any record of who accessed your files.

TELNET ATTACKS   Telnet attacks are possibly the oldest form of data crime. With older mainframe and Unix systems, Telnet was the only way to gain access to the system. Early electronic criminals seized upon this open door to crack logins and passwords and thus gain access to the system's data. Now that any Win2K product has the ability to act as a Telnet server, the threat is very real for Win2K systems.

To close this type of security vulnerability, only run the Telnet service on those machines that absolutely need it. If you run the Telnet service, however, make absolutely sure that your user accounts have adequate passwords, that the Guest account is disabled, and that any unnecessary user accounts are removed. You should also rename the Administrator account to ensure that an attacker cannot count on that login name as a way to gain entry through Telnet.

> **NOTE:** A recent security vulnerability was discovered with Telnet that allows a malicious user to obtain logon credentials using an HTML page. For more information, refer to Microsoft's Security Bulletin at **http://www.microsoft.com/technet/security/bulletin/MS00-067.asp**.

Protocol Security Solutions

With many of the vulnerabilities listed in the previous section, the best security is to follow the best practices for using a particular protocol. For example, secure your SNMP agents, disable anonymous FTP, and disable the Telnet service. These common-sense approaches will repel most of the attacks perpetrated on or within your network.

However, with IP spoofing, session hijacking, man-in-the-middle, sniffers, and source-routing attacks, some of the most effective security solutions involve configuring and managing your routers to recognize and repel such attacks. Once upon a time, routers were not much more than network links and were not "smart" enough to perform the necessary security tasks to thwart such attacks. However, as network devices come with more built-in security features, routers not only can, but should perform the security tasks necessary to repel these common data communication attacks.

And with older versions of WinNT, reconfiguring your network devices was the only way to provide a higher level of network communication security. With the introduction of Win2K, however, network administrators have another important tool in the security arsenal—IP Security.

INTERNET PROTOCOL SECURITY (IPSEC)   Encryption and its algorithms have long been used before the advent of the computer to hide the contents of confidential messages. And when the computer rolled onto the scene, many of these encryption methods were adapted to hide confidential electronic data. However, many of these methods and tools used to encrypt computer data exist at higher levels of the OSI model and therefore do not have a chance to affect both the data and headers of a network packet. For example, Secure Sockets Layer version 3/Transport Layer Security (SSL3/TLS) is used by browsers to protect confidential data, but this solution exists higher in the application layer to protect documents transmitted over the Internet. The packet headers of this data, however, are left unprotected and thus vulnerable to attack.

It is only recently that IPSec has become widely available to hide both the contents of network data and the packet itself. The greatest benefit to IPSec is that it offers end-to-end security, meaning that the sender and receiver have to have IPSec-aware systems. However, any intermediate routing device just forwards the packet on. These intermediate devices are oblivious to the fact that the packet is encrypted.

NOTE: When routing IPSec traffic, a network device does not need to have the same IPSec settings as your hosts since these devices will simply pass the encrypted packets on to their final destination. If, however, you must send IPSec traffic through firewalls, secure gateways, or proxy servers, IPSec traffic may be blocked by default. You should refer to Microsoft's Knowledge Base article at **http://support.microsoft.com/support/kb/articles/Q233/2/56.ASP** for information to configure your network systems to allow IPSec traffic.

There are currently two basic types of IPSec modes: *tunnel mode* and *transport mode*. When using transport mode, only the data carried by each packet is encrypted. Tunnel mode, on the other hand, encrypts both the header information and the data. Obviously, tunnel mode is more effective in thwarting attacks such as IP spoofing and sniffers because your IP address and various other pieces of IP addressing information are encrypted during transmission. This way, even if your packet is intercepted, the malicious computer user must break the IPSec encryption to discover any information.

VIP: See Chapter 16 for details on IPSec and how to configure it for use with Win2K.

Other Popular Protocols

Although TCP/IP is becoming the standard for network communications, many home and corporate networks do not have the luxury of switching cold turkey from other protocols that might currently be in use. For this reason, it is equally important to familiarize yourself with other popular protocols, their uses, and potential security pitfalls.

NOTE: One of the major reasons TCP/IP is exploited so frequently is its ability to connect systems to the Internet. Attackers can literally sit at home and remotely break into remote systems using the Internet. Because other protocols are not used for connectivity to the Internet, they present fewer security threats.

IPX/SPX

IPX/SPX (Internetwork Packet Exchange/Sequenced Packet Exchange) was developed by Novell for data communication to and from NetWare servers. Until NetWare 5, all NetWare servers used IPX/SPX to communicate. IPX is the lower connection-less communication protocol, which lies within the OSI model's network layer. In other words, like IP, it is very fast and does not require acknowledgements from packet transfers. SPX is the higher connection-oriented protocol, which lies within the transport layer. In contrast, SPX, like TCP, requires packet ordering and acknowledgements from successful data transfers.

IPX/SPX's major security issues are similar to those of TCP/IP. IPX versions of sniffers, man-in-the-middle attacks, and session hijacking are all potential threats to this protocol. Luckily, since the Internet uses TCP/IP for communication, it is less likely that malicious computer users will break into your network electronically by exploiting

IPX/SPX. The threats for IPX/SPX usually come from a system with access to your local area network or hosts.

Unfortunately, Win2K does not offer tools to directly close security holes with IPX/SPX.

To install Microsoft's implementation of IPX/SPX, NWLink, manually on a particular Win2K system, follow these steps:

1. Right-click the Network Places desktop icon and choose Properties.
2. Select the network connection where you would like to install IPX, and then right-click and select Properties.
3. Click the Install button, select Protocol, and click the Add button.
4. Select NWLink IPX/SPX/NetBIOS Compatible Transport Protocol, then click OK.

After the installation of NWLink is complete, you will see it installed within the Properties dialog box along with NWLink NetBIOS.

NetBEUI

NetBEUI will often be found in older Windows networks or mixed WinNT/Win2K environments. Additionally, homes and small business offices may use NetBEUI for network communication because there is almost no administrative overhead to maintaining NetBEUI communications.

NetBIOS (Networked Basic Input-Output System) was developed by IBM and Sytek as a networking add-on to PC BIOS. This protocol ran on top of lower-level protocols such as IPX and TCP/IP. Consequently, it is rarely used in current operating systems. NetBEUI (NetBIOS Extended User Interface) was developed by Microsoft to add more functionality to NetBIOS. NetBEUI does not map cleanly on the OSI model because it covers the transport, network, and data link layers. One big benefit to NetBEUI is that it can be used by all current Windows platforms. However, its poor routing capabilities and network performance have caused this protocol to slowly disappear.

Since NetBEUI cannot be routed between networks, all attacks on your critical systems have to take place from the attached network segment. For this reason, a NetBEUI network poses a lesser security threat to your computer systems. Again, a sniffer is always a real threat, but in the case of NetBEUI, the attacker must have access to the segment.

To install NetBEUI on a particular Win2K system, follow these steps:

1. Right-click the Network Places desktop icon and choose Properties.
2. Select the network connection where you would like to install IP, and then right-click and select Properties.
3. Click the Install button, select Protocol, and click the Add button.
4. Select NetBEUI, and then click OK.

After the installation of NetBEUI is complete, you will see it installed within the Properties dialog box.

NETWORK SERVICES

While network protocols form the lower layers of network communication, network services facilitate that communication by providing necessary information to network servers and workstations. As with WinNT, Dynamic Host Configuration Protocol (DHCP), Domain Name System (DNS), and Windows Internet Name Service (WINS) form the core network services available to network clients. However, in Win2K, the emphasis has shifted from WINS to Dynamic DNS for name-to-IP address resolution.

DHCP

Dynamic Host Configuration Protocol (DHCP) is designed to automatically provide TCP/IP settings to network workstations. As a network administrator, DHCP is a godsend, allowing the administrator to avoid assigning and maintaining static IP addresses for all workstations on the network. In addition to IP addresses, a DHCP server can dynamically dole out important information such as WINS server addresses, DNS server addresses, default gateways, and other IP settings. So if any of these settings were to ever change, the network workstation will receive the updated information the next time an IP address is requested. For more information on DHCP, refer to RFC 1541.

Because network clients merely lease an IP address, each workstation must go through a process to obtain that IP address, establish the lease, and renew the lease. The process involves five important phases:

▼ **Discovery** The network client broadcasts a message over the network to locate all of the DHCP servers located on the network. This discovery request includes the client's MAC address for the DHCP server response since the client does not yet have an IP address.

■ **Offer** All DHCP servers on the network respond back to the client's MAC address with an available IP address. The Offer message is also a broadcast message. However, the message includes the requesting client's MAC address. All other network clients ignore the broadcast message.

■ **Request** The network client then responds via broadcast message to accept the offered IP address and notify other DHCP servers that their offers are rejected. The other rejected DHCP servers return the offered IP addresses back to their available address pools.

■ **Acknowledgement** The DHCP server leasing the accepted IP address then responds to the client with another broadcast message acknowledging the lease of the IP address. The message is sent again via broadcast since the client still does not have an IP address. The network client will not accept the IP address until the Acknowledgement message is received and processed from the DHCP server. Once the ACK message is received, the client accepts and assigns the offered IP address.

▲ **Renewal**   Since a network client is only leasing the IP address, the client must renew its lease to continue using the assigned IP address. This lease period is configurable at the DHCP server and is generally set at the longer possible period to avoid a deluge of network traffic. (In Win2K, the lease period is set at eight days by default.) The client will attempt to renew its IP address when 50 percent of the lease period has expired. For example, if the lease period is ten days, then the client will attempt a renewal at five days. If the server is not available, the client will keep its current IP address and retry the renewal process when 87.5 percent of the lease period has expired. Using the previous example, the client would retry renewal three quarters of the way during the eighth day. If the DHCP server is again unavailable, the client will start the process from the beginning, trying to discover all DHCP servers and obtain a new IP address.

Installation and Configuration

To install the DHCP service on a Win2K server, perform these steps:

1. From the Control Panel's Add/Remove Programs tool, select Add/Remove Windows Components.

2. Select Networking Services and click the Details button.

3. Select Dynamic Host Configuration Protocol (DHCP) and click the OK button.

   To configure various DHCP settings, select the DHCP tool from the Administrative Tools folder. The DHCP tool will allow you to define a pool of IP addresses, default TCP/IP settings for clients, excluded IP addresses, reserved IP addresses, and other DHCP settings, as shown here.

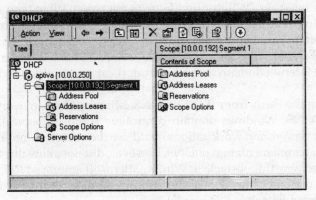

Security Concerns

The biggest security concern involving DHCP server is the idea of a *rogue DHCP server*. Either through malicious actions or inadvertent DHCP service installation by an employee on a network server, a rogue DHCP server interrupts DHCP requests from clients from the legitimate DHCP servers. Although a rogue DHCP server is not as damaging as other security attacks, its presence on your network can still cause the considerable disruption of network communications.

To avoid this type of situation, Win2K allows you to set up a list of authorized DHCP servers. Unfortunately, there are two major drawbacks to this new security feature. The first drawback is that you must install the first DHCP on a domain controller or a member server—the DHCP server authorization requires Active Directory to operate. After the first DHCP server is installed, however, you can install DHCP on workgroup servers or any other type of server. The second drawback is that only Win2K DHCP servers can be on the authorized list. WinNT servers or other types of operating systems cannot be added.

To add a DHCP server as an authorized server, perform these steps:

1. Within the DHCP tool, right-click DHCP | Manage Authorized Servers.

2. Click the Authorize button, specify the IP address of the desired DHCP server, and click OK.

DNS

With the introduction of Win2K, Domain Name System (DNS) has replaced Microsoft's WINS implementation to resolve computer names to IP addresses. DNS has always been the directory service of choice for the Internet, Unix systems, and other types of networks. But it was not until Win2K that DNS became the standard for Windows networks. In fact, Active Directory relies on DNS to provide its name space. When you create a domain within Active Directory, the domain name is actually a DNS name. For example, your company may set up a domain named *ourcompany.com*. This name follows the standards set forth for DNS names regardless of whether or not you have this domain name registered through an Internet domain name registrar. (Learn more about Active Directory in Chapter 8.)

When shifting the focus from WINS to DNS, Microsoft had to overcome one major obstacle. With WINS, Windows domain controllers could dynamically register their presence so other servers and workstations could use their services for network authentication. The typical implementation of DNS, however, did not allow this type of dynamic update. So to overcome this obstacle in Win2K, Microsoft embraced RFC 2136 to create a DNS that allows domain controllers to dynamically update records. This new system is appropriately named Dynamic DNS, or DDNS.

TIP: Because a discussion of DNS could consume an entire book, you may want to check out *Windows 2000 DNS Server*, by William Wong (Osborne/McGraw-Hill, 2000), for more details on installing, configuring, and administering DNS within Win2K.

WINS

The Windows Internet Name Service (WINS), like DNS, translates computer names into IP addresses. However, WINS translates NetBIOS names to IP addresses instead of the Fully-Qualified Domain Names (FQDN) that DNS uses. As mentioned previously, Win2K was the first Microsoft operating system to move away from WINS toward the new Windows standard of Dynamic DNS. If, however, you must integrate your Win2K server into a heterogeneous environment with previous versions of Windows, you will probably have to install, configure, and maintain WINS for quite a while.

Win2K, however, does improve on the WINS of WinNT with the following new features:

▼ **Persistent Connections** WINS servers can maintain a persistent connection for replication purposes, thus eliminating the overhead in opening and terminating replication connections.

■ **Manual Tombstoning** When a deleted WINS record was removed from one WINS server, it was possible under WinNT that another WINS server would re-replicate the deleted record around the network before the deletion instruction took place. Manual tombstoning eliminates this problem.

■ **Enhanced Search** The new WINS server allows better record searching by offering a set of search criteria.

■ **Record Verification** You can now quickly compare the entries for a particular WINS record across WINS servers.

▲ **Export Function** You can now export your WINS list to a comma-delimited file for import into other applications for reporting purposes.

TIP: Since a discussion of WINS could consume an entire book, you may want to check out *Admin911: DNS & WINS*, by Dustin Sauter and Scott Hall (due out Spring 2001 from Osborne/McGraw-Hill), for more details on installing, configuring, and administering WINS within Win2K.

Installation and Configuration

To install the WINS service on a Win2K server, perform these steps:

1. From the Control Panel's Add/Remove Programs tool, select Add/Remove Windows Components.

2. Select Networking Services and click the Details button.

3. Select Windows Internet Name Service (WINS) and click OK.

To configure various WINS settings, select the WINS tool from the Administrative Tools folder. The WINS tool will allow you to view registered computer systems, define WINS replication partners, and establish other WINS settings.

Security Concerns

As with DDNS, one of the biggest security threats for WINS is unauthorized computer users making updates to the WINS tables. However, unlike DNS, WINS must manually configure which servers can modify, update, or delete records. These trusted systems are called *replication partners*. Replication partners ensure that all workstations and servers on the network receive the same NetBIOS name-to-IP address resolution.

To add a WINS replication partner, open the WINS tool. Expand your WINS server, right-click Replication Partners and select New Replication Partner.

RECAP

Network protocols and services form the basis for successful network communication. Their use is critical for all network users to access data, run programs, and communicate over the network. You should understand these critical components and protect their operation. This chapter has provided you with a general overview of some of the more popular network protocols and services and security measures to protect each.

CHAPTER 7

Windows 2000 Security Risks and Solutions

"Understanding all the security risks in Windows 2000 is like herding crickets. Have you ever tried to herd crickets?"

—Phil Cox

In Chapters 2 and 3, we talked about generic security threats and countermeasures. This chapter is going to revisit some of the concepts introduced in the earlier chapters but it is going to focus on Win2K issues. Our viewpoint in the chapter remains at a strategic level instead of addressing specific tactical details. Because of the high-level view used here, much of the information in this chapter can easily be generalized to other operating systems, but the intended focus is Win2K. Subsequent chapters in the book focus on detailed information specific to Win2K subsystems and services.

Two aspects of Win2K distinguish it from Unix when considering the possible threats to security. First, Win2K contains a great deal of support for older Microsoft operating systems. Second, Win2K integrates features and subsystems across a wide variety of services that it offers. Each of these very desirable features may also be exploited to form the basis of an intrusion.

THE FOCAL POINTS

It is pretty safe to assume that the vast majority of potential attackers must rely on one or more of three factors to gain control of your systems:

- ▼ A user account that has a guessable password
- ▧ A system that is improperly configured or administered
- ▲ A published exploit for which a hotfix or administrative fix is available

Most administrators in the world can assume that there are very few attackers in the world that will develop a new method that will be used to specifically target and exploit their particular systems. Doing so would generally take detailed knowledge of the internal systems and often the internal business practices as well.

It turns out that even if you are vulnerable to one or more of the three problems in the previous list, an attacker without some knowledge of your systems will find them difficult to exploit without detection if you are using good auditing policies and practices, or you are using a suitable intrusion detection system. This is because an attacker who has no specific knowledge of your systems will normally have to repeat an attempt many, many times. This should either generate an audit trail or set off an alert.

How Does an Attacker Gain Knowledge About Your Systems?

Information can be difficult to restrict. It is even more difficult when one of the primary functions of your computer systems is to facilitate the sharing of information. Win2K's

Active Directory is designed to provide a central repository of data for your domain. Although it supports strong authentication and access control, the default configuration may not be adequate for all customers.

Typically, unauthenticated users can make some AD queries about users or groups. For example, if an attacker has a Security ID (SID) of a user or group he can probably query the AD to find out the descriptive name that is associated with the SID. This might not sound like much of a threat but it can still be useful information. Suppose, for example, that an attacker has a SID that has a descriptive name of "purchasing administrators." This tells the attacker that it might be useful to compromise accounts that have this SID as a group membership.

There are many other avenues that may present themselves to a determined attacker:

▼ Unauthenticated users may be able to get access to information that may be exploited.

■ Users may be able to log on as guests and gain access to resources available to the Everyone group.

■ Administrative users might log on at insecure remote locations.

■ Unattended Windows (9x, NT, 2K) desktops can be doorways into the network for attackers.

■ Network sniffers can capture traffic.

▲ Captured mail may contain sensitive information.

How Can You Prevent an Attacker from Gaining Knowledge About Your System?

If you know (or believe) that attackers are trying to gain knowledge about your system, you need to figure out how to prevent it. Most of the information gained by an attacker is gained via querying services that should not be accessible, in one way or another, to them. The most important overall strategy in preventing attackers from getting information is to not provide it to them. This may sound too simplistic, but many people overlook the obvious. As a standard practice, you should take the following precautions:

▼ Limit information in DNS (you may need to run an internal and external DNS if you are using the AD).

■ Disable unnecessary services.

■ Secure the data in transit (that is, through encryption).

■ Filter services with routers.

▲ Apply appropriate Win2K access controls on the data itself.

How Do You Decide What Level of Information Is Acceptable to Disclose?

One of the biggest problems is that people do not think about what they actually want to give out. It tends to happen by default. For example, you may not want your employee list publicly available, but someone else decides to place the "old" corporate Web server out on the Net to be the "new" e-commerce server and does not remove the old information. Part of the security process is to decide what can and can't be disclosed.

One problem with this concept is that a number of Win2K servers do not allow you to granularly define what you do and do not want to let out. For example, you cannot limit the type of MSRPC calls that will be allowed. You either allow them all or none, so you can't say "I'll let the user info out, but not the password information." The only way to limit this is with Win2K ACLs.

The bottom line is to understand the services and what they offer and then only allow those services that you want.

BACKWARDS COMPATIBILITY IS THE BANE OF SECURITY

Microsoft has a huge installed base of users and systems. To their credit they have provided lots of backwards compatibility so that organizations can easily migrate to Win2K over time. However, these features can also cause problems for people that are responsible for system security.

If your domain must support legacy operating systems, some of the security features that Win2K offers may not be available to you. In other cases, the security may be downgraded only when one of the older operating systems or applications is actively being used. For example, some applications may not support Kerberos authentication and a weaker form of authentication may end up being used. In the case of FTP, this will mean that clear text passwords are being sent over the network.

Many organizations might decide to upgrade their existing systems to Win2K instead of performing a clean installation of the new operating system. This can save a lot of time and effort but upgraded systems will not necessarily end up with the same security permissions that are put in place during a clean installation. The upgrade procedure usually preserves the security settings that were on the original system as much as possible. If the security configuration of the system was poor before upgrading, it will likely be poor after the upgrade as well. You should be very cognizant of this point when upgrading critical network and application servers at your organization.

TOO MUCH INTEGRATION CAN BE A BAD THING

Microsoft product literature often highlights how well integrated their applications are with the operating system. From the perspective of a typical user "who just wants to get the job done," the level of integration that Microsoft provides is a wonderful thing. From the perspective of the people responsible for security, it can be a frightening aspect of the system.

By now, probably everyone involved with Microsoft operating systems and security is aware that the Microsoft scripting services can be used by Microsoft Outlook and that this feature can be exploited by attackers. This is just one example of how features that are developed to meet the demands of the typical customer can be used against the very same customers.

Since Microsoft has made Internet Explorer part of the desktop, every attacker knows that IE will be available on each user's desktop. If an exploit of IE is discovered then you have a race between the attackers and your system administrators to see who can get the desktops secured before the exploit is used. If you have a site that is very interesting to attackers, your system administrators might find themselves outnumbered and facing daunting odds.

Another area of integration that worries many system administrators who are new to Windows is Microsoft's use of Remote Procedure Call (RPC) and named pipes. Many Unix administrators are used to each network protocol using a well-defined and controlled port number. Most firewall administrators depend on this behavior. Microsoft applications and services frequently use the Microsoft RPC. This means that many different applications use the same port numbers for at least part of their communication or initialization. It also means that a large number of application and services depend on the Microsoft RPC service. If this service could be exploited, it might be used as an entry point into other areas of the system.

AUTHENTICATION

When we think of authentication-based attacks or attacks on the authentication mechanism, we usually mean acquiring a password or compromising the authentication protocol. Passwords are a primary target for attackers, and for some, acquiring passwords is the primary goal itself. It is usually much easier than trying to compromise the authentication protocol. It is not uncommon for attackers to run network sniffers, steal files, social engineer, or dive into dumpsters to get the information they need. The other method, compromising the protocol, is much harder, yet potentially more "information" rich because once you compromise it, you can use it wherever you go. Once the information is obtained, your systems and possibly those of your business partners, customers, and employees are at risk. We will discuss both of these methods of authentication-based attacks a bit more in depth.

NOTE: See Chapter 11 for more details on authentication.

Reusable Credentials

Although there are many ways to get access to a reusable credential (such as stealing a smartcard, the public-private key-pair, or a SecureID card and PIN from a user), for Win2K it usually means getting a username and password. This can be done a couple of ways:

▼ Use the Anonymous and Guest accounts.

■ Obtain a username then attempt to guess the password using a dictionary attack.

■ Obtain the password representation from a local SAM database and try to "crack" them.

▲ Sniff the usernames and passwords off the network.

Using the Anonymous and Guest Accounts

Anonymous access (a.k.a. *null session*) is defined as a connection with a blank (that is, null) username and a blank password. As discussed in the last chapter, the IPC$ share is used for authentication purposes for SMB/CIFS-based traffic. When someone makes an anonymous connection to the IPC$ share, the anonymous user is placed in the Everyone group (this is a Win2K local group and is described more in Chapter 10). This means that any permission that the Everyone group has on the system, the anonymous user has as well. Once this anonymous authentication is made, the user may issue MSRPC calls to obtain information (such as a user list) or attempt to access any files that are shared by the Everyone group. The Guest account is a member of the Everyone group as well and poses the same problem. While WinNT was vulnerable to information enumeration via the null session connection, Win2K installs with the RestrictAnonymous key enabled. This key prevents a majority of the MSRPC calls to fail with "access denied."

It should be obvious that this type of functionality could be very dangerous if used by an attacker. It would be nice if you could just get rid of it, but you can't. This type of connection was, and is, a staple of many network communications in the Windows networking environment (see Chapter 11 for more details). Suffice to say that the need for anonymous connections will not be going away anytime soon. This means that we need to restrict these accounts as much as possible. The primary target when using these accounts is the Registry, file shares, and MSRPC calls.

Obtaining a Username, Then Attempting to Dictionary "Guess" the Password

With this method, an attacker can get one or more legitimate usernames through one of many mechanisms:

▼ Anonymous connections, using MSRPC to enumerate the user list

■ NBTSTAT against a domain controller

■ SNMP via the LANManager MIB

■ LDAP queries against an Active Directory Server

■ E-mail addresses and mail servers (remember that Win2K usernames are *<username>@<domain>*)

▲ Default accounts: Administrator, Guest, IUSR_*systemname*, and so on

Once the attacker gets a username, he or she can attempt to guess (a.k.a. *dictionary attack*) or "bruteforce" legitimate passwords until one works. Once the attacker gets a valid username and password, he or she can use it to access system resources.

THE ADMINISTRATOR ACCOUNT: A FOCAL POINT   The Administrator account is the first account targeted because it has unlimited privileges. The attacker will tend to focus on the administrative shares (C$, D$, WINNT$) on your servers and execute administrative MSRPC commands (such as adding a user), as this would prove to be very fruitful if access can be gained.

Obtaining the Password Representation from the Local SAM Database and Trying to "Crack" It

This type of attack is focused on getting access to information stored in the local SAM database on a machine. This could provide local account information and passwords that could potentially (and very likely) be the same as a domain-based account. The goal tends to be accessing an archived/backup copy of the SAM database from one of the following:

▼ The %Systemroot%\Repair directory.

■ A live SAM database (via pwdump2).

■ An Emergency Repair Disk.

■ Backup tapes.

▲ Local API calls to extract information. (Note that you already need administrative access on the machine, but this could allow you to get information on other accounts local to this machine, which could potentially yield an account with a duplicate domain account.)

Once the attacker gets the information, he or she can use a password cracker, such as L0phtcrack, to attempt to crack the passwords. The likelihood that at least one password on a system with more than just default accounts will be cracked is very high (greater than 80 percent).

By definition, this is a single machine attack, *unless* the attacker can get the information from a Win2K domain controller, then the information in the SAM is for the domain accounts. Please see Chapter 8 for details on Win2K and WinNT domain integration.

Sniffing the Usernames and Passwords Off the Network

This type of attack is focused on getting usernames and passwords from network traffic. There are two primary methods: getting cleartext and getting SMB authentication packets. The first, and easiest, method is getting the information in cleartext when a user authenticates to a service that allows it. This would be sniffing the cleartext username and password that is passed in the authentication traffic from such services as Telnet, FTP, SMTP, POP, IMAP, and HTTP Basic Authentication. Once attackers have this information, they have something they can use right away to attempt to authenticate with. The second method would be sniffing older Win2K-based SMB authentication packets with programs such as readsmb (from L0pht). This information is available when operating in a "mixed mode" domain (see Chapter 8) or if using the NTLM authentication in the Win2K Telnet server. Although this information is not immediately useful, an attacker can use a password cracker such as L0phtcrack to "crack" these passwords as well.

Authentication Protocol Risks

Compromising the authentication protocol is not a trivial task. Most of the protocols have had significant peer review at this point in time, so the risks are limited. Most of the risk comes from Microsoft supporting backward compatibility and their own extensions to current standards.

Kerberos

Just because the Kerberos protocol has been around for quite some time and has been through numerous peer review cycles, you should not assume that it is bullet-proof. There are a number of potential weaknesses:

▼ Running an insecure Key Distribution Center (KDC) could allow account data to be compromised. By default, each domain controller is also a KDC.

■ The default Kerberos authentication is reusable passwords, so it is still vulnerable to password attacks.

■ There has been no independent code review on the Microsoft implementation of the protocol.

■ Microsoft's "embrace and extend" mentality and how it affects Kerberos.

▲ Trust relationships: one-to-many (client) and many-to-one (server).

NOTE: See Chapters 8 and 11 for more information on Kerberos.

MSV1_0

MSV1_0 is used for local and workgroup authentication in Win2K and is the default WinNT authentication protocol. By default MSV1_0 uses NTLMv1 and LM as the authentication levels. This means that Win2K has the same authentication vulnerabilities as WinNT when it uses MSV1_0. This really only matters in network-based authentication. The potential risks are

▼ Exposing LM challenge-response packets on the network

▲ Susceptibility to downgrade attacks

Public Key

Public keys are not a panacea, as they are subject to the same problems as passwords in the sense that they can be used for unauthorized access. With passwords, you just have to guess the right username and password, and this can be done against a central database of users (that is, the domain). With public keys, on the other hand, a hacker would have to attack the end node systems to compromise the users. What a hacker needs to compromise a public key is its associated private key, and usually to get this, the hacker has to attack a specific end node. This makes the target much harder for the hacker to specifically identify. This type of attack tends to be focused on a specific target, as the likelihood of a large number of accounts/keys being broken is small. The main problem is that the likelihood of a single public-private key pair being compromised is fairly high, since most end-user computers are fairly insecure. In Win2K, the private key could potentially be compromised in a number of ways:

▼ Through Certificate Services with inadequate ACLs and authentication requirements

▧ By compromising the server running the Certificate Services

▲ By getting access to the user's key store via programmatic methods

PPTP

PPTP will allow remote users to attempt to establish a Virtual Private Network (VPN) with the PPTP server. The authentication is done against the local accounts database, a domain, RADIUS, or other third-party authentication. Win2K implements PPTPv2 (that is, it uses MS-CHAPv2), which does not appear to be as vulnerable as PPTPv1 (that is, using MS-CHAPv1). However, it does support MSCHAPv1 for compatibility. The risks associated with PPTP include

▼ Susceptibility to downgrade attacks to MS-CHAPv1

▧ Lack of strong authentication by default

▧ Ability to attack user accounts with potentially no auditing

▲ Ability to bypass firewall restrictions since many firewalls allow VPNs (that is, PPTP) through to an internal VPN server

NOTE: See Chapter 16 for more information on PPTP.

Cleartext

FTP, HTTP Basic Authentication, Telnet, POP, and IMAP are supported by Win2K services. They all pass user and authentication data in the clear. The risk with these services are

▼ Sniffing of confidential data

▲ Sniffing of authentication credentials

AUTHORIZATION

All Win2K authorization happens through Access Control Lists or User Rights. The Win2K security model enforces the authorization model on the system. The weaknesses associated with authorization occur on systems that are configured in such a way that they cannot enforce the authorization rules or they have programmatic flaws that allow the authorization mechanisms to be bypassed. Some of the areas of vulnerability in authorization are

▼ Access Control Lists

■ The Security Reference Monitor

■ Weak client security

▲ The security subsystem

Access Control Lists (ACLs)

ACLs provide one of the primary methods by which authorization to objects (that is, files, directories, and AD objects) is determined. We will look at a couple of risk areas with ACLs.

File Systems

Selection and configuration of file systems is a critical part of the Win2K security model. The ability of Win2K to properly authorize access to objects deals with its use of the NTFS file system. Win2K supports two types of file systems: FAT32 and NTFS. They are described briefly here (for more details, see Chapter 12).

▼ **FAT32** This file system provides no security controls whatsoever. For example, if you create FAT32 partitions on your Win2K Server, anyone who can log on to the system will have full control of any file on the FAT32 partition.

▲ **NTFS** This file system provides the ability to assign Discretionary Access Control Lists (DACL) and System Access Control Lists (SACL) to the objects stored on it (see Chapters 5 and 12 for more details). It is required for any level of real security on a system. The major risks with NTFS are not that an attacker will bypass the NTFS driver or exploit a bug in it, but that the administrator will improperly set the ACLs or not set them at all!

EFS   The NTFS file system supports the Encrypting File System, as described in Chapter 5. This encrypted file service provides protection from prying eyes, even when booted from another operating system, and the only way to compromise the system is to get hold of the keys that were used to encrypt the information in the first place. Potential risks include

▼ Corrupting the key store or EFS information on the file, as no one would be able to read the file contents after that.

■ A bug in the EFS recovery agent (RA).

▲ Disclosure of the user password or administrative password for the system on which the files are encrypted. By default, the RA for any file on the system is the Administrator account, so anyone with the Administrator (or other designated RA) access, may be able to get access to any file.

NOTE: See Chapter 12 for more details.

PHYSICAL ACCESS   If an attacker can get physical access to a client computer without anyone's knowledge, he or she can boot your system to a different OS and use a low-level disk scanning program to view disk information. The potential risks include

▼ The ability of an attacker to use the client computer to gather information on the local system (such as cached passwords)

▲ The ability of an attacker to boot an alternative OS to gain connectivity to the network in order to attack other systems

Security Reference Monitor (SRM)

The SRM is another key component in the authorization process. It actually makes the determination to allow or deny access, so if an attacker can get by it, he or she is home free! Some of the potential ways an attacker can do this include

▼ Exploiting programming bugs to get elevated privileges such as Debug a Process.

▲ Getting another process that is running at a higher privilege level (such as IIS as LocalSystem) to execute his or her code. (IIS is notorious for this.)

Exploiting the Security Subsystem

A similar risk as those inherent in the SRM is the ability to get a malicious piece of code into the path of the security subsystem, for example, by replacing the Graphical

Identification and Authentication (GINA) or adding a Notification Package. An attacker can use any piece of code that is placed in the path of the security subsystem to compromise the entire system by

▼ Gathering usernames and cleartext passwords

■ Modifying the access token when it is created

▲ Executing code as the LocalSystem

Weak Clients Compromise Security

Any system that can participate in the domain has the potential to gather extensive information about resources on that domain. If an attacker can get access to a client on a domain, it might give him or her just enough information to get into a server, then from there into a domain controller, then anywhere in the network. Attackers can exploit weak client systems by

▼ Installing a keyboard reader on an insecure client.

■ Gathering usernames and passwords (although local, there is a high likelihood that they will have matching domain accounts).

▲ Accessing confidential information stored locally.

To state the obvious, systems that run DOS, Windows for Workgroups, and Windows 9x are inherently insecure. They do not provide the strong logon and authentication protections that Win2K and WinNT computers provide.

NOTE: See Chapter 17 for more information.

AUDITING

One of the things attackers will target is the auditing data. If they can corrupt, change, or delete their tracks, then it is highly unlikely that they will be identified. The following situations offer attackers the opportunity to exploit the auditing data:

▼ **Auditing Is Never Turned On**   By default, security auditing is not enabled on Win2K. This is by far the greatest risk.

■ **Inadequate Data Capture**   One weakness in Win2K auditing is that you cannot customize the data that is captured. There are many instances where the Win2K auditing is totally inadequate for your needs, such as the complete inability to record IP addresses in the security audit data.

- ■ **Full Audit Logs**   The attacker will attempt to generate security events that will fill the logs, which can be used to overwrite the data that may indicate the attack. This is very effective, since the default EventLog rotation is to overwrite events when necessary.

- ■ **Permissions to Manage Logs**   Attackers will attempt to gain access to an account that has the Manage the Security and Audit Logs user right. This way, they can delete the security events as needed.

- ▲ **Auditing Bugs**   Attackers will use bugs discovered in the auditing functions of Win2K or the services it is providing to mask their attacks or presence. For example, by default IIS logging will stop when the disk is full, but a bug in the IIS auditing code causes a change to what got logged when the disk space was freed up and logging was resumed.

An attacker's main focus will be on deleting the logs if they exist, but most of the time they don't exist, so it is a non-issue.

NOTE: See Chapter 13 for more details.

OTHER RISKS

This section describes the high-level risks associated with other Win2K services and features. These services fall into four categories: OS programming bugs, network services, BackOffice services, and other core services. You can really break it into two general categories: functions and services that Win2K relies on (such as the Active Directory) and those that provide functions to external clients (such as the Exchange server).

OS Programming Bugs

There are a number of programming bugs that exist, and more will be discovered over the course of time, that will provide a mechanism to breach the Win2K security shell. The best examples are from WinNT currently, so we will look at them for reference.

BeSysAdm, SecHole, and their predecessor GetAdmin, are three of the most commonly used local privilege escalation attacks against WinNT. These programs will add any user to the Administrators group. GetAdmin worked by using a buffer overflow in the WinNT kernel to add the Debug user right to the access token of the user executing the program. Then the program, now with the modified access token, will "debug" the Winlogon process and attach a "suspended thread." This thread is actually just a piece of code that will add the user to the Administrators group. Once Winlogon "resumes" the suspended thread, it will execute the command. Since Winlogon runs in the context of the LocalSystem account, the SRM will allow the command to complete. Then the user just logs out and back in again. Now he or she is a member of the Administrators group.

The original uses of these bugs were only via a local console, but many sites have demonstrated the ability to use them remotely with servers either running attacks against a Web site or using the Telnet server to get remote access and run the exploit.

These attacks are very simple to exploit, but also *very* devastating. You can see why it is so important to have bullet-proof code in the trusted portion of the operating system. The one good thing is that Microsoft tends to be pretty timely in issuing patches for those bugs, so with a good maintenance program you should be able to fix the bugs before they get too widespread. Obviously, this does not help if you are the first site to be exploited, but then you are working on the law of averages.

Networking Services

Win2K supports many networking services, and they all elevate the risk to Win2K. The following are some of the more attractive network services from an attacker's standpoint.

NOTE: See Chapter 6 for more details.

TCP/IP

The Microsoft TCP/IP stack has been notorious for coding bugs. There have been numerous denial of service–based attacks directed at sending malformed packets to the stack to attempt to crash the machine. There is no reason to expect that the code is now bullet-proof, especially with all of the new, added features. The only problem is that there is little that can be done outside of keeping an eye on the hotfixes and applying them as needed. Here are some of the potential risks:

▼   Denial of service attacks.

▲   Improper security decisions based on flawed packet data. (For example, does the IPSec security filter properly re-assemble fragmented packets *before* it makes its filtering decision? If not, then an attacker might be able to bypass filtering rules using fragmented packets.)

DNS

Win2K is very dependent on valid DNS information. DNS replaces WINS as the primary name service in Win2K, and the Active Directory is directly tied to the DNS namespace. Any compromise/corrupt/spoof information regarding DNS is potentially devastating in a Win2K network (and on any network for that matter). Here are some of the potential risks to the DNS data:

- ▼ Poisoning the DNS data
- ▣ Forging DNS response
- ▣ Gathering DNS information
- ▲ Corrupting or forging dynamic updates

DHCP

DHCP has become a staple of the network infrastructure for many organizations. It eases administrative burden and helps with mobility. Here are some of the potential risks associated with DHCP:

- ▼ Spoofing of the DHCP server to provide clients with invalid settings
- ▲ Gathering detailed information from the DHCP server itself, or sniffing it off of the network

WINS

Although Win2K theoretically does not use NetBIOS, the reality is that non-Win2K systems (such as WinNT and Win 98) will be around for quite a while. Because they use NetBIOS, the requirements for NetBIOS name service will continue to be there, and thus we will have issues with WINS. WINS provides attackers with the following opportunities:

- ▼ The ability to gain valuable service-related information from machine names
- ▣ The ability to corrupt WINS server data
- ▲ The ability to inject invalid entries into the WINS server

SNMP

Not much attention is given to SNMP, but it has the potential to be a very serious security hole in your network. SNMP not only provides a way to gather detailed information about a wide variety of information on your systems, but it can also allow you to set a number of configuration options as well. Please see Chapter 6 for more details. Here are some of the potential risks associated with SNMP:

- ▼ Default community strings of "public" and "private"
- ▣ Ability to set configuration parameters
- ▲ Ability to gather detailed system (and potentially domain) information

Some BackOffice Services

BackOffice provides a number of services, such as e-mail, relational database, Web server, and Internet proxy. These services provide significant functionality, and also provide potential exposures. We will look at the risks of the most frequently used services here.

Microsoft Proxy Server (MPS)

Since MPS potentially guards the gates to your internal network, this is a very likely target for attack. Compromise of this box can expose the entire internal network to the untrusted networks. Here are some of the potential risks associated with Proxy Server:

▼ It is an ISAPI DLL, so any fundamental flaw in IIS will also be in the Proxy Server.

■ Improper configuration can allow the system to become a "router" as well as a Proxy Server.

▲ The machine could become an entry point into a domain.

The configuration issues are a very likely scenario if you don't have an experienced MPS administrator.

NOTE: See Chapter 15 for more details.

RRAS

Much like MPS, RRAS provides a potential path into your internal network. This can be accomplished with the routing, remote access, or VPN services. There are many ways to abuse RRAS to gain access to a network that you would not normally get access to. Here are some of those potential risks:

▼ Improper configuration could provide a direct "route" to your internal network.

■ Unrestricted VPN allows bypass of routers.

■ RRAS provides an avenue to attempt username and password attacks.

▲ If a connection is made, all traffic is encrypted, so detection is unlikely.

NOTE: See Chapters 14 and 16 for more details.

Internet Information Server

IIS is probably the most widely deployed BackOffice service. Its functionality is tremendous and integration with Win2K is fabulous, from a functionality standpoint. From a security standpoint, IIS provides ample opportunity to crack Win2K wide open. It is continually being tested and poked and prodded, and vulnerabilities keep popping up. It is arguably the most exploited application on the Net. Some potential risks associated with the IIS server are

▼ Sniffing of valid usernames and passwords when using generic HTTP (that is, no SSL) and Basic Authentication.

- Overflow or improper validation of input data from client, caused by Web applications not having proper code review and allowing execution of commands or access to files that is undesirable.

- Improper configuration (that is, default).

- Unsecured FTP, SMTP, and/or IISADMIN services.

- An exploit in the actual IIS server code. The code base is huge, the functionality is extensive, and the peer review for security is minimal.

- Being a point to attempt username and password cracking against.

▲ Inadequate logging for intrusion attempts. Since so much data goes through the server, there is a high likelihood that any attacks against the server will go unnoticed.

NOTE: See Chapter 19 for more details.

SQL Server

The SQL Server is a prime candidate for exploitation. It is a staple service that will be found in almost any Microsoft shop, so will be a "first round" service that attackers will look for. Chances are that it will have some level of valuable data, potentially the most important data the company has, and more than likely be less secure than many of the other services on the network. There is a tendency for database servers in general (and SQL specifically) to be needed by a wide variety of users, so the access is typically open for anyone with a legitimate database username and password. Since the database server is almost always considered to be on the "inside," the network controls will be typically less than stellar. Some potential risks associated with the SQL Server are

▼ Unauthenticated queries.

- Improper DB table access permissions.

- Poor passwords on privileged accounts.

- Improper validation of SQL commands allowing undesirable query results.

- Improper configuration (that is, default).

- Username and password cracking, if the SQL Server is authenticating against the domain.

▲ Inadequate logging for intrusion attempts. Since so much data goes through the server, there is a high likelihood that any attacks against the server will go unnoticed.

Exchange Server

The popularity of Exchange makes it a likely target for attack, and the fact that it provides so much functionality increases the potential that the attack will succeed. Exchange provides robust support for e-mail. Like the SQL Server, it too will be a "first round" service that attackers will look for. With this great deal of functionality, some potential risks associated with the Exchange server are

▼ Improper configuration.

■ Sniffing of valid usernames and passwords over cleartext (that is, no SSL), POP, or IMAP connections.

■ Mail relay or SPAM initiation due to improper configuration.

■ An attack on the actual Exchange server code. The code base is huge, the functionality is extensive, and the peer review for security is minimal.

■ Username and password cracking.

▲ Inadequate logging for intrusion attempts. Since so much data goes through the server, there is a high likelihood that any attacks against the server will go unnoticed.

Core Services

There are a number of services that can be considered "core" to a Win2K network. This section discusses some of the risks associated with those "core" services.

SMB and CIFS (File and Printer Sharing)

The file and printer sharing system in the Win2K environment is the Server Message Block (SMB) protocol. This is implemented in two ways: first, with the Common Internet File System (CIFS), which implements the SMB protocol using TCP/IP services (such as DNS for name resolution), and second, with the NetBIOS protocol, which is supported for backward compatibility. For all intents and purposes, the two implementations have the same security risks, as the main difference is in the method used for name resolution (CIFS uses DNS, while NetBIOS uses NetBIOS names). We will be referring to both of them in their general form of SMB.

NOTE: See Chapter 6 for more details.

SMB is implemented as the Server and Workstation service on Win2K computers. However, SMB is generally considered a security problem if you are connected to an untrusted network. Some of the potential risks associated with the SMB are

▼ Using anonymous connections to access SMB "shares" that do not have appropriate ACLs

■ Having a session "hijacked" by someone who then masquerades as the real client

▲ Sniffing the data out of the SMB packets

NOTE: See Chapter 12 for more details.

Active Directory

The AD is the central nervous system of a Win2K network. An attacker who wants to get the "crown jewels" will go after this. If the AD is compromised, the entire network is effectively compromised. This will be a service or primary attack focus not only because it holds valuable data, but also because a change here could potentially touch every Win2K system on the network. Some of the potential risks associated with the AD are

▼ Administrators not applying adequate ACLs on AD objects, thus allowing attackers the ability to access information that they should not have access to.

■ Attackers utilizing the transitive trust to gain access to a resource that was not properly secured. (Many administrators are used to WinNT trust and will not be cognitive of the nuances in transitive trust.)

■ Attackers getting access to AD information through a WinNT domain in *mixed-mode* operation.

■ Attackers using a compromised user account to gain access to the AD and exploit improper permission settings.

■ Attackers using an anonymous LDAP query to gather information.

▲ Attackers attempting to change Group Policies.

NOTE: See Chapter 8 for more details.

MICROSOFT WINDOWS INSTALLER (MSI)   Win2K integrates MSI and the AD. This integration allows users to automatically download and install applications that are not already existent on their systems. The calling program must be MSI-aware, and most Win2K applications are. A program can be automatically downloaded and installed, by creating an *installation package* (this is defined in the Microsoft Platform Software Development Kit). This *installation package* has all the information that MSI needs to install or uninstall an application or product.

The Microsoft Management Console (MMC) is a good example. If a user performs an action that requires a snap-in that is not installed, and the AD shows that there is an *installation package* for the snap-in, the snap-in will be downloaded automatically and installed on the user's local machine.

One of the major risks associated with MSI is the fact that if an attacker can get privileged access to the AD, they can configure it to support software distribution and then make an MSI installation package that contains a Trojan Horse. From this point on, they can send a user e-mail with an attached file that would cause that application to be installed. This would work on any system in the domain.

Individual System Registries

Although Win2K uses the AD as a repository for many of its settings, each machine still has a Registry, and its security is vital to the security of the system. Unlike WinNT before it, Win2K does not allow anonymous access to the entire Registry by default. The risks associated with the Registry are

▼ Improper settings that allow the Everyone group (that is, anonymous connections) to connect to any portion of the Registry.

▲ Improper ACLs on the critical Registry keys and values.

COM+/COM/DCOM/RPC

Win2K brings with it a large focus on client-server models and e-commerce. To facilitate these goals, there exist a number of programmatic ways to accomplish the same goal. Because there are so many ways to "cut a potato" per se, this also means that there are more ways to get into the system. You have to ensure that all the "code" running on your system is designed with security in mind, and that it adequately reflects the security level that you have implemented on the system. Some risks associated with these technologies are

▼ A user acting as an Administrator could execute a malicious ActiveX control.

■ A program or service that is written insecurely and running as LocalSystem could be the catalyst that provides a crack in the Win2K armor.

▲ The fact that one little program that is not written correctly can jeopardize your entire installation.

Certificate Services

Certificate Services are a likely target, because they potentially hold the keys to the Win2K PKI. Compromise of this service or system will mean the ability to compromise the PKI integrity. This is a *big* problem! Some risks associated with Certificate Services are

▼ Improper configuration of the service

▲ Exploit of the underlying Win2K OS

NOTE: See Web Chapter 1 at **www.osborne.com** for more details.

Terminal Services

Terminal Services will be a very likely target because they provide the ability to get an "interactive" session on the remote machine. Since all Win2K servers come with Terminal Services, and all Win2K systems will have clients, there will be many more people wanting to use it "because it's there." Some risks associated with Terminal Services are

▼ Exploit of the bugs in the Terminal Services to gain access to other user's session and data

■ Improper configuration of the service

■ Exploit of the underlying Win2K OS

■ Exploit of weak usernames and passwords

▲ Inexperienced administrators configuring for usability and not security

Telnet

Win2K now comes with a Telnet server installed, but not started, by default. When it is started, it requires NTLM authentication to connect (that is, no cleartext passwords). This is all well and good, but one of the main purposes of a Telnet server is to allow cross-platform access, thus you will need to enable the cleartext authentication for use by any client other than Win2K or WinNT. The risks associated with the Telnet server are

▼ Cleartext authentication for a large number of clients.

▲ NTLM passwords can be sniffed for use in a password cracker when authenticating a Win2K or WinNT client.

ATTACKS AGAINST USERS

Attacks directed against users are becoming much more prevalent. The most common form of attack is a computer virus, and they have been around for ages. Like viruses, the newer attacks can range in scale from annoying, to very destructive, to detrimental in terms of information leakage.

NOTE: Many of these types of attacks were described in more detail in Chapter 2.

Viruses and Trojan Horses

A virus is a malicious program that is run by a user, usually not on purpose. When executed, a virus will *infect* and/or attach itself to another piece of code, so as to reproduce itself. Viruses usually perform some type of action along with the replication. As stated earlier, this action ranges from the malicious (such as erasing files) to the annoying (flashing things on a screen). There are many different types of viruses, such as:

▼ **File Infectors**   Infect regular programs, such as COM or EXE files. They get invoked each time the infected program runs.

■ **BIOS and File System Infectors**   Infect/modify the actual file system or the boot sector (that is, the master boot record). These are invoked either by file system access or system boot. They are not attached to any particular program.

▲ **Macro Viruses**   Exploit the auto-execution macro capabilities in programs such as Microsoft Office and Microsoft Word. Simply by opening an infected document, the virus, written in a product's macro language, can spread.

Viruses are usually spread, perhaps unwittingly, by user actions. Some ways in which this occurs include

▼ Booting from an infected floppy

■ Running an infected program

■ Opening an infected e-mail attachment

▲ Downloading infected files

NOTE: A worm is a self-propagating virus.

A relative of the virus, and a potentially much more devastating exploit in the long run, is the Trojan Horse. Since the Trojan Horse usually performs some action that is expected and something that is not (i.e. the Trojan part), they may be very hard to detect. Trojan Horses can be introduced in much the same way as a virus.

> **VIP:** The authors believe the auto-download and execution of downloadable content will be a primary method of exploitation in the next decade.

Holes and Backdoors

As large teams of programmers rush products to competitive markets, bugs and holes are inevitable. When putting programs through test loops, programmers will bypass certain functions (like security checks) to make the tests run faster. Unfortunately, hackers may find and exploit these holes. Sometimes their discoveries become widely known. Sometimes the hacker guards them like trade secrets to prevent vendors from plugging the holes. Some risks are

▼ Bypass mechanisms left in by mistake

▲ Lack of understanding of the security requirements for running programs on Win2K

You should carefully consider the potential ramifications of backdoors and holes when installing any program or service on a computer system that holds sensitive information.

Security Zones

Microsoft's Internet Explorer 4.0 introduced *security zones*. These zones allow you to designate different levels of "trust" to systems in different security zones. The basic premise is that you allow more information and functionality to more "trusted" zones. Thus, your security policy might allow "active scripting" from Web servers on your intranet, but prohibit it from Internet-based Web servers.

The problem then arises if the attacker can "trick" your security zone–enabled application (such as Internet Explorer, Outlook, and so on) into thinking the attacker is in a more trusted zone. Security options enable you to assign specific Web sites to various zones, depending on how much you trust the content of the specific Web site. For example, the "dotless IP address" issue in IE 4 involved a vulnerability that would allow an attacker to use an all numeric host name (such as 031713501415) instead of a real DNS name. IE would assume that the address that was given back was in the "Local Intranet Zone," which potentially could have many more permissions than the "Internet Zone."

> **VIP:** This is a prime example of a programming or logic bug that was described in the previous section. Security needs to be in layers, and this is a great example.

BEST PRACTICES

While there are a number of things that increase the risk to Win2K systems and networks, there are relatively few things that can be done to reduce the risk significantly. They tend to fall into four major categories:

▼ Architecture

■ System setup and installation

■ System administration

▲ User accounts

Architecture

A secure network starts with a secure architecture. If you want a secure Win2K network, you should design it around the Win2K security architecture. This entails running a complete Win2K or "native" mode network so as to get the most benefit out of Kerberos, Active Directory, Group Policies, NTFS, and other Win2K security services.

Authentication

The following best practices deal with authentication issues:

▼ Use strong third-party authentication if possible. If this is not an option, then implement a mechanism that requires strong passwords.

■ Use switched media to raise the bar for sniffers.

■ Run a time-synchronization protocol.

■ Don't allow SMB/CIFS over untrusted networks.

▲ Don't allow any cleartext-based authentication over untrusted networks.

Authorization

The following best practices deal with authorization issues:

▼ Use domains and Organizational Units to delegate the administration authority for systems in your Win2K domain.

■ Use Group Policies to set appropriate file system permissions and user rights for similar systems.

■ Use EFS for any files and directories that hold sensitive information.

■ Implement physical security; it is essential to the security of Win2K. This may be as simple as a lock and key, or you may need to post guards after hours.

▲ Don't dual-boot systems.

Auditing

The following best practices deal with auditing issues:

▼ Enable auditing.

■ Use a third-party log analysis tool to gather multiple logs to a central location for analysis.

▲ Set appropriate audit log settings.

nstallation and Setup

There are a number of things you can do to protect your system during the installation and setup phase.

▼ Use high-quality equipment to avoid downtime.

■ If you are upgrading an older system, check the hard drive for defects.

■ Use NTFS for all file systems.

■ Physically secure the Kerberos Key Distribution Center (KDC).

■ Harden the OS on the KDC.

■ Ensure that clients that store public keys are running Win2K and are hardened.

■ Validate file system ACLs.

■ Set up auditing for critical files and directories.

■ Perform fresh installs of Win2K, as opposed to upgrading hosts from NT4.

▲ Do not weaken permissions over the Active Directory.

System Administration

Mismanagement is probably the biggest security concern. If you don't fully understand the security system and, as a result, set options inappropriately, intruders will take advantage of your system. Here are some guidelines to follow:

▼ Use only Win2K computers for your administrative activities because the logon security is more secure than some other operating systems and it will not open you up to downgrade issues.

■ Use a common configuration for similar systems. This will allow you to better manage and secure them as the number of systems grows larger. This is the only real way to scale security. You may want to use a system duplication utility like Ghost or opt for the "Unattended install" method.

■ Use the Win2K Resource Kit (available in bookstores or directly from Microsoft) because it provides additional administration tools that make your job easier. Some of the tools are useful for evaluating security and the settings of user accounts and file permissions.

- Use a VPN if you will be doing administration over an untrusted network.
- Secure your backups because they contain valuable information.
- Use NTFS for all shared file systems, set appropriate NTFS ACLs, use explicit share permissions, do not allow anonymous connections, use SMB packet integrity (and possibly encryption).
- Tighten ACLs on the AD; use your AD server only for AD functions and secure appropriately (that is, harden).
- Use authentication and security mechanisms provided for the COM and MSRPC family of technologies. Perform a security-based code review for all applications that use them.
- Ensure ACLs settings and restrict anonymous access to the Registry.
- Do not use the Telnet server.
- Run virus checkers.
- Educate your users not to execute or open files indiscriminately.
- Disable the "Server" service (that is, file and printer sharing) on client workstations. Clients will still be able to access other servers using the "Workstation" service, but won't be able to share information from their own systems.
- Use security zones if your application supports them.
- ▲ Test all new programs on a quarantined system.

User Accounts

The out-of-the-box configurations for user accounts and file permissions may be inappropriate for some installations, but unlike WinNT, Win2K does set the permissions in a much stricter manner (*if it is a clean install and not an upgrade*). You will still need to take a close look at the default properties on files and directories and the rights of user accounts to ensure that it is adequate for your site.

Be sure to differentiate between administrative and general user accounts and the activities associated with each. Administrative users should use non-administrative accounts for normal network activities. Win2K includes some built-in groups such as Administrators, Account Managers, and Server Managers that are appropriate for most management activities. Predefined user groups are Users and Guests, but in most cases, you'll create your own groups to fit the requirements of your network.

A regular user can log in to a Win2K system and use the Run As command. This command allows the user to run specific applications in the context of another user ID (that is, alternate user credentials). It is good practice for administrators to use regular user accounts for normal non-administrative use, then use the Run As command to perform administrative-level operations without logging off and back on.

By default the Guest account is disabled, but you should check to ensure it is anyway. As for the anonymous access, many services (such as Microsoft RPC, File Sharing, Printer Sharing, and the Registry) allow anonymous connections by default. What is potentially worse is that many of those services also have a high level of privileges for the Everyone group. You should be very cautious about allowing the Everyone group access to network services, and you should restrict access only to needed files on the actual system.

NOTE: See Chapter 21 on hardening Win2K, and Chapter 10 on user and group management.

Administrator Account

Your best protection is to change the name of the Administrator account and use a very hard-to-guess password, one that includes a long string of alphanumeric and meta characters and no discernible words. Set lockouts on all other user accounts. Set the lockout value to whatever your security policy defines (you do have a security policy, don't you?). If you don't, then a good rule of thumb is to allow four mistakes in typing or improperly selecting domain or local logon.

NOTE: The Administrator account can't be locked out from logging into the console. This is to avoid complete loss of access to the server, should the account be locked out over the network. If this was not the case, someone could lock the Administrator account through failed network logon attempts and cause the server to become unavailable—essentially a denial of service attack.

RECAP

We have looked at quite a bit of information in this chapter. It is important not to get too discouraged, but to have a realistic understanding of the risks. Here are some of the overlying reasons that Win2K is and will continue to be a vulnerable platform:

▼ **Huge OS**   With upwards of 50 million lines of code, Win2K is an extremely huge piece of code. Based on the history of bugs in large pieces of code, the probability that Win2K will have bugs is high. Add to that the code base of all the different services that will probably be run on the system, and you have the makings of a venerable smorgasbord of potential vulnerabilities.

■ **Almost "Too Many" Security Features**   When Microsoft heard the plea for more security features, they may have gone overboard. It is kind of like drinking from a fire hose, rather than a garden hose. Given the fact that the security system is now so vastly complex, albeit thorough, getting all settings correct is a rather arduous and time-consuming task. For the general Win2K system administrator, we believe that this will potentially lead to frustration and a complete opening of systems just to get them to work. This is *not* what Microsoft had in mind!

■ **Vast Amount of "Undocumented" Features** There are literally hundreds, if not thousands, of undocumented API calls in Win2K. Security through obscurity is no security at all.

■ **Backward Compatibility with LAN Manager** The bane of Win2K and, for that matter, WinNT. LAN Manager is the source of some of the most egregious WinNT security problems. You will still be vulnerable to these in as much as you have to keep non-Win2K systems working together. The only real hope is to set up a *native-mode* (that is, homogeneous Win2K) network, and then turn all NetBIOS and LAN Manager compatibility off.

▲ **Default Configuration Is Oriented to Ease of Use, Not to Security** Realize that ease of use is (and will always be) job #1 for Microsoft products; to think otherwise would be foolish. This is especially true if you upgrade instead of doing a clean install, as Microsoft does not want to tighten a system down if there is a chance that things may stop working.

We have seen that there are numerous potential vulnerabilities in Win2K. They range from the simple (using a FAT32 file system) to the complex (man-in-the-middle attacks against SMB). It can almost seem like a daunting task to secure Win2K, but alas, don't lose hope. There *really* are just a few things that you can do to get you 80 percent of the way to a secure system:

▼ Don't use default configurations.

■ Require strong passwords.

■ Disable unneeded services.

■ Use security options in Local or Group policies.

■ Disable NTLM.

▲ Disable NetBIOS (native mode only).

VIP: You are only as secure as your weakest link, so if you configure your network to allow non-secure clients (such as Win 9*x*) to interoperate, you have exponentially reduced the level of security in your network.

Here is a final analogy to keep in mind.

Win2K security should be viewed as an egg. If you try to crush an egg lengthwise in the palm of your hand by applying pressure to the pointy ends, it takes a great deal of effort (relatively). Whereas if you turn the egg sideways and apply pressure to the sides, the egg breaks with very little pressure. Similarly, with Win2K (and its predecessor WinNT), you can configure it to be strong and it will take a great deal of effort to "crush" it. But turning one little thing sideways can cause it to become a mess all over your hands.

Be systematic and diligent at what you do!

PART III

Securing Windows 2000

Securing Windows 2000

CHAPTER 8

Active Directory

Active Directory (AD) is arguably the crown jewel of Microsoft's Win2K Operating System. Almost all of the other touted security and administrative features of Win2K, such as Intellimirror or Group Polices, will not function without it. The AD brings the ability to scale administration and security to a large number of systems. It also provides the service by which Microsoft has integrated many network-based services.

At its heart, the AD is a directory service that has been integrated with Win2K. A directory service includes not only the directory itself (that is, the location where the information is stored), but also the services that make that information available to other users and computers on the network. The AD that is included with Win2K leverages previous Microsoft directory services (such as Exchange) with new functionality and robustness.

There are two security aspects of the AD. First is the actual securing of the AD itself (that is, the services and data it provides). The second is the use of the AD as a vehicle to securely manage other services. We will be focusing on the first aspect in this chapter and discussing the others in their respective chapters. Also, because there are entire books written on how to design an AD, we will only be touching on nonsecurity design issues at a high level. For the intricate details about all aspects of AD, you should refer to *Windows 2000 Active Directory,* by Joe Casad. We will cover the basics of design, especially those that directly affect security, but the focus will be on what is required to manage the AD securely.

WHY A DIRECTORY SERVICE?

As networks have grown over the years, information about people, applications, and resources have been scattered throughout entire enterprises and are continuing to proliferate. Because most applications need information, they provide some method of storing it, and as the number of applications increase, so does the information and places where it is stored. This causes a problem, in that the information needs to be managed and kept up to date. For example, if an employee leaves a company, their credentials need to be disabled or removed. If you have a large number of information stores, then you have to ensure that this is done in each one. Also a significant amount of this information is duplicated in the information stores. Another simple fact is that any distributed network needs a centralized repository of certain information (that is, a directory), such as user accounts, or else it does not scale. Due to the critical nature of the information in the directory service, it will be the center of any network implementation.

To address these issues, companies seek to provide what is called an enterprise-wide *directory service*. This directory service provides a common location to store, access, and manage the information that is needed. This is where the Active Directory fills the niche for Microsoft. In Microsoft's "Planning for a Global Directory Service" they see the Active Directory as "the focal point of the Microsoft directory service strategy." They built the AD using Internet-standard technologies and fully integrated it with the operating system. Microsoft also designed the AD for other uses such as "isolating, migrating, centrally managing, and reducing the number of directories that companies have."

The directory services provide repositories for information like people and resources. They also provide a consistent way to name, describe, locate, access, manage, and secure information about these resources. Some of the other functional parts of a directory service are the ability to set and enforce the security of the information and administration, as well as the ability to partition and distribute the information and replicate it. The AD supports all of these.

WHAT IS THE ACTIVE DIRECTORY?

The AD is an attempt to make a scalable domain structure—it replaces the old WinNT domain model with one that is hierarchical and scalable. It is a standards-based (that is, it supports LDAP) directory service, and like any other directory service, it provides a location to store objects and attributes about those objects, as well as services to get at that data. In a limited sense, you can think of it as a complete trusted WinNT domain and a globally shared registry. Any of the information that was previously stored in the registry in WinNT (that could have been used on multiple machines) can now be stored in the AD. In this way, remote systems can use the AD as a centralized repository and controlling agent for the domain.

Some of the benefits and functionality that the AD provides are

▼ **Win2K Integration**   By being integrated in the Win2K OS, Microsoft has been able to optimize the use and performance of the AD for use by Win2K.

■ **Integrated Security**   The use of Kerberos and/or public key certificates allows a true single sign-on. The AD provides information storage for those services.

■ **Centralized Administration**   Since Win2K can store information about system configuration, user profiles, and applications in the AD, you can use it to centrally manage that information. By using Win2K Group Policy, an administrator can manage user configurations, computer configurations, network services, and directory-enabled applications from a central location.

■ **Customized User Environments**   Using Group Policy, you can use the AD to set where users store their documents, where their personal settings are saved, and the general configuration of their environment. You can also use the AD to enable on-demand application installation, logon and logoff scripts, and security settings.

■ **Directory-Enabled Applications**   Applications can use the AD to store and locate information they need, such as configuration and installation information.

■ **Software Installation**   The AD can be used to install software on Win2K systems.

▲ **Service Configuration**   The AD allows you to configure certain services-related settings on an enterprise level.

Some of the features that the AD uses to accomplish these functions are

▼ Lightweight Directory Access Protocol (LDAP)

■ Hierarchical Domain Structure

■ Transitive Trust

■ Multimaster Replication

■ Global Catalog

▲ Group Policies

We will be describing each of these features in greater detail throughout the rest of this chapter.

COMPONENTS

The AD is made up of many different components and operations; this section will give a brief coverage of them and how they relate to the security of the AD.

Namespace and Naming Contexts

For any set of information, there must be a namespace. A *namespace* is defined as a space where a given name can be resolved. For example, the Domain Name System (DNS) is a namespace, because a given DNS name can be resolved within it. Much the same way, the AD is a namespace as well, because a name can be resolved to an object. *Resolving* is a process by which a name is translated into an object or the information the name represents.

In the AD, the namespace is divided into three naming contexts. The first is the *Domain* (a.k.a. User) naming context (herein referred to as just a Domain). This naming context holds things that are applicable to an individual domain (that is, user, groups, computers, and Organizational Units). The Domain naming context holds all objects and attributes that are applicable to the domain and is only applicable to the domain that it exists in. Every domain controller (DC) in that domain has a copy of it. The second naming context is the *Configuration* naming context (herein referred to as just the Configuration). This defines the replication topology and other data concerning the configuration of the AD (that is, what domains actually exist in it, where DCs are located, and so on). It is a forest-wide naming context, so every DC in the forest (that is, the AD) has a copy of this naming context. The third naming context is the *Schema* naming context (herein referred to as just the Schema), and it defines objects and attributes that can be stored in the AD. Along with what can be stored, it also defines operation rules. Like the Configuration naming context, it is forest-wide and is stored (that is, replicated) on every DC in the forest.

VIP: The term "naming contexts" can be a bit misleading as they sound abstract; however, they are actually locations (that is, partitions) that exist in the AD. Thus, for our discussions the Domain naming context and the domain it refers to are one in the same. They actually make up the directory and are the actual things that are replicated. You may also see these referred to as Domain "container," Schema "container," and Configuration "container."

Objects and Object Naming in the AD

The Active Directory contains many objects. Each object represents a unique piece of data within the enterprise. These pieces of data can be either individual items (such as a username), or containers (such as a collection of users). (Individual items are also called *end nodes* or *leafs*.) Each object (whether leaf or container) has a set of associated properties or *attributes* that may contain security and/or file system data about the object.

There are two ways to find things in the AD. The first is using a *distinguished name (DN)*. The DN of an object uniquely identifies the object and contains enough information to retrieve the object from the directory. It is basically the full path from the AD directory root to get to the object itself. The DN for the user Phil Cox in the example.com domain would be: /O=Internet/DC=COM/DC=Example/CN=Users/CN=Phil Cox, where "O" is an organization name, "DC" is a domain component, and "CN" is a common name for the container. These are abbreviations for the directory naming attributes. There is another term called the *relative distinguished name (RDN)*. This is the portion of the DN that is relative to the container that it lives in. It is unique in its relative context. This is also referred to as the *common name (CN)*. A good rule of thumb to help remember the DN is that the DNS names get the DC label, Organizational Units get the OU label, and all others get the CN label. Everything always starts in the "Internet" organizational name.

TIP: Most of the common directory service query keys (that is, O, DC, CN) are all defined in RFC 2253.

The second method to find something in the AD is by searching on object attributes. The AD schema defines object attributes that can be used to locate an object. Two of the special ones are

▼ **Globally Unique ID (GUID)** The GUID is a 128-bit identifier that is unique to an object within a namespace. With the GUID, any object in the AD can be uniquely identified, and the GUID never changes, even if the object is moved within the AD. It is important to note that GUIDs are not unique across namespaces (that is, Active Directories), but for all intents and purposes this does not matter.

▲ **User Principal Name**   Principals (users and groups) each have a "friendly" name—the *User Principal Name (UPN)*, which is shorter than the DN and easier to remember. The User Principal Name is similar to an Internet e-mail address in that it has a username and the domain name the account is in. So for the user pcc in domain example.com, the UPN would be Phil.Cox@example.com.

Virtual Containers (VC)

We touched on containers a bit earlier, and they are pretty straightforward, but there is a special container or *Virtual Container (VC)*. VCs allow you to expose other LDAP-compatible directories via the AD. It basically holds a pointer to the other directory, and the AD will send the information to the client. The information stored in the AD is known as "knowledge information," and it describes where the directory should appear in the AD, the DNS name of the other directory server, and the DN where searches should begin.

Global Catalog

The primary purpose of the Global Catalog (GC) is to assist in searching for objects in the entire AD. It allows users and applications to find objects in any domain in the AD, as long as they know at least one of the searchable attributes (such as the username) of the target object. The GC is a partial replica of all the Domains in the AD and a full replica of the Schema and Configuration naming contexts. The reality is that the GC has a replica of every object in the AD, but only a small number of their attributes. The GC is built automatically when the AD replicates. By default there is one GC per site, but that is configurable.

TIP: There are default sets of properties that are replicated into the Global Catalog, but administrators can specify additional properties if they so desire.

Schema

The Schema defines what objects and attributes can be stored in the AD. It maintains all the object classes and attributes held in the AD. For each object class, the Schema defines where the object class can be created in the AD and a list of attributes that the class must or may contain. If you want to add an object class or an attribute to an object, you have to first define it in the Schema. This is the template by which the entire AD is built. From a security standpoint, this is one of the most critical components, as modifications here will be reflected throughout the entire AD.

Domain

A domain is a group of computers that are grouped together to form an administrative boundary for Users, Groups, Computers, and Organizational Units that exist in the domain. They share the same Domain, Configuration, Schema, and Global Catalog. Domains form the foundation of the AD. The AD is made up of one or more domains, and each domain has its own security policies and security (that is, trust) relationships with other domains in the AD. The namespace of a Win2K domain corresponds to a DNS domain, and the Root domain is the first domain created in an AD. Because Win2K domain structures are tightly coupled to the DNS structures, they are not only the roots of the Win2K AD domain, but of the DNS domains as well. The example.com domain is shown next.

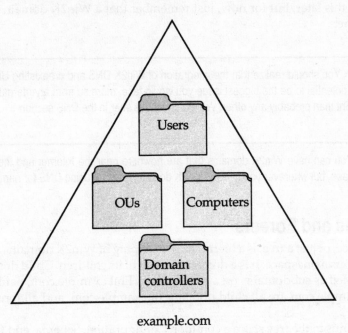

example.com

Partitions in the AD

Domains are actual physical partitions of the database that make up the AD. There is a Directory System Agent (DSA) process that runs on every DC, which actually holds the Domain, Configuration, and Schema information on the server. The DSA is used to provide access to the actual store of data. The DSA provides functions such as maintaining GUID-to-object associations, validating changes to the Schema on the Schema master, enforcing access control in the directory, supporting Replication, and providing "referrals" to other domains in the forest.

The DSA process manages the physical storage for the directory. Systems connect to the DSA, and then search for, read, and/or write directory objects and attributes. The DSA provides an abstraction between the client and the physical format of the directory.

Domain Names

In WinNT, the domain structure was flat, and thus the use of a flat namespace (NetBIOS) was simple: Make the NetBIOS domain name a name that is not already used in the Microsoft network you are running. When Microsoft moved to a hierarchical domain structure, they needed a new namespace. The best bet would be to use one that is well tested, already widely supported and accepted, scalable and distributed. Well, DNS fit the picture, and thus the AD domain namespace is directly tied to a DNS namespace. We will discuss this later, but for now, just remember that a Win2K domain name *is* a DNS domain name.

NOTE: You should realize that the integration of Win2K DNS and preexisting Unix DNS hierarchy has the potential to be the biggest issue you would face, more so from an internal business-political standpoint than probably any other. We will cover this later in the DNS section.

VIP: You can have Win2K domains that are nowhere near the Internet and the well-known DNS namespace, but wherever you have a Win2K domain, it *will* be using DNS for name resolution.

Domain Trees and Forests

A domain tree, or just a tree, is a hierarchical grouping of Win2K domains that are all part of a contiguous namespace. It is a domain with all of its children. Child domains are those that are created as subdomains on a root domain. Phil.example.com, paul.example.com, and tom.example.com are all child domains of example.com, and all form a contiguous namespace.

All domains in the tree share a common Configuration, Schema, and Global Catalog. The structure of the tree is determined by the DNS names of the domains, and all the domains in the AD are linked together with transitive trust relationships.

A forest is a collection of discontiguous domain trees that are linked together with bi-directional transitive trust. Like the domain trees, all domains in a forest share the same Schema, Configuration, and Global Catalog. The difference is that the trees do not form a contiguous namespace. The first domain created in the AD is known as the Forest Root Domain and can never be deleted without destroying the forest. A forest does not have a distinct name, but is actually just a set of cross-reference objects and Kerberos trust relationships. All the member trees know the cross-references and trust relationships.

The following illustration shows the logical AD layout for the example.com and example.org domains. The example.com domain has child domains of phil.example.com, paul.example.com, and tom.example.com. The domain phil.example.com also has a child domain, Win2K.phil.example.com. The example.org domain has only one child domain, brad.example.org, which has a child of its own, nt.brad.example.org. The example.com was the first domain placed in the forest.

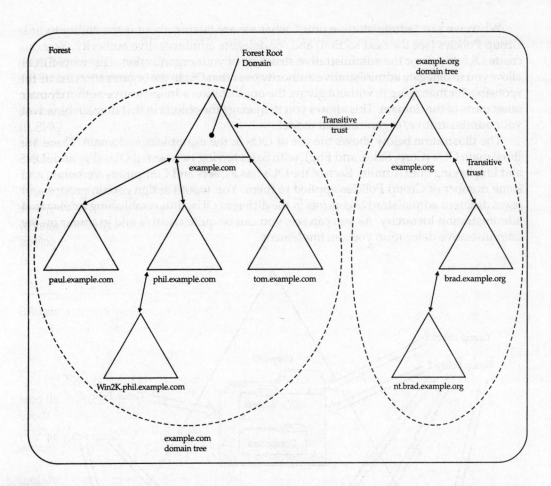

Forest

Forest Root Domain

example.org domain tree

Transitive trust

example.com

example.org

Transitive trust

paul.example.com

phil.example.com

tom.example.com

brad.example.org

Win2K.phil.example.com

nt.brad.example.org

example.com domain tree

VIP: It is important to understand that because of transitive trust, and the fact that the domains all share the same Schema, Configuration, and Global Catalog, they also share all their information. Thus, if I am sitting in nt.brad.example.org, and there are no controls on a system in Win2K.phil.example.com, I can have free roam of that system. This will be discussed more in the "Trust" section later in this chapter.

Organizational Units

An Organizational Unit (OU) is a type of directory object that is contained within a domain. OUs are "special" containers in the AD into which you can put users, groups, computers, and other OUs. They are "special" in that they can have Group Policies linked to them, whereas regular containers cannot. They are intra-domain objects, which mean they cannot span domains. They are the smallest atomic administrative units that exist in the AD and form what are called *security boundaries*. By default, because a domain is an administrative boundary, and an OU can only exist within a domain, the domain *is* the outermost OU.

When we say "administrative unit," what we are talking about is the ability to link Group Policies (see the next section) and/or delegate administrative authority. You can create OUs to mirror the administrative structure of your organization. This would then allow you to delegate administrative authority over that OU to the organization that is responsible for managing it, without giving the organization administrative authority over other parts of the domain. This allows you to manage the objects in that domain based on your administrative/organizational model.

The illustration below shows the use of OUs in the example.com domain. There are three main OUs (Corp, Sales, and Eng), with Sales having two nested OUs (Pre and Post) and Eng having one (Admin). Each of the OUs has a Users and Computers container, and some number of Group Policies applied to them. You would assign certain groups and users different administrative controls in the different OUs, thus establishing a delegated administration hierarchy. As you can see, you can be quite creative and granular on the administrative delegation you can implement.

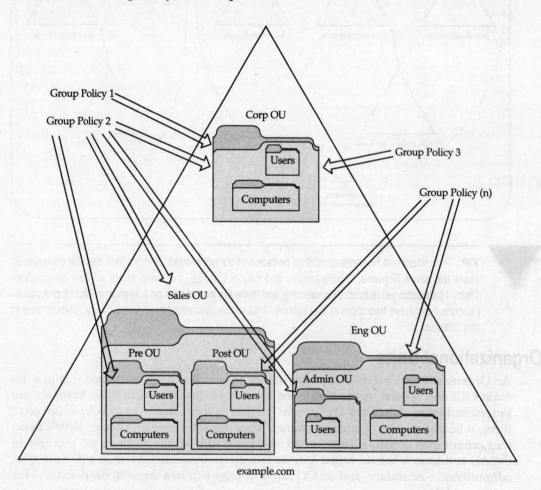

example.com

As stated earlier, OUs can contain other OUs, so you have significant flexibility in the granularity that you delegate administrative authority. This allows you to model the administrative structure of your domain almost exactly to how it actually operates.

Group Policies

Group Policies provide the ability to group security and configuration settings into templates, which can then be applied to individual systems, domains, or OUs. This is the primary method for applying global security and configuration settings to systems within a Win2K network. Group Policies are discussed in depth in the next chapter.

Sites

A site is defined as one or more TCP/IP subnets that are connected with a high-speed link (such as T1 or Ethernet). They are primarily used in determining the replication topology to allow for efficient and fast replication. Within a site (intra-site), Remote Procedure Call (RPC) is used for replication, and between sites (inter-site), you can use RPC or messaging (that is, SMTP). If you run Exchange, then you can use any of the messaging transports supported by Exchange (such as SMTP, X.400, and others). Win2K systems also use site information to locate an AD server that is "close" to the system. The locator service running on the system will attempt to locate an AD server that is on the same subnet or within the same site.

OPERATIONS

The AD is made up of many different components and operations. This section will cover them briefly and how they relate to the security of the AD.

Trust

A *trust relationship* allows information, such as user security IDs, in one domain to be used in another. The default trust in the AD is bi-directional and transitive. *Bi-directional* in this case means that if you establish a Win2K trust relationship between domain A and domain B, they will both implicitly trust each other. For the AD, this means that when you add a child domain it will trust the parent and the parent will trust it. *Transitive trust* means that if domain A trusts domain B, and domain B trusts domain C, then domain A trusts domain C. The trust model in Win2K is based on the Kerberos trust model. This transitive, bi-directional trust ensures that you do not have to have additional trust relationships among forest members.

Contrast this with WinNT trust, which was uni-directional, meaning that you had to explicitly establish directions of trust, and non-transitive, meaning that you only trusted domains for which you had a direct trust relationship.

> **VIP:** Trust does not establish authorization. Trust is just a single part of the Win2K security model. You must take the time to set up appropriate rights and permissions in all domains in the forest.

How Trust Works

Win2K uses "trust paths" to pass authentication requests between domains in the forest. It does this to ensure the legitimacy of the account and its credentials before it is granted access to a resource that is not in its home domain. This means that each time an account tries to access a resource in a remote domain, the Win2K server will traverse (that is, walk up) the trust links until it gets to the domain the account is in. This is a heavy performance hit for authentication with nonlocal domain accounts. Please see Chapter 11 for details on trust.

FOREIGN SECURITY PRINCIPAL AND PHANTOM RECORDS   If you add a member of a trusted domain that is in a different AD (that is, forest) to a group in your domain, the AD will put an object in the ForeignSecurityPrincipal container. This object represents the real object, but the AD does not have the authoritative information on the object because it exists elsewhere. This provides linkage for membership listing and ACLs.

Phantom Records are references to objects that do not exist in the same domain. If one object references another object that is outside of its domain, a phantom record containing the GUID, SID (if applicable), and DN of the referenced object is created. This allows the referenced object to be located when detailed information is needed.

Other Types of Trust

There are two other types of trust that can be established in Win2K: shortcut trusts and external trusts. *Shortcut trusts* are used to reduce the performance hit you take when traversing the "trust path." You can create a shortcut trust between two non-adjacent Win2K domains in the same forest. They must be nonadjacent, because adjacent domains would already have this link. They are one-way transitive trusts (just like WinNT), so if you want them to be bi-directional, you will need to create one in each direction. *External trusts* are used to create trust relationships with domains in another forest or a Kerberos realm. Like shortcut trusts, these are also one-way and non-transitive by default.

Replication

Unlike WinNT, which used single-master replication where only one server held a writeable copy of the domain data (that is, the PDC) and many read-only copies (that is, BDCs), the Win2K AD uses *multimaster replication*. Multimaster replication means that every DC contains a writeable copy of the domain information. This allows updates to be applied to any DC in a domain. The AD then replicates the changes to other DCs in the domain. Replication is automatic and transparent. In order to manage changes originating from multiple sources, DCs rely upon information from replication objects, described in the next section.

AD replication is done over what are called *replication transport protocols*. By default, the AD supports two replication transport protocols: RPC and SMTP. Both protocols run over IP as the underlying network layer. The RPC protocol is used for inter- and intra-site replication. RPC is used over higher-speed links and to replicate all domain information between sites. The inter-site RPC replication is performed on a scheduled basis and is compressed. The SMTP protocol is only used for inter-site replication, and only replicates nondomain directory partitions between sites (that is, Schema and Configuration). This is configurable, and you can choose to use one or the other for specific purposes, but the defaults usually work the best.

Replication Objects

There are certain values stored with objects and attributes that are used during replication. They are documented here:

▼ **Update Sequence Numbers (USNs)**   Server-specific, 64-bit numbers stored with every attribute and object. All DCs maintain a table of the highest USNs received from their replication partners.

■ **Property Version Numbers (PVN)**   Global version numbers for the attribute or object. Unlike USNs, they are not server-specific values. When an object is created in the AD, the PVN is initialized and stays with the object through its lifetime.

▲ **Timestamp**   A time and date placed on an object or attribute when a change occurs.

How Replication Happens

When an object or one of its attributes are changed, the DC that makes the change performs what is known as an *originating update* on the object in the AD (an originating update increments the PVN and the USN). The changes are then replicated to other DCs in the local domain and then throughout the AD with what is known as a *replicated update* (replicated updates only update USN). This propagation occurs until all the DCs have been updated.

When a DC gets an update, it needs to decide if it will apply it. All incoming objects and attributes (that is, those being replicated to the DC) with USNs that are greater than those stored on the DC will be updated. When a replication partner notifies the DC that replication is required, that DC asks for all changes with USNs greater than the values it has stored. The USN table is updated atomically as the DC applies the changes. If the USNs are the same (a.k.a. a *collision*), then the update with the highest PVN will take precedence. If both the USN and PVN are the same, then the latest timestamp will take precedence. Finally, if the USN, PVN, and timestamp are the same, but the data is different, the data that came from the DC with the highest GUID (created when the machine account was created) will take precedence (this appears to be a random design decision by Microsoft). This AD replication is based on replicating attribute changes and not the entire object, which makes it much more efficient.

NOTE: Collisions occur when the same property is updated at two or more DCs at roughly the same time.

Operational Roles

Although multimaster replication is a very effective and scalable way of managing changes to the AD, it does have its limitations. There are some types of changes that need to be replicated in a different manner, mostly because of time criticality. To deal with these anomalies, Win2K has defined *operational master roles*. There are five roles, two of which are forest-wide in scope, and three which are domain-wide. By default, the first DC in the AD (that is, the first DC created in the first domain) has all of these roles assigned to it. As you get more systems, you should look at distributing these roles out to different DCs. You will have to manually distribute these roles, as it does not happen automatically.

Roles That Are Forest-Wide

The following operational master roles are forest-wide. The roles can be split amongst DCs in the forest, but no more than one DC in the forest can be defined for the role at a time.

▼ **Schema Master** This is the only DC that can perform write operations to the directory Schema, and thus controls any modifications or changes to the Schema. You need access to the Schema Master to make changes to the Schema. Any updates are then replicated from the Schema Master to all other DCs in the forest.

▲ **Domain Naming Master** This is the DC that can add or remove domains to or from the forest, and add or remove cross-reference objects to external directories.

Roles That Are Domain-Wide

The following operational master roles are domain-wide. The roles can be split amongst DCs in the domain, but no more than one DC in the domain can be defined for the role at a time.

▼ **Primary Domain Controller** This DC provides PDC functions (password changes, replicating updates to BDCs, and Domain Master Browser) for compatibility with down-level WinNT systems. Even when running in native mode, this role master still performs some very important functions such as being the first DC to which password changes get replicated. Also, when there is an authentication failure (that is, a bad password), the authentication request is retried at this DC. This is because a new password change might not have been replicated to the authenticating DC yet, and since this DC gets password changes first, it can ensure this problem does not happen.

■ **Relative Identifier (RID) Master**   The DC with this operational role allocates RIDs to the other DCs in the domain. It will allocate them in blocks of 100 to each DC in the domain. These RIDs are used when generating a new Security ID (SID) for a User, Group, or Computer on the DC. An object SID is the Domain SID plus the RID. If a DC runs out of RIDs, and the RID master is unavailable, then you will not be able to create new security principal objects on that DC.

▲ **Infrastructure Master**   The DC with this operational role is responsible for maintaining references to objects in other domains. It must update any changes to those objects in its domain. For example, if a group from another domain is included in a group in this domain, any changes to the remote group (such as adding a new user) must be reflected in this domain. That is the responsibility of the Infrastructure Master. The Infrastructure Master updates these references on its copy of the directory and replicates the changes to other DCs in its domain. If this DC is not available, then the changes will only be updated through the replication process (read: it will happen, but it may take a while).

Modes of Operation

Win2K domains can run in one of two operational modes: native or mixed. Mixed mode is the default installation mode, and allows you to support down-level Windows clients (that is, WinNT and Win98). What it really does is provide the PDC role (described earlier) for WinNT networks. An interesting thing about mixed mode is that Win2K clients will first attempt to go to a Win2K DC using Kerberos, but if they can't find one, they will fall back to a WinNT DC using NTLM authentication. Mixed mode also limits you on the size the AD can be, because 40MB is the largest SAM that can be replicated to a WinNT BDC.

Native mode is a Win2K-only mode. It does not provide PDC support for WinNT domains, but does allow the AD to "grow." There are three other *very* desirable new features: universal groups, nested group membership, and inter-domain user moves. These will be detailed in Chapter 10. Native mode is what you want to be in, but in reality, mixed mode is the operational requirement for most organizations, at least for a while.

NOTE: We use the term "grow" because there are conflicting numbers as to how big the AD can really get, both from a theoretical and a practical standpoint. The ranges we have heard are 1–10 million objects, as opposed to the 40,000 or so in WinNT.

Table 8-1 lists the differences between Win2K native mode and mixed mode.

Domain Name System (DNS): The Win2K Name Service

As we briefly discussed earlier, DNS is the name service (and thus the namespace) for Win2K and the AD. What we did not discuss was how it was done. WinNT used NetBIOS, which had dynamic updates and NetBIOS name types. The NetBIOS name

Operation	Native	Mixed
Groups	Supports all group types and operations, including universal groups and group nesting	Does not support universal groups or group nesting
Replication	Single-master support (that is, PDC) to replicate to WinNT BDCs. Win2K uses multimaster	All multimaster
NetBIOS	Optional (on by default)	Required
Authentication	Kerberos only	NTLM with WinNT

Table 8-1.   Major Differences Between Mixed and Native Modes

types were used to locate services in WinNT. For example, name type 0x1C was a domain controller. This presents a problem, since DNS names historically have not indicated service locations, and it has been a static namespace. So now we have a problem with service indication and dynamic updates.

VIP: Remember that Win2K still supports NetBIOS, but it can be disabled. If you are not running an AD, then the system will fall back to NetBIOS.

Extensions to the DNS standards have been made to deal with these problems: Dynamic DNS (DDNS, RFC 2136), incremental zone transfers (IXFR, RFC 1995), and Service Resource Records (SRV RRs, RFC 2052). DDNS, a recent addition to the DNS standard, define a protocol extension for dynamically updating DNS records with new or changed information. Incremental zone transfers just allow you to update information that has changed, as opposed to transferring the entire zone information. SRV RRs provide the "locator" that Win2K needs to find services. Using DDNS, servers publish their addresses and services with SRV RRs. The Win2K SRV RR looks like

```
_<service>._<protocol>.<domain>
```

The typical example is finding the LDAP server associated with the AD. So continuing with the example.com domain, we would find the following TCP-based LDAP server for that domain:

```
_ldap._tcp.example.com
```

Additional information may be provided on the SRV RR to help set a priority for the server. This assists clients in selecting the best server.

NOTE: The underscore (_) is a required prefix to prevent potential namespace collisions.

By default, when any server is installed, it will attempt to publish itself and its services via DDNS. Because some networks use dynamic IP allocations as well (a.k.a. DHCP), servers check their registration information periodically to make sure it is correct. If it is not, it will use DDNS to update it.

The Win2K server can store its authoritative DNS data in the AD or in local files. If it stores it in the AD, then it can be replicated among all the DNS servers that use the AD. This replaces the traditional zone transfer method of updating information. You can still use zone transfers if you are using local text files or a non-Win2K DNS server.

NOTE: You do not have to run DDNS; you can manually configure the records stored by DNS servers, but this is a major headache and is not recommended for larger ADs.

Win2K Default SRV RRs

Microsoft uses the _msdcs subdomain to list Microsoft-specific services and their well-known pseudonyms. By default, Win2K published a number of default SRV RRs for clients to find services on. Here is a partial listing for the example.com Win2K domain with the default site "Default-First-Site-Name."

_ldap._tcp.example.com	An LDAP server accessible via TCP
_ldap._tcp.Default-First-Site-Name._ sites.example.com	An LDAP server accessible via TCP in the site named "Default-First-Site-Name"
_ldap._tcp.dc._msdcs.example.com	A DC accessible via TCP
_ldap._tcp.Default-First-Site-Name._ sites.dc._msdcs.example.com	A DC in the site
_ldap._tcp.pdc._msdcs.example.com	A PDC accessible via TCP
_ldap._tcp.gc._msdcs.example.com	A GC accessible via TCP (remember that the GC is forest-wide, and thus the domain here is the root domain in the forest)
_ldap._tcp.Default-First-Site-Name._ sites.gc._msdcs.example.com	A GC for the site
_kerberos._tcp.example.com	A Kerberos server for the Domain via TCP
_kerberos._udp.example.com	A Kerberos server via UDP

Secure Updates

Win2K uses the Generic Security Service Application Program Interface (GSS-API) to secure dynamic updates to DNS. GSS-API is defined in RFC 2078. It specifies a way to establish a secure communications channel using security tokens. The following comes from the RFC:

> *This Generic Security Service Application Program Interface (GSS-API) definition provides security services to callers in a generic fashion, supportable with a range of underlying mechanisms and technologies and hence allowing source-level portability of applications to different environments.*

The Win2K DDNS uses Kerberos v5 as the underlying security provider protocol, as defined in the IETF Internet-Draft "GSS Algorithm for TSIG (GSS-TSIG)." Please see the draft and RFC for details of the protocols and mechanisms (**http://www.ietf.org/html.charters/dnsext-charter.html**).

NOTE: The recommendation for Secure Dynamic Update is specified in RFC 2137. At this point in time, Microsoft does not implement this method because it uses the security in the AD.

Using a Non-Win2K DNS Server or Static DNS

The DNS server that the AD uses must conform to the DNS specifications (that is, RFCs), implement SRV RRs at a minimum and ideally DDNS as well. DDNS is highly recommended because of the administrative burden in maintaining up-to-date static DNS entries. As discussed earlier, the AD will attempt to automatically register itself and services with DDNS in the DNS server defined for it. Disabling this feature is discussed later in this chapter.

NOTE: Bind 8.2.2 and later supports all the extensions that are required by the AD.

ACTIVE DIRECTORIES AUTHENTICATION, AUTHORIZATION, AND AUDITING

The authentication, authorization, and auditing (3 A's) of the AD is controlled by its integration into the OS. The AD is part of the Win2K Security Subsystem, which makes it a part of the Win2K Trusted Computing Base. Thus, it participates fully in the Win2K Security model. This means that the same mechanisms that are used to control the 3 A's for Win2K are applicable to the AD.

Authentication

Any access of an object in the AD is subject to authentication of the user who is requesting the access. The AD uses the integrated Win2K authentication. This is Kerberos authentication by default, but can be any authentication method supported by the Win2K system that you are connecting to.

The AD is a Win2K service and is accessed via certain protocols. It is the authentication mechanism supported by the protocol that is used for authentication to the AD. For example, if you are trying to perform an ADSI query (that is, an MS-RPC call), the protocol will attempt to authenticate you using those protocols defined for MS-RPC (Kerberos by default). If you were using LDAP, however, you could authenticate with a Bind operation. See Chapter 11 for details on authentication.

Authorization

Like all of Win2K, all objects in the AD are protected by ACLs. The ACLs provide a mechanism by which you can grant or deny access and operations on any object and/or its individual attributes. One of the best ways to think of the AD is like a Win2K file system. It has objects, that is, containers (directories) and leafs (files). For each object, it has ACLs that apply not only to the object itself, but also to the attributes of the object. The objects in the AD support delegation of administrative authority (remember OUs?) and inheritance of ACEs from parents. Also, any access to the object is validated by the SRM that resides on the system being accessed. So authorization is done with ACLs and user rights, just like in the base OS.

VIP: Just as a point of reference, on just a single User object, there are 17 different object permissions that can be set, and 146 different attribute permissions that can be set. The scope of object ACLs is almost daunting.

Supported Protocols and APIs

As with almost all Microsoft-based services, there is more than one way to get access to the information. For the AD, there are a number of protocols as well as APIs that can be used to get at the information in the AD. The primary protocols used to access the AD include

- ▼ **LDAP**   Lightweight Directory Access Protocol, the AD core protocol. LDAP version 2 and version 3 are supported.

- ■ **MAPI-RPC**   The remote procedure call (RPC) interfaces supporting the MAPI interfaces. This is why the Exchange messaging transports work—they implement the MAPI interfaces.

- ■ **Replication RPC**   A Microsoft proprietary RPC interface to access the AD for replication.

- ▲ **Replication SMTP**   Replication using SMTP.

The supported Application Programming Interfaces to access the AD include

- ▼ **Active Directory Service Interfaces (ADSI)**   Supports many different programming languages (Java, VB, C, C++, and others). ADSI is built on

LDAP and is used to hide the LDAP details from the programmer. This interface uses COM.

- ■ **LDAP**   The LDAP API for the C programming language (RFC 1823).
- ■ **Messaging API (MAPI)**   Supported for backward compatibility, and should not be used for future development.
- ▲ **WinNT Net and SAM**   Supports WinNT methods for accessing the SAM.

All of these protocols and APIs use the Directory System Agent (DSA) to access the AD data (that is, database store). MAPI can also access the AD at the database layer as well. The following illustration shows the APIs and services that are used to access the AD and the layers that provide the services they are accessing.

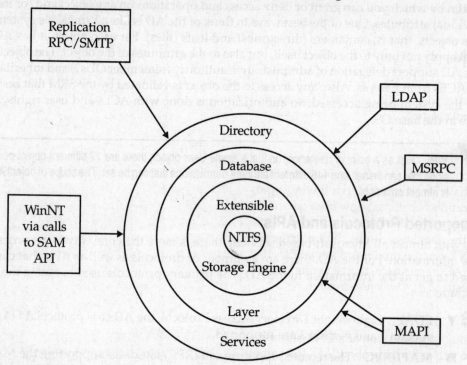

SID Tracking

One feature to note is SID tracking (a.k.a. SID History). When an object with a Security ID is moved from one domain to another, it gets a new SID, but with the AD, the object will remember its old SID. This ensures that SIDs used in ACLs are not made invalid if the account is moved. This is good in some respects, but maybe not so good in others. Let's say that a user is in a DB administrator role in a certain company, and the administrators had granted that user special rights to the database in DBDomain. Then that user switched jobs, and his account was moved to the WidgetDomain. The account has a new SID, but keeps the old one. Although the user is no longer a DB admin, the fact that he has his old SID and that trust is transitive—that is, the DBDomain server will accept authenticated users in the WidgetDomain—means that the user still has all the access he had before. This is a good reason to use groups in ACLs and not individual users.

Auditing

Just like authentication and authorization, auditing is integral to the Win2K OS and is not something that is set separately. The AD auditing occurs just like file system auditing: you enable auditing on objects, and then you set the SACL on AD objects that you want audited. The audits will end up in the Security EventLog or the Directory Service EventLog. Please see Chapter 13 for details on setting up auditing in Win2K.

DESIGN

Now that we have a good handle on the basic components, operations, and issues surrounding the AD, we will look at some basic design issues that we must take into consideration.

Namespace

The best rule of thumb here is to limit the amount (that is, the number) of domains that you have to administer. For the most part, domains have been used for administrative separation, which can now be accomplished by OUs. This means that we can shrink the number of domains that you have and make that part of your life easier. You should design the namespace to be similar to the structure of your business. Most of all, forget the WinNT domain model and think DNS. It would be better to have your DNS group design your AD namespace, then let your Win2K group set up the administrative model on the namespace that was just created.

DNS

Although the selection of a DNS server may not seem to be directly security-related, it is when you are talking about AD. It is something that needs to be done very carefully, and can have long-lasting consequences if not chosen correctly. It also has a direct bearing on the structure that your AD can have, so make your choice only after careful planning.

You have four basic options:

▼ **Use a Win2K-Based DNS Hierarchy**   This option has the advantage of being integrated with Win2K. Another large advantage is that it is integrated into the AD (as discussed earlier). The disadvantage is that it puts all your DNS eggs in one Microsoft basket. This is the best solution if you have a very large homogeneous Windows network.

- **Use a Primary Win2K DNS and Integrate Unix Into It** This option has the advantage of leveraging existing DNS infrastructure, but a disadvantage in that it requires you to make your current DNS structure as a subcomponent of the new Win2K domain. This option is the least desirable of all.

- **Keep Your Existing DNS Structure, and Make a Win2K-Specific Child Domain** This option has the advantage of keeping your existing DNS structure and placing the Win2K DNS structure under it. The disadvantage is that all your Win2K systems will need to be a part of that domain for logins, and thus those systems will have a different domain name than other (non-Win2K) systems on the same network. This is probably the overall best solution if you already have an existing DNS hierarchy.

- ▲ **Use a Unix-Only DNS** If you have the DDNS infrastructure already established, then this is an easy move. The disadvantage is that you lose the ability to distribute zone data via the AD. Otherwise, it should work fine.

Administration Space

As alluded to in the "Namespace" section, you will need to define how objects in your new AD will be administered. The easiest way is to use OUs and delegation of administrative control. The ability to nest OUs and granularly delegate administrative control over the objects in that OU provides the mechanism that you will need to accomplish this. This will allow you to apply administrative control in a manner consistent with your business needs and organizational structure.

When you design your OU structure, you should attempt to use a *breadth-first approach*, because nesting OUs cause a performance hit when accessing the objects in the AD. Another problem you might run into is the limit on nesting OUs. OUs can only be nested to ten levels; you can't go any deeper. I have yet to see an organization that needed ten levels of OUs, as most of the companies that span that deep actually have multiple subdomains, which take care of the problem.

Global Catalog

You must design the placement of GC servers in your AD structure. The GC will be used extensively if you have more than one domain, as it has pointers to all the critical information in the entire forest. If a system needs information about an object in another domain, it will go to the nearest GC server. This could be a major problem if you don't allow for this. How would your WAN link hold up with hundreds or thousands of Win2K boxes trying to get the GC on the other side of it?

It is a wise move to put at least one GC server in every "site" that you have defined when a domain spans multiple sites. It would be better to have two or three in a larger network (that is, hundreds of hosts), but not too many. Remember that the GC holds a full replica of the Configuration and Schema and all objects and attributes that matter in all the domains in the forest. This could grow to be quite large, and the replication to many servers could become a performance issue.

Replication

We touched on replication with the GC issues, but there is more to replication design than the GC. Although the GC is big, it holds just a small percentage of the information that a domain holds. When designing the AD for replication, you want to design domains around sites if at all possible. The two largest replication operations are replicating a domain between its controllers and replicating the GC to all the GC servers. By far the bigger of the two is the domain replication. Because it is the biggest replication issue, if you can structure the domains in your AD so that they fall on site boundaries, you will be better off in the long run.

You may think, "But he just said to run a single domain if possible." This is still the best rule of thumb, because while you may lose some performance, the ease of use gained is well worth it.

Limits on Design Decisions

You may have some requirements that limit the options that you have with respect to design of your AD. Table 8-2 may serve as a guide when designing your AD structure. The horizontal lists are potential attributes and functions that you may require. The vertical list is the potential domain configurations that you can use. The table has values that denote the ability to perform the function (top row item) given the domain structure (left side item). The "N" denotes that you cannot perform the function; a "Y" denotes that you can.

	Delegation of Administration Authority	Different Security Policies (i.e. Group Policies)	Multiple DNS Domains	Different Schemas and/or Configurations
Single Domain	N	N	N	N
Single Domain with OUs	Y	Y	N	N
Directory Tree	Y	Y	Y (child domains)	N
Forest	Y	Y	Y (non-contiguous namespace)	N
Separate AD	Y	Y	Y	Y

Table 8-2.   Active Directory Structure Matrix

ADMINISTRATION

We don't want to be redundant, but the administration that we will be covering is that of administering the AD securely, not using it to administer other things securely. With that in mind, we will press on to talk about tools that are used to administer, install, and set up the AD, then some common configurations.

Tools

There are many tools that can be used to administer the AD. Some are graphics-based, and others are command line-based. We will detail a number of the more useful ones.

Active Directory Domains and Trusts

The Active Directory Domains and Trusts snap-in (Figure 8-1) displays all domain trees in the forest. By default it is accessible from the Start | Programs | Administrative Tools

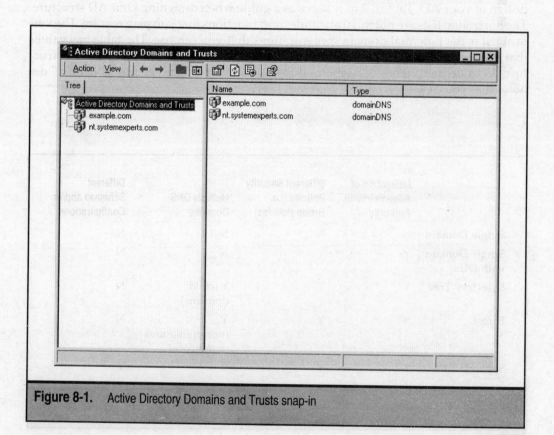

Figure 8-1.   Active Directory Domains and Trusts snap-in

section on every DC. It can also be added to any MMC by adding the snap-in. The tool is used to

▼ Launch the Domain Manager

■ Manage trust relationships

■ Set the operating mode

▲ Define alternative User Principal Name (UPN) suffixes for the forest

Active Directory Sites and Services

The Active Directory Sites and Services snap-in (Figure 8-2) is used to administer the replication topology. These topologies cover both intra- and inter-site replication. By default it is accessible from the Start | Programs | Administrative Tools section on every DC. It can also be added to any MMC by adding the snap-in. The tool is used to

▼ Add and remove sites

■ Move computers into a site

■ Add a subnet to a site

■ Associate a site with a subnet

▲ Create a site link

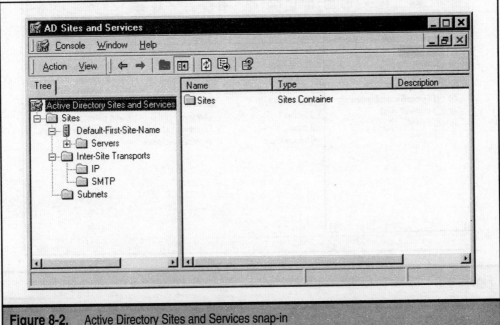

Figure 8-2.   Active Directory Sites and Services snap-in

Active Directory Users and Computers

The Active Directory Users and Computers snap-in (Figure 8-3) is used to manage the objects in the domain. By default it is accessible from the Start | Programs | Administrative Tools section on every DC. It can also be added to any MMC by adding the snap-in. The tool is used to perform the following operations on AD objects such as Users, Groups, Computers, and Shared Folders:

▼ Add attributes and objects

■ Move attributes and objects

■ Delete attributes and objects

▲ Modify attributes and objects

The following containers are available:

▼ **Built-in**   Default container for built-in groups.

■ **Computers**   Default container for computer objects.

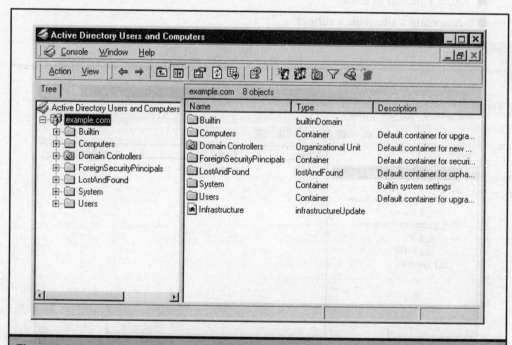

Figure 8-3.   Active Directory Users and Computers snap-in

- **Domain Controllers** Default container for Win2K DCs.
- **ForeignSecurityPrincipals** Default container for objects from trusted domains outside of the AD (that is, forest) that have been added to groups in the domain, such as WinNT domains, Kerberos realms, or other Win2K AD forests.
- ▲ **Users** Default container for user objects.

There are two containers that can be displayed with the View | Advanced Features option:

- ▼ **System** Default container for built-in system settings.
- ▲ **LostAndFound** Default container for domain objects whose container was deleted elsewhere at the same time that the object was created.

ADSIEdit

The ADSIEdit is a snap-in that allows you to perform LDAP operations against any of the directory partitions (that is, Domain, Configuration, or Schema). ADSIEdit accesses the AD via the ADSI and allows you to add, delete, and move objects within the AD. Also, object attributes can be viewed, changed, and deleted.

NOTE: You can install Active Directory Administrative Tools on your Win2K Pro or Server with the Windows Components Wizard, or from the ADMINPAK on the Win2K Server or Professional CD.

Other Tools

There are other useful tools that come on the Win2K Server CD in the Support subdirectory. Most of them just provide another way (either graphically or from a command line) of providing the functionality of the tools. Please see the online documentation for the details of some of the commands. A number of these tools have limited or no documentation, and can only be learned by trial and error.

- ▼ **Ldp** A graphical tool that allows users to perform LDAP operations.
- **Ntdsutil** Provides command-line management facilities for the AD, including database maintenance, management of operational roles, and more.
- **MoveTree** Allows you to move objects from one domain to another.
- **DNSCMD** Allows you to perform a number of DNS operations and checks, such as Secure DNS update and de-registration of resource records.
- **DSACLS** Allows you to view or modify the ACLs of directory objects. This can be used remotely as well.
- **NETDOM** Allows you to manage domain objects from the command line.

- **REPAdmin and REPLMon** Allows you to administer replication-type issues, such as replication consistency, replication status, and forced replication. REPLMon is a GUI-based tool.

- **SDCheck** Allows you to view the security descriptor information on an object.

▲ **ACLDiag** Allows you to view the ACLs on a directory object.

NOTE: You can install Active Directory Support Tools on your Win2K Pro or Server from the `Support` subdirectory on the Win2K Server CD.

NETDOM: A Kitchen Sink Tool

NETDOM is the crescent wrench of domain administration. It can perform a large number of tasks and is very versatile. This tool is a very effective command-line tool for administrators to manage Win2K domains and trusts. Some of the things it can be used for include

▼ Joining a computer to a domain

■ Managing computer accounts

■ Establishing and managing trust relationships (uni-directional or bi-directional) between domains (Win2K, NT, Kerberos)

■ Validating and resetting the secure channel

▲ Synchronizing time

It is installed as part of the Win2K Support Tools mentioned earlier.

Setup and Installation

The setup and installation of the Active Directory is a separate process than the installation of Win2K Server. You must install the server first, then at some later time, you can perform the AD setup. The following section details the initial installation and setup tasks associated with the AD. We will detail the steps to set up a fresh AD, which is setting up the first domain in a forest, then cover the differences when adding a child to a domain tree, a new domain tree to an existing forest, and an additional DC to an existing domain. Again, the basic thrust will be covering issues that deal with security during these operations, not a detailed step-by-step guide, which can be found online in the Microsoft TechNet articles, or the Microsoft Win2K Resource Kit.

The implementation process starts by selecting a system that will be the first DC in the AD. Once you have selected it (as part of your design criteria, I hope), you will run the DCPROMO command. Unlike in WinNT, you can promote and demote servers as DCs without restriction. There are really only two steps that need to be taken when setting up an AD:

1. Set up a secure server to run the DC on.

2. Start the conversion process. This can be done by using the Active Directory option in the Windows 2000 Configure Your Server dialog box. (It is there by default after installing or running DCPROMO from the command line.) Note that you can run a "quiet" installation with DCPROMO by supplying an answer file (dcpromo /answer:<answerfile name>); see the online help for the file format.

Let's get started!

NOTE: When a Win2K Server is converted to a DC, the existing SAM database is replaced by a more streamlined version. This SAM is only used when the server is started in Directory Services Restore Mode.

What Are My Options?

There are certain limitations on what you can set up, given the system you are planning on installing the DC on. If you have a Win2K Server that is a member server or standalone, either through a new install or upgrade, then you can create a DC in a new domain or add it to an existing domain. If you are upgrading from a WinNT PDC, you have to make a new domain. If it is a WinNT BDC, then it can become a DC or member server in an existing domain.

Setting Up the First Domain, Forest, and AD

As an administrative-level account, run DCPROMO from the command line. This will start the Active Directory Installation Wizard. Click Next to start the process. The first option that you will have to set is the type of DC to create (see Figure 8-4). You can set up a DC for a new domain, or add it to an existing domain. When you create a new domain, the existing SAM user accounts become users in that domain. Local groups are converted to groups with type "local group," and the built-in local groups are converted to groups with type "built-in local group." For our example, we will select a DC for a new domain.

If we would have selected to add the DC to an existing domain, we would have been prompted for a Domain Administrator level account and the domain to add it to.

Because we have selected a new domain, we are asked if it is to be a child of an existing domain in the AD, or if we want to create a new domain tree (see Figure 8-5). Ours is the first domain, so we are creating a new domain tree.

Now we are asked if we want to create or join a forest (see Figure 8-6). When you are setting up an AD, there is no pre-existing forest, so you have to create one. If there were another AD already set up, this option allows you to create a separate forest, just in case you needed a different Schema or Configuration (that is, replication) setup. If you create a new forest, you should realize that there is no inherent trust between different forests.

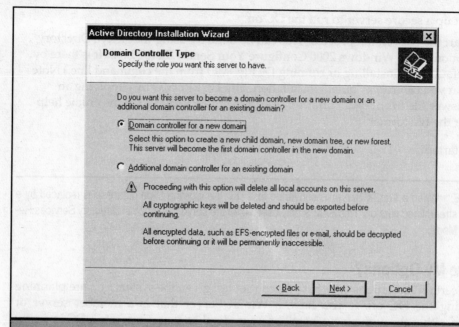

Figure 8-4. Domain Controller type selection

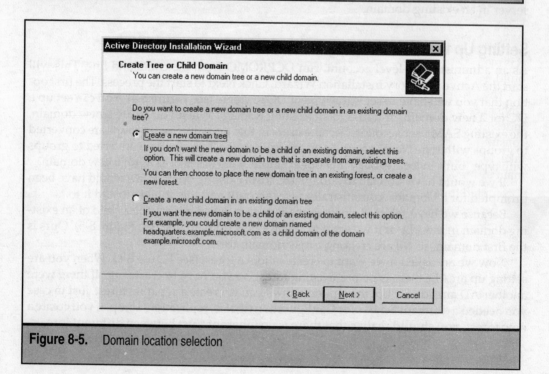

Figure 8-5. Domain location selection

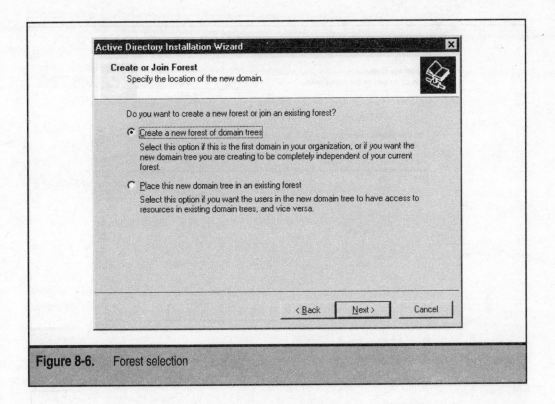

Figure 8-6.   Forest selection

It is really setting up an entirely separate AD namespace. Because we are doing the initial build, we will Create a New Forest of Domain Trees.

Then we are asked for the new DNS domain name (see Figure 8-7). This will be the DNS name that we will link to the active directory. Although the screen in Figure 8-7 alludes to the fact that you can just use your organization's DNS name, using it without consulting the group who provides DNS service to your organization would be a mistake. Refer back to the "Design" section for DNS tips. Needless to say, we have our domain example.com (properly registered, of course).

VIP: Don't just grab a domain name—go through the proper channels and register it correctly *before* you set it up! A good place to start is **www.internic.net**.

Next you are asked for the NetBIOS name. This is for compatibility with Windows Explorer and other NetBIOS-centric applications, as well as Windows systems that use NetBIOS. You should keep the default for this, as it makes it a bit easier to correlate the DNS domains and the NetBIOS domains.

Next you are prompted for the locations to store the actual AD database and its associated log. Note that the log is a Transaction Log, not an event and auditing log. The default is C:\WINNT\NTDS\. The defaults are okay, but if you can, you should store them on separate partitions (like the screen says).

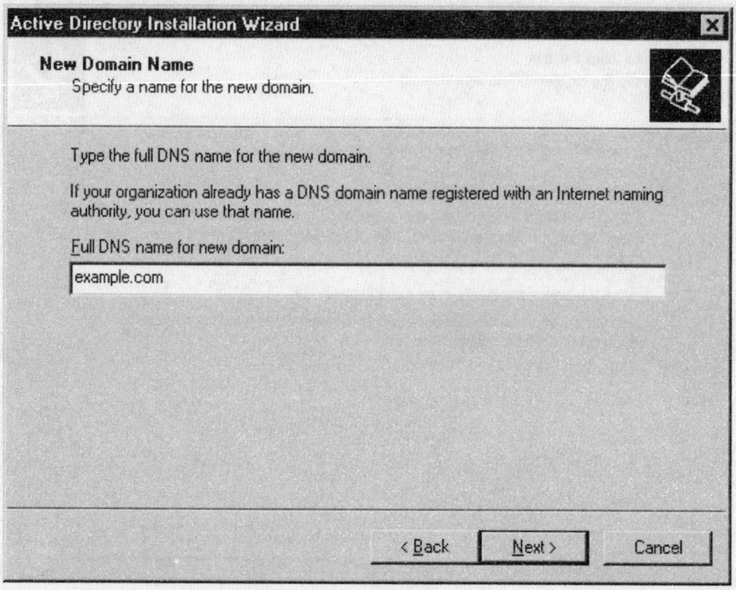

Figure 8-7. Domain name selection

The major security issue here is making sure the NTFS permissions on the directories are secure. By default the directory does *not* inherit (its children do), and only Administrators and LocalSystem have access to the directory. This is a good thing to validate periodically.

The next screen asks for the location of the SYSVOL folder. The SYSVOL holds the domain's system policies and logon scripts. Because this folder holds critical data, it is important to validate the NTFS as well as share permissions on a periodic basis.

By default the directory does not inherit (but its children do), and it has the following NTFS permissions:

▼ Administrators: Full Control

■ LocalSystem: Full Control

■ Authenticated Users: Read, Read&Execute, List

■ Server Operators: Read, Read&Execute, List

▲ CREATOR OWNER: blank

Share permissions are

▼ Administrators: Full Control

■ Authenticated Users: Full Control

▲ Everyone: Read

NOTE: SYSVOL is replicated with the File Replication Service (FRS). Changes are replicated immediately within a site, and are scheduled between sites.

The next screen prompts for the DNS configuration (Figure 8-8). If you have the DDNS structure set up as described in the earlier DNS sections, then you can say No; otherwise, you should set up an AD-integrated DNS structure. For our example, we will set it up. It does not really ask you anything; it just sets up the DNS information and moves you on to the next step. We will cover making sure the DNS server is secure a bit later in this chapter.

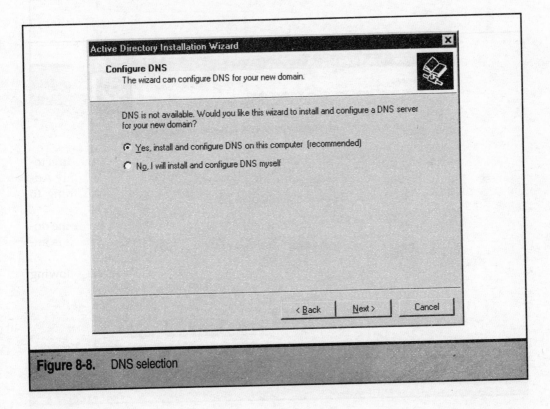

Figure 8-8. DNS selection

The next option is a big security issue. You will have the opportunity to "loosen" the access to the AD to allow anonymous connections to gather user data. There is a Built-in group called Pre-Windows 2000 Compatible Permissions that has read permissions to all critical domain user and group attributes. Older Windows applications (such as WinNT RAS) require anonymous read access to particular user and group attributes. By selecting the Permissions Compatible with Pre-Windows 2000 Servers option (see Figure 8-9), the Everyone group is made a member of this group, and thus allows the required access. We will select the more secure option for our example.

If you do not need to support applications that require anonymous read access to these attributes, select the Permissions Compatible Only with Windows 2000 Servers option. If you do select this, you can secure it later by removing the Everyone group from the Pre-Windows 2000 Compatible Permissions built-in group. This may potentially break older applications, but will significantly increase the security of your Win2K system

The last and final option (but not the last screen) will have you set the password for recovery. Win2K supports the restoration of System State data (that is, restoring the SYSVOL directory and AD directory service database) on DCs. Booting in the Directory Services Restore Mode does this. This password is needed to authenticate in this mode.

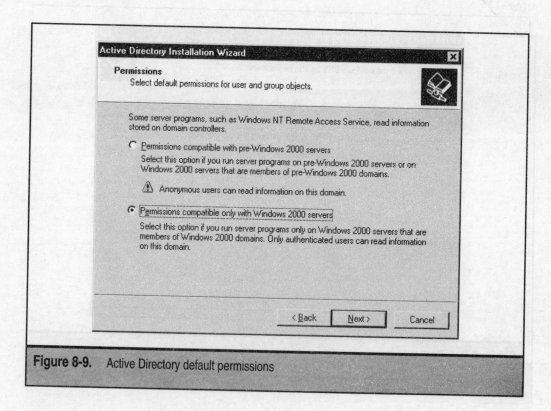

Figure 8-9.   Active Directory default permissions

The next screen is just a summary of the options you have selected and the option to proceed with the installation or to cancel out of it. It will take awhile for the process to complete; then you will be prompted to "Finish" the installation, which just means rebooting.

That's it. Now you have a fully functioning AD. In the next few sections we'll discuss the steps to add other types of DCs to the AD.

Adding a DC to an Existing Domain

The initial steps are the same, but you should choose to add a DC to an existing domain in the screen shown in Figure 8-4. When you add the DC to an existing domain, the local accounts in the SAM are deleted (as alluded to by the warning icon). The accounts from the existing domain will be replicated to the new DC.

Then you are prompted for the credentials to use to perform the operation to set up this DC as a trusted DC in the domain and add it to the AD (see Figure 8-10). We need to enter a Domain Admin level account here.

Then you are prompted for the domain that you want to add the DC to (see Figure 8-11).

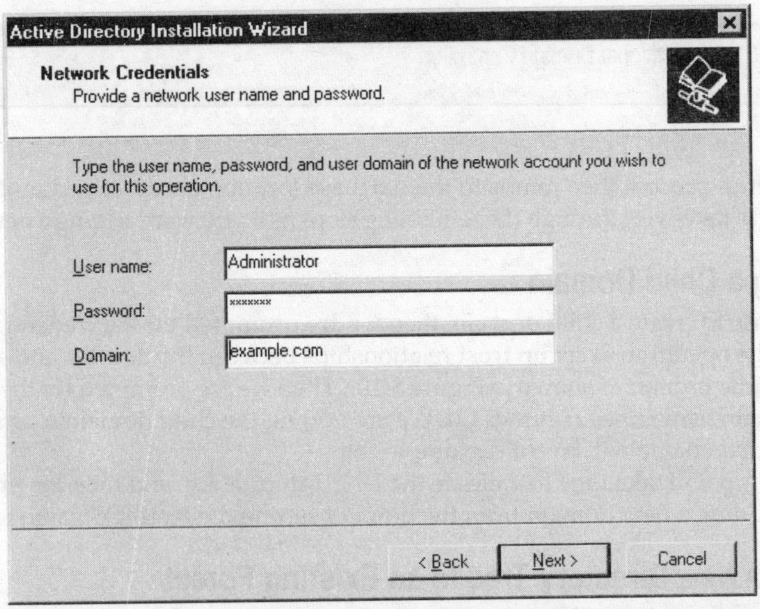

Figure 8-10.   Network credentials

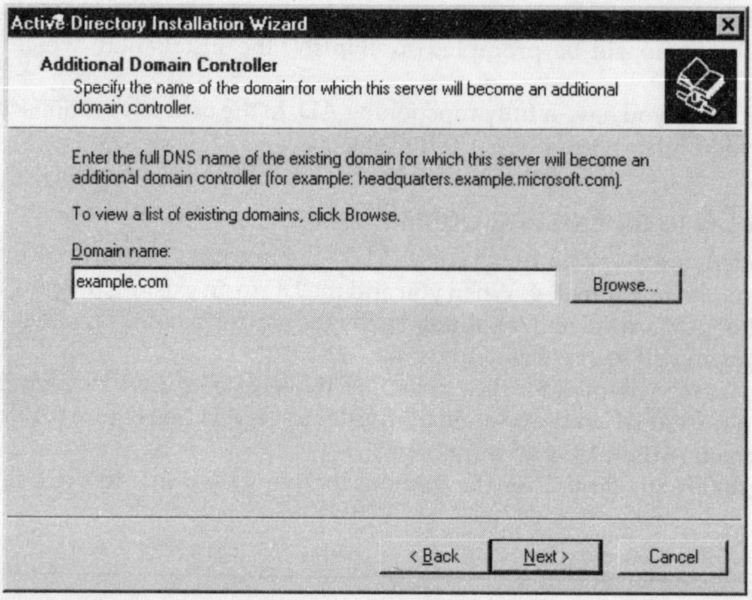

Figure 8-11.   Additional Domain Controller

The setup process then jumps to the database location (as described in the previous section) and takes you through the remaining steps as if you were adding a new domain.

Creating a Child Domain

If we choose to create a child domain, then we are prompted for the credentials to use to perform the operation to set up trust relationships between the domain and add it to the AD (the same prompt as shown in Figure 8-10). Then we are prompted for the parent and child domain names (see Figure 8-12). We are adding the child domain to example.com, so our domain name will be child.example.com.

The setup will take time to validate the DNS information, and then the process is the same as adding a new domain from the point of setting the NetBIOS name to the end.

Adding a New Directory Tree to an Existing Forest

Let's say we wanted to add the example.org domain to the AD. Since it is not a contiguous namespace with example.com, we would have to create a separate domain tree, and then place it in the existing forest (that is, AD). We would have selected a new domain (see Fig-

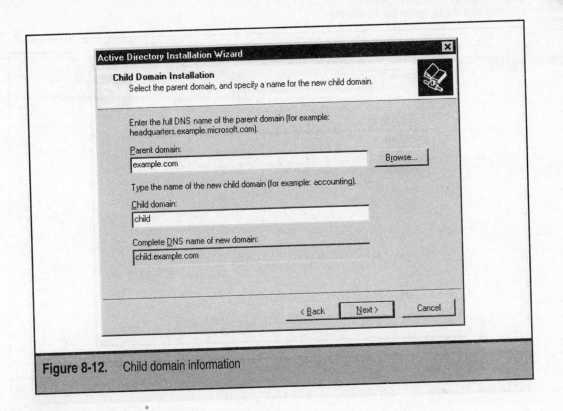

Figure 8-12.   Child domain information

ure 8-4), a new domain tree (see Figure 8-5), and then an existing forest (see Figure 8-6). We would then enter the credentials (Enterprise Admin level) to use to perform the operation to set up trust relationships between the domain trees and add it to the AD (the same prompt as shown in Figure 8-10). Then we are prompted for the new root domain name for the tree (see Figure 8-13).

⋅ As when adding a child domain, the setup will take time to validate the DNS information, and then the process is the same as adding a new domain from the point of setting the NetBIOS name to the end.

Securing the AD

For the most part, if you took the time to install the AD correctly (that is, not loosening up permissions), it is fairly secure. The reality of AD security is that is rests on multiple factors. This section will address those factors and give guidance on what to do to mitigate them.

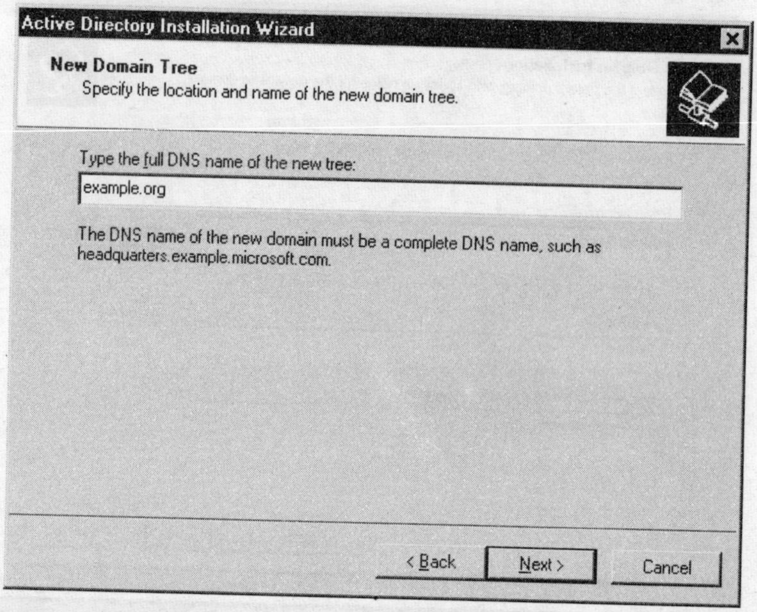

Figure 8-13. New domain tree name

When we think about a secure AD, we need to think in layers. There are six layers of security that we need to worry about:

▼ Securing the system

■ Securing the database

■ Securing the replication

■ Securing the normal access methods

■ Securing the objects

▲ Auditing

Securing the System

To have a secure AD, the underlying OS must be secure. This means good passwords, NTFS partitions, only necessary services, and so on. Chapter 21 goes into the details of securing (that is, hardening an OS) and discusses the services required for different types of system setups.

Once this is set up, then we can use the Group Policy functionality to maintain the security (Group Policies are discussed in depth in the next chapter). The Group Policy is replicated from the first DC in a domain to all other DCs in that domain. The default Group Policy is developed from three security templates, `DCFirst.inf`, `DefltDC.inf`, and `DCUp.inf`, which are located in `%Windir%\Inf`. There are two default Group Policies that are set up: Default Domain Policy, which is applicable to all systems in the domain, and Default Domain Controller Policy, which is applicable only to DCs in the domain. The Default Domain Controller Policy has precedence, and it is not very tight. For example

▼ No auditing is defined.

■ It allows the Everyone group from the network.

▲ Any Authenticated User can add a workstation to the domain.

You should take the time to restrict the Default Domain and Default Domain Controller Group Policies to ensure an adequate level of security. Here are some recommendations (see Chapter 9 for implementation details):

▼ **In Account Policies** Set password and account lockout policies in accordance with your security policy. Enable password complexity. Set Kerberos Policy to enforce user logon restrictions and set a clock synchronization tolerance.

■ **In Local Policies** Enable auditing (successful and failed) of account logon and logoff events, policy changes, and account management. Remove the ability of the Everyone group to access this computer from the network. Restrict who can add workstations to the domain. Restrict anonymous connections and set LM Authentication Level to 3.

VIP: Setting LM Authentication Level to 3 will only allow Win2K and WinNT SP6a and later to communicate over SMB.

■ **In Event Log** Set appropriate event log file settings. See Chapter 13 for detailed recommendations.

▲ **Registry and File Systems** Validate/tighten the ACLs on the critical Win2K directories (`WINNT` and subdirectories, wherever you put the AD files and logs).

The biggest issue is running unnecessary and unsecure services such as Telnet. The most important thing to do when securing a DC is to remove or disable any unnecessary services.

Securing the Database

Attackers will attempt to get "under" the AD layer to access the data. They will attempt to use file-sharing exploits or other "access" methods to get to the AD server. The two primary methods will be network CIFS/SMB access or local/interactive access.

As far as local/interactive access goes, the physical file that holds the AD data is `Ntds.dit`. The live copy resides in the `%SystemRoot%\NTDS\` directory. The LocalSystem account exclusively locks this file, much like the locking of the SAM file in WinNT. Thus the only way to get at the data is through API calls, a security flaw in the file-locking mechanism, or getting the LocalSystem to access the file for you. If you do have administrative level privileges, then you could use a tool like LDIFDE to dump the domain database or use pwdump2 (a third-party tool) to extract usernames and password hashes.

When the AD is installed, the process applies ACLs for the NTFS and share permissions for the directory service and file replication directories. By default only Administrators and LocalSystem have Full Control to `%SystemRoot%\NTDS\Ntds.dit`, and no other access is defined. Care should be taken to ensure the permissions on this file do not change. You should audit this file for change in permissions or ownership.

CIFS/SMB access is restricted to the administrative shares by default, except for the `SYSVOL`, but that has appropriate NTFS and share permissions (as noted earlier in the section on `SYSVOL` setup). So unless you take actions to place the AD data at risk via CIFS/SMB, it won't be accessible. Besides, the exclusive locking would deny access anyway.

VIP: You can always dual-boot the computer and use a disk reader to get the information also, so physical security is always a must. Remember the offline copies of the database in the form of backups and database dumps as well.

Securing the Replication Process

The replication traffic is encrypted with the secure channel, so anyone looking for the information will have to break the secure channel first. The security of the process is dependent on the security of the transport. The replication process will happen over one of two transports: RPC or SMTP. So as long as the secure channel is kept "secure," so is the data.

Securing Normal Access Methods

Securing access will take into account blocking access to the ports that can be used to access the AD, such as LDAP (389, 636), Global Catalog (3268, 3269), SMB (139), and CIFS (445). Then, you can use Group Policies to control what actions are allowed on the domain objects, much like you would use them for critical file system objects.

There will no doubt still be some access that anonymous users will always have, such as enumerating a given SID to a username or a username to a SID. These tend to be simple operations, in that they don't do the heavy security checking that more in-depth queries may require. This is a performance issue for the most part, because if you have a SID or a name, you have what you need anyway. By performing the blocking of access to the query ports, you eliminate this exposure as well.

Securing the Objects

Object security in the AD is completely dependent on the ACLs on the object. If you don't have proper ACLs on the objects in the AD, then all bets are off. The reality is that there are numerous ways to get to information in the AD, and your last layer of defense is the individual object/attribute ACL.

By default, the object ACLs are pretty tight. The one exception to that is anyone in the Pre-Windows 2000 Compatible Access group, which has a high level of access to domain User and Group objects (described earlier). This group will have the Everyone group in it if you had selected the default installation options. Figure 8-14 shows that this group allows a much broader access to User and Group information to anyone who is in it. Take the time to validate the high-level ACLs on the containers that are in the AD, and then use inheritance to propagate them down.

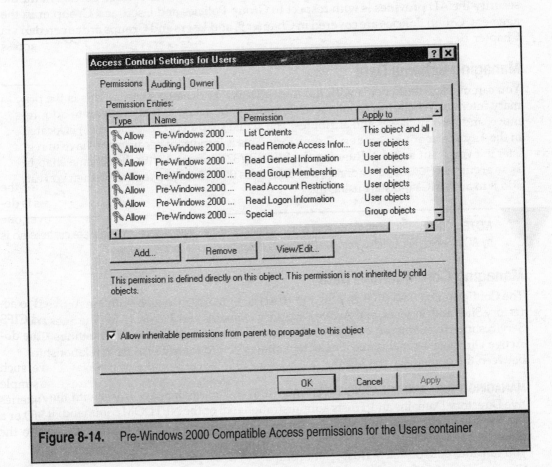

Figure 8-14. Pre-Windows 2000 Compatible Access permissions for the Users container

Auditing the AD

We will actually cover the specifics of this later in the chapter, but too many people think that security is just getting things set up correctly. That is not the case; setting up correct auditing on the system is just as important as setting proper object permission ACLs. You need to ensure that you are auditing critical operations and data, such as changes to policy data or critical files in the WINNT, NTDS, and SYSVOL partitions.

Common Administrative Tasks

There are a number of administrative tasks that can be done with the AD. We will look at some of the most common tasks associated with managing the AD and how to do them securely. This chapter is not about illustrating all of the tasks, as that is an entire book in and of itself, but only the steps needed to secure the AD. A large portion of the security the AD provides is with respect to Group Policies and Users and Group management. Group Policies are covered in Chapter 9, and Users and Groups are covered in Chapter 10.

Managing Schema Data

You can manage the Schema with the Active Directory Schema snap-in. This is the primary interface Win2K has to interactively modify the schema. It allows you to add, remove, and modify classes and attributes. The actual snap-in (schmmgmt.dll) is located in the %systemroot%\System32 directory. This is important because you have to register it if you want to use it. Running the REGSRV32 command with the Schema snap-in as an argument (REGSRV32 schmmgmt.dll) does this. Once you register it, then you can add it to an MMC, and start using it.

NOTE: The security of all the objects in the Schema and the Configuration container are controlled by ACLs, which are settable from the Properties dialog box on any of the objects.

Managing Configuration Data

The Configuration data (that is, sites and trust) is regularly managed with the Active Directory Sites and Services, and Active Directory Domains and Trusts. Using the Sites and Services interface, you can configure and manage the sites and replication settings. The Active Directory Domains and Trusts tool allows you to manage the trust relationships between the domains in the forest.

MANAGING TRUST AND CREATING EXTERNAL TRUST   You can manage trusts with the Active Directory Domains and Trusts administration tool or the NETDOM command. If using the AD admin tool, you would open the Properties dialog box for the domain in question by right-clicking and selecting Properties, then selecting the Trusts tab. Then you can add, edit, or delete trust relationships.

You can use these same tools to set up an external trust (that is, an explicit trust relationship with a domain outside of the forest). This trust is uni-directional and non-transitive by default. If you use the NETDOM command, there are a couple of options that assist in creating external trusts:

▼   **REALM**   Indicates that the trust is to be created to a non-Windows
Kerberos realm.

▲   **TWOWAY**   Specifies that a trust relationship should be bi-directional.

SETTING UP REPLICATION TOPOLOGY   You set up a replication topology by using the Active Directory Sites and Services administration tool. This tool is used to set configuration parameters that will be used by the *Knowledge Consistency Checker (KCC)*. The KCC is the process that creates the replication topology for the forest (it runs on all DCs). The KCC creates replication connections between DCs in the same site automatically and uses configuration data to configure links between the sites. There are two things that need to be done to give the KCC the information it needs to build the replication topology:

▼   **Set Up Sites**   This provides the basis for knowing which DCs are highly
connected.

▲   **Set Up Subnets**   When placed in a site, it allows the KCC to know how best to
replicate between the DCs. When you set up subnets, you define them and then
determine which subnets provide the best connectivity for replication and add
them to the same site. These should mirror the IP subnets and subnet masks
that exist on your networks.

You can use Active Directory Sites and Services to create sites and subnets, then associate the subnets with the sites. You create them by selecting the sites container, then right-clicking and selecting New Site. Then you can configure the option for the object you just created. Like all AD-related objects, sites, subnets, and servers all have a Security tab for setting ACLs on the objects. You can also use Group Policies and delegation to better manage them.

Switching to Native Mode

When a domain is initially installed, it is installed (by default) in mixed mode. When you are no longer required to support down-level clients such as WinNT, or you want to use the full-blown features of the AD, you can convert the domain to native mode. Realize that once you do this, it is not reversible. Using the Active Directory Users and Computers or the Active Directory Domains and Trusts administrative interface, you can open the Properties page (see Figure 8-15) on the domain you want to switch. Then click the Change Mode button in the Domain Mode section of the screen. You will see a warning stating that the process is non-reversible. Once you have switched modes, you will be able to utilize such features as universal groups and group nesting.

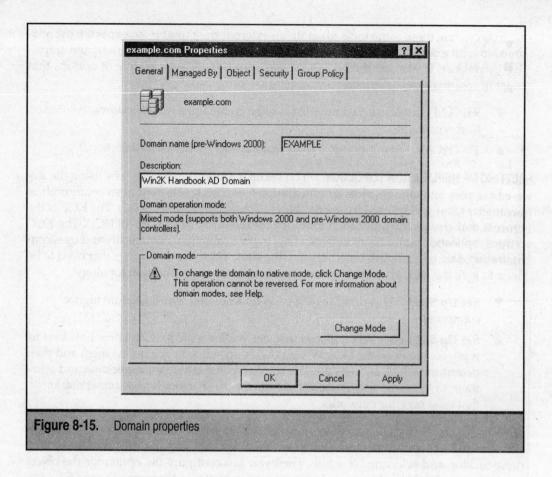

Figure 8-15. Domain properties

Adding an Organizational Unit

We have talked about OUs. Now we will look at creating one in the example.com domain. We will use the Active Directory Users and Computers interface to perform the operation. From the interface, on the domain you want to add the OU to, right-click and select New | Organizational Unit.

You will then be prompted for the OU name. Once you enter it and click OK, the new OU appears in the console. Now we need to configure the OU, which is done by right-clicking and selecting Properties. By default, all of its descriptive information is blank (such as who manages it, where it's located, and so on), so you will need to fill that out. The use of OUs and Group Policies together are what give the AD such an administrative appeal. From the Group Policy tab in the Properties sheet (see Figure 8-16), you can choose the following options:

▼ **New**   Create a new Group Policy and make a link to this OU.

■ **Add**   Add a link to an existing Group Policy.

▲ **Block Policy Inheritance**   Allows an administrator to block Group Policies that are flowing down from higher-level domains or block OUs from applying to the current OU and its children. *One caveat: You can't block Group Polices that use the No Override option.*

Let's say that we added a new Group Policy: TestOUGroupPolicy (this process is detailed in the next chapter). We would then link it to the OU, using the Add button. Then we could perform OU operations on it like setting the No Override bit, disabling it (mostly for testing), editing it, or setting the properties on the Group Policy itself (see Figure 8-16). The Group Policies are cumulative for all those listed in the window, as well as inherited Group Policies, so a more restrictive policy always wins over a less restrictive one.

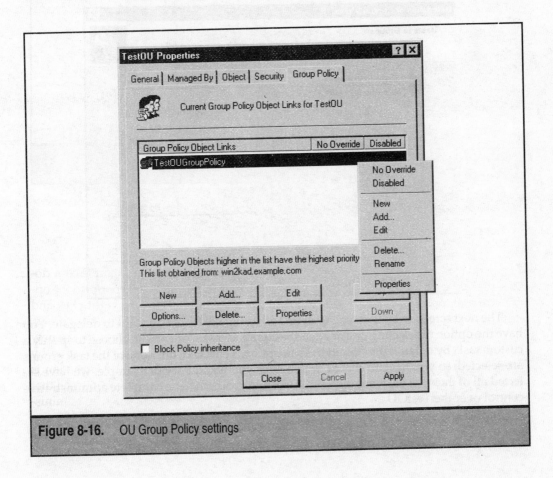

Figure 8-16.   OU Group Policy settings

NESTING OUS   Nesting OUs is a simple matter of expanding the OU, and then performing the same process as was just described for adding an OU. Nesting OUs are mostly used to more granularly define the administrative ability of the parent OU. This is mostly for very large or splintered organizations.

Delegating Control

We have discussed the benefit of being able to delegate control over domains, OUs, and other special containers. Now we will see how to do it. When you find the object that you want to delegate control over (TestOU for our example), right-click and select Delegate Control, which will bring up the Delegation of Control Wizard.

You will then be asked to select Users and/or Groups (from any domain in the forest) that will have control over the object. You should always use Groups for permissions and administrative control, as Users will come and go but Group functions usually are pretty constant. The results of adding the TestOUAdmin group to the list are shown below.

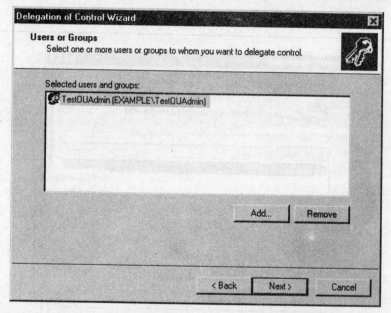

The next screen will allow you to define what type of tasks you want to delegate. You have the option of selecting one or all of the common tasks, or you can choose to specify a custom task. By default, the Common Task option is checked, but none of the task groups are selected, so you have to choose which ones you want. For our example, we have selected all of them, as we want the TestOUAdmin group to have complete administrative control over the TestOU.

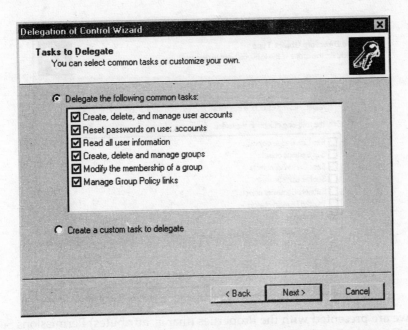

Once you have selected the common tasks, you are taken to an acknowledgment screen, and the Delegation of Control Wizard finishes its operation.

The best and easiest option is to choose one of the common tasks, as the custom task definition can be very complex. One of the main axioms in security is to keep it simple, as complexity leads to errors, and errors lead to compromise. We will look at the custom task delegation next.

CUSTOM TASK DELEGATION We will take a look at the custom task delegation to demonstrate the power and granularity of the delegation ability in Win2K, but to emphasize it is best not to use custom task delegation, we will use a ridiculous example.

We have a group of people that we have hired to validate the Job Titles of all the people in TestOU. To do this, we will add them to a special Group, TestOUJobTitleAdmin, and give them the ability to read and write the Job Title attribute (that is, property) for all users in the TestOU.

We start the Delegation of Control Wizard the same as before, and then add our Group (TestOUJobTitleAdmin). Then we select the custom tasks, and we will be brought to the Object Type Delegation page (shown next). Here we will select *only the following objects in the folder* (that is, container), and the specific object class *User objects*. The other option just allows you to select properties (described next) for the current folder and objects that exist in the folder currently, as well as the ability to create new objects in the folder.

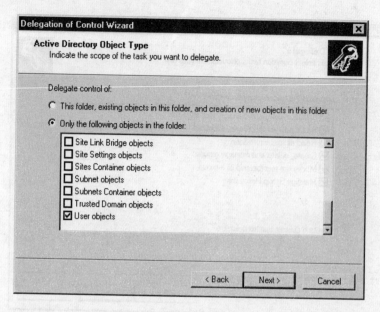

Then we are presented with the Properties (that is, attributes) Permissions Selection sheet. The General tab includes properties that may be generalized for that object class. The Property-Specific option allows you to get to the specifics of this object type, and the last option allows the creation of child objects. We are being very specific, so we will use the Property-Specific option, and select the Read Job Title and Write Job Title properties (shown next). In reality, most all of the properties are selected by default, so we had to clear them.

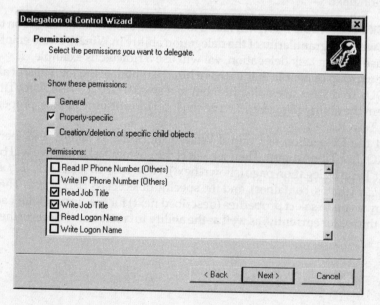

The Delegation Wizard is just an easy way of applying ACLs on the objects. To validate what we have just done, we can look at the Access Control Settings for TestOU (on TestOU, select Properties | Security | Advanced). We see that the two groups are now in the ACL for TestOU (shown below).

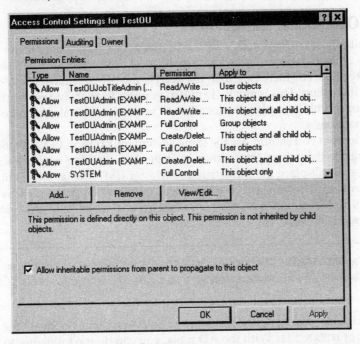

> **VIP:**   Delegation of other types of objects, such as domains or special containers (that is, Users), is very similar to the process we just finished.

Renaming, Moving, and Deleting Objects

Every object in the AD can be renamed and deleted, and most objects can be moved to different containers. The one exception is the forest root domain (that is, the first domain created in the AD). It cannot be deleted, renamed, or moved without irreversibly damaging the AD. To move an object, you need to right-click the object, then select Move. A browser-type window will be displayed so that you can select the container to move the object to. To rename or delete, just right-click the object and request the desired operation.

You cannot use any of the graphical tools to move objects across domains; you need to use a tool like NETDOM.

Demoting a DC

You use the same tools to demote DCs as you did to promote them: DCPROMO. When you demote a DC, the shortcuts to Group Policy security settings are removed, and the links in the Administrative Tools menu to the local security settings for the member server or for the standalone server are added. When the demoted DC is not the only DC in the domain, the server becomes a member server in the domain it was just demoted from. If it is the only DC, it becomes a standalone (that is, workgroup) server.

Managing Operational Master Roles

When you initially set up a Win2K AD, it will place the operational master roles on the first DC. This tends to be acceptable for a small forest with a few DCs in a single site. As the complexity of the AD increases, then the need to move operational master roles to different DCs is important. This is mostly to match your replication and network topologies. A good rule of thumb is to plan the location of your operational master roles on a domain-by-domain basis.

For each domain you should use the same system for RID and PDC functions in small domains; separate them for performance in large domains, but ensure they are in the same site. Also, don't place the Infrastructure Master (IM) role on a DC with a GC, but make sure they are in the same site. For the forest, you should put the Schema Master and Domain Naming Master roles on the same system and make sure the system is a GC server. This ensures timely and accurate updates.

VIP: If the IM is placed on a GC server, cross-domain object references in that domain will not be updated because the IM will think that everything is up to date. This is not an issue if all DCs are GC servers also.

If you need to transfer an operational master role, you can use some of the AD administration tools or NTDSUTIL. With the AD tools, you can do the following to transfer:

▼ **The Domain Naming Master** Use the Active Directory Domains and Trusts. Start the tool and select the top level (Active Directory Domains and Trusts), and then right-click and select Connect to Domain Controller. Then select the DC that you want to *transfer the role to*. At the top again, right-click and select Operations Master. This will bring you to the screen to change the role; select Change. This will change transfer the role to the new DC.

■ **The Schema Master** Use the Active Directory Schema snap-in (described earlier). Start the tool and select the top level (Active Directory Schema), and then right-click and select Change Domain Controller. Select the DC that you want to *transfer the role to*. Then at the top again, right-click and select Operations Master. This will bring you to the screen to change the role; select Change. This will change transfer the role to the new DC.

■ **The Per-domain Masters (RID, PDC, Infrastructure)** Use the Active Directory Users and Computers administration tool. Start the tool and select the top level (Active Directory Users and Computers), then right-click and select Connect to Domain Controller. Select the DC that you want to *transfer the* *role to.* Then at the top again, right-click and select Operations Master. This will bring you to a screen with three tabs, one for each of the roles. Pick the role to transfer, then select Change. This will transfer the role to the new DC.

▲ **Any Operational Master Role** Use NTDSUTIL to transfer any of the roles to another system. From the command line, run **NTDSUTIL** and select the "Roles" option, then use the "Connections" option to connect to a DC. Once the connection is made, use the "TRANSFER <ROLE>" command to transfer that role to the DC you connected to.

With NTDSUTIL, you can not only transfer roles, but seize them as well. It is a bit handier also, because you can perform all the functions from the command line, instead of multiple windows. If you use the tools to seize a role, it will attempt a nice "transfer" first, then if that does not work, it will perform the seizure. See the command help (type **NTDSUTIL /?**) for more information.

GRANTING ROLE TRANSFERS To perform a transfer, you must have the right permissions. Role transfers are granted by object permission for each role:

▼ **Change Schema Master** Granted to the Schema Admins group by default

■ **Change Domain Master** Granted to the Enterprise Admins group by default

■ **Change RID Master** Granted to the Domain Admins group by default

■ **Change PDC** Granted to the Domain Admins group by default

▲ **Change Infrastructure Master** Granted to the Domain Admins group by default

If you need to change these permissions, you will need to use the ADSIEdit tool. You use the tool to find the role object, and then find the appropriate property (that is, attribute) and change the permissions.

To seize a role, you have to have one of the transfer permissions that were just described, plus the Write fsmoRoleOwner property permission on the DC you are transferring the role to. By default, the Write fsmoRoleOwner property permission is granted to the same groups that are granted transfer permissions.

Setting up Auditing

To enable auditing on AD objects, you first must set the Domain Policy to allow it. This is done by enabling the Audit Directory Service Access option, which is accessed by selecting Default Domain Policy | Computer Configuration | Windows Settings | Security Settings | Local Policies | Audit Policies. Once that is enabled, you can set auditing on an object by selecting the object (preferably a high-level container), then right-clicking and selecting Properties | Security | Advanced | Auditing. Then select Add to set up auditing for a new User or Group. See Chapter 13 for details on the entire auditing process and tools.

TIP: Your energies would be much better spent monitoring policy changes and account management rather than auditing specific AD object access, although there may be some objects that you would want to watch.

Backing Up and Restoring

There is no secret to backing up the AD data; just ensure that your software will do it! The default Win2K backup program, `ntbackup.exe` (see Figure 8-17), will back up the System State data (that is, the AD data). Restoring it is a bit different. You have two options for restores: non-authoritative and authoritative.

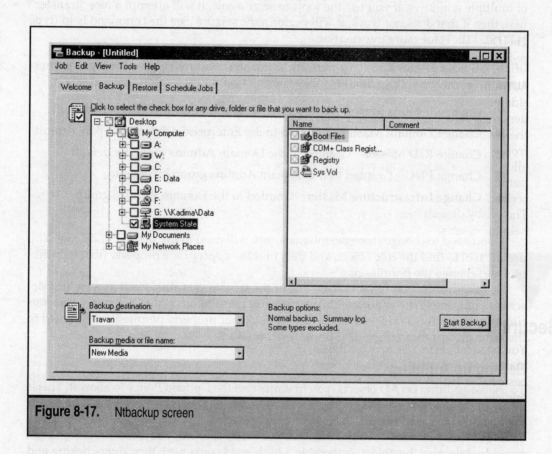

Figure 8-17. Ntbackup screen

NON-AUTHORITATIVE In a non-authoritative restore, the DC is restored from backup, then the restored data is updated through normal replication. It is non-authoritative in the sense that any updates that were in the database are considered invalid, and the data is updated with what is incoming. The Ntbackup tool can be used to restore in this mode. To restore in this mode, you need to

1. Boot into the Directory Services Restore Mode (press F8 during the boot process). You will need to log in (remember the Directory Service Repair Mode password you set during install?).

2. Start Ntbackup and restore the System State.

3. Once the restore is completed, the File Replication service is reset so that it is ready for replication, and the AD database is verified for restore.

The DC then reboots into normal mode, checks AD database files for consistency and re-indexes them, replicates FRS data, and restores the Certificate Services database.

AUTHORITATIVE An authoritative restore just means that the restored data can be considered authoritative for replication matters (that is, its data *is* designated to take precedence over any other instances of those objects on other DCs). So when replication occurs, the restored data will be propagated out. This type of restore is usually used to restore from a known good state, for example, before objects were deleted. The Ntdsutil tool allows you to perform this type of restore. You perform an authoritative restore after you perform a non-authoritative restore. You perform the non-authoritative restore as described earlier, then you use the Ntdsutil tool to mark restored objects as authoritative. The process to perform this restore is detailed and very site-specific; see the ntdsutil help for details.

TIP: Most of the restores that you will do will be non-authoritative.

Securing DNS

You need to make sure the DNS system that you are using is secure. It really does not matter what you use (that is, Unix or Win2K), as long as it is secure and functional. The basic functionality of any DNS server will be adequate for operation, but some make administration much easier. For our purposes, we will talk about securing Win2K DNS.

To configure the security, we will use the DNS administration tool (that is, DNS snap-in). This can be accessed via the Start | Programs | Administrative Tools | DNS.

There are two sets of security-related configurations that we will be setting: the first is dealing with the properties of the DNS server itself, and the second is the properties on the individual zones.

DNS Server Properties

We will look at the server-specific properties first. From the DNS administration tool, select the DNS server to administer, and open the Properties dialog box (right-click and select Properties). You will see a screen with the following tabs:

▼ **Interfaces** Allows you to select the IP address that the DNS server will listen on. By default, it will listen on all interfaces.

■ **Forwarders** Allows you to set the servers to which this server will forward any unresolved queries.

■ **Monitoring** Allows for connectivity and data validation testing of the server.

■ **Root Hints** Used to find other DNS servers on the Internet.

■ **Logging** Defines what events are saved in the logs.

■ **Security** Defines auditing and permissions for the server and data.

▲ **Advanced** Allows you to set advanced features.

We will look at the security-related options (Security, Advanced, and Logging) in more depth in the following sections.

SECURITY The Security options provide the same interface for object ACLs that we have seen in every other service. The interesting part about this is that these are actually inherited from the AD. If you look at the System container in the Advanced view of the Active Directory Users and Computers administration tool, you will see the DNS data and the ACLs that are applied to it. The default permissions are adequate, and if you want to tighten them, you can do it here or in the AD admin tool.

ADVANCED The Advanced tab (shown next) provides a number of options, and the defaults are fine. The security-related settings that should be enabled are described here:

▼ **Fail on Load If Bad Zone Data** Sets the DNS server to parse files strictly. This option should be set if you decide not to use AD integrated zones or if you are a secondary server for another DNS zone.

▲ **Secure Cache Against Pollution** This option should be enabled, as it will attempt to determine if the extra data not in response to the original query should be cached. Its decision is based on the fact that the extra data is part of the exact related DNS domain name tree for which the original query was made. For example, a response to a query for phil.example.com that contained "referral" data for systemexperts.com would be discarded.

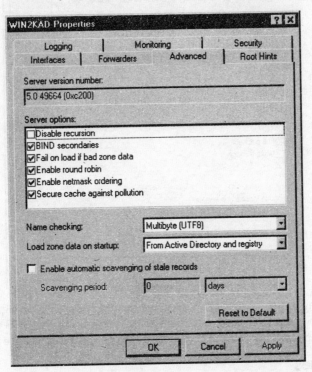

LOGGING   This allows you to define what DNS-related events are logged to the debugging log (shown next). Note that if you are using an AD integrated DNS, then you can also audit the data in the AD instead of or in conjunction with this log. There is a performance hit for logging, but that is true for any service, so you need to be selective about what you enable. By default, logging is off, but when it is enabled, the log file (dns.log) will be found in %Systemdir%\System32\Dns. The Update logging option, which logs dynamic updates, is the only one that should be enabled all the time; all the rest can be enabled for troubleshooting only.

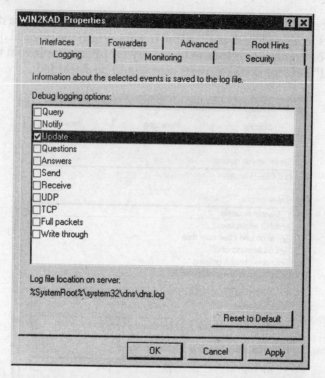

If we are going to use Win2K DNS, then we should use the AD integration for performance and security reasons. If we use the AD for distributing the DNS data, then the security mechanisms that replicate AD data will also be used to replicate DNS data.

Zone Properties

We will now take a look at the security-related properties that can and should be set for the specific DNS zones. To get the zone properties up, you open the DNS administration tool, and then expand the DNS server and zone container (that is, Forward Lookup Zones) you are managing, then right-click the zone to configure and select Properties. The next screen shows the properties for the example.com domain. The security-related options are located in the General, Name Servers, Security, Zone Transfers, and WINS sections (that is, all of them except Start of Authority). The Security tab is like the server properties, and the WINS tab enables DNS to use WINS resolution if a name is not resolved via DNS (it is disabled by default, and should be left that way), so we will cover the others.

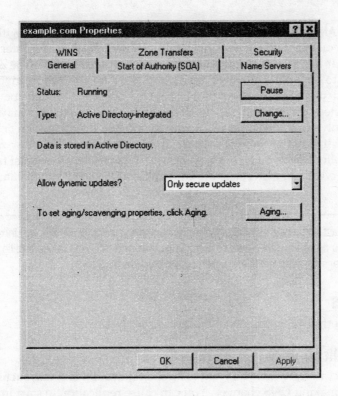

GENERAL   This screen allows you to define two security-related settings: the type of server and the dynamic update requirements.

▼ **Type of Server**   You can make the server an AD integrated server or allow it to read zone information from regular files. AD integration is recommended, as it provides not only security, but also a method of maintaining multiple primary name servers by means of the data in the AD. If you choose to use an AD integrated DNS, then you can have all DCs in a domain that run DNS servers be primaries for that domain.

▲ **Dynamic Updates**   This allows you to specify if dynamic updates are allowed, and if so, whether or not they must be secured. The current implementation of Secure Updates is only applicable to Win2K DNS servers, and as the secure update method used, is not supported by non-Win2K servers.

NAME SERVERS AND ZONE TRANSFERS   The security-related issues with the Name Servers option come into play when you combine it with the Zone Transfers options. The Name Servers tab has a list of all known (that is, trusted) DNS servers. The Zone Transfers tab allows you to limit zone transfers. By default, they are allowed to anyone; this is too permissive and must be changed. Zone transfer should definitely be restricted on Internet-connected servers as this is one of the first things an attacker may look for.

First, you only need zone transfers if you do not use AD integration *or* you have secondary servers. If either of these is the case, then you will need to allow zone transfers, but you should limit them to the hosts you trust. The easiest way is to list trusted servers in the Name Servers tab, then select the Only to Servers Listed in the Name Servers Tab option.

TIP: The fact is that currently the security mechanisms in place for Win2K and Unix are not compatible, so if you do use a Unix-based DNS infrastructure, you will need to use traditional DNS security mechanisms, such as router filters, limiting zone transfers, and so on.

Tips and Tricks

Here are some other operations that you may need to perform.

Forcing Replication

There may be occasions when you want to force a replication to occur, such as when troubleshooting or making DNS changes. You can cause replication to start immediately by using the Active Directory Sites and Services administration tool. Open up the admin tool, expand the Sites container, and then open the specific site and server that you want to replicate *from*. Select the NTDS so that the right-hand side of the window shows the replication partners. Right-click the replication partner you want to replicate to, and select Replicate Now. This will cause the replication to start.

Validating Structure and Trust

You can use the Active Directory Domains and Trusts administration tool or the NETDOM command to validate trust relationships. Both of these tools will validate that a secure channel can be established between the DCs. The secure channel is one of the vehicles used for replication, and can thus be used to validate the trust relationship. Using the AD tool, you edit the trust for the domain you want to validate (right-click the domain and select Properties | Trusts | Edit). Then you click the Verify button. This will take you through steps to "verify" the trust relationship.

Setting Up Win9x Clients to Use the AD

Win95/98 clients can be updated so they can use some of the features of the AD, such as searching the AD, using DFS, and changing passwords on DCs. To update the clients to support this functionality, you install the Directory Services Client Update that is found on the Win2K server CD in `CLIENTS\WIN9X`. The installation is simple and adds quite a bit of functionality to the clients. You need to realize, though, that allowing insecure client systems like Win95/98 will also weaken your entire network security by using older insecure protocols such as LAN Manager and share level security.

Using ADSIEdit

Once you have installed the snap-in, then you can use the ADSIEdit tool. Once you open it up, you connect to an "LDAP path" (that is, a server) to perform operations. To connect, you select the ADSIEdit tool, and then right-click and select Connect, which will bring you to the screen shown next. This allows you to specify the connection point (that is, Schema, Configuration, Domain Naming Context, RootDSE, or a DN) and the server to connect to.

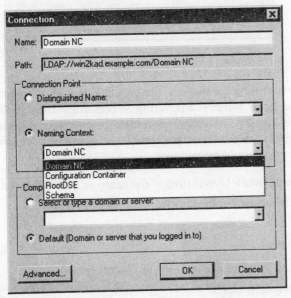

Clicking the Advanced button will allow you to specify credentials and protocols to use. The resulting connections to the example.com Schema, Configuration, and Domain

NC are shown next. From this point, you can perform operations on the objects in those containers.

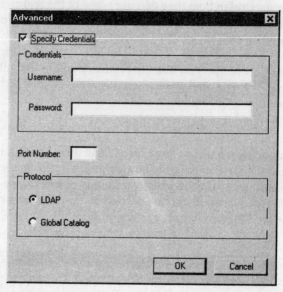

Migration

The simple fact is that most people are not creating Win2K domains from scratch, but they are migrating from WinNT. Migrating successfully from a WinNT domain to a Win2K AD requires careful analysis of your current system and in-depth planning. This section cannot begin to cover all the issues, but it can get you started in the right direction. Here are the steps you should be taking:

1. Plan a new network layout (this is the same as a new installation):
   - DNS structure
   - OUs
   - Group Policies
   - Physical: Replication and Server placement
2. Migrate domain models:
   - Decide if resource domains are OUs in a single domain or separate domains (see Table 8-1 in the "Design" section earlier in this chapter).
   - Try to structure DNS with what matters most: business and administration (one domain) or many little centers of power (multiple domains).

- If WinNT Resource domains were used for administration purposes, then merge them into a single domain and replace them with OUs. If they were used for accounts as well as resources, then make them a child domain.

3. Start the process:

- Take one BDC from the domain offline, just in case you need it back.
- Take PDC that will be in the root domain and convert it.

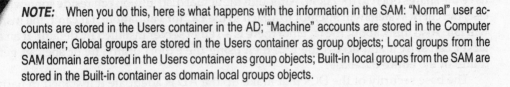

NOTE: When you do this, here is what happens with the information in the SAM: "Normal" user accounts are stored in the Users container in the AD; "Machine" accounts are stored in the Computer container; Global groups are stored in the Users container as group objects; Local groups from the SAM domain are stored in the Users container as group objects; Built-in local groups from the SAM are stored in the Built-in container as domain local groups objects.

- Update remaining PDCs in the forest.
- Update BDCs.
- Update member servers and workstations.
- Change to native mode.

Active Directory Migration Tool (ADMT)

Microsoft provides a tool called the Active Directory Migration Tool (ADMT). This tool allows you to migrate from a WinNT domain(s) to a Win2K AD. It will also allow you to restructure Win2K domains. It is a graphical tool, and like most of the other Microsoft tools, uses a wizard-based approach. Some of the things that it will allow you to do include

- ▼ Migrating users, groups, and computers.
- Setting file permissions.
- Migrating Microsoft Exchange Server mailboxes.
- Using reporting tools to help assess migration impact.
- ▲ Using a rollback feature. (Use this with caution. You know the old saying—you can never really go home, because home is never how you remember it.)

You can find the tools and detailed documentation at **http://www.microsoft.com/ WINDOWS2000/library/planning/activedirectory/admt.asp**.

RECAP

The AD is the crown jewel. If you can take it down, you have the entire Win2K network, and potentially every other network that trusts it. This is definitely a single point of security failure! Security of the DCs that hold the AD data is of primary importance in a Win2K network.

When you use the AD with other services, usually the overall security from the AD standpoint is diminished. For example, when you use MSI, it requires that the AD server have the shares open to the client. Although the actual distribution can reside somewhere else, the client system will attempt to attach to the DC for validation; if it can't, the install will fail. Also think about the fact that there is a Telnet server installed by default. If an attacker can start it and access the DC, then using the export utility, he or she can get a dump of the entire database.

The base security of the DCs that make up the AD is adequate if installed in native mode; otherwise, there is a significant amount of information that can be obtained from the directory. When you go about securing the DCs, the most important concepts in order are

1. Group and User permissions on the top level containers
2. OUs and delegation
3. Trust relationships
4. Replication structure
5. DNS integration
6. Global Catalog
7. Extensibility of the Global Catalog and the Schema

TIP: For details on managing all aspects of the AD, we suggest the *Windows 2000 Active Directory* by Joe Casad, which is part of the Network Professional's Library series from Osborne/McGraw-Hill (2000).

CHAPTER 9

Group Policies

In this chapter, we will be looking at Group Policy (GP). This is one of the key additions to Win2K that assists in what Microsoft calls *Change and Configuration Management* (*CCM*). In regular terms, the primary purpose is to reduce system administration effort. The system administrator can use GP to deploy configuration settings that allow for distributed management of desktop configurations. These configurations can be applied to individual or groups of computers and users. By default the GP can be used to distribute Registry-based policy settings, security settings, software installation, scripts, and folder redirection.

This chapter is not about detailed GP design and deployment, but about gaining a general understanding of what GPs can do and some of the features associated with them. We will be focusing on securing GP itself, and using GP to secure computers and users. We will be discussing design and implementation, but in a general manner. If you have a detailed Active Directory, with many sites, domains, and Organizational Units (OUs), this chapter will probably not be enough. We recommend the *Windows 2000 Active Directory* by Joe Casad (Osborne/McGraw-Hill, 2000).

WHAT IS A GROUP POLICY?

Group Policies (GPs) are the primary method for enabling centralized change and configuration management in Win2K. They are tightly coupled with the AD and can be applied locally, at the site level, at the domain level, and at the OU level. They are processed by User and Computer objects that are located in the containers (for example, site, domain, or OU) that the GP is linked to.

GPs can be used to provide things such as software installation services, configuring and locking down user desktops, and configuring computers. You can configure logon and logoff scripts for users, run startup and shutdown scripts for computers, or deploy kiosk computers by restricting options available to the desktop and their ability to connect on the network, and many other things.

A GP is an enterprise object, in that it can be applied to site, domain, or OU containers. Multiple GPs can be associated with these container objects, and they can effect more then just Registry settings. In contrast with WinNT, which uses a single system policy file (that is, `ntconfig.pol`) to contain all the functionality to enforce a limited policy (that is, the policy was limited to User and Computer Registry settings), you can use GPs in Win2K to specify settings for

▼ Registry-based policy settings (similar to NT)

■ Security settings that affect the local computer, domain, and network settings

■ Software installation using MSI

■ Folder redirection

▲ Computer startup and shutdown scripts, and user logon and logoff scripts

NOTE: The following abbreviations for the Registry hives are used throughout this chapter:
HKEY_Local_Machine is commonly seen as HKLM
HKEY_Current_User is commonly seen as HKCU

For example, you can use GPs to push down user rights to each machine in the selected container (OU, and so on).

ser and Computer Configurations

The GP is split into two sections: User and Computer. The User Configuration includes all user-related policies. These configure the user environment settings that are applicable to things like OS behavior, desktop settings, security settings, and logon/logoff scripts. The user-related settings are defined under the User Configuration tree of the Group Policy, and are applied when a user logs on and when the GP is refreshed.

The Computer Configuration includes all computer-related policies. These configure the running system environment (as opposed to user environment) for things like OS behavior, service settings, security settings, and startup/shutdown scripts. The computer-related settings are defined under the Computer Configuration tree of the Group Policy and are applied when a computer boots and when the GP is refreshed.

Types of Policies

There are three different types of policies that can be found in a Win2K network: Local Group Policy, Active Directory Group Policy, and WinNT System Policy.

Local Group Policy (a.k.a. Local Policy)

Every Win2K computer has a local Group Policy Object (LGPO). This policy is managed and resides on the system that it applies to (that is, it is not centrally managed and it resides on the file system of the local computer). The LGPO is primarily provided to allow you to assign policy on a system that does not participate in an AD domain. For example, for security reasons, you might not want to install a publicly available kiosk machine on an AD domain. With LGPO, you can modify local policy to provide security and desktop restrictions without the use of an AD-based Group Policy Object (GPO). The LGPO supports all the default extensions (that is, functionality) except software installation and folder redirection.

Active Directory Group Policy

When you set up an Active Directory (see Chapter 8), one of the objects that is now available is the GPO. Much like the LGPO, the Active Directory GPO (herein referred to as the GPO), allows you full access to the entire suite of Group Policy functions. The GPO can be linked to any site, domain, or OU in the AD. There can also be multiple GPOs linked to those objects as well. The GPO uses inheritance, blocking and override functionality, and tree disabling to perform their function.

NT System Policies

System policies are policies that were created using the System Policy Editor (`Poledit.exe`) in WinNT and are still usable with Win2K. If you upgrade a WinNT DC, the system policies that reside in the *Netlogon* share will be moved to the Win2K `SYSVOL` (the *Netlogon* share on the PDC is now the `SYSVOL\Sysvol\`*domain*`\Scripts` on the PDC emulator in the domain). When downlevel clients (that is, WinNT and Win 9*x*) connect to the *Netlogon* share, they will attempt to access these policies and not access the Win2K GPOs. Note that the upgrade does not convert the system policies to GPOs, as there is such a fundamental difference in their structure. What you can do, though, is migrate the old template files (`.adm`) that were used to create the `.pol` file to the GPO, as the ADM files used by the GPO have the exact same format.

NOTE: If you upgrade a WinNT domain and you use policy files in the login script, then you need to either migrate the `.adm` file or delete the policy stuff and create a GPO.

Group Policy Objects

You will see many references to Group Policy Objects (GPO) in this chapter, as well as any other document that you read on Group Policy. The GPO contains the Group Policy settings that you create; you could say it provides a virtual storage area for policies. The Active Directory (AD) then links the GPO to one of the site/domain/OU container objects in the AD. By using multiple GPOs, you can define multiple policies, and then link one or more of the GPOs to the selected containers. You can also use a GPO to specify if the User Configuration or Computers Configuration portion of the GPO is enabled or disabled.

4LSDOU?

There is a notation that you will see used with Group Polices quite a bit—it is some form of the string 4LSDOU. This string stands for the order in which policies are applied. "4" denotes the WinNT 4.0 system policy; "L" denotes a LGPO; "S" is for the site GPO(s); "D" is for the domain GPO(s); and "OU" is for the Organizational Unit GPO(s). We will also use it to indicate where a particular setting can be set/applied, as you will see later in the chapter. For example, if a certain setting can be applied at the site, domain, and OU level and not with WinNT system policies or a local GPO, then that setting would be denoted as SDOU; if just the domain and OU, then DOU.

Group Policy Object Internals

A GPO is made up of two components—the Group Policy Container (GPC) and the Group Policy Template (GPT). The GPC is an AD object that is associated with the GPO. It is stored in the System | Policy container for the domain that the GP is defined in (CN=*policyGUID*,CN=Policy,CN=System,DC=<*domain*> in directory speak, as defined in Chapter 8 on the Active Directory). The GPC holds a version number, an indicator as to which components have settings associated with them, and the state (enabled or disabled) of the component/setting. There is no GPC for the LGPO.

The GPT is a set of files residing in the SYSVOL folder (%systemroot%\System32\SYSVOL\sysvol\<*domain*>\Polices by default), which is replicated on all DCs. The GPT has three subdirectories that are used to hold the gpt.ini file, administrative templates (that is, .adm files), security configuration files (.pol files), logon/logoff and startup/shutdown scripts, and software installation information. The gpt.ini file holds different information depending on the GPO. If it is the LGPO, then it has which client-side extensions are needed, the status (enabled/disabled) of the User or Computer Configurations, and the version number. The SDOU GPO has only the version number. The three top-level directories in a GPT are the ADM directory, which holds the .adm files, and the User and Computer directories that hold all security information and settings (that is, .pol files) and scripts that apply to their respective configuration trees.

NOTE: Replication of the GPT occurs under the control of the Win2K File Replication Service (FRS).

GPT AND GPC STORAGE EXAMPLE   As an example, let's say there is a GP defined in the example.com domain that has the GUID 9C5A22F6-9D47-439E-9552-8140B4699505 (the name is never used in the GPT or GPC, only in the GUID). We would then see the following GPT directory tree:

```
C:\Winnt\System32\SYSVOL\Sysvol\example.com\Policies
\9C5A22F6-9D47-439E-9552-8140B4699505
    \ADM
    \Machine
    \User
```

The GPC would be stored in the AD as the following (line broken for readability):

```
CN={9C5A22F6-9D47-439E-9552-8140B4699505},CN=Policies,
CN=System,DC=example,DC=com
```

TIP: Remember that a GP is only defined in one location. You can define identical GPs, but they are different and have different GUIDs.

VERSION CONFLICT   Since the GPC and GPT are separate entities (with separate file system objects and AD objects), there is a potential that they will be refreshed/updated at different times. To ensure that there is not an application of a GPO that has mismatching GPC and GPT, the version numbers in the GPC and GPT must agree. If they do not, an error will be logged and the GPO will not be applied.

GP Registry Areas

GP Registry areas are persistent Registry settings that govern things such as the way a computer is configured and will operate, as well as how a user's desktop and environment is configured, and the rights the user has. While the settings persist throughout a boot or logon cycle, they are validated often, and if there is a change, the entire tree is applied new. Computer GP values are stored in `HKLM\Software\Policies` and `HKLM\Software\Microsoft\Windows\CurrentVersion\Policies` on the computer it applies to. The User GP values are stored in `HKCU\Software\Policies` and `HKCU\Software\Microsoft\Windows\CurrentVersion\Policies` on each computer the user logs into. Values that are set by specific GPOs are cleaned up when the GPO no longer applies (that is, when it is unlinked or disabled). Only LocalSystem and Administrators can edit or change these keys in `HKLM` by default.

> **NOTE:**   The terms "Group Policy" or "GP" are commonly interchanged with "Group Policy Object" or "GPO" because when we are talking about actually using them, the GPO is the actual implementation of the GP.

Local Group Policy Storage

The LGPO is stored in a different location than the SDOU GPO. You will find the Local Group Policy in the `%systemroot%\System32\Group Policy`. It has the same structure and contents as the GPs on the `SYSVOL`.

PROFILE AND POLICY—A REFRESHER

There is sometimes a bit of confusion about the difference between profiles and policies. This short section is to refresh your memories.

Profiles are user-specific and are used to hold configuration preferences for each user's desktop settings and work environment. Profiles restore the settings of the desktop from the last logon session for a user. This feature allows several people to use the same computer, each customizing it for his or her own use. In a nutshell, profiles are used to provide a user environment. Profiles are by default stored in the *Documents and Settings* directory (WinNT used *Winnt\Profiles*). See Chapter 10 for details on user profiles.

In WinNT, a manager could create a mandatory profile, which could not be changed by a user. These profiles were denoted by the obligatory .man suffix on the user profile file `ntuser.man`. When mandatory user profiles are set, a user can change the desktop during any logon session, but those changes are not saved for the next session. This provided some level of administrative fault tolerance in that if a user misconfigured his desktop and then called for support, the administrator could simply have him restart his computer or logon session to restore previous settings. *This functionality is still available, but is better accomplished with Group Policy.*

Policies are network-wide profile settings that can be applied to users and computers. They can be combined with or supercede the user's own profiles to provide a custom configuration that is controlled by network managers.

So what is the difference between profiles and policies? Polices are both a user and a computer configuration tool that can be global in nature. Profiles, on the other hand, are linked to a single user account, and provide not only user-centric configuration (that is, not computer-centric), but file storage and application setting information.

NOTE: You can use both profiles and policies simultaneously.

DEFAULT GPOs

When you set up an AD, there are two default GPOs that are created: Default Domain Policy and Default Domain Controller Policy.

Default Domain Policy

The Default Domain Policy is applied to the domain container. Thus it will be evaluated and potentially applied to all ojects in the domain, such as Users, Computers, and DCs. The default settings are listed in Table 9-1.

Default Domain Controller Policy

The Default Domain Controller Policy is applied to the "special" Domain Controller container in the domain. Thus it will be evaluated and potentially applied by every object (that is, DCs) in the container. Because it is "closer" to the actual objects (for example, DCs) that it contains, it takes precedence over the Default Domain Policy if there are any conflicts. The default settings are listed in Table 9-2.

HOW THEY ARE APPLIED

GPOs can be defined and applied to computers, users, or both. For each of those areas, the GPOs are evaluated in order starting at the site, then the domain, and finally the OU. For each of the settings in the policy, you can specify if the setting is Enabled, Disabled, or Not Configured. By default, the settings are Not Configured, which means that there is no change to be made by this GPO and thus they will have no effect on that setting when the policies are actually applied to the system. As described later, inheritance flows from top to bottom, but precedence flows from bottom to top, unless there is a Block, No Override, or specific *deny* ACL for the GPO.

Account Policy | Password Policy	Value
Enforce password history	1 passwords remembered
Maximum password age	42 days
Minimum password age	0 days
Minimum password length	0 characters
Passwords must meet complexity requirements	Disabled
Store password using reversible encryption for all users in the domain	Disabled
Account Policy | Kerberos Policy	**Value**
Enforce user logon restrictions	Enabled
Maximum lifetime for service ticket	600 minutes
Maximum lifetime for user ticket	10 hours
Maximum lifetime for user ticket renewal	7 days
Maximum tolerance for computer clock synchronization	5 minutes

Table 9-1. Default Domain Policy Active Settings

Account Policies | Account Lockout	Value
Account lockout duration	30 minutes
Account lockout threshold	5 invalid logon attempts
Reset account lockout counter after	5 minutes
Local Policies | Audit Policy	**Value**
Audit account logon events	Success
Audit account management	Success and Failure
Local Policies | User Rights	**Value**
Access this computer from the network	Everyone, Administrators, Authenticated Users
Add workstations to domain	Authenticated Users

Table 9-2. Default Domain Controller Policy Active Settings

Local Policies | User Rights	Value
Back up files and directories	Administrators, Backup Operators, Server Operators
Bypass traverse checking	Everyone, Administrators, Authenticated Users
Change the system time	Administrators, Server Operators
Create a pagefile	Administrators
Debug programs	Administrators
Enable computer and user accounts to be trusted for delegation	Administrators
Force shutdown from a remote system	Administrators, Server Operators
Increase quotas	Administrators
Increase scheduling priority	Administrators
Load and unload device drivers	Administrators
Log on locally	Account Operators, Administrators, Backup Operators, *<domain>*\Domain Users, Print Operators, Server Operators, TsInternetUser
Manage auditing and security log	Administrators
Modify firmware environment values	Administrators
Profile single process	Administrators
Profile system performance	Administrators
Remove computer from docking station	Administrators
Restore files and directories	Administrators, Backup Operators, Server Operators
Shut down the system	Administrators, Backup Operators, Account Operators, Server
Take ownership of files or other objects	Administrators
Local Policies | Security Options	**Value**
Digitally sign server communications (when possible)	Enabled

Table 9-2.   Default Domain Controller Policy Active Settings *(continued)*

The following is the flow of GP evaluation, profile loading, and script events for a computer startup and user logon:

1. Upon system startup, the computer evaluates any WinNT system policies that are applicable to it.

2. The Computer Configuration portion of the LGPO, if one is defined, is evaluated.

3. The Computer Configuration portions of the site-related GPO(s) in order of preference, from lowest to highest, are evaluated.

4. Then the Computer Configuration portions of the domain-related GPO(s) in order of preference, from lowest to highest, are evaluated.

5. Then the Computer Configuration portion of the OU-related GPO(s) in order of preference, from the outer- to innermost OU and within an OU from lowest to highest, are evaluated.

6. Once all the GPs are evaluated, their cumulative settings are applied to the system.

7. The computer runs the startup script(s) that are defined for it.

8. The user logs on and the profile is loaded.

9. Then the User Configuration sections of the applicable GPOs are applied.

10. The system runs the logon script(s) that are defined for the user.

The Registry section where the Group Policy is stored is wiped clean and rewritten to hold the cumulative GPO data if any of the GPO version numbers have changed.

TIP: Beware of using WinNT system policies on a Win2K system, as they may write Registry entries outside of the GPO scope (that is, the GPO Registry trees described in the "Group Policy Object Internals" section) to an unexpected location.

Synchronous Versus Asynchronous

By default, GPOs are applied synchronously during startup and logon. This means that each of the steps listed in the previous section would be completed before the next step is started. Thus you would not see a Logon screen until all GPOs were applied to the system and the startup script had completed. You can, however, have them processed asynchronously (that is, in parallel). When you apply GPOs asynchronously, the computer will display the logon prompt before it finishes updating computer Group Policy, and a user logging on will get the desktop before all the User GPOs are applied. In this case, the system does not coordinate loading the desktop and applying user Group Policy.

You can enable the asynchronous processing by selecting the Apply Group Policy for Computers Asynchronously During Startup and/or the Apply Group Policy for Users Asynchronously During Logon settings by choosing Computer Configuration | Administrative Templates | System | Group Policy (see "Configuration Settings in the Group Policy" later in this chapter).

How NT System Policies Affect Policy Application

By default, Win2K will not use WinNT system policies, but they can be enabled. You can turn off the processing/viewing of NT 4.0-style system policies using the Administrative Templates section of the GP. But if you decide to enable them for Win2K systems, there are some issues:

▼ They will potentially overwrite what a GPO has set when a user logs on.

■ When a GPO is updated, it will change the values back, potentially causing a conflict.

▲ WinNT policies can set Registry settings outside of the GPO limits, and they are persistent.

If you do have downlevel system policies, and they are enabled for Win2K systems, then they will be evaluated by not only the downlevel clients (WinNT and Win 9*x*), but also any Win2K workstation or member server that will use them. Here is a breakdown:

▼ Mixed-mode domain workstations and member servers will evaluate System Policies, then LGPO, then Site, then Domain, and then OU. (4LDSOU)

NOTE: Native-mode domains do not process downlevel system policies.

■ Standalone Win2K workstations or servers will evaluate System Policies, then LGPO. (4L)

▲ Downlevel clients *only* evaluate System Polices. (4)

Table 9-3 lists, using 4LSDOU notation, which policies apply, when they apply, and where they apply.

Environment	Downlevel Client	Win2K Workstation	Win2K Member Server	Win2K DC
Standalone	None	L	L	N/A
Domain member	4	4L	4L	N/A
Mixed-mode domain	4	LSDOU	LDSOU	LSDOU
Native-mode domain	N/A	LSDOU	LSDOU	LSDOU

Table 9-3.   Policy Table

CONFIGURATION SETTINGS IN THE GROUP POLICY

Now that you know the basics of Group Policies—what they can do, where they can be applied, and so on—we need to look at what they actually allow us to set/configure. As stated earlier, each GPO has two basic trees of configuration data (or maybe better put as "areas of coverage"): the Computer Configuration (HKLM) and Users Configuration (HKCU). These covered areas are shown as two distinct sections in the Group Policy Editor (Figure 9-1).

This section is not intended to describe every option in detail, as the online documentation is very helpful. The coverage here is to give you an overall scope of what is covered by Group Policies. Knowing what their function is and what they cover by default will set you on the road to utilizing them in an efficient and effective manner.

This section is an overview of the default configuration settings that can be applied with GPOs. The specific settings that deal with using and managing GPOs are covered in this chapter, as well as designing GPO structures. The specifics of other service-related settings, such as File Systems, will be covered in the respective service-related chapters (for example, the settings for the File System in the GPO is covered in Chapter 12).

Computer Configuration

This section of the GPO is specific to every computer that resides in the container that the GPO is linked to, independent of the user at the machine. Figure 9-2 shows a mid-level expansion of the Computer Configuration section of a GPO.

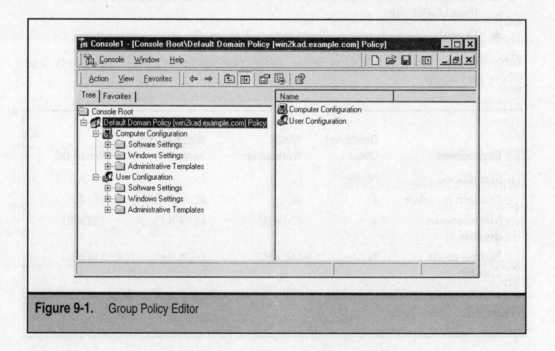

Figure 9-1.   Group Policy Editor

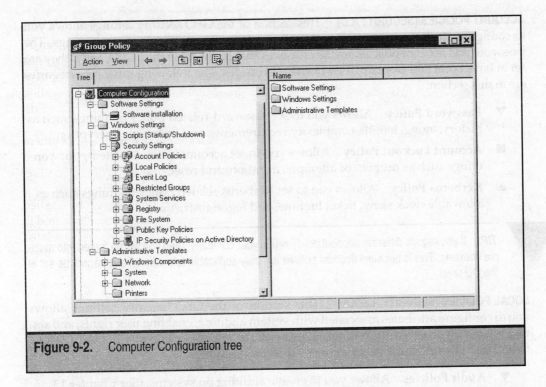

Figure 9-2. Computer Configuration tree

Software Installation (SDOU)

This option allows you to utilize the Microsoft Installer (MSI) functionality to centrally manage software distribution in your company. By *assigning* the policy to the Computer section of the GPO, it will cause the software to be automatically installed when the computer boots. Unlike the User section (described later), the computer section does not have a "publish" option (that is, an optional setting) for installation; all software added here is automatically installed by default. As with all objects in Win2K, you can, however, use ACLs to limit whom this applies to and thus only have the software be installed on computers in a certain group.

Windows Settings (LSDOU)

This part of the GPO is used to hold computer-related security settings, as well as startup and shutdown scripts. When we say "computer-related" we are referring to the fact that the settings defined here are applicable to the computer, regardless of the user that is using it.

SCRIPTS (LSDOU)   This policy allows you to specify startup and shutdown scripts. These scripts will be run at system startup and shutdown, and they are run in the context of the LocalSystem account (so be careful). You can use any of the Windows Script Host (WSH) languages to write the scripts. By default, these languages are VBScript and JavaScript (JScript).

ACCOUNT POLICIES (SECURITY, LD)   This section of the GPO security settings allows you to configure attributes associated with passwords, accounts, and Kerberos settings. The password and account policies are the only ones that can be set in the LGPO, and if they are set in both Local and Domain, then Domain overrides. The following three subcategories are in this section:

▼ **Password Policy**   Allows you to set password-related policy on things such as history, aging, length, complexity requirements, and reversible encryption.

■ **Account Lockout Policy**   Allows you to set account lockout-related policy on things such as number of attempts, duration, and reset.

▲ **Kerberos Policy**   Allows you to set Kerberos-related policy on things such as allowable clock skew, ticket lifetime, and logon restrictions.

TIP: If you require different account policy within your company, then you will be forced into multiple domains. This is because account polices are only applicable to a domain and cannot be set at the OU level.

LOCAL POLICIES (SECURITY, LSDOU)   This section of the GPO Security Settings allows you to configure attributes associated with system auditing, enabling user rights, and setting miscellaneous security settings. These policies are applicable to all of the LSDOU flow. The following three subcategories are in this section:

▼ **Audit Policies**   Allows you to enable auditing on systems. (See Chapter 13 for details on auditing settings.)

■ **User Rights Assignment**   Allows you to assign user rights to Users and Groups, including rights to debug a program, log on locally, log on from the network, create a process level token, and many more (34 by default).

▲ **Security Options**   Allows you to set many different security-related policies, including SMB signing, secure channel restrictions, automatic logoff, LANManager authentication level, logon text banner and notice, and many more (40 by default).

EVENT LOG (SECURITY, SDOU)   This section allows you to configure the Event Log settings for each of the logs (application, system, and security).

■ **Settings for Event Logs**   Allows you to set Event Log–related policy on things such as log capacity, access restrictions, retention settings, and whether to shut down the system if the logs fill.

RESTRICTED GROUPS (SECURITY, SDOU)   This section lets you define, by policy, who are members of certain Groups, and which Groups are members of other Groups.

There are two basic options:

▼ **Members of Restricted Group** Enforces the membership in the group. If a User or Group is in that restricted group's member list, but is not in the Group, it is added to the Group. If a User or Group is a member of the group, but is not in the restricted groups' member list, it is removed.

▲ **Restricted Group Is Member Of** If the restricted group is not in a group it should belong to, it is added. Unlike the membership enforcement, if the restricted group belongs to a group not listed here, it is *not* removed.

> *VIP:* If you place a group in the restricted groups, and the member's list is empty (which it is by default), all current members of the group are removed. *So be careful!*

SYSTEM SERVICES (SECURITY, SDOU) This section allows you to configure the start-up settings and permissions for each of the listed services:

▼ **Start-up Settings** Allows you to specify the mode in which the service will start. The options are Automatic, Manual, or Disabled.

▲ **Permissions** Allows you to specify what permissions are applicable for the service. The permissions that can be set are Full Control, Read, Write, Delete, and Start/Stop/Pause.

> *NOTE:* See Web Appendix A on the Web at **http://www.osborne.com** for more details on the services and their functions.

REGISTRY (SECURITY, SDOU) This section allows you to configure the ACLs for Registry keys. This will allow you to configure User and Group permissions, as well as auditing for any and all Registry keys in the HKEY_Local_Machine, HKEY_Users and the HKEY_Classes_Root trees.

FILE SYSTEM (SECURITY, SDOU) Much like the Registry policy, the File System policy allows you to configure User and Group permissions, as well as auditing for any and all directories and files on the system. The reality is that the configuration of this is very dependent on the system on which you are configuring it. It will look at the system on which you are configuring the GPO to determine the file system structure. Therefore, it is really only practical if you are using it to lock down well-known or available files and directories (such as boot.ini or C:\Winnt).

PUBLIC KEY POLICIES (SECURITY, LSDOU) This section defines the interaction with the Win2K Certificate Services. These are just Group Policies that help distribute certificates to computers, establish Certificate Trust Lists, establish common trusted Certification Authorities, and manage key recovery policies for the encrypting file system. Their primary purpose is to make an easier job of deploying a Public Key Infrastructure. See Web Chapter 1 at **http://www.osborne.com** for details on Certificate Services and Public Key Policies.

IP SECURITY POLICIES (LSDOU)   This section allows you to set IPSec security policies, which are used to determine the IPSec interaction between two systems. It is used to configure filter lists and actions, policy rules, security and authentication methods, connection types, and key exchange settings and methods. See Chapter 16 for details on IPSec and IPSec policies.

Administrative Templates (LSDOU)

This part of the GPO is used to hold policy changes that will affect the HKEY_Local_ Machine Registry tree. The configuration options in this section are all derived from template files that live in the SYSVOL partition on the DCs. Because they are derived from templates, they are extensible. We will discuss this a bit later, but for now on to the descriptions.

WINDOWS COMPONENTS (LSDOU)   This section of the Policy deals with things related to Windows components:

- ▼ **NetMeeting**   Disables the remote desktop-sharing feature of NetMeeting. Users will not be able to set it up or use it for controlling their computers remotely.
- ■ **Internet Explorer**   Allows you to set IE-related policy on things such as security zones, proxy settings, preventing automatic installation of components, and more.
- ■ **Task Scheduler**   Allows you to set task-related policy on things such as viewing and changing the properties of an existing task, starting and stopping tasks manually, creating new tasks, and more.
- ▲ **Windows Installer**   Allows you to set installer-related policy on things such as disabling the installer, disabling rollback, enabling user controls, logging, and more. This will apply to all applications installed on the computer the GPO is applied to.

SYSTEM (LSDOU)   This is a placeholder container for things that don't seem to fit elsewhere:

- ▼ **Logon**   Allows you to set policy related to system operations during logon such as logon/logoff scripts, set how long the system waits for scripts applied by Group Policy to run, delete cached copies of roaming profiles, and more.
- ■ **Disk Quotas**   Allows you to set policy related to disk quotas such as enabling and enforcing them, what will be logged, what to do with removable media, and more.
- ■ **DNS Client**   Allows you to set the primary DNS suffix for all affected computers.
- ■ **Group Policy**   Allows you to set policy on Group Policy, such as refresh interval, background refresh, loopback processing mode, and many others.
- ▲ **Windows File Protection**   Allows you to set Windows File Protection policy to manage the service. Settings determine things such as scanning protected files, the maximum amount of disk space that can be used for the file cache, alternate location for the cache, and others.

NETWORK (LSDOU) This configuration section deals with those services that are network-based:

▼ **Offline Files** Allows you to set offline files policy to manage the service. Settings include options for enabling the service, disabling user configuration of offline files, synchronizing all offline files before logging off. In addition, you set the action on server disconnect, files you don't want cached, event logging level, and much more.

▲ **Network and Dial-up Connections** Allows you to set whether administrators can enable, disable, and configure the Internet Connection Sharing feature of a dial-up connection.

PRINTERS (LSDOU) This section allows you to set printer policies, such as allowing printers to be published, automatically publishing new printers in the AD, printer browsing, printer pruning, checking published state, Web-based printing, and others. See Chapter 12 for details on printers and sharing.

User Configuration

As was described earlier, these sets of configurations are applied to users independent of what system they are on. When we say "User Configuration," we are referring to the fact that the settings defined here are applicable to the User profile, regardless of who is using it. Figure 9-3 shows a mid-level expansion of the User Configuration section of a GPO.

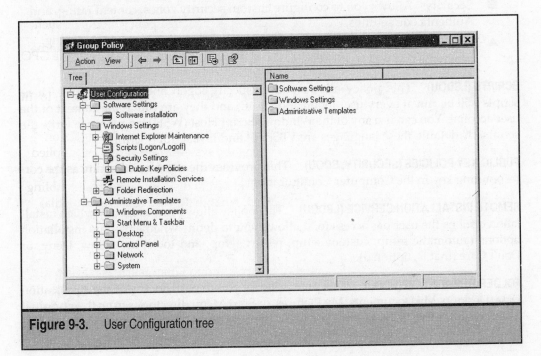

Figure 9-3. User Configuration tree

Software Installation (SDOU)

This section provides the same functionality as the Computer Configuration option of the same name. The major difference is that the User version has the Publishing option, as well as the Assign option:

▼ **Assign** Causes the application to be automatically installed upon system boot.

▲ **Publishing** Allows the user to optionally install the application through the Add/Remote Program option in the Control panel.

Windows Settings (LSDOU)

Because this is in the User Configuration, this part of the GPO is used to hold User-related security settings, as well as logon and logoff scripts.

INTERNET EXPLORER MAINTENANCE (LSDOU) This section deals with configuration and security settings for Internet Explorer:

▼ **Browser User Interface** Allows you to set browser title, animated bitmaps, custom logo, and browser toolbar buttons.

■ **Connection** Allows you to configure connection and proxy settings, user agent strings, and auto configuration.

■ **URLs** Allows you to configure Favorites & Links, Important URLs, and Channels.

■ **Security** Allows you to configure custom security zones, content rating, and Authenticode settings.

▲ **Programs** Allows you to configure the default Program settings and external programs that will be displayed.

SCRIPTS (LSDOU) This policy allows you to specify logon and logoff scripts. These scripts will be run at every user logon and logoff, and they are run in the context of the user account. You can use any of the Windows Script Host (WSH) languages to write the scripts. By default, these languages are VBScript and JavaScript (JScript).

PUBLIC KEY POLICIES (SECURITY, SDOU) This provides the same functionality as the corresponding key in the Computer Configuration.

REMOTE INSTALLATION SERVICE (LSDOU) This policy allows you to specify which installation options the user has access to. It allows you to define whether certain installation options (automatic setup, custom setup, restart setup, and tools) are Allow, Deny, or Don't Care (that is, optional).

FOLDER REPLICATION (SDOU) This policy allows you to redirect any of the Application Data, Desktop, My Documents, My Pictures, or Start Menu directories from their original locations to another. It also allows you to configure settings for those redirected folders.

Administrative Templates (LSDOU)

This part of the GPO is used to configure how the system is displayed to the user. It provides administrators the ability to lock down many aspects of the user's desktop and environment.

WINDOWS COMPONENTS (LSDOU)   This section of the policy deals with things related to Windows components:

- ▼ **NetMeeting**   Allows you to configure user-specific settings on things such as application sharing, audio, video, and the options page.

- ■ **Internet Explorer**   Allows you to configure user-specific IE settings on things such as Internet control panel, offline pages, browser menus, toolbars, persistence behavior, and administrator approved controls.

- ■ **Windows Explorer**   Allows you to configure user-specific settings for the Explorer. Settings include things such as the common open file dialog, enabling the classic shell (that is, disabling Active Desktop), removing the File menu from Windows Explorer, removing Map Network Drive and Disconnect Network Drive, hiding the Hardware tab, requesting credentials for network installations, and many more.

- ■ **Microsoft Management Console**   Allows you to configure user-specific settings on things such as restricting or explicitly permitting the loading of specific snap-ins and Group Policy configurations, as well as restricting the user from entering author mode, or restricting users to the explicitly permitted list of snap-ins.

- ■ **Task Scheduler**   Allows you to configure user-specific settings on things such as preventing run or end options, disabling task creation or deletion, and others.

- ▲ **Windows Installer**   Allows you to configure user-specific settings on things such as always installing with elevated privileges, disabling rollback, preventing users from installing from removable media, and others.

START MENU & TASKBAR (LSDOU)   Allows you to configure the Start Menu & Taskbar by performing such actions as removing the user's folders from the Start Menu; disabling and removing links to Windows Update; disabling Logoff on the Start Menu; disabling and removing the Shut Down command; removing certain menus such as Network & Dial-up Connections, Search and Run; and many more.

DESKTOP (LSDOU)   This section is similar to the Start Menu & Taskbar configuration in that it is used to lock down the user's desktop. It can be used to configure such things as hiding all desktop icons, prohibiting users from changing the My Documents path, saving or not saving settings at exit, and more. It is also used to configure items associated with the Active Desktop, as well as user interaction with the Active Directory.

CONTROL PANEL (LSDOU) This section of the policy deals with things related to items and operations in the Control Panel:

▼ **Add/Remove Programs** Allows you to configure user-specific settings such as disabling Add/Remove Programs, hiding the Change or Remove Programs page, hiding the Add New Programs page, hiding the Add/Remove Windows Components page, and disabling Support Information, and others.

▦ **Display** Allows you to configure user-specific settings such as disabling the Display Control Panel, password protecting the screen saver, hiding the Settings tab, setting the screen saver executable name, and others.

▦ **Printers** Allows you to configure user-specific settings such as disabling the ability to add or delete printers, allowing users to browse the network to find printers, and others.

▲ **Regional Options** Allows you to configure user-specific language by disabling the menus and dialogs control in the Regional Options Control Panel.

NETWORK (LSDOU) This section of the policy deals with things related to items and settings for the Network configuration:

▼ **Offline Files** These are the same options that are in the Computer Configuration section, with identical meanings.

▲ **Network and Dial-up Connections** Allows you to configure user-specific settings such as enabling deletion of RAS connections, enabling connection and disconnection of a RAS connection, enabling access to properties of a LAN connection, allowing connection components to be enabled or disabled, allowing TCP/IP advanced configuration, and many others.

SYSTEM (LSDOU) This section of the policy deals with things related to operations and configurations of the system. It allows you to configure user-specific settings regarding welcome logon screens, drivers with invalid or non-existent signatures, command prompts, Registry editing tools, and others. There are two subsections that contain a number of configuration parameters themselves:

▼ **Logon/Logoff** Allows you to configure user-specific settings to disable the Task Manager, lock the computer, or change a password; and other settings that limit a user's profile size, disable the Run Once list, and more.

▲ **Group Policy** Allows you to configure user-specific settings such as the refresh interval for users, domain controller selection, automatic update of ADM files, and others. This is very important to how GPOs are applied to individual users.

That is it—the entire list of things that GPOs cover and can configure by default. Because they are extensible, there may be configurations we have not covered, but as you can see, there is quite a bit there already. Now that we have a basic scope of what can be covered, we'll take a look at just how we set it up and what exactly we should focus on.

Loopback Processing Policy

By default GPOs are applied on the basis of the location of the object being configured. For a user, GPOs are applied based on the location of the User object (that is, what site, domain, and OU the User object is in). This means that when a GPO is applied on the basis of the User object, the User Configuration is used, but the Computer Configuration of the GPO is ignored. The same goes for a computer. It will have GPOs applied to it based on the location of the Computer object (that is, what site, domain, and OU the Computer object is in). This means that when a GPO is applied on the basis of the Computer object, the Computer Configuration is used, but the User Configuration of the GPO is ignored.

In this default scenario, users have appropriate policies applied to them regardless of what system they are logged into, and computers have a consistent set of configurations, regardless of the user using it. Well, what if you want to apply a specific user policy based on the computer the user is logging into? This is where the loopback processing comes into play. With loopback processing, you can apply a GPO based on the computer the user is logging into.

Loopback processing tells the computer to apply the User Configuration portion of the GPO as well as the Computer Configuration based on the location of the Computer object. In this way, every user that logs into the computer gets the User Configuration from the GPOs for that computer. If you enable this option, you can choose one of two methods for processing:

▼ **Merge** This will apply the regular User Configurations (that is, user object-based), and then the regular User Configurations based on the computer object location. The result is a "combined" configuration from all of the GPOs. Because the computer GPOs are evaluated later in the process, they will take precedence if there is a settings conflict.

▲ **Replace** This will *only* apply to the regular User Configurations based on the computer object location. The result is a replaced policy based on the computer GPOs only.

Figure 9-4 shows the policy setting key that must be configured to use this option.

FEATURES

Group Policy uses many features to provide its functionality, such as inheritance, policy blocking, blocking override, filtering with groups, disabling GPOs, delegation, multiple policy linking, and refreshing. We need to understand these features before we get into the details of Group Policy. This section focuses on those functions.

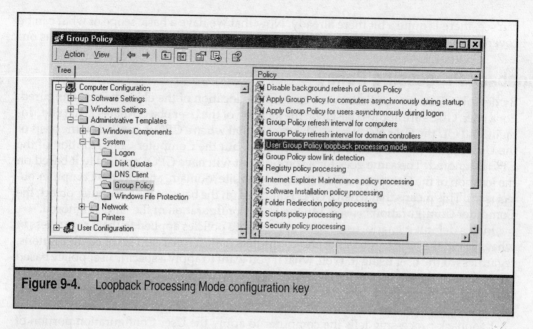

Figure 9-4.   Loopback Processing Mode configuration key

Inheritance

Inheritance is a feature of Win2K in general and has been discussed at length throughout this book. Much like the inheritance of ACLs, GPO settings flow from the top down, or may be better described as from furthest to closest, with *closer/lower having a higher precedence*. The order of evaluation is local GPO, site GPO, domain GPO, then OU GPO. Once all the GPOs have been evaluated, the cumulative values for all the settings are applied. Also, any GPO that is linked to a higher object (SDOU) in the AD tree will flow down to its child objects (and grandchildren, and so on). It is important to understand that it *evaluates* the settings in each GPO to a cumulative total then applies them, versus applying each setting as each GPO is evaluated. This is very much like the old carpenter's rule of "measure twice and cut once."

For example, looking at the following illustration, when a DC in the example.com domain boots, the following process happens:

1. The Computer Configuration portion of the LGPO is evaluated.

2. Then the Computer Configuration portion of GP2 (the site GPO) will be added, with its values overriding any conflicting values.

3. Then the Computer Configuration portion of the Default Domain Policy (the domain GP) will be added, with its values overriding any conflicting values.

4. Next, the Computer Configuration portion of the Default Domain Controller Policy (the OU GP) will be added, with its values overriding any conflicting values.

5. The resulting GP is applied to the HKLM Registry portion of the DC that just booted.

6. If a user in the corporate OU then logged on to a DC in the phil.example.com domain, the User Configuration portion of the LGPO is evaluated.

7. Then the User Configuration portion of GP2 will be added, with its values overriding any conflicting values.

8. Next, the User Configuration portion of the Default Domain Policy *for the example.com domain* (because the user account is in example.com, *not* phil.example.com) will be added, with its values overriding any conflicting values.

9. The User Configuration portion of the Corp GPO (the OU the user is in) will be added, with its values overriding any conflicting values.

10. The resulting GP is applied to the HKCU portion of the Registry for the DC the user is logging into.

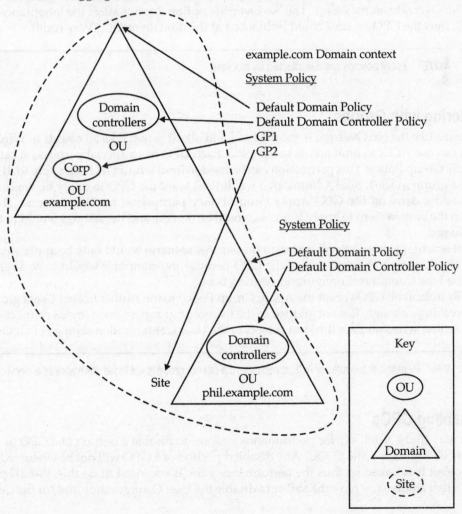

Blocking and No Override

There may be times when you don't want to inherit settings. If this is the case, there is an option to *block policy inheritance*. This will allow you to block GPOs that are linked to higher-level sites, domains, or OUs from applying to the current site, domain, or OU and its children. That is to say if you block at an OU, then no site or domain or parent OU GPOs will be evaluated on that OU. It basically says "start fresh from here and work down."

That's great, now you can block all those policies that the top-level domains are trying to push down on you. Well, there is a high probability that there will be some top-level domain policies (such as Minimum Password Length) that should be forced down; for these there is the *No Override* option. You can set the No Override option to prevent any child container from overriding, which includes blocking, the policy.

Blocking and No Override are not specific to a GPO, but to the link that is using the GPO. For example, you can link the same GPO to two different sites, site1 and site2, and set No Override on only site1. The No Override option doesn't affect the inheritance on site2, thus the GPO on site2 could be blocked at the domain or OU. (Way cool!)

NOTE: Local policies are not affected by blocking.

Filtering with Groups

It seems like the No Override is the final say, but alas it is not. Like all objects in Win2K, you can use ACLs to limit access to the GPO. Each GPO has a special permission called Apply Group Policy. This permission can be used to limit who a GPO can apply to. If we had a group in site1, Site1Admins, that we did not want the GPO to apply to, we could just add a deny on the GPO Apply Group Policy permission for Site1Admins. Thus, when the system went to apply it, access would be denied, and the settings would not be evaluated.

It is actually more convoluted than this, as this scenario would only be applicable to the User Configuration portion of the GPO because the computer would have already applied the Computer Configuration during boot.

By default all GPOs grant the Apply Group Policy to the Authenticated Users group. Interestingly enough, it is not granted to the Everyone group, so anonymous connections are denied access and are thus not subject to the User Configuration settings of GPOs.

VIP: Remember the rules of ACL application: If a user or group is not listed, then access is denied.

Disabling GPOs

You may find a need, say for performance reasons, to disable a portion of a GPO or the entire GPO on a specific SDOU. Any disabled portion of a GPO will not be evaluated on the object it is linked to, thus the performance gain. If you need to do this, Win2K provides that ability. You have the ability to disable the User Configuration and/or the Computer Configuration for that GPO. This will affect anything that links to this GPO; that is, it affects the GPO attributes and is not specific to the SDOU that it is linked to. You also have the option to disable a GPO for a specific SDOU. With this option, you disable the GPO on the SDOU, which will cause it to not be evaluated on the SDOU or any of its children or below. It is of interest to note that you can actually get a GPO to be applied to a child even if it is disabled at the parent—you have to explicitly link it on that SDOU.

An Interesting Observation

An interesting thing about GP inheritance is that although inheritance is supposed to flow down the SDOU trees, the fact that a domain established an administrative boundary poses a problem. We have found that there really is no "inheritance" across sites or domains. Only the GPOs that are linked to the specific site or domain the user or computer is in will be evaluated. *The OU is the only container in which inheritance truly flows down the tree.* Most of the documentation that you will read does not allude to this, but it has been our experience.

Delegation

As described in the last chapter, the AD can delegate control of portions of the AD. With the AD, you can delegate the following Group Policy tasks:

▼ The ability to manage Group Policy links for AD objects

▲ The ability to create and/or edit GPOs

This can be a very useful management tool when used correctly. It allows you to give administrative control over GPO in conjunction with other administrative responsibilities on sites, domains, and OUs.

Multiple Policy Linking

The AD provides the ability to link multiple GPOs to an SDOU, or link one GPO to multiple SDOUs (one-to-many or many-to-one). This is useful when you need to explicitly ensure that certain SDOUs have the same set of policies applied to them. You may be able to get the same desired results with less performance problems if you just make duplicate GPOs and place them in the SDOU that you are trying to configure.

Cross-Domain Linking

Cross-domain linking is what happens when a GPO created in one domain is applied to an SDOU in another domain. While this is certainly technically possible, it comes with a potential showstopper: performance! The remote link will be accessing GPO objects and file shares in the domain where the GPO resides. As stated earlier, it is usually recommended to duplicate GPOs instead of cross-domain linking them, especially over slow links. There is also a security risk, in that there has to be share access to the DCs in the domain where the GPO resides. This would preclude any GPO linking that would potentially flow over an untrusted network.

> **NOTE:** Linking is possible because GPO links are held in the GC, so they can be referenced anywhere in the AD.

Refreshing GPOs

Win2K will refresh the GPOs linked to a User and Computer without the user logging off, then back on, or the computer shutting down and then restarting. By default, DCs check for policy changes every five minutes, and all other computers and all users check every ninety minutes (+/- an offset that can be configured). Software installation and folder redirection are only checked at system startup and user logon. These values are customizable using Group Policy.

A Redux

Here are the Group Policy inheritance and use guidelines:

▼ LGPOs have the least precedence and reside on the system itself.

■ A GPO exists in one domain. That is to say that different GPOs can be in different domains, but the same GPO (that is, the same GUID) will not exist in two domains. They can be linked to any site, domain, or OU in the AD. Thus a GPO in one domain can be linked to an OU in another.

■ A GPO that is linked to a site will be evaluated by any computer or user in the site, regardless of domain membership or domain location of the GPO.

■ The domain and site members (that is, not child domain members) will only evaluate a GPO that is linked to a domain or site. Thus, domain and site GPOs do not flow down the inheritance tree.

▲ A GPO that is linked to an OU is only evaluated by the OU members and their children (that is, nested OUs). An OU GPO does flow down the inheritance tree.

GROUP POLICY AUTHENTICATION, AUTHORIZATION, AND AUDITING

Authentication, authorization, and auditing (the 3 A's) for Group Polices is the same as those of the OS. This is because Group Policies are just "things" that are implemented and protected by the AD and local system protections. This means that the same mechanisms that are used to control the 3 A's for Win2K are applicable to the Group Policies.

Authentication

Because Group Policies exist as both file system objects and objects in the AD, any access of those objects is subject to authentication of the user who is requesting the access. Both the AD and the server providing the file shares use integrated Win2K authentication.

This will be a Kerberos authentication by default, but can be any authentication method supported by the Win2K system that you are connecting to.

Authorization

Group Policies are made up of objects, whether in the AD or a file on the SYSVOL, and thus are protected by ACLs assigned to the objects. By default, only Domain Administrators, Enterprise Administrators, Group Policy Creator-Owners, and the SYSTEM account can create a new GPO. If you want to allow a User or Group to be able to add GPOs, then you should place them in the Group Policy Creator-Owners group.

Like all objects in Win2K, the user who creates an object becomes the Creator-Owner, which gives him or her Full Control of the object; this is the same with GPOs. So anyone who creates a GPO has full control over that GPO by default. It is important to note that being a member of the Group Policy Creator-Owners group only gives you the ability to add GPOs; it does not give you any implicit rights to modify or delete existing GPOs. The rights that you have as an individual user or member of another group would have to grant you those permissions. For example, if user PCC is a member of the Group Policy Creator-Owners, then he can add a GPO, and because he added it, he owns it and has full control over it. By default Authenticated Users have read access to all GPOs; thus, the user pcc would have read access as well, but nothing else.

There is also the ability to delegate, which is really a fancy term for applying the proper permissions to an object and using inheritance to help them flow. By default, Enterprise Administrators have Full Control on all GPOs. If you desire to have a user or group be able to administer all GPOs, then you would have to add them to the Enterprise Administrators group, or make a new group and add it to all GPOs.

Auditing

Just like authentication and authorization, auditing is something that happens integral to the Win2K OS and is not something that is set separately. The Group Policy auditing occurs just like file system auditing; you enable auditing on objects, then you set the SACL on the objects that you want audited. The audits will end up in the Security Event Log or the Directory Service Event Log. Please see Chapter 13 for details on setting up auditing in Win2K.

ADMIN

This section will cover the setting up and managing of Group Policy, and the tools used to do that. We will also cover some rudimentary discussion on design and planning issues that revolve around Group Policy.

Tools

There are a number of tools that can be used to create and manage Group Policies. The most commonly used tools are the Active Directory Tools (Active Directory Users and

Computers and Active Directory Sites and Services), the Group Policy Editor, and ADSIEdit. We will cover those tools in this section.

AD Tools

You get to the Group Policy interface by selecting Properties | Group Policy for the object (site, domain, or OU) that you want to manage. See Figure 9-5 for the Group Policy page on the TestOU. With this page, you can add, delete, edit, and set options and properties for the GPOs on the OU. To set up a GPO on a site, you would use the Active Directory Sites and Services. For domains and OUs, use the Active Directory Users and Computers.

Group Policy Editor (GPE)

An alternative is to use the Group Policy Editor MMC snap-in. This snap-in allows you to select any Group Policy Object in the AD to edit. By default, it has settings for Registry-based policies, security settings, software installation, scripts, and folder redirection. You cannot use this tool to create a new policy, only to edit existing policies. To use this tool, you open the MMC (Start | Run | MMC.EXE). Then go through the process of adding a snap-in, and select the Group Policy snap-in. The next screen you see (Figure 9-6) is the default and will edit the LGPO. If you select the Browse option, you can select an SDOU GPO or a LGPO for another system (see Figure 9-7). As you can see, this allows you

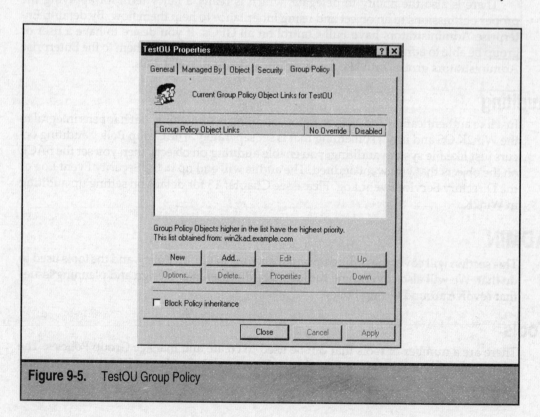

Figure 9-5. TestOU Group Policy

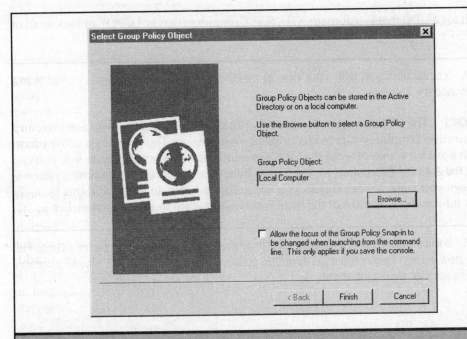

Figure 9-6.   Default Group Policy focus

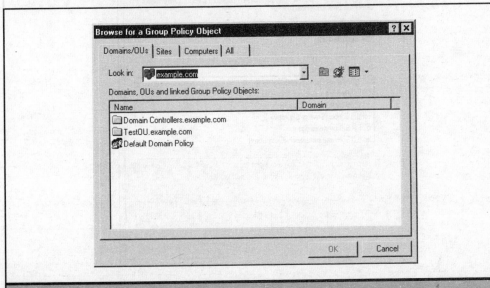

Figure 9-7.   Group Policy selection

to search for a GPO that is a domain/OU, Site, Computer (that is, LGPO), or look at all of them at once.

TIP: You can launch the GPE with a focus on the LGPO, simply by running `gpedit.msc` from a command line.

EXTENSIONS The GPE functionality (that is, Windows Settings, Security Settings, and Administrative Templates) is provided by snap-in extension. The extensions allow you to extend or limit the scope of what the GPE can manage. As shown in Figure 9-8, you can uncheck the Add All Extensions for the Group Policy snap-in, and then selectively choose which ones you want to use. Unless you are going to write an extension, this is really more for information, as most of the time you will not want to limit functionality.

TIP: If you are getting error messages about finding a Group Policy server or opening a Group Policy, there is a high likelihood that you have DNS problems. Ensure that your DNS is working correctly before you start down another trail.

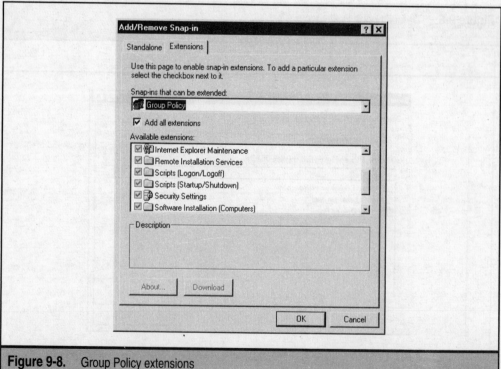

Figure 9-8. Group Policy extensions

ADSIEdit

You can use ADSIEdit (Figure 9-9) to perform LDAP operations against the System | Policies portion of a domain. This is mostly useful for setting permission on the AD objects that reside there. It allows you an alternative method of deleting objects, as well as managing object attributes.

Planning Group Policies

The best Group Policy design is a top-down approach. It should mirror your security policy, with the broadest policies being defined at the upper portion of the hierarchy and becoming more specific down the tree. The reality is that Group Policy design and Organizational Unit design go hand in hand and can't be done separately. The structure of your AD—the depth, use of sites, and OUs—all play a factor in when and how you will use Group Policy.

Before you start creating GPOs, consider where you need to apply the policy. Does the policy apply to all of your users or computers? If so, perhaps you need to apply the policy at the site level. If the policy is relevant to only one domain or to users within one OU, applying the policy at the domain or OU level might be more appropriate.

You also need to consider how to determine effective policy at any given level in the hierarchy. You need to take time to figure out what the combination of policies are at each hierarchy level. Also the more Group Policies that need to be applied, the slower the computer startup or user logon, which will play in to the design as well.

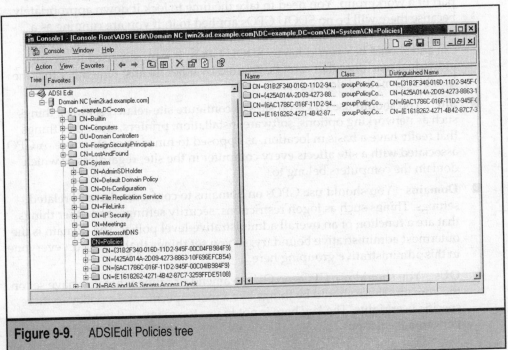

Figure 9-9. ADSIEdit Policies tree

You should consider the following issues when designing your Group Policy deployment:

▼ **When to Use Blocking** Use this to block things you don't want set by a higher-level policy.

■ **When to Use No Override** Use this when you want to ensure that the settings you define will be propagated down and applied.

■ **When to Use Group Filtering (Limiting with ACLs)** Use this for special circumstances where you want to block a No Override or you don't want a particular GPO to apply to a group of users.

■ **Use Cross-Domain Links Sparingly** The systems will have to access the SYSVOL on the remote DC, and this takes time and affects performance. You should use them within sites if needed and *very* sparingly across sites.

▲ **Determine Multiple Policy Interaction Before Deployment** Take the time to flow chart the effective policy settings at different levels in the AD hierarchy.

When to Use Different Types of GPOs

We have discussed the different types of GPOs (LSDOU); now we need to look at when and where to use them:

▼ **Local** You should absolutely define a LGPO if the system is standalone or part of a workgroup. You need to take the time to lock it down appropriately, because there will be no SDOU GPOs applied to it. If you are running as a domain member, then don't spend a lot of time on this, as all of the settings can and should be overridden by SDOU GPOs. It is mostly used to secure individual machines that can't be secured by other means; remember that the Local GPO method does not scale well.

■ **Site** You should use GPOs on sites to configure site-related settings, things such as networking options, software installation, printers, and other things that really have a basis in location, as opposed to function or structure. A GPO associated with a site affects every computer in the site, regardless of which domain the computers belong to.

■ **Domains** You should use GPOs on domains to configure domain-related settings. Things such as logon restrictions, security settings, and other things that are a function of an overall administrative-level policy. The domain is the outermost administrative boundary, so you set things that will affect everyone in this administrative grouping here.

▲ **OUs** You should use GPOs on OUs to amend or refine what you have set on the domain. These should be things like a more specific audit policy or more specific user rights. The key here is not to use too many of them for performance reasons.

Unlike sites, where physical location is the primary issue, domains and OUs are administrative in purpose and should be used for such. Use domains to set most, if not all, of what you want, and then use OUs to supplement your domain GPOs.

TIP: If you have multiple domains in a site, consider creating identical GPOs at the domain level, so that the computers will get the GPO from its own DC. This will help in performance.

Defining a Group Policy

Once you have defined what needs to be configured and where you want to configure it, you can start the process of defining the actual GPOs. We will go through the process of creating a Group Policy for the example.com domain that we used in Chapter 8.

Creating a GPO

When creating a GPO on an SDOU, you use the appropriate AD tool (described earlier), then go to the object you want to create the GPO on and select it. Once it is selected, you go to Properties | Group Policy | New. You will get a new GPO called New Group Policy Object (Figure 9-10), which you can now select and edit.

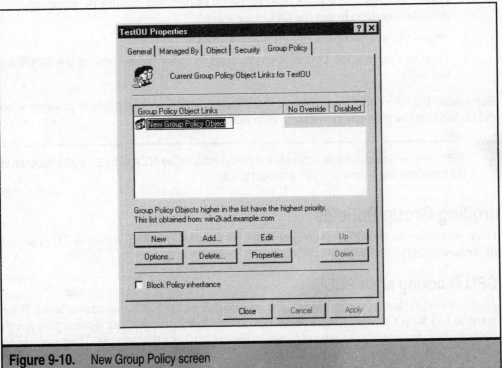

Figure 9-10.   New Group Policy screen

Editing a GPO

You can edit a GPO during its initial setup, or at any time after that. To do this, you can use the GPE or the AD tools described earlier. The AD tools just open up the GPE on the specific GPO that you select if you go that route, so it is probably best to just use the GPE to start with. If you do, you will be able to select the GPO you want, as described earlier. By either means, you will end up in the GPE with the ability to configure the GPO. The screen that you will see is the same as the one shown in Figure 9-2 or 9-3. They are updated in real-time and then replicated in the manner specified in the refresh intervals.

You can now start walking down the Computer or User Configuration trees, setting the values you need. You can use the Next Policy and Previous Policy buttons while editing policies in the Administrative Templates section of the User or Computer Configuration, for ease of navigation.

Adding a Second GPO

This process is simple; you just do the following:

1. Go to the object (SDOU) that you want to add the GPO to.
2. Open the Properties | Group Policy on that object.
3. Either click Add (to add an existing GPO) or New (to create a new one, as described earlier) to get the GPO you want.
4. Press OK, and you have linked it to the object.
5. You can then use the Up or Down buttons to order the priority of the GPOs on the object.

Remember that the GPO listed first in the window will have the highest priority when evaluated (that is, its settings will override any of the others).

VIP: You need read and write access to the Policy section in the AD, and the SYSVOL folder on the DC to perform any actions on a GP, even just to read.

Controlling Group Policies

Once you have set up GPOs, then you must set about controlling their use. This section describes issues in controlling GPOs.

GPO Blocking at an SDOU

As described earlier, you can block GPO inheritance at the SDOU container level. If you want to block GPOs from higher-level containers from propagating down, you set the Block Policy inheritance checkbox shown in Figure 9-10. It's that simple. Then none of the GPOs linked to the parent or higher will be evaluated at this container or its children. When you set this, it is applicable to the container (SDOU), not a specific GPO.

No Override, or Disable at an SDOU

To set the No Override option (described earlier) for a GPO, you select the GPO that you want, then click the Options button (shown previously in Figure 9-10). This will bring up the screen shown in Figure 9-11. Then you can select the No Override button. The extreme opposite of this is the Disabled option. As described earlier, this will cause this GPO not to be evaluated on this specific object, however, it *will* be evaluated on its children and below.

DISABLING SUBTREES   A further disable option is that of disabling the User or Computer subtrees of a specific GPO. To do this, you select the GPO that you want, then click the Options button (Figure 9-10). Then in the Disable section, shown in Figure 9-12, you can check one or both of the following options: Disable Computer Configuration settings or Disable User Configuration settings. The effect of disabling both is the same as disabling the entire GPO for the SDOU (described previously).

Using Group Filtering

One of the ways to actually block, or for that matter explicitly grant, access to a GPO is with the Apply Group Policy permission (that is, ACL) to the GPO on the specific SDOU. If you set a *deny* for this permission for any group, then when the GPO is to be evaluated, Win2K will deny access to it, thus preventing it from being merged with the other GPOs that are evaluated at the SDOU. This could potentially be used to block a No Override, if you really didn't want it applied to a specific group. Understand that to set this, you must have write permissions on the GPO in the domain in which it is stored (that is to say, only administrators in the domain that holds the GPO can set this by default). Thus, you can't use this to thwart higher-level mandates.

The converse is to set an explicit *allow* to a specific group to ensure that they are the only ones that it gets applied to. You may use this to set specific user rights for some super

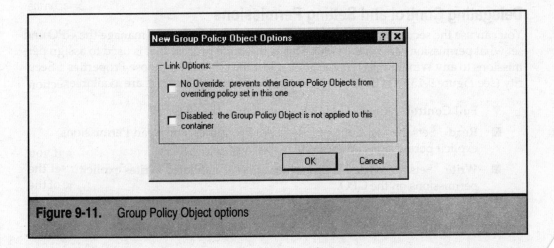

Figure 9-11.   Group Policy Object options

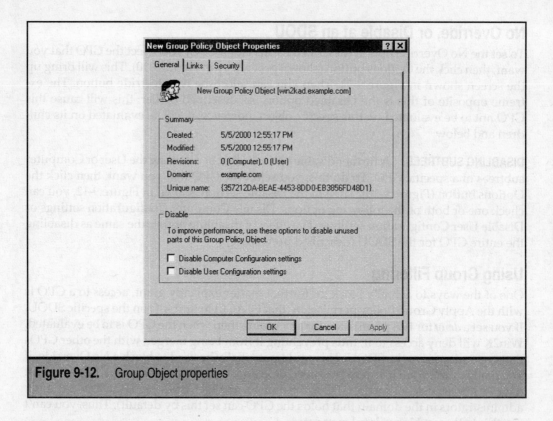

Figure 9-12.   Group Object properties

administrator group. Figure 9-13 shows that the SuperAdmin group has the allow on the Apply Group Policy permission. We have cleared it on all the others listed, and thus they will be the only ones that have that policy evaluated for them.

Delegating Control and Setting Permissions

You can use the security properties on a GPO to delegate who can manage the GPO and set what permissions are on the GPO. This is the same process that is used to assign permissions to any Win2K object. For a GPO, select the GPO, then choose Properties | Security (see Figure 9-13). The following general permission groupings are available:

▼ **Full Control**   Allows complete control over the GPO.

■ **Read**   Sets the List Contents, Read All Properties, and Read Permissions explicit permissions on the GPO.

■ **Write**   Sets the Write All Properties and All Validated Writes explicit permissions on the GPO.

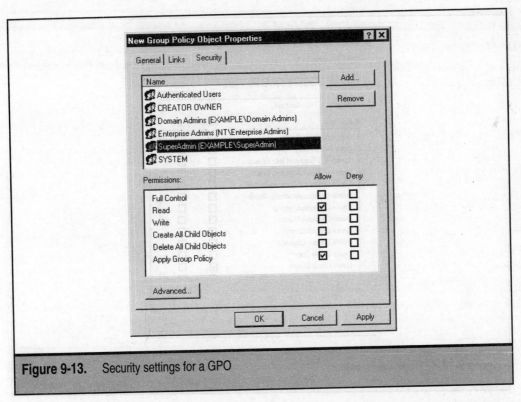

Figure 9-13.   Security settings for a GPO

- **Create All Child Objects**   Sets Create All Child Objects and the Create *<object type>* Objects explicit permissions on the GPO.

- **Delete All Child Objects**   Sets Delete All Child Objects, and the Delete *<object type>* Objects explicit permissions on the GPO, the only relevant *<object type>* being groupPolicyContainer.

▲ **Apply Group Policy**   Sets the List Objects and Apply Group Policy explicit permissions.

Selecting Advanced | *<entry>* | View/Edit will take you to the explicit permissions for an individual entry (Figure 9-14). There are 38 explicit object permissions and 10 explicit property permissions that can be set on a GPO. A portion of the object permissions are shown in Figure 9-14.

Controlling Group Policy with Group Policy

There are a number of settings that are specific to GPOs that are configured in the Administrative Templates | Group Policy portion of the GPO. They are discussed here.

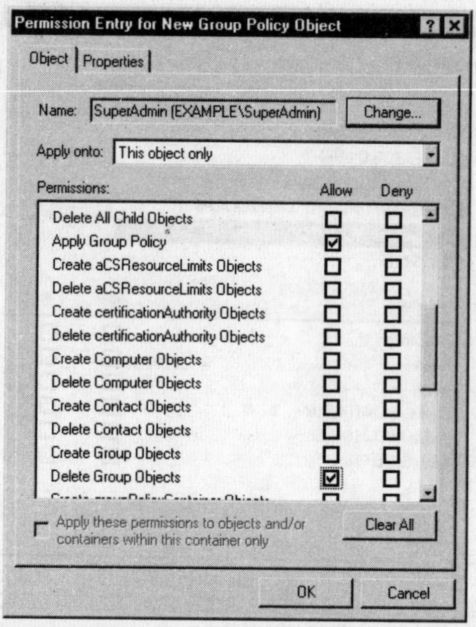

Figure 9-14. Explicit permissions

COMPUTER CONFIGURATION   In the Computer Configuration section you can configure the following settings:

▼ **Disable Background Refresh of Group Policy**   Prevents refreshing of Group Policies while a user is interactively logged into a computer.

■ **Apply Group Policy for Computers Synchronously During Startup**   Ensures the Computer Configuration portion of the GPOs is evaluated and applied before allowing a user logon.

■ **Apply Group Policy for Users Synchronously During Startup**   Ensures the User Configuration portion of the GPOs is evaluated and applied before allowing a user logon.

■ **User Group Policy Loopback Processing Mode**   Puts this GPO in loopback mode for this SDOU.

■ **Group Policy Slow Link Detection**   Lets you set the connection link speed that you deem as slow.

▲ **Registry Policy Processing**   This sets when Registry policies are updated. It affects all policies in the Administrative Templates folder and any other policies that store values in the Registry.

The following configurations allow you to set when the specific service policies are updated:

▼ Folder Redirection Policy Processing

■ Disk Quota Policy Processing

■ Scripts Policy Processing

■ Security Policy Processing

■ EFS Recovery Policy Processing

■ Software Installation Policy Processing

▲ IP Security Policy Processing

Two other options, Group Policy Refresh Interval for Computers and Group Policy Refresh Interval for Domain Controllers, are discussed later in this section.

You will see the following options in a large majority of the Computer settings we just covered:

▼ **Allow Processing Across a Slow Network Connection**   Allows updates even if using slow links. This is a potential performance problem.

■ **Do Not Apply During Periodic Background Processing**   Prevents updating of these policies while there is a user interactively logged onto the system.

▲ **Process Even If the Group Policy Objects Have Not Changed**   Normally, if a value has not changed in the GPO, the setting is not updated on the remote computer. This will reapply the policy even if it did not change.

USER CONFIGURATION   In the User Configuration section you can configure the following settings:

▼ **Group Policy Refresh Interval for Users**   Allows you to set how often Group Policies for users are updated while the user is logged in.

■ **Group Policy Slow Link Detection**   Same purpose as for Computer Configuration.

■ **Group Policy Domain Controller Selection**   Determines which DC is used by the Group Policy snap-in.

■ **Create New Group Policy Object Links Disabled by Default**   Allows you to set the state of a newly created GPO.

■ **Enforce Show Policies Only**   Allows you to display only true policies from the `.adm` files. This means that only settings that reside in the `Software\Policies` or `Software\Microsoft\Windows\CurrentVersion\Policies` Registry subkeys of `HKLM` or `HKCU` will be shown.

- ■ **Disable Automatic Update of .adm Files** Allows you to control the update of the .adm files when opening the GPE.

- ▲ **Download Missing COM Components** Allows you to have the computer search the AD COM components that a program requires.

Operational Issues

This section takes a look at the things that need to be configured from an operational standpoint. It is not in-depth, but should be enough to get you started in the right direction.

Setting Refresh Intervals

Using the Administrative Templates/System/Group Policy settings in either the User Configuration or Computer Configuration sections of the Group Policy, we can configure the refresh intervals.

GROUP POLICY REFRESH INTERVAL FOR COMPUTERS (COMPUTER CONFIGURATION) For non-DC computers you can specify a background update rate for Group Policies in the Computer Configuration folder. You can configure the refresh range from 0–64,800 minutes (45 days) with a "variable" window. This "window" allows the updating of many systems to happen at semi-varied times and not be a load all at once on the system or the network.

The 0 minutes actually translates into a refresh every 7 seconds. This low of a value would pose a very high load on the system and is not recommended. If this policy is disabled or not set, the default is set to 90 minutes with a 30-minute "window."

GROUP POLICY REFRESH INTERVAL FOR DOMAIN CONTROLLERS (COMPUTER CONFIGURATION)
This allows you to specify a different refresh interval for DC computers. The settings can have the same values as the non-DC computers, with a "window" also. If this policy is disabled or not set, the default is set to 5 minutes. This is only used for SDOU.

GROUP POLICY REFRESH INTERVAL FOR USERS (USERS' CONFIGURATION) This allows you to specify the GP refresh interval for users when they are logged on to a computer. This only applies to the User Configuration tree of the GP. Like the refresh of the non-DC computers, the users' default is 90 minutes, with a 30-minute "window."

DISABLING BACKGROUND REFRESH There is also a setting that allows you to disable the refreshing of Group Policy. By enabling the Disable Background Refresh of Group Policy in the Computer Configuration section, you are preventing the updates to Group Policy while the computer is in use. The Group Policy will still be updated, but only when the computer is not in use (that is, no user is logged on).

Customizing the GPO

There are two ways to extend what a GPO can be used to configure. You can write a template file (.adm), but this will only allow you to make changes to Registry-based information. The second method is to write a GPE snap-in extension. With this second method, you can create an extension that can store both Registry and non-Registry policy (that is, file-based) settings.

Adding a Template

Once you have created a template file, you can add it to either the User or Computer Configuration by selecting the Administrative Templates container in either User or Computer. Then right-click and select Add/Remove Templates. You will then see the screen in Figure 9-15. This shows the Current Policy Templates that exist. Then you can select Add to add the new one.

By default the templates live in `%systemroot%\inf`. When you "add" the `.adm` file, the actual file is added to the `Sysvol\<domain>\Policies\<GUID>\ADM` folder of the GPO you are adding it to.

Enabling Auditing

By default, the GPO has auditing entries for Successful and Failed: Writes, Deletes, Modifications, and Creates. Although it has the entries, by default auditing is *not* enabled on a system. To enable auditing on a GPO, you first must set the Domain Policy to allow it. This is done by enabling the Audit Directory Service Access by selecting Default Domain Policy | Computer Configuration | Windows Settings | Security Settings | Local Policies | Audit Policies. Once that is enabled, you can set auditing on a GPO by selecting the GPO (preferably a high-level container), then right-clicking and selecting Properties | Security | Advanced | Auditing. Then select Add to set up auditing for a new User or Group. See Chapter 13 for details on the entire auditing process and tools.

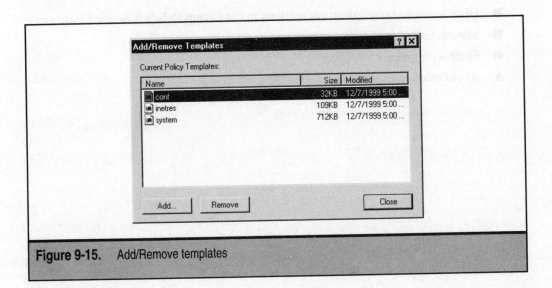

Figure 9-15.   Add/Remove templates

Enabling Verbose Logging

You can enable a more verbose logging on the GP client-side. To enable this, you need to set the `RunDiagnosticLoggingGroupPolicy` Registry values under the `HKLM\Software\Microsoft\Windows NT\CurrentVersion\Diagnostics` key.

RECAP

We have covered quite a bit about Group Policies, what they are, what they are used for, how to use them, and so on. Out of all of it, you should come away with a good understanding of the purpose of Group Policy and a feel for what they cover. If you understand that, you are well on your way to actually being able to use them. There are a number of functions that you can do with Group Policy that are not covered here, such as software installation, managing offline folders, and setting user desktops. They will be discussed in some measure in other chapters.

There are two primary concerns that you should have when embarking on the Group Policy trail. The first is security-related: figuring out the *effective policy*. You need to take time to figure out what all the inheritance, blocking, no override, and ACL settings really mean when the GPOs are finally applied to a system. The second is a performance issue and deals with *GPO processing*. If you use too many GPOs, you will undoubtedly cause serious performance issues. Be efficient with your use of policies, and don't use them when you don't have to.

Here are some best practices that will help you in implementing your Group Policy architecture:

▼ Use Organization Units and Group Policies together. Design them at the same time.

■ Disable unused configuration sections in the Group Policy (User or Computer).

■ Minimize Group Policies in domains and OUs for users.

■ Filter with groups.

▲ Avoid cross-domain links.

CHAPTER 10

User and Group Security Management

In order to achieve a high level of security in Win2K, it is critically important to have a thorough understanding of two of its foundational components—user and group accounts. In fact, the bulk of what is checked and evaluated by security-analysis tools, such as the Kane utilities, is the proper setup of user and group accounts, excessive user rights, and user account policies. While *some* of the concepts and material in this chapter will be old hat to veteran WinNT managers, the nuances and functionality that Win2K brings to the table will be of interest to everyone.

TERMINOLOGY

It's easy to get lost and confused in the terminology of workstations, local groups, global groups, universal groups, local and remote domains, and such. As you read this chapter, make sure to differentiate among these different systems and objects. This discussion is primarily concerned with domains rather than workgroups, and servers more than workstations. Also note the following:

▼ A *Win2K Server computer* operating as a domain controller maintains the domain name context (that is, the domain) for that portion of the Active Directory (see Chapter 8).

■ A *member server* is a Win2K Server that is not a domain controller, but is a member of a domain. It maintains its own user account database (SAM) in addition to accessing users and groups from other domains in the forest.

■ A *Win2K Workstation computer* maintains its own SAM and can be a member of a domain.

▲ User and group accounts are associated with a *Security ID (SID)*. This SID is automatically generated when the user or group is created, and cannot be re-created if the group or user is deleted. The SID can be stored in an object ACL to define an authorization level for any number of users and groups.

USERS

To gain access to a Win2K resource, you have to have a user account. All Win2K computers provide access (authentication and authorization) through user accounts. This is because the SIDs associated with the user accounts are an integral part of the security functionality of Win2K. Without them, the security does not work, so they are mandatory.

User accounts are used in conjunction with groups (covered later) to control the authorization a user has. For most users, an account will be created, then that account will be added to a group that already has the rights and permissions you want to grant to the user. It is possible to grant rights and permissions to individual user accounts, but adding users to groups that already have permissions is the most efficient management practice.

When you think of users and the access they need, keep in mind that there are two major types of access—Normal and Administrative:

▼ **Normal Access**   Every user needs access to programs, data files, and other system resources for everyday tasks.

▲ **Administrative Access**   A subset of users will need access to the system so they can manage user accounts, servers, peripherals, and other network resources.

There are also two types of users that can be used to provide that access—Computer Local and Domain:

▼ **Computer Local Users (CLU)**   The local users are located in the local SAM database on Win2K Workstation or member servers. This is the same as it was in WinNT. Logging on to one of the accounts gives you access to resources on the local computer; you do not have access to resources elsewhere in the domain.

▲ **Domain User (DU)**   The Domain user account is defined in the domain and is held in the Active Directory. Logging on to a Domain account gives you access to resources in the entire forest.

Default Accounts

There are a number of default accounts that are created at the time of system installation. This section takes a look at three of those accounts: Administrator, System, and Guest. There are other accounts that are created by specific services that you may install (i.e. KRBTGT, the Kerberos Account, when you set up an Active Directory server).

The Administrator Account

The Administrator account (not to be confused with the Administrators group) is a built-in account that is installed when a Win2K system is set up. In a domain environment, the Administrator account is set up simultaneously with the first domain controller in the domain. The person setting up the system specifies the initial password for the Administrator account. The Administrator account should be renamed, because of the proliferation of scripts that directly target that name. It can never be disabled or deleted, and it can't be locked out.

The Administrator can do the following:

▼ Create and manage user and group accounts

■ Create and connect to shared directories

■ Establish trust relationships

■ Manage all aspects of hard drives

■ Manage all aspects of printers and printer sharing

■ Manage security policies

- Manage auditing and security logs
- Modify the operating system and install new drivers
- Take ownership of files and other objects
- ▲ Lock, log on to, and shut down servers

In domain environments, the Administrator account for the domain permits you to manage servers and workstations in the domain, including domain controllers, member servers, and Win2K Workstation computers. The Administrator account is a member of the built-in Administrators group, as well as of the Domain Admins and Domain Users groups. Through this membership, the Administrator account potentially has full access to every system in every domain on the network.

Here are some guidelines for the Administrator account:

▼ For security reasons, the Administrator account should be renamed to something obscure.

■ To enhance Administrator account security, create a two- or three-part password, with each part known only by one person, as discussed later in this chapter.

■ Because the Administrator account has full access to the system, the administrator should log on to the account only when necessary and log off immediately.

■ Use Organizational Units and other groups, such as Account Operators and Server Operators, to create sub-administrators.

■ Consider revoking all network access by Administrators. This means all administration must be done from the server console in a controlled environment.

■ If there are multiple administrators, create a separate administrative account for each so you can audit their individual activities. If unauthorized activities are occurring, it will not be possible to ascertain which administrator is the perpetrator unless separate accounts are used.

■ Avoid logging in to the Administrator account at mistrusted computers or at computers in unfamiliar settings. Your activities could be monitored electronically or photographically to capture passwords and other secure information.

■ Any user who is a member of the local Administrators group on a Win2K computer can take ownership of files and access the data in those files, no matter what the current permissions are on the files. Because of this, you need to closely monitor and audit the activities of users with administrative rights.

▲ Seriously consider whether you really can trust your administrators and sub-administrators. For security's sake, be a pessimist. Your job and your company's assets may be at stake.

VIP: For security reasons, the owners of the administrative accounts need to have their own personal accounts to use when they are accessing the network for non-administrative tasks. This will allow them to perform their user tasks in a non-privileged account.

The System Account

The System account (a.k.a. LocalSystem) is not a user account, but an account that the operating system uses to run programs, utilities, and device drivers. The System account has unlimited power, so rogue Trojan Horse services that manage to infiltrate your system and run under the System account have the ability do just about anything. They could also create and change user accounts or perform other activities that wreak havoc on your system.

System-type accounts are common in other operating systems, and one of the most famous Unix security attacks was a worm that took advantage of a bug in TCP/IP services to take over Unix's equivalent of a System account.

The System account provides a way to run services without the need for an actual administrative user to be logged on. The System and Administrator accounts have similar powers, but the System account is used by the operating system and by services that run under Win2K. The System account is an internal account that does not show up in the user account administration tools.

Some services will only run under the System account, such as Server and Workstation. If you are installing a new service, especially if it is one that is untrusted, you should run that service under a special account that has the lowest level of access rights and permissions that the service requires. This will prevent an infected service from doing damage to your system. You create the account (described later in this chapter), then use the Services utility to configure a service to start up under the account.

New to Win2K is the ability for System accounts to perform tasks requiring network capabilities. (Previous versions of NT would not allow the System account to perform any tasks that required network privileges.) Use this feature with caution.

The Guest Account

The Guest account allows people to access a Win2K computer without logging in to a specific user account. The Guest account is like an anonymous logon. Be aware that the Guest account, like any other account, has access to every directory where the Everyone group has permissions, which may be a problem for data and application directories. This access is what makes people edgy about using the Guest account. The Guest account is disabled by default on Win2K computers and should stay that way.

If the Guest account is enabled in a domain, users can access any computer in the forest that allows all legitimate accounts to access the system (that is, the Everyone group described later in the chapter) as the Guest account from the domain in which it is enabled. Using the Guest account, users can log on and view a list of resources, but rights and permissions limit access to those resources. If you decide to use the Guest account, you could create a directory for public files and give guests Read Only access to the directory. Remember, because it is a Domain account, every computer in the forest trusts it, which is an obvious security hole.

TIP: If you need some type of shared access, consider a Role account, which is limited to a certain functional role that needs to be accomplished.

USER ACCOUNT SETTINGS

You need to make sure that all accounts have appropriate security settings. This is accomplished in two different ways. First, you can set specific Account Policy via Group Policy on the domain the account is in. Second, you can set individual restrictions for any user by setting specific User account properties on the specific user object.

Account Policies

Account Policies are applied via the Group Policy Object (GPO) mechanism on the domain they apply to (as described in the last chapter), or they are applied via the Local Security Policy for the system you are managing. These are configurations and settings that will be applied to users and groups that are members of the domain that the GPO is linked to or are local to the computer for the Local Security Policy. It is important to understand that it may appear that non-local Account Policies can be applied on SOU containers (as defined in Chapter 9), but in reality, they can only be applied on D (domain) containers. We will be focusing on the domain-level policies.

There are three types of account policies: password policies, account lockout policies, and Kerberos policies. Each of the account policies can be used to configure different security or operational aspects of an account. This section describes the policies that can be set.

TIP: Please refer to Chapter 9 for details on using and deploying Group Policies.

Password Policies

The Password Policies section is where you set policies that control how passwords are handled in the domain. The settings you make here are critical to protecting passwords and your password security scheme. Your policy settings should be consistent with your written policy. Implemented policy protects the network from hacker attacks and written policy defines the responsibility of users who have been given access to the organization's information system. You should have users read and sign such policies as part of their employment contract.

Password Policies (see Figure 10-1) are used to control security requirements for passwords. They include the following settings:

▼ **Enforce Password History** Prevents users from toggling among their favorite passwords and reduces the chances that a hacker/password cracker will discover passwords. This setting configures how frequently old passwords can

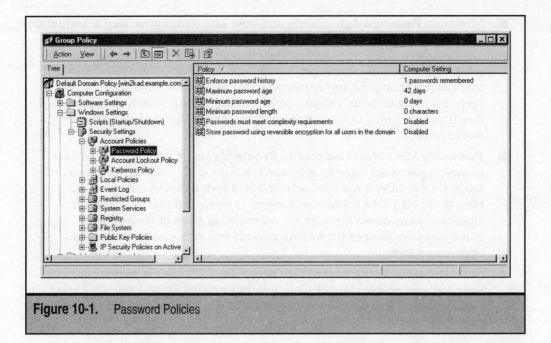

Figure 10-1.   Password Policies

be reused. By default, Win2K stores one password in the password history, but this can be configured to store up to 24. You should use this to prevent users from reusing common passwords. This is also a critical security feature because it can prevent hackers from logging in to an account using a password that they previously discovered. To use this option effectively, do not set the Minimum Password Age parameter to zero.

NOTE: Because of the way passwords are saved in a table, users cannot reuse a password until they have changed passwords *n*+2 times, where *n* is the number of passwords remembered. So if Enforce Password History is set to 3, users cannot revert to the first password until they have changed their password five times (3+2).

- **Maximum Password Age**   Denotes the maximum time a user *can* keep a password before it *has to* be changed. By default Win2K will require a new password every 42 days. This value should be changed to something consistent with your security policy. A good rule of thumb is to decrease the time as the security requirements increase. Note that the user will get a warning box when the aging date is less than 30 days away. In a secure environment or if you suspect frequent break-in attempts, you might want to set this value to 7 so users need to change their passwords every week. However, keep in mind that passwords should be difficult to guess and that frequent password changes will burden your users. They may be tempted to write the latest password down, and that's the worst thing that can happen.

■ **Minimum Password Age**   Configures how long a user *must* keep a password before it *can* be changed. This is just the opposite of the prior setting and is used to prevent users from immediately changing their password back to what it just was. If this is not set, but Enforce Password History is, then a user can just change his or her password the number of times the history keeps it +1 and enter the original password. By default Win2K does not set this. If you are going to set an Enforce Password History value, do not set this to zero.

■ **Passwords Must Meet Complexity Requirements**   Configures the system to use the password filter for password changes and creations, *not* password usage (that is, after it has been set). This will install the default password filter (PASSFILT.DLL), which will enforce a password that is at least six characters long, doesn't contain the username or parts of the user's full name, and uses three of the following: numbers, symbols, lowercase, and uppercase letters.

▲ **Store Password Using Reversible Encryption**   Allows the passwords to be stored in a reversible manner. This is mainly needed if you are using Digest Authentication (see Chapter 16). By default the passwords are stored as hash functions (that is, they are irreversible).

Account Lockout Policies

The Account Lockout feature is your key to preventing brute-force password cracking/guessing attacks on your system. Consider this: The default setting is No Account Lockout; if you retain this setting, someone could execute a dictionary attack against your server. Such an attack will attempt, over an extended period of time, to log in to a user's account using different passwords with the expectation of actually guessing the correct password. In a dictionary attack, thousands of well-known passwords are tried. If your users don't create hard-to-guess passwords and you don't have Account Lockout set, someone could use this method to break into a valid user account.

Account Lockout Policies (see Figure 10-2) are used to control security requirements for how and when accounts are locked out due to failed logon attempts. They are also used to configure account-reset settings. They include the following settings:

▼ **Account Lockout Threshold**   Configures the number of failed logon attempts (that is, bad logon count) that are allowed before an account is locked out. The primary use of this is to thwart password-guessing attacks against an account. The default value is 0 in Win2K, which means there is no lockout, but it can have a range of 0–999. A good rule of thumb is about 5, but this should match your security policy. It should be noted that this is only applicable to initial logons and not screen savers or desktop locking.

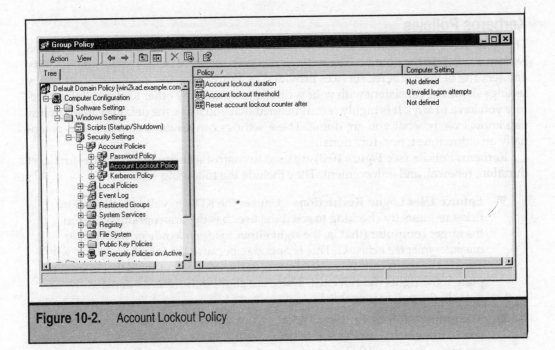

Figure 10-2. Account Lockout Policy

- ■ **Account Lockout Duration** Configures the number of minutes that the account will be locked out before it is unlocked. The value can range from 0–99,999. If it is set to 0, then the account must be unlocked manually (that is, by an administrator). Any other value will unlock the account after that many minutes. By default the setting is 0, but has no meaning because there is no account lockout. A good rule of thumb is 30 minutes, as this is usually an adequate length to thwart a hacker attempt when used with a fairly low Account Lockout Threshold. If you set the value low, valid users will be able to retry logging in to their accounts much more quickly and not hassle you to unlock them, but intruders will also be able to retry attempts more often to gain access to accounts.

- ▲ **Reset Account Lockout Counter After** Configures the number of minutes that must pass between failed logon attempts before the "bad logon" count is reset. The "bad logon" count is also reset on a successful login. By default the setting is 1 with a range of 1 to 99999, but as with Lockout Duration, it has no meaning because there is no account lockout. Keep in mind that an intruder could try a different password every half-hour for days at a time to bypass lockout, so set this value appropriately.

Kerberos Policies

The Kerberos Policies section is where you set policies that control the parameters on Kerberos tickets in the domain. The settings you make here are critical to the functionality and security of the Kerberos services provided by Win2K. For the most part, your policy settings should be consistent with your written policy and any other Kerberos infrastructure you have (if any). It is highly recommended that you leave the default values, unless you know exactly what you are doing. These settings can render a domain, and potentially an entire forest, non-functional.

Kerberos Policies (see Figure 10-3) are used to control security requirements for ticket duration, renewal, and enforcement. They include the following settings:

▼ **Enforce User Logon Restrictions**   Causes the KDC to validate all session ticket requests by checking to see if the user has the appropriate rights on the target computer (that is, the right either to *log on locally* or to *access the computer from the network*). This is optional, because the target computer will also do the check, but this would prevent the issuance of the ticket in the first place if the rights did not exist. There is a slight performance penalty. By default, the policy is enabled.

■ **Maximum Lifetime for User Ticket**   Configures the maximum duration, in hours, for which a user (a.k.a. ticket granting) ticket (TGT) is valid. The value can range from 0–99,999, and a 0 value turns off expiration. By default, the policy is set at 10 hours.

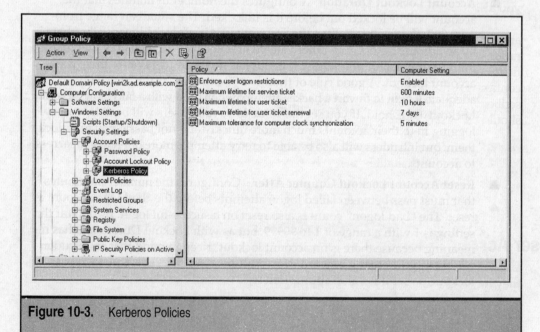

Figure 10-3.   Kerberos Policies

■ **Maximum Lifetime for Service Ticket** Configures the maximum duration, in minutes, for which a service (a.k.a. session) ticket is valid. The value must be greater than 10 minutes, but less than or equal to the Maximum Lifetime for User Ticket setting. The value can range from 0–99,999, and a 0 value turns off expiration. By default, the policy is set at 10 hours.

■ **Maximum Lifetime for User Ticket Renewal** Configures the maximum duration, in days, for which a service ticket or user ticket *cannot* be renewed. By default, the policy is set at 7 days.

▲ **Maximum Tolerance for Computer Clock Synchronization** Configures the maximum deviation, in minutes, between the KDC clock and Kerberos client's clock. If the difference is greater than the value here, tickets are not issued for the client. This is to prevent replay attacks, but if your times are not synchronized, authentication *will* fail. The value can range from 0–99,999, and a 0 value turns off expiration. By default, the policy is set at 5 minutes.

NOTE: Only domain member computers use the Kerberos Policies; standalone and workgroups use NTLM.

Other Group Policy Settings

There are a number of other settings in the Administrative Templates that can be applied via Group Policy that affect the security of user accounts. There are a significant number of them, and their recommended settings will vary by organization. This is just to make you aware of them, as you should evaluate the security ramifications for all of them.

The entire User Configuration tree is very important in securing user accounts. There are over 377 different configuration options that can be configured just in the User Configuration tree alone, so it is well beyond the scope of this book to detail each of them. Let it suffice to say that they are pretty straightforward, but that over 60 percent of them should be configured at some level, so you will need to look over them all. Each of the settings was described in Chapter 9. For the Computer Configuration | Administrative Template tree, you should focus on the following settings (as they relate to users and groups):

▼ **Windows Components** NetMeeting, Internet Explorer, Task Scheduler, and Windows Installer

■ **System** Settings in this container, Logon, Group Policy

▲ **Network** Offline files

User Account Properties

User account properties are set on individual users. Since these are specific to the user, they have nothing to do with Group Policy or local security settings; they are attributes on the user object. You can use the Active Directory Users and Computers tool to administer domain users or the Local Users and Groups tool to administer local users. These tools are described later in the Administration section.

This section will take you through the security-related configurations that can be set for users. There are five configuration tabs in the User Properties that we will cover in depth: General, Account, Profile, Member Of, and Security.

General

The General tab (see Figure 10-4) is used to set general user information. The one setting that is important from a security and management standpoint is the Display Name option. In Win2K, user accounts have both a *display* name and a *logon* name. By default the display name (a.k.a. User Account Full Name) is the user's first name, initial, and last name (as you would see it regularly written). You can change it, but display names must be unique in the database in which they are stored (that is, unique in the SAM if local, or unique in the domain if a domain account). They have to be 64 characters or less, and can only contain alphanumeric and special characters. This is the main name you will see displayed in the Active Directory tools.

Account

The Account tab is used to set a majority of the security settings for the user account, such as User Logon Name, Account Options, Logon Hours, Log On To, Account Is Locked Out, and Account Expires.

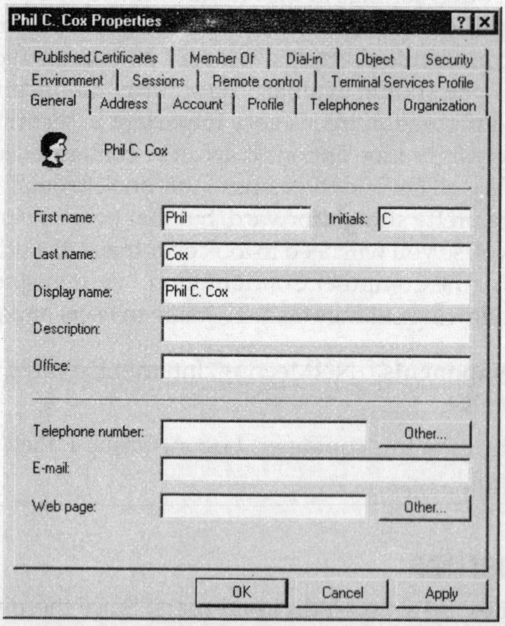

Figure 10-4. User Object Properties General tab

USER LOGON NAME   The user logon name (a.k.a. User Principal Name, UPN) is what is used for authentication. By default, the logon name is a combination of an administrator-set username concatenated with the domain name, thus resulting in a logon name with the form *user@Win2Kdomainname*. When creating logon names for new accounts, make sure to follow a naming scheme. As your site grows, you want to ensure that you are not scrambling to figure out how to name users in a consistent and coherent manner, but you want a naming policy (or scheme) in place before hand. The most commonly used methods use some derivation of the user's full name, such as the user's first name and last initial; first initial and last name; first initial, middle initial, and last name; and so on.

As with display names, local logon names must be unique on a workstation and domain logon names must be unique throughout the domain. The settable portion (that is, user part) of the logon name can be up to 64 characters, but if it is over 20, the down-level WinNT name will be the first 20 characters. The logon names can contain all characters except

   " / \ [ ] : ; | = , + * ? < >

Usernames are stored case-sensitive, but are used with no case sensitivity.

Sometimes it makes sense to make usernames hard to guess. In minimum-security environments, you can create usernames that are the first letter of the first name, middle initial, and last name, such as pcc. In more secure environments where you want to hide usernames from potential intruders, you can set up naming schemes or use cryptic codes that have no logical meaning except to you. Here are some naming schemes; remember to make sure your scheme is not easy to figure out.

PcamSKM990	First letter of the following words: Phil Cox administrative manager Smoothie King Multimedia 990 (start date)
Am0001-990PCC	A coded username: am = administrative manager 0001 = employee number 999 = employee start date PCC = employee initials

ACCOUNT OPTIONS   The Account Options section gives you the ability to control the status of a user account, some authentication characteristics, and account sensitivity. For example, if the User Cannot Change Password option (described in the following list) is not set, users may simply change their existing strong password to something easy to remember. Here are the options that you can set on the dialog box to enforce your password policies and improve security:

▼   **User Must Change Password at Next Logon**   You must create an initial password for any account, but giving this password to a user may compromise security—someone could capture it in an e-mail transmission or overhear it on the phone. This option forces the user to change the initial password and avert any unauthorized logons with the initial password (unless of course the hacker who illegally obtains the password logs in to the account before the user).

■ **User Cannot Change Password**   You may prefer to create a hard-to-guess password for an account. By setting this option, you prevent the user from changing the password to something that is easy to remember or type.

■ **Password Never Expires**   Password history, discussed earlier in the "Password Policies" section, lets you set a password expiration time for user accounts. This option lets you override that expiration time for a specific account.

■ **Store Password Using Reversible Encryption**   This option allows the passwords to be stored in a reversible manner. This has the same effect of the identical setting in the Group Policy Password Policy.

■ **Account Disabled**   You can set this option to disable accounts if a user goes on vacation or on temporary leave. It prevents anyone else from accessing the user account through illegal means.

■ **Smartcard Is Required for Interactive Logon**   You can set this to prevent a user from using a password only to log on to the account, interactively or from a command line. Although the policy name implies that it applies to interactive logons only, it is applicable to both interactive and network logons. It does not apply to remote access logons (see Chapter 16 for details on remote access policies). Microsoft recommends not setting this for any user who will be performing administrative-type commands; it will break some of the administration tools because certain tools require the use of username and password and do not support public key authentication.

■ **Account Is Trusted for Delegation**   This allows a service to gain access to resources on other computers on behalf of the user. See Chapter 11 for details on Kerberos and delegation.

■ **Account Is Sensitive and Cannot Be Delegated**   This allows you to specify that an account is too sensitive (that is, powerful) to allow it to be used in a delegated manner.

■ **Don't Require Kerberos Preauthentication**   This is primarily an option that is to be used if you are using a non-Win2K version of Kerberos for authentication. If you are using a non-Win2K version of Kerberos and it does not support preauthentication, then enable this. See Chapter 11 for details on Kerberos.

▲ **Use DES Encryption Types for This Account**   This option allows you to specify the use of DES as the encryption algorithm.

LOGON HOURS   The Logon Hours option is used to restrict the logon hours during which the user can log on to the domain and connect to a domain controller. Logon Hours can be used to prevent users from logging on to a system after hours when their activities are less likely to be monitored. This option can also thwart hackers from breaking into an account after the rightful user has logged off.

The Logon Hours dialog box pictured here has all hours enabled:

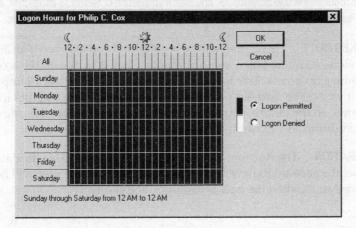

To change the hours, click and drag a box around a specific set of hours, then click Allow or Disallow. If a user doesn't have privileges for a particular time period, black bars do not appear in that period.

LOG ON TO   This option, shown here, is used to specify the NetBIOS names of the computers that the user can log on to. This is a useful security feature, because it forces users to log on to systems where their activities can be physically monitored. It also prevents hackers from logging on to an account from their base of operation, which might be outside your company. Click the radio button for The Following Computers and type in the NetBIOS names of the computers that users can log on to.

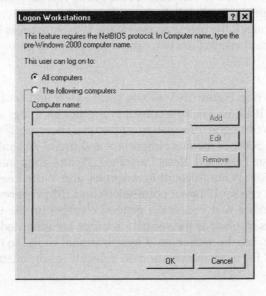

VIP: This requires the use of NetBIOS, and thus if you get rid of NetBIOS altogether, as is the future, this option will become ineffective. This should be considered in a depreciated status.

ACCOUNT LOCKED OUT?   This option will be highlighted and checked if an account locks because there were too many failed logon attempts. Click it to free up the account so that the user can again gain access. This is an indication that someone has attempted to break into an account unless the user simply forgot her password. The user obviously knows the account name, so the culprit may be someone who works near the original account owner. Set up auditing so you can track the activities of suspected users.

ACCOUNT EXPIRATION   The Account Expires option allows you to set the date of account expiration or set the account to never expire. If you set a date, the user will be warned of the pending expiration when the date is less than 30 days away.

Profiles

The Profile tab allows you to specify a logon script and home directory for the user as well as a profile, which includes the environment settings for the user. Profiles let users log on to a familiar environment from other computers in the domain. A user's home directory is where personal files and programs can be stored. If the directory should be located on the computer where the user logs on, click the Local Path button and type the path to the directory. If the directory is on a network server, click Connect and specify the drive letter and path for the directory. These are discussed later in this chapter.

Group Membership

The Member Of tab allows you to view and set the group membership of the user, as well as setting the primary group the user belongs to. This tab allows you to add or remove the specific user from a group. If the user is accessing the Win2K services from a Macintosh or another POSIX-compliant client, then you can set the primary group as well.

Security

The Security tab, shown in Figure 10-5, allows you to view and set the ACLs associated with this user account. It allows you to set object properties for things such as changing the password, Read and Write logon information, and so on. There are 27 general permissions groups that can be set. Some of the most important and useful general permission groups are Full Control, Change Password, Reset Password, Write Group Information, Write Remote Access Information, Write Account Restrictions, and Write Logon Information. On the Advanced tab, you can set 17 object permissions and 152 property permissions.

It is not recommended that you make general changes on the user objects, but on higher-level containers instead, as the security settings are inherited from the container that they are located in. See the section on "Organizational Units" in the Active Directory discussion (Chapter 8) for more information on delegating administration tasks.

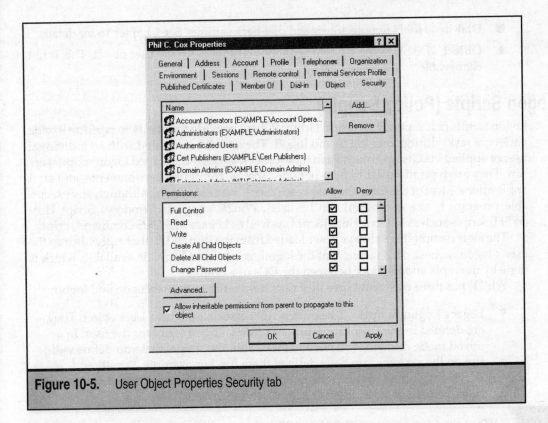

Figure 10-5.   User Object Properties Security tab

The Rest of the Settings

There are ten configuration tabs in the User Properties that we will not cover in depth. Most of the settings are related to information that is normally carried in Microsoft Outlook contact information. Here is a brief list of them and their functions:

▼ **Address**   Holds information about the location of the user, such as street, P.O. box, city, state, and so on.

■ **Telephones**   Holds information about the phone numbers of that user, as well as any notes that you may have.

■ **Organization**   Holds information about the organization the user is in, such as title, department, and company. There is also a link for the manager of the user, but the manager must already be defined as a user.

■ **Remote Control, Environment, Session, and Terminal Services Profile**   Hold settings for the user when using Terminal Server. See Appendix A for details.

■ **Published Certificates**   Holds all public key certificates that are published for the user. See Web Chapter 1 at **www.osborne.com** for more details.

- **Dial-in**   Holds remote access and dial-back settings. See Chapter 16 for details.
- **Object**   Displays the Update Sequence Numbers for the user object. This is not changeable.

Logon Scripts (Policy Scripts)

Logon scripts (a.k.a. policy scripts in Group Policy) provide the ability to perform a wide variety of tasks during user logon and logoff. They can be associated with an individual user or applied via Group Policy. Each time a user logs on, the assigned logon script(s) are run. They are typically used to map network shares, configure environments, and start applications. Most of the time, they are batch files (`.bat` extension), although any executable program (`.exe` extension) can be used. Win2K supports Windows Script Host (WSH) scripts such as VBScript and JScript, as well as Legacy MS-DOS command scripts.

The logon script(s) are always downloaded from the Win2K DC that authenticates the user's logon request. This means that the logon scripts must be made available, which is done by the replication service between the DCs of a domain.

Win2K has three different types of scripts associated with user logon and logoff:

- **Legacy Logon Scripts**   These are scripts associated with a User object. They are defined in the User Properties | Profile | Logon script for the user. In a mixed mode domain, you need to make sure the scripts that you define will run on the systems you have defined them for. For example, Win2K and Win98 know how to run `.vbs` and `.js` scripts natively, whereas they must be embedded in `.bat` files for WinNT and Win95.

VIP: Legacy logon scripts run last, after all GPO, and can override anything that was configured with the User Properties portion of the GPO.

- **Group Policy Logon and Logoff Scripts**   These are scripts associated with a Group Policy Object. They are defined in Group Policy | User Configuration | Scripts.

Using Logon Scripts

Logon scripts can be created with any text editor, and then saved with the appropriate extension. You then assign the scripts to individual users, or to multiple users via GPO. There are several default environment variables that you can use when creating logon scripts:

%HOMEDRIVE%	Local drive letter connected to the user's home directory
%HOMEPATH%	Full path to user's home directory
%OS%	The operating system of the system
%PROCESSOR_ARCHITECTURE%	The processor type of the system

%PROCESSOR_LEVEL%	The processor level of the system
%USERDOMAIN%	Domain the user is authenticated from
%USERNAME%	The username

Controlling with Group Policy

In the Logon/Logoff section of the Group Policy (User Configuration | Administrative Templates | System | Logon/Logoff), you can define parameters that control the way in which scripts are processed for the user:

▼ **Run Logon Scripts Synchronously**   All scripts are run to completion, in the order evaluated, then the user desktop appears. An equivalent option is under the Computer Configuration portion of the Group Policy and has precedence over this setting.

■ **Run Logon Scripts Visible** and **Run Logoff Scripts Visible**   These options run the scripts in a command window.

▲ **Run Legacy Logon Scripts Hidden**   Legacy logon scripts will not be seen running. If you run in this mode and user input is required (say because of a script malfunction or server problem), the script will wait ten minutes before completing.

Best Practice

Use scripts sparingly. When or if you do use them, use Group Policy scripts and avoid using Legacy (that is, user) scripts, and minimize the total number of scripts you use. If you use Legacy scripts, and you process GPO asynchronously (see Chapter 9), then there is no definite order in which the scripts will be run (that is, GPO, then Legacy), and you may have unpredictable results. So if you use Legacy scripts, ensure that processing of Group Policy is synchronous; this will ensure that GPO scripts are processed first, and then Legacy scripts.

Profiles

User profiles are used in conjunction with Group Policy to define the user environment. The user profile resides on each and every computer, and will exist even if you don't use Group Policy. User profiles contain user-specific settings such as video resolution, program items, network connections, printers, desktop settings, and so on. Profiles allow more than one user to have a customized environment on the same computer, since each user has his or her own settings stored in his or her profile.

The profile maintains the state of the desktop between user sessions. That is to say that when users log on to their workstation, they receive the desktop settings as they existed when they logged off. In WinNT, profiles provided a way to administer settings for groups of users. In Win2K, Group Policy accomplishes many of these functions, so the use of profiles as an administrative tool is reduced. Profiles can be set in the Profiles tab of the User Account Properties.

Profile Creation and Storage

The *standard* User Profile is created the first time you log on to a computer, or when you log on to a system and there is no existing profile. All user profiles are created from the Default User profile, which is stored on each and every Win2K computer. The profile is created in a directory, named after the username, in the `%userprofile%\Documents and Settings` directory (usually `C:\Documents and Settings`) on the local computer. The Default User directory and `NTuser.dat` file is the basis for the profile that will be created for the user. The `NTuser.dat` file is the portion of the user profile that is used to configure the Registry on the computer for the user. If any changes are made to the settings that are associated with the profile, they are saved to the local user profile.

Roaming Profiles

A *roaming profile* is a profile that is stored on the profile server and is downloaded to any computer you log into. The administrator will create the profile on the profile server, then when you log on to any computer with the account associated with the roaming profile, that computer will download the profile to its local disk. When you log off, any changes to the profile are then uploaded to the profile on the profile server and thus saved for your next logon. In this manner the profile is available every time you log on to any computer on the network.

If the server is not available, for any reason, the local cached copy of the roaming user profile is used. If the user does not have an already existing profile on the computer, and the server is not available, a new local user profile is created. Note that if the profile is not "downloaded" from the server, say because of a problem, it will not be "saved back" when the user logs off.

Mandatory Profiles

A *mandatory profile* is a regular roaming profile for which changes made during the user's logon session are not saved to the Profile. The mandatory profile performs that same function as a regular profile, with the exception that it will not save changes made by the user to the desktop settings. Users make changes while they are logged on, but when they log off, the changes are not saved to the profile. To create a mandatory profile, you change the extension to `.man`, thus a mandatory user profile would be `Ntuser.man` instead of `Ntuser.dat`.

It is highly recommended that you use Group Policy to customize your user profiles rather than mandatory user profiles. They can be applied to individuals or an entire group of users.

CAUTION: If you use roaming or mandatory profiles, you need to be careful that the video settings that the user has will not damage the settings on the computer that user is logging into.

Managing Profiles

You can do a number of things with user profiles, such as copying, deleting, and changing between local and roaming. All these operations are performed via the User Profiles tab in the System control panel. The COPY command allows you to copy an existing profile to a new location and then change the user associated with the new profile. You can delete or change the profile type from the same tab. To perform these operations, you must be logged on as an administrator to the local computer.

GROUPS

Groups are just collections of users and potentially other groups. There are two types of groups in Win2K: security groups and distribution groups. Security groups are used to grant rights and permissions to resources. When added to a security group, the user obtains the rights and permissions that are already granted to the group. Distribution groups, on the other hand, have no security relationships at all. They are e-mail distribution groups, and thus are only used with e-mail applications (that is, Exchange) to send e-mail to groups of users.

Win2K has default and built-in administrative and user groups. By making a user a member of one of these groups, you automatically grant him or her the rights and permissions assigned to the groups for administering the system or for accessing it for everyday tasks.

We will be focusing on the security groups in this chapter. For our purposes, we will be using the term "group" to refer to a security group.

Type and Scope

There are two terms—type and scope—that need to be understood before pressing on any further. This is important because the term meanings have changed since WinNT.

▼ **Group Type**   Defines whether the group is a security or distribution group.

▲ **Group Scope**   Defines where the group applies, or what used to be the group type in WinNT. People familiar with WinNT will remember that group types were Global or Local.

Group Scopes

As previously described, the scope of a group determines the extent to which the group is applied in the Active Directory. There are three group scopes in the Win2K environment: *Domain Local*, *Domain Global*, and *Universal*. They are described next.

DOMAIN LOCAL   A group using the Domain Local (a.k.a. local) group scope can be used in any ACL in its own domain, and *only* its domain. It can contain members from any domain in the forest, but may not be used in any other domain. A local group allows you to place Domain Users, Domain Local, Global, and Universal groups together. The local group is stored in the domain it is created in, and only replicated in that domain. They do *not* appear in the GC. A good rule of thumb for using local groups is to start membership size as small and use nesting (described later). They are available in both mixed mode and native mode domains.

DOMAIN GLOBAL   A group using the Domain Global (a.k.a. global) group scope can be used in any ACL in the forest, but can only contain members from its own domain. They cannot contain local or universal groups. They can only contain other global groups or users; thus, they are only really usable for cross-domain use. Global groups are stored in the domain they are created in, and only replicated in that domain. They appear in the GC, but their members do not. As a rule of thumb, you should keep the size manageable (that is, a couple thousand) by using nesting. Global groups are available in both mixed mode and native mode domains.

UNIVERSAL   A group using the universal group scope can be used to contain members from any domain in the forest and can be used in any ACL in the forest. Universal groups are stored in the Global Catalog (the group and its members), so replication is an issue. The main goal in using universal groups is to reduce replication traffic. Each time a universal group is updated, the GC servers in every domain need to be updated; this can cause a significant amount of traffic. With this in mind, you should try to keep the membership as static as possible, nest only Domain Local and Domain Global groups in universal groups, and keep the total number of objects in a universal group to as small a number as possible. Although you can put in other universal groups and individual users, it is not recommended. They are only available in native mode domains.

Nesting

While nesting was available in WinNT (Global in local), hierarchical nesting is a new feature of groups in Win2K. It provides the ability to place one group inside of another, and thus gives the ability to mimic a hierarchical structure. When you have a Win2K domain in native mode, it supports group nesting for Universal, Global, and Domain Local groups. There is no technical limitation on how deep you can nest groups, but if you nest them too deep, it will result in a performance hit. This is very similar to the nesting of OUs.

Computer Local Groups

Computer Local groups (CLG) are defined in the local SAM database on Win2K Workstations or member servers. They are only usable on the machine they are defined on. Being in one of these groups gives you access to resources on the local computer, not domain wide. They cannot be nested.

Domain Controller Built-in Local Groups

Built-in Local groups are defined for use only within the domain controllers of a domain. They are not seen on any system that is not a DC for the domain that they are in. Being in one of these groups gives you the rights and permissions the group has on every DC in the domain.

Group Inclusion

There is a definite method for using the groups efficiently. Microsoft likes to call global groups, "export" groups, and local groups, "import" groups, in that global groups are imported into local groups. They leave universal groups out of it, because they are used in special circumstances. Table 10-1 shows the group inclusion rules for a mixed mode domain, and Table 10-2 shows the rules for a native mode domain.

Group Type	Stored In	Contains	Used In
Computer Local	Local SAM	Local user accounts (that is, in local SAM) Domain user accounts Domain Local groups from the domain the system is in	Object ACLs Cannot be used in other groups
Domain Local	Domain portion of the AD	Domain users Domain Global groups from any domain	Object ACLs Computer Local groups
Domain Global	Domain portion of the AD	Domain users from the domain it is in	Object ACLs Any Domain Local group
Universal	N/A	N/A	N/A

Table 10-1.   Mixed Mode Domain Rules

Group Type	Stored In	Contains	Used In
Computer Local	Local SAM	Local user accounts (that is, in local SAM) Domain user accounts Domain Local groups from the domain the system is in	Object ACLs Cannot be used in other groups
Domain Local	Domain portion of the AD	Domain users and Domain Global groups from any domain Domain Local groups from the local domain Any universal group	Object ACLs Computer Local groups Domain Local groups in local domain
Domain Global	Domain portion of the AD	Domain users and Domain Global groups from any domain	Object ACLs Computer Local groups Domain Local groups in local domain Any Domain Global or universal group
Universal	Global Catalog (actually, AD storage is in the domain in which it is created)	Domain users and Domain Global groups from any domain Any universal group	Object ACLs Computer Local groups Domain Local groups in local domain Any universal group

Table 10-2. Native Mode Domain Rules

VIP: If groups have members from other domains, known as *cross-domain membership*, it results in a performance hit. You should minimize this to the greatest extent possible. It should not be minimized such as to lose security, but because of the performance issues, group members from other domains should not be used unless they are needed.

Using Groups

So how do you take advantage of these groups and use them to promote security? You can start by creating very precise global groups that will hold users with very specific job titles and tasks. Then it's easy to set rights and permissions. In WinNT, Microsoft recommended that you assign permissions by placing the user Account in a Global group, then store the global group in a Domain Local group, and store the Domain Local group in the object Permissions (that is, the ACL). This is also referred to as **AGDLP**. *This is still the recommended way in Win2K with a mixed mode domain.*

WinNT Issues

WinNT supports two domain level groups: Domain Local and Domain Global. It is important to use similar group strategies as in mixed mode domains, as NT BDCs will be replicated from the PDC operations master.

NOTE: During migration, WinNT Domain Local will become a Win2K Domain Local, and the WinNT Domain Global will become a Win2K Domain Global.

Native Mode

If you are running a native mode domain, then your options increase significantly. You can do things like making groups based on OU memberships, and then using those groups in a Domain Local group to provide access by OU membership. Another scenario is to use universal groups instead of the global groups in the AGDLP strategy. The total opposite of the AGDLP is to use a total universal group strategy. In this, you would place the user Account in a Universal group, then store the universal group in the object Permissions (that is, the ACL). This is also called an **AUP** strategy. This has some definite drawbacks in terms of replication, as every user and group would be replicated throughout the forest.

Maybe the best strategy is to place the user in global groups, using nesting when you need it, say at the OU level. Then place those global groups in universal groups for use within the forest. Then place the universal (or global from the same domain) in a local group for object permissions.

As you can see, there are a number of different group strategies that you can use. Just be careful not to get too carried away. All this nesting and cross-domain group inclusion comes with a performance price and potentially a security price. Remember, security usually varies inversely with complexity. When you are developing a strategy for using groups, remember to think about OUs. The strategies must be linked. Consistency is key to making things understandable and manageable. If you implement things in a consistent manner, you will win in the end. Think streamlined—enough to get the jobs done, but not too much. Don't get sloppy.

Default Groups

Win2K has a set of default groups that are appropriate for the most common types of system access, but you can create and manage new groups for your specific needs. The default groups fall into two categories: local and domain.

The Local Groups

Throughout this discussion, keep in mind that three types of Win2K computers may exist in a domain (DC, member server, and workstation), and that there are slight differences among the local groups that exist on these systems.

Win2K domain controllers (DCs) have the following Built-in Local groups:

▼ Account Operators

■ Administrators

■ Backup Operators

■ Guests

■ Pre-Windows 2000 Compatible Access

■ Print Operators

■ Replicators

■ Server Operators

▲ Users

Win2K Workstation computers and member servers have the following groups. Note the Power Users group and the absence of DC-related operator groups.

▼ Administrators

■ Backup Operators

■ Guests

■ Power Users

■ Replicators

▲ Users

The rights assigned to each of the groups are discussed later in this chapter. First, each of the groups is discussed along with some security precautions for using the groups.

ACCOUNT OPERATORS GROUP   Members of the Account Operators group have the ability to create user accounts and groups. However, they can change and delete only the accounts and groups that they create. Account operators can also log on to servers, shut down servers, and add computers to the domain. This group has enough power to pose a serious security threat; its membership must be monitored. An unauthorized person who obtains Account Operator status can create and change user accounts.

Note that account operators cannot modify higher privilege groups, or add members to them. Groups such as the Domain Admins global group, the Administrators group, the Account Operators group, the Backup Operators group, the Print Operators group, or the Server Operators group fall into the "can't" touch category.

ADMINISTRATORS GROUP   The Administrators group, which exists on all Win2K computers, has full control of the computer. No other group has such extensive abilities. The Administrator user account gains these rights by being a member of this group, and it can't be removed from the group (this prevents accidental lockouts). In domain environments, administrators manage the configuration of the entire domain.

Even though administrators have full control of a system, they only have access to every file on a server at first. As users start to create files, they become the owners of those files.

Ownership of objects allows the owner to set all permissions and have complete access to the object. A user who creates a file or directory owns it. In contrast, if a member of the Administrators group creates a file or directory, all the members of the Administrators group own it.

BACKUP OPERATORS GROUP   Members of the Backup Operators group have the ability to back up and restore files on any directory in the system, even if they do not have permissions to access the files. Users who have both Backup and Restore rights can read, change, and write any file using the backup and restore APIs. The permissions of this group override other permissions. Normally, a user who creates a directory or file is the owner of that entity and can set permissions, but the Backup Operators group can override these permissions in order to back up the server to tape or other medium.

Obviously, membership in this group must be tightly controlled. A rogue user could steal information from the server, or an industrial spy could convince your backup operator to steal the files for her or grant her access to the account. A hacker who breaks into the account can also take advantage of the rights to steal valuable information, including files that contain passwords and user account information.

Designate only trusted people to this status, and make sure their rights are limited to only those files and directories they need to back up. In addition, log all backup operator activities in the Audit log. Remember that data on backup tapes is not encrypted. Someone with Restore privileges could restore the tape on another Win2K system (such as her personal workstation).

GUESTS GROUP   The Guests group is very similar to the Guest account with regard to its rights and permissions on the system.

PRE-WINDOWS 2000 COMPATIBLE ACCESS   Members of the Pre-Windows 2000 Compatible Access group have the ability to read access to particular user and group object attributes. This group has access to the user and group object attributes that existed in WinNT and that are required by WinNT applications to function with Active Directory.

POWER USERS GROUP   The Power Users group exists on Win2K Workstation computers or member servers. Members of the group have a set of extended rights and privileges that can be considered subordinate to the Administrator rights. They can perform such system administration tasks as

▼ Sharing directories over the network

■ Installing printers and sharing them over the network

■ Creating, modifying, and deleting user accounts (but not Administrative accounts)

■ Adding user accounts to the Power Users, Users, and Guests groups

▲ Performing other tasks such as setting the system's clock and monitoring performance

The typical management procedure for handling user accounts on Win2K Workstations that participate in domains is to add the user's domain account to the Power Users group. Then users have their normal rights on the domain and the rights of the Power Users group on their workstation. Using this technique, domain administrators can decide which users should have Power User status on a particular workstation.

PRINT OPERATORS GROUP   Members of the Print Operators group can manage printers. They have the ability to create, change, and delete how printers are shared in the domain. Print Operators can also log on to servers and shut them down.

REPLICATORS GROUP   Win2K servers on a network can replicate (copy) information among themselves. The contents of one directory can be copied to a similar directory on another server automatically so that information is continually backed up in real time. This group should include Domain User accounts that are allowed to log on to the Replicator services of the primary domain controller and the backup domain controllers in the domain.

SERVER OPERATORS GROUP   Members of the Server Operators group have the ability to create, change, and delete shared printers, shared directories, and files. They can also back up and restore files, format hard disks, change the system time, lock the computer, and shut down the system. Note that the server operator does not have the ability to unlock a *workstation* that has been locked by another user. Only the administrator and the currently logged-on user can unlock a workstation.

To create sublevel administrators to manage domain servers, add users to the Server Operators group. As members of the group, they can shut down servers, share and stop sharing directories, and back up and restore files. However, they cannot change user attributes, add drivers, or take ownership of files.

Because of the extended rights and permissions of this group, you should follow all the security precautions that you follow for all other administrative accounts. Users who are members of this group should have a separate personal account that they log in to for doing normal non-administrative work. Hackers who obtain access to accounts in this group can steal information and perform other malicious activities.

USERS GROUP   Members of the Users group (not to be confused with Domain Users) do not have local or network access rights on servers, but can log on locally at Win2K workstation computers. The rights at workstations include the ability to log on locally, shut down the system, create local groups, and manage the groups that they create. Note that network users gain the ability to log on to servers by being members of the Everyone group, not members of the Users group. Everyone has the Access This Computer from Network right by default on servers. If you remove Everyone from this right, you need to assign a new group of network users to the right.

OTHER GROUPS   The following groups do not have members in the same sense as the groups discussed earlier. Instead, any account that uses the computer in a specific manner will automatically be a member of the group. Note that these groups reflect resource access but do not refer to the privilege level of the user.

- ▼ **Interactive Users**   Any user who only logs on to the computer using an interactive logon.

- ■ **Network Users**   Any user who connects to the computer over the network.

- ■ **Everyone**   Any user who accesses the computer, including interactive and network users. Administrators must pay special attention to the Everyone group. By default it has permissions that may not be appropriate in secure environments. In particular, Guest users have access to all directories available to Everyone, as discussed previously.

- ■ **Creator/Owner**   Any user who creates or takes ownership of a resource.

- ■ **Dial-up**   Any user who is logged on to the system through a dial-up connection.

- ■ **Batch**   Any user who is logged on through a batch queue facility such as the Task Scheduler.

- ■ **Service**   Any user who is logged on as a service.

- ■ **Enterprise Controllers**   All DCs in the Active Directory.

- ▲ **Terminal Server Users**   Any user who is logged on via the Terminal Services server.

Domain Groups

When you set up a domain, several predefined groups are automatically created and placed in the Users folder for Active Directory Users and Computers. When you add a computer to the domain, these groups are then added to the local groups on those computers. These domain groups are described in the following sections.

DOMAIN ADMINS (GLOBAL SCOPE) The Domain Admins group allows its members to manage all aspects of the domain. This includes adding and deleting users, computers, and OUs; setting permissions on any and all objects in the domain; and so on. Throughout this discussion, be sure to differentiate among the *Administrator user* account, the *Administrators local* group, and the *Domain Admins global* group. Though quite different, they are used in concert with OUs to create a hierarchy of administrative control for resources within a domain.

When Win2K is initially set up, the Administrator account is created and made a member of the Administrators local group. This membership is what gives the Administrator account some of its power. Then when the system is added to the domain, the Domain Admins global group is automatically added to the Administrators local group. Because the domain Administrator account is a member of the Domain Admins group, anyone who logs in to the domain Administrator account has administrative rights on the local domain.

If you want to give another user administrative rights in the domain, just add her user account to the Domain Admins global group. You can also put the Domain Admins group into the Administrators local group on systems in other domains to grant the members of the group administrative rights in those domains. To grant a user administrative rights to a Win2K computer that is not a domain controller, add him to the Administrators local group.

DOMAIN USERS (GLOBAL SCOPE) The Administrator account and all new user accounts are automatically added to the Domain Users global group. This group is a member of the Users local group for the domain and the Users local group for every Win2K Workstation computer and member server in the domain. Note that, by default, the Users group itself does not start out with any permissions. Also, on Win2K Workstation computers, the Users group has the right to log on locally at the keyboard of the computer, shut down the system, and create and manage local groups.

DOMAIN GUESTS (GLOBAL SCOPE) The Domain Guests global group has no permissions or rights. It is designed to be used as a group for Guest-type accounts and in reality is hardly ever used. Initially, it contains the Guest user account for the domain.

CERT PUBLISHERS (GLOBAL SCOPE) This group contains all computers that are running an enterprise certificate authority. This allows them to publish certificates for User objects in Active Directory. By default this group is empty until Certificate Services are installed on a computer.

DOMAIN COMPUTERS (GLOBAL SCOPE)   The Domain Computers global group contains all computers that are members of the domain. This group can be used to grant permissions or rights to every computer in the domain. DCs are not members of this group by default, as they have their own special group.

DOMAIN CONTROLLERS (GLOBAL SCOPE)   The Domain Controllers global group contains all DCs in the domain. It is used to grant permissions or rights to every computer in the domain.

GROUP POLICY CREATOR OWNERS (GLOBAL SCOPE)   The Group Policy Creator Owners group permits its members to create new GPOs. The Group Policy Creator Owners group does not give full control to all GPOs in the domain, just the ability to create them. Once they are created, the owner then has full control. By default, only the Administrator account in the domain is a member of this group.

ENTERPRISE ADMINS (GLOBAL—MIXED, UNIVERSAL—NATIVE)   The Enterprise Admins group is defined in the forest root (that is, the first domain created in the forest) and has permissions to create sites and configure subnets in Active Directory directory services. By default, only the Administrator account in the forest root domain is a member of this group. Membership in this group must be restricted to prevent unauthorized modifications to sites and trust relationships. By default, the Enterprise Admins group is granted full control over all objects in a forest.

SCHEMA ADMINS (GLOBAL—MIXED, UNIVERSAL—NATIVE)   The Schema Admins group is defined in the forest root (that is, the first domain created in the forest), and has permissions to modify the directory schema. By default, only the Administrator account in the forest root domain is a member of this group. Membership in this group must be restricted to prevent unauthorized modifications to the schema. If the schema is corrupted, the entire directory will stop functioning.

Primary Group

There are certain services that require a Primary Group indication. The POSIX and Macintosh are two services that are supported by Win2K that require that you have this set. The group must have a global or universal scope and by default, is the Domain Users group for users and Domain Computers for computers.

Group Review

For security reasons, the members of groups must be reviewed on a regular basis. Because global/universal groups can be added to local groups, thereby obtaining the rights and privileges of the local groups, some members of those groups may obtain inappropriate access rights. For example, assume a former member of your management team moves to another department in another domain. If that person is a member of a global group that is added to your local Administrators group, she will gain administrative rights that might be inappropriate in her new job, especially since she knows a lot about your department.

You might consider some users in other domains untrustworthy. One approach is to remove the user from the global group in the other domain if you have permissions to do so. You could also create a new global group with only appropriate users, or remove the global group from the local group and add only the accounts of users that should have access to the local group.

It's a good idea to keep an active document of the global groups that are available on the network and of the lists of members for those global groups. Fully document the rights and permissions available to all groups.

USER RIGHTS

A *right* is an authorization to perform some action on a system. These actions are often related to tasks that system administrators need to do, but there are some basic rights that all users need in order to access a system. They can be assigned to either users or groups, but are mostly effective with groups. They give the members of a group the access they need to perform management tasks or simply to access a system as a normal user. You need to know about rights if you are trying to figure out the access levels of local groups and if you need to grant special rights to your own custom groups. You can configure user rights on any of the LSDOU containers. They are defined as part of the Local Policy in the GPO that is associated with the LSDOU.

Table 10-3 describes the standard user rights for Win2K and how these rights are implemented in Win2K Server and Win2K Workstation. Note that Win2K Workstation computers have a Power Users group but do not have the Server Operators group, Account Operators group, nor the Print Operators group, which are server-oriented management groups.

If you study Table 10-3, you'll see that the rights assigned to groups make sense. If you need to grant a user a right, you should add her to a group that already has the right rather than grant her a right directly.

Rights	Description	Groups That Have This Right by Default
Access this computer from network (SeNetworkLogon Right)	Allows a user to connect to the computer from the network (a.k.a. a Network logon).	Everyone, Administrators, Power Users

Table 10-3. User Rights Default Assignments

Rights	Description	Groups That Have This Right by Default
Act as part of the operating system (SeTcbPrivilege)	Allows a user or group to run a process as a trusted part of the operating system. The LocalSystem account has this as a built-in right.	None
Add workstations to a domain (SeMachineAccount Privilege)	Allows the user to add a computer to the domain he or she has the right in.	Authenticated Users
Back up files and directories (SeBackupPrivilege)	Allows the user or group to use the NTFS backup application programming interfaces (APIs) to bypass normal file and directory permissions to back up the files.	Administrators, Backup Operators, Server Operators, Power Users
Bypass traverse checking (SeChangeNotify Privilege)	Allows the user or group to traverse folders for which they may have no access, while attempting to get at a child object that they do have access for. This does not allow them to view files in those directories, just pass though them.	Everyone, Administrators, Authenticated Users
Change the system time (SeSystemTimePrivilege)	Allows the user or group to set the system time of the computer.	Administrators, Server Operators, Power Users
Create a token object (SeCreateTokenPrivilege)	Allows a user or group to use the **NtCreateToken()** API call to create an access token.	Administrators

Table 10-3.   User Rights Default Assignments *(continued)*

Rights	Description	Groups That Have This Right by Default
Create permanent shared objects (SeCreatePermanent Privilege)	Allows a user or group to create an object in the Win2K object manager space. By default, processes that run in Kernel mode have this privilege.	None
Create a pagefile (SeCreatePagefile Privilege)	Allows the user or group to create and/or change the size of a pagefile.	None
Debug programs (SeDebugPrivilege)	Allows the user or group to attach a debugger to any process that is running on the system.	Administrators
Deny access to this computer from network (SeDenyNetworkLogon Right)	Prohibits a user or group from performing a Network logon.	None
Deny local logon (SeDenyInteractive LogonRight)	Prohibits a user or group from performing an Interactive logon.	None
Deny logon as a batch job (SeDenyBatchLogon Right)	Prohibits a user or group from performing a batch-type logon.	None
Deny logon as a service (SeDenyServiceLogon Right)	Prohibits a user or group from performing a Service-type logon.	None
Enable computer and user accounts to be trusted for delegation (SeEnableDelegation Privilege)	Allows the user or group to change the Trusted for Delegation setting on a user or computer object in the AD. This has great impact on Kerberos.	Administrators

Table 10-3.   User Rights Default Assignments *(continued)*

Rights	Description	Groups That Have This Right by Default
Force shutdown from a remote system (SeRemoteShutdown Privilege)	Allows a user or group to shut down a computer over the network.	Administrators, Server Operators, Power Users
Generate security audits (SeAuditPrivilege)	Allows a user or group to create a process that can generate entries in the security log.	None
Increase quotas (SeIncreaseQuota Privilege)	Allows a user or group to create a process that can increase the processor quota for another process.	Administrators
Increase scheduling priority (SeIncreaseBasePriority Privilege)	Allows a user or group to create a process that can increase the execution priority of another process.	Administrators
Load and unload device drivers (SeLoadDriverPrivilege)	Allows a user or group to install and uninstall Plug and Play (PnP) device drivers. This is not applicable to non PnP drivers.	Administrators
Lock pages in memory (SeLockMemoryPrivilege)	Allows a user or group to create a process that can keep data in physical memory, thus no paging occurs.	None
Log on as a batch job (SeBatchLogonRight)	Allows a user to log on by using a batching facility.	Administrators
Log on locally (SeInteractiveLogonRight)	Allows a user to perform an Interactive logon.	None

Table 10-3.   User Rights Default Assignments *(continued)*

Rights	Description	Groups That Have This Right by Default
Log on as a service (SeServiceLogonRight)	Allows a user to log on as a service. The LocalSystem account has this as a built-in right.	Administrators, Account Operators, Backup Operators, Print Operators, Server Operators (also Everyone on Workstations)
Manage auditing and security log (SeSecurityPrivilege)	Allows a user or group to manage the audit and security logs (that is, clearing them). It also allows the user or group to set object access auditing options.	Administrators
Modify firmware environment values (SeSystemEnvironment Privilege)	Allows a user or group to perform modifications to the system environment variables.	Administrators
Profile a single process (SeProfileSingleProcess Privilege)	Allows a user or group to monitor the performance of non-system processes, usually with the Performance Monitor.	Administrators
Profile system performance (SeSystemProfile Privilege)	Allows a user or group to monitor the performance of system processes, usually with the Performance Monitor.	Administrators
Remove computer from docking station (SeUndockPrivilege)	Allows the user or group to undock a computer using the Eject PC option on the Start menu.	Administrators

Table 10-3.   User Rights Default Assignments *(continued)*

Rights	Description	Groups That Have This Right by Default
Replace a process-level token (SeAssignPrimaryToken Privilege)	Allows a parent process to replace the access token on one of its child processes.	None
Restore files and directories (SeRestorePrivilege)	Allows the user or group to use the NTFS restore application programming interfaces (APIs) to bypass normal file and directory permissions to restore files and directories.	Administrators, Backup Operators, Server Operators, Power Users
Shut down the system (SeShutdownPrivilege)	Allows a user or group to shut down the local computer.	Administrators, Backup Operators, Account Operators, Server Operators, Print Operators, Power Users (also Users on Workstations)
Synchronize directory service data (SeSynchAgentPrivilege)	Allows a user or group to perform directory synchronization tasks. Also allows for a service to perform them as well.	None
Take ownership of files or other objects (SeTakeOwnership Privilege)	Allows a user or group to take ownership of any object with an ACL, thus anything with an "ownership" attribute, typically files and directories.	Administrators

Table 10-3. User Rights Default Assignments *(continued)*

NOTE: The LocalSystem account has almost every right on the local system.

Keep in mind that rights are slightly different on Win2K Workstation computers. A Power Users group exists in which users can create user accounts and modify or delete only the accounts that they create. Power users can also create local groups but modify or delete only the groups they create.

Also remember that rights apply to the individual system, for either the domain or a local computer. Rights may be passed via the Group Policy, but they are applied and evaluated on the local system. Permissions, on the other hand, apply to specific objects. Rights will often override the permissions set on objects. This is true in the case of the Backup Operator, which has the right to back up even files on which the owner has revoked access to all users.

In a secure environment, make sure that the Everyone group and the Guests group are not assigned the Log On Locally and Shut Down the System rights. The first option would allow anyone to log on at the computer, where he would have more resources available to perform malicious activities. The latter option would allow someone to shut down a server and deny service to others.

Some Caveats on Rights

The following rights have a high degree of security risk associated with them. Some of them can be used to place processes in the trusted part of the operating system, while others can be used to launch a denial of service attack. Most of them can be used in one manner or another to totally subvert the security of the system. It is important that you limit the assignment of these rights to only those users and groups that must have them. The rights are:

▼ Act as part of the operating system
■ Create a token object
■ Add workstations to a domain
■ Back up files and directories
■ Change the system time
■ Debug programs
■ Enable computer and user accounts to be trusted for delegation
■ Increase quotas
■ Increase scheduling priority
▲ Load and unload device drivers

AUTHENTICATION, AUTHORIZATION, AND AUDITING

The authentication, authorization, and auditing (the 3 A's) that apply to user and group security are the same as those that apply to the OS. This is because users and groups are objects in the AD or local SAM, and thus are implemented and protected by the AD and local system protections. Thus the same mechanisms that are used to control the 3 A's for Win2K are applicable to managing users and groups.

Authentication

Because users and groups, as well as the configurations that control them (Group Policy and Local Policy), exist as objects in the AD or local SAM, any access of those objects is subject to authentication of the user who is requesting the access. Both the AD and the system use integrated Win2K authentication. This will be a Kerberos authentication by default, but can be any authentication method supported by the Win2K system that you are connecting to or logged in on.

Authorization

Users and groups are just objects in the AD or SAM, and their configurations are either in Group Policies or Local System Policy, and thus are protected by ACLs assigned to the objects. By default, only Domain Admins, Account Operators, Power Users, and the System accounts can manage user accounts (the Account Operators has limited management ability at that). If you want to allow a user or group to be able to manage user accounts, you will first have to determine what level you want them to have. If you want to give them full control over all users and groups in the domain, then add them to the Domain Admins group. If you want them to have a lesser level, then your best bet is to make an OU for the resources that you want to manage, and then create a new group with the permissions and rights that you want and add the user or group to that.

For example, the illustration below shows that the user pcc is a member of the Domain Admins group, which gives him the ability to manage all aspects of the domain. This includes all users and groups in the domain. The user pbh has been placed in the SalesAdmin group, which was given full control over the SalesOU. Thus, pbh can manage all aspects of the SalesOU, which includes users and groups.

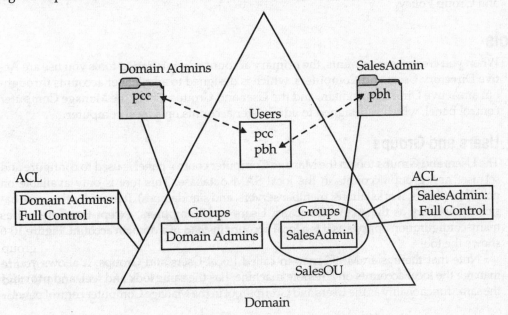

Auditing

Just like authentication and authorization, auditing is something that happens integral to the Win2K OS and is not something that is set separately. The user and group auditing occurs just like file system auditing; you enable auditing on objects, then you set the SACL on the objects that you want audited. The major user- and group-related audit settings to have configured are

▼ Audit of account management

■ Audit account logon events

▲ Audit logon events

The audits will end up in the Security EventLog or the Directory Service EventLog. Please see Chapter 13 for details on setting up auditing in Win2K.

NOTE: The auditing system only tells you what user accounts were used for the audited events. If someone has misappropriated an account, you might wrongly think the owner of that account is responsible for unauthorized activities.

ADMINISTRATION

This section details the basic administration of the user accounts and groups. It will cover the setup and management of accounts and groups and the tools used for those purposes. We will also cover some rudimentary discussion on using groups in concert with OUs and Group Policy.

Tools

When you create user accounts, the primary account administration tools you use are Active Directory Users and Computers, which is designed to administer accounts throughout an Active Directory domain, and the User and Groups tool in the Manage Computer control panel, which is designed to administer accounts on a local computer.

Users and Groups

The Users and Groups tool in the Manage Computer control panel is used to configure and set user and group accounts in the local SAM database. This tool is only available on non-DCs (that is, workstations, member servers, and standalones). It provides the same basic functionality as the Active Directory Users and Computers, except there are not as many configuration options as it is a local account instead of a domain account. Figure 10-6 shows the tool.

Note that there is an MMC snap-in called Local Users and Groups. It allows you to manage the local accounts on a remote machine, has the same look and feel, and provides the same functionality as the Users and Groups tool in the Manage Computer control panel.

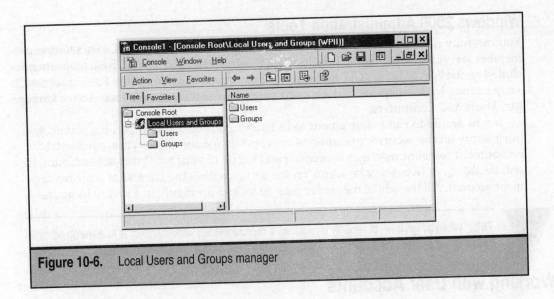

Figure 10-6. Local Users and Groups manager

Active Directory Users and Computers

The Active Directory Users and Computers snap-in (Figure 10-7) is used to manage the users, groups, and other things like OUs for domains in the forest. By default it is in the Start | Programs | Administrative Tools section on every DC. It can also be added to any MMC by adding the snap-in.

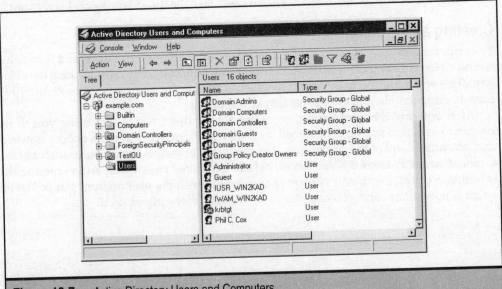

Figure 10-7. Active Directory Users and Computers

Windows 2000 Administration Tools

You can fully manage remote servers from a computer running Win2K Workstation or member server by installing the Windows 2000 Administration Tools. These tools are included on the Win2K Server CD, in the AdminPak.msi file located in the i386 directory. They include MMC snap-ins that are used to manage servers, such as the Active Directory Users and Computers.

If you decide to run management tools from a computer other than the server, you must apply all the security precautions appropriate for servers to your administrative computer. If someone manages to access it and log on to your administrative account, he will be able to do whatever he wants on the server within the context of your management account. All the while, the server may be locked up tightly in a secure location.

TIP: When a high level of security is required, a recommended security policy is to allow no administrators to log on from the network; instead, have them log on only at a server console.

Working with User Accounts

This section covers administrative tasks related to user accounts, such as creating, copying, disabling, deleting, setting account policy, viewing effective policy, and changing properties. You can perform these operations on the local or domain level—the process is the same, but the tools are different. We will be covering the domain accounts, that is using the Active Directory Users and Computers administration tool instead of the local Users and Groups management tool, but will note any major differences in the local tasks.

The best way to understand this is to do an example. We will walk through adding Tom Sheldon to the example.com domain. Then we will take the time to configure his account.

Creating a User Account

To create the new user account in the domain, select the Users container, and then select Action | New | User (note that the Action items can be accessed by right-clicking the object also). This will bring you to the screen in which you fill in the information (see Figure 10-8), remembering that the User logon names are important.

After entering the information, press the Next button, which will bring you to the password selection and options screen, as shown in Figure 10-9. Enter a good password, and potentially any of the restrictions that you want to put on the account, such as User Cannot Change Password if you have machine-generated passwords. After entering this information, press Next, and you are prompted to finish the user account setup. The account is now set up, and you can start to configure other options on it.

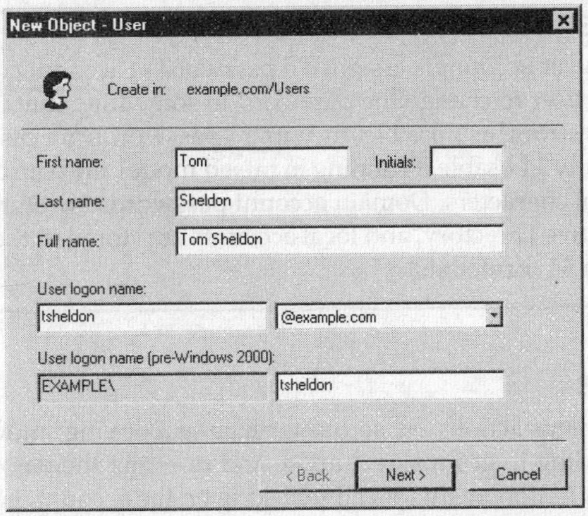

Figure 10-8.   New Object - User screen

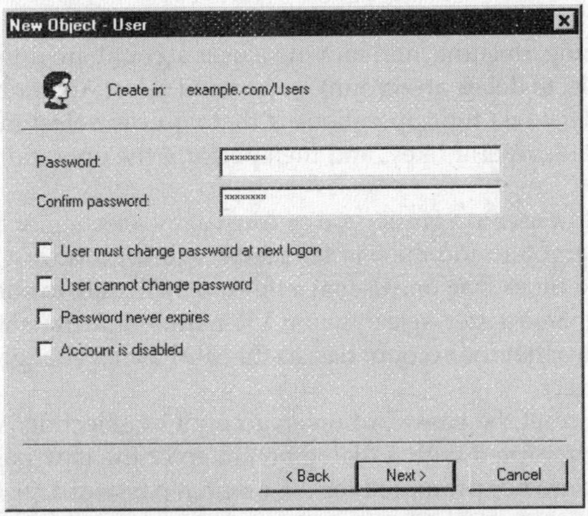

Figure 10-9.   Password selection and options screen

A Note on User Account Password Strength

By default, each user account is assigned a password at account creation. You want to encourage the user to change the password to something that is a hard-to-guess password and as strong as possible. In Win2K, passwords are case-sensitive, up to 104 characters (only 14 usable if running in mixed mode), and can contain alpha-numeric and symbol characters. Domain account passwords are stored in the domain portion of the Active Directory, and local accounts are stored in the local SAM database (see Chapter 11 for details).

Account Actions

You can perform many actions on accounts, such as copying, moving, disabling, enabling, deleting, adding to groups, renaming, and resetting the password. These are all done by clicking the Action menu (or right-clicking on the account on which you are performing the action).

Copying an account is done by selecting the account you want to copy and then selecting Action | Copy. This creates a new user, copying information from the selected user. The settings associated with the Account Options, Account Expires, Profiles, and Members Of options are copied to the new account; all the other information will be default settings. You would use this to configure template accounts and use them to add users that require certain configurations.

Disabling, enabling, deleting, and moving a user account are done in much the same manner. For example, to delete an account, you would select Action | Delete. The one interesting fact about the last four operations is that you can select multiple accounts by holding down the CTRL or SHIFT key, and then perform the operation on all the selected accounts.

If you want to add a user to a group, you can do that by selecting Action | Add Members to Group. This allows you to add the selected user(s) to one group at a time. You can select multiple users to add more than one user at a time, but still only to one group at a time.

If you want to rename a user, select Action | Rename. Note that this will do nothing to the security associates that the account has, as the SID has not changed, just the name associated with the object.

Finally, you can reset the password on an account by selecting Action | Reset Password. You will be prompted with a dialog box to enter the new password. By using a password reset, you are not prompted for the original password, just the new one.

Setting Account Policies

The best bet for setting Account Policies is to set them from the GPOs linked to the domain. As discussed earlier, there are just too many settings to look at, so we will look at an example of setting the Logon/Logoff policies to disable the Run and RunOnce registry values.

Select the Disable the Run Once List policy in the User Configuration | Administrative Templates | System | Logon/Logoff section of the Group Policy. You can then choose to keep it not configured, enable it, or disable it. You would then do the same for the Disable Legacy Run List policy. Figure 10-10 shows the resulting GPO.

It is interesting to note some of the other settings in this section, such as Disable Lock Computer and Disable Logoff, which seem to be almost anti-security, in that the ability to lock the computer when you leave it, as well as allowing users to log off of a system when they are done with it, are usually associated with "good" security practices.

Viewing Effective Policies

Once you have spent the time to actually define and configure the policies for a user, it is nice to be able to see how they actually flow down to the local user on the system. One way of doing this is to log on as the user you are potentially testing, and use the Local Security Policy tool (select Start | Programs | Administration Tools | Local Security Policy) to view the *effective* policy at the local machine.

If we look at the Local Security Policy | Password Policy (Figure 10-11), we will see that on this particular computer, there is no password history defined on the local computer, but the effective policy is that one password is kept in history. This shows us that on the domain that this computer is a member of, there is a GPO that has the Enforce Password History value set to 1. You can use the Local Security Policy tool to look at Account Policies, Local Policies, Public Key Policies, and IP Security Policies as well.

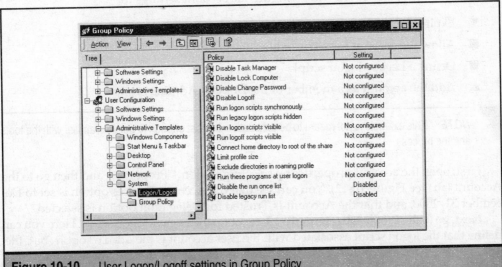

Figure 10-10. User Logon/Logoff settings in Group Policy

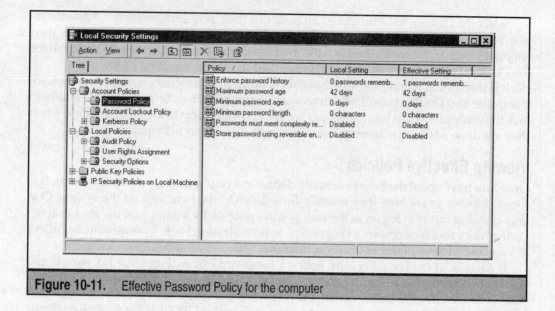

Figure 10-11.   Effective Password Policy for the computer

Changing Account Properties

The specific settings are described in the "User Account Properties" section earlier in this chapter. In this section, we will continue with our Tom Sheldon account to show how we would set the properties. We will configure the account settings to

▼ Expire the account on Dec 31, 2000

■ Allow the account to be trusted for delegation

■ Define a Legacy logon script

▲ Add the account as a member of the Domain Admins group

NOTE: This example is not meant to be exhaustive, but just enough to get you familiar with the tools and the process.

First, open the account properties by selecting Action | Properties, and then go to the Account tab (see Figure 10-12). You can see that the Account Expires option is set to December 31, 2000, and that the Account Is Trusted for Delegation option is selected.

Next, go to the Profile tab (Figure 10-13) to set up the Legacy logon script. Here you can define that the logon script associated with the user account is the `adminlogon.bat` file. The scripts are located in the `SYSVOL` share on the DC for the domain the account is in.

Next, go to the Member Of tab (Figure 10-14) to set up groups that Tom is a member of. By default, every domain user will have the Domain Users group listed here. Since you want to add Tom to the Domain Admins group, click the Add button to add the Domain Admins group here. Figure 10-14 shows the resulting group membership for the user.

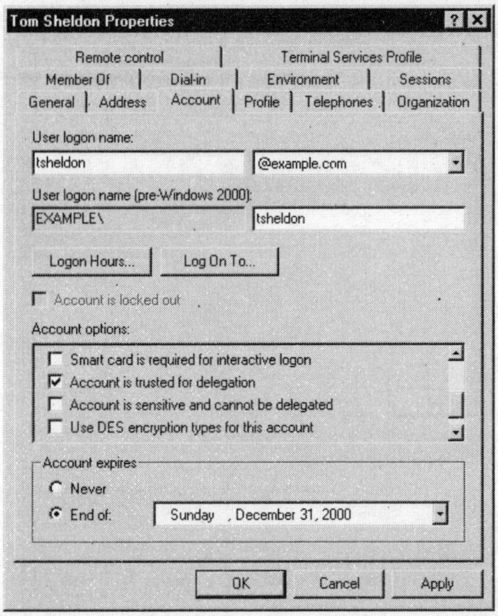

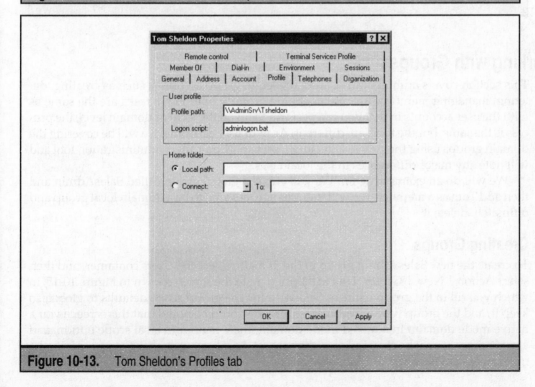

Figure 10-12.   Tom Sheldon's Account Properties tab

Figure 10-13.   Tom Sheldon's Profiles tab

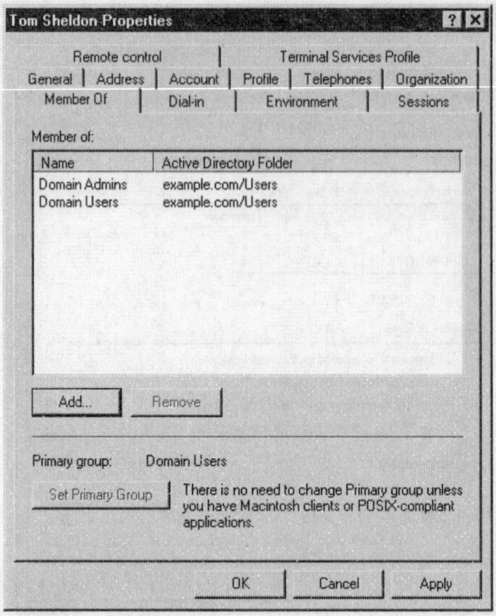

Figure 10-14. Tom Sheldon's Member Of tab

Working with Groups

This section covers administrative tasks related to group accounts, such as creating, deleting, managing membership, and changing group scope. These tasks are the same as with the user accounts in that you can perform them on the local or domain level; the process is the same, but the tools are different. As with user accounts, we will be covering the domain groups using the Active Directory Users and Computers administration tool and will note any major differences in the local tasks.

We will do an example again. We will create a global group called SalesAdmin and then add Tom as a member. We will then change its scope to be a domain local group and ultimately delete it.

Creating Groups

To create the new SalesAdmin group in the domain, select the Users container, and then select Action | New | Group. This will bring you to the screen shown in Figure 10-15, in which you fill in the group name as SalesAdmin. The group scope defaults to global, so keep it, and the group type is a security group. It should be noted that this screen is for a native mode domain. In a mixed mode domain, there is no universal scope option, and group scopes cannot be changed once they are set. Local groups only have you specify the name; there are no scope or type settings.

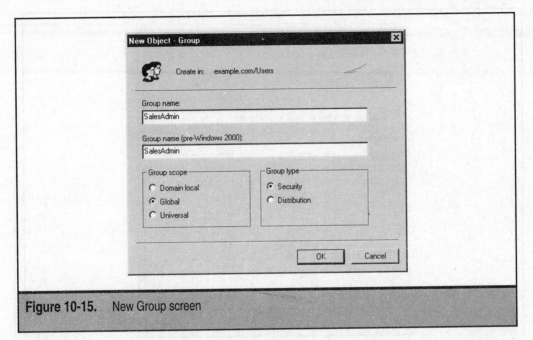

Figure 10-15. New Group screen

After entering the information, press the OK button, which will complete the group account setup. Now we can manage the group by double-clicking it to bring up the Properties dialog box (Figure 10-16). The tabs allow you to manage different aspects of the group:

▼ **General** Manage descriptive information, change the group scope, change the group type, and add any notes that you want to make on the group.

■ **Members** Manage what users and groups are members of this group.

■ **Member Of** Manage what groups this group is a member of.

▲ **Managed By** Allows you to link an account to the management of this group. This is only for informational purposes and provides no special control over the group.

MANAGING MEMBERSHIP WITH RESTRICTED GROUPS You normally manage group membership with the Members tab, but there is another way. For groups that are *very* security-sensitive (that is, Domain Admins or Enterprise Admins), you may want to ensure that the membership of those groups is mandated in a automated manner. You can do this with the Restricted Groups configuration in the Group Policy.

To add a group to the Restricted Groups policy, edit the GPO (see Chapter 9), and then select the Restricted Groups option in the Security Settings section of the Computer Configuration tree. Select Action | Add Group to add the group that you want to manage. This will add the group to the policy, and now you can double-click it to configure the memberships. Figure 10-17 shows that the Domain Admins group in the example.com domain *contains* the user accounts Administrator and tsheldon. It *also* shows that it is a *member of* the Enterprise Admins group. Restricted Groups are only valid for domain groups; they cannot manage local groups.

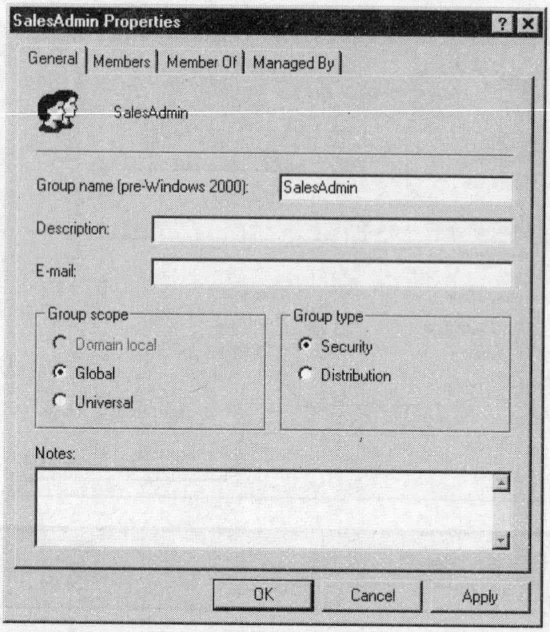

Figure 10-16. SalesAdmin Properties dialog box

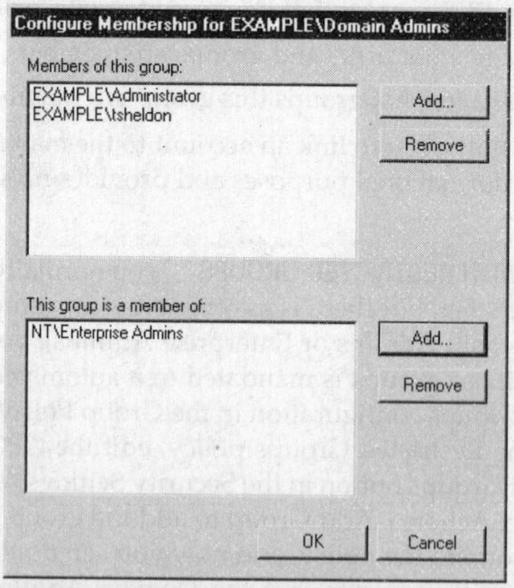

Figure 10-17. Domain Admins Restricted Group Policy

VIP: Restricted Groups are arguably the best way to maintain membership in groups with high security functions and those with strict membership requirements. But you need to ensure that you don't mess up group membership with them. They *will* remove any group that is not listed. This is an easy way to lock yourself out of a system.

Account Actions

You can rename, move, or delete groups in the same manner you did user accounts—using the Action menu or right-clicking the group on which you are performing the action.

If you want to rename a group, select Action | Rename to change the group name. Just as with user accounts, this will do nothing to the security associates that the group has, as the SID has not changed, just the name associated with it. Deleting and moving a group is done in much the same manner by selecting Action and then selecting Delete or Move. You can select multiple groups for moves and deletes.

Group Creation Pointers

When setting up accounts and groups, be sure to identify all of the requirements that users have of the system and create accounts accordingly. The following steps outline the general procedure for creating groups:

1. Create local groups with access to the object, such as directories that hold programs or devices (for example, printers).

2. Grant appropriate rights to the group.

3. Create one or more global or universal groups that should have access to the object.

4. Add users to the global or universal groups.

5. Add the global or universal groups to the local groups in any of the domains or computers where the users in the global group should have access to resources.

6. If you no longer want a user to have access to a resource, remove her account from the global or universal group. If you no longer want all the members of a global or universal group to have access to resources assigned to a local group, remove the global or universal group from the local group.

When designing and creating your group hierarchy, think of global and universal groups in terms of the departments, workgroups, and/or divisions of your company. This will help you create meaningful groups that correspond appropriately to the resources of the network. For example, you could create a management group that has access to directories that hold reporting information throughout the network. Because some of those directories might exist in other domains, you would want to create a global group for the managers.

Another example might be the need to allow a user in a domain to administer some Win2K computers but not others. To do this, you would create an OU in the domain in which you could place the computers you wanted the user to admin. Then you would create a global or universal group called something like WSAdmins. In the GPO on the OU, you could use the Restricted Groups setting to make the WSAdmins group a member of the workstation's Administrators local group, which would give you full control over the computers. To add additional administrators, you would just add them to the WSAdmins group. Then, when you want to remove the ability, you just remove the WSAdmins group from the Restricted Groups on the OU.

THREE KEYS TO USING GROUPS FOR GENERAL ADMINISTRATION   There are three keys to a successful administration strategy:

1. Use group policy to set configurations and rights.

2. Use OUs to assign different levels of administration hierarchy for delegation.

3. Use groups to assign different levels of permissions and authorization on the OUs.

Working with Rights

User rights are defined in the Group Policy | Local Policies node for the SDOU and the Local Security Policy | Local Policies node for local. These can be configured for the LSDOU; see Chapter 9 for details on Group Policy. You should note that you can configure local policies and save them and then import them into a SDOU Group Policy.

You can configure user rights in one of two manners: globally or locally. *Global* configuration refers to setting the rights on an SDOU; *local* refers to setting it locally on that system. Remember that there are precedence rules, discussed in Chapter 9, which determine which settings actually get applied.

Setting User Rights Policies

To configure User Rights policies on an SDOU, open the GPO you are administering, then select Computer Configuration | Windows Settings | Local Policies | User Rights Assignments. Now you can manage any and all user rights that will be applied via this GPO. To configure a specific user's rights, double-click it, select Define These Policy Settings, and then add the groups that you want to have the right.

As described a bit earlier, you can select Local System Policy | Local Policies | User Rights Assignments to configure the local settings on a single system.

RECAP

Administering user rights is pretty straightforward, with the exception of getting the Group Policy settings initially configured for the User Configuration tree. After that, most of the administration has to deal with groups and using them effectively to distribute rights and permissions.

As you can see, there are a number of different group strategies that you can use. The thing you have to watch for is getting too carried away. All this nesting and cross-domain group inclusion comes with a performance price. When you are developing a strategy for using groups, *remember to develop the strategy using Group Policy and OUs as well*. The strategies must be linked. Consistency is key to making things understandable and manageable. If you implement things in a consistent manner, you will win in the end. Think streamlined. Enough to get the jobs done, but not too much. Don't get sloppy.

The following are some "best practices" that should be applied when creating and using users and groups in Win2K:

▼ Use strong authentication when possible.

■ Enable Account Policies such as password aging and account lockout.

■ Assign rights on a group basis, not to individual users.

■ Assign rights as high in the group hierarchy as possible. This maximizes the use of inheritance and nesting.

■ Validate high privilege group membership, such as Enterprise Admins, using Restricted Groups.

▲ Use the "least privilege" rule when adding users to groups and granting groups certain rights. You only want to allow the "least" amount of access that a user requires to accomplish his or her function and no more. The granting of excess privileges has a tendency to lead to security or administrative problems.

CHAPTER 11

Logon and
Authentication

"Trust does not exist in a blind alley."

—*Dallas N. Bishoff*

This chapter brings several of the other chapters together. It provides information on how Windows validates attempts to gain access—how Win2K provides the mechanisms to keep the wrong people out and how the same mechanisms allow the right people to access the resources you want. To do this, Win2K has to have a way to create trust. If you're going to trust Win2K to manage your information, this section will help you understand whether your trust is misplaced, or well founded.

IN THE BEGINNING

Before anyone can access your Win2K resources—even anonymous access to your Web site—an authentication process has to happen. Most system administrators never really give this much consideration; they just take the default implementation options, set up the permissions for access control—assuming that they didn't just leave "everyone" with "full control"—and never think about whether they are using appropriate authentication mechanisms. You may not fit into this category, but you probably know someone who has a system configured without much thought about authentication. This section will help you understand what decisions you need to reflect on regarding authentication, including the what, why, and when, as well as how authentication relates to Win2K security.

Authentication Today

On a daily basis, and in many different ways, you are authenticated in society. When you greet friends, they respond with your name because they recognize you. You have to present a driver's license when you are paying by personal check. Your ATM transaction requires you to have an ATM card and remember your personal identification number (PIN). You enter a building and a guard asks you for identification. Computer systems provide similar challenges to users and have technical mechanisms to process your attempt to gain access to system objects and resources.

Computer-based authentication is not as simple as it used to be. In the legacy days, we had centralized systems, the users worked inside the building, and very few people had access to a computer terminal. Today, we have highly distributed heterogeneous systems accessed from inside and outside of the galaxy by employees, business partners, customers—even my dog can attempt to use the computer. The face of the modern networks is constantly changing.

So, to protect you from my dog, Win2K provides some excellent ways to support authentication. It does this by supporting various forms of a challenge-response process. It includes mechanisms for the parties to validate each other, and some of the authentication processes even provide ways to ensure integrity. However, the different authentication processes are not appropriate for use in all cases, and you need to make choices. Really, you need to make two choices.

Identification and Authentication (I&A)

Generally, Microsoft simply uses the term "authentication" instead of the more proper terms "identification and authentication." Technically, this is inaccurate and it limits the considerations that are appropriate to address both areas. *Identification* is essentially how the users will present themselves—their credentials—to Win2K, which you control. After which, *authentication* is the mechanism that Win2K will use to validate the identity of the user using the credential presented, which you can also control. They are two separate formal decisions that dictate how you configure your Win2K environment.

Win2K requires users to identify themselves. It may be a fairly common method—a standard user ID with a password—or the Win2K system may be configured to accept a smartcard as the only form of credential. It may be configured so that a user can use a password when accessing the network from the inside, but the same user must present PKI credentials when accessing the network remotely. It may allow anonymous access—which is still authenticated—to browse a corporate public Web site, but may require a two-factor security token authentication process to access the internal intranet site.

Regardless of the identification method that is configured, you still have to determine what will be the appropriate authentication mechanism to evaluate user identity, validate their credentials, and determine whether access will be allowed. When an individual enters a user ID and password, will the system use NTLM, or does it require Kerberos to authenticate the user? Does the system have a trusted third-party SSPI mechanism installed? Is Win2K using its own PKI Certificate Authority, or will the identity of the user be validated using an external Certificate Authority? You also need to understand how the identification and authentication process is tied into your authorization controls—like the Windows 2000 Access Control Lists built into NTFS.

The Relationship to Authorization

Authorization, of course, is the level of permissions a user has to interact with the system objects and resources. However, the system first has to go through the identification and authentication process. If the system doesn't know who the user is and what role or groups the user belongs to, how can the system determine what security token to issue, and how will the user access the objects and resources that you intend to make available to them? Surprise! The system won't know. The user will not get access—and now you know why we have this chapter.

Of course, successful identification and authentication does not imply or require communication with the system access controls. For instance, you can have a firewall issue a challenge to a user attempting to access a Web site. The user's ID and password may match the identity information that the firewall has, allowing authentication and access. However, it is not automatic that the identification and authentication process is tied to your network system access controls—without integration in some fashion, it's not. If the firewall doesn't know how to interact with the internal system access controls, it won't—and in most cases, because of security architectures, it doesn't. In such cases, the firewall works in binary fashion; you either have full access or you have no access.

There are various reasons why you may not want your users authenticating directly onto your firewall. In such cases, you can consider using an identification and authentication "pass-through" process that can integrate with your access controls—solutions like LDAP, RADIUS, and TACACS+, for instance. The point of all of this is to ensure that you understand there are alternatives, and they have different evaluation considerations. The implementation, integration, and management of the alternatives can be very different.

NOTE: Authenticating directly onto your firewall has positive and negative evaluation points. Generally, the firewall operating system should not be configured to interact with your internal network to avoid compromise. Your accounts tend to be static on a firewall, which may not conform to mandatory password rotation requirements. Your users may have problems remembering their passwords, causing increased administrative costs. Large firewall-based account databases can significantly impact performance because of the memory required to cache the accounts. On the other hand, separate account challenges may be part of a multilevel security architecture. Again, security is a matter of informed decision-making.

AN IDENTIFICATION AND AUTHENTICATION PRIMER

Authentication is really about trust, and how trust is established, and the process of how trust is sustained. The security model inside of Win2K controls and sets the architecture for how authentication will occur. It does this by providing Security Support Provider Interfaces (SSPI), which support third-party implementations. The identification and authentication support ties directly into access controls in the kernel, the file system, and the services. It also provides support for various forms of encryption within the operating system, including support for authentication systems. This is done using the CryptoAPI (CAPI) facilities.

The Local Security Authority

The principal mechanism for processing identification and authentication is the Local Security Authority (LSA). The LSA interacts with `Winlogon.exe` and the Graphical Identification and Authentication (GINA) DLL to collect the credentials and present them to the installed Security Support Provider Interfaces to achieve authentication. If the Security Support Provider accepts the credential, then the system builds your security token, which you then use to access objects and resources. As Figure 11-1 represents, Win2K allows you to refine certain settings for the Local Security Authority. To access it, select Start | Programs | Administrative Tools | Local Security Policies. You can also access this through the MMC using the GPO to configure domain-wide settings.

The important aspect for you to understand about the Local Security Authority is tied to the concept of impersonation, which we'll cover next. The Local Security Authority, act-

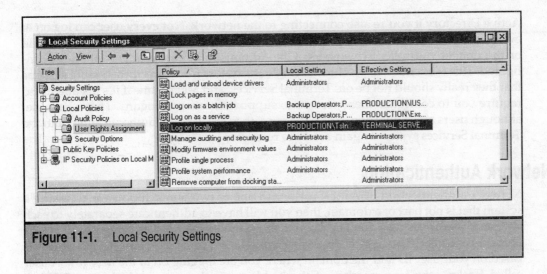

Figure 11-1.   Local Security Settings

ing on your behalf, maintains the integrity of the identification and authentication process by ensuring that you cannot alter the manner in which your credentials are validated, nor how your session security token will be constructed. It also controls the process of accessing other resources on your behalf.

Impersonation

This is going to seem odd to you, but you never directly access any of the objects or resources that Win2K or WinNT controls. Through the LSA process covered in the previous section, the Win2K system takes care of that for you. When you attempt to access a folder located on your application server, Win2K acts on your behalf. It collects your request, takes your security token, validates that you have permission to access the folder, and returns the results back to you. This process is called *impersonation*, and this is the way it happens all the time.

It is really an excellent model when you think about it in terms of integrity and trust. Users, computers, resources, and objects can be temporary, that is, they change with your network environment. The Win2K security model, which is static, knows how to establish trust within its components, and it knows how to interact with a potential user. While users can change and be deleted, the Win2K security model is always there, and it knows how to maintain trust within itself. Regardless of whether you are accessing a system directly, called *interactive logons*, or accessing a system across the wire, called *network authentication*, impersonation within Win2K can sustain the trusted nature of the operating system and service your access requests.

Interactive Logons

When you log on to a system directly, it's called an "interactive logon" and you are using the "log on locally" permission. The LSA will process you against a machine SAM or the

Active Directory if you're also connecting to the network. Not every user can log on to every system with an interactive session. For instance, Win2K restricts the ability to log on to a domain controller to members of the Administrator group, unless otherwise configured. This is intended to preclude non-administrators from directly accessing systems that they really should not be on. Terminal Services, and MetaFrame if it's installed, also require you to configure these servers to support interactive logons. That's because, although users are connecting across the wire, they are actually authenticating onto the Terminal Services system to gain access to resources.

Network Authentication

Network authentication in Win2K is done in one of two ways. If you are accessing a system that is not part of a domain, then you will have to authenticate separately to each system. If you are using a domain account, then your credentials are processed against a domain controller. This is done by using your User Principal Name (UPN), which is based on your user ID and the domain where you are logging on to the network. A user called Rocky, who is a member of the baddog.com domain would have a UPN of rocky@baddog.com, a format that supports the DNS locator constructs of Active Directory.

During the network logon process, the LSA will work with the Active Directory domain to create your security token (SID). If Kerberos is being used, it acquires a Kerberos ticket from a Kerberos Distribution Center (KDC), located on every domain controller. This is covered later in the "Kerberos Authentication" section of this chapter.

Delegation

The capability to support delegation in Win2K is an interesting feature, accomplished by using yet another wizard. It can also be dangerous, so let's take a look at it. *Delegation* is essentially the ability to let someone else use your authority or act on your behalf. Win2K also supports the ability to delegate authentication.

Delegation of authority can be done in a number of areas. You can delegate the ability for someone to read the mail in your Inbox and respond for you in Exchange, or you can delegate administrator permissions inside of a domain. The place where this can go wrong is in failing to establish reasonable roles and policies and not tracking the delegation. If a person leaves the company or is reassigned, the delegation permissions frequently are not altered. So, essentially, someone has permissions that are no longer appropriate. If you're going to use delegation, make sure you have a way to track and control it.

Delegation of authentication is actually a necessary feature inside of Win2K. If you are accessing a system, let's say a Web server, and it has to query a database server to get the data that you are requesting through a Web-based form, which credential should it use—the credentials of the Web server or yours? Well, if you want to control who gets access to what type of information stored on the database server, the Web server has to present your credentials for authentication. This is done through delegation of authentication. The Web server takes the same credentials that you presented upon access, and forwards this onto the database server. The database server then determines whether you have the permissions necessary to supply you with your information request.

Factored Authentication

What is factored authentication, you ask? Well, you and your users have been doing factored authentication since the first time you were prompted to log on. The term "factored" comes from the alternatives, and the combinations, you have to ensure the integrity of the identification and authentication process. Mainly, it deals with the identification process—or how the user presents credentials for authentication. It basically comes down to how you mix the alternatives for identification to create credentials you require to ensure trust. Those alternatives are based on the following criteria:

▼ **Something the User Knows** A simple example is a user ID or a password.

■ **Something the User Has** This could be a security token or smartcard.

▲ **Something the User Is** This might be some form of biometric solution.

NOTE: You could also argue that a system host could be challenged and authenticated based on something it is—an IP address. An example of this could be found in a DNS server that only communicates zone transfer information with another system that it can identify and authenticate. This is done using an IP address.

If you require only one of these criteria, you're using single-factor authentication. If you use any two of the criteria, you're using two-factor authentication. Of course, if you use all three criteria, now you're using three-factor authentication. The intent is to enhance the trust factor in the identification and authentication process. The chance of a password being compromised is actually high—especially if the password is not periodically required to be changed. The chance of compromising a user account with two-factor or three-factor authentication that incorporates a retinal scanner is pretty remote.

Security Token Systems

Security token products are regarded as a two-factor authentication solution and require a Security Solution Provider component installed on Win2K. Networks that require enhanced security controls use this type of solution frequently because it provides substantial protection against weak or stolen credentials. While there are other security token products on the market, RSA Security is the leading source, and we'll use them as an example for this section. Support for RSA Security's SecurID Agent is already installed on Win2K.

The RSA Security product line is generally referred to as SecurID, but is really comprised of ACE/Servers, ACE/Agent, and SecurID tokens (see Figure 11-2) for the clients. The ACE/Server component is installed as a service on a Windows NT/2000 or Unix system daemon. ACE/Server administration (see Figure 11-3) is done through a Windows client installed locally or remotely. System access controls use an ACE/Agent installed on each host that is being protected by the ACE/Server. For example, this could be a client, server, firewall, or network access server (NAS).

Figure 11-2. RSA SecurID tokens

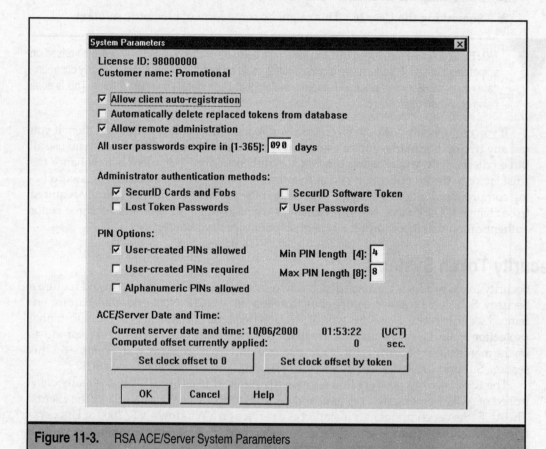

Figure 11-3. RSA ACE/Server System Parameters

Here's how it works, as shown in Figure 11-4. When a user attempts to log into a host protected by an ACE/Agent, the user is prompted for a PASSCODE. The PASSCODE is a combination of a personal identification number (PIN) that the user knows and a six-digit, randomly generated number that changes periodically, usually every 60 seconds. The combination of both of these two items—something you know and something you have—forms the PASSCODE. Clearly, brute force attacks aren't going to work here. The authentication request is sent to the ACE/Server, where the PASSCODE is validated. While Figure 11-4 presents this as a remote access scenario, the process is the same for remote access or internal network access, and can be integrated into firewall and VPN solutions if the vendor supports SecurID—and most do.

One of the interesting things about this process is the ability to mix the security controls. If a user is not a member of a group that requires authentication by the ACE/Server, the LSA will process the user with one of the other mechanisms such as NTLM or Kerberos. So, it's not uncommon to see implementations where administrator-level access is challenged by the ACE/Server, but regular users on the system never see an ACE/Server challenge. For instance, let's take a public Web server sitting in a DMZ. Anyone can access the Web site to view content and never know that it's protected by an ACE/Server. However, if an administrator or someone trying to update the Web pages attempts to access the system using his own credentials, he will see an ACE/Server challenge and have to successfully authenticate himself. Because we're using two-factor authentication, the possibility of compromised passwords pretty much goes out the window.

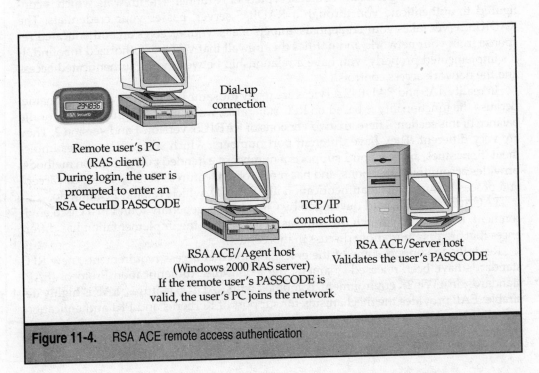

Dial-up connection

Remote user's PC
(RAS client)
During login, the user is
prompted to enter an
RSA SecurID PASSCODE

TCP/IP
connection

RSA ACE/Agent host
(Windows 2000 RAS server)
If the remote user's PASSCODE is
valid, the user's PC joins the network

RSA ACE/Server host
Validates the user's PASSCODE

Figure 11-4. RSA ACE remote access authentication

If you're interested in testing this type of security solution, RSA Security (**www.rsasecurity.com**) offers a free evaluation pack that includes the ACE/Server software and two SecurID tokens. It's an excellent opportunity to see this type of technology in action.

Pass-Through Authentication

This form of authentication is usually implemented with remote access or Internet-based access. You probably know it as the Internet Authentication Service (IAS), RADIUS, or TACACS+. Most folks don't understand what it is, but it's not complicated.

Most pass-through authentication implements are addressing controls over internal access from the outside world. You don't want to expose the IP ports of your network authentication systems to the world, but your users need to have some way to present their credentials and get authenticated. This is where pass-through authentication comes into play. The pass-through system is acting as your proxy, basically taking your credentials in a format that the pass-through system can support, and presenting them on your behalf to the authentication systems on your network. They collect the information for the credentials, then package and communicate it in a manner that your authentication system will accept, process, and authenticate. For instance, let's go back to the firewall example at the beginning of the chapter where we talked about having a disconnect with your internal access control environment. You present your cleartext user ID and password to the firewall, protecting it inside of an encrypted VPN tunnel. The firewall, which is configured to authenticate you through a RADIUS server, passes your credentials. The RADIUS server takes your credentials, impersonates you, receives an authenticated response from your network, and notifies the firewall that you are authorized inbound. If it's implemented properly, you have a relationship between your authenticated access and the network access controls.

In reality, IAS and RADIUS services are really the same thing under a different name. Because the functionality is based on RFC standards, we'll use the term RADIUS for the balance of this section. There are two versions of RADIUS: version 1 and version 2. They are very different. They have different port numbers, which sometimes causes implementation issues, and version 2 supports a number of extended authentication methods, provides accounting extensions, and has more robust features. Version 2 also can accept and process security token authentication like SecurID, which version 1 cannot do.

TACACS+ is a standard developed by Cisco, and is generally found in a Cisco environment. It works very much the same as RADIUS, but the implementation has differences that aren't important to discuss in this context.

Recently, to support some of the emerging Internet access requirements, new RFC standards have been released—namely, the Extensible Authentication Protocol (EAP) standards. In a Win2K environment, combined with RADIUS features, EAP is highly desirable. EAP provides the mechanisms for support of Kerberos and PKI authentication, including the ability to support a smartcard logon from outside of your network. It can do this a number of ways, including encryption by various means such as Transport Layer Security (TLS). You can think of TLS as SSL version 3.1, because that's what it really is.

When Netscape transferred SSL to the IETF, it was determined that SSL would be re-named TLS. It has some additional new features, like smartcard logon support, but it is basically the same SSL you know and love.

To enable Extensible Authentication Protocol, follow these steps:

1. Open the Microsoft Management Console and from the Console menu item, select Add/Remove Snap-in.

2. Add Routing and Remote Access.

3. Right-click the Routing and Remote Access icon and select Add Server.

4. Right-click on your new server and select Configure and Enable Routing and Remote Access.

5. Right-click on Properties, select the Security property tab, and select the EAP settings that are appropriate for your network. This is depicted in Figure 11-5.

Mutual Authentication

This is an important authentication consideration. You may not always need to use it, but you need to understand that it is available and know when it can be used. The concept of mutual authentication is simple: Both parts to the session, the client and the server, have the ability to require authentication of the other party before they contract any busi-ness—hence, the term "mutual authentication." Mutual authentication is available in

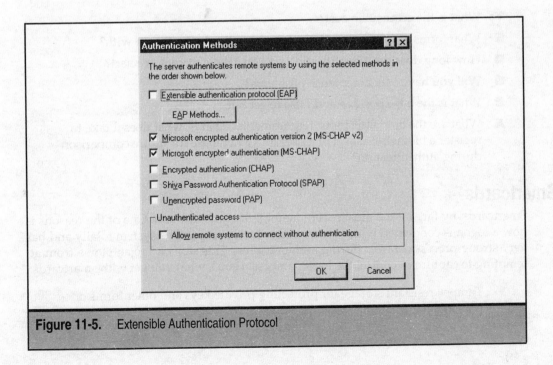

Figure 11-5. Extensible Authentication Protocol

IPSec sessions, and to a certain degree in PPTP sessions (challenge and response has to use MSCHAP version 2), DNS-based challenges, and SSL or TLS sessions.

The session authentications can be based on host-to-host, host-to-gateway, and gateway-to-gateway configurations. That is, you can have your workstations mutually challenge each other. You can have a workstation and a firewall mutually challenge each other, and you can have two firewalls challenge each other. A common example of the second two situations is an IPSec-based VPN tunnel. In the case of IPSec, the two parties will not start to exchange data unless they can go through successful mutual authentication.

The concept of having your Internet browser challenge a Web server is not an uncommon practice, especially with SSL. However, with SSL and TLS, it is possible to also configure the Web server to challenge the Web browser. In the case of an intranet server, this may be something you should consider. It depends on the information being served up to the intranet client and whether you need to validate access.

Considerations with Biometrics

Biometrics is one of the least used, yet more interesting methods of creating user credentials. Biometrics is essentially the "something you are" part of factored authentication, and is rarely used as a single-factor authentication process.

Forms of biometric systems include fingerprint, hand geometry, voice recognition, signature recognition, and retinal scanners. They can be very strong forms of authentication, especially when combined with another factor. At the same time they can be expensive. Here are things to think about when you're evaluating biometric systems.

▼ What is the acquisition cost?

■ What forms of factored authentication can they be combined with?

■ How long does the authentication process take to accept or reject?

■ Will you have user acceptance problems?

■ What is the false positive and false reject rate?

▲ What are the biometric input requirements? That is, what does it take to register a biometric aspect of a user into a database for future comparison during authentication?

Smartcards

Smartcards, by far, are the most secure method of authentication. One of the reasons is how a logon is conducted with a smartcard, which bypasses the system totally and has very strong process controls during authentication. This stops a Trojan Horse from attempting to capture or control the logon process. Here's what you get with smartcards:

▼ Tamper-resistant storage for protecting private keys and other forms of personal information.

- Isolation of security-critical computations involving the private key from other parts of the system that do not have a "need to know."

▲ Portability of credentials and other private information between computers at work, home, or on the road.

Microsoft publishes which smartcard products can be used with Win2K. You should review the hardware compatibility list (HCL), and look for a vendor statement that it is Win2K certified. Those products will be integrated circuit cards (ICC) and smartcard readers that are certified to work using an RS-232, PCMCIA, or USB interface.

Smartcards can store the digital identity of users, so they can be implemented as part of a secure PKI project on your network. They can be used with remote access solutions, except as noted. You can integrate them with building access systems, so a user has to have the same credentials (his or her smartcard) to pass through building control points, as well as to log on to computer systems—and you can configure sessions to automatically implement logoff or lock computer terminals if the smartcard is withdrawn from the reader. Again, if users have to have their credentials to move through the building, they'll have to remove their smartcard when leaving their terminals.

All of these seem like great access controls. Well, you'll also have to consider the days when users forget their smartcards at home, and now they can't move around the building, and they can't log onto their computers until you issue them a temporary card. That card may only be good for that day, but still, someone is going to have to issue it to them. There are resources and human factor considerations to smartcard implementation, so planning is essential.

On the other hand, it will really be hard for someone to break into a system that requires a smartcard for access. Let's take an extreme case. Let's say that someone compromises your Web server and because of weak access controls the intruder is moving through your network. He happens to stumble across your Research and Development application server with highly confidential company designs that the company invested millions into over the past year. If the only means of authenticating onto that system is a smartcard, you just got your money's worth when you decided to require this type of authentication to sensitive systems.

Microsoft will tell you that some of the limitations to using smartcards occur during interactive logons. Smartcards are not appropriate for the following scenarios:

▼ The user is required to join his or her computer to a domain.

- The user must perform administrative tasks such as promote a server to be a domain controller.

▲ A user needs to configure a network connection for remote access.

Each of these scenarios is an issue because the security model inside of Win2K needs to register the user, computer, or object as a trusted party before it can associate a smartcard authentication to it.

NOTE: The Microsoft Windows 2000 Server Resource Kit points out that smartcards cannot be used with Terminal Server or MetaFrame authentication. It's simple; your smartcard reader is connected to your computer with the Terminal Services client, not the Terminal Server where the authentication is actually taking place—something to think about when planning your authentication model for Win2K.

METHODS AND CRITERIA

In this section we try to identify some of the evaluation criteria, some of the different authentication methods that Win2K presents you with, policy considerations, and the different types of logon methods. There are really a number of choices, as indicated in Figure 11-6, which shows a property page in Internet Information Server 5.0.

Here is a quick review of the alternatives, which are covered in more detail within this section, as well as in other parts of the book.

▼ **Anonymous**   This is basically the same authentication you use to freely access the many Web sites you visit. Even though it doesn't imply it, there is actually an account and authentication still takes place.

■ **Basic Authentication**   This method provides basic password authentication on Web servers. During the authentication process, the user is prompted for a user ID and password. If the credentials match, then the user will be authenticated and allowed to enter the Web site or network. Note, the user ID and password are transmitted openly, and there is no protection provided by this form of authentication. This issue is covered in depth later in the Basic Authentication section.

■ **Digest Authentication**   This is a new authentication method that uses regular passwords, encrypted by using a hash process. It is new to Win2K. If you use this method of authentication, you'll find that it only works with Win2K domain accounts, and the accounts must store the passwords as encrypted text.

▲ **Integrated Windows Authentication**   This method includes NTLM, Kerberos, PKI, and even security tokens like SecurID. Please note, your users may need to use Internet Explorer to ensure proper authentication through a Web server.

Evaluation Criteria

Identification and authentication systems, like other security considerations, should be weighed against the value achieved and the risk mitigated. They should be the product of independent testing and validated integrity. Kerberos v5, for instance, has managed to stand up over time, while Kerberos v4 had a number of problems. The NTLM hash has suffered from its own heritage, having never been intended for use as an Internet-based authentication protocol. PKI, when properly implemented, is amazing, allowing for clear or encrypted transmission without compromising the integrity of the credentials and creating new possibilities for legally binding commercial transactions.

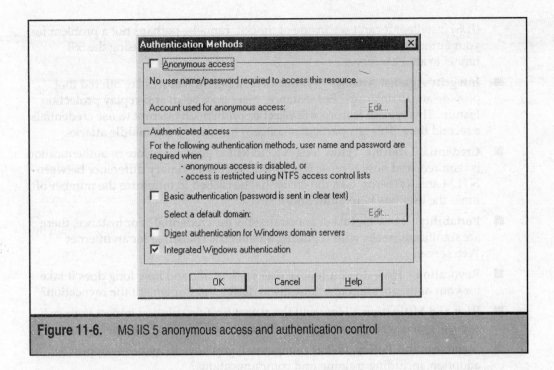

Figure 11-6. MS IIS 5 anonymous access and authentication control

If a compromised password could create significant loss, you should really be looking at your alternatives, and this section is intended to help you evaluate your options, and set your requirements. In the end, one of the best yardsticks is a simple question: Do I trust the identification and authentication process given the resources that it is protecting? It's all about trust.

To answer that question, first you have to identify which one of the several identification and authentication alternatives within Win2K is appropriate for your needs. You get to use anonymous, basic (cleartext), message digest, NTLM, Kerberos, and PKI credentials. We cover these in a moment after we identify how we're going to evaluate our options. This is what you should be thinking about:

▼ **Integrity in Storage**   Can the integrity of the credential be compromised while in storage, and what protective measures or features are available to preclude this? Do not underestimate this consideration. If someone is successful in attacking the SAM, the KDC, or the PKI store, how does that impact your system?

■ **Integrity in Transit**   How is the integrity of the credential impacted as it transits the network? A cleartext password has little protection across the Internet, but add in an SSL tunnel, and now the cleartext password isn't exposed, even though you haven't changed the authentication process. On the other hand, you just created an issue if you have an Intrusion Detection System

(IDS) installed. It can't see inside of the SSL tunnel—perhaps not a problem for your authentication solution, but it's an issue if someone is using the SSL tunnel to attack a server.

- **Integrity Against Attacks**   What native, inherent features are offered that provide attack defenses? For instance, there may be an anti-replay protection feature. This type of feature will reject or prohibit an attempt to use credentials a second time. This is a particular concern for man-in-the-middle attacks.

- **Credential Lifetime**   How long is a credential good for before re-authentication is required, and how is reuse controlled? This is a primary difference between NTLM and Kerberos. Can the credential be cached to minimize the number of times the user has to re-authenticate?

- **Portability**   How mobile or constrained is the credential? For instance, there are significant issues with requiring a biometric challenge for an Internet Web server.

- **Revocation**   How do you revoke user credentials, and how long does it take for your authentication mechanisms to detect and implement the revocation?

- **Risk and Mitigation**   How will the authentication solution impact your risk exposure, and what new mitigation changes will have to be made?

- **Standards and Policy**   What changes will you have to make to support adoption, including training and communications?

- **Security Architecture**   What network changes will have to be made to provide for adaptability, including integration within your current environment?

- **User Acceptance**   Will users reject the new authentication system? This comes up mainly with biometric systems like retina scanners.

- **Authentication Processing Time**   How long does it take to process authentication? If it takes too long, your users aren't going to be happy, and you're creating lost productivity. Make sure it's worth it.

- **Reliability**   How reliable is the system, both for up time and for accuracy? If the authentication server isn't available, can your users still successfully log on? Does the solution have a predictable false positive accept and false reject rate that is acceptable to you. False rejects are better than false accepts, generally speaking. This issue comes into play with biometric systems.

▲ **Cost of Ownership**   Can you afford it? Don't implement authentication systems because you can; increased security generally translates into increased costs. However, if your business requirements dictate increased authentication integrity, then evaluate that against your cost of ownership. By the way, in a full analysis, user ID and password systems do not have inexpensive cost of ownership. Look at your help desk records for resetting passwords, and think of the cost of having a sensitive, proprietary research and development project file stolen because of inappropriate, weak integrity in your authentication system.

The balance of this section provides a brief overview of the authentication methods, and then specific evaluation information for your benefit. It does not provide detailed information on each of the authentication methods, which is available on the Microsoft Web site at **www.microsoft.com/windows2000/library/howitworks/default.asp**.

Anonymous Authentication

Anonymous authentication really isn't anonymous at all—it's just shared. On the Web server, you identify an account that is associated with anonymous access, and that account can be used by anyone visiting the site. However, the Anonymous Access checkbox must be selected, indicating that it is an approved authentication method. By default in IIS 5.0, it is not selected. You have to enable it if that's what you want.

How Anonymous Authentication Stacks Up

Anonymous authentication has its place. It's not secure, but then there is plenty of information that doesn't require the burden and overhead of the other authentication methods discussed. This is a definite advantage. The help desk is not going to get calls asking to have a password changed because the user forgot it. Here's a breakdown of evaluation characteristics: It's portable; it's reliable; account integrity issues are generally not a concern; and you can easily revoke anonymous access by changing permissions.

On the down side, if you don't configure the access controls associated with the anonymous account properly, your Web site visitors may give your home page a new look, or access other parts of your network. Pay attention to the authorization afforded to anonymous users. The time spent will save you embarrassment and the dubious honor of becoming an incident response veteran.

Basic Authentication

Basic authentication is used for external access, both on Web sites and even on firewalls, to gain access via Internet connections. It is a popular choice with system administrators, and a hated method by security administrators. It's easy to use, easy to configure, and doesn't have the browser restrictions associated with Integrated Windows Authentication. Basic authentication is sometimes referred to as cleartext, which isn't far from the truth. In reality, the user ID and password are forwarded using Base64 encoding. Encoding is not the same as encryption. Encoding has a known decode value, so a strong password like *tEa-4-2* will decode just as fast as, well, a really weak password like *password*.

How Basic Authentication Stacks Up

Just about every major security reference on the topic warns against this type of authentication without some form of added protection like SSL or TLS. Remember, this type of authentication is exposing your internal accounts and passwords—that may not be a good idea. Still it is done frequently. In fact, you probably have users accessing public

Web sites, like **hotmail.com**, using their internal network account name and password. A little guidance to your users can go a long way here.

So let's evaluate Basic Authentication against the criteria we listed earlier. It is portable; revocation can be accomplished easily; user acceptance is not an issue; it's reasonably reliable; and cost of ownership is negligible. On the other hand, it definitely has broad credential integrity issues, creates standards and policy concerns, and may impact adversely on security architecture.

So, how can we mitigate the risks created by using Basic Authentication? Simple, require the credentials to be transported inside of an encrypted IPSec, PPTP, SSL, or TLS tunnel. Then, the credentials are protected in transit; standards and policy can be controlled. We do have a security architecture issue, though. An Intrusion Detection System (IDS) cannot monitor encrypted connections. The problem isn't so much the fact that the IDS system can't see the identification and authentication process. It's that it can't see anything—including an attempt to hack a system. This is your trade-off, and you have to evaluate the risks and benefits along the way.

Message Digest Authentication

In contrast to some of the issues presented with Basic Authentication, this new method provided by Win2K is wonderful to see. Basically, the Message Digest method is implemented by hashing the password, addressing integrity. However, if you use this method of authentication you'll find that it only works with Win2K domain accounts, and the dialog box will tell you that the accounts must store the passwords as encrypted text. Message Digest is configured in the GPO, as reflected in Figure 11-7.

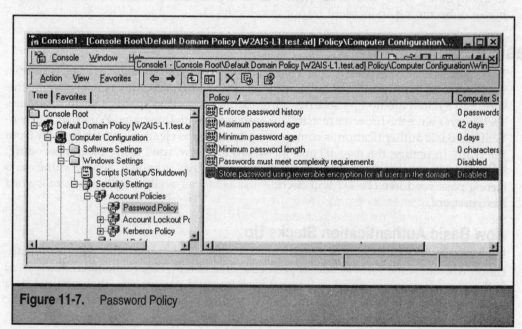

Figure 11-7.   Password Policy

How Message Digest Authentication Stacks Up

Let's compare Message Digest directly against the Basic Authentication criteria evaluation results, and then expand on it. It is still portable on a Win2K network; revocation is just as easy; it's reliable; and cost of ownership is only slightly higher. Reviewing the Basic Authentication down side, Message Digest does not have the credential integrity issue, acceptable standards and policy can be addressed, and it has limited impact on your security architecture.

On the other hand, if you don't have a Win2K network implementation that provides standardization and architecture, you can't use it—another reason to consider upgrading the entire network to Win2K.

NTLM Authentication

As part of the selections that fall into Integrated Windows Authentication, NTLM is one of the alternatives that provides for a client to log on directly to the network. NTLM is a combination of the more secure NT authentication mechanism and the legacy LAN Manager authentication mechanism, which is weaker. The combination is referred to as NTLM, but you can disable the LM portion in the registry.

NTLM is generally not appropriate for Internet-based access. The reason is simple—to allow NTLM authentication from the Internet, you have to open up the principal IP ports that are used to attack a Microsoft network. Yes, you'll be able to have network authentication, browse your network resources, and retrieve your files, but so will just about everyone else on the planet. The people that can't don't have Internet connections.

Inside of the network, NTLM is still a reasonable alternative. However, because of the proprietary nature of NTLM, it may not integrate well as an authentication mechanism with your other systems, certainly not in the single sign-on sense. Sure, you can integrate it with Novell networks and even Apple Macintosh networks, but when it comes to Unix, or the emerging Internet, remote access, and mobile users everywhere in the world today—well, it was never intended to be a distributed, modern authentication mechanism. It suffers from its LAN Manager heritage, which pre-dates modern Internet requirements. Configuration of NTLM authentication is administered in the GPO, as represented in Figure 11-8.

How NTLM Authentication Stacks Up

Here's a fast rundown on NTLM, which we'll compare to Kerberos and then PKI. NTLM has a number of integrity issues. There are known ways to attack integrity in storage. Yes, there are ways to secure the SAM, but frankly few administrators actually use such measures. There have been successful in-transit integrity attacks, and there is no anti-replay feature. Credential lifetime has limited controls. It is not portable in an Internet world without putting the whole network at risk. It creates a number of problems for security architecture, though these can be addressed.

On the plus side, revocation can be achieved in a reasonable manner. Standards and policies can be provided without significant technical issues. User acceptance is not a

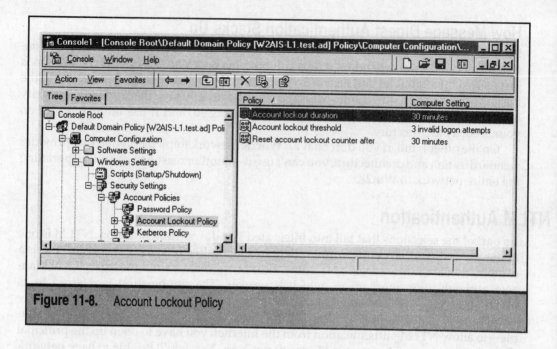

Figure 11-8. Account Lockout Policy

problem, nor is authentication processing time. It is just as reliable as most password-based systems, and cost of ownership can be argued either way. Then, of course, there is the legacy Windows question. Until Microsoft has released a Kerberos client for the rest of the Windows family, NTLM may be the only reasonable way for you to provide a common authentication model.

In summary, take a look at the history of vulnerabilities and attacks, consider the Internet and e-commerce, and ask yourself: How much further can you continue to rely on NTLM as a principal authentication method? Win2K gives you new opportunities—take them.

Kerberos Authentication

Microsoft has some excellent white papers that cover Kerberos, and the Windows 2000 Server Resource Kit covers a number of considerations for implementing Kerberos in your network. The concepts surrounding Kerberos are not hard to grasp, but they do take time to read in detail. So you can evaluate Kerberos against the other alternatives, we'll spend some time trying to describe the fundamentals of what it is, how it works, and the heritage of Kerberos. However, the major focus of this section is identifying what you need to know about Kerberos in contrast to other Win2K authentication alternatives. You need to know when to use it, whether it is a better choice, and how to evaluate it. This section will help you do that.

Kerberos Principals, Services, and Tickets

Kerberos has the following components, which we'll cover:

- ▼ The Kerberos Distribution Center
- ■ The Kerberos Authentication Service
- ■ The Ticket-Granting Ticket
- ▲ The Ticket-Granting Service

Kerberos parameters are administered in the GPO as represented in Figure 11-9.

First, Kerberos is based on tickets, which are controlled by the Kerberos Distribution Center (KDC). Every Win2K domain controller is a KDC. The tickets are like vouchers that you use to acquire things. Tickets can be issued to users, machines, services, and applications, which are regarded as "principals." With Kerberos, there are two fundamental types of tickets. There is the ticket that is issued to a principal, which is called a Ticket-Granting Ticket (TGT) and is unique for each principal. The other type of ticket is used by a principal to request services. This type of ticket is called a Ticket-Granting Service (TGS); it is unique for each session and can only be issued to a principal with a TGT. So each principal may have several session (TGS) tickets.

The KDC is an intermediary that all of the Kerberos principals trust. Communication between the KDC and principals is based on pre-shared secrets, which are unique for each principal. When a principal wants to communicate with another principal across the

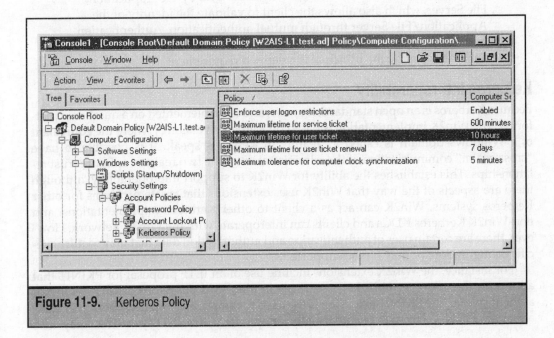

Figure 11-9. Kerberos Policy

network, it presents the unique ticket (TGT) assigned by the KDC as part of the request. The KDC issues the principal a session ticket (TGS), which the principal uses to initiate communications with the other intended principal. The target principal, in turn, gets its copy of the session ticket (TGS), which allows the principals to mutually authenticate each other. Hence, the intermediary nature of the KDC, which acts as the mutually trusted party and controls communications between the principals.

So, the process represented in Figure 11-10 is accomplished in the following manner:

1. KRB_AS_REQ is the authentication service request made by the principal to the KDC for a Ticket-Granting Ticket (TGT).

2. KRB_AS_REP is the authentication service response to the principal with a Ticket-Granting Ticket (TGT).

3. KRB_TGS_REQ is the request by the principal, based on possession of a TGT, to the KDC for a Ticket-Granting Service (TGS) ticket so that it can access a specific resource on the Application/File Server, which is also a known principal.

4. KRB_TGS_REP is the response to the principal, issuing the Ticket-Granting Service (TGS) ticket to the principal for the specific resource on the Application/File Server.

5. KRB_AP_REQ is the transmission of the TGS ticket to the Application/File Server.

6. KRB_AP_REP is the acknowledgement of the TGS by the Application/File Server, which also allows the client to validate the identity of the Application/File Server through mutual authentication. Authentication in step 6 is dependent on the Kerberos implementation, and whether mutual authentication by the principal is a defined requirement.

Kerberos Interoperability

Because Kerberos is an open standard, it can be, and is, implemented on a number of platforms. The Win2K implementation is based on Kerberos version 5, where the equivalent of a Windows domain is called a "realm" in Kerberos speak. It is possible to have "cross-realm" communication, if the administrators of the two realms configure trust relationships. This establishes the ability for Win2K to support interoperability, although there are aspects of the way that Win2K uses extensions that create problems for other Kerberos systems. Win2K can act as a client to other Kerberos implementations, and non-Win2K Kerberos KDCs and clients can interoperate with the Win2K network. However, there are certain uses of authentication and authorization data that may require specific configuration, or may not be supported.

For instance, the Win2K extensions include use of an IETF proposal for PKINIT that allows for the use of a public key certificate in place of a password during the initial authentication. The PKINIT extension is the basis for smartcard logon support in Win2K, although PKINIT has not been formally adopted by the IETF yet. This may also

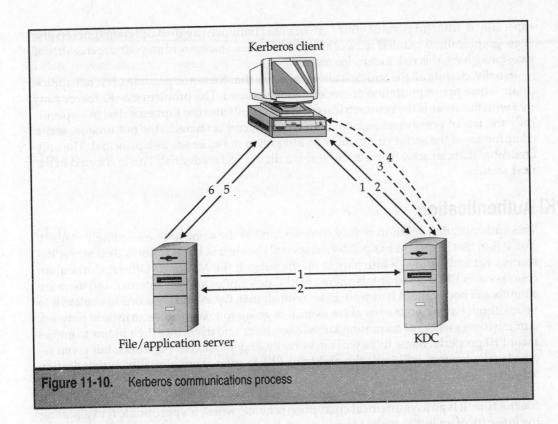

Figure 11-10. Kerberos communications process

cause interoperability issues with other Kerberos implementations. If you need to establish interoperability, Microsoft has a number of papers that cover the issues and the process to configure this. In particular, look at the Step-by-Step Guide to Kerberos 5 Interoperability and the Windows 2000 Kerberos Interoperability white paper.

How Kerberos Authentication Stacks Up

In an Internet world, you'll find Kerberos to be a very interesting authentication mechanism, designed to address the authentication needs of distributed networks—perfect for Win2K environments designed with the Internet in mind.

Kerberos has a very effective design that ensures integrity. It has built-in anti-replay protection and controls for credential lifetime. It is portable. It supports timely revocation of credentials, and can integrate into your security architecture with minimal changes. It is reliable, to the extent that the network architecture is reliable, and it has excellent cost-of-ownership considerations.

One of the concerns with Kerberos is its sensitivity to time—it uses a timestamp, and by default operates within a five-minute window. If your network is not maintained inside of this window, it could actually break authentication. You need to watch this, especially if different parts of your network are configured against different timeservers. A geographically separated network with multiple domains within your organizational forest may have this risk factor, for instance.

Finally, despite all the truly excellent qualities that Kerberos provides, it is not appropriate where non-repudiation of credentials is required. The problem that Kerberos runs into with this issue is the symmetrical encryption built into the Kerberos design—specifically the use of pre-shared secrets. Because the secret is shared, it is not unique, and a compromise of the secret could allow an attempt to masquerade as a principal. The only credential that can actually meet this test is a digital PKI credential. This is covered in the next section.

PKI Authentication

This authentication solution is very complex, and at the same time exceedingly elegant. You'll find that Microsoft has published several chapters in the Windows 2000 Server Resources Kit and various white papers on the subject; the Microsoft Official Curriculum courses cover PKI fundamentals; there are RFC descriptions on the Internet; and there are a number of books about it as well. Even with all that, try to find someone to explain it to you without having your eyes glaze over. It is going to take most security and network administrators weeks of cramming knowledge, facts, and trivia into their brains to implement PKI properly. Some folks will never really understand how it works, but given recent legal adoption, will trust the ability of PKI to offer them a quality authentication solution.

Let's start with the acronym and work our way forward. PKI stands for Public Key Infrastructure. It is an asymmetrical encryption scheme, which is appropriate for validating the integrity of an individual's identification. It has two essential components—a public key and a private key. The basis of PKI can be summarized by the following—proof of identity is based on possession of the public and private keys, without which identity cannot be validated. The essence of PKI is to bind a digital credential to an entity, like an individual. You can also have digital credentials for hosts. PKI is the product of years of open standards development. It has been rigorously tested and has not yet been broken. So, while you may not understand PKI yet, you can reasonably determine that PKI is a secure authentication mechanism. You can also take comfort that recognition of PKI has progressed to the level where a number of countries have laws stipulating that PKI, when properly implemented, managed, and controlled, is legally acceptable as a means of proving identity, and therefore legally acceptable as an authentication mechanism—although, the laws may not be the principal reason why you elect to use PKI on your network.

Some of the components to PKI include significant documentation, like Certificate Practice Statements (CPS), and other policy and legal instruments. You will have to determine whether you'll implement a standalone Certificate Server or an enterprise version. You'll have to identify whether you'll trust outside certificate servers and use certificate trust lists (CTL). You'll need to purchase infrastructure and ensure that it has proper fault-tolerance built into your design. Most of all you're going to need a plan and talent.

These blueprints illustrate the four major factors in building a scalable, robust, and secure Win2K network with proper Active Directory and DNS structure, as well as proper Organizational Unit and Group Policy usage.

Windows 2000 Security Handbook Blueprints

Table of Contents

The following illustrates a central corporate admin unit with subunits for Manufacturing (MFG) and Sales. This drawing illustrates one potential Organization Unit (OU) structure to delegate admin control.

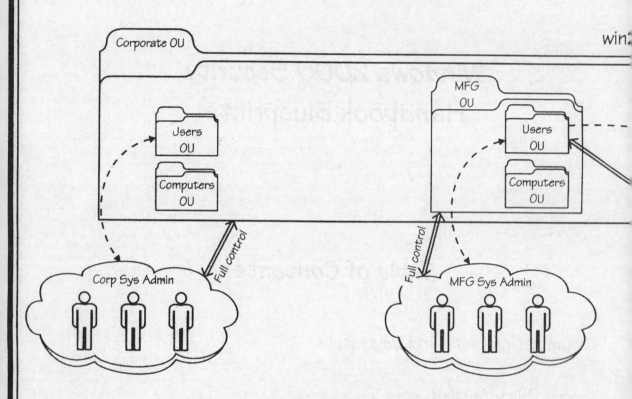

OUs are created to abstract the organizational structure and hierarchy.

Administrative groups are located in the OUs that they serve.

nd Delegation

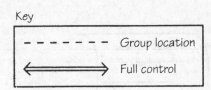

Key

- - - - - - - Group location

⟵═══════⟶ Full control

.example.com

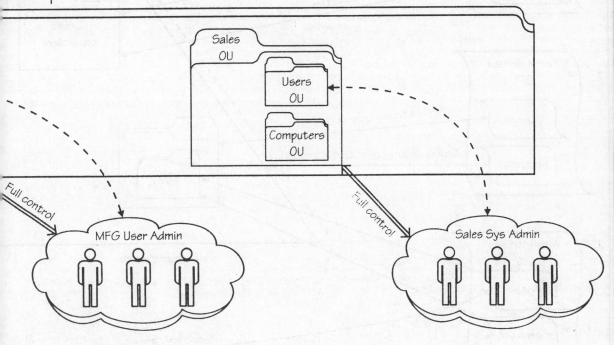

The Delegation wizard is used after structure and groups are created.

Groups must have permissions revoked on child OUs. For example, the MFG SysAdmin will have Full Control (FC) of the User OU in the MFG OU, unless they are removed with the ADSIEdit utility.

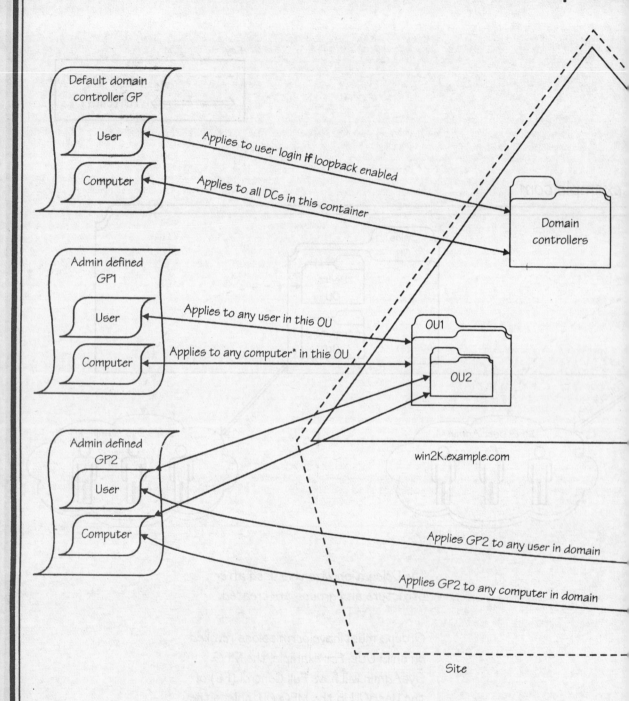

Default domain controller GP
User — Applies to user login **if** loopback enabled
Computer — Applies to all DCs in this container

Domain controllers

Admin defined GP1
User — Applies to any user in this OU
Computer — Applies to any computer* in this OU

OU1

OU2

Admin defined GP2
User
Computer

win2K.example.com

Applies GP2 to any user in domain

Applies GP2 to any computer in domain

Site

4

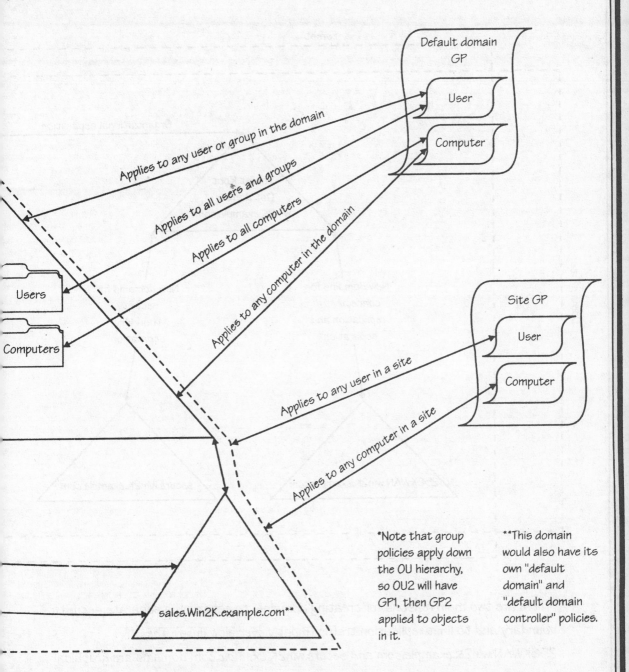

Default domain
GP

User

Computer

Applies to any user or group in the domain

Applies to all users and groups

Applies to all computers

Applies to any computer in the domain

Users

Computers

Site GP

User

Computer

Applies to any user in a site

Applies to any computer in a site

sales.Win2K.example.com**

*Note that group
policies apply down
the OU hierarchy,
so OU2 will have
GP1, then GP2
applied to objects
in it.

**This domain
would also have its
own "default
domain" and
"default domain
controller" policies.

Remember precedence: 4LSDOU (NT4, Local, Site, Domain, OU)
and domains from administrative boundaries.

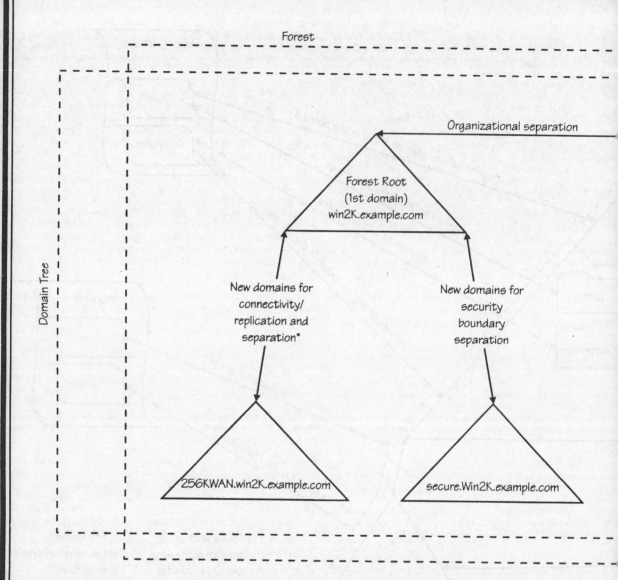

Forest

Organizational separation

Domain Tree

Forest Root
(1st domain)
win2K.example.com

New domains for
connectivity/
replication and
separation*

New domains for
security
boundary
separation

256KWAN.win2K.example.com

secure.Win2K.example.com

*There are two main reasons for creating domains: to establish a separate security boundary and to limit replication traffic (mostly over slow links). The 256KWAN.win2K.example.com and secure.win2K.example.com domains are graphical illustrations of these principles. Please refer to Chapter 8 for a detailed discussion of these issues.

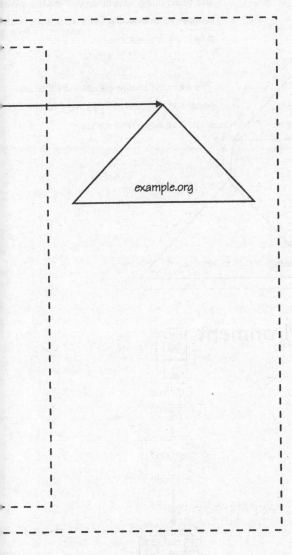

example.org

Design Factors

- ∞ Geographical and connectivity
- ∞ Support model
- ∞ Political structure of organization
- ∞ DNS namespace ownership
- ∞ Namespace requirements
- ∞ One or more global catalog servers in a site

Tips

- ∞ Keep only administrative accounts and computers in the Forest Root.
- ∞ Limit reliance on trust to limit referrals.
- ∞ Use Group Policies to control.
- ∞ Limit replication.
- ∞ Limit to one Forest.
- ∞ Limit nesting to not more than five levels.
- ∞ Use domains to make security boundaries and limit replication traffic.

Win2K DNS Structure in Heterogeneous Networks

Win2K Forest uses secure dynamic
DNS updates and AD integrated DNS.

The best, most workable solution for a Win2K
domain in an existing DNS structure is to
add it as a subdomain.

This example shows Sales and MFG as
separate domains, as opposed to the OU
structure described earlier.

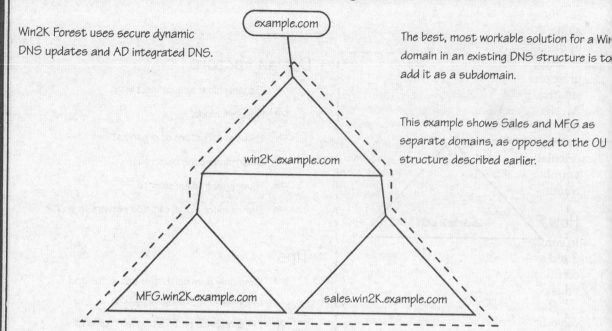

Win2K DNS in a Firewalled Environment

Set up Win2K DNS servers to "forward"
external requests to external DNS server.

Configure firewall to only allow DNS traffic to
Win2K DNS servers from external DNS
server(s).

This also limits the availability of Service
Resource Records (SRV RR) to external sites.

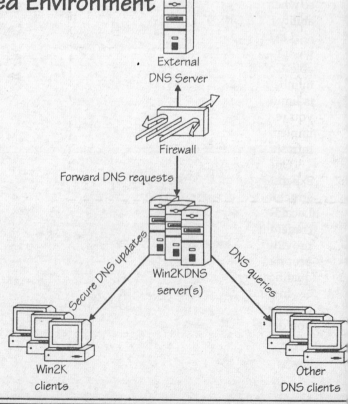

For those of you who don't believe in planning, who think you're just going to learn it along the way—invest in aspirin, your favorite flavor of stomach medicine, and start updating your resume.

So, if it's going to be so hard, why do it? Well, it has remarkable payoff. You can integrate and control your authentication into VPN tunnels and network resources and use smartcards for factored authentication to improve security. PKI provides support for digital signatures in e-mail messages and supports encrypted e-mail. It is the only way you can really get to non-repudiation, and therefore is excellent for commercial transactions in a digital world. Done right, it can actually make you money and save you money. The calculation for that is different for each environment and should be based on addressing your business objectives, and not as a cool opportunity for spending the network staff's training budget.

How PKI Authentication Stacks Up

In contrast to the other solutions, PKI is more secure, more expensive, and more complicated to implement properly. Sure, you can turn on a Certificate Server and start issuing certificates, but you'll find in short order that a lack of understanding and planning on your part may cause you to have to start all over.

Here's a review of our evaluation criteria. You need to protect the private key storage of your PKI implementation, but aside from that, integrity is a proven attribute that you can rely on. You do not have an issue with the integrity of credentials in transit, and there are no known integrity attacks on the keys themselves. The credentials are portable, more so when implemented with smartcards. User acceptance should not be an issue, and reliability is excellent.

On the down side you'll find the following: Credential lifetime can be controlled, but it is important to note that the revocation time period may have delays that are not acceptable. Consider this during planning. Cost of ownership, at least initially, will be high. The number of technical folks out there who are qualified to conduct a large implementation is limited, and you can expect to pay premium rates. Even if you use your own staff, you're going to burn significant staff hours during the planning phase—and do not implement without conducting a successful pilot program. PKI can also have significant infrastructure costs to integrate into your security architecture.

One of the ways to save on the implementation costs, infrastructure costs, and other expenses of getting PKI up and running is to find someone who will manage the infrastructure and process for you—an outsourced PKI solution. In such cases, you'll act as the Local Registration Authority (LRA)—meaning you'll identify and control who gets PKI credentials, and the outsourcing company will act as the Certification Authority (CA), providing the infrastructure and staff to manage your PKI system. You should spend appropriate time reviewing the outsourcing firm's credentials, infrastructure, and staff qualifications, but this may be a better alternative for you.

In summary, PKI is the future of a digital economy, like it or not. If you haven't started planning for PKI yet, now is a good time to start, because you won't have as much time as you'd really like when it becomes a business or organizational requirement.

It's also exciting, and if you get into it now, your annual revenue opportunities are going to be brighter. So, invest in yourself—start looking at PKI.

SECURITY POLICY CONSIDERATIONS

While each of the areas in this chapter are important, I want to spend a little time helping you reflect on how the identification and authentication process and security policies lose touch with each other. As we covered in the beginning, most administrators do not reflect on this topic. I say that because you'll almost never see identification and authentication covered in the security policies for an organization.

As a result, most networks have users with sensitive accounts using the same user ID and password on Internet sites—administrators falling into this category. You will also see a high incidence of network administrators or power users violating the doctrine of "least privileged access," by connecting to a remote Web site while logged into the system as an administrator, instead of going through a separate user account. This allows a rogue Web site, a piece of malicious code, or a virus to use your credentials, your current active sessions, and do any number of things that you aren't aware of and certainly can't control. A better practice, which Win2K supports, is to run your network sessions under your own personal credentials, and use administrator credentials only for the tasks that you need. If you need to act as an administrator for a particular task, press the SHIFT key, select the item, right-click, and choose Run As.

You may not realize that this is a big concern. Believe me, there are folks out there who have Web sites waiting for you and your users. Folks who will send your network users, including your administrators, interesting SPAM e-mail with an attractive offer—just click the hyperlink, said the spider to the fly.

There is one last thing to consider. Authentication records, properly maintained and controlled, have legal considerations. If you have the staff to achieve this, which most large networks do, you want to separate the administration and auditing functions in your Win2K system. Your administrators should be restricted from deleting event logs or other features that would allow them to alter records that would reflect abuse. This doesn't stop them from saving logs to a file during log rotations, but they shouldn't be allowed to delete authentication records captured in the Security event log.

RECAP

In this chapter we have covered a lot of ground, which is not to say that we have covered everything in detail. You will probably have to pursue additional reference material to enhance your understanding of the logon and authentication process, and its importance in your overall security posture. However, you should have a better understanding of what the landscape looks like, and awareness is an essential starting point. Here's what we hope you learned along the way.

▼ Authentication actually has two parts. The first part is how users present their credentials—which is called the *identification* process. The second part is how the system validates the credentials—which is called the *authentication* process.

■ We covered the relationship of authentication to authorization, which is what the users are allowed to do after they are authenticated successfully.

■ We reviewed the role of the Local Security Authority (LSA), how impersonation works, issues associated with delegation, pass-through authentication, and the benefits of mutual authentication.

▲ Criteria and methods of authentication were covered. This included some head-to-head reviews, and identification of when different methods are appropriate.

While other reference material can go into more detail on each of the authentication alternatives you have, we hope that you've gained a better understanding of how to select the proper alternatives for your network environment.

CHAPTER 12

File System and Network Share Security

Windows system administrators spend most of their time managing users and groups, folder and printer shares, and files and folders. And since these tasks usually have to occur yesterday, most administrators become too hurried to incorporate security into their everyday tasks. "Slap it in and worry about the details later" is the motto of the day. And although this scenario is understandable, ensure that you do not fall into this trap. Try to consider the security details as you perform your tasks, not after your systems or network have been exploited.

This chapter is designed to help you think about the security details during your daily administrative duties so, hopefully, security becomes second nature (if it is not already). Specifically, this chapter addresses the security involved in the daily tasks of managing your files and folders and your network shares. For more information on managing users and groups and the associated security concerns, see Chapter 10.

ACCESS-CONTROL MODEL

Before you delve into the details of securing your files, folders, and network shares, it may be helpful to peek under the hood and see how objects are secured within Win2K.

As you may already know, processes and threads do all of the work within any operating system. A *process*, in simple terms, is a series of commands that have been copied into memory and are currently being executed by the operating system. A *thread* is considered a lightweight version of a process in that it also executes a series of commands, but it does not allocate its own resources within the operating system—it shares the resources of the calling process. In practical terms, an application, utility, or service can execute multiple processes and each process can execute multiple threads.

The *Access-Control Model* is Win2K's overall security framework that governs how these processes and threads access *securable objects*. And unlike Windows 9x, all processes and threads must authenticate themselves to gain access to Win2K resources. To do so, processes and threads take on the security rights of the directing user or operating system component. For example, when you send a document to your printer, your application and its associated processes and threads take on the same rights as your user account.

A securable object, on the other hand, is simply any Windows object that can contain security information. Here is a list of some of the securable objects within Win2K:

- ▼ Files and folders
- ■ Network shares
- ■ Printers
- ■ Pipes
- ■ Processes and threads
- ■ Registry keys
- ▲ Services

Securable objects all share one common characteristic in that they have a *security descriptor*. The security descriptor identifies who owns the particular object, which users or groups have access to the object, and how Windows should handle auditing the object. For example, whenever you create a file, Win2K automatically names you as the resource owner, grants you access to the file (if this has not already been accomplished at the parent folder) and determines if this is a file that Windows needs to audit. (For more information on auditing, refer to Chapter 13.)

NOTE: The part of the security descriptor that contains information about which users and groups have access to an object is called a *discretionary access-control list (DACL)*. The part of the security descriptor that holds instructions on how Windows should audit the object is called the *system access-control list (SACL)*.

As you can see, the security descriptor is responsible for securing Win2K objects. So how does Win2K determine if any given user or group matches the information contained within the security descriptor? Win2K compares the *access token* to the security descriptor. An access token is created each time a user successfully logs into Win2K and contains the following:

▼ A Security Identifier (SID) for the logged-on users

■ The SIDs of groups that the user belongs to

■ The current logon session SID

■ A list of privileges held by the user or user's groups

■ The owner's SID

▲ The source of the access token

This access token is then associated with every thread and process started by that user. The token is compared to the security descriptor and access is either granted or denied for a particular action.

WIN2K FILE SYSTEMS

One of the most vital uses of the Access-Control Model is protecting your Win2K file system. The file system is a framework that the operating system uses to organize, manage, and keep track of your files. Win2K offers support for three different types of file systems: FAT16 (also known as FAT), FAT32, and NTFS. Each file system has its benefits and drawbacks, as shown in the Table 12-1.

As you can see, NTFS offers the greatest number of benefits—especially in terms of security. It offers file and folder permissions, encryption, and disk quotas. One of the major (if not only) benefits of FAT16 or FAT32 over NTFS is support for Windows 9x. This is critical for computers dual-booting Win2K and a 9x version of Windows. Normally,

	Largest Logical Volume Supported	Smallest Default Cluster Size for a 1GB Hard Drive	Largest Number of Root Directory Entries	File and Folder Security Support	Encrypting File System	Disk Quotas	Support for Windows 9x
FAT16	2GB	32KB	512	No	No	No	Yes
FAT32	2TB	4KB	Unlimited	No	No	No	Yes
NTFS	16EB	512 Bytes	Unlimited	Yes	Yes	Yes	No

Table 12-1. File System Comparisons—Major Features

dual-boot systems are confined to workstations that need backward compatibility for specific applications. You should never use Windows 9x on a critical network server! So in most cases, NTFS is the only real choice for Win2K servers.

If you are still not convinced of NTFS' superiority, here is a list of benefits:

▼ **Efficient Use of Disk Space**   Because NTFS uses smaller default cluster sizes, smaller files do not consume large amounts of disk space unnecessarily.

■ **NTFS Permissions**   NTFS has built-in security to secure files, folders, and drives. Neither FAT16 or FAT32 offers the native ability to allow or deny access to files and folders.

■ **File Compression**   NTFS offers file compression that is built into the operating system. Native compression is far more reliable than DriveSpace, which is included with the Win9x operating systems. You can compress files, folders, or drives.

■ **Encrypting File System**   With the introduction of Win2K, Microsoft offers encryption built into the operating system. This allows you to encrypt individual files or entire folders.

■ **Indexing**   By tightly integrating indexing with NTFS, Win2K allows you to search for files or folders using file system attributes as search criteria (for example, creation date, filename, and so on). You can control indexing to specific files, folders, or drives. The Indexing Service uses the NTFS *Change Journal*, which tracks additions, modifications, and deletions to files and folders. This modification to indexing improves file performance by eliminating entire volume rescans for these types of file changes.

NOTE: Although the Indexing Service's performance is improved in Win2K, you should limit indexing to only those files, folders, or drives that absolutely need it. The additional overhead associated with indexing can consume significant resources on your Win2K system.

▲ **Disk Quotas** Long missing in previous versions of Windows, disk quotas allow you to limit the amount of disk space used by specific users or groups. Win2K's implementation of disk quotas allows you to set a threshold to warn the user before violating the disk quota and also set a specific action once the user has crossed the limit.

FILE-LEVEL SECURITY

As mentioned previously, NTFS is the only logical choice for Win2K systems—especially those that do not need to dual-boot with Windows 9x. And in security terms, it is the only choice. Permissions, Encrypting File System (EFS), and disk quotas are all valuable tools to fight off potential attacks. The following sections assume that you agree and have installed NTFS on your Win2K system.

NTFS Permissions

The ability to secure your critical data is perhaps the most compelling reason to choose NTFS as your file system. *NTFS permissions* allow you to do this by controlling access to files, folders, or drives within the operating system and avoiding the use of third-party utilities. There are two overall recommendations when setting NTFS permissions:

▼ Grant access to groups, not users. In small organizations, you can still afford to manage permissions on a user-by-user basis. If you administer a network within a medium- to large-size business, you cannot. The sheer magnitude of managing files, folders, and drives by granting access to individual users would overwhelm a team of network administrators, let alone one administrator. Even if you are part of a smaller business, get in the habit of using groups. They will save you time and energy.

▲ Use inheritance. By default, files and folders inherit permissions from their parent container. For example, if you have granted Read Only access to the DOMAIN USERS group to your server's C: drive, all files and folders will inherit the same permission. The exception to this rule is if permissions have already been set (by you or Win2K) on a particular file or subfolder; those permissions take precedence and will not be changed.

Special Permissions

When you think of NTFS permissions, you probably think of the Read, Write, and Full Control rights that are popularly used to secure files and folders on a Win2K system. Those NTFS permissions, however, are comprised of a combination of *special permissions*. In addition to using the usual NTFS permissions, you can modify the special permissions to allow you more granular control over file and folder security. Table 12-2 outlines the various special permissions and their descriptions.

Permission	Description	Applies To...
Change Permissions	Grants or denies the ability to change NTFS permissions.	Files, folders, and drives
Create Files	Grants or denies the ability to create files within the folder or drive.	Folders and drives
Write Data	Grants or denies the ability to change data within files or overwrite any existing content.	Files
Create Folders	Grants or denies the ability to create subfolders.	Folders and drives
Append Data	Grants or denies the ability to add data to a file.	Files
Delete	Grants or denies the ability to delete a file or folder.	Files, folders, and drives
Delete Subfolders And Files	Grants or denies the ability to delete subfolders and files—even if the Delete permission has not been granted on a particular subfolder or file.	Folders and drives
List Folder	Grants or denies the ability to see file or folder names listed within a particular folder.	Folders and drives
Read Data	Grants or denies the ability to view data within a file.	Files

Table 12-2. Special Permissions

Permission	Description	Applies To...
Read Attributes	Grants or denies the ability to view the attributes of a file or folder (e.g., Hidden, Read Only, etc.).	Files and folders
Read Extended Attributes	Grants or denies the ability to view extended attributes of a file.	Files and folders
Read Permissions	Grants or denies the ability to view the NTFS permissions.	Files, folders, and drives
Synchronize	For multithreaded or multiprocess programs, this permission grants or denies the ability for multiple threads to wait for the use of the file or folder.	Files, folders, and drives
Take Ownership	Grants or denies the ability to change an owner of a file or folder. An owner can always change permissions regardless of the rights that already exist.	Files, folders, and drives
Traverse Folder	Grants or denies the ability to move through folders and subfolders. By default, everyone is granted the ability to ignore this right. To change it, you must modify the Group Policy.	Folders and drives

Table 12-2.   Special Permissions *(continued)*

Permission	Description	Applies To...
Execute File	Grants or denies the ability to run a program file.	Files
Write Attributes	Grants or denies the ability to change attributes.	Files and folders
Write Extended Attributes	Grants or denies the ability to change any extended attributes.	Files and folders

Table 12-2.   Special Permissions *(continued)*

MODIFYING SPECIAL PERMISSIONS   To modify special permissions, perform these steps:

1. Within the Windows Explorer or a similar Win2K tool, right-click the desired file, folder, or drive and select Properties.

2. Within the Properties dialog box, click the Security tab.

3. Click the Advanced button.

4. Within the Access Control Settings dialog box, select the permission that you would like to modify and click the View/Edit button. Win2K will display the Permission Entry dialog box shown here.

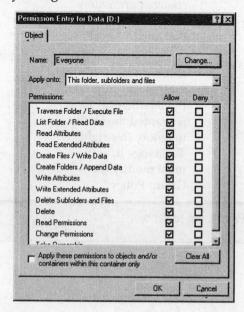

Within the Permission Entry dialog box, select the Allow box for any special permission that you would like to explicitly allow or the Deny box for any permission you would like to explicitly deny. The Apply Onto drop-down box also allows you more granularity in how those special permissions are applied. For example, you can choose to apply the permissions to this folder only, this folder and subfolders, the files contained within this folder only, or other combinations.

NTFS Permissions and Descriptions

As mentioned previously, NTFS permissions combine the rights and abilities of the special permissions. NTFS permissions are more commonly used because they usually suit most security purposes and situations. In addition, using the NTFS permission saves the administrative work of modifying special permissions for each secured file, folder, or drive.

Table 12-3 outlines the various NTFS permissions and their unique combination of special permissions.

NTFS Permission	Combination of Special Permissions	Applies To...
Read	List Folder/Read Data Read Attributes Read Extended Attributes Read Permissions Synchronize	Files, folders, and drives
Write	Create Files/Write Data Create Folders/Append Data Write Attributes Write Extended Attributes Read Permissions Synchronize	Files, folders, and drives
Read and Execute	Same as Read permission with the addition of: Traverse Folder/Execute File	Files, folders, and drives

Table 12-3.   NTFS Permissions

NTFS Permission	Combination of Special Permissions	Applies To...
List Folder Contents	Same as Read and Execute permission	Folders and drives
Modify	Same as Read and Execute permission with the addition of: Create Files/Write Data Create Folders/Append Data Delete Write Attributes Write Extended Attributes	Files, folders, and drives
Full Control	Same as Delete permission with the addition of: Delete Subfolders and Files Change Permissions Take Ownership	Files, folders, and drives

Table 12-3. NTFS Permissions (continued)

MODIFYING NTFS PERMISSIONS   To modify NTFS permissions, perform these steps:

1. Within the Windows Explorer or a similar Win2K tool, right-click the desired file, folder, or drive and select Properties.

2. Within the Properties dialog box, click the Security tab. Win2K will display the Security sheet, as shown here.

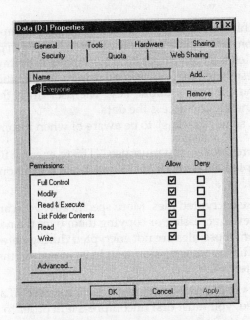

Within the Security sheet, click the Add button to grant new users or groups access to this file, folder, or drive. Select a particular user or group and click the Remove button to deny users from accessing this file, folder, or drive. To modify the rights associated with a particular user or group, highlight the user or group account in the Name field and select the Allow box for any special permission that you would like to explicitly allow or the Deny box for any permission you would like to explicitly deny.

NOTE: You can modify NTFS Permissions from the command prompt using the resource kit XCACLS command. Type **XCACLS /?** for more information.

Encrypting File System (EFS)

One of the major security holes with Windows NT 4.0 was (and still is) the vulnerability of data once an attacker has physical access to your computer. For example, if your laptop were stolen, normal user authentication and NTFS permissions could effectively block an attacker from logging into Windows NT 4.0 and accessing your data. However, using another operating system (such as Linux), an attacker could bypass Windows NT 4.0, mount the NTFS volume, and access your files and any sensitive data stored within.

In order to combat this type of security weakness, Win2K's implementation of NTFS was built with encryption native to the operating system. The *Encrypting File System (EFS)* allows you to encrypt files as a native operating system feature—much like file compression. Using EFS, each designated file is encrypted using a combination of a Win2K-generated encryption key and the user's public key. The user must then use his/her own private key to decrypt the file and access the data.

There are, however, some "gotchas" to be aware of when it comes to EFS:

▼ As mentioned previously, you must use NTFS to encrypt files and folders. If you have encrypted a file under NTFS and move it to a non-NTFS volume, the file is decrypted.

■ You cannot share encrypted files. More specifically, you can share files that are encrypted; however, accessing or copying them over the network will decrypt them. In addition, those files are not encrypted during network transmission. To protect files during transmission, you have to use another method such as IPSec (see Chapter 16).

■ You cannot encrypt files or folders that are compressed. If a volume, folder, or file is compressed, you must first uncompress it in order to use encryption.

■ Only the user who encrypted the file or a data encryption recovery agent (see "Disaster Recovery" a bit later in this chapter) can decrypt it.

■ System files cannot be encrypted.

▲ Encrypted files can still be deleted.

It is important to keep these "gotchas" in mind when planning how and where data encryption is employed. In addition, to help you plan a data encryption policy, here is a list of recommended best practices when using EFS:

▼ Encrypt the folder where a user stores most of his/her documents. This ensures that all user documents are encrypted by default.

■ Encrypt any folders that hold applications' temp files. Since temp files often contain the same sensitive data as your original document and are not always promptly removed from the system, encrypting them should be a priority.

▲ Encrypt folders instead of files to ensure the greatest number of files are protected and to reduce administrative overhead.

Encrypting a File or Folder

To encrypt a file or folder, follow these steps:

1. Within Windows Explorer or a similar tool, right-click the desired file or folder and select Properties.

2. Within the General sheet, click the Advanced button.

3. Within the Advanced Attributes sheet, select the Encrypt Contents to Secure Data checkbox, as shown here.

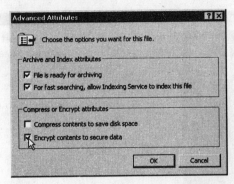

If you have chosen to encrypt a file that does not reside within an encrypted folder, Win2K will display the following warning message. This dialog box gives you the opportunity to encrypt the parent folder or simply encrypt the file.

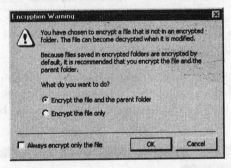

To decrypt a file, follow the same procedure and simply uncheck the Encrypt Contents to Secure Data checkbox.

NOTE: You can also encrypt and decrypt files from the command prompt using the CIPHER command. Type **CIPHER /?** for more details.

Disaster Recovery

Because, by default, only the user who encrypted a file can open it, it is important to have a backup strategy in case the file encryption certificate and associated private key are damaged or lost. For an individual Win2K system, this is a straightforward task. Follow these steps:

1. Using the MMC snap-in Certificates, select Personal | Certificates.

2. From the right pane, select the certificate issued to you with the intended purpose of Encrypting File System.

3. Right-click the certificate and select All Tasks | Export. Win2K will start the Certificate Export Wizard, as shown here.

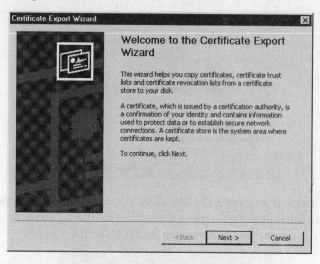

4. Use the wizard to export the certificate and associate private key to a floppy disk. Then store the floppy disk in a secure place.

If the certificate is ever lost or damaged, restore the certificate and associate private key using Certificates. Select Personal and right-click Certificates and select All Tasks | Import. Win2K will start the Certificate Import Wizard (shown here) to restore the lost certificate and key.

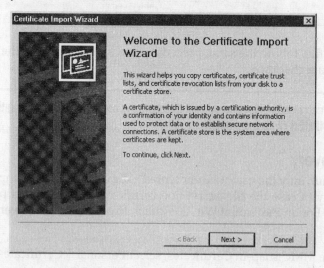

However, in a business environment, it is equally important that administrators have a backup method to access data if a network user has encrypted it—especially in situations where the employee has left the company and has left encrypted data behind. At the domain, organizational unit, or computer level, administrators can set three different types of *encrypted data recovery policies*:

▼ **Recovery Agent Policy** Designated users and certificates can recover encrypted data within their area of responsibility (that is, domain, OU, and so on). The default recovery agent for the domain is the domain administrator.

■ **No Recovery Policy** When the Encrypted Data Recovery Agents policy is removed, a no-recovery policy is in place. No recovery agents have been designated to recover encrypted data; however, each computer's local policy is in effect. The default recovery agent in this case is the local administrator.

▲ **Empty Recovery Policy** When all recovery agents and associated certificates are removed, EFS is effectively turned off. No one can encrypt or decrypt data within the scope of the policy.

To enact any of these policies, launch the MMC snap-in Group Policy. Connect the domain you would like to enact a policy. Select Computer Configuration | Windows Settings | Security Settings | Public Key Policies | Encrypted Data Recovery Agents. Right-click and select Add to add recovery agents. Right-click and select Delete Policy to enforce a no-recovery policy. Right-click and select Delete All Listed Users and Certificates to enforce an empty recovery policy.

Disk Quotas

Disk quotas limit the amount of disk space any user or group of users can utilize on a particular Win2K system. Normally, disk quotas are used on servers where network users share data and consume disk space. You may not normally think of disk quotas as a security feature. However, much like a credit card limit, they can be an effective way to limit the damage of a malicious user.

Specifically, disk quotas can thwart denial of service attacks that create a large number of files or large-sized files filling up precious disk space, thereby denying disk space to other network users. Although this type of attack is not permanently damaging to your system, if it occurs on a volume that contains the Win2K system files, an attack can shut down the Win2K system.

To enable disk quotas on a particular drive, follow these steps:

1. Right-click the drive and select Properties | Quota.

2. Select Enable Quota Management.

3. To help fend off denial of service attacks, you should also check the Deny Disk Space to Users Exceeding Quota Limit option. Set the appropriate quota options as shown here.

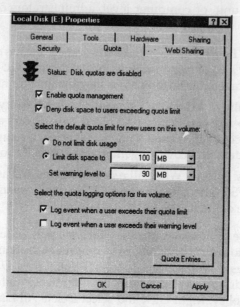

NETWORK SHARES

The ability to share resources is not new to Win2K, so a good portion of this section will probably be a review for most Windows administrators. However, for those of you new to the Windows platform, a *network share* is a vital feature that allows network users to share a particular Windows resource. In particular, this section will focus on sharing folders and printers and using the *Distributed file system (Dfs)*.

Shared Folders

A *shared folder* is simply a drive or folder that is shared out to other network users. With the proper permissions and access, other users can access information on your Win2K workstation or server. For example, if you need to create one data location where the Accounting department can store its files, you could create the folder D:\DEPT\ACCT on your Win2K server to store those files. However, in order for the accounting folks to be able to access the directory, you must share it out to them. In this case, you might create a share named ACCT that they can easily find within their copy of My Network Places.

To create a share, perform these steps:

1. Within Windows Explorer or a similar tool, right-click the desired drive or folder and select Sharing.

2. Select the Share This Folder option.

3. Enter a share name and any desired comments and set a user limit as shown here.

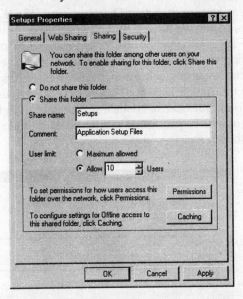

To modify the share permissions, click the Permissions button. Use the Add button to add users or groups and the Remove button to remove users and groups. Once you have the correct users and groups, explicitly grant access by checking the Allow checkbox or explicitly deny access by checking the Deny checkbox.

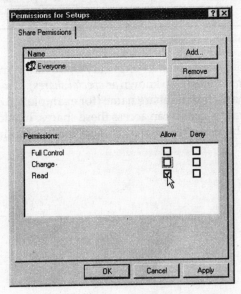

Publishing Network Resources

Another spectacular feature of Active Directory and Win2K is that you can *publish* network resources, including shared folders. Publishing is like listing a business in the yellow pages—it allows potential customers the ability to quickly and easily find your resource. Using the Find feature, network users can search for shared folders regardless of which server or workstation the shared folders reside on. To publish a shared folder, use the Active Directory Users and Computers tool. Navigate to the container where you would like to create a shared folder, right-click and select New | Shared Folder. You will be prompted to enter a new name and the UNC path of the shared folder, as shown here.

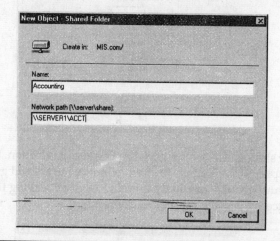

In addition to folders that you may explicitly share out, Win2K creates default shares known as *administrative shares* (also known as *special shares*). These shared folders are usually distinguished by a $ after the share name (for example, C$ or ADMIN$). Only members of the Administrators group can access these shares. In addition, you can only view these types of shares by using the Shared Folders MMC snap-in shown here.

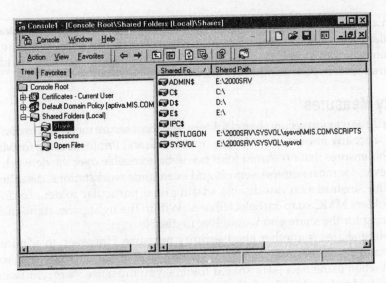

Here is a list of the typical administrative shares:

▼ **Drive$**   Win2K creates this default share for each drive on your system—for example, C$, D$, E$, and so on.

■ **ADMIN$**   This share is used during remote administration tasks and points to the \WINNT folder.

■ **IPC$**   This share is used by programs to share Windows named pipes.

■ **NETLOGON**   This is used by Win2K servers only. It points to the \WINNT\SYSVOL\SYSVOL*domain*\SCRIPTS folder.

▲ **SYSVOL**   This is used by Win2K domain controllers to store a copy of a domain's public files among domain controllers. It points to \WINNT\SYSVOL\SYSVOL.

NOTE: You can add a dollar sign to the end of any specified share name to turn it into a *hidden share*. The advantage to a hidden share is that it will not be displayed within My Network Places or Network Neighborhood among network users. Note, however, that you will still have to (and definitely should) restrict the access on hidden shares. Just because they are hidden does not mean they are secure.

From a data access standpoint, shared folders are a great way to share one instance of a particular file (or files) among all users on the network. This eliminates multiple copies and versions of files stored on individual computers. From a security standpoint, however, shared folders pose another security threat.

Security Measures

There are three ways to secure shared folders. The most secure method is to disable Win2K's ability to share any resources. To do this, disable File and Printer Sharing for Microsoft Networks. This ensures that no shared folders will be accessible over the network.

However, for most network servers and even some workstations, disabling sharing is not possible. Instead you can disable sharing on a particular folder. To do so, use the Shared Folders MMC snap-in. Select Shares. Within the right pane, right-click and select Stop Sharing for the share you would like to disable.

Disabling shares is another good security measure. However, to administer Win2K remotely and for some programs, you cannot disable administrative shares. In these cases and when using necessary shared folders, you must use *share permissions* to secure the shared folder. Like NTFS permissions, share permissions provide another level of security to allow only authorized users to access your data. However, unlike NTFS permissions, there are only three permission levels:

▼ **READ**   Allows a user or group to view file and subfolder names, traverse subfolders, view files, and run programs.

■ **CHANGE**   Grants the same permissions as Read but also allows a user or group to add files and subfolders, change data in files, and delete files and subfolders.

▲ **FULL CONTROL**   Grants the same permissions as Change but also allows a user or group to change NTFS permissions and take ownership of files and subfolders.

SHARE PERMISSIONS VERSUS NTFS PERMISSIONS   Share permissions specify restrictions (or the lack thereof) on how network users can view and manipulate data on your computer. They do not apply to any user who might physically log on to your computer. In addition, share permissions specify the maximum rights available to users connecting to the shared folder over the network.

NTFS permissions, on the other hand, specify the restrictions on how *any* users can view and manipulate data on your computer—including users who log on locally. NTFS permissions also serve to further restrict access to any files and folders within a shared drive or folder. For example, if the ACCT share has the Read share permission, but the NTFS permission is Full Control, a connected network user will only have Read access. If the ACCT share has the Read share permission, but the NTFS permission is No Access, a connected network user will have no access to the files and folders.

NOTE: The largest threat posed by shared folders or drives is that whenever you create a folder share, the share is shared out to the Everyone group with the Full Control permission—by default! It is absolutely critical that you modify this setting. The best situation would be to remove the Everyone group and only include necessary users and groups. If, however, you have to use the Everyone group to provide universal access, set the permission to Read. If network users need Change or Full Control access, only grant those permissions to specific users and groups.

Distributed file system (Dfs)

The Distributed file system (Dfs) is an excellent administrative tool introduced with Windows 2000. Dfs allows you to publish shared folders from a number of servers into one namespace that is transparent to network users. This means that users can access one share over the network that actually points to a number of shares on a number of different Win2K systems.

In addition, administrators can use Dfs for fault-tolerance and load balancing. Dfs allows you to replicate Dfs roots and shared folders to multiple servers on the network. In case of server failure, users still have access to their critical files and folders. Or if one server is inundated with network traffic, replication allows another server (or servers) to pick up the slack.

NOTE: To install, configure, and manage Dfs, use the Distributed file system tool located within the `Administrative Tools` folder.

As far as security is concerned, Dfs itself poses no additional security risks. Instead of implementing another set of permissions or access requirements, Dfs uses the permissions already implemented on a particular shared folder. For example, if you publish SERVER1's ACCT share through Dfs, it still retains the same share and NTFS permissions that you have previously set. Publishing the folder over the network via Dfs changes nothing.

Shared Printers

A *print server* used to be a necessary component of a network when sharing printers among network users. The print server usually ran on a centralized server and serviced multiple printers. Because printers generally do not have enough memory to store every user's document, a print server's main responsibility was to receive, prioritize, and queue documents that need to be printed. These documents waited in the *print queue* until the printer was ready. Once the printer had enough memory, the print server would then send a document to the printer.

In many of today's networks, however, the centralized print server is slowly disappearing. Instead, each workstation is queuing user documents and waiting to connect to network printers. This type of situation reduces the administrative overhead associated with centralized print servers and offloads the printing tasks from the file servers.

Win2K, however, still offers the ability to share printers and act as a centralized print server. This can be especially useful in peer-to-peer network environments. Simply physically connect a printer to a Win2K system, share the printer out, and all network users can use that one printer.

To share a printer, perform these steps:

1. Within the `Printers` folder, right-click and select Sharing for the printer you would like to share.

2. Select the Shared As option and enter a share name as shown here.

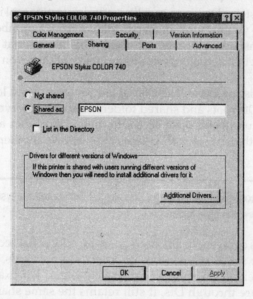

Security Measures

Shared printers do not work like shared folders in that they offer no shared permissions. Instead, you must use NTFS permissions to secure printers and ensure that only authorized users can print, manage documents sent to the printer, or manage the printer itself.

To modify NTFS permissions on a printer, perform these steps:

1. Within the `Printers` folder, right-click and select Properties for the desired printer.

2. Select the Security tab.

3. Within the Security sheet (as shown here), click the Add button to grant new users or groups access to this file, folder, or drive. Select a particular user or group and click the Remove button to deny users from accessing this file, folder, or drive. To modify the rights associated with a particular user or group, highlight the user or group account in the Name field, and select the Allow box for any special permission that you would like to explicitly allow or the Deny box for any permission you would like to explicitly deny.

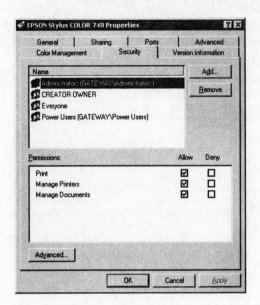

RECAP

Since most of your day is probably consumed with managing files, folders, drives, and network shares, it is important that you learn the security risks. This chapter introduced you to some of the existing risks and provided ways to thwart would-be attackers. Incorporating sound security practices into your administrative tasks may cost you a little extra time now, but in terms of passing security audits and preventing data theft, it will save you loads of time in the future.

CHAPTER 13

Auditing

A uditing does not prevent a potential security problem, but the data gathered may alert you once an event has occurred. Auditing is critical to maintaining the security of your servers and networks because it lets you track events that occur on the machines within your environment—events triggered by both authorized users and by intruders. In addition to *authentication* and *authorization*, Win2K provides a number of tools that enable the system administrator to audit events and wade through the data that may be generated.

The auditing capabilities of Win2K are an evolution of those provided since the earliest version of NT. However, there are some new additions that this chapter will cover. Before we go into the new capabilities let's consider some of the implications of gathering audit information. If you are going to gather information, you should have some ideas about how it is intended to be used and think about how it might be misused.

POLICIES

The default Win2K audit policy collects no information. Most other operating system vendors take a similar approach. No data is gathered until someone at the customer site has put at least a little thought into what should be collected. The defaults are optimized for the convenience of the typical customer or end user, not for the security-conscious system administrator.

Since you are reading this book, you probably are concerned about the security of your computer systems. You may be tempted to configure auditing as one of the first tasks that you perform when you first install a new computer or new Windows domain. In general, this is what you should do. However, if you don't have a policy for your systems, you should take some time to think about the issues before you even turn on your computers.

You should consider auditing a practice that requires strict controls and procedures. Most large corporations have an existing auditing policy. Some industries have their policies imposed by external regulators. Your Win2K auditing practices should conform to your company's standards. If your company or site does not have any existing standards, you should consider creating some.

RFC 2196, also known as the Site Security Handbook, has some sections that cover these same concepts. Section 4.6.5 states, "If you collect and save audit data, you need to be prepared for consequences resulting both from its existence and its content." Our coverage of these concepts is not intended to be comprehensive, but your organization should consider the legal issues involved with audit data.

The auditing data that you gather should help you secure your environment and troubleshoot problems. However, it is possible that this data could be put to many other uses. It might get subpoenaed during a criminal investigation or civil litigation. It might be used to monitor what employees are doing while using the computers. Audit logs might be used by intruders to determine which users have elevated privileges or where interesting data resides. The data might even be used by a competitor to determine who your customers are.

When creating a policy you should also decide what will be done with the auditing information if a security incident occurs. Will immediate backups be made? Will the logs be handed over to a law enforcement agency without a court order? Will additional steps be taken to create a chain of evidence for future prosecution? Suppose that a senior vice president of your corporation has read an internal memo that has a filename of `Mutagenic Effects of Our Product XYZ`. It's a safe bet that someone in the company cares about who should have access to that information and how long it should be kept around.

You may want to have a separate policy for each type of machine in your environment:

▼   End user's desktop and laptop computers

■   Application servers

■   Domain Controllers

▲   Machines located on your perimeter networks such as a Web server used for e-commerce.

Some of the areas that should be covered in your policy are

▼   Log disposal and rotation

■   Log retention time

■   Log contents

▲   Log accessibility

OVERVIEW OF WIN2K AUDITING

Hopefully, the previous section got your attention, and you are now convinced that this is an important chapter. Let's now take a step back and get a better of idea of what Win2K provides for auditing. Then we can make some informed decisions about what and how we want to configure things.

Like NT, Win2K includes an Event Logging Service; it is not an active detection system, but instead a consumer of information provided by other objects. Each computer that has auditing enabled stores the data on its local disk. All Win2K computers have at least three log files: Application, Security, and System. Win2K servers may have an additional three log files: Directory Service, DNS Server, and File Replication Service. The Directory Service and File Replication Service event logs are only displayed in Event Viewer when looking at a domain controller, and the DNS logs are only available on servers running the DNS service.

Each of these logs has a physical file that holds the data. By default all logs are located in the `%WINDOWS%\System32\Config` directory.

▼   `Appevent.evt`   Contains the Application event log data. This file contains the data generated by user-mode applications. All users can write to the application event log via the event API. By default all users are also able to view this log using the Event Viewer application.

- `Sysevent.evt` Contains the System event log data. This file contains the data generated by system processes and kernel-mode device drivers. Again, all users may write to this log and by default all users may view the data using the Event Viewer.

- `Secevent.evt` Contains the Security event log data. This file contains audit events messages from privileged processes that are running as the LocalSystem or as Administrator. By default only members of the Administrator group can read and clear this log. Additional users can perform these tasks if they have been granted the Manage Auditing and Security Log user right or the SE_AUDIT_NAME privilege.

- `DNSEvent.evt` Contains data that is generated by the Microsoft DNS server. The DNS Server event log is only available for viewing on servers that are running the Win2K DNS server. The file contains information such as when the DNS server successfully completes a zone transfer to another server and the IP address of the remote server; when the local DNS server writes a new version of the zone file; and when the DNS server has detected bad or unexpected packets or excessive replication traffic.

- `NTDS.evt` Contains the Directory Service log events generated by the Active Directory Server that relate to the running and maintenance of the service. At this time Microsoft has not provided a file that describes all of the event IDs that may appear in this log. Hopefully, a future resource kit will include this, or the user community will independently create it. By examining the filter property sheet for the event log in the Event Viewer, it is possible to view the currently registered event sources and categories. Some of the individual events that can be logged include information about defragmentation operations on the database, when they start and when they complete; LDAP authentication negotiation problems; unavailability of LDAP over SSL due to a missing or invalid certificate; failure to contact the global catalog; intersite messaging problems; and modifications to intersite topology.

- ▲ `NTFRS.evt` Contains the events that concern the File Replication Service. Like the DNS log, the filter screen of the Event Viewer won't give you a lot of information about what types of events may appear in this log. But individual events may include information about starting the File Replication Service and when the File Replication Service stops, which also prevents the computer from acting as a domain controller.

While the Win2K operating systems generate events that appear in the Application and System event log it should also be pointed out that any third-party applications may normally do this as well. When your company evaluates third-party software for purchase, outsources custom development, or develops software internally, the logging capabilities should be considered or specified. Proper integration with the existing system can improve overall system administration.

Types of Security-Related Events

From a security analyst's perspective, the three broad categories that can be monitored are logon and logoff, object access, and process tracking. The logon and logoff information is generated by the Local Security Authority (LSA). The operating system provides support for object auditing. These objects include files, directories, printers, and Registry keys. Using this feature, we can monitor which users have accessed which files. Process tracking, sometimes called *detailed tracking,* is also built into the operating system. This feature provides us with the ability to record which programs a user is running on a computer and which programs a server is using.

It is important to note that auditing relies heavily on the NTFS file system. The log files cannot be properly secured if another file system such as FAT or FAT-32 is being used. Also, file system auditing cannot be enabled if NTFS is not being used.

The Event Logging Service

All access to the event log files is mediated through the Event Logging Service that is encapsulated in the EVENTLOG.EXE file. The service cannot be paused or stopped once it has been started. However, an administrator can configure the service not to start on the next system reboot. This is not recommended. Also, direct access to the log files is possible if the system is restarted under another operating system that has NTFS support, for example, DOS or Linux.

The Event Logging Service opens the event log files when it first starts. These files remain open and are locked for writing by the Event Logging Service only. A sharing violation will occur if another process attempts to write directly to the event log. Furthermore, the service sets bits in the header of an open event log file so that if another process attempts to copy the file, it will be interpreted as being corrupt and the copy will fail.

User-mode applications communicate with the Event Logging Service through the event logging API. This is provided within the ADVAPI32.DLL file. Kernel-mode programs communicate with the service through the I/O Manager and may only write events.

Any program that is properly registered may send an event report to the Event Logging Service by using the event logging API. The Event Logging Service formats the event report and writes it into the appropriate event log. The native user account audit data and file system audit data are generated by the *Security Reference Monitor (SRM).* This is a kernel-mode component that does the actual access validation, as well as the audit generation. The data still gets written to the logs via the Event Logging Service.

Protocols and Ports Used to Access the Event Logs Remotely

Examination of the traffic generated by the Win2K Event Viewer shows that all of the traffic is a mixture of the MSRPC and SMB protocols. Like many Microsoft applications, the Event Viewer uses RPC over SMB. The SMB connections will use simple protected negotiation (SPNEGO) to negotiate the authentication method. This should normally lead to using Kerberos. You will see MSRPC traffic over port 445 or 139 (SMB ports are described in Chapter 6). Traffic going from the queried machine travels back to the original machine on the initial source port. This is the same mechanism that is used on WinNT.

Managing the Audit Logs

You don't want to gather all of the data that it is possible to collect. If you have too much data you will find it difficult to review the information. Collecting the data does take some CPU and disk access time. It also requires disk storage. It is possible to misconfigure the audit-gathering capabilities so that a computer spends almost all of its time filling up the audit logs and has no spare cycles to process user commands or requests. You don't want to create your own denial-of-service attack—it wouldn't look good on your resume.

USING THE GATHERED INFORMATION

Once your system has been configured to log information, you will need to know how to use the data. If you are concerned about security you probably want to have some idea about the overall logon activity on the computers under your control or within the domain. Since Windows saves the information locally, how do you do this without visiting each and every event log on each and every computer? Note that domain logons do get recorded on the DC that was used to authenticate the user. There are some time-saving tips, but in the long run you should consider using tools that

▼ Consolidate the information centrally

■ Programmatically review the information

▲ Generate notifications if a potential problem is detected

If you have to review the information manually, one thing to remember is that most user's logon scripts, or profiles, perform standard drive mappings to remote file servers as soon as a user logs in. A good place to get started is by looking at the logs for the central file servers and checking for events with a *type 3* logon. A type 3 logon indicates a network (remote) logon, as will be generated by mapping a file. Assuming that the file server only performs this function and that it is not normally used for interactive logins, it is even more important to see if there are any *type 2* (interactive) logons, since this would tend to be even more unusual.

Another helpful fact to remember is that domain controllers don't record all failed logins, but they will record account lockouts. If your site uses common practices look for event ID 644 (see Figure 13-1) on the DC's security logs. These are the result of several failed login attempts in a short period of time, as defined by your account policies. Remember, your administrator accounts won't get locked out so this is not an effective method of determining if someone is using a brute force password-guessing attack on the administrator accounts.

If you have many users executing software from the file server, then you should consider enabling object access auditing on the executable files. Of course you have already made the files read-only so that nobody can replace or modify the files to introduce a Trojan Horse or virus. However, if you enable object access auditing on the files, you will be able to determine if someone has attempted, or been able to, open the files with write ac-

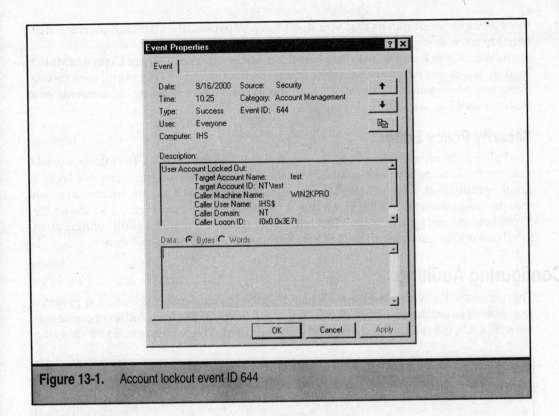

Figure 13-1.   Account lockout event ID 644

cess. But remember, Win2K doesn't tell you what the user did to the file, only the type of access that was used to open the file. Don't jump to conclusions too quickly. Take your time and determine the facts.

ADMINISTRATION

This section introduces you to the tools used to administer and view the event logs.

Tools

We need to introduce the tools before we describe more of the features and uses. These tools will be referenced throughout this chapter, so knowing about them in advance is a must.

The Event Viewer

The Event Viewer application displays the logged data by communicating with the Event Logging Service via the event logging API. It may be used to view logs on the local computer, or it may communicate over the network to view remote logs. This has some advantages. It means that you don't have to personally visit each machine that needs to have its logs reviewed.

In Win2K the Event Viewer has become a Microsoft Management Console (MMC) snap-in. If it doesn't appear as a choice in your Administrative Tools menu, then choose Computer Management. The MMC, with the Event Viewer showing the contents of a System event log, is shown in Figure 13-2.

Security Policy Editor

The Policy Editor is used to manage the security policy in the LSDOU. The interface to administer the local policy (L) is available via the Control Panels | Administrative Tools | Local Security Policy menu selection. The Group Policies (SDOU) are administered on the specific containers (SDOU) Properties | Group Policy section. Figure 13-3 shows the Event Log settings for the Default Domain Policy Group Policy. The audit configuration interfaces are the same for all the LSDOU settings, so a local one is not shown.

Configuring Auditing

This section will cover using the tools just described to configure the event log parameters, as well as set the auditable events. If you are going to use only AD level configurations (SDOU), then all can be configured from the Group Policy interface. If you are going

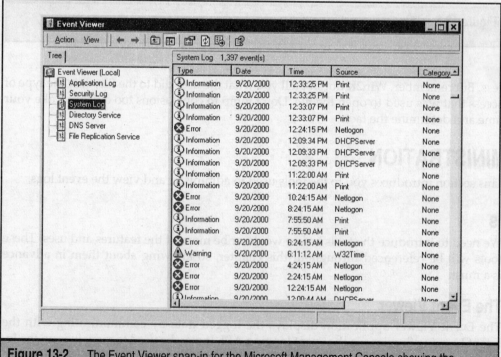

Figure 13-2.   The Event Viewer snap-in for the Microsoft Management Console showing the contents of a System event log

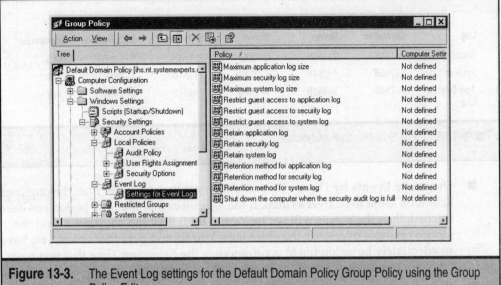

Figure 13-3. The Event Log settings for the Default Domain Policy Group Policy using the Group Policy Editor

to configure the local settings, you will use the Event Viewer to set the Event Log settings, and the Local System Policy to set the actual Audit Policy (events to audit). Our discussion and description will be on AD-based auditing. If you do have to use the Event Viewer, it is the exact same interface that WinNT used for the Event Log settings.

VIP: Although the default configuration does not enable any auditing, we offer some suggested base auditing configurations for users and domains. These settings may not be the best practices for your particular company or industry. You should refer to the "Policies" section of this chapter before implementing any of these configurations.

Setting Event Log Parameters

First we need to set what we will have in terms of our Event Log settings. The settings that can be configured (for the Application, System, and Security), as shown in Figure 13-3, are as follows:

▼ **Maximum Size**   Sets the maximum size the log will grow to. This can be set for the three main (Application, Security, and System) logs. The effect of this value really is dependent on your log review process as well as what you do when the log fills. Log size recommendations are listed in Table 13-1.

■ **Retention Time**   Defines the *Retain* parameter, which is the number of days that events should be maintained until they are allowed to be overwritten.

■ **Retention Method**   Determines what to do with the logs *if* the event log fills up. Retention methods and times are specified in Table 13-2.

Log	Domain Controller	File and Print Server	Database Server	Web Server	RAS Servers	Workstation
Security Log	5–10MB	2–4MB	2–4MB	2–4MB	5–10MB	1MB
System Log	1–2MB	1–2MB	1–2MB	1–2MB	1–2MB	1MB
Application Log	1–2MB	1–2MB	1–2MB	1–2MB	1–2MB	1MB

Table 13-1. Log Size Recommendations

- **Overwrite Events by Days** Causes the events that are older than the required Retention Time to be overwritten. If the logs fill before the time period has been reached, then the events will not be logged until the time has passed, and the service can now overwrite the older logs. You should note that unless you have an adequately large log file to accommodate the Retention Time that you have set, you are setting yourself up to miss critical audit data.

- **Overwrite Events as Needed** Causes the oldest events to be written over, regardless of the Retention Time requirement. This is the safest method, but can be exploited by an attacker by flooding the logs to overwrite potential critical information. This should be used only if you do not have any log maintenance programs in place.

- **Do Not Overwrite Events (Clear Logs Manually)** Requires you to clear the logs manually. This will ensure that anything that is logged is there until the administrator clears it. It has the same problem as Overwrite Events by Days in that once the logs are full, there are no more events written until the log is cleared. This method works well if you have a regular review method and an intrusion detection system that will alert you if your logs are almost full.

- **Restrict Guest Access** Removes the ability of the Everyone group to access the logs. Normally, the Application and System event logs are accessible by any user. The Security log is normally only viewable by administrative level accounts.

Log	Overwrite Policy Setting
Security Log	Overwrite events older than 21 days
System Log	Overwrite events older than 14 days
Application Log	Overwrite events as necessary

Table 13-2. Log Retention Recommendations

▲ **Shut Down the Computer When the Security Audit Log Is Full**   Also known as the CrashOnAuditFail registry key. If you have this set, and your logs fill up (that is, you have Do Not Overwrite Events or Overwrite Event Older Than X Days and it is less than that number) and can't be written to, the system will halt (literally). If this happens, only administrative users will be able to log in. *This setting is not recommended for systems that must be highly available.*

Setting Audit Policy

After we configure the Event Log settings, we need to set the actual Audit Policy. This is where we define what we will actually be capturing. There are nine different audit categories that we can select, and they are shown in Figure 13-4. Table 13-3 lists recommended Audit Policy settings.

NOTE: All values can be set to audit Success or Failure. Success will generate an audit entry when the given action is successful. Failure will generate an audit entry when the given action fails.

▼ **Audit Account Logon Events**   Audits user logon/logoff events where this computer was used to validate the account. For example, if a user logs into a workstation with a domain account, the DC that was used to validate the credentials will make an entry in its Security event log.

■ **Audit Account Management**   Audits account management events on the system. Events are things such as creating or deleting a user or group or changing a user password.

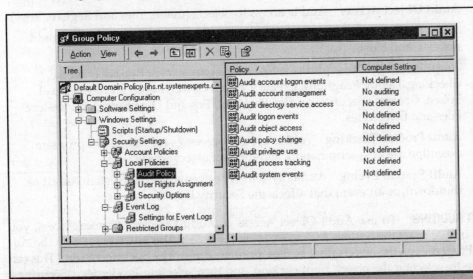

Figure 13-4.   Default Audit Policy (no auditing)

Event Category	Success	Failure
Audit Account Logon Events	X	X
Audit Account Management	X	X
Audit Directory Service Access		X
Audit Logon Events	X	X
Audit Object Access		X
Audit Policy Change	X	X
Audit Privilege Use		X
Audit Process Tracking		
Audit System Events		X

Table 13-3. Recommended Audit Policy Settings

- ■ **Audit Directory Service Access** Audits access objects in the Active Directory.

- ■ **Audit Logon Events** Audits user logon and logoff on the machine the user is logging into. This will audit logon types (such as network, interactive, batch, and so on). An important note is that if you use this in conjunction with Audit Account Logon Events, then you will have an audit trail that has an event in the domain the account exists in, as well as the system the account logged into.

- ■ **Audit Object Access** Audits access to objects (that is, files and Registry keys).

- ■ **Audit Policy Change** Audits all changes to user rights assignments, audit policies, and trusts.

- ■ **Audit Privilege Use** Audits use of user rights, except Bypass Traverse Checking, Debug Programs, Create a Token Object, Replace Process Level Token, Generate Security Audits, Back Up Files and Directories, and Restore Files and Directories.

- ■ **Audit Process Tracking** Audits system processes for things like program execution, process termination, and indirect object access.

- ▲ **Audit System Events** Audits system-type events, such as system restart or shutdown, or an event that affects the Security log.

OBJECT AUDITING To use Audit Object Access or Audit Directory Service Access, you will also have to set the System ACL (SACL) on the object. The SACL is set with the Auditing Properties on the objects (that is, files, printers, directory object, and so on). This can be done by selecting the object, right-clicking, and then selecting Properties | Security | Advanced | Auditing. Figure 13-5 shows the audit properties that can be set on a file or folder object (note that the one property that is cut off in the figure is Take Ownership).

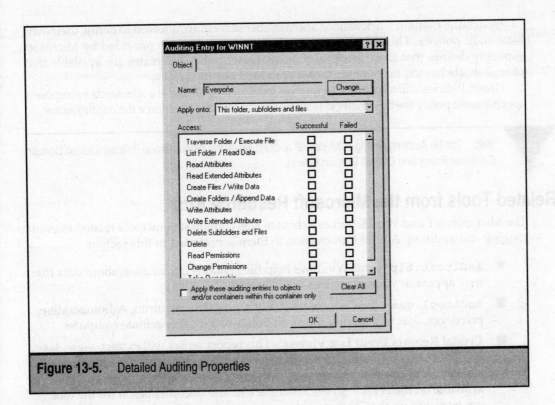

Figure 13-5.   Detailed Auditing Properties

NOTE: The System ACL (SACL) also uses inheritance, so audit settings can/will flow down the hierarchy as well.

Using Active Directory to Control Auditing

As with almost every other feature in Win2K, auditing can be centrally controlled via Group Policy and the Active Directory. Thus, the previous auditing configurations can be applied via Group Policy at the LSDOU level, as described in Chapter 9. So configuring which events will be audited can be done with a very fine granularity by assigning a configuration to a single computer within the domain. Or a uniform configuration can be made for every computer within the domain.

Some domains may create organizational units (OUs) for their computers. In this case different audit policies could be applied to each organizational unit. This could be very useful if the organizational units did not represent geographic or political divisions within the domain, but instead represented operational categories such as desktop, application server, print server, file server, database server, and Web server. The most efficient method of doing this is by using Active Directory Group Policies. The management of Group Policies is covered in Chapter 9 of this book.

By default, domain workstations and member servers are allowed to define their own local audit policies. This is because the default policy definition provided by Microsoft explicitly defines that these are local policies. Other policy templates are available that change this behavior, or you may create your own custom policy.

Group Policies will take precedence over local audit policies. If a site needs to impose a specific audit policy the best method is to use Group Policies to enforce the configuration.

VIP: The No Auditing setting is the default auditing set by the default Group Policies (Default Domain Controller Policy and Default Domain Policy).

Related Tools from the Microsoft Resource Kits

The Microsoft NT and Win2K Server Resource Kits contain several tools related to event logging and auditing. A brief introduction to them is provided in this section.

▼ **Auditcat.hlp** This Windows help file contains information about data that may appear in your event logs.

■ **Auditpol.exe** This is a command-line program, requiring Administrative privileges, that will modify the audit policy of a local or remote computer.

■ **Crystal Reports Event Log Viewer** This report writer will extract, view, save, and publish information from Windows event logs. A variety of formats are available and some are suitable for importing into a database. This tool is available on the NT 4.0 Server Resource Kit. The documentation for the tool can be found on the CD that contains the program.

■ **Elf.exe** The Event Log Filter tool comes with the Microsoft BackOffice Resource Kit. It is used to monitor multiple servers for certain events and log them to a text file.

■ **Evtscan.exe** The Event Log Scan tool also comes from the Microsoft BackOffice Resource Kit. It is used to monitor specific servers for a certain event. This can be used in a situation where a problem is occurring intermittently. The tool can be configured to poll a Server event log at predefined intervals and then take a specified action once a specific event has been detected, such as restart a service or send mail to notify a user of the event.

■ **Dumpel.exe** The Dump Event Log is a command-line utility that can be used to dump an event log for a local or remote system into a tab-separated text file. This utility can also be used to filter for certain event types and to filter out certain event types.

■ **Logevent.exe** The Log Event is a command-line utility that can be used to write event data to a local or remote event log. It can be useful when creating scripts or batch jobs whose execution you want to monitor.

- **Ntevntlg.mdb**   This is an Access database file that contains the Windows Event Log Messages. It is sometimes useful when someone has reported an event ID to you without sending you more information.

▲ **Audit.exe**   This tool is from the Microsoft Win2K SDK, not the Resource Kit. It is provided in source form in the SDK. It is able to query the current audit status and change the audit state of an audit event type. The source code also demonstrates how to enable and disable all auditing.

NOTE: Most commands support the / ? command-line switch to show acceptable parameters.

CREATING AN AUDITOR ACCOUNT: SEPARATING DUTIES

Win2K does not come with an account that is specifically configured to have access and control over the audit information, but limited functionality in other areas of system administration. Some other operating systems, such as Novell Netware, provide this functionality. Many organizations find this level of control extremely useful.

An auditor account should be able to track all the activities of the Administrator, as well as all other users, and have full control of the auditing logs. Once the auditor account has been configured and assigned, the Administrator cannot touch the auditor account or the auditing logs. Therefore, all activities of the Administrator can be tracked by an independent auditor.

The Specifics

Although Win2K does not have an auditor account, you can create one. You will need to treat the Administrator account as *the* auditor account. All other administrators must then be assigned to lower-level administrative groups such as Account Operators, Print Operators, or your custom groups. Do not add anyone to the Administrators or Server Operators groups because members of these groups can change or delete the auditing logs. Also, do not give any user or group the Manage Auditing and Security Logs right.

CAUTION: This is not a trivial task and should be performed in a test network to ensure that it does not break your production environment.

The basic steps for creating an auditor account are as follows:

1. Designate two or three people as auditors.
2. Rename the Administrator account to **Auditor** or some obscure name to prevent detection.

3. Remove all members of the Administrators and Sever Operators group and reassign them to custom management groups that do not have the right to change and delete the audit logs.

4. Gather the three new auditors at the server and open the Properties dialog box for the Administrator account.

5. In the Password field, have auditor 1 enter her password, then write that password on a card marked 1 and slip it into an envelope. The envelope will eventually go to some trusted party.

6. Have auditors 2 and 3 do the same thing as auditor 1.

As a test, go through this procedure using some low-level account to make sure that everyone understands it and that you can reopen the account by combining the parts of the password. In particular, don't use spaces in the password.

If everything works, follow the procedure again using the real auditor account and real passwords. Seal the envelope and give it to a trusted third party, such as the CEO of your company, or put it in a safe deposit box. If you're really paranoid, you could put each part of the password in separate safety deposit boxes with specific instructions as to how they are to be retrieved.

From this point on, all high-level administration and monitoring of the auditing logs can only be done by the auditors, who must all be present to access the system. Granted, this procedure may seem a bit complex and may be unnecessary in your environment, but the basic procedure should give you an idea of what you need to do to set up secure auditing.

Keep in mind that the password you gave to the trusted party might be compromised. To prevent unauthorized access to the account, make sure that no one can log on to it from the network. This is good practice anyway because it means that all administration must take place at the console of the server where other people are presumably present to monitor the activities of that person. To revoke network access for auditors (and administrators), open the User Manager and choose Policies | Rights, then remove Administrators and Everyone from the Access This Computer from the Network right.

Note that removing Everyone will mean that no one can access your servers from the network. You will need to reassign the right to the groups that should have network access. Don't use Domain Users since its members include the Administrator account that you can't remove. Instead, create new custom groups, such as Network Users.

PROTECTING THE LOGS

There is a less cumbersome method to isolate your audit logs from modification by your system administrators. It provides other important features as well. Your logs should reside on a computer other than where the original event took place. By separating the logs from the machine, or even the domain, you can create a configuration that enables you to effectively monitor the actions of your administrators. The machine(s) that store the accumulated information should have a different set of administrators than the other computers.

There are many other benefits to doing this. Let's assume that you've configured auditing, and you are even gathering the right data for your needs. Suddenly, one of your servers disappears from the network. One of the first things you want to do is check your logs to see what was happening just before you noticed the problem. Maybe it's a network outage; maybe it's a denial-of-service attack. Maybe your machine room got broken into and your server is now in the back of some truck. You can't look at the events leading up to the disappearance from the network because you can no longer look at the logs without visiting the server.

Let's look at a different scenario. Suppose that you have a Web server sitting between two firewalls in your corporate DMZ. You deal with sensitive data and you want to limit the types of traffic that the server will accept. Event Viewer uses the normal RPC ports to communicate with the remote event service to view the logs. You want to limit what machines the server will accept connections from, but at the same time you want to be able to administer your network from any machine that you happen to be near. If the server could push the audit data to a known central location, it would make the configuration a lot simpler.

Finally, suppose that you do have an intruder who successfully gains entry with administrator access. One of the intruder's goals will be to avoid detection. Once he has administrator access on the machine that contains the logs, you have a pretty good chance that the logs will be erased or modified to hide the intruder's tracks. If the logs reside on a different machine to which he has not yet gained access, the job of avoiding detection is a lot harder.

As was mentioned earlier, Win2K does not natively provide the ability to store the logs on a remote machine. However, there are methods and tools that allow you to implement this important feature. Some commercial host-based intrusion detection applications such as Intruder Alert from Axent, System Secure from Internet Security Systems, and Centrax from CyberSafe perform this type of log consolidation.

INTEGRATING WINDOWS AUDITING INTO THE ENTERPRISE

Auditing is not a concept that was invented by Microsoft. Similar facilities are built into other operating systems. Existing heterogeneous computing environments often have tools policies for managing their audit logs from these other operating systems. Some third-party tools are available for integrating the Windows event log data into the systems being used by other operating systems.

Using WMI

The Win2K WMI Event Log Provider provides access to data and notifications of events from the Win2K event log service. Using this provider, you can use WMI to write a centralized logging service for Win2K and for that matter WinNT. WMI has other event providers as well that could possibly be integrated in a home-grown system, such as the SNMP Trap Provider and the Registry Event Provider. See the Event Log Provider information in the MSDN library.

Perl or C(++) and SQL

Another method of providing enterprise logging solutions is to use the Perl Event Log module (or some other means of getting logs from the event log, say a C or C++ program) and a centralized database (i.e. MS SQL) for log/event storage. You would have to write a program that would extract data/events from the Win2K logs and send them reliably and securely to a central storage location. This is the basic premise of most commercial IDS systems, plus a large portion of wrapping and report generation tools.

Using syslog

Unix provides a logging facility called syslog, which can be used to save information locally or configured to save the log information to a remote machine. The protocol normally used is based on UDP and is unsecured. Another problem with syslog is that the format of the message is not standardized. This inhibits the development of automated tools that can review the logs and generate notifications when a problem is detected that needs human intervention. Of course, others might point out that this lack of standardization helps to keep many people employed maintaining analysis tools.

There are many tools available that can help integrate Unix and Windows log information. Using third-party tools, Windows events may be sent to a remote Unix syslog daemon. Or, if a site prefers to manage and review its audit information on Windows, there are third-party syslog daemons for Windows. These can accept data from remote Unix systems.

Recent Developments

Various groups are trying to improve the syslog situation. The abstract of the IETF draft document "Universal Format for Logger Messages" states: "This document presents a format to describe system events for logging purposes. Some of the features presented here are already in use with the common syslog facility, but most of them are lost in the crowd of syslog format freedom."

Other groups are trying to provide secure forms of the protocol so that the logs don't get overwhelmed with false information or disclosed to inappropriate eavesdroppers. In 1998 Derren Reed presented a paper on the topic at the USENIX Security Symposium. He has written a version of syslog that uses TCP and allows for SSL encryption of the data delivery.

RECAP

This chapter has covered the basics of Win2K auditing, and some overall requirements if you are going to actually use the information for anything useful. There are a number of things that need to be done, and here is a summary list:

▼   Decide what data needs to be collected.

■   Decide what data should not be collected.

■   Decide who should have access to the data.

■   Configure the system as appropriate to your environment.

■   Use a third-party log consolidation product if you cannot realistically review all of the logs on the machines you have.

▲   Review the data and act upon the information.

One important audit "rule to live by" is that if you are going to log it, then look at it!

PART IV

Securing Windows 2000 Networks

PART IV

Securing Windows 2000 Networks

CHAPTER 14

Firewalls and Proxy Servers

firewall, as shown in Figure 14-1, puts up a barrier that controls the flow of traffic between networks. The safest firewall would block all traffic, but that defeats the purpose of making the connection, so you need to strictly control selected traffic in a secure way. Application-level proxy servers today provide the highest level of protection. In Figure 14-1, proxy services run at the application level of the network protocol stack for each different type of service (FTP, HTTP, and so on).

A *proxy server* is a component of a firewall that controls how internal users access the outside world (the Internet) and how Internet users access the internal network. In some cases, the proxy blocks all outside connections and only allows internal users to access the Internet. The only packets allowed back through the proxy are those that return responses to requests from inside the firewall. In other cases, both inbound and outbound traffic is allowed under strictly controlled conditions. Note that a virtual "air-gap" exists in the firewall between the inside and outside networks and that the proxies bridge this gap by working as agents for internal or external users.

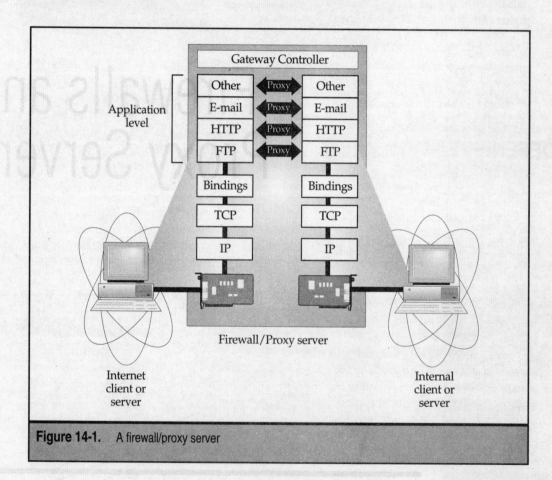

Figure 14-1.   A firewall/proxy server

This chapter is broken into two major sections: The first section covers firewalls in general, and the second section, "Windows 2000 Home-Grown Firewalls" describes two scenarios that use Win2K and default services to deploy a firewall. Chapter 15 covers Microsoft's Proxy Server.

Readers who want to explore firewall concepts and architecture in more detail should refer to the following books:

▼ *Firewalls and Internet Security: Repelling the Wily Hacker* by William R. Cheswick and Steven M. Bellovin

▲ *Building Internet Firewalls* by D. Brent Chapman and Elizabeth D. Zwicky

The books and their authors are the usual reference sources for just about any article or book you're likely to read on modern network security. Although the authors are UNIX experts, the books deal primarily with TCP/IP networks and the Internet—the focus for almost any discussion of firewalls.

Discussions about protecting networks usually focus on threats from the Internet, but internal users are also a threat. Indeed, surveys indicate that internal users perpetrate most unauthorized activities. In addition, organizations that connect with business partners over private networks create a potential avenue for attack. Users on the business partner's network may take advantage of the inter-company link to steal valuable information.

DEFENSIVE STRATEGIES

The first decision you will have to make is the security "stance" that will be used in your network. There are two basic stances, with endless variations:

▼ **That Which Is Not Expressly Permitted Is Denied** With this stance, security is a priority, and you will validate services before they are allowed. This stance assumes that you do not know where all the holes are, so you will only allow services you have validated or feel comfortable with. The object of this stance is to "fail closed" if something should happen. This is the "exclusive" stance discussed in Chapter 4.

▲ **That Which Is Not Expressly Denied Is Permitted** With this stance, functionality is a priority, and you will allow all services unless they are found to have vulnerabilities. This stance assumes that you know where all the holes are —a *very* poor assumption to make—so you allow services until you have a reason to remove them. The object of this stance is to "fail open."

The stance you choose will affect your entire architecture, so make sure you take the time to make this decision wisely.

Firewalls are often described in terms of perimeter defense systems, with a so-called "choke point" through which all internal and external traffic must pass. This is a logical location to implement the "stance" you have chosen. The usual metaphor is the medieval castle and its perimeter defense systems, as pictured in Figure 14-2. The moats and walls provide the perimeter defense, while the gatehouses and drawbridges provide "choke points" through which everyone, including storming hordes of marauders, must travel to enter or leave the castle. You can monitor and block access at these choke points.

While the storming hordes and other such medieval analogies might be appropriate in some cases, the real threat is often the stealthy spy who slips over walls in the dark of night and scales every barrier undetected to reach his target of attack. Or the sneaky spy who walks around behind the castle and slips in the unlocked garden door.

If a firewall is like a castle, how far do you let people into it, and what do you allow them to do once inside? Local townspeople and traders were usually allowed to enter the market yard of the castle with relative ease so they could deliver or pick up goods. At night, the gates were closed, and goods were brought into the castle—usually after close inspection. Following this analogy, the market yard could be compared to the public Web and FTP servers that you connect to the Internet for general availability.

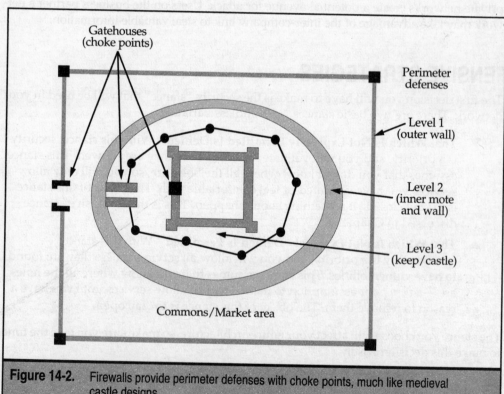

Figure 14-2. Firewalls provide perimeter defenses with choke points, much like medieval castle designs

While just about anybody could enter the market yard, only trusted people and people with special credentials were allowed into the inner perimeters of the castle. Within these walls is the *keep*, a heavily fortified structure that provides the last defense against attackers.

> **NOTE:**   Interestingly, the castle proved quite capable of withstanding attacks until the cannon came along. In the 16th century, Essex and Cromwell overran many castles in Ireland with little artillery. They simply blew the parapets off the tops of castle walls to make them indefensible, then scaled the walls. What similar weapons will our network defenses face?

In Europe, there were many different types of strongholds. Tower homes were relatively simple defensive structures designed to protect residents from marauding bands of looters and neighboring clans. Still larger castles with massive walls and bastions were built by the wealthiest of clans. Similarly, businesses with the biggest budgets or the most valuable information to protect build the strongest defenses.

In times of peace, the rulers of a castle would meet with local townspeople, tradesmen, and dignitaries from other areas. Any direct meeting with the king or queen was usually preceded by a strip search. But if the political situation was tense, the ruler might prefer to avoid direct contact with visitors. In this case, the protocol was for all visitors to meet with the agent of the king or queen, who would then relay messages between parties. The agent provided proxy services.

Firewalls have been designed around these two approaches. A *packet filtering firewall* uses the strip-search method. Packets are first checked and then either dropped or allowed to enter based on various rules and specified criteria. A *proxy service* acts as an agent for a user who needs to access a system on the other side of the firewall. A third method, called *stateful inspection*, is a variation of the packet filtering firewall. This method would be analogous to a gatekeeper remembering some defining characteristics of anyone leaving the castle and only allowing people back in with those same characteristics.

Like the multiple perimeter defenses of the castles, multiple firewall devices can be installed to keep wily hackers out of your networks. The spies or assassins vaulted moats and scaled walls to reach their targets. Of course, it helped them if the castle guards were sleeping, so don't slack off on your own defense. You can build a "trip wire" defense by putting "relatively weak" devices on the outer edge of your defense that sound alarms when attacked.

Once in place, a firewall, just as a castle, requires constant vigilance. If someone can climb your fence at night when no one is looking, what good is the fence? Security policies and procedures must be put into place. In defending a castle, the archers and boiling oil men need a defensive strategy, and they need regular drills to ensure that the strategy works. If flaming arrows hit your internal systems, you'll need a disaster recovery plan to quench the flames and get the system back online.

Castle parapets and towers protect the soldiers who defend the castles. Without defenders, the castle is vulnerable to attackers that scale walls or knock down doors. Likewise, your firewall is not a standalone device. You need to manage and monitor it on a regular basis and take action in the event of an attack. It is also only one part of your defense. If the attackers do get inside, you need to keep them from looting your systems by implementing security measures at each domain and server.

This brings up another point. While firewalls are keeping Internet intruders out, your internal users might be looting your systems. You may need to use your firewall technology to segregate your separate departments, workgroups, divisions, or business partners. You may also need to implement encryption throughout your organization. Firewalls also do not protect against leaks, such as users connecting to the outside with a desktop modem. In addition, if some new threat comes along, your firewall might not be able to protect against it. Viruses and misuse of security devices are also a threat.

FIREWALL POLICIES

If an intruder can find a hole in or around your firewall, then the firewall has failed. There are no in-between states. Once a hacker is in, your internal network is at his or her mercy. If he or she hijacks an administrative account, you're in big trouble. If he or she hijacks an account with lesser privileges, all the resources available to that account are at risk.

No firewall can protect against inadequate or mismanaged policies. If a password gets out because a user did not properly protect it, your security is at risk. If an internal user dials out through an unauthorized connection, an attacker could subvert your network through this backdoor. Therefore, you must implement a firewall policy.

Obviously, the firewall and the firewall policy are two distinct things that require their own planning and implementation. A weakness in the policy or the inability to enforce the policy will weaken any protection provided by even the best firewalls. If internal users find your policies too restrictive, they may go around them by connecting to the Internet through a personal modem. The firewall in this case is useless. You may not even know your systems are under attack because the firewall is guarding the wrong entrance.

CLASSIFYING FIREWALLS

Any device that controls network traffic for security reasons can be called a firewall, and in fact the term "firewall" is used in a generic way. However, there are three major types of firewalls that use different strategies for protecting network resources. The most basic firewall devices are built on routers and work in the lower layers of the network protocol stack. They provide packet filtering and are often called screening routers. High-end *proxy services* operate at the upper levels of the protocol stack (that is, all the way up to the application layer). They provide proxy services on external networks for internal clients and perform advanced monitoring and traffic control by looking at certain information inside packets. The third type of firewall uses *stateful inspection* techniques, which is just a derivative of a filtering firewall.

Routers are often used in conjunction with proxy servers to build a multitiered defense system, although many commercial firewall products may provide all the functionality you need.

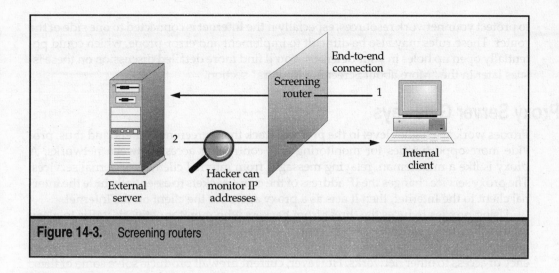

Figure 14-3.   Screening routers

Figures 14-3 above and 14-4 below illustrate the differences between screening routers and proxy servers, both of which are described in the next few sections.

Screening Router (Packet Filters)

The router connects two networks and performs packet filtering to control traffic between the networks. Screening routers can look at information related to the MAC (hardware) address of a computer, its IP address (Network layer), and even the types of connections (Transport layer) and then perform filtering based on that information. A screening router may be a standalone routing device or a computer that contains two network interface cards (a *dual-homed system*).

Administrators program the device with a set of rules that define how packet filtering is done. Ports can also be blocked; for example, you can block all applications except HTTP (Web) services. However, the rules that you can define for routers may not be sufficient

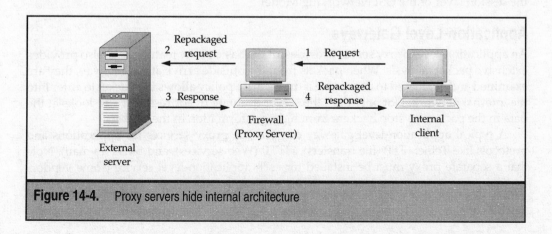

Figure 14-4.   Proxy servers hide internal architecture

to protect your network resources, especially if the Internet is connected to one side of the router. Those rules may also be difficult to implement and error-prone, which could potentially open up holes in your defenses. You'll find more detailed discussion on these issues later in the "More about Screening Routers" section.

Proxy Server Gateways

Proxies work at a higher level in the protocol stack than screening routers, and thus, provide more opportunities for monitoring and controlling access between networks. A proxy is like a middleman, relaying messages from internal clients to external services. The proxy service changes the IP address of the client packets to essentially hide the internal client to the Internet, then it acts as a proxy agent for the client on the Internet.

Using proxies reduces the threat from hackers who monitor network traffic to glean information about computers on internal networks. The proxy hides the addresses of all internal computers. Traditionally, using proxies has reduced performance and transparency of access to other networks. However, current firewall products solve some of these problems.

There are two types of proxy servers:

▼ Circuit-level gateways

▲ Application-level gateways

Circuit-Level Gateways

This type of proxy server provides a controlled network connection between internal and external systems (that is, there is no "air-gap"). A virtual "circuit" exists between the internal client and the proxy server. Internet requests go through this circuit to the proxy server, and the proxy server delivers those requests to the Internet after changing the IP address. External users only see the IP address of the proxy server. Responses are then received by the proxy server and sent back through the circuit to the client. While traffic is allowed through, external systems never see the internal systems. This type of connection is often used to connect "trusted" internal users to the Internet. These proxies operate at the session layer of the OSI Networking Model.

Application-Level Gateways

An application-level proxy server provides all the basic proxy features and also provides extensive packet analysis. When packets from the outside arrive at the gateway, they are examined and evaluated to determine if the security policy allows the packet to enter into the internal network. Not only does the server evaluate IP addresses, it also looks at the data in the packets to stop hackers from hiding information in the packets.

A typical application-level gateway can provide proxy services for applications and protocols like Telnet, FTP (file transfers), HTTP (Web services), and SMTP (e-mail). Note that a separate proxy must be installed for each application-level service (some vendors achieve security by simply not providing proxies for some services, so be careful in your evaluation). With proxies, security policies can be much more powerful and flexible because all of the information in packets can be used by administrators to write the rules that determine how packets are handled by the gateway. It is easy to audit just about everything that happens on the gateway. You can also strip computer names to hide internal systems, and you can evaluate the contents of packets for appropriateness and security. These proxies operate at the application layer of the OSI Networking Model.

NOTE: Appropriateness is an interesting option. You might set up a filter that discards any e-mail messages that contain "dirty" words.

Stateful Inspection Techniques

One of the problems with proxies is that they must evaluate a lot of information in a lot of packets. In addition, you need to install a separate proxy for each application you want to support. This may affect performance and increase costs. A new class of firewall product is emerging that uses stateful inspection techniques. Instead of examining the contents of each packet, the bit patterns of the packets are compared to packets that are already known to be trusted.

For example, if you access some outside service, the server remembers things about your original request like port number, and source and destination address. This "remembering" is called *saving the state*. When the outside system responds to your request, the firewall server compares the received packets with the saved state to determine if they are allowed in.

While stateful inspection provides speed and transparency, one of its biggest disadvantages is that inside packets make their way to the outside network, thus exposing internal IP addresses to potential hackers. Some firewall vendors are using stateful inspection and proxies together for added security.

The debate over whether proxies or stateful inspection techniques are better rages on. If you are choosing a firewall, talk to vendors and read the product reviews. In the meantime, some router vendors such as Bay Networks, Cisco, and Ascend are implementing firewalls in their router products, closing the gap between inexpensive hardware-based devices and high-end application-level servers. These types of firewalls operate at the networking layer of the OSI Networking Model. This is the same layer as screening routers.

Network Address Translation (NAT)

As described in earlier chapters, the Internet uses the IP protocol and specifically IP addresses as a method of delivering packets from one host to another. For these packets to be allowed over the Internet, the addresses must be valid "public" IP addresses (addresses allocated by InterNIC are known as public addresses). This was not a problem a few years ago, as the number of addresses was plentiful, but with the advent of the Web, available addresses are becoming scarce. This coupled with the fact that every Internet Service Provider (ISP) is trying to gobble up as much of the IP address space as possible to sell to their customers leads to a shortage. It is because of this shortage that "private" addresses were defined. Private addresses are a portion of Public addresses given special features. For more information, see RFC 1597 (**http://www.ietf.org/rfc/rfc1597.txt**).

All addresses with the following features are known as "private" addresses:

▼ **10.0.0.0–10.255.255.255**   This is 10.0.0.0 with the subnet mask 255.0.0.0

■ **172.16.0.0–172.31.255.255**   This is 172.16.0.0 with the subnet mask 255.240.0.0

▲ **192.168.0.0–192.168.255.255**   This is 192.168.0.0 with the subnet mask 255.255.0.0

Since "private" addresses cannot receive traffic from the Internet (that is, they are not routed across the Internet), there needs to be a way to "translate" these into "public" addresses. In steps network address translation!

NOTE: NAT is documented in RFC 1631.

An IP router that is implementing NAT (a.k.a. a NAT box), can translate "private" addresses into "public" addresses (that is, Internet-routable addresses). By doing this translation, only internal addresses that are defined in the NAT table mapping will be reachable by external hosts. Thus, NAT provides protection from Internet-based attacks, because packets that have private addresses as their destination will not be routed across the Internet, so any attacker will have to know the current mapping of the internal (private) IP address to external (public) IP address that the NAT box has in its tables for a successful attack to work.

There are two basic methods of NAT:

▼ Many-to-many

▲ Many-to-one (a.k.a. *IP masquerading*)

Many-to-Many

In this scenario, a small business has received a "public" class "C" address space (x.y.z.0–255) from their ISP. Class "C" networks have 256 addresses, 254 of which are useable. They have 500 internal hosts and assign these hosts to a portion of the 10.0.0.0 pri-

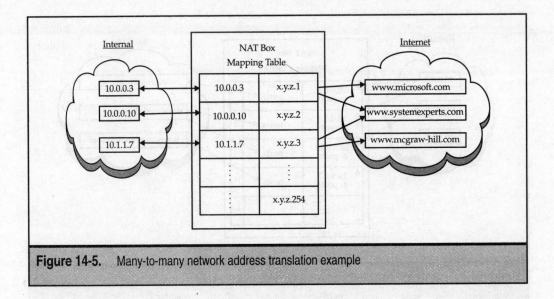

Figure 14-5. Many-to-many network address translation example

vate network range. To do this, they set up their NAT box to support many-to-many mapping. This will allow up to 254 hosts to access the Internet at one time. Each time a machine needs to access the Internet, the NAT box will map one of the public addresses (out of the class "C") to an internal address, and then forward packets back and forth. Figure 14-5 above shows how this looks.

Many-to-One (IP Masquerading)

This is a typical scenario in which a company has set up a proxy firewall or a router that supports a single NAT address (x.y.z.w). Every request that comes into the NAT box will leave with the external address of the NAT box as its source address. Thus every Internet-based machine thinks it is talking to a single IP address, the external interface of your NAT box. The number of hosts that this method can support is theoretically unlimited, whereas the many-to-many can only support as many hosts as you have external addresses. This is the most common type of NAT setup and is shown in Figure 14-6.

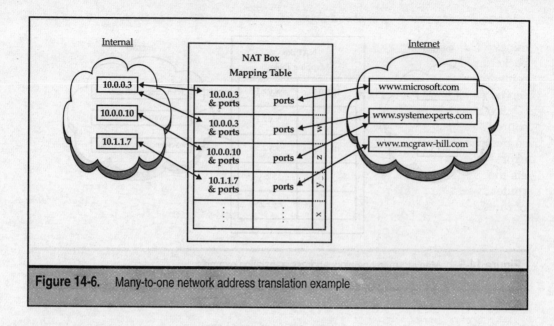

Figure 14-6. Many-to-one network address translation example

MORE ABOUT SCREENING ROUTERS

Routers are used to join individual network segments that have different network addresses as shown here:

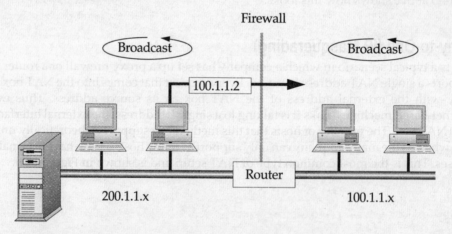

You can purchase standalone routers from vendors like Cisco, Nortel, and 3Com, or you can build a router in a Win2K Server computer by installing two network interface cards and enabling the Routing and Remote Access Service (discussed later). The latter is a dual-homed system.

A router actually looks inside packets to see what the target IP address is and determines whether it should forward the packet across the link. In the previous illustration, a packet in network 200.1.1.x is addressed to a workstation on network 100.1.1.x, so the router forwards it across the link. In the absence of any security provisions, the router has served its purpose by doing this simple task.

Screening routers have the additional capability of filtering packets based on the source and/or destination IP address of the packet. If a packet is from an undesirable source, the router can be programmed to drop it. The basic filtering rule is "all that is not expressly permitted is denied." That means that all packets are dropped except for packets that the router has been specifically programmed to allow onto the network. The router looks inside each packet and evaluates any of the following, depending on the type of router:

▼ The *source address* of the IP packet can be evaluated to determine whether the person sending it is someone you want to access the network. For example, you could block all IP packets that originate from your competitors' IP address range.

■ The *destination address* of the IP packet can be evaluated to restrict packets from reaching a particular system. For example, you could block all packets from the Internet that are destined for an internal system that is supposed to be secure and should be accessed only by internal systems.

▲ Specific *service ports* can be evaluated to prevent someone from using an application such as Telnet, FTP, SMTP, or various other Internet services. This process is discussed in the next section.

Ports and Port Filtering

In addition to filtering based on IP addresses, screening routers can look at information available at the Transport layer of the protocol stack and make forwarding decisions based on that information. The Transport layer is responsible for delivering packets in a reliable way between systems and for managing multiple sessions over the same network connection. Each session has its own channel. For example, if you use FTP to request a file from a server, the requests are sent over one channel and the file is transmitted back to you over another channel. The endpoint of the channel is called a *port*. FTP normally uses ports 20 and 21. A list of TCP/IP ports can be found in Web Appendix B at **www.osborne.com**.

The basic idea is to block a port if you don't want someone to use it in some inappropriate way. For example, if you don't run FTP services, you can configure your screening router to block ports 20 and 21. Looking at this a different way, if you want to provide only World Wide Web services on a server that is directly connected to the Internet, you can block all other ports except port 80, which is the HTTP port.

In conjunction with port filtering, a screening router also looks at the TCP flags in a segment (packet) header. Each segment has a flag that defines its purpose in the "conversation" that is taking place over the channel between the client and server. Flags are used in conjunction with port filtering to provide a more extensive rule base.

How Secure Are Screening Routers?

While screening routers have their place, they are not likely to provide the protection you need when connecting internal networks to the Internet. First, they directly expose your internal network to the Internet as a route that can possibly be traversed by a wily hacker. Someone can monitor the packet stream that emerges from your organization and glean valuable information, such as internal IP addresses of systems to attack! The more advanced proxy servers discussed later hide your internal network addresses from the Internet.

Screening routers may be an easy target for experienced hackers. A single port left open may provide all that the hacker needs to breach your security. Screening routers are usually configured via a difficult and error-prone process. For example, you must first define a set of rules based on your security policy that specifies exactly which packets are allowed. You then translate this set of rules into the syntax required to program the router, often writing multiple lines of scripting code. Put simply, there are a lot of chances to make dangerous mistakes. In contrast, many firewalls let you set similar rules with just a few commands.

However, despite their shortcomings, screening routers may be useful in some network configurations where you are connecting internal networks to other internal networks, assuming there is some level of trust involved. It all depends on your security requirements and the level of protection you can get from the router.

Some other disadvantages or problems with screening routers are as follows:

▼ Most commercial routers do not run higher-level applications that can detect suspicious activities.

■ Some routers do not generate alerts that can warn you of attacks on your system.

▲ Some devices do not even know how to detect and log an actual break-in.

HIGH-END FIREWALLS

Application-level gateways provide proxies that control access through the firewall in a unique way. They fully understand the protocols of the applications that are allowed to interoperate through the gateway and fully manage both inbound and outbound traffic at a level that is not possible with screening routers. This tends to be more secure, because the application gateway need only understand the specifics of what they pass, allowing developers and designers to be much more precise in the security design of their code.

The FTP service provides a good example of how an application-level proxy server can provide advanced filtering. The application-level server can allow users from the outside to access an FTP server, but it will look in each packet and block any packets with the PUT command for specific users. This prevents just anyone from writing files to the server.

Another important feature of application-level servers is authentication. You can allow only specific users through the firewall on the basis of their credentials. Doing this is useful for trusted mobile users or people from affiliated organizations who need to access specific systems on your networks.

Also keep in mind that firewalls can hide your internal network addresses from the Internet for security reasons and so that you can implement any IP addressing scheme you need without having to register with Internet authorities. This feature is increasingly important as registered IP addresses become scarce.

Proxy services can provide additional functions of interest to network administrators:

▼ Tracking all the sites that users access on the Internet and keeping records can help reduce Internet activities. Mailing these records to users on a periodic basis will let them know they are being monitored.

■ Screening of specific hosts and URLs can be used to restrict the sites that internal users access.

▲ Caching often-accessed Web pages can reduce requests and responses to the Internet (discussed under "Proxy Server Caching," later in this chapter).

Firewall Implementations

The Cheswick/Bellovin and Chapman/Zwicky books mentioned at the beginning of this chapter provide the material that most firewall vendors use when describing their firewall implementations. This section outlines the basic architectures that are described in Chapter 4 of Chapman and Zwicky's *Building Internet Firewalls*.

Note that these texts refer to the firewall as the *bastion hosts*. A bastion host is a system that is "hardened" against security breaches. The term "hardening" refers to removing unused/unneeded services, as well as securing the services that are running to the tightest possible extent.

Of course, a firewall installation must consist of several devices, including the packet filtering routers discussed previously. Often these routers are used for "perimeter defense," providing the first wall that attackers must scale in order to reach the bastion host. They may also be used for other lines of defense inside the network, as you'll see.

Dual-Homed System

The dual-homed system is a computer that includes at least two network interface cards, as pictured here. Win2K supports this configuration, and you can enable or disable routing between the cards, depending on your requirements. Routing is disabled between the network interface cards in the dual-homed system so that the application-level software can control how traffic is handled between networks.

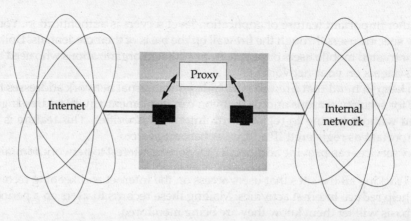

There is one other use for this type of configuration. Assume that the dual-homed host runs an HTTP (Web) service. If routing is disabled, then the host on either network can still access the Web services but packets cannot travel past the server. For example, if several departments in an organization need to share the same Web server but you don't want to create a routable link between the departments, you could use this configuration.

Screening Host Architecture

In this scenario, pictured in Figure 14-7, the screening router only allows Internet users to connect with a specific system on the internal network—the application-level gateway (bastion host). The gateway then provides inbound and outbound control as described earlier under the discussion about such devices.

The packet filtering router does a lot of work in this configuration. Not only does it direct packets to a designated internal system, it may also allow internal systems to open connections to Internet systems or disallow these connections. You set these options based on your security requirements. Chapman and Zwicky note that this architecture may be risky because it allows packets to move from the Internet to the internal network, unlike the dual-homed architecture, which blocks all packet movement from the external network to the internal network.

Screened Subnet Architecture

This architecture is similar to the screening host architecture described in the previous section, except that an extra layer of security is added by putting up a perimeter network that further separates the internal network from the Internet.

A reason for doing this is to protect the internal network if the bastion host succumbs to an attack. Since the bastion host is connected to the Internet, hackers will target it.

Variations

Chapman and Zwicky offer some variations on the designs described in the previous section, along with some warnings. For example, they mention that using multiple bastion hosts attached to the perimeter network is okay. You might run different services in each

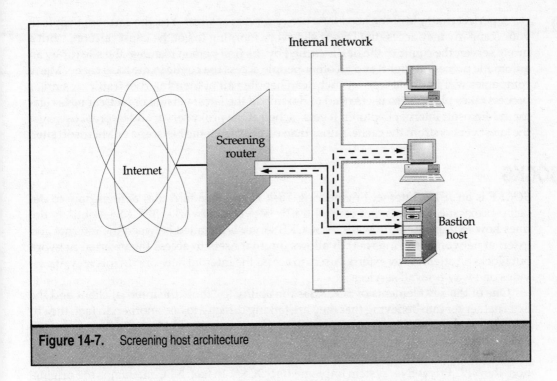

Figure 14-7.   Screening host architecture

of these hosts, such as HTTP (Web) services, e-mail services, or an external DNS service. Of course, each system must be hardened against attacks.

Another option is to combine the interior and exterior routers in screened subnet architecture if you use a router that has more than two ports, although this configuration is vulnerable if the single router is attacked. You can also merge the bastion host and the exterior router in the screened subnet architecture as well. However, do not merge the bastion host and the interior router.

If multiple interior routers are used, a situation could occur in which the internal router decides that the fastest way to another internal system is via the perimeter network, thus exposing internal network packets on the perimeter network.

For more information about these configurations and others, refer to the previously mentioned books.

Proxy Server Caching

A proxy server usually manages a disk cache that holds frequently accessed Web pages that other people in your company are likely to access. If someone requests a page, the proxy server intercepts the request and returns the appropriate page in the cache. This procedure reduces traffic on your Internet connection. Bottlenecks are reduced and people who need to get real work done on the Internet are not held up.

A perfect example of the need for a proxy server is *Dilbert*. Yes, the cartoon. People in your company may access the *Dilbert* site every morning to get the latest cartoon. With a proxy server, the comic of the day is cached by the first person to access the site (or by an automatic process at night) and all other people access the comic in the local cache. Many companies will find that a proxy cache can handle half of their Internet traffic. A similar process takes place when users need to download the latest version of Netscape Navigator or Microsoft Internet Explorer. It gets cached at the proxy server and internal users get the latest version from the cache, rather than directly from the Netscape or Microsoft site.

SOCKS

SOCKS is an IETF (Internet Engineering Task Force) standard that defines how to develop proxy mechanisms that control traffic between networks. SOCKS essentially defines how to implement firewalls. A SOCKS server is installed between the internal and external networks (the Internet). It allows internal users to access the external network but blocks all attempts by external users to access the Internal network. In this way, it provides one-way firewall services.

One of the key elements of SOCKS is the ability to "fool" the internal client and the external server into believing that they are talking directly to one another. In fact, the client talks to the SOCKS server and the SOCKS server talks to the target server on the external network.

The Microsoft Proxy Server implements SOCKS, as discussed in Chapter 15. In addition, the NEC PrivateNet system implements SOCKS. In fact, NEC maintains the original implementation of SOCKS developed by Dave Koblas and has developed its own advanced versions.

In order for a client application to use SOCKS, it was once necessary to build the support directly into the application. Companies such as Aventail and Hummingbird have developed programs that make any application SOCKS-aware.

The latest version of SOCKS (version 5), which was finalized in 1996, includes interesting features such as authentication, the ability to go through multiple firewalls, improved security policies, and more flexible filtering methods.

COMMERCIAL FIREWALLS

As mentioned, firewalls that provide circuit-level proxy services, application-level proxy services, and stateful inspection techniques are available. You can refer to Chapter 15 for more information about the Microsoft Proxy Server.

If you need to allow some access to internal systems, then you'll need to look beyond screening routers to application-level gateways and other high-end firewall products like those discussed in this section, although routers should still be included in your defensive system. There are a number of important features to look for in such products:

▼ **Address Translation/Privacy**   Prevents internal network addresses from appearing on the Internet (see earlier section on NAT). The firewall itself appears to be the originator of all traffic as it makes the Internet available to internal users. This is also referred to as IP masquerading.

■ **Alarms/Alerts**   Warns administrators when an attacker is attempting to breach the system. Threshold settings must be available and properly tuned to warn of attacks without triggering unnecessary alarms. Notification of attacks should be done with real-time messages, pagers, electronic mail, and other means.

■ **Logs and Reports**   Provides valuable information that helps you evaluate and detect potential security problems.

■ **Transparency**   Allows internal users to access the Internet without having to deal with the firewall. Its purpose is to make access for the user, or more appropriately for the application the user is running, just as if the firewall was not there. The firewall cannot be seen; from a usability level it is transparent to the user.

▲ **Virus Checking**   Checks for viruses and looks for Trojan Horse executable programs (available in some commercial firewall products). However, this feature can affect performance.

For more information about what to look for in firewalls, consult the many reviews and lab reports presented in industry journals and magazines. A good resource for overall comparisons is the "CSI's Firewall Product Resource" at the Computer Security Institute (**www.gocsi.com**).

The firewall market has exploded since 1996 and many vendors have their own features and selling points. You will have to have a requirements document *before* you start looking for a solution. Vendors have a tendency to sell you what they think you think you need. When you are evaluating a solution (yes, a solution—never buy a product, but a solution) make sure you get references of companies that are using the current product, and have the vendor "prove" what they are telling you works; don't take a marketing slick as validation. There are many great features in today's firewalls, and you should use them to your best advantage.

WINDOWS 2000 HOME-GROWN FIREWALLS

It is entirely possible to use a Win2K Server on the Internet as a gateway for your internal clients or as an internal separator for your intranets. Although it is feasible, it is not the best option. You should find a commercial firewall to meet your needs, but alas, this might not be possible for everyone. This section is for those people.

The two Microsoft solutions for building firewalls are the Microsoft Proxy Server or Routing and Remote Access Service (RRAS). The Proxy Server, discussed in depth in the next chapter, provides the "proxy" functionality that has been discussed here and falls into the "commercial firewall" category. The RRAS server, on the other hand, provides routing and filtering services. RRAS allows you to set up your Win2K Server to be a router, and potentially a Remote Access Server (RAS). The setup of the RAS server is discussed in Chapter 16.

You may be tempted to provide Internet users with other services such as Web or FTP on your Win2K firewall box. Be aware that you must carefully evaluate your goals and the security implications of that decision. It is vital that your firewall be a *very* secure machine, so running non-firewall-related services (like Web or FTP) on your Win2K firewall is highly discouraged. Use your firewall for its purpose, and set up other machines to accomplish the other functions you need. In most cases, you will set up the firewall to allow access to an *extranet* that is not connected to your full corporate network, but a small LAN that some industry people call the "dirty net." That means that untrusted packets flow on it.

NOTE: An extranet is a semi-private network that is used to securely share part of a company's private information with suppliers, vendors, partners, customers, or other businesses. It is used to limit access to your private (i.e. internal) network. An extranet can be viewed as part of a company's intranet that is extended to users outside the company.

In this section we will be discussing two scenarios in which RRAS can be used to provide a firewall service for internal users to the Internet. The first is a basic "filtering router." The second is a "NAT box." Though there are many other configurations that RRAS supports, and we will mention them in the RRAS setup section, we will be focusing only on those two.

NOTE: The issue of allowing Internet users into your internal network is *very* complex and, as such, beyond the scope of this book. If this is your scenario, a detailed book on firewalls should address the issue.

If we are going to use a Win2K system as a firewall, two things must be done:

▼ You must "harden" the Win2K Server itself.

▲ You must install and configure the Routing and Remote Access Service.

Hardening Win2K Server

As with any security-related services, you must ensure that the underlying operating system is as secure as possible. To do this, you will harden the Win2K Server. This section gives an overview of this process, but details can be found in Chapter 21.

Architectural Requirements

If you are going to harden a Win2K Server for a firewall, there are some basic architectural requirements that you need to ensure:

▼ The system is standalone (that is, it is *not* part of a Win2K Active Directory domain or a Windows NT domain).

- It has at least two network interface cards. A third card would be used for an extranet.
- This machine will be running only firewall services (that is, no Web, FTP, or file services).

With those architectural requirements in place, you can start to build a hardened Win2K Server.

Starting from Ground Zero

The process starts by setting up a new server. Do not try to convert an existing system—it will take much longer, and there are potential unknowns about the software and state of applications on that system. You will save yourself a lot of time and potential frustration if you do a clean install.

SETUP The setup is straightforward and is used to get a minimally installed system with security features such as NTFS and EFS. The system will only be running the minimally required services, and will not be using any file sharing. The system will also be in a workgroup or part of an isolated domain.

UP AND RUNNING Once the system reboots, you need to go to the second phase of "hardening," which is disabling services that you did not have a choice to install (and there are a number of them). It is easier to define what should be enabled and turn off the rest, rather than trying to turn off what is bad.

> **TIP:** When you're not dealing with firewalls, but just wanting to generally secure systems, this still applies. The general premise of not installing services unless you need them and then disabling the ones you cannot uninstall is still valid. You will have to take some time and effort to understand the exact setup for any architecture you need, but this should give you a good feel for how to go about it.

Caveat to the Pristine System

Many people will not heed this advice, and will run systems that support multiple functions because either they do not see the problem with it or they have financial constraints that prohibit them from doing it the right way. Chapter 21 details some allowable workarounds for these situations.

Installing Routing and Remote Access

Now that the server is "hardened," you will set up the Routing and Remote Access Server to provide the LAN-to-LAN connectivity that you are trying to achieve.

A Bit About the "Routing" Part of Routing and Remote Access

The Win2K Server running the routing portion of RRAS is called a *Win2K router*. It provides multiprotocol routing, Virtual Private Networks (VPN), and network address translation (NAT) services. It provides a very functional routing platform for small LANs and has built-in filtering capabilities. One of the main advantages of Win2K RRAS, as compared to the WinNT version, is that it is integrated more completely with the Win2K operating system. Some of the more important features of Win2K RRAS include

▼ Support of Open Shortest Path First (OSPF)

■ Routing Information Protocol (RIPv1 and RIPv2)

■ Internet Group Management Protocol (IGMP) router and proxy mode

■ Network address translation (NAT)

■ IP and IPX packet filtering

■ Virtual Private Networks (VPN) with the Point-to-Point Tunneling Protocol (PPTP) and the Layer Two Tunneling Protocol (L2TP) over Internet Protocol security (IPSec)

▲ Both a GUI and command-line interface for remote monitoring and configuration

There are many other features in RRAS, most of them dealing with using Win2K router as a general router, and not in the context of a firewall. This chapter looks at NAT and the filtering capabilities.

The underpinnings of RRAS are installed by default in Win2K. To get RRAS up and running, all you have to do is configure it, and that's described next.

Enabling the Routing and Remote Access Service

The following steps are used to enable the RRAS services on a Win2K system.

1. Open the Routing and Remote Access configuration tool by selecting Start | Programs | Administrative Tools | Routing and Remote Access.

2. Select the server where you want to enable it. By default, it is the localhost, and that is what you are configuring.

3. Then right-click Configure and Enable Routing and Remote Access.

4. The wizard will take you through the steps.

Figure 14-8 shows the default configuration options that you can choose. In these scenarios, you are using the Network Router configuration as a basis for the screening router, and the Internet Connection Server for the basis of the NAT box. You will look at the "screening router" first.

Screening Router

In this scenario, your ISP has given you a range of valid IP addresses that are "routable" across the Internet. This means that potentially all of your internal addresses can be

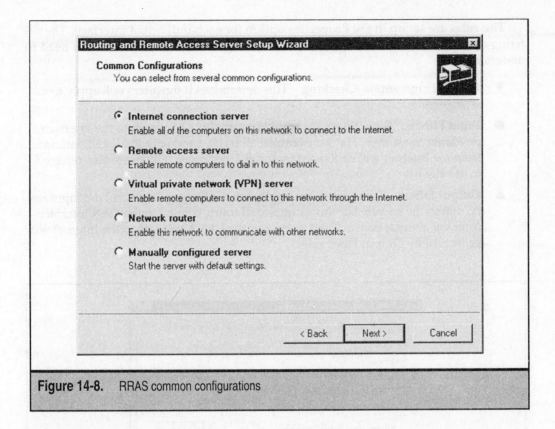

Figure 14-8. RRAS common configurations

reached from anywhere on the Internet. You may want to set up a filtering router to prevent this access, while allowing internal users unlimited access to the Internet.

As stated earlier, you should choose the Network Router configuration option shown in Figure 14-8. Then select TCP/IP as the protocol to use. Once the wizard finalizes the setup, you'll need to make your own configuration modifications.

Setting Up Filtering Rules

The main issue to worry about now is setting up the filtering rules. All of the RRAS administration can be done from the GUI, which is what is recommended. In the GUI, you select the server to administer, and the IP Routing | General option. This will give you a listing of the interfaces that are used on this server.

NOTE: For the purposes of these examples, consider the Local Area Connection to be the internal interface and refer to it as "LAN." The external interface will be on Local Area Connection 2; refer to it as "LAN2."

The rules are set up in the Properties option for each individual interface. The filtering options are on the General tab shown in Figure 14-9. The options you need to understand are

▼ **Enable Fragmention Checking**   This determines if the filters will apply to all IP fragments.

■ **Input Filters**   These filters are applied to anything coming into the interface, no matter the source. For our example, all traffic coming in the LAN2 interface from the Internet will be filtered by Input Filter rules. (Filters are also referred to as *rules*.)

▲ **Output Filters**   These filters are applied to anything going out of the interface, no matter the source. For this example, all traffic coming in the LAN interface from the internal network and going out the LAN2 interface to the Internet will be filtered by Output Filter rules.

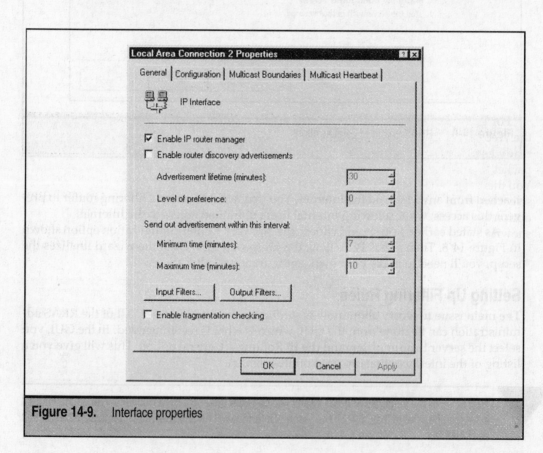

Figure 14-9.   Interface properties

For this example, we want to be able to accomplish the following:

▼ Internal users need to get anywhere on the Internet.

▲ Internet users need to access the Web server on the firewall.

You have four filters that you can set up: 1) inbound on internal interface (LAN), 2) outbound on internal interface, 3) inbound on external interface (LAN2), and 4) outbound on external interface, as shown in the following illustration and Table 14-1. To set up the rules you want, you will use inbound on internal interface and inbound on external interface. Pretty simple, so let's do it!

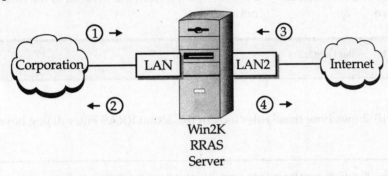

For LAN, just let all packets flow. For LAN2, you will need to allow connections to the Web server (port 80) on the firewall (IP address 128.32.7.39), connections that are already established (if you don't allow already established connections, then any reply packet to an internal client going out will be blocked), and allow all outbound traffic. You then select the Input Filters option, and then add the rules from Table 14-2. You then select the Drop All Packets Except Those That Meet the Criteria Below option. This last option is what causes the Allow action defined in the table. The resulting traffic flow is shown here.

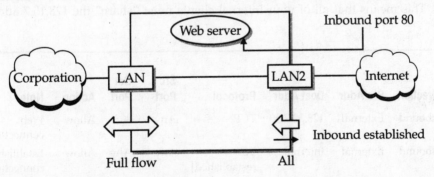

Direction	Meaning
1. Inbound on internal interface	Packets flowing from the internal network into the firewall
2. Outbound on internal interface	Packets flowing from the firewall to the internal network
3. Inbound on external interface	Packets flowing from the external network into the firewall
4. Outbound on external interface	Packets flowing from the firewall to the external network

Table 14-1.   Filter Directions

Figure 14-10 shows how these rules look in the actual RRAS Filter dialog boxes.

NOTE: If you look over the options carefully, you will see that there is really no way to explicitly put an IP spoofing rule in, because of the either/or limitations.

NAT Box

Let's start by saying that RRAS in general and RRAS NAT specifically are designed for SOHO (small office/home office) and small office LANs.

In this scenario, you have a DSL (Digital Subscriber Line) and "public" addresses 128.15.7.32–47 from the ISP and are using 192.168.0.0–192.168.255.255 for the internal network. This means that all of your internal clients must "share" the 128.15.7 addresses

Direction	Src Addr	Dest Addr	Protocol	Src Port	Dst Port	Action	Note
Inbound	External	128.32.7.39	TCP	Any	80	Allow	Web connections
Inbound	External	Internal	TCP [established]	Any	Any	Allow	Established connections

Table 14-2.   LAN2 Filter Rules

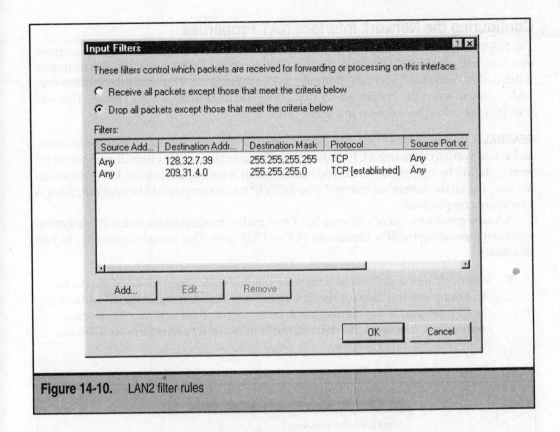

Figure 14-10. LAN2 filter rules

when they go out on the Internet. RRAS NAT supports both the many-to-many and the many-to-one NAT configurations. RRAS NAT also provides a limited DHCP server for the internal clients. It will send an IP address, subnet mask, default gateway, DNS server, and WINS server to the DHCP client. It will also act as a DNS server and WINS server for the internal network. When name-resolution requests are received by the network address translation computer, it forwards the name-resolution requests to the Internet-based DNS and WINS servers for which it is configured and returns the responses to the home network computer.

Setup

To set up a NAT box, follow these steps:

1. Use the Internet Connection Server configuration shown in Figure 14-8.
2. Select the NAT option.
3. Select the interface that is connected to the Internet (LAN2 in these examples).

It's that simple; now you have to configure it!

Configuring the Network Interface NAT Properties

The NAT box must be configured to use the external address range that the ISP has given you. You will use the RRAS administration GUI to configure these settings. If an interface is defined as "external," you can configure NAT ranges for it. This example only has one, LAN2, so you select the Properties for that under the IP Routing | NAT option. This will give you the dialog box shown in Figure 14-11.

GENERAL   In the General tab, you define whether the interface is external or internal, and if you want to translate TCP/IP headers. The selection of the internal or external interface should be straightforward. The interface that is connected to your ISP is the external one, and all the others are internal. The TCP/IP translation should be enabled, but it is a bit more complicated.

A *header translation* occurs when a NAT box makes modifications to the IP packet beyond just translating the IP address and TCP or UDP port. This happens primarily in two situations:

▼   When address and/or port information is stored in the payload of the packet. An example is the data for the FTP PORT command; it stores the IP address in the FTP header. If this translation does not occur, then you may experience connectivity problems. By default, the Win2K router can do this for FTP and ICMP, but not other services.

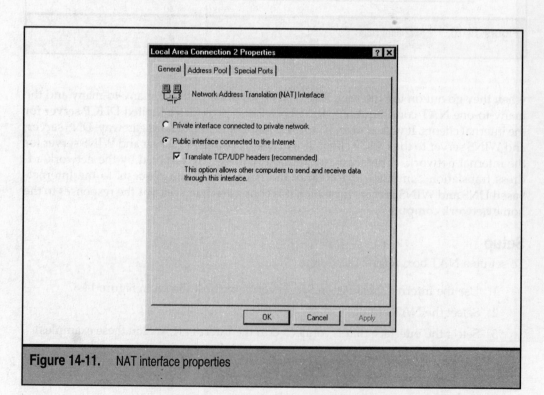

Figure 14-11.   NAT interface properties

RRAS Filtering Limitations

The filtering capabilities of RRAS are primitive, and nowhere near that of conventional routers. Most routers allow a mixture of allow/deny and directional (inbound vs. outbound) rules on a given network interface. RRAS rules do not support the former. They are an either/or conditional. This means that for a given direction of traffic, you can either accept all the packets that match the rules and deny the rest, or deny all packets that match and accept the rest. This is *very* limiting. An example of this limitation is the prevention of IP spoofing. IP spoofing is when a user on an external network sends a packet to your internal network, with a source address that is internal to your network. This is done in hopes that an internal machine will accept a packet that appears to be from another internal machine without question or authentication.

Any good firewall or router looks for Internet-based packets that have source addresses that are internal to that network (see the following illustration), and drop them if they do.

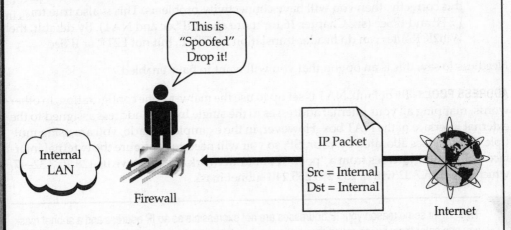

The logic to drop this packet is something like "if the packet is inbound from the Internet and the source address is an internal address, then drop the packet." For the Internet interface, this would be represented as:

Direction	SrcAddr	Dest Addr	Protocol	Src Port	Dst Port	Action	Note
Inbound	Internal	Internal	Any	Any	Any	Drop	Spoofed packets

With the limitations of RRAS, you can only make an explicit IP spoofing rule in a rule-set definition if you use the "accept anything that is not explicitly denied" security stance. This is because once you make a drop rule, all the others must be of the same type.

To actually get this IP spoofing rule to work in our example and still use a "that which is not expressly permitted is denied" security stance, you would have to put a rule on the LAN's outbound or Internet interface. The problem with this is that it would drop any packet originating on the firewall with an internal destination. You are probably getting a clearer picture of the lack of robustness and flexibility of the RRAS filtering functionality.

▲ When a non-TCP/UDP transport is used. As an example, PPTP does not use TCP or UDP; it uses GRE. So NAT will have to translate the Tunnel ID (which identifies the data stream) stored in the GRE header. If the NAT does not do this correctly, then you will have connectivity problems. This is also true for L2TP and IPSec (see Chapter 16 for more about IPSec and NAT). By default, the Win2K Router can do header translation for PPTP, but not L2TP or IPSec.

Needless to say, this is an option that you will want to have enabled.

ADDRESS POOL   By default, NAT is set up to use the many-to-one configuration, in other words, mapping all your internal addresses to the single Internet address assigned to the external interface of the NAT box. However, in the example scenario, you are using multiple IP addresses allocated by your ISP, so you will need to configure the external interface to allocate addresses from a "pool." For our network, the ISP gave us 128.15.7.32–47, which is 128.15.7.32 with a 255.255.255.240 subnet mask.

TIP: If for some reason your IP addresses are not expressible as an IP address and a subnet mask, you can enter them by indicating the starting and ending addresses.

To configure this, select the interface you want to administer under the IP Routing | NAT tree in the RRAS administration GUI. Select the properties for the interface you will be administering (see Figure 14-11). On the Address Pool tab, select Add. Enter an IP address and a subnet mask, or a Start and End address.

SPECIAL PORTS   By default, a NAT box will only map for outbound connections, that is, connections initiated from the internal network to the external network. There may be a need to allow Internet users to access resources on your private network (that is, to allow limited inbound connections). To do this, you can use the special ports option. This allows a "reverse" mapping of sorts.

CAUTION: This can completely subvert your internal network security. If you use this option, be sure that you have done a complete design review.

To use this feature, you must:

▼   Allocate and configure a static internal IP address for the internal server you will be mapping to.

■   Map an external port and IP address to that internal address and port.

▲   Exclude the external IP address from the NAT address pool on that interface.

What this feature does is provide a static mapping of a public address and port number to a private address and port number. This may be used to map to an internal host such as a Web or Mail server.

This option is configured on the Special Ports tab in the properties for the interface you are administering (see Figure 14-11).

Configuring NAT Properties

The NAT portion of the router has its own properties that can be set. The options deal with logging (general), translation, address assignments, and name resolution (see Figure 14-12).

▼   **Translation**   This option defines how long the mappings remain active. The UDP is set to 1 by default, which is adequate. The default TCP mapping will remain in the tables for 24 hours by default—this is too long. We recommend that you decrease the TCP to 60 minutes. This only takes effect if the connection is not actively being used. Another option in this tab is the network Applications settings. This provides the ability to map external servers to an internal address.

■   **Address Assignment**   This option allows you to become a DHCP server for the internal network.

▲   **Name Resolution**   This option enables the NAT box to be a DNS and/or WINS "proxy" of sorts. It will accept requests from clients, forward them on to external servers, and then send the replies back to the clients.

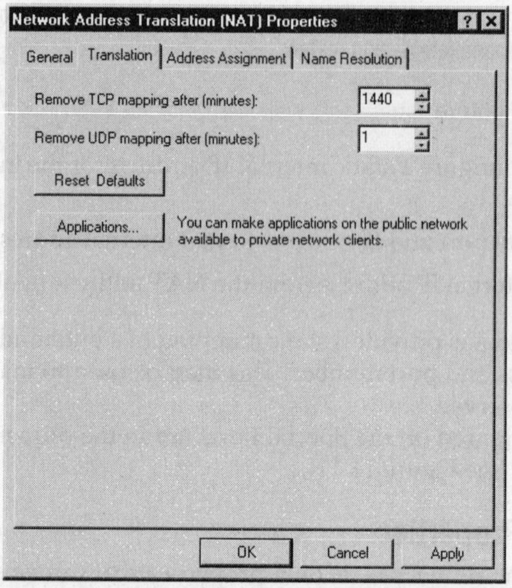

Figure 14-12. NAT Translation options

RECAP

As you can see, there is a great deal of functionality in RRAS. The questions you must ask yourself are: "Is it worth it?" and "Is there a better, more effective solution?" For most, the answers are "No" and "Yes" respectively, but not for all.

Although we have been discussing the importance of firewalls for blocking the front door, it is important to evaluate and identify *all* your network access points when deciding where to put your firewall. There have been more than one instance of a company who spends a hundred thousand dollars for firewalls, just to have them bypassed by someone who dual-homes his or her server or has a dial-up connection that circumvents all the firewalls.

One of the most important parts of security effectiveness is architecture. Make sure that you architect, then implement—not vice-versa. As the parable goes:

A wise man who built his house on the rock. The rain came down, the streams rose, and the winds blew and beat against that house; yet it did not fall, because it had its foundation on the rock. ... Whereas the foolish man built his house on sand. The rain came down, the streams rose, and the winds blew and beat against that house, and it fell with a great crash.

As with a house, you must build on a strong foundation. Make your decisions wisely!

CHAPTER 15

Microsoft
Proxy Server

"If all you have is a hammer, then everything looks like a nail."

—Unknown

Proxy servers have one main function: to pass packets back and forth between networks. This "passing back and forth" can be implemented in any number of applications or services. Two of the most common types of proxy servers are Web proxy servers (which usually perform caching also) and proxy firewalls. These are the two that Microsoft has implemented in the Microsoft Proxy Server (MPS).

The Web caching feature is the driving force behind the popularity of the MPS, and it is by far the most touted feature of the product. The majority of the development effort appears to be in this direction, evidenced by the simple fact that the MPS is not a standalone application, but an ISAPI DLL that runs inside the Internet Information Server (IIS).

The security features (a.k.a. firewall features) are much less robust, but still very functional for certain environments. They are complimentary to the Web caching feature and are used to help secure it.

Because this is a security book, this chapter will focus mainly on the security (that is, firewall) functionality of the Microsoft Proxy Server, with a brief discussion of the caching feature.

NOTE: One very important thing to note about the MPS is that it is *not* integrated into the Win2K Security Model. I say that because the MPS functionality operates the same when running on Windows NT or Win2K. There is no integration in the Active Directory or link to group policies, and administration is proxy-centric, not domain-centric. I believe this will change in future versions, but for now this is what we are working with.

FEATURES

This section covers the major features of the MPS. These are not meant to be exhaustive in detail, just enough to give you an understanding of what they are. For a detailed look at the features, please refer to the online Microsoft documentation on the MPS. This is usually located at `C:\msp\docs`.

NOTE: We are not sure why Microsoft uses the abbreviation "MSP" for the proxy server. This book uses the actual initials for the abbreviation "MPS."

Web Caching

Along with the standard Web caching functionality of a single machine, the MPS provides *distributed caching*. This feature allows you to distribute a cache across multiple

MPS in an array or chained configuration. The caching provides a significant performance benefit by allowing clients to access cached documents from the fast internal network rather than having to retrieve the original over a potentially slower Internet connection.

MPS supports distributed caching using the Cache Array Routing Protocol (CARP). CARP is a new IETF standard that supports array-based and chain-based content caching. The implementation of CARP allows the MPS to perform automatic load balancing, set up distributed content caching, and provide fault tolerance. The MPS implements CARP in two structures:

▼ **Proxy Arrays (Parallel Structure)**   A group of servers that function in parallel to each other. From the client's perspective, they function as one machine (entity), but in reality there are two or more servers providing the service. To separate this further from the proxy chains described next, it is safe to say that each proxy server may contain separate data and that they do not leverage each other's information. They exist solely to provide a load-balancing function.

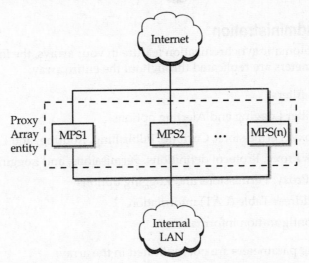

▲ **Proxy Chains (Hierarchical Structure)**   A group of servers that work in a hierarchical structure. When one server sends a request to the "upstream" server, if that server doesn't have the information cached or local, it forwards the request up the chain, and so on. The client is not aware of the "chain," as the servers do all of the forwarding and management. SSL-based chaining is supported.

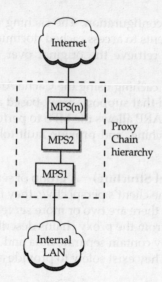

Arrays and Administration

If you use the automatic synchronization feature in your arrays, the following MPS configuration parameters are replicated throughout the entire array:

▼ Domain filters

■ Packet filter Logging and Alerting options

■ Web Proxy: Permissions, Caching, Publishing, Routing, and Logging options

■ WinSock Proxy: Protocol definitions, Permissions, and Logging options

■ SOCKS Proxy: Permissions and Logging options

■ Local Address Table (LAT) information

▲ Client configuration information

The following parameters are not replicated in the array:

▼ Web Proxy: Cache "Enable" option, cache size, or cache location

■ Logging directories

■ Packet filters

▲ IIS service password settings

NOTE: Using Internet Service Manager (ISM), you can manage IIS settings in the WWW service. Also, you should use the "Everyone" account instead of the IUSR_*computername* account because the IUSR_*computername* (anonymous) account is not correctly replicated across an array, unless the machines are part of the same Win2K domain.

Security

The security features of the MPS provide secure connectivity between trusted (usually internal) and untrusted (usually external) networks, as well as security between members of an array or chain. MPS provides:

▼ Packet filtering

■ Detailed logging

■ Authentication: proxy-to-proxy and user-to-proxy

■ Reverse proxying

■ Reverse hosting

▲ Server hosting

 NOTE: Both Routing and Remote Access Service (RRAS) and MPS have packet filtering capabilities. This chapter only deals with those of MPS.

Packet Filtering

MPS packet filters exist to determine which packets get passed to the Web Proxy, WinSock Proxy, SOCKS Proxy, or another service running on the MPS. MPS *will not* pass packets unless there is an application proxy or service available to accept the packet.

MPS supports both inbound and outbound packet filtering and will do dynamic filtering if it's enabled. This filtering is not like a dynamic filtering router, but is a filter to determine which packets can be passed through to the internal network's circuit and application layer proxy services. Individual packet filters are configured to allow only specified packets to be passed "through" MPS.

The ISAPI integration into Win2K (and Windows NT) is so tight that it allows the MPS packet filter (through IIS and ISAPI) to intercept packets before they are passed to other higher services or applications on the MPS. When the MPS packet filter intercepts the packet, it evaluates it and determines if it should be passed to an upper-level service or application. Once the MPS filters permit the packet, it is passed to one of the three MPS services (discussed next) or to another service running on the MPS.

 NOTE: This is only applicable if you have enabled packet filtering. If you are not using packet filtering, then the MPS will "allow" all packets to the upper-level services by default.

MPS Is Not a Router: An Important Fundamental

An important fact to understand is that the MPS is not a router. It does not have routing functionality. You can install the RRAS, which was discussed in the last chapter, on the MPS and thus combine MPS and RRAS onto a single box to make a router out of the proxy. If you decide to do this, you are *strongly* encouraged to use MPS packet filtering. If you do not, then external users will be able to use your MPS as a router to your internal network. As described momentarily, the MPS packet filter can be used to protect the RRAS service from rogue packets. Remember though, the best security stance is "minimalist"—only run what you need to. Mixing services in Windows 2000, such as RRAS and MPS, tends to weaken security in the sense that the interaction and the reliance of one protocol on the basic security stance of another usually leads to a weakest common denominator. This applies to any OS.

NOTE: It should be noted that if you are running RRAS and MPS packet filtering on the same box, the packet filter evaluates the packet before it is passed to the RRAS service. If you are not running the MPS packet filter, the MPS will route any and all packets that it receives; this is potentially dangerous and the reason why having RRAS and MPS on the same server is not advisable.

MPS is the epitome of the application gateway described in the last chapter. If there is not a specific application proxy written to accept a packet, then MPS will not pass it! The MPS has three "services" that provide its proxy functionality:

▼ **Web Proxy** Acts as an HTTP application proxy, working at the application layer in the OSI model.

■ **WinSock Proxy** Will proxy any application that is written to the WinSock API, working at the transport layer of the OSI model.

▲ **SOCKS Proxy** Will proxy any application that is written to the SOCKS 4.3a protocol specification, working at the transport layer of the OSI model.

As you will note, none of these work at the network layer where routing happens. Since the MPS is not functioning as a router, it should not be set as a default gateway either. Used as a Web Proxy, the MPS host will be specified as a "proxy server" in client browsers. The MPS will process packets that it can do something with, that is, those destined for the proxy services (Web, WinSock, and SOCKS proxies).

DYNAMIC PACKET FILTERING Rather than requiring you to manually predefine (that is, permanently open) a set of ports for every different application, dynamic filtering opens ports (based on source and destination ports in the initiating packet) automatically when needed. After the communication session ends, the ports are automatically closed.

The dynamic filtering will only open ports for communication requests initiated from "internal" or "trusted" clients (see discussion on LAT later in this chapter). When an internal client initiates a request, the MPS notes the IP address and port numbers in the packet and will set up a rule "dynamically" to allow those packets. This removes the need for an admin to create static rules for every possible connection combination. This also reduces the need for unbinding specific services from the external network adapters, since only an internal host can initiate the connection to that service. Note that if we manually predefined the ports, they would then be open for communication requests that were initiated from "untrusted" clients.

TIP: If you are running an actual client on the MPS itself that needs to get to the Internet and you have enabled packet filtering, you will need to configure static filters. The steps required to configure this are specified later in the chapter.

 NOTE: Packet filtering applies only to the external network adapter.

Logging and Alerts

The MPS supports logging for all MPS services (Web Proxy, WinSock Proxy, and SOCKS Proxy) and Packet Filtering. It allows you to send logging information to

▼ Text files

▲ ODBC database

 NOTE: Some of the MPS events will show up in the "System" EventLog.

The MPS packet filter logging allows you to keep a detailed audit trail for later use in troubleshooting or security incidents, while the MPS services (Web, WinSock, and SOCKS) logging allows you to keep a large range of information about service usage. These service logs are discussed in greater detail in the actual configuration section of the chapter.

 TIP: To get any really useful data out of the MPS logs, you need to use a third-party log redux tool. See Chapter 13 and Appendix A for more information on third-party tools.

MPS also supports setting alert thresholds for specific events, such as dropped packets. These are standard Win2K alerts, which can use SNMP or Windows Pop-Ups to send information to users or machines.

Authentication

MPS uses the authentication methods and restrictions that are defined for the IIS server. You must set them for the IIS server running the MPS; they cannot be set in the MPS itself. The authentication options are described in detail in Chapter 19, but here is a quick summary:

▼ **Allow Anonymous** Allows any user to use the services on the IIS server.

■ **Basic (Clear Text)** Requires users to enter a user name and password.

■ **Digest Authentication** Offers the same basic functionality of Basic authentication, but it does not transmit the password in clear text over the network.

▲ **Integrated Windows Authentication**   Uses Kerberos v5 authentication protocol and/or the NTLM authentication protocol.

PROXY TO PROXY   In an arrayed or chained environment, you can carry the same client authentication throughout the route taken, including Windows NT challenge/response authentication and SSL tunneling.

USER-BASED   MPS allows you to restrict service to authenticated Users or Groups. This, of course, requires that they authenticate to IIS. This is discussed in greater detail in the configuration section for each of the services.

Proxy Features

Along with the services and functions that we have been discussing, there are three features that really don't fall neatly into a category, so we will discuss them here. They are Reverse Proxy, Reverse Hosting, and Server Proxy. They are very similar in their basic function, but they are used in different situations. Sometimes it is really hard to tell which one you are using; the best way to know is by how you have configured the functionality.

REVERSE PROXY   This feature allows you to publish information from an internal Web server to the Internet. The MPS is configured to accept URL requests on a port (usually 80) from any host, internal or external. The MPS then "reverse" proxies the requests to whatever Web server you have configured it to pass to. This allows an Internet-based client to get Web-related data from an internal Web server without having a physical connection to it. Setting this up is described in the "Web Proxy: Publishing" section, later in this chapter.

NOTE: Using this feature can be problematic if you are running a Web server on the MPS, as only one service can be listening on a port at a time. You will have to decide which one you want. You can set the Web server to listen on a port other than 80, but you can't have the Reverse Proxy listen on a port other than 80.

REVERSE HOSTING   This feature allows you to "map" internal Web trees to specific URLs that the MPS will respond to. This is very similar to the Reverse Proxy, except that you can map to multiple internal Web servers and even certain portions of the Web trees on those servers. The MPS is configured such that when a URL request is received, it will use the mapping table to determine which internal Web server and path to make the request to. From that point on, it is just like the Reverse Proxy in that it will query the internal Web server for the "mapped" URL, and return the response to the external client. There does not have to be any correlation between the URL the MPS receives and the internal Web server tree structure. It may get confusing if there is not, but it is not required. The other thing to remember is that from the external network, this all looks like one Web server, so if two internal servers have the same path portion of the URL, the MPS will have to have two different mappings. For example, the MPS named Proxy will reverse host the schedule trees from the internal Web servers' web1 and web2:

MPS URL	Internal URL
http://Proxy.example.com/schedule	http://web1.int.example.com/schedule
http://Proxy.example.com/other_schedule	http://web2.int.example.com/schedule

Like the Reverse Proxy, this feature also allows an Internet-based client to get Web-related data from many internal Web servers without having a physical connection to it. Setting this up is described in the section Web Proxy: Publishing, later in this chapter.

SERVER PROXYING   This feature uses the WinSock Proxy server and WinSock Proxy client to allow internal services to "bind" to external ports on the MPS. The internal host will have the MPS "bind" to a specific external port, and then when any packets come into that port, the MPS forwards them to the internal host that made the binding. For example, you may want your internal Microsoft Exchange server to receive any SMTP mail from the Internet, but you don't want to place it physically on an Internet connection. You can configure the WinSock client on that Exchange server to "bind" to the MPS' external port 25. This would ensure that any traffic received on the external port 25 by the MPS would be directed (proxied) to the internal Exchange server.

The function of server proxying is similar to reverse hosting, except it is used for general services, not just Web traffic. Setting this up requires service-specific modification on the internal server running the service.

NOTE: There are multiple Knowledge Base articles describing the setup for different services. The Microsoft Knowledge Base can be found at **http://www.microsoft.com/kb**.

Microsoft Proxy Server Services

We have talked about some of the features of the proxy server. Now we need to talk about what mechanisms the MPS uses to implement those. Think of the MPS as providing connections between networks in different ways. Primarily the connections are between trusted and untrusted networks. It uses three mechanisms to do this: a general Web Proxy, a SOCKS-based TCP Proxy, and a Windows or a Sockets-based TCP-UDP Proxy.

THE WEB PROXY SERVICE   The Web Proxy service supports proxy requests from clients that are compatible with the CERN proxy protocol (all major Internet browsers support it). The Web request goes to the proxy server, the MPS makes the request on behalf of the client, and then returns the results to the client. Along with CERN proxy support, the MPS supports HTTP and FTP object caching, reverse proxying, and reverse hosting. The Web Proxy and WinSock Proxy do support user-level authentication; the SOCKS Proxy only supports authentication based on IP address. You also have the ability to restrict access to different Internet sites based on domain name and IP address; this is known as *domain filtering*. The Web Proxy has logging and alerting functions. The proxy can be used by browsers running on any computer on your internal network, regardless of the operating system (such as Windows 95, Windows NT, Macintosh, or UNIX).

> **TIP:** Administrators need to know how to force a clearing of the cache. What does the administrator need to do when you discover that someone made a confidential file available via HTTP or FTP? If it is cached, a simple deletion or change of access control on the file system may not be enough. On MPS, you can set the cache size to zero, restart the Web Proxy services, and then put the size back to the original value.

The proxy also performs IP masquerading, which means that all packets going to the Internet have the IP address of the MPS external interface card regardless of the internal source address. This is a basic feature of most proxy type systems, and thus all of the services (Web, WinSock, and SOCKS) support it.

THE WINSOCK PROXY SERVICE   The WinSock Proxy service performs redirection of the WinSock system APIs. It allows clients written to the WinSock API, such as Microsoft Telnet or FTP, to be able to use the WinSock Proxy to access the Internet. The client application makes a WinSock API call; this call is intercepted by the WinSock Proxy client, and redirected to the WinSock server on the MPS. The MPS then creates a circuit-level connection to the external host, and thus a communication path from the internal application to the Internet application is established.

The WinSock Proxy service, as well as supporting TCP/IP, will accept requests from IPX/SPX-based networks. The WinSock Proxy will also support challenge/response authentication between the client and remote server. The service will perform inbound and outbound access control. You can control access by port number, protocol, end-user, or group. Each port can be enabled or disabled for communications by a specific list of users or user groups, and the list of users that can initiate outbound connections at a port can be different from those that can listen on the same port.

Along with the ability to restrict inbound and outbound access, you can perform "domain filtering" as described previously. It also performs IP masquerading and supports logging and alerts. The client compatibility is limited to those clients who use the WinSock API *and* have the WinSock client installed (this means Windows operating systems only).

THE SOCKS PROXY SERVICE   SOCKS clients work in much the same way as the WinSock clients: API redirection. The SOCKS Proxy service supports SOCKS version 4.3a and exists purely for cross-platform support. The one caveat about this version of the SOCKS Proxy is that it only offers TCP-based services. It does not proxy UDP, IPX/SPX, or anything else. Microsoft makes the WinSock functionality much more desirable, so most Windows client applications are written to the WinSock API to get the added features not supported by *this version* of SOCKS. Since this is the case, when you are using the MPS, the majority of clients that use this service are UNIX, Macintosh, and other types of operating systems.

> **NOTE:**   The more recent version of SOCKS is much more robust and supports UDP, but this version is not supported by MPS.

The SOCKS service uses IP addresses along with identification (Identd) for authentication (it has no facility to do user authentication). Note that Identd authentication is by assertion. For example, here is an authentication exchange: "I'm Phil because I say I'm Phil! You had better believe me!" As you can tell, it is really stretching it to call this "authentication" at all.

It does perform IP masquerading and supports logging and alerts. As far as client support, if you have UNIX and Macintosh clients, this is the only option you have with MPS that will allow you to support non-HTTP-type protocols. Since SOCKS is not a proprietary protocol, it has very wide client support.

THE DECISION TO USE THE MICROSOFT PROXY SERVER

At this point, you might be asking yourself: Why would I use the Microsoft Proxy Server in the context of a firewall? It appears that the major features deal with performance (that is, caching) as opposed to a full-featured firewall that supports multiple operating systems and all sorts of TCP/IP/UDP-type protocols.

The MPS becomes a very valid firewall option in the right situations, such as the following:

▼ A small business connecting to the Internet

▲ A medium-size company connecting to the Internet that has a homogeneous Microsoft-based infrastructure and wants to allow internal clients to access external resources and potentially a small number of inbound connections

The MPS works well in an environment that is largely Windows-based or where almost all traffic is Web-based. It is not the best option in a very heterogeneous-type environment. Your infrastructure and architecture should determine if you are going to use the MPS at your site.

▼ If you have a large heterogeneous environment, then you should probably look for another solution.

▲ If you have a Windows-based environment, the Microsoft Proxy Server, even in a large corporation, may be a viable option.

In the context of when to use it and where to use it, there really is no cut-and-dry answer; it very much depends on your organization and the base operating systems that you have installed.

ADMINISTRATION

Now that you've decided to use MPS (you have, haven't you?), this section steps you through the recommended installation procedures (the performance and caching features are mentioned, but not described in detail). This section also focuses on several configuration options for clients using MPS services. All installation and configuration recommendations will be discussed in reference to three common scenarios:

▼ A network dialing up to the Internet

■ A network using a dedicated link

▲ Adding a DMZ to the foregoing

Tools: The Internet Service Manager

The administration of the MPS is done with the Internet Service Manager (ISM). This is the same tool that is used to administer the IIS server. Note that the ISM is just the MMC with the Internet Information Server (IIS) snap-in loaded. To start the ISM with the MPS administration additions, select Start | Programs | Microsoft Proxy Server | Microsoft Management Console. The ISM is shown in Figure 15-1.

Each of the three Microsoft Proxy Services—the WinSock Proxy, Web Proxy, and SOCKS Proxy—all have their own configuration panels, as seen in Figure 15-1.

Installing Server Software

Installing MPS consists of six main steps:

1. Start setup.
2. Install components.
3. Set the cache drives.
4. Define the LAT.
5. Configure client setup information.
6. Set access control.

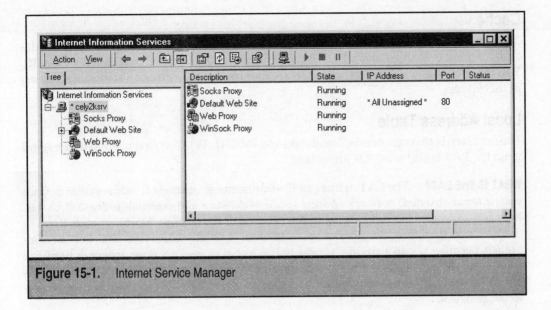

Figure 15-1.   Internet Service Manager

We will discuss steps 2, 4, 5, and 6. The rest are very evident as to what to set and do not deal with security per se.

Startup

To start the setup, download the Win2K update for MPS, which can be found at **http:// www.microsoft.com/proxy**, and use that to start the install.

NOTE: You must have a valid MPS or BackOffice disk containing MPS distribution to perform the setup.

On the Installation Options window, the following options appear:

▼ **Proxy Server**   Installs the MPS ISAPI DLLs into the IIS server on this machine, as well as the client software.

■ **Administration Tool**   Provides the MMC Snap-in to manage the MPS.

▲ **Documentation**   This will install the MPS on-line documentation.

You can select any or all of these options. If you drill down on the Change Options tab on the Proxy Server, you'll see that you can install the server as well as clients for Windows NT Intel, NT Alpha, and Windows 3.*x* clients. Note that you can install the Administration Tool to set up a remote machine to administer the MPS.

You then are prompted for the location to install the MPS. By default, it is in C:\msp. You can change that folder as well as select installation options.

Cache

Next, you set the cache options: enabled, where, and what size (see Figure 15-2). By default, caching is enabled and a 100MB cache file is created on the C partition (by default). You can choose other partitions and increase the size as well. You can also disable caching in this option.

Local Address Table

The next step is to construct the Local Address Table (LAT). You first need to understand what the LAT is and why it is important.

WHAT IS THE LAT?   The LAT defines an IP address range or single IP address that defines your internal (trusted) network address space. Make sure that external (untrusted, that is, Internet) addresses are not entered in the Internal IP Ranges list. Doing so adds them to the LAT and therefore identifies them as internal (trusted) addresses. This is a security breach because it can provide unwanted external access to your internal network computers. Also, if a client attempts to connect to an IP address defined in the LAT, it is not redirected through Proxy Server, and therefore won't be able to reach it from the internal network.

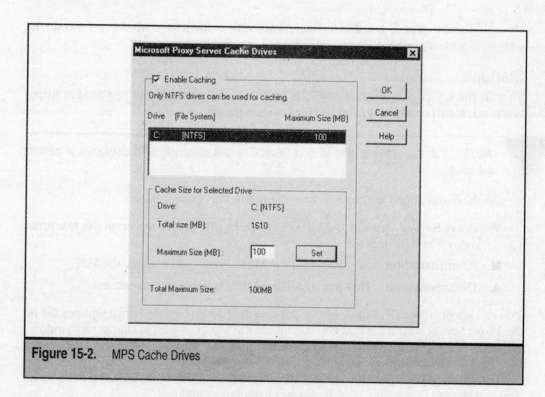

Figure 15-2.   MPS Cache Drives

TIP: You can edit the LAT at a later time using the Internet Service Manager (ISM) or by directly editing the `Msplat.txt` file, which is located in the MSP "Clients" directory.

CAUTION: Getting this correct is fundamental to the security of your network. If you configure this incorrectly, you can let the entire Internet into your LAN.

SETTING THE LAT   Figures 15-3 and 15-4 show the screens associated with setting up the LAT. You have two options to configure the LAT: You can type in IP address ranges, or you can construct the table from the currently existing network interface cards that are on the MPS machine. The latter option is preferred, as there is less of a chance for mistakes.

The Construct Table button shown in Figure 15-3 will bring up the window shown in Figure 15-4. You can then select the desired interfaces that are internal (trusted) and ensure that the external interfaces are *not* selected. You will be prompted with a Setup Message reminding you that the LAT should only contain internal addresses.

CAUTION: By default, this option will load *all* interfaces into the LAT. This is *not* what you want if you are using MPS for security, so be careful! However, it may be okay if you are using it for caching only or have only one interface.

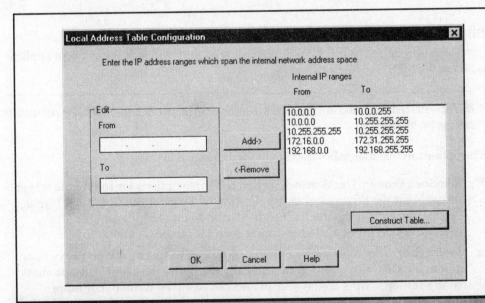

Figure 15-3.   Local Address Table Configuration

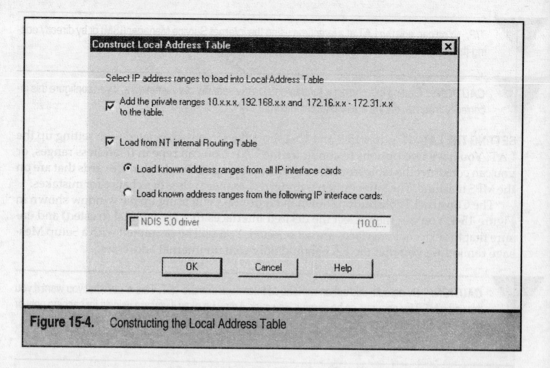

Figure 15-4. Constructing the Local Address Table

Configuring Client Setup Information

The next step is to define how the client Web browser and WinSock Proxy client applications access the MPS (see Figure 15-5).

NOTE: You can modify this at a later time with the Internet Service Manager (ISM), the tool used to manage the IIS server.

The options in this dialog box can be divided into two areas:

▼ **WinSock Proxy** The WinSock section has three options for setting the server (proxy) that the WinSock client application will connect to: Computer Name (that is, the NetBIOS name), IP Address, and Manual configuration. The Manual option is not available during setup; it can be set later.

▲ **Web Proxy** The Web proxy options allow you to specify a Web Proxy or an automatic URL to be used to dynamically configure the client. The automatic configuration scripts are JavaScript and can easily be written. For more information on writing automatic configuration scripts, see the online MSP help files.

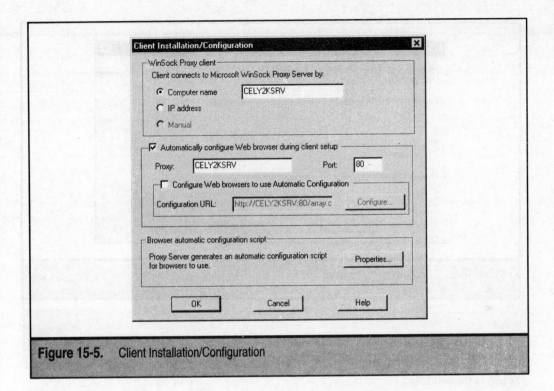

Figure 15-5. Client Installation/Configuration

You may find a need for some clients to have additional IP addresses defined as internal (that is, in the LAT). This may be a set of special machines that only a few clients should access or know about. You can do this by creating a permanent "client LAT" by adding the IP addresses to a file named `Locallat.txt`, which is stored in the client's `Mspclnt` directory (`C:\msp\clients`, by default). The client computer uses both the `Msplat.txt` and `Locallat.txt` files, if they exist.

Setting Access Control

You will then be prompted to set access control requirements for the Web Proxy and WinSock Proxy services. Both are enabled by default (see Figure 15-6), so the Web and WinSock Proxy services will try to validate connections from clients. By using this option, you have enabled access control security for these services.

NOTE: It is important to understand that although access control is enabled, it is enabled for everyone. This has the effect of essentially being disabled.

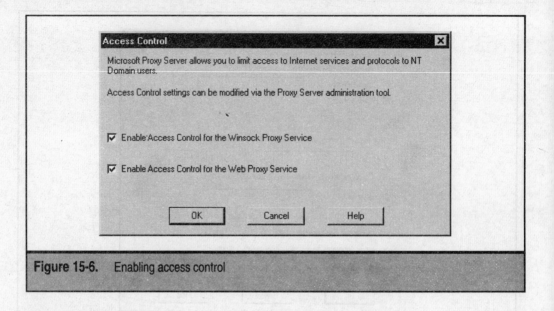

Figure 15-6. Enabling access control

Finishing Up

Once these have been defined, you've finished the installation and the MPS is installed. Setup is that simple.

POST-INSTALLATION

Now that the MPS is installed, we will want to go back to validate, as well as set some configuration parameters that we couldn't set during the installation.

Setting the Properties

The first step in the post-installation process is to configure the MPS. The following sections detail the configuration settings of the MPS.

Services Tab

Before discussing the configuration of the individual MPS services, let's discuss one set of configurations that is applicable to all the services and the MPS in general. You will view the WinSock Service tab for this example, but you could use the Web or SOCKS Properties as well. The Service tab (Figure 15-7) on the Properties dialog box for each of the MPS services sets configuration parameters that are applicable for all of the MPS-specific services. It provides the ability to configure two global categories of services and one operational service.

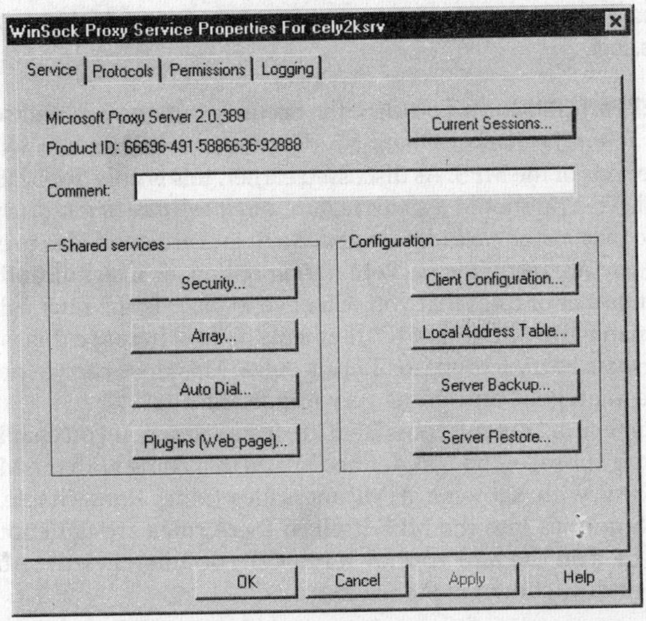

Figure 15-7. WinSock Proxy Service Properties

The global categories include

▼ **Shared Services** Parameters that affect all three services (Web, WinSock, and SOCKS). This allows you to set security properties, set up and manage arrays, set up auto dial parameters, and add Web plug-ins.

▲ **Configuration** Parameters that are specific to base operation of the server and clients. This allows you to back up or restore the server configuration, change the LAT (using the LAT configuration that we saw earlier), and set client configuration (as described earlier).

The operational category includes

■ **Current Sessions** Shows which clients are currently connected to the service and what User they are authenticated under. This will be specific to the service that the session is currently connected to (i.e. WinSock, Web, or SOCKS).

This section covers the Shared Services' security configuration in more detail. The other options have either been covered already (for example, LAT and client configuration) or deal mostly with daily operations and not security specifically.

TIP: The best information on the proxy server is from the Proxy FAQ found at **http://proxyfaq. networkgods.com**.

SECURITY: PACKET FILTERING   If you click the Security button, you will see the window shown in Figure 15-8. The Packet Filters tab determines whether you will be using the packet filtering options of the MPS. As discussed earlier, this is only applicable to interfaces that are *not* in the LAT. You should use this feature, *but it will take time to determine your filtering requirements, so you must be meticulous and patient*. It is also a good idea to enable dynamic packet filtering if you are using the packet filtering option, as it significantly eases the administration and number of rules that you will have to place in the filter rule set.

You should enable the filtering of IP fragments as well because this is a very sneaky way that attackers use to try to bypass filtering rules. This does carry a performance hit, but security is the main goal, and this is very important.

There are a number of "default rules" that are installed when you enable packet filtering; these rules are a subset of the "predefined" rules that come with the MPS and cannot be edited. They deal with allowing ICMP messages (ping, unreachable, timeout, and quench) and DNS queries into the MPS itself. If these rules are not enough, and most likely they won't be, you can add your own rules. To do this, click the Add button, and you will see the window shown in Figure 15-9.

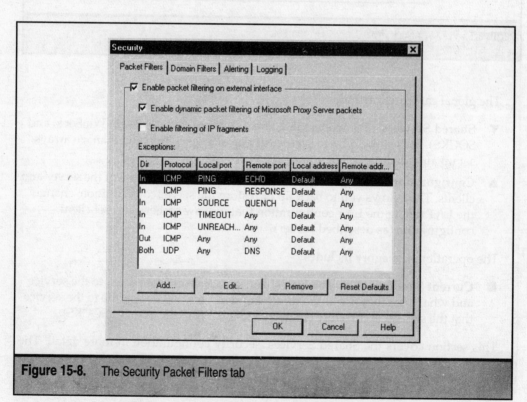

Figure 15-8.   The Security Packet Filters tab

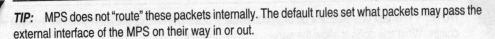
TIP: MPS does not "route" these packets internally. The default rules set what packets may pass the external interface of the MPS on their way in or out.

This screen allows you to select one of the predefined rules or set up a custom (a.k.a. static) filter based on the following criteria:

- ▼ **Protocol ID**   Any, TCP, UDP, or ICMP. What IP protocol type will be allowed by this rule.

- ■ **Direction**   Inbound, Outbound, or Both. Apply the rule on packets entering the interface, leaving the interface, or both.

- ■ **Local Port**   Any, Fixed Port, or Dynamic Port (1025-5000). Which MPS port is being used.

- ■ **Remote Port**   Any or Fixed Port. Which port on the remote host is being used.

- ■ **Remote Host**   Single Host or Any Host. What the IP address of the remote host is.

- ▲ **Local Host**   Default Proxy External IP Addresses, Specific Proxy IP, or Internal Computer. What the destination IP address is.

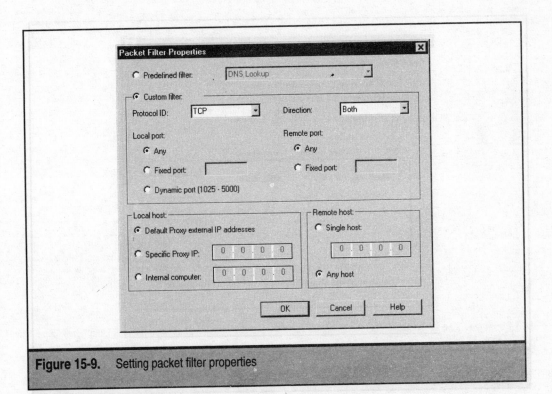

Figure 15-9.   Setting packet filter properties

NOTE: This last one needs a bit of explanation. It does *not* enable packet routing for internal machines. What this does is allow the server proxying to work.

SECURITY: DOMAIN FILTERS   Domain filters enable us to filter requests based on either IP address and subnet mask or domain name; they may be explicitly granted or explicitly denied (this is the same as IIS). The screen shown in Figure 15-10 shows an example of denying access to any host that is in the "example.com" domain or in the 198.178.0.0–198.178.255.255 IP address range. Figure 15-11 shows the screen for adding domains to the list.

TIP: It is important to understand that the entries in this window are exclusive, in that the list has either all the hosts you want to allow access to or all the hosts you want to block access to. You cannot mix grant and deny filters.

SECURITY: ALERTS   You can set up alerts on specific events like rejected packets, protocol violations, or disk full, as shown in Figure 15-12. If an alert is triggered, you can specify an automatic action that the MPS will perform, such as sending mail to a specified SMTP mail server.

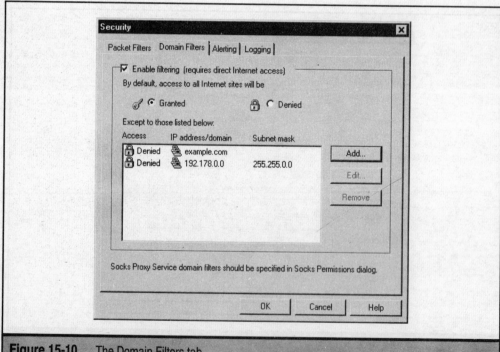

Figure 15-10.   The Domain Filters tab

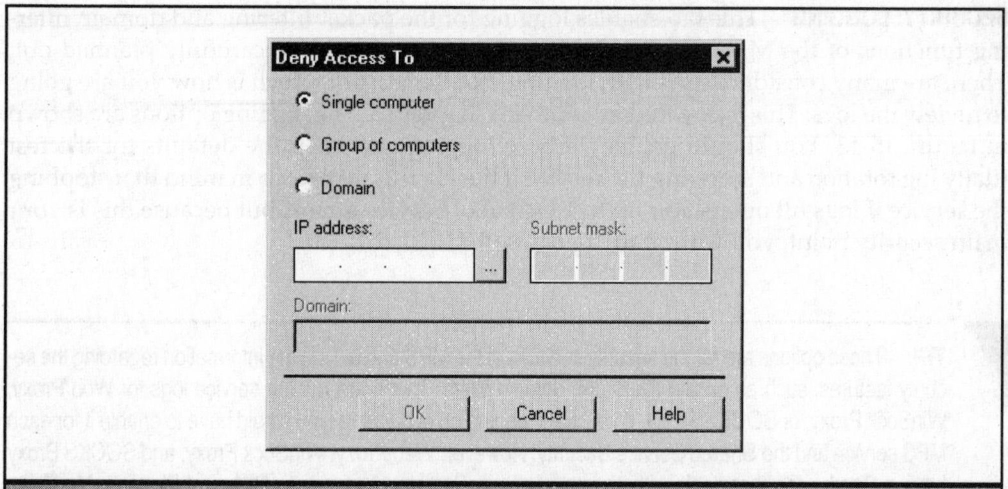

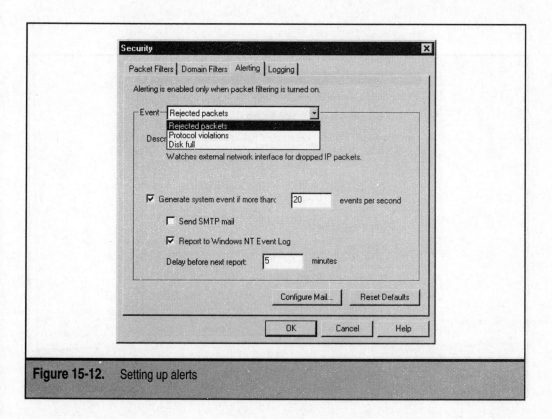

Figure 15-11.   Adding domains to the domain filters list

Figure 15-12.   Setting up alerts

SECURITY: LOGGING This tab enables logging for the packet filtering and domain filtering functions of the MPS. The logging configuration should be carefully planned out. There are many considerations with logging, not the least of which is how you are going to review the logs. This is covered in depth in Chapter 13. The logging options are shown in Figure 15-13. You should enable verbose logging and keep the defaults for the rest (daily log rotation and stopping the service if the log fills up). Keep in mind that stopping the service if logs fill opens you up to a Denial of Service attack, but because this is your main security point, you want it to "fail closed."

TiP: These options are for the security services of the MPS and will log the information regarding the security features, such as packet filters and domain filters. These are *not* the service logs for Web Proxy, WinSock Proxy, or SOCKS Proxy. If you want logging on everything, you would have to enable it for each MPS service and the Shared Service Security. However, Web Proxy, WinSock Proxy, and SOCKS Proxy have a Service tab that deals with shared services: Security, Array, Auto Dial, and Plug-ins. Modifying these on any service will modify them for all services.

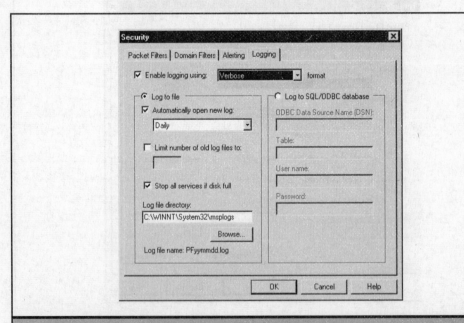

Figure 15-13. Setting logging options

Service Configurations

Now we will look at the specific service-related properties.

WinSock Proxy Service Properties

For the WinSock Proxy service there are four tabs: Service, Protocols, Permissions, and Logging. The Service parameters are the same as discussed earlier, so this section will cover the Protocols, Permissions, and Logging options. The main security issues are what protocols you will proxy and what permissions you apply to those protocols.

WINSOCK: PROTOCOLS   The Protocols tab is shown in Figure 15-14. Protocol definitions determine which application protocols can be used to access the Internet. Figure 15-14 shows that the Net2Phone service is selected. If you edit that service, you come to the window shown in Figure 15-15 (this is the same screen that you would get if you were adding a protocol). This screen allows you to set the protocol name, define the port numbers that the initial connection comes in on, specify whether it's a TCP or UDP port, specify whether it's inbound or outbound, and indicate port ranges for any other connections. You can also save the protocol definitions to or load them from a text file.

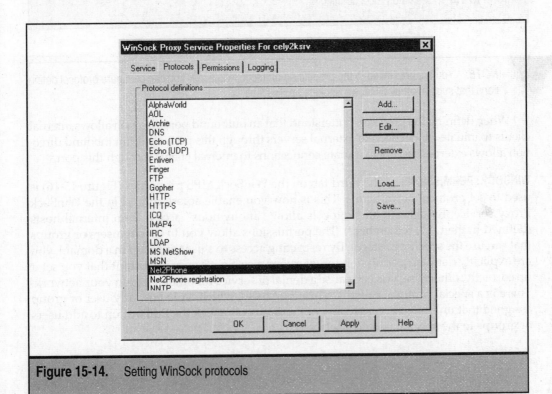

Figure 15-14.   Setting WinSock protocols

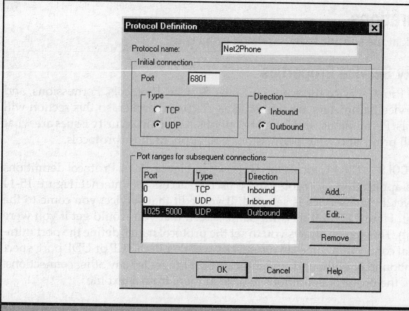

Figure 15-15. Setting protocol definitions

NOTE: You are not limited to the predefined protocol definitions. You can configure protocol definitions that support other Windows Sockets applications.

When defining the protocol, understand that an outbound port direction allows internal clients to initiate connections to external servers through this port, while an inbound direction allows external servers to initiate connections to internal clients through this port.

WINSOCK: PERMISSIONS The third tab on the WinSock MPS properties (Figure 15-16) is used to set protocol permissions. This is how you enable access control in the WinSock Proxy service. By default, all protocols allow "anonymous" access from internal hosts (defined in the LAT, remember?). The permissions allow you to specify users or groups that can use the specific protocol. By restricting access to a user or group in a domain, you are explicitly denying permission for everyone else. So it's very important that you set it up correctly; otherwise, you can cause a denial of service for other users on your network. There is a special protocol called Unlimited Access, which will allow any user or group assigned to it unlimited access to any of the protocols. Click the Edit button to add users or groups to the specific protocol selected.

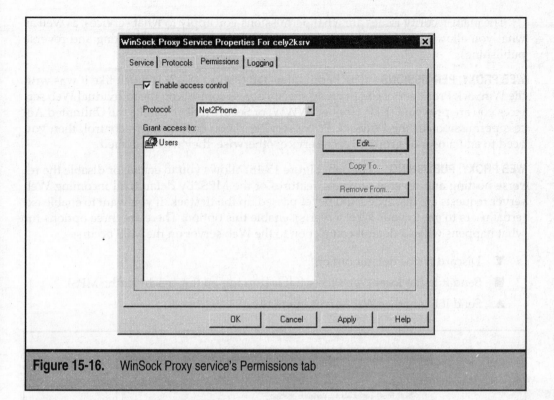

Figure 15-16.   WinSock Proxy service's Permissions tab

WINSOCK: LOGGING   Logging is enabled by default and is set on the fourth tab. The interface and options are the same as shown in Figure 15-13. You have two options for logging location: a File or an SQL/ODBC database. If you choose to log to a file, you can also set automatic rotation of log files, limit the number of old logs to maintain, and indicate the location of the file. For the SQL/ODBC logging, you will need to set up a server to log to.

NOTE: WinSock logging is not integrated into the Windows 2000 Event Logging Service, but it has similar features. Please see Chapter 13 and Appendix A for more details on logging and third-party tools related to their management.

Web Proxy Service Properties

For the Web Proxy service there are six tabs: Service, Permissions, Caching, Routing, Publishing, and Logging (see Figure 15-17). The Service parameters are the same as discussed earlier. The Caching tab allows you to enable or disable caching, define and set a cache expiration policy, and enable or disable active caching. The Routing tab allows you to configure Proxy Array routing (not IP routing). Logging configuration is identical to the others. So that leaves us with the Permissions and Publishing tabs to discuss.

The main security issues are what permissions you apply to what services, as well as what you allow in and out via the Publishing tab (that is, reverse hosting and reverse publishing).

WEB PROXY: PERMISSIONS　The Permissions tab (Figure 15-17) is much like it was with the WinSock Proxy service in that you specify access controls on the individual Web services you are proxying (FTP, Gopher, WWW, or Secure (SSL)). Unlike the Unlimited Access permissions in the WinSock Proxy service, if you enable access control, then you need to add a user or group to each service; otherwise, they will be denied.

WEB PROXY: PUBLISHING　This tab (Figure 15-18) allows you to enable or disable the reverse hosting and reverse proxying features of the MPS. By default, all incoming Web server requests are discarded and never passed up the IP stack. If you want to enable external users to get to your Web server(s), enable this option. There are three options for what happens when a default connection to the Web server on the MPS occurs:

▼　Discard it (the default option).

■　Send it to the local Web server if it is running on this machine (the MPS).

▲　Send it to another Web server internally.

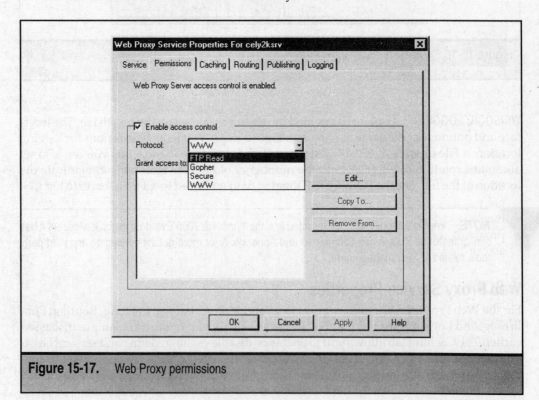

Figure 15-17.　Web Proxy permissions

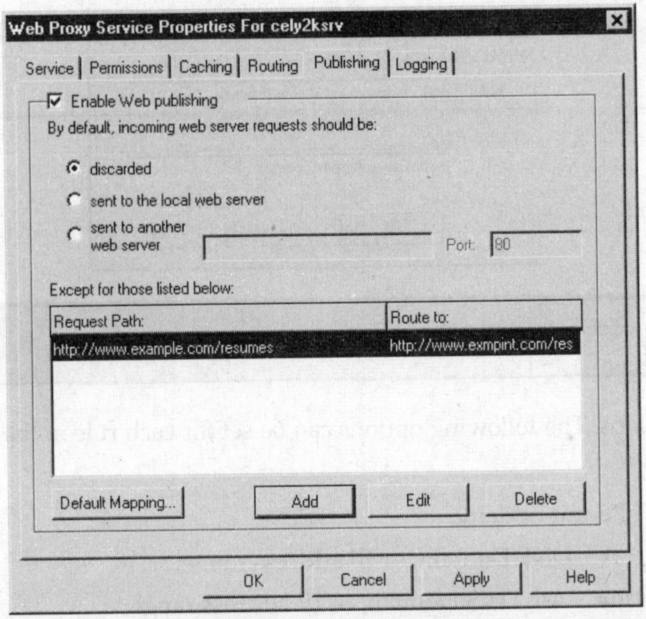

Figure 15-18.   Web Proxy publishing options

This last option, if selected, only happens if there is not a mapping for that specific URL in the mapping table.

Mappings (see Figure 15-19) are a way to granularly define multiple reverse proxies. You can define which URL will be returned (most likely an internal one) for a given external request. The mapping in Figure 15-19 will cause any request to the MPS for documents starting with the URL **http://www.example.com/resumes** to be mapped (that is, proxied) to **http://www.exmpint.com/res** (note that Figure 15-18 shows the resulting screen after clicking OK).

SOCKS Proxy Service

The SOCKS Proxy service has three tabs: Service, Permissions, and Logging (see Figure 15-20). Service and Logging have been described before. The Permissions tab (Figure 15-20) defines which hosts you allow for which TCP ports. Figure 15-21 shows the screen for

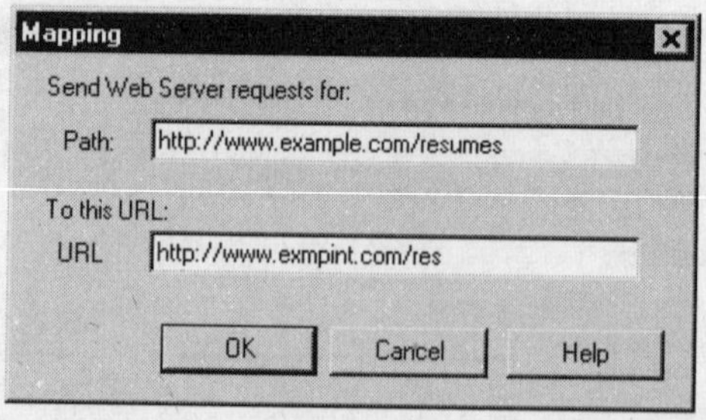

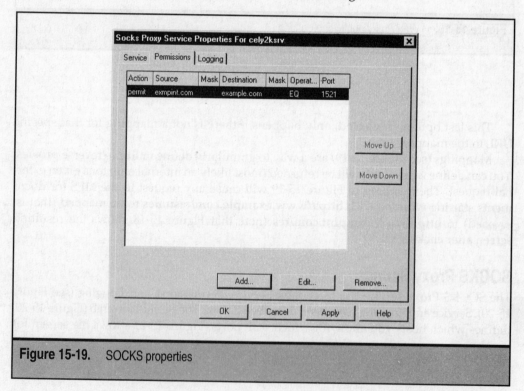

Figure 15-20. Web Proxy mapping

adding permissions. The following options can be set for each rule in the SOCKS Permissions dialog box:

▼ **Action** Permit or deny.

■ **Source** All, DNS Domain, or IP address range.

■ **Destination** All, DNS Domain, or IP address range.

Figure 15-19. SOCKS properties

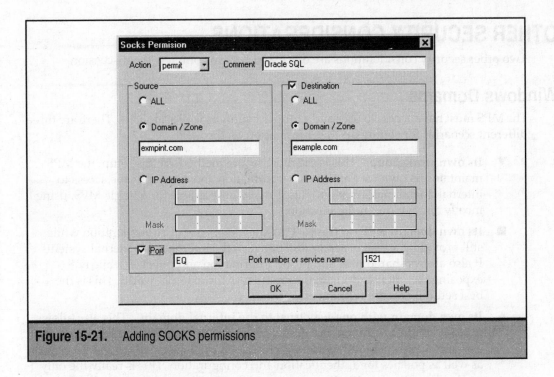

Figure 15-21. Adding SOCKS permissions

▲ **Port**   Port number or service name and a relative range associated with that
value (equal, not equal, greater than, less than, greater than or equal, less than
or equal).

In Figure 15-21, there is a rule that would "permit" any host in the **exmpint.com** domain to connect to any host in the **example.com** domain using a port equal to 1521 (note
that Figure 15-20 shows the resulting screen after clicking OK).

Using IIS to Set Authentication

We have covered the security-related configuration options that can be set with the MPS
properties. The only other security-related option that needs to be set is actually set on IIS,
and that deals with what type of authentication is required to connect to the server. If you
want to require Win2K authentication, then you must do it on the IIS server and not on
the MPS. See Chapter 19 for details on IIS authentication settings.

NOTE: The fact that MPS is actually an ISAPI plug-in to the IIS server is why we have to define authentication at the IIS server and not at the MPS.

OTHER SECURITY CONSIDERATIONS

Two other security considerations are discussed here to complete the discussion.

Windows Domains

The MPS must have access to user and group accounts as well as policies. There are three different scenarios for setting up this information on the MPS:

▼ **Its own workgroup**   This is the most secure method. In this setup, the MPS maintains its own user and group information and does not have access to internal domain information. This is really only usable for a single MPS, using mostly anonymous authentication.

■ **Its own domain with no trust**   This allows for ease of administration while still providing a wall of separation between the internal and external systems. It also allows shared user and group information and policies, while not exposing the internal domain information to the external world. This is the best setup if you are running arrays.

▲ **Its own domain with one-way trust to the internal domain**   This also allows for ease of administration, but does expose part of your internal domain to the external world. This allows the MPS to use internal user and group information as well as policies for authentication and configuration. This is really the only workable option for sites that require user authentication for most services. If you do not use this setup, then you have to duplicate all user and group information on the MPS anyway.

TIP: If you use this last method, ensure that you are using a good filtering router to prevent unwanted external queries for information to the MPS.

The Identd Simulation Service

MPS provides a "fake" Ident server (`identd.exe`), which supplies a false, random user name to those who require Ident for connections. It must be installed manually, and is located on the MPS CD. After it is installed, you can find it by selecting Start | Control Panel | Services.

INSTALLING CLIENT SOFTWARE

Your options for client software will vary depending on the MPS service you are planning on using. Here are your options:

▼ **Web Proxy**   No client software needed. All of the current browsers can be used through the Web Proxy by just setting the proper configurations in the browser.

■ **SOCKS Proxy**   You will have to ensure that your client software is SOCKS-enabled, but there is no client software per se to install.

▲ **WinSock Proxy**   You will have to install the WinSock client software that comes with the MPS. You will only need to install software on the client if you are using the Microsoft-based clients.

Following are guidelines for installing the WinSock client software.

Installing the WinSock Client

You will need to be able to access the MPS with traditional Microsoft networking (SMB/CIFS) to install the software. On the client, connect to the Mspclnt share on the MPS. Run `Setup.exe` from that share and follow the instructions. There is a Web interface to this also, but it just downloads a batch file, which runs the real `Setup.exe` from the network share. You would access this via **http://proxyservername/Msproxy**.

Figure 15-22 shows the WinSock client configuration screen. With this configuration, you can select which MPS to attempt to connect to and the protocol to connect with. The configuration also allows you to "update" the client LAT from the designated MPS. You configure this with the WinSock client Control Panel.

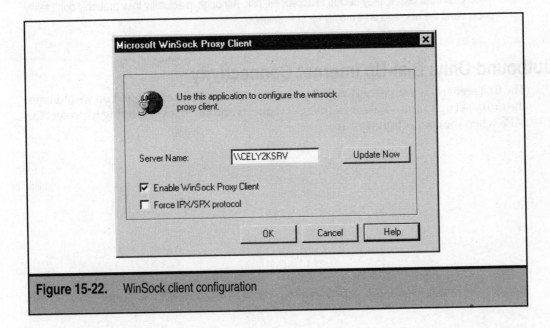

Figure 15-22.   WinSock client configuration

COMMON USES

The three common security configurations that you see the MPS used in are

▼ **Outbound Only**   Dial-up Internet connectivity
■ **Inbound and Outbound**   Business using a dedicated link
▲ **Inbound and Outbound**   With a DMZ

NOTE: In computer networks, a *DMZ* (*demilitarized zone*) is a network that separates the company's internal (private) network from an external (public) network, such as the Internet. It is used to separate networks with different trust levels and is sometimes called a *neutral zone* or a *perimeter network*.

The problem with the MPS is that it doesn't have great support for non-Windows platforms, and this keeps many large corporations from committing to it as an enterprise solution. In large environments, the MPS is usually used as a distributed caching service. There are many organizations that use multiple MPSs in an array configuration as their Web proxy.

NOTE: The Small Business Server is probably the most popular platform for the MPS because you have Win2K, Proxy, Exchange, and SQL all on one server. This has its own security problems, but for most small businesses, they decide to accept the risk. Although in actuality they probably don't really understand the risk, and do it mostly for convenience.

Outbound Only: Dial-Up Internet Connectivity

The first scenario is a small network that is using dial-up Internet access. You would have the proxy set up to auto-dial for all Internet requests and use packet filtering to protect the MPS when the connection was up.

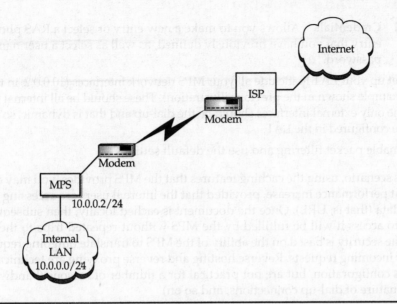

CAUTION: Make sure that the MPS has no default gateway defined on any of its network interfaces. This will prevent rogue packets from being routed to the internal network. If the MPS receives a packet that it does not know what to do with, then it should drop it. If the default route were set to an internal network, the MPS would then forward that packet to the default gateway on the internal network. This is a security breach waiting to happen. If you have more than one internal network, then you will need to define static routes for each of them on the MPS. Otherwise, the MPS will drop traffic that is not on directly connected internal networks.

For this configuration, you would need to do the following:

▼ Set up a RAS (Remote Access Service) phonebook entry for the Internet Service Provider that you are dialing into (that is, set up Win2K dialing properties).

■ Configure the auto-dial settings on the MPS. You do this in the Shared Services: Auto Dial section. There are two tabs: Configuration and Credentials.

   ■ **Configuration** Allows you to specify dialing services for the WinSock and SOCKS Proxy or for the Web Proxy.

- **Credentials** Allows you to make a new entry or select a RAS phonebook entry that you have previously defined, as well as select a user name and a password.

- Set up your LAT to include all your MPS network interfaces (10.0.0.2, in the example shown in the previous illustration). These should be all internal because the only external interfaces should be the dial-up and that is dynamic, so it won't be configured in the LAT.

▲ Enable packet filtering and use the default settings.

In this scenario, using the caching features that the MPS provides, you may observe a significant performance increase, provided that the internal users are accessing the same external data (that is, URL). Once the document is cached locally, then subsequent user requests to access it will be fulfilled by the MPS without repeated trips to the external source. The security is based on the ability of the MPS to translate outgoing requests and block any incoming requests. Reverse hosting and reverse proxying are technically feasible in this configuration, but are not practical for a number of reasons (bandwidth, dynamic IP nature of dial-up connections, and so on).

Inbound and Outbound: Small to Medium Business Using a Dedicated Link

This scenario, shown here, uses a dual-homed Microsoft Proxy Server. The organization has a dedicated link to the Internet on the external side (usually DSL or Frame Relay) and a connection to the local network on the internal side.

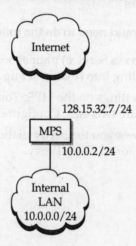

CAUTION: Make sure that the MPS only has a "default gateway" defined on the external interface. Like the preceding scenario, if you have more than one network internally, then you will need to define static routes for each of them on the MPS. Otherwise, the MPS will drop traffic that is not on directly connected internal networks.

Using this configuration, you would need to do the following:

▼ Configure the internal network to be in the LAT configuration and ensure that the external network is not. LAT would contain 10.0.0.0–10.0.0.255 in this example.

■ Set up the clients to use the MPS for Web Proxy and potentially the WinSock and/or the SOCKS Proxy.

■ Enable packet filtering.

▲ Keep the default packet filtering rules and security settings (these are adequate for a dual-homed proxy machine).

TIP: If you decide to use more elaborate packet filters, you will need to validate that the rules are doing what you want them to. This can be very tedious and time consuming.

VIP: For any of the MPS configurations, and especially those with direct connections to the Internet, the most important security settings are the IP addresses in the LAT and proper IP filtering rules.

Inbound and Outbound: With a DMZ

This configuration, shown here, will build a MPS as a tri-homed machine with a DMZ. This configuration, however, violates one of the fundamental security rules for the MPS: Never enable routing.

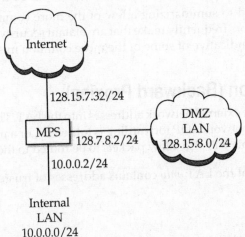

CAUTION: Make sure that the MPS only has a "default gateway" defined on the external interfaces. Like the preceding scenario, if you have more than one network internally, then you will need to define static routes for each of them on the MPS. Otherwise, the MPS will drop traffic that is not on directly connected internal networks.

In order to set up a DMZ using the MPS, you will need to do the following:

▼ Enable RRAS as a LAN router on the machine.

■ Configure the MPS DMZ interface to have an external IP address.

■ Configure the LAT to contain the IP addresses for the internal network card *and* the DMZ network card (not the DMZ network). In this example, the LAT would contain 10.0.0.0–10.0.0.255 and 128.7.8.2.

VIP: Ensure that the IP addresses of the machines on the DMZ network and the MPS external address are *not* in the LAT.

■ Configure static routes on the MPS for the DMZ network.

▲ Set up static packet filters to allow the Internet-based machines to access the DMZ-based machines. To allow HTTP connections to 128.15.8.3, you would set a filter as you would expect, but you would set the internal host to the 128.15.8.3 address. This configuration will allow internal clients to access the Internet, and internal and external clients to access hosts on the DMZ. The MPS packet filtering will prevent packets from originating from the DMZ back into the internal network; this is because the DMZ hosts are not in the LAT, and thus cannot initiate connections to internal hosts.

FREQUENTLY SEEN MISCONFIGURATIONS

This section is devoted to summarizing a few of the more common configuration mistakes that administrators frequently make that are blatant security no-no's. It is not meant to be exhaustive, but indicative of some of the more common mistakes.

LAT Misconfiguration (Backward Proxies)

PROBLEM Putting the external network addresses into the LAT. This allows Internet users to browse the internal network. If IP forwarding is turned on, or a malicious client used the WinSock Proxy, then this will also allow packets to be routed to the internal network.

SOLUTION Ensure that the LAT *only* contains addresses of trusted internal hosts.

Misconfigured Default Gateways

PROBLEM   Having the default gateway pointing to the internal network interface. This would allow an attacker to send packets to the MPS that would be sent to the internal network.

SOLUTION   Ensure that the default gateway for the MPS is set to the Internet interface (the one connected to the ISP).

Running All BackOffice (BO) Services on One Host

PROBLEM   It is usually a combination of small service-related vulnerabilities that lead to catastrophic compromises. If you are running a large number of different services on the BO server, then you have significantly increased the risk that small vulnerabilities in each service can be used together to compromise the entire machine (sometimes called *cascading*). There are two aspects of this problem when dealing with the MPS. The first aspect is running MPS as a part of a BO server that is hosting other potentially sensitive resources. This means that a compromise of the MPS would immediately compromise any and all services on that server. The second aspect is that if you are reverse proxying/hosting multiple services to a single machine on the internal network, then a cascade attack could be mounted against that server. This could potentially lead to a complete compromise of the internal network *through the properly functioning MPS*.

SOLUTION   Isolate functionality to individual machines if possible. If this is not possible, then limit the number of services that each machine runs.

Bad Filter Rules

PROBLEM   Confusing the inbound versus outbound filtering logic. This can cause either a denial of service, in that the services you want to support are now filtered, or worse, it can allow traffic that you do not want to be allowed into the MPS.

SOLUTION   Validate rules *prior* to placing them on the MPS. This validation should be done in a test network to ensure that the rules do what you want them to. Also, unless you need a filter for ICMP, you should disable it for security reasons.

Allowing Access to Microsoft Networking Ports (135, 137–139 TCP and UDP)

PROBLEM   If you're either not implementing packet filtering or are only blocking specific ports and you forget to block the Microsoft Networking ports (see Web Appendix B (**www.osborne.com**) for port listings), then you have opened the MPS up to direct attacks against the underlying operating system. This is probably one of the most common and yet devastating misconfigurations.

SOLUTION   Use MPS filtering, Router ACLs, or Internal Port filtering (described in Chapter 21 on hardening the system).

SOCKS Misconfiguration

PROBLEM   Configuring the SOCKS proxy to allow inbound access from the Internet.

SOLUTION   Ensure the SOCKS proxy does not allow inbound connections from the Internet.

Enabling Analysis of UDP Packets Option

PROBLEM   A Denial of Service attack can be mounted against the MPS with a UDP flood.

SOLUTION   Do not enable the Analysis of UDP Packets option in the packet filter.

RECAP

We've looked at the Microsoft Proxy Server, some of its setup characteristics, and some scenarios where it might be applied. The security-related features were reviewed and explained. Some of the more performance-related issues and caching were briefly discussed. Your decision to use the MPS, or not, should depend on the specific security requirements you have. If you require a very secure, highly configurable box, then the MPS is not something that you should consider as an ideal solution. If you do require a high-performance caching proxy that provides some good basic security features and you don't have unusual protocol requirements, then the MPS is a viable candidate. If you're running a majority of Windows-based clients, the MPS is very much something that you should look at and something that you should consider in your firewall and security efforts.

For more information on this, Microsoft has a proxy Web site (**www.microsoft.com/ proxy**) as well as the proxy FAQ (**proxyfaq.networkgods.com**). Both of these provide a vast amount of detail on the services, both security- and performance-related, as well as many other features, and they're a great place to keep up to date on this technology. The scope of this book precludes us from covering all of the details of the proxy server. Hopefully, this chapter has given you a basic understanding of its abilities, where it can be used, and at least an idea of what the services provide; you can go from here to make a better decision.

We have not covered the performance details of MPS in this book sufficiently for any reader to make an informed decision in this regard. If performance is a requirement, you should get a book devoted specifically to MPS and the caching features.

CHAPTER 16

Remote Access and Virtual Private Networks

This chapter covers the technologies that are used to connect private systems and networks together over a public infrastructure. Collectively, we will be referring to these technologies as Remote Access and Virtual Private Networks.

WHAT'S THE PROBLEM?

The problem, or maybe better phrased the "issue," is that we have more mobile users and remote networks than ever before. And all those users and networks need to be connected to our internal corporate networks. This explosion of remote connectivity has come about for a number of reasons:

▼ Corporate mergers have caused a significant rise in the need to physically join disparate networks.

■ In the same vein, global companies require that their nationally separate networks be connected together into a single "corporate" network. This poses a very complex problem because of the different encryption laws in each nation.

■ Geographically separate workers are using the public Internet as a "virtual" office.

■ More road warriors. There are more people traveling and needing access to data in their corporate networks.

▲ The boom of national ISPs now allows workers to telecommute from almost anywhere in the world.

WHAT ARE WE TRYING TO ACCOMPLISH?

We know we have a problem—disconnected users and networks. Our obvious inclination is to say "Let's connect them!" This is all well and good, but first, we have to know who we want to connect, and then, second, what we need out of the connection. The "who" is usually pretty straightforward, and it deals with remote offices/networks, partners, or mobile users. The "what" can be a bit more complicated and is described in the next section.

So we all agree on the right thing to do: solve the problem. But by solving the connectivity problem, we have introduced a potentially greater problem—compromised security. By making the connection, we have now started passing our network traffic over someone else's physical network. If you don't take the time to ensure the security of the traffic, it will cost you in the end.

The Requirements Matrix

Knowing that we need to connect the users is fine, but finding the proper solution is not always easy. The nice thing about this problem is that there are some well-established technologies that can provide the answers you need. Although the technologies exist, it is very important that you first determine your requirements *before* you select the solution. The requirements for all traffic on your network should be spelled out in your security plan. If you do not have one, then: Stop. Do not pass GO. Go directly to Chapter 4. A policy is fundamental to a successful security strategy; without it, you will fail! It is not a matter of *if*, but *when*. The requirements should specify what level of security is needed for "User" data as well as "System" data.

NOTE: We differentiate User and System data. System data is stuff like connection setup, authentication, and management. User data is stuff like e-mail, files, and Web traffic.

For the data categories, you will need to evaluate the requirements for confidentiality, integrity, availability, and management. For each of them, you will need to know if it is required or optional, and you will need to determine the priorities. We like to use a simple table as an example of what we call a "requirements matrix." As shown in Table 16-1, you will need to determine if all data or just System data is encrypted.

Your matrix will be specific to your situation. For example, the matrix in Table 16-1 shows that a software development company providing access to its employees listed confidentiality as required and priority #1 for both User and System data, while they listed integrity as required and priority #2 for User data and availability as required and priority #2 for System data, and so on. On the other hand, an ISP probably does not care about confidentiality, but would rank availability #1 and management #2. Obviously, this matrix is very general, and you should make it more specific to your situation, but it gives you a feel for the process.

Remote Access: Possibility #1

For the purpose of this book, we will define *remote access* as "an unencrypted connection from a single machine or network, across a public network (dial-up, leased lines, or the Internet) to another trusted machine or network." The important point to pull out of this is "unencrypted connection." One major difference between remote access connection

	Confidentiality	Status	Integrity	Status	Availability	Status	Management	Status
User Data	1	Req	2	Req	3	Opt	4	Opt
System Data	1	Req	4	Opt	2	Req	3	Opt

Table 16-1.   Requirements Matrix

and a Virtual Private Network is the encryption of the connection. We know this is not a perfect definition, but it gets the point across.

NOTE: Remote Access Server (RAS) is not the same as *remote access server*. The *remote access server* is a generic term used for a system that provides the remote access service, whereas *RAS* is the Microsoft-specific server.

Remote Access Is Not Remote Control

One important point to remember is that remote access does not mean remote control. *Remote access* deals with providing a network connection between different systems; this is a Layer 2 and 3 (data link and network layers) function in the OSI model (see Chapter 6). *Remote control* deals with actually controlling some aspect of the system you are connecting to, usually at Layer 7 (application layer). Symantec's PCAnywhere is an example of a remote control product that can be run over a Point-to-Point (PPP, to be discussed later) remote access connection.

Virtual Private Networks: Possibility #2

For the purpose of this book, we will define a Virtual Private Network (VPN) as "an encrypted connection from a single machine or network, across a public network (dial-up, leased lines, or the Internet) to another trusted machine or network. This connection emulates a point-to-point connection and is usually viewed as an extension of the private network." The important points to pull out of this is definition are "encrypted" and "point-to-point connection." Along with the encryption difference mentioned earlier, the other major difference between remote access connection and a Virtual Private Network is that the VPN is point-to-point.

Properties

All VPN technologies have certain traits or characteristics. Those traits allow the VPN to accomplish the function of the emulated point-to-point link that is encrypted. Those traits are described in the following sections.

TUNNELING (A.K.A. ENCAPSULATION)   All VPN technologies provide a method of tunneling data that resides on the private network in such a manner that it can be sent over the intermediate network(s). Placing the private network data packet into a packet for the intermediate network usually does this. Then, when the packet gets to the other end of the connection, the receiving side removes the private packet from the "transit" packet, and places it on the internal network.

AUTHENTICATION   VPN authentication has two forms:

▼   Client authentication

▲   Data authentication and integrity

Client authentication would fall into the System data that was described earlier in the section on the requirements matrix. The data authentication and integrity would be the User data.

Client authentication takes place when the VPN connection is being established. The VPN server will authenticate the client and, if the client is configured to do so, will authenticate the server. This last authentication is called *mutual authentication* and will protect the client from communicating with a masquerading VPN server.

Data authentication and integrity is used to ensure that the data that went in one side of the connection is the same data that is coming out the other side. Confidentiality and integrity are the keys here. The authentication trait will cause both sides of the connection to validate the data that is sent. This is usually done with cryptographic checksums.

ENCRYPTION   Along with tunneling and authentication, all VPN technologies provide encryption of the traffic flowing over the tunnel. This is to ensure that the data traversing the connection is confidential (that is, only viewable by the end points). In a VPN, the data is encrypted with a shared key by the sender, and decrypted with the same shared key by the receiver. This means that packets that are sniffed (that is, captured) in the middle of the connection are not viewable by the sniffer, *unless* he or she knows the shared key. That is why the "P" in VPN stands for "Private" and not "Public." Neither the type nor the strength of the encryption is specified. You should ensure that whatever is selected is adequate for your needs.

Types of VPN Structures

There are three types of VPN structures.

HOST TO HOST (TRANSPORT)   In a host-to-host structure, there is a VPN client (a single end-user computer), which connects to a VPN server. All traffic is between the client and server, which means that there is no forwarding of traffic (that is, packets) off of the server to another machine on the network. For this structure all traffic *is* or *is not* encrypted between the two points.

GATEWAY TO GATEWAY (TUNNELING)   A security gateway makes a gateway-to-gateway VPN connection that connects two portions of a private network. Computers running Windows 2000 Server and Windows NT Server 4.0 with the Routing and Remote Access Service (RRAS) can create gateway-to-gateway VPN connections. Thus, multiple packets that are destined for systems on the network of the other gateway will be tunneled. All data packets traveling from one gateway to another are encrypted.

HOST TO GATEWAY (TUNNELING)   A host will make a secure connection to a gateway (i.e. router) to another network. Then all traffic originating from the host, with a destination on the remote network, will be passed over the secure, encrypted connection (VPN).

When Do We Use Them?

This is an obvious question that arises when discussing these technologies. It gets back to the requirements matrix discussed earlier. Once you have **identified your requirements**, the selection is much easier. One rule of thumb that you **should keep in mind** is that remote access solutions tend to be less secure, but easier to manage than VPN solutions. With that in mind, Table 16-2 lists some common "**rules of thumb**."

	When to Use	Pros	Cons
Remote Access	When you just want network connectivity. When security is not a requirement. When you only need security for the authentication portion of the connection (confidentiality of the data does not matter).	Accessibility for mobile users is excellent since connection is usually via dial-up. Manageability.	Data transmission may not be secure.
VPN	When you already have network connectivity. When security of data across the connection is required. When you want to tunnel traffic from one network to the other.	Security. Avoidance of long-distance and 1-800 telephone charges. Global availability of the Internet. Maintenance-free network infrastructure between companies.	Scalability. Management. Susceptibility to Internet disruption.

Table 16-2. Remote Access Versus VPN

NOTE: You can use a VPN over a dial-up connection, but the link (PPP) must already be established.

TIP: Do not forget that the Internet has no guaranteed level of service. If you are going to build your corporate networks over it, this point should not escape you.

LEASED LINES AND VPNs   It is obvious to most people that a VPN is beneficial over a public or untrusted network such as the Internet. What some do not think about, though, is using a VPN over leased lines. Although leased lines "belong" to the company you lease them from, they are no less of a threat. If you encrypt your communication over the Internet, then you should think long and hard before you let the same communication go over your leased lines in an unencrypted fashion.

With the basic understanding of remote access and VPNs, let's look at some protocols that are used to implement them.

PROTOCOLS AND STANDARDS

The following section covers some of the protocols used to supply remote access and VPN services on Win2K.

Remote Access

When we think of remote access, there are two specific protocols that are widely used to provide the service. They are the Point-to-Point Protocol (PPP) and Serial Line Interface Protocol (SLIP). PPP is the de facto standard used today. SLIP is generally not used anymore but it is covered here for completeness.

Point-to-Point Protocol (PPP)

PPP is an industry standard protocol, which uses point-to-point links to transport multiprotocol datagrams as described in RFC 1661 and 1171. It is the mainstay of all dial-up connectivity and is the primary protocol used in Microsoft's RAS client and server.

Serial Line Interface Protocol (SLIP)

SLIP has been around for years. It is the predecessor to PPP and as such, has much less functionality. Its primary purpose was to provide a link over which a single protocol could be transmitted. It has no mechanism to dynamically assign address-related information (that is, IP address, routing information, and so on) to the client; this means that the client and server may be configured beforehand. SLIP has no ability to transport more than one protocol. This is not a problem if you are just using one protocol, but many sites use both TCP/IP and IPX. For all intents and purposes, SLIP is limited to TCP/IP. There is no error detection/correction capability, and no compression (CSLIP is a specification that allows compression of just the IP header portion of a TCP/IP data packet). SLIP is not supported on any Microsoft RAS server. However, it is supported on Microsoft RAS clients.

Point-to-Point Tunneling Protocol (PPTP)

PPTP is a communication protocol that supports the creation of a VPN across a TCP/IP network to PPTP servers. PPTP is just an extension of PPP, which tunnels datagrams (primarily IP) over an intermediate network. This intermediate network is usually the Internet, but could also be your LAN. PPTP has all of the characteristics of a VPN: It supports tunneling, authentication, and encryption. PPTP is defined in the IETF draft "Point-to-Point Tunneling Protocol" (**http: www.ietf.org/html.charters/pppext-charter .html**). PPTP was the default VPN protocol for Windows NT.

PPTP is supported by Microsoft (Win2K and Windows NT support PPTP servers), Ascend Communications, ECI Telematics, 3Com, and U.S. Robotics. As implemented by Microsoft, PPTP uses analog, ISDN, or X.25 communication lines to create a tunnel directly to a specific server on a network.

IP Security (IPSec)

This section on IPSec is not a detailed reference on IPSec, but just enough to understand the basics. IPSec is designed to provide a high-quality, interoperable, secure network-level (at the IP layer) connection for IPv4 and IPv6. IPSec accomplishes this by offering security "services" such as access control, connectionless integrity, data origin authentication, replay protection, and confidentiality. All of these services are provided by three main security protocols: the Authentication Header (AH), Encapsulating Security Payload (ESP), and key management (Internet Key Exchange, IKE). IPSec does not dictate which of the three protocols are used, or how they are used; it allows the communicating systems to negotiate what they want to use. This is true for both protocols and algorithms. This also means that there is no dictated algorithm to be used in each of the protocols; thus, you can use your own if you so desire and if the party you are communicating with supports the same algorithm.

NOTE: There is a standard set of default algorithms to ensure interoperability in the global Internet.

One of the design features is that you should still be able to communicate with entities that do not use IPSec. In as much as you and they agree not to use the IPSec protocols, there should be no effect on the traffic between you.

The following are fundamental components of the IPSec security architecture:

▼   **Security associations**   How the systems will determine the protocols and algorithms that are used. What they are, how they work, and how they are managed.

- ■ **Security protocols** Authentication Header (AH) and Encapsulating Security Payload (ESP).
- ■ **Key management** Manual and automatic (the Internet Key Exchange (IKE)).
- ▲ **Algorithms** For authentication and encryption.

Security Associations

A *security association (SA)* is a set of policy and key(s) that are used to protect information on the network. Security associations are fundamental to IPSec as they are used to define the common security services, mechanisms, and keys used to protect the communication from end to end. AH and ESP make use of SAs to get the keys they need to perform their function. Also, one of the jobs done by IKE is establishing and maintaining the SAs. An SA consists of a unique combination of a Security Parameter Index (SPI), an IP destination address, and a security protocol (AH or ESP) identifier. The destination address may be one of the following:

- ▼ Unicast address
- ■ IP broadcast address
- ▲ Multicast group address

Before any secured data can be exchanged, an SA must be established between the communicating systems. The systems must agree on how to exchange and protect information. There are two types of SAs that are defined: transport mode and tunnel mode. A *transport mode* SA is a security association between two hosts. The *tunnel mode* is used when either end is a security gateway.

> **NOTE:** These are implemented as IP Security Policies in Win2K.

COMBINING SECURITY ASSOCIATIONS If a security policy needs to use more then one SA to implement the required security policy, the traffic will have to go through multiple SAs (a.k.a. *security association bundle* or *SA bundle*).

SA and Key Management

All IPSec implementations must support both manual and automated SA and key management. Although AH and ESP are pretty much independent of the management techniques, the techniques can affect some of the functionality that each provides (that is, the granularity of key distribution determines the granularity of authentication provided).

- ▼ **Manual** An individual manually configures each system with keying material and security association management data. This works for a limited number of connections.

▲ **Automated** SA and keying material are automated. This is the only viable technique for a large-scale deployment. The default automated key management protocol selected for use with IPSec is Internet Key Exchange (IKE).

Security Protocols

Security services can be provided between a pair of communicating hosts, between a pair of communicating security gateways, or between a security gateway and a host. IPSec has three specific protocols that are used in different configurations to provide those security services.

AUTHENTICATION HEADER: AUTHENTICATION ONLY AH is a new IP protocol type. It is used to provide message integrity, authentication, and optional anti-replay service or IP datagrams. It does all of this without the concept of confidentiality (encryption). It can be used in conjunction with ESP (described next) to provide confidentiality, though. Any and all of these options are determined during the SA negotiation.

ENCAPSULATING SECURITY PAYLOAD: AUTHENTICATION AND ENCRYPTION ESP is another new IP protocol. It may be used to provide the same security services as AH, but it also provides a confidentiality (encryption) service. The main differences between the authentication provided by ESP and AH is that ESP encrypts the data and does not do anything with the header information (that is, covers the data and not the IP header fields). Currently, ESP relies on a minimum 56-bit DES encryption strength, but can be used with almost any symmetric encryption algorithm. Because ESP is used to encrypt a data into a blob, which is then stuffed into another IP packet, it can be used on legacy networks today.

KEY EXCHANGE FUNCTIONS: INTERNET KEY EXCHANGE Because AH and ESP use shared secret values to provide their services, there needs to be a way to negotiate keys; this is where IKE comes in. IKE is the default key exchange and security negotiation protocol used in IPSec implementations. Its purpose is to establish security associations and crypto keys. For the SA, it will negotiate, establish, modify, and delete SAs and their attributes. For key management, IKE supports both manual and automatic distribution of public (asymmetric) and private (symmetric) keys. IKE is defined in IETF draft document found at **http: www.ietf.org/html.charters/ipsec-charter.html.**

Security Association Modes

As stated earlier, AH and ESP support two modes of use: transport mode and tunnel mode. IPSec allows very specific control over the connections that are allowed. You may have host-to-host, host-to-security gateway, and security gateway-to-security gateway. The administrator controls all this. The two modes are described here.

TRANSPORT (HOST TO HOST) Transport mode will protect the IP packet payload, but not the IP header. Think of this as protecting upper layer protocols. *Remember: IP payload but* *not header*. This will mostly be used in a host-to-security gateway, implementing a mobile user VPN connection to a corporate network.

TUNNEL (SECURITY GATEWAY-TO-SECURITY GATEWAY AND HOST-TO-GATEWAY)   This will perform Layer 3 tunneling—the tunneled payload is a Network layer packet. The entire IP packet is encapsulated and secured for transfer by one of the IPSec security protocols. *Remember: Entire packet.*

▼   **ESP Tunnel Mode**   The original IP header (which is the original packet header) usually carries the ultimate source and destination addresses, while the outer IP header contains the address of a security gateway. The original header is placed after the ESP header, and an ESP trailer is appended prior to encryption. Everything following the ESP header, except for the ESP authentication trailer, is encrypted. Now the entire original packet is secured (encrypted). This encrypted blob becomes the data of a new packet (that is, encapsulated), and the new IP header is used to route the packet from origin to the next destination, usually a security gateway.

▲   **AH Tunnel Mode**   Very similar to ESP, but no encryption for the packet, only authentication and integrity. The whole packet is signed for integrity, including the new tunnel header.

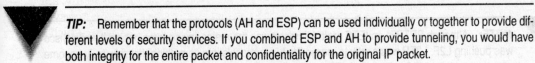

TIP: Remember that the protocols (AH and ESP) can be used individually or together to provide different levels of security services. If you combined ESP and AH to provide tunneling, you would have both integrity for the entire packet and confidentiality for the original IP packet.

IPSec and Network Address Translation

It is the job of Network Address Translation (NAT) to look at packets and translate the address information in them, whereas it is IPSec's job to make packets unintelligible and unalterable. Thus we have a fundamental incompatibility (as was noted with Kerberos in Chapter 11). This fundamental incompatibility means that you cannot establish end-to-end IPSec *through* NAT gateways. The NAT gateway can be used as the security gateway, then back-end IPSec connections to the internal hosts. It cannot tunnel them because it has to be able to see the address information of the original datagram (taking the IPSec wrappings off, so to speak), but then it can wrap it back up before sending it in or out.

Architecture Is Key

IPSec is not a fix-all; it requires good implementation and a complete security architecture. To quote from RFC 2401:

"... the security offered by use of these protocols ultimately depends on the quality of the their implementation...Moreover, the security of a computer system or network is a function of many factors, including personnel, physical, procedural, compromising emanations, and computer security practices. Thus IPSec is only one part of an overall system security architecture.... Finally, the security afforded by the use of IPSec is critically dependent on many aspects of the operating environment in which the IPSec implementation executes. For example, defects in OS security, poor quality of random number sources, sloppy system management protocols and practices, etc. can all degrade the security provided by IPSec."

IPSec Drafts and RFCs

IPSec is a very complex topic, and cannot be done justice in such a short time. You are encouraged to follow the IETF development of this set of standards. The Web site for the IETF IPSec working group is at **http://www.ietf.org/html.charters/ipsec-charter.html**. They have links to all the relevant IETF drafts and RFCs (1825-1829).

Layer 2 Tunneling Protocol (L2TP)

Much like PPTP, L2TP can tunnel PPP frames over multiple types of networks (IP, X.25, Frame Relay, or ATM). Currently, though, it is only defined for use over IP. This is not much of a problem, because IP is used over the majority of all networks. L2TP uses the UDP protocol for all tunnel operations (maintenance and data). It is defined in RFC 2661. *Win2K uses IPSec ESP for the encryption within L2TP.*

NOTE: Although PPTP is an IETF draft, Microsoft was the major driving force behind it while Cisco was pushing L2F. L2TP was a way to merge the two protocols into something that may truly become an industry standard. Supposedly L2TP has the best of both protocols.

Since the L2TP is currently only defined for IP, it assumes that there is an IP connection between the sender and receiver. If the connection does not already exist, it will need to be established before the L2TP session can be established. L2TP uses the same authentication mechanism as was used to create the PPP session between the sender and receiver.

Win2K L2TP relies on IPSec for encryption services and is known as *L2TP over IPSec*. L2TP over IPSec provides the primary VPN services of encapsulation and encryption.

Encapsulation

Encapsulation for L2TP over IPSec packets consists of two layers, as illustrated here. First, a PPP frame is encapsulated with an L2TP header and a UDP header. Then, the L2TP message is encapsulated with an IPSec ESP (this is described next) header and trailer, an IPSec authentication trailer, and finally an IP header. The IP header has source and destination IP addresses that correspond to the VPN sender and receiver.

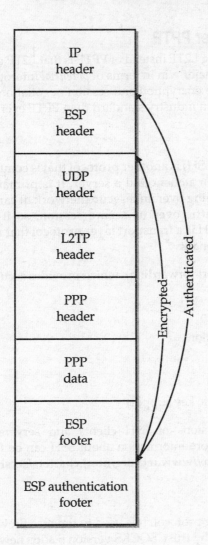

Encryption

L2TP uses IPSec encryption mechanisms by using encryption keys generated from the IPSec authentication process.

> **NOTE:** It is possible to have a non-IPSec-based (unencrypted) L2TP connection where the PPP frame is sent in plain text, but, as stated before, this takes the "Private" out of VPN.

Advantage of L2TP over PPTP

The main advantage of using L2TP instead of PPTP is that L2TP uses IPSec as the encryption mechanism. This is a major win in terms of *potential* interoperability, as well as the security associated with the encryption and session negotiation. L2TP also has a much better chance of becoming an industry standard than PPTP ever did.

SSH

The Secure Shell protocol (SSH) is another protocol that is commonly used to establish secure connections between a client and a server. It is primarily used for secure remote login and secure copying over an insecure network. It can also perform "tunneling" of network-based traffic over its secure session, so it can provide a secure network service as well. SSH is a transport layer protocol that runs on TCP/IP. It provides the following functionality:

▼ Tunneling (a.k.a. port forwarding), which provides secure network services

■ Strong encryption

■ Server authentication

■ Message authentication

■ Packet compression

■ Key exchange

▲ Public and symmetric key support

There are commercial versions of SSH clients and servers that run on Win2K (**www.datafellows.com**). More information about SSH can be found in the IETF draft document SSH found at **http://www.ietf.org/html.charters/secsh-charter.html**.

SOCKS5

SOCKS is a generic proxying protocol. It is used to traverse firewalls and other network boundaries that are defined by trust. SOCKS version 5 adds new features, two of which are very notable: authentication and UDP. SOCKS v5 is described in IETF draft document found at **http://www.ietf.org/html.charters/aft-charter.html**.

HOW DO WE CHOOSE?

Now that we have seen the options, at least from a protocol and standards standpoint, we will need to determine what we will use. This is potentially a very easy *or* very hard decision; it all depends on how well you know your requirements. Since the requirements are such an integral part of getting this right, we will go over some of the more critical things you should have answers for. Then we will look at Win2K services that provide solutions, as well as some third-party options.

Looking at the Requirements

As stated earlier, you need requirements to get anything right, but especially security solutions. Don't even attempt to implement a solution without having a good grasp on the following areas, both in terms of your requirements and the proposed solutions' ability to meet them.

The Security Level

You need to evaluate what level of security you need, particularly in terms of authentication and encryption.

AUTHENTICATION   You will need to determine what level of authentication will be required. Will you allow reusable passwords, even though they are not transmitted in the clear? Will you require SecureID, or smartcards, or token-based authenticators? Will you require two-factor authentication? Or maybe even biometrics?

NOTE: *Two-factor authentication* just refers to making a user authenticate at two different points.

ENCRYPTION   You will need to determine what level of authentication and data encryption will be required. The authentication encryption is not thought about much, but it is important to ensure that the solution you are looking at does not compromise the authentication mechanism in any manner, such at the early PPTP implementations (see **http://www.counterpane.com/pptp.html**). One example is sending reusable authenticators (that is, passwords) over the network in clear text. As far as data encryption goes, you will need to determine if you need it or not. This makes the split between a remote access and a VPN solution. If you do not need encryption, then you can look at remote access solutions; if you do need it, then you will need a VPN solution. Once you determine that encryption is needed, you will need to determine the "strength" that you will need.

It is beyond the scope of this book to determine the security "strength" you need, but you should understand that strength is a measure of many factors. Two of these you usually have control over: encryption algorithm and key length. As far as selecting an algorithm to use, you should consult your local cryptographer (you mean you don't know one?). If that is not an option, seek the advice of a reputable organization to provide you with proper guidance.

The key length is a much simpler matter: Given the same algorithm, a longer key is a stronger key. Remember, though, that you will use these keys in computations, so a longer key is also more computationally expensive (that is, uses more CPU), so it could affect performance significantly.

CAUTION: U.S. residents and companies should refer to the International Traffic in Arms Regulations (ITAR) for information on encryption and export controls.

The Availability Requirement

What type of availability do you require? If you have a 7x24 requirement and must have accountability for the connection, then the Internet is *not* an option. You will need to go with leased lines. Even with leased lines, there is no guarantee, but you should have a Service Level Agreement (SLA) with your leased line provider that details compensation if any outage should occur.

The Cost Requirement

In terms of costs associated with remote access and VPNs, the following items always come into play and should be considered:

▼ Who is required to control the links? Can it be outsourced?

■ Which are the one-time costs?

▲ What are the ongoing (i.e. maintenance) and administration costs?

Should You Use a Proprietary Solution?

Most solutions from vendors implement some portion of a proprietary system. Watch out! While this may make some things better, it may lock you into a solution that you will be wishing you had never gotten into in the future.

NOTE: You need to take all of these "requirement" areas into consideration when looking at a solution; if you do not, you will find that it was short-sighted, and most likely you will not get the solution you need. It is important to understand that you may need multiple solutions. If that is what you need, then do it! Don't go for a one-size-fits-all solution if you don't have a one-size-fits-all problem.

AUTHENTICATION

As we discussed in Chapter 7, there are numerous security-related risks when dealing with any type of authentication: replay attacks, client impersonation, server impersonation, and so on. In this section, we will describe the authentication mechanisms that are used in Win2K RAS and VPNs in more detail.

Levels of Authentication

To start, we need to understand that authentication takes place at two levels in the protocols that we have been discussing:

▼ **Machine-level** Authenticates machines during the establishment of the security association, such as with IPSec.

▲ **User-level** Authenticates the username and password, such as with PPTP or L2TP tunnel, which use a Point-to-Point Protocol (PPP) authentication method.

Protocols and Mechanisms

Win2K uses the following protocols and mechanisms for authentication in the various remote access and VPN services that it provides.

Password Authentication Protocol (PAP)

This is a basic plain text (that is, not encrypted) authentication scheme. It is defined in RFC 1334. In the PAP authentication exchange, the client sends an "Authenticate-Request" message to the server. The server validates the information received from the client (username and password) against what it has, then returns a reply: "Authenticate-Ack" if the authentication was successful, "Authenticate-Nak" if not.

PAP is here to allow Win2K clients to connect to non-Win2K remote access servers and to allow non-Windows clients to connect to Windows RAS servers. This is truly the universally supported protocol.

TIP: Do not allow PAP over anything but dial-up lines. The risks of having a password sniffed on a dial-up line are *significantly* less than over an IP-based network.

Shiva Password Authentication Protocol (SPAP)

SPAP is a reversible encryption mechanism used by Shiva Remote Access Servers. The purpose of this protocol is to allow Windows clients to authenticate against a Shiva Remote Access Server. The only difference between SPAP and PAP is that the password is encrypted by the client, then decrypted by the Shiva server, so the password does not go over the wire in clear text. This method is of very limited use, because it will only talk to a Shiva server.

Challenge Handshake Authentication Protocol (CHAP)

CHAP is a challenge-response authentication protocol described in RFC 1994. CHAP uses the RSA Message Digest 5 (MD5) hash function (one-way encryption) to generate the response to a challenge issued by a remote server. The flow goes like this:

1. The client makes the connection request.

2. The server replies with a CHAP Challenge message, which contains a session ID and a random challenge string (prevents replay attacks).

3. The client uses MD5 to create a hash (that is, challenge-response) of the challenge, session ID, and user password.

4. The client sends the challenge-response and the username back to the server.

5. The server performs step #3, generates its version of the challenge-response, and compares that to what the client sent back.

6. If they match, then the client must have known the correct password. The server sends a CHAP success message. If they do not match, the server sends a CHAP failure message.

CAUTION: The CHAP specification requires that passwords be stored in a decryptable form. This is because the same value needs to be used by the client and server in the hash generation.

CHAP is a widely supported industry standard used by many dial-in clients and servers. CHAP is supported in all Windows clients and the RAS servers. The main benefit of CHAP is that the password, whether clear or encrypted, is never passed over the network. Although the password is never passed over the network, the challenge is, so a weak password can still be easily guessed.

Microsoft Challenge Handshake Authentication Protocol (MS-CHAP)

MS-CHAP is very similar to CHAP in its foundation. It relies on a challenge and challenge-response for authentication. It is different in the method used to generate those values. There are currently two versions of MS-CHAP: MS-CHAPv1 and MS-CHAPv2. Version 2 (MS-CHAPv2) is much more secure than version 1, but is only supported by Win2K and Windows NT 4.0 SP6a and later.

NOTE: The functionality supposedly came in SP4, but did not work properly until SP6a.

MS-CHAPV1 MS-CHAPv1 uses the RSA Message Digest 4 (MD4) hash algorithm to create the challenge-response, instead of MD5 that is used by plain CHAP. The same general packet exchange as CHAP is used, with one exception: MS-CHAPv1 uses the stored hash (NTLM and LanMan, as defined in Chapter 11) of the password to generate the challenge-response. Thus, there will be two challenge-response values in the return packet. MS-CHAPv1 authentication exchange uses the same challenge-response calculations as described in the NT authentication (see Chapter 11). The basic flow is as follows:

1. The client makes the connection request.

2. The server replies with a MS-CHAPv1 challenge message, which contains a session ID and a random challenge string.

3. The client creates the challenge-response (remember, there are usually two, but you can configure the systems to never use the LAN Manager hash) using the password representation(s), the session ID, and the challenge string.

4. The client sends both challenge-response values, the username, and a domain name back to the server.

5. The server performs step #3, generates its version of the challenge-response, and compares that to what the client sent back. If they match, then the client must have known the correct password. The server sends an MS-CHAP SUCCESS message. If they do not match, an MS-CHAP failure message is sent.

6. If data encryption is enabled, then symmetric (shared secret) encryption keys are generated by the client and server using the information from the authentication exchange.

MS-CHAPV2   This is the same as MS-CHAPv1, except

▼ LAN Manager hash is never used in generating the challenge-response.

■ It allows for mutual authentication for both sides of the connection. The remote access client authenticates against the remote access server and the remote access server authenticates against the remote access client. This ensures that the remote access client is dialing into a remote access server that has access to the user's password, which through inference provides protection against remote server impersonation.

▲ Separate session keys are used in each direction of the connection.

The authentication exchange is the same as MS-CHAPv1, with the following exceptions related to how the challenge-response is generated and the response packet sent back from the server on a successful authentication:

▼ After the client receives the challenge string, it will generate a challenge-response using the Secure Hash Algorithm (SHA) to hash the challenge string it received, a new challenge string it creates (a.k.a. *peer challenge string*), the session identifier, and the NTLM version of the user's password.

■ The client will send the challenge-response, username, and the peer challenge string to the server.

■ The server validates the challenge-response and will send back a success or failure notice, along with an authenticated response based on the sent challenge string, the peer challenge string, the client's encrypted response, and the user's password.

▲ The client then validates the authentication response. At this point, both the client and server have authenticated to one another.

Extensible Authentication Protocol (EAP)

EAP is an extension to PPP that provides the ability to define (plug in) various authentication schemes to be used in the authentication of a PPP connection. Unlike the previous methods, which lock you into an authentication protocol during PPP setup, EAP allows you to agree to "negotiate an authentication protocol" during the authentication phase. The client and server will negotiate to use EAP, which will be used to negotiate the specifics during the authentication phase of the connection. When that phase is reached, the client and server will negotiate the specific method to use, and if no method is agreed upon, the connection is terminated. Currently, Win2K only supports EAP-MD5 and EAP-TLS by default.

EAP-MD5   EAP-MD5 is just the CHAP authentication described earlier, except it is used as a plug-in to the EAP extensions. This allows clients to use the flexibility of EAP (in that they can wait until a later time to declare the protocol they want to use), but still support the CHAP authentication mechanism. Once the connection authentication phase is reached, the following exchange happens:

1. The server sends an EAP-Request message to the client.
2. The client sends the user ID to the server in an EAP-Response message.
3. The server sends an EAP-Request message, which has the MD5 challenge string.
4. The client sends the MD5 hash of its user ID and password to the server in an EAP-Response message.
5. The server validates the response and sends a success or failure message to the client.

NOTE: EAP-MD5 is a required EAP type and can be used to test EAP interoperability.

EAP-TLS   EAP-TLS uses Transport Layer Security (TLS) when establishing a PPP connection. When EAP-TLS is used, the client and server use certificates to authenticate each other. This provides for mutual authentication of the client and server. The client sends the user certificate, and the server sends the machine certificate. TLS is described in detail in RFC 2246, and EAP-TLS is defined in RFC 2716.

NOTE: EAP-TLS is only supported on Win2K servers that are members of Win2K domains.

Remote Authentication Dial-In User Service (RADIUS)

RADIUS is an industry standard method of providing authorization, identification, authentication, and accounting services for distributed dial-up/remote access networking.

A RADIUS client, usually a remote access server, sends a user authentication request to a RADIUS server, and the server validates the request.

Like EAP, RADIUS can be configured to support multiple authentication methods. By default, CHAP and PAP are supported. This means that the authentication information in the packet will be dependent upon the authentication mechanism that has been defined. The authentication exchange using CHAP is as follows:

1. The remote access user sends authentication information to the RADIUS client (that is, the remote access server).

2. The RADIUS client then creates a RADIUS Access-Request packet containing information such as the user's name, the MD5 hash of the user's password, the ID of the client, and the Port ID the user is using.

3. The RADIUS client then sends the Access-Request to the RADIUS server and waits for a reply. The Access-Request can be sent to more than one server and can be resent if no response is received.

4. The RADIUS server will validate the legitimacy of the Access-Request by checking to ensure that it was sent from a configured RADIUS client. If digital signatures are enabled for the client, then they are validated as well.

5. After the client is validated, the server will validate the user information in the Access-Request. This is where authentication and authorization take place in the RADIUS model.

6. If all conditions are met, the list of configuration values for the user are placed into a RADIUS Access-Accept packet that is sent back to the RADIUS client (that is, the remote access server).

NOTE: For more information about the RADIUS protocol, see RFCs 2138 and 2139.

INTERNET AUTHENTICATION SERVICE (IAS)   IAS is the Microsoft implementation of a Remote Authentication Dial-In User Service (RADIUS) protocol. IAS performs centralized authentication, authorization, auditing, and accounting of all connections using the service (dial-up and APN, currently). It can be used with RRAS, which allows user authentication, authorization, and auditing data to be stored at a central server, rather than on each network access server (NAS). If you use it, you should centralize the IAS server.

Unauthenticated Connections

Win2K supports unauthenticated PPP connections. To do this, the authentication phase of the PPP connection establishment is skipped. This is a very serious security risk, and should be used with extreme caution. If you allow this type of connection, the Guest account is used, so you would have to enable it.

Remote Access Authentication

The remote access portion of the RAS server just supports a PPP link for the clients, and it provides two options for authentication: RADIUS or Windows Authentication. If you select RADIUS, then the RADIUS server dictates which authentication mechanisms you use. The default is Windows Authentication, and it supports Extensible Authentication Protocol (EAP: MD5, TLS, and smartcard), Challenge Handshake Authentication Protocol (CHAP), Microsoft Challenge Handshake Authentication Protocol (MS-CHAP v1 & v2), Shiva Password Authentication Protocol (SPAP), Password Authentication Protocol (PAP), and anonymous authentication. All of these methods are described in detail in this chapter. There is also an ability to perform some level of mutual authentication with EAP-TLS and MS-CHAPv2.

Callback and Caller-ID as Authentication

RAS supports both callback and caller-ID. Callback allows the server to call the client back *after* a successful user authentication. The callback number can be preset, or can be specified by the user after authentication. The former is more secure, but the latter is more flexible for mobile users.

Caller-ID simply verifies, or attempts to verify, that the incoming call is from a specific phone number. This is really only valid for fixed locations or cellular connections. To state the obvious, caller-ID requires that the Win2K modem driver and all the phone system equipment support caller-ID.

TIP: If you configure caller-ID and the call cannot be ID'd for some reason, the connection is dropped.

While neither of these are truly considered security features, as a semi-knowledgeable user can bypass them, they do raise the bar with respect to ease of compromise.

PPTP Authentication

PPTP authentication is the same as that used by the Win2K RAS server that is running the PPTP service. You can select EAP, which would give you the option of EAP-MD5 or EAP-TLS, or you can select one or more of PAP, SPAP, CHAP, and MS-CHAP (v1/v2). You cannot have EAP and any of the latter listed protocols.

L2TP and IPSec Authentication

The Win2K implementations of L2TP and IPSec can use one or more of the following authentication methods: Kerberos (default), certificates issued by a certain CA, or a shared key that you define. On the default rule for the IPSec policy you are setting, you can define multiple authentication methods, using different combinations of the three methods listed. Note that Microsoft IPSec is a proprietary implementation, as it defaults to using Kerberos as a way of distributing keys.

CAUTION: Microsoft strongly recommends that you do not use PAP or LAN Manager protocols for authentication, unless you absolutely have to support clients running legacy software and there is absolutely no way your users can authenticate with other protocols.

AUTHORIZATION

The following section discusses the authorization methods that are used in Remote Access and Virtual Private Networks.

Remote Access Policies

In Windows NT, RAS authorization was based on a user having dial-in permissions. In Win2K, authorization is based on dial-in properties and remote access policies. Remote access policies allow you to define conditions and connection settings that will affect remote access permissions and connection attributes. You can use remote access policies to require the following:

▼ Different sets of authentication and encryption requirements for VPN and dial-up users

■ Strong authentication

▲ Encryption attributes for connections

Using conditions (described in the next section), you can grant remote access based on any or all of the following:

▼ Time of day and day of the week

■ Group membership

▲ Type of connection being requested (dial-up or VPN)

NOTE: Both RRAS and IAS use remote access policies to determine whether to accept or reject connections. The individual service tools (that is, Routing and Remote Access or Internet Authentication Service) administer remote access policies.

In Win2K, users are authorized to connect only if they match *at least* one of the remote access policies *and* have dial-in permissions.

Remote Access Policy Parts

A remote access policy is a rule that has three elements:

▼ **Conditions** A set of attributes that must match for a connection to be authorized. Some conditions are: User group (no built-in local groups), tunnel type, and client IP. See the online documentation for a complete list.

■ **Remote Access Permission** Grant or Deny (default). If all the conditions of a remote access policy are met, you either grant or deny access permission.

▲ **Profile** Properties that are applied to the connection after it is authorized. This deals with what happens after the connection. It is the heart of the security of the connection, in the sense that it deals with authentication and encryption.

PPTP

PPTP Authorization is the same as RAS. It is determined with the dial-in user properties and the remote access policy. By default, if the user account has dial-in privileges, then a PPTP connection can be established. If the user does not, then it can't. In addition to the authorization to establish a connection, PPTP allows you to define if the connecting user is authorized to connect to the entire internal network, thus acting like a tunnel, or only to the destination, thus using a direct connection.

IPSec Security Policy

For clients that will be using IPSec, you will usually configure an IPSec security policy. This policy is defined as part of the security settings that are applied either to an individual system (via the local security settings) or to a group of systems (via group policies). The IPSec security policies allow you to set rules that govern the connections to that machine. Each policy allows you to set

▼ **Security Methods** Options to use AH, ESP, or both; integrity and encryption algorithms to use; and session key generation settings

■ **Authentication Methods** Kerberos, digital certificates, or even a shared secret (password)

▲ **Connection Type** Remote access, LAN, or all network connections

You can have more than one rule per policy, and more than one policy per system. Like all things in Win2K and NT before it, the policies "aggregate" together, unless there is an explicit "deny."

Account Lockout for Remote Access

RAS has an option that will allow you to lock out an account after a specified number of failed authentication attempts. This lockout is only for RRAS (that is, remote access and

VPN connections), and does not affect the regular Win2K logon. But like the account lockout policy in Win2K, you must determine the number of failed attempts that will lock out the account and how often the "failed logon" counter is reset.

Registry keys that need to be set to enable this are located in the HKEY_LOCAL_MACHINE\ SYSTEM\CurrentControlSet\Services\RemoteAccess\Parameters\ AccountLockout registry key. Their names are:

▼ **MaxDenials**   The maximum number of failed attempts before the account is locked out. By default, account lockout is disabled (that is, value is 0).

■ **ResetTime**   The amount of time before the failed attempts counter is reset. By default, it is 48 hours. Time is in minutes.

▲ **Domain name:**user name   If account is locked out, you must manually delete the registry subkey that corresponds to the user's account name.

TIP: This can be used to cause a denial of service, as there is no way to differentiate a malicious attack from a forgotten password. Thus, if you set account lockout, an attacker could attempt to guess usernames and passwords and potentially lock out all RRAS users. The likelihood of this succeeding depends on the attacker's ability to guess your usernames, which is not extremely hard to do.

Remote Access Secure Encryption

While a remote access connection is not typically encrypted, RRAS has the ability to encrypt the remote access link. This is unlike a VPN, because it really deals with dial-up sessions. The RAS server (Win2K and WinNT) and RAS clients (Win2K, WinNT, and Win 9x) support the Microsoft Point-to-Point Encryption Protocol (MPPE) for this link security. MPPE uses the Rivest-Shamir-Adleman (RSA) RC4 stream cipher to encrypt the data passing over the dial-up line. It can use 40-bit, 56-bit, or 128-bit encryption keys with RC4. MS-CHAP or EAP-TLS authentication is required, as they can be used to generate the keys. Setting this up will be covered during the installation and configuration portion of this chapter.

AUDITING

It seems that Microsoft just does not get it when it comes to the need for robust auditing/logging of services. As you will soon see, the ability to configure the auditing for VPNs and remote access has a lot to be desired. Although there is a significant amount of security features and functionality in the VPA and RAS services for Win2K, the logging configurations are totally inadequate.

As with the auditing section of previous chapters dealing with specific services, this section covers the available auditing technology and features that are available with Win2K.

Remote Access and PPP Logging

You can enable remote access logging for "errors," "errors and warnings," or "maximum amount of information." We were not able to find a complete description of the specific errors logged at each level. Needless to say, regular logging of "errors and warnings" is prudent, but "a maximum amount of information" probably is not. Note that this last option would be very useful in troubleshooting situations. The logs can be written either in a database format or UTF-8.

You can also enable PPP logging, which logs information on the PPP connection establishment process. All interaction after that process would be generated by another service.

PPP Tracing for RRAS

PPP tracing is an option to gather very detailed information about the PPP programming code and network events to either a console window or to a file on the disk. To enable PPP tracing to either a file or console, you will need to change the following registry values (located in `HKEY_LOCAL_MACHINE\SOFTWARE\Microsoft\Tracing\PPP`) to 1:

▼ **EnableFileTracing**   Places logging information in `%SystemRoot%\tracing\PPP.log`.

▲ **EnableConsoleTracing**   Displays logging information in a console window.

Logging for PPTP, L2TP, and IPSec

There is no specific auditing for PPTP, L2TP, or IPSec. Their auditing is integrated with the Win2K security subsystem. For example, if a user connects to a PPTP server, that connection is logged as a regular authentication in the Security EventLog (if you have auditing enabled).

NOTE: Since this book is on Win2K, the rest of the chapter will be discussing only Win2K-based options for Remote Access and VPN solutions. This is *not* because Win2K is the best or only solution in every circumstance, but because we are focusing on leveraging out Win2K investment to the greatest possible extent. As with any service you are trying to implement, find the right solution for your problem and do not just use a solution just because you "have it."

ADMINISTRATION

This section will cover the tools used to administer the services that we have talked about, as well as the service installation and post-installation configuration.

Tools

As with almost every service-related administration tool that we have encountered in this book, the MMC pokes its head in again. It is used as the interface to administer RRAS, IPSec policies, IAS, and virtually every other RAS- and VPN-related configuration.

Routing and Remote Access Service (RRAS)

The RRAS administration MMC is used to manage all RAS/PPTP/L2TP configuration settings (as well as routing configurations) on the Win2K system. You can access the MMC interface in two manners. You can select Start | Programs | Administrative Tools | Routing and Remote Access, or you can add the Routing and Remote Access snap-in directly into an MMC console that you have defined (this procedure was described in Chapter 5).

IPSec Security Policies

As mentioned earlier, IPSec security policies are what determine the IPSec interaction between two systems. They are managed with—you guessed it—the IPSec Security Policy MMC snap-in. The IPSec policy will be applied from both the Local Security Policy and any Group Policy that is applied to the machine. Thus, the settings for IPSec are configured as part of the Local Security Policy or the Group Policies that are applied to the system. The IPSec Policy configuration snap-in can be used to configure the following information:

▼ IPSec filter lists

■ IPSec filter actions

■ IPSec policy rules

■ Security methods

■ Authentication methods

■ Connection types

▲ Key exchange settings and methods

Internet Authentication Service (IAS)

As mentioned earlier, IAS is Microsoft's implementation of the RADIUS protocol, and needs a bit more discussion.

IAS FEATURES   IAS is an integrated component of the Win2K server(s). It is designed to provide central authentication, authorization, auditing, and accounting for VPN and dial-up services. With the centralized authentication, IAS supports the majority of authentication protocols that were discussed, with the exception of SPAP. IAS uses Remote Access Policies and is integrated into the AD in the sense that it can use the AD to authenticate users, and uses the User Principal Names (UPNs) and Universal Groups in the AD. This allows you to use group membership to allow or deny access to users.

By using RADIUS, IAS can control connection parameters for any network access server that uses the RADIUS protocol. RADIUS also allows IAS to gather usage records and logging information at a central location. The auditing/logging setup *is* the same as the RRAS server. IAS is *tightly* integrated with RRAS, in that they share remote access policies and logs. This allows you to set up RRAS at small sites without needing a separate IAS server. IAS is also scalable.

IAS is administered with the Internet Authentication Service MMC snap-in.

NOTE: The online documentation for each of these services is very complete and helpful. You are highly encouraged to use it as a reference as you are setting up the services. There are also checklists that may prove helpful.

Installing Remote Access Server Using RRAS

Now that we have a basic understanding of what technology is available for remote access and VPNs in Win2K, we will look at installing and configuring these services. We will look at each service, and the security-related components that it supports. In the following sections, we will tie this all together into recommendations as to when, or if, to use a Win2K technology.

The Win2K solution for remote access and VPN is the Routing and Remote Access Service (RRAS). RRAS supports generic remote access, PPTP, and L2TP VPNs. The service is installed, but not enabled, by default. It is integrated with the Win2K security model (that is, AD and access controls), and thus has access to the authentication mechanisms of Win2K. It should be noted that the RRAS service supports routing as well as remote access. This is covered in Chapter 15. For this section we will refer to the service as just RAS (Remote Access Server) so as to not confuse the routing capabilities.

Since it is installed by default, to enable RRAS, all you have to do is run the RRAS admin tool (Start | Programs | Administrative Tools | Routing and Remote Access), then follow the directions to set up the Routing and Remote Access Server. This will start the Configuration Wizard. Once the wizard starts you will get to a page that asks you what type of server you want to set up. For our purposes, we select Manually Configured Server (Figure 16-1), so we can walk through the actual MMC configuration steps. You may want to select a more specific configuration, which will allow the wizard to help you in your configuration.

Installing Internet Authentication Service (IAS)

IAS is installed as a component of the Networking Services either in the initial setup or through the Add/Remove Programs control panel. Once you have selected it, you will be prompted to install IAS.

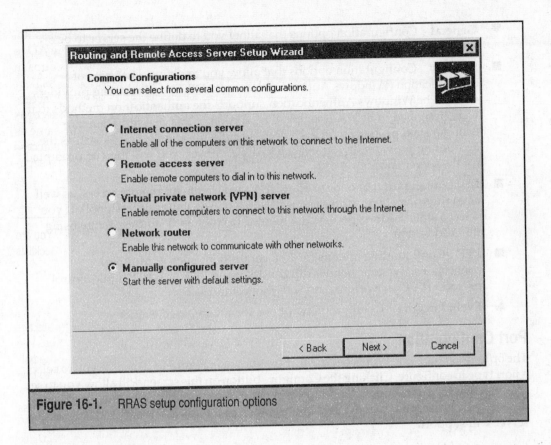

Figure 16-1.   RRAS setup configuration options

Configuring RRAS

Once you have it up and running, you need to configure RRAS. We have spent the bulk of this chapter talking about the specific features and technical details. We will now look at what is supported where and how to enable or configure each component.

Defining the RRAS Properties

In the Properties dialog box of the RRAS server that you are configuring, you will see the options described next. It may seem that there are only a few settings, but don't be fooled; this is just a small portion of the configuration ahead of us. Outside of RRAS Properties, we have Port Properties, Remote Access Policies, and Remote Access Logging Properties.

TIP: For a more detailed explanation of each option, you can right-click on the option to get a context-sensitive description of the option.

▼ **General**   Configuration options that allow you to define the server to be a remote access server, a router (not covered in this chapter), or both.

■ **Security**   Configuration options that allow you to define what type of authentication (Windows Authentication or RADIUS) and auditing providers to use. The Windows Authentication supports the authentication methods that were described in the "Authentication" section of this chapter. There are configuration properties for each of these authentication types, as well as the accounting provider. If you select a RADIUS server, you will then be prompted for the server specifics.

■ **IP**   Configuration options to allow IP-based clients for remote access, as well as configuring client address allocation (DHCP or static address pool). If you select a static address pool, you will need to enter an IP address range using the Add button.

■ **PPP**   Configuration options for PPP connections such as Multilink connections, dynamic bandwidth control using BAP or BACP, Link control protocol (LCP) extensions, and software compression.

▲ **Event Logging**   Configuration options for RRAS-based events.

Port Configuration

The options on the Ports Properties dialog box (shown in Figure 16-2) enable you to select a port type to configure. Clicking the Configure button on this screen will allow you to set the direction for connections (inbound or inbound/outbound), the phone number (for devices which use phone lines), and the number of logical PPTP and L2TP ports the server will support.

Remote Access Policies

Remote access policies are stored locally on the RRAS or an IAS server. Since these policies are very important to the whole Win2K remote access service and affect both remote access and VPN, we will go though the details of the security-related settings. As an example, we will define a policy that will only allow users of the VPN group who have dial-in permissions to connect. (We will only be reviewing security-related tabs.)

TIP: All the settings that we will look at can be set on the properties of any existing policy.

The first step is to define a new security policy. You do this by right-clicking the Remote Access Policies, then selecting New Remote Access Policy. This will start the Policy Wizard, which will ask for a policy name. Then after defining the name, you can set up conditionals. Figures 16-3 and 16-4 show a conditional that requires that users be in the Global group "NT\VPN Users."

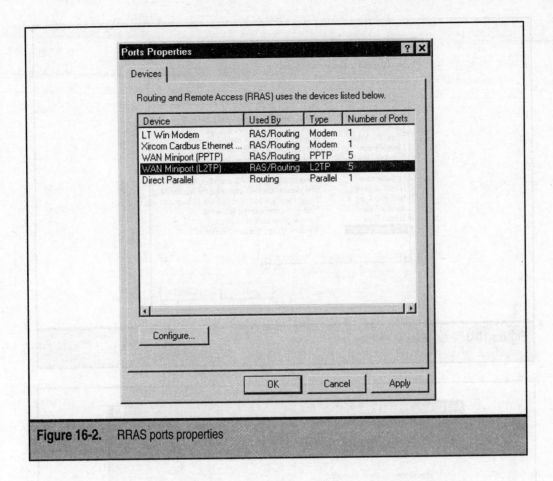

Figure 16-2.   RRAS ports properties

Next you will set either "grant remote access permissions" or "deny remote access permissions" that are in effect when the conditionals apply. You can then edit the profile that is associated with the policy that you are defining. The following is a description of the settings that can be configured.

DIAL-IN CONSTRAINTS   The Dial-in Constraints tab allows you to set the following options:

▼   **Disconnect If Idle For**   This is an inactivity timeout. You can define that any connection that is inactive for 15 minutes gets disconnected. This is mostly used to prevent people from connecting and just leaving it up, consuming resources (a port, modem line, and so on) while not actually utilizing the resource.

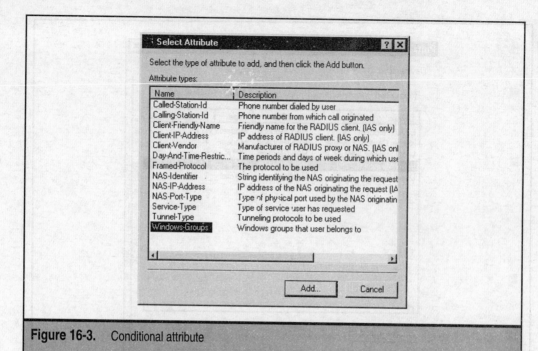

Figure 16-3. Conditional attribute

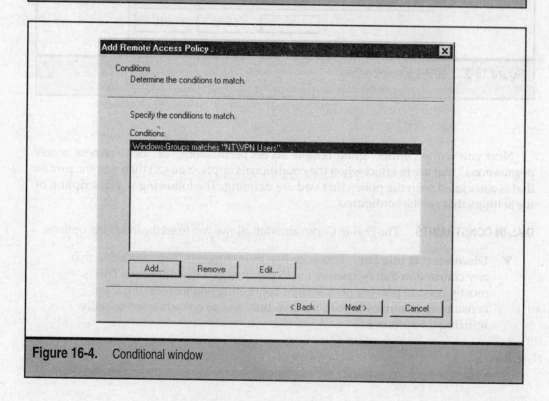

Figure 16-4. Conditional window

CAUTION: This does not close user data files and exit applications cleanly. It just disconnects, so be careful if you use it. This is disabled by default.

■ **Restrict Maximum Session To**   This is the maximum amount of time, in minutes, that a connection can be established. This is another way to limit resource wasting, but this again just closes the connection. This is disabled by default.

■ **Restrict Access to the Following Day and Times**   This option sets day of week and hour of day limits. This is applicable during the initial connection only. The RAS server will not disconnect an active connection that continues in to the restricted time. You may want to use this to limit the ability of a hacker to try to connect to resources when others would not be using them. For example, you would not expect users to be dialing in from home during the workday if they are supposed to be in the office. This is disabled by default.

■ **Restrict Dial-in to This Number Only**   This option specifies the phone number that the call must originate from. This allows you to ensure that users are using local access numbers instead of more expensive toll numbers. This is disabled by default.

▲ **Restrict Dial-in Media**   This option specifies the type of connection that must be used. You may want to use this to ensure that only a select group of users can actually connect to your VPN server. This is disabled by default.

IP   The IP tab allows you to set the following options:

▼ **IP Address Assignment Policy**   This setting determines the IP address negotiation option. Options can allow the client to request a specific IP, ask the server to supply an IP, or use whatever the specific server has set in its properties (this is mostly for use in a centralized setup). By default, the local server setting takes precedence.

▲ **IP Packet Filters**   These filters can be used to specify which packets will be received and forwarded on from the client, as well as which packets that are received for the client will be passed back to it. You could use this to say that you would not allow any Telnet attempts from a host to the remote client or vice versa. By default, these are blank. Figures 16-5 and 16-6 show an IP filter that will permit all traffic except that which is destined for 128.115.3.0/24.

AUTHENTICATION   In the Authentication tab you can set the authentication methods (discussed in the "Authentication" section) you want to use. It is important to make sure the RRAS server has the corresponding authentication types enabled. If it does not, the profile cannot enforce them (obviously).

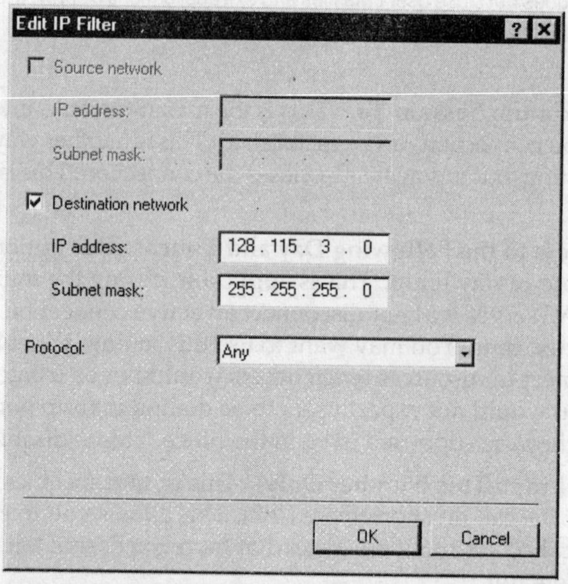

Figure 16-5. Remote access IP filter editor

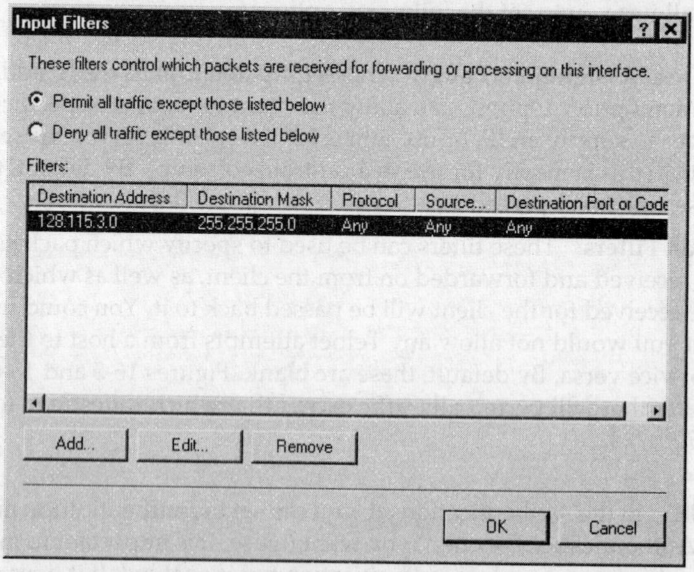

Figure 16-6. Remote access IP input filter list

ENCRYPTION   On the Encryption tab, you can set the encryption options (that is, strengths) you desire. All of the options are enabled by default.

▼ **No Encryption**   If other policies are set, encryption will be negotiated, but if the negotiation fails, it will allow a non-encrypted connection. This is only applicable to a remote access session and IPSec, not VPNs (that is, PPTP and L2TP). *The option is enabled by default, and should be disabled unless there is a business need for it.* If that is the case, make a special remote access policy for this type of connection only, and severely limit its use.

■ **Basic**   Connections can negotiate an MPPE 40-bit key for PPTP and dial-up, or a 56-bit DES IPSec ESP key for L2TP.

■ **Strong**   Connections can negotiate an MPPE 56-bit key for PPTP and dial-up, or a 56-bit DES IPSec ESP key for L2TP.

▲ **Strongest**   Connections can negotiate an MPPE 128-bit key for PPTP and dial-up, or a 56-bit triple DES IPSec ESP key for L2TP. *This option is only available on North American versions of Windows 2000.*

ADVANCED   The Advanced tab can be used to specify a set of RADIUS attributes that are sent back to the RADIUS client by the IAS server. Most of these are specific to RADIUS and are ignored by the RRAS server. There are five attributes that are used by RRAS: Account-Interim-Interval, Framed-Protocol, Framed-MTU, Reply-Message, and Service-Type. For more information, please see the online context-sensitive help.

TIP: To create a centralized set of remote access policies for multiple servers, you need to set up an IAS server as a RADIUS server. Then set up all servers to use RADIUS and have them all point to that server. This, in effect, will cause the IAS server to make the policy decisions and just let the servers know the outcome. If you use a RADIUS server, the local remote access policies stored on the server are not used.

REMOTE ACCESS POLICY SUMMARY   Once you install the policies that you need, you can set the order in which they are applied. If you match a deny, then access is automatically denied. Otherwise, as long as you have a match, you can connect. You need to take time and set this up correctly. We recommend that you look into setting up a central IAS server.

Remote Access Logging Policy

These options allow you to configure logging of authentication, accounting, and status information. It also allows you to specify a file location. The file can be a local file, a network share, or a named pipe. The options also allow you to specify log file format, which can be IAS (that is, RADIUS) format or database-import format. With the database format, you can import your data into a database instead of reviewing the raw data.

Configuring IAS

The setup of IAS is about as easy as the installation and is extremely quick (especially if you already have a RRAS server setup). There are only a few properties for the IAS server that you have to configure, and they are described next. Since IAS shares the Remote Access Policies and Logging settings with the RRAS server that is installed on the same machine, you should not have to configure them. If you have not installed RRAS on the system that you are running IAS on, then you will have to configure these options (see the earlier section "Configuring RRAS" for more information).

IAS Settings

To configure IAS, you will need to open the Properties dialog box (right-click and select Properties). The Service tab, shown in Figure 16-7, allows you to set the service description as well as logging settings. You should realize that enabling the Log Successful

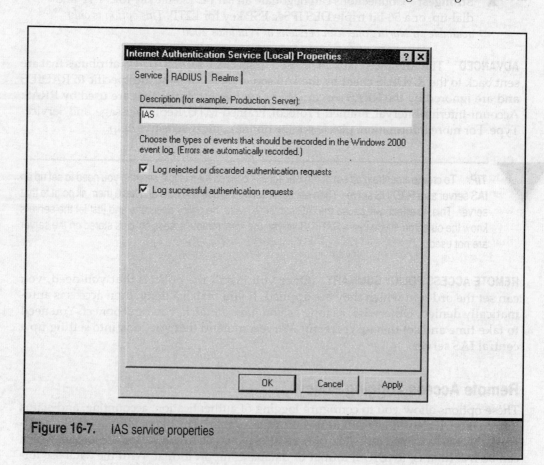

Figure 16-7.   IAS service properties

Authentication Requests option can result in extremely large amounts of data being logged. Make sure that you have appropriate EventLog settings to handle the data.

The Radius tab allows you to specify UDP ports that your RADIUS server will accept requests on for Authentication and Accounting. You can specify multiple port settings by using a comma-separated list of ports.

IAS uses realm names to figure out which server holds the user's credentials, so it can forward authentication requests to that server. Realm names can be a prefix format such as NT4DOMAIN/ or a suffix such as @Win2KDomain. The Realms tab allows you to re-place realm names (that is, identifiers), which will allow you to forward authentication requests to a potentially different authentication server. For example, you can configure any user attempting to authenticate with *user*@example.com to be re-written to *user*@ras.example.com and thus forwarded to the authentication server for ras.example.com instead of example.com.

Setting Up IAS Clients

The other operation that you can perform is to set up RADIUS clients (that is, servers that will be using the IAS server for authentication). To do this, right-click the Clients selection in the IAS MMC snap-in, then select New Client. This will initiate a wizard process that will ask you to enter the following information.

FRIENDLY NAME AND PROTOCOL The friendly name that you use should be descriptive of the client that you are adding and can be used in remote access policies to restrict access. The Protocol has only one option and that is RADIUS.

CLIENT INFORMATION Figure 16-8 shows the client information setup screen. The Client Address is for the Network Authentication Server that will be using the IAS server for authentication. If you specify a DNS name, you can verify it (actually resolve it) by clicking the Verify button. This will allow you to select an individual IP address for a given server if it has more than one (and you don't know them). Otherwise, any request coming from that DNS name will be processed.

If you choose a specific vendor, you can use remote access policies that are specific to a certain vendor Network Authentication Server. If you do not know or do not want vendor-specific policies, then just use the default RADIUS standard.

The shared secret is the password used by the IAS and Network Authentication Server to communicate securely. The shared secret is case-sensitive and should be very complex.

Firewalling Your IAS Server

Since your IAS server is so critical to the security of your remote access services, you want to make sure it is safe and secure. One way of doing this is by firewalling it. You will need to make sure that your RAS servers can access the IAS. This would require you to allow UDP to/from the RAS servers to the IAS server. Since it is UDP, you would be wise to monitor it continuously.

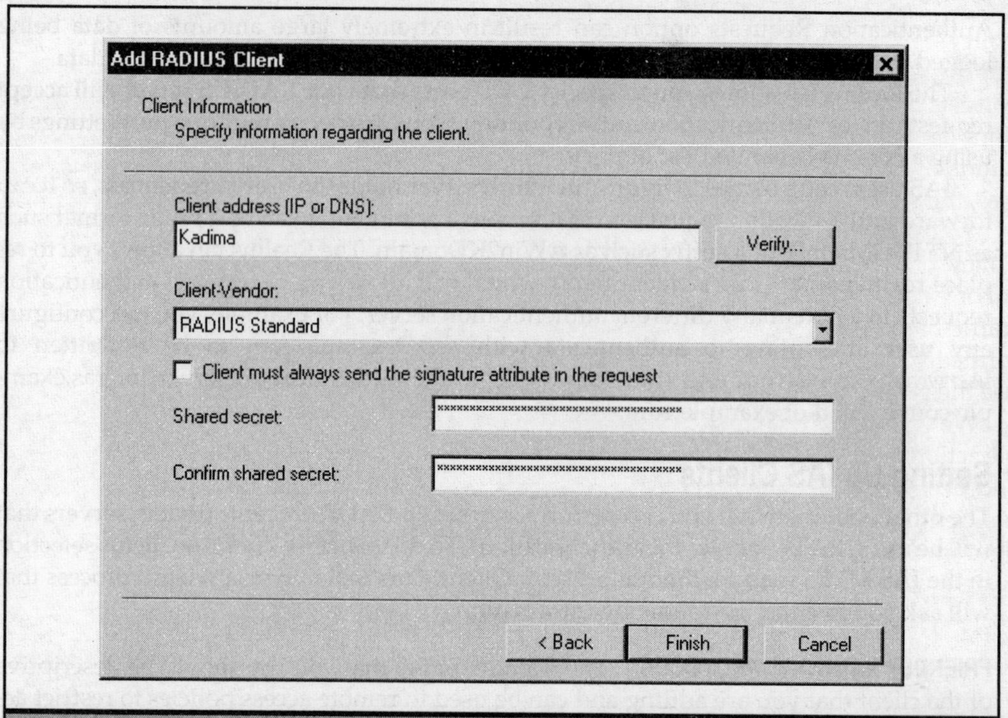

Add RADIUS Client

Client Information
Specify information regarding the client.

Client address (IP or DNS):

`Kadima`   Verify...

Client-Vendor:

`RADIUS Standard`

☐ Client must always send the signature attribute in the request

Shared secret: `xxxxxxxxxxxxxxxxxxxxxxxxxxxxxxxxxxxxxxx`

Confirm shared secret: `xxxxxxxxxxxxxxxxxxxxxxxxxxxxxxxxxxxxxxx`

< Back   Finish   Cancel

Figure 16-8.   Client information

Configuring IPSec Security Policies

You may have noted that there is no "installation" procedure for IPSec. This is because IPSec is built into Win2K. Although it is built-in, like most other security features in Win2K, it is disabled and must be manually enabled and configured.

Before we jump in, let's briefly review what is where in Win2K regarding IPSec configurations. In Win2K, there are three fundamental configuration "items": *IP filter list*, *IP filter actions*, and *IPSec policy*. IP filter lists and filter actions can be configured independently of the IPSec policy, and they are used to define who the rule applies to and an action (permit, block, or security negotiation) if it applies.

The IPSec policy has two configuration sections. The first is a General setting that allows you to configure the name, description, and key exchange settings for that particular policy. The second is the Rules setting, which allows you to define one or more rules that apply to that particular policy. There will be one or more rules per policy, and each rule consists of one IP filter (from the IP filter lists), one IP filter action (from the IP filter actions list), one or more authentication methods, whether the connection is host-to-host or a tunnel, and the type of connection (RAS, IP, or both). After you have defined the policies, they are applied (that is, made active).

You can manage IPSec policies from either the Local Security Policy, Group Security Policy, or the individual IPSec Policy snap-in. You can only activate it with either the Local or Group policy. We will go through configuring an IPSec policy that secures all TCP traffic between two networks (10.0.0.x and 10.0.1.x). Most of what we will do is performed via the wizards for setting up a new policy. If you are editing an existing policy, use the Properties dialog box for the configuration you are modifying.

We will use the Default Domain Security Policy for our examples. You get two possible actions by right-clicking on the IPSec policy: Manage IP Filter Lists and Filter Actions, and Create IP Security Policy. Filters are applicable to (that is, will be used in) all IPSec policies on a machine or a Group policy, so we will look at them first. The rest of the configurations we will look at are on a per policy basis.

How IPSec Handles Packets

Each packet, inbound or outbound, is evaluated against the active IP filter list and its active IPSec policies (remember the rules we mentioned earlier). When a packet matches a filter, which was part of a rule, it then applies the filter action. If the action is "permit," then the packet is accepted or forwarded with no changes. If the action is "block," then the packet is rejected. If the action is to negotiate, then it calls IKE to negotiate. After IKE completes the negotiation, it returns the SA parameters and the session keys to the IPSec driver.

If the packet was inbound, then IPSec will verify the packet integrity (and decrypt it if needed), then transform it back into the original IP format. The IPSec driver will validate the new IP packet to make sure it is traffic that should be accepted. If it is, it will pass it up the stack. Note that for a normal IP session (that is, unsecured), the IPSec filters are still used just to ensure that we are not accepting a plain packet from a system that we should be blocking packets for or only be accepting secure packets from.

NOTE: Filters applicable to tunnels are evaluated first, then host-to-host filters.

IPSec Filter Lists

The IP filter lists allow you to define when traffic will be secured. A match on source, destination, and type of IP traffic will cause the defined type of security negotiation. Each filter list contains at least one filter (which defines IP addresses and traffic types). Because you can have more than one filter in the list, one IP filter list can be used to secure many different communication scenarios.

You must have both an inbound and outbound filter between the computers specified in the filter list. Each filter must contain a policy for all traffic that flows between two hosts. For example, since we want to secure all TCP traffic between 10.0.0.x and 10.0.1.x, there will need to be four rules: 10.0.0.x inbound and outbound, and 10.0.1.x inbound and outbound. Inbound filters apply to incoming traffic. Outbound filters apply to traffic leaving a computer. *You must have a filter to enable the security.* These filter lists are used later in the actual policies that are defined.

Using the IP Security Policy of the Default Domain Security Settings (see Figure 16-9), we use the Manage IP Filter Lists and Filter Actions dialog box to set the IPSec filters and associated actions for those filters.

To set up our desired security, we will need to *add* a new filter. We'll call it "Secure10," with a description of "Secure 10 net" (see Figure 16-10). We then need to add a filter rule, but we will not use the wizard (uncheck Use Add Wizard). We will get a screen with three tabs: Addressing, Protocol, and Description. We will detail these next.

ADDRESSING You must define a source and destination address, which can be one of the following: address of the machine (My IP Address), Specific IP Address, Any IP Address, or Any IP Subnet. The mirror option allows you to have a dynamic rule that allows packets in the reverse. For our purposes, we will define a specific IP subnet as seen in Figure 16-11. We will also add a corresponding rule for 10.0.1.x as the source.

PROTOCOL You can define the protocol that the traffic is using. This automatically defaults to cover all protocols in the TCP/IP protocol suite. You can specify protocol and port numbers, and you can define a custom protocol if you need to. For our example, we will define it to use TCP, but will not define specific ports. See Web Appendix B at **www.osborne.com** for a listing of IP protocol numbers.

DESCRIPTION This tab is used to set the description. When all is finished, we have the final screen shown in Figure 16-12.

IPSec Filter Actions

The actions are just that: actions that are to be taken if a given filter is matched. By default, there are three actions defined:

▼ **Permit** Allows any unsecured communication. This is basically to support the "don't break things that don't have IPSec running on them" rule.

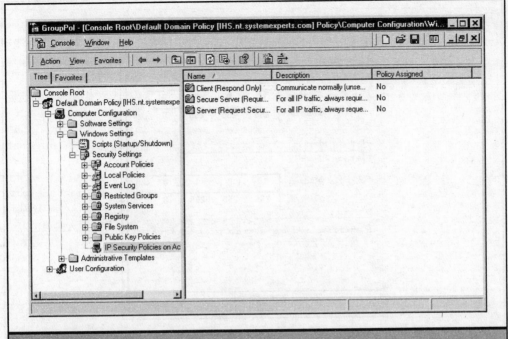

Figure 16-9.   Default Domain Security Settings

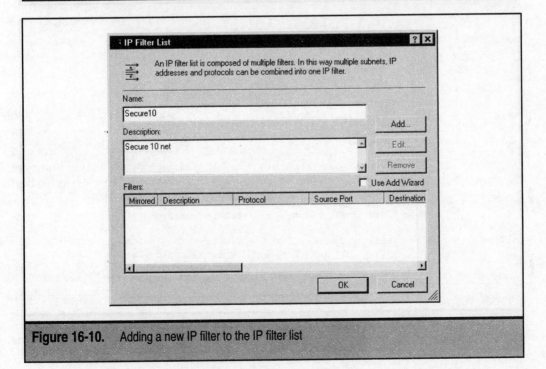

Figure 16-10.   Adding a new IP filter to the IP filter list

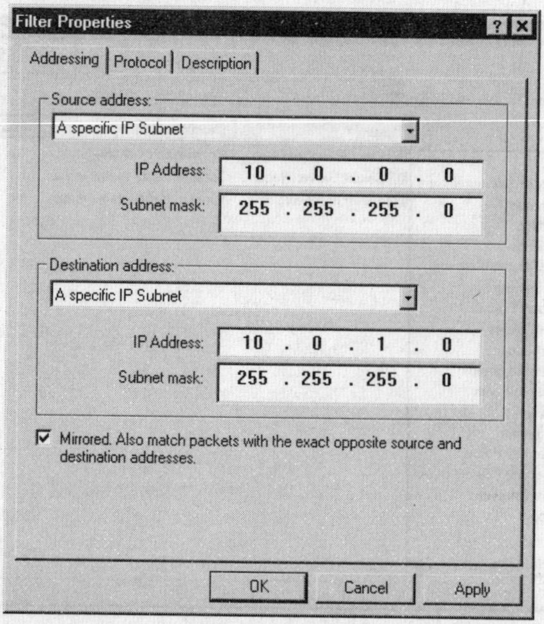

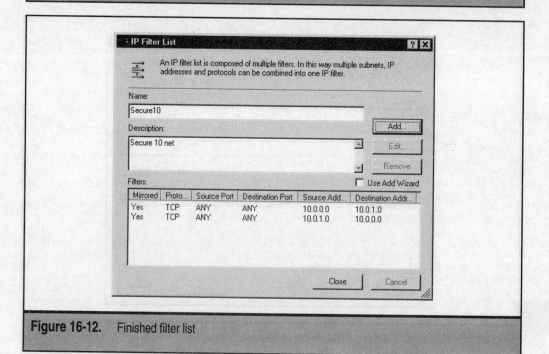

Figure 16-11.   IP filter addressing properties

Figure 16-12.   Finished filter list

■ **Request Security**   Tries to negotiate security, but will accept unsecured communication. This provides security when available, but does not require it.

▲ **Require Security**   Always negotiates with IPSec; thus, if a client does not support IPSec, they cannot communicate. This method *will not* accept unsecured communication. The client must establish trust and negotiate security methods.

These actions will be adequate for most uses, but in our scenario, we do not want any unsecured (that is, not encrypted) traffic between the two subnets, so we will need a rule that requires security. Again, we will not be using the wizard, but you might want to. You would add an action that would

▼ Negotiate security

■ Use a custom security method that will use SHA1 for message integrity and triple DES for message confidentiality (encryption), and generate a new session key every 100K bytes or 3600 seconds

■ Use Perfect Forward Secrecy

▲ *Not* allow unsecured connections

TIP: Perfect Forward Secrecy (PFS) means that if an attacker had the long-term key, it wouldn't help him read a message he had in hand, whether freshly intercepted or cached from a while ago. This is useful to be sure, and it is possible only where the keys used to encrypt are negotiated at the outset of each conversation and the long-term key figures only in their negotiation, not their value.

The following is an example of adding a filter list to accomplish our previous example.

1. We add a new Filter List with the Add button on the Manage Filter List tab.

2. We then use the Security Methods tab to require security negotiation, not allow unsecured communications, and set Perfect Forward Secrecy. Notice that there is no "unsecured" option selected in Figure 16-13, because we want to "require" security.

3. We then add a new Security Method via the Add button on the Security Methods tab.

4. We then use the Custom option, and set the Integrity algorithm (SHA1 in this case), the Encryption algorithm (3DES in this case), and Session Key generation settings for the security method being defined. Note that you could use ESP if you wanted to provide security.

TIP: If you do not want to take the time to set these up at the outset, you can define IPSec filters and actions during the process of defining the IPSec policy. These methods just differentiate the major configuration steps.

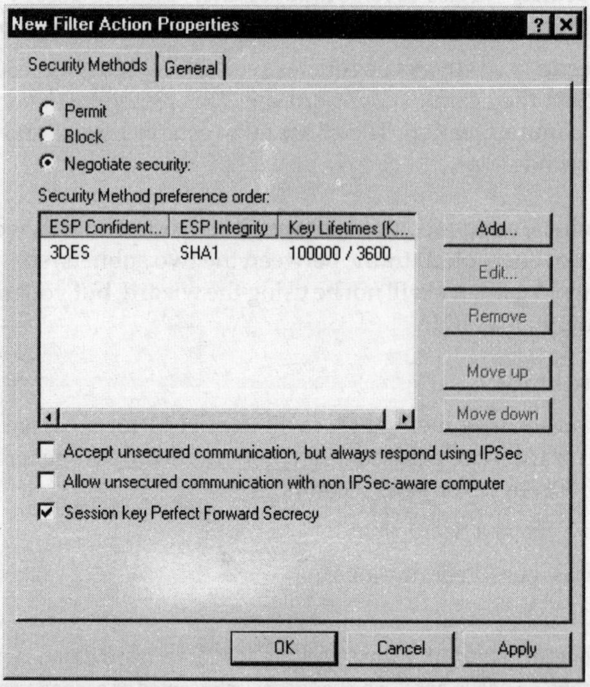

Figure 16-13. Security methods list and actions

IPSec Policies

As we mentioned earlier, the third basic configuration component of IPSec is the policy. The policy is where we take the filter rules and actions, add the user authentication methods we require, select the connections to use it on, and choose the type of IPSec connections we will be using. From the policies that we will be looking at, we can select

▼ One of the IP filters from the IP filters list, or add a new one

■ One or more of the authentication methods: Kerberos (default), certificates, or shared secrets

■ The mode of the connection: transport or tunnel

▲ The connection type this applies to: RAS, IP, or both

In our example, we will be creating the Net10 IPSec policy. In that policy, we will be using the Secure10 filter, Only Secure action, Kerberos authentication, transport mode, and making it apply to any and all connection types.

1. Add a new security policy (make sure to edit at the finish).

2. Check the General tab to validate the name and description of the policy, as well as the default time to check for policy changes (see Figure 16-14).

3. If you need to set any advanced key exchange settings, you can use the Advanced button on the General tab (you probably won't have to mess with this).

4. On the Rules tab, add the new rule.

5. Select Secure10 as the IP Filter rule to use.

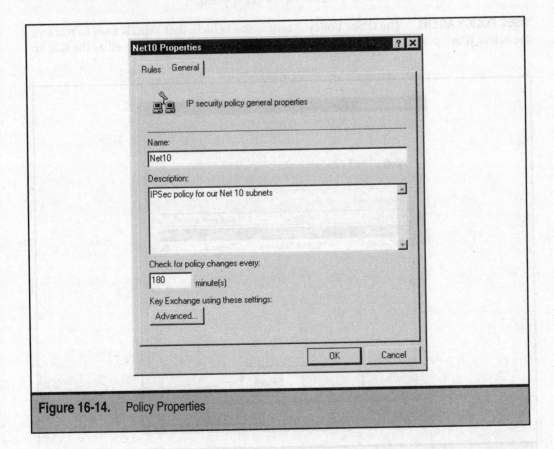

Figure 16-14.   Policy Properties

6. Select Only Secure for the Filter Action.

7. On the Authentication method tab of the new rule Properties sheet, select Kerberos as the Authentication method. You can add others here as well.

8. In the Tunnel Setting tab, specify that we are *not* using tunnel mode.

9. Then select the All Network Connections option in the Connection Type tab.

10. Now in the Rules Properties, check that Secure10 is selected (checked), and the Dynamic rule disabled (unchecked). See Figure 16-15.

11. The last part is to activate (i.e. via right-click) Net10 in the IPSec policy settings.

Note that we do *not* want the default dynamic rule to apply; we are being explicit in our configurations. Also note that because this is a domain-wide policy, the Net10 machines should be in this domain. If not, it would never get applied.

IPSEC POLICY AGENT   The IPSec Policy Agent is the vehicle that Win2K uses to retrieve the active IPSec policy information from the Local Security settings as well as the Group

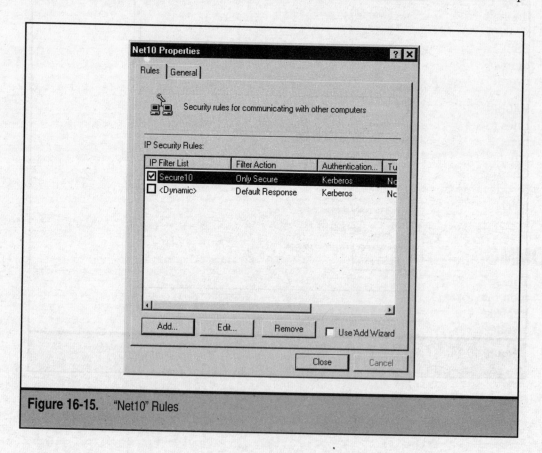

Figure 16-15.   "Net10" Rules

Policies (via the AD). If there is not an active policy at system start time, the agent will continue to check (poll) the AD and the Local policy. Also, any changes that are applied to these policies while the system is running will be applied.

A Closing IPSec Comment

We have spent a significant amount of time on the IPSec category, but we have still left a lot of stuff out, such as arguments for certain cryptographic algorithm strengths, session key generation time, certificate use, and many other things. If you are going to implement this in anything other than a small-scale manner, *you need a book written especially about IPSec*. We cannot cover the topic in depth in such a short space. Also, if at all possible, find someone else who has actually used the Win2K version of IPSec on a large scale.

L2TP and IPSec

Win2K uses IPSec and L2TP in combination to provide both tunneling and security for IP packets across any network. Win2K is designed and tuned to use L2TP as the link and the IPSec ESP features for security. In essence, Microsoft recommends that you use L2TP to do the tunneling and IPSec to secure the data.

Note that you can create an unsecured L2TP connection in Win2K (that is, not using ESP). However, this would not be a VPN, because it would not be private. Microsoft recommends that you only use such a connection "…temporarily to troubleshoot an L2TP over IPSec connection by eliminating the IPSec authentication and negotiation process."

MACHINE CERTIFICATES FOR L2TP OVER IPSEC   You are required to use machine certificates to support machine-level authentication for L2TP over IPSec-based VPN connections. Each machine, both clients and servers, must have a valid machine certificate. You will need to have access to a certificate authority to get the certificates. Please see Web Chapter 1 at **www.osborne.com** for more information about setting up an in-house certificate authority. Once you have it set up, then you can install the certificates on the machines.

COMMON USES

This section will describe the configurations needed to implement four of the most common remote access and VPN architectures you will encounter. They rely heavily on the information contained throughout this chapter, so you may have to refer back. The four architectures are

▼ Mobile user dial-up to corporate network

■ Mobile user using external ISP to access corporate network

■ Remote office VPN to corporate network

▲ Partner networks (extranets)

General Remote Access and VPN Recommendations

Before we begin, we need to cover a couple of architectural "defaults" that we will use for all of the scenarios.

▼ **Use a Specific Remote Access (RA) Domain** We will use a specific domain in the Active Directory to control user access. That domain would contain an account for each user that is allowed to use the remote access service. *This will require that you remove the default bi-directional trust in Win2K domains or to create a totally separate AD forest (see Chapter 8).* You do not want accounts in the RA domain to be trusted anywhere else.

■ **Create Access Based on Group Membership** All access capabilities are based on the group membership of the authenticating user.

■ **Use Remote Access and IPSec Policies** Use the policies to implement the security requirements that you desire.

■ **Use Two-Factor Authentication** This means that you will authenticate once to the RRAS server to get a connection, be it remote access or VPN, then you will have to authenticate again, with domain authentication, to access domain resources.

■ **Enable Auditing and Logging** You will need these for tracking and intrusion detection.

■ **Lock Down the Clients** It is imperative that you secure your clients, especially laptops. What happens if they are stolen? How will this affect your service?

■ **Use L2TP Over PPTP** L2TP is a much better protocol and is the recommended method. Only use PPTP if you have clients that cannot support L2TP *or* you do not have the ability to issue certificates (that is, you have not read Web Chapter 1 at **www.osborne.com**).

■ **Keep It Simple Stupid (K.I.S.S.)** The more complex, the harder to secure.

▲ **Develop a Remote Access Network (RAN)** All remote access and VPN servers will sit on this segregated network.

Why a Remote Access Network (RAN)?

You may ask yourself why you want a segregated, not isolated, network. As we noted in Chapter 7, there are a number of risks associated with remote access connections. As such, we will assume that the remote access servers are minimally trusted, in that we only want to be able to monitor the traffic that is flowing from the machines. The easiest way to do this is by having them located together. We can also use a RAN to limit the type of traffic that will flow between the RAN and the corporate network. It is entirely possible that you will allow all traffic. Even if this is the case, a RAN is a good idea just in case you change your mind later.

NOTE: This section, which could be a book in and of itself, is meant to provide basic information. You will need to architect your solution.

Mobile User Dial-Up to Corporate Network

This is a very typical scenario, where we have mobile users (a.k.a. road warriors) that need to access the corporate network. We will provide a remote access server using a RRAS server running on a Win2K server platform, using an IAS server for authentication to a Win2K domain. We will set the RRAS server up with high-speed analog modems to provide the dial-in capability. After you have the lines and modems working correctly (not a trivial task itself), you will need to do the following:

1. Ensure that the remote users are in the appropriate groups or have the appropriate dial-in permissions. Note that you will need to make sure that the IAS server is registered in the AD and that it has permission to read the user objects in the RA domain.

2. Set up one or more RRAS servers on a RAN. You could use any NAS, but because we are dealing with Win2K, we will be using RRAS. This server will act as a router, so you will need at least one network interface along with the modems.

3. Configure the remote access policy.

4. Set up an IAS server on the RAN. It is advisable that you set up a backup IAS server as well (redundancy is key for security and reliability). The IAS server will use the RA domain to obtain user accounts and groups that are used in the remote access policies.

5. Set up the router filters for the RAN to the corporate network to allow any desired traffic to and from the corporate network.

6. Set up each user computer to dial-in.

When done, your network setup will look something like the following illustration.

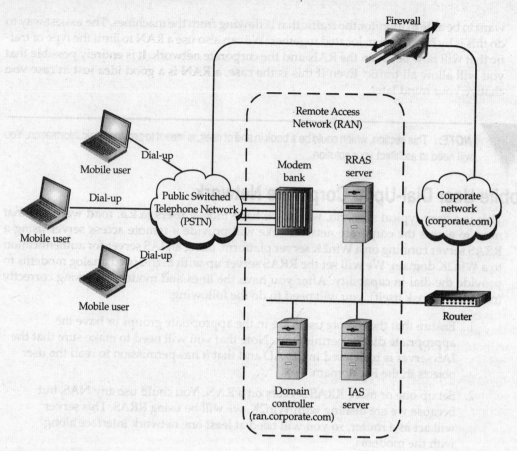

What Happens?

When a user connects to an RRAS server, he or she presents his or her credentials (username and password). Then the RAS sends a RADIUS authentication request to the IAS server. The IAS forwards the authentication request to the DC to check those credentials. If you are not using the IAS service, then the RRAS server will perform the authentication and authorization checking.

The IAS server then uses the information (user properties) in the response from the DC and the remote access policies to determine if dial-up access is allowed. If access is allowed, then IAS sends an access-accept packet to the RRAS server. The RRAS server will then grant access and establish the connection parameters, such as an IP address. It will also start routing the packets sent to and received from the client. When the user disconnects, the RRAS server sends an accounting-stop packet to the IAS server, indicating the end of the user session.

Should You Use It?

There are some problems with this architecture, not the least of which is cost. Depending on the number of mobile users, we will have to maintain multiple servers, modem pools, phone lines, and long-distance lines. This type of implementation can be quick to set up, but very costly in the long run.

ANOTHER OPTION: OUTSOURCING LINES   There is a service, which is provided by some ISPs, that will allow you to control the ISP access. This is similar to the current configuration (as well as what we will look at next) with one exception: You control the user account access. When an employee connects to the ISP's NAS, the authentication and usage records are forwarded to the IAS server on the RAN. The IAS server allows the company to control user authentication, track usage, and manage which employees are allowed to access the ISP's network. Once the user is connected to the ISP NAS, then the user establishes a VPN into the RAN.

Mobile User Using External ISP to Access Corporate Network

This is becoming a much more typical scenario as telecommuting becomes more popular. This allows all remote users (both mobile and home) to access the corporate network, without the expenses of maintaining dial-up lines and services. In this scenario, we will provide an L2TP/IPSec VPN using RRAS running on a Win2K server platform. We will again use IAS for authentication to the RA domain. The RAN in this case becomes what is commonly referred to as an extranet or DMZ. In this scenario, auditing and intrusion detection become of the utmost importance.

The steps to set it up are very similar to the previous scenario:

1. Ensure that the remote users are in the appropriate groups, or have the appropriate dial-in permissions. Note that you will need to make sure that the IAS server is registered in the AD and that it has permission to read the user objects in the domain.

2. Set up one or more RRAS servers on a RAN, which is *only* providing VPN services. This server will act as a router, so it will need at least two network interfaces.

3. Ensure the server acts as a gateway and not an endpoint.

4. Configure the remote access policy to only allow VPN connection types.

5. Set up the RRAS server to support VPN clients (preferably only L2TP) and configure the L2TP and PPTP ports. *This is where you could set the PPTP ports to zero to prevent any use of PPTP.*

6. Set up L2TP over IPSec filters to ensure that only VPN traffic is sent and received by the RRAS server on the Internet interface.

7. Set up an IAS server on the RAN.

8. Set up the router filters for the RAN.

9. Set up each user computer to use the appropriate VPN client to attach to the RAN.

When done, your network setup will look something like this:

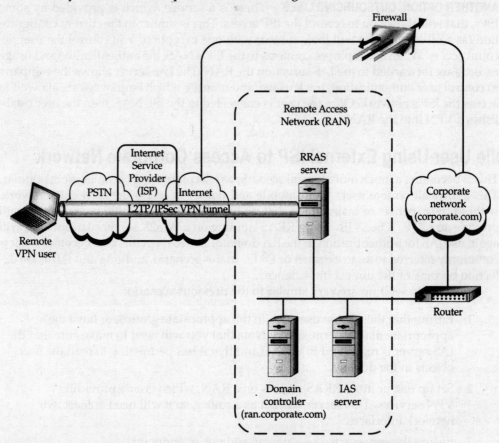

Should You Use It?

This appears to be the up-and-coming solution for this type of access. The Internet is becoming more reliable, and the VPN solutions are becoming more robust. This is definitely something you should consider using.

Remote Office VPN to Corporate Network

This scenario is very similar to the last one, with the exception that you will be implementing a gateway-to-gateway VPN as opposed to a host-to-gateway VPN. In this scenario, we are going to enable traffic to be able to initiate in either direction (that is, from the RAN to remote, or vice versa). Most of the setup is the same as the previous VPN configuration, so we will only detail the differences.

1. Set up the RAN in the same manner as before.

2. Set up a domain controller that will serve both the corporate and RA domains on the remote office network. This will allow IPSec policies (via Group policies) to be consistent.

3. Set up the RAN server to initiate and receive L2TP connections from the remote office VPN gateway.

   ■ *Configure demand-dial interfaces for each branch office router.* You can create a demand-dial interface by using the Demand-Dial Interface Wizard. Set the Connection Type to be VPN. Set the VPN type to be L2TP. Set the Destination Address to be the remote office VPN gateway Internet IP address. Set the Dial-out Credentials that will be needed to authenticate you to the remote VPN gateway. Set the Dial-in Credentials that the remote VPN gateway will use when connecting to you. Also, you should enable the Add a User Account So a Remote Router Can Dial In option.

   ■ *Configure static routes* so that traffic to and from the remote office will be forwarded by using the appropriate demand-dial interface. For each network at the remote office you will need to define: the interface (which is the demand-dial interface that corresponds to the remote office), the destination network and mask, and the metric.

4. Set up the remote office VPN gateway to initiate and receive L2TP connections from the RAN VPN gateway. This is the same as before, just in reverse.

   ■ You will need to perform the same basic setup as on the RAN. Since it is assumed to be a small network, you may not have segregation between the remote access network and the office network.

   ■ *Configure demand-dial interfaces for the RAN.* Set the Connection Type to be VPN. Set the VPN type to be L2TP. Set the Destination Address to be the RAN VPN gateway Internet IP address. Set the Dial-out Credentials that will be needed to authenticate you to the RAN VPN gateway. Set the Dial-in Credentials that the RAN VPN gateway will use when connecting to you. Also, you should enable the Add a User Account So a Remote Router Can Dial In option.

   ■ *Configure static routes so that traffic to and from the remote office will be forwarded by using the appropriate demand-dial interface.* For each network in the corporate office you will need to define: the interface (which is the demand-dial interface that corresponds to the remote office), the destination network and mask, and the metric.

When done, your network will look like the mobile user described previously, but will have a corporate network on both ends, instead of a remote VPN user.

Should You Use It?

Remote office VPNs are a valuable tool and should be considered. The one point to remember is that the Internet has no guaranteed level of service; that is determined by availability or bandwidth. If the Internet goes down, so does your link. If the performance is acceptable, and you can live with the availability issues, then this solution is viable.

Partner Networks (Extranets)

An *extranet* environment is one in which one or more business partners need access to a specific set of services or servers. You provide those services by extending your corporate intranet to provide those services. When you do this, you must ensure that there is adequate authentication, authorization, and auditing.

We will build an extranet using the same basic architecture as the RAN, but this time, we may put other partner-specific servers and services on it, versus just having VPN or remote access services. Here is how we propose you set it up:

1. Make a separate subnet for the partner network.

2. Set up a new domain in the AD called "partner."

3. Configure a one-way trust from the partner domain to the corporate domain (that is, the partner domain *trusts* the corporate domain, but not vice versa).

4. Set up the VPN services like you did on the RAN, except this time all authentication is to the partner domain.

5. Configure the router to block all traffic, then open it up to potential traffic that you will allow from the partner network to your corporate network.

6. Using Win2K domain groups, we will limit what services and servers that each partner can access.

When done, your network setup will look something like this:

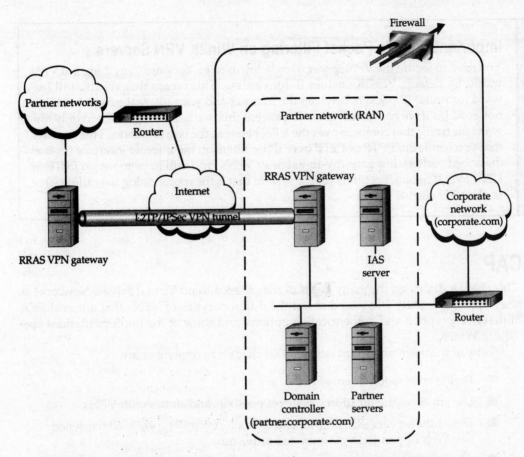

A derivation on this configuration would be to allow all the partners to have a domain that was trusted by the partner domain. This would allow partners to manage their own accounts and services. This is very risky, but may be acceptable in many circumstances.

Should You Use It?

In a word: Yes! The alternative to extranets is letting users roam around your entire internal network. This is unacceptable! Whether you use this design or another, do not allow partners unrestricted access to your internal networks.

> ## Important: Enable Packet Filtering on Win2K VPN Servers
>
> You need to secure the VPN server from being used to "forward" anything but VPN traffic. By default, Win2K enables IP forwarding. This means that Win2K will forward (or route) IP packets between the Internet and your internal network. This is not good (as if we had to tell you). To prevent this, we will set up filters to only forward the traffic that comes in over the VPN between the two networks. This requires that you configure PPTP or L2TP over IPSec filters on the Internet interface (as was described earlier). For gateway-to-gateway VPNs, you will have to set up PPTP or L2TP over IPSec packet filters for the system that is the router doing the calling (that is, the VPN client).

RECAP

This chapter discussed the many facets of remote access and Virtual Private Networks as they apply to Win2K. We talked about the different types of VPNs that are available, different encryption and authentication options, and some of the implementations specific to Win2K.

Some of the more important items in this chapter to remember are

▼ Define your requirements *first*.

■ Use strong authentication whenever possible, and *always* with VPNs.

■ *Ensure* the servers (RRAS, IAS, and domain controllers) are well hardened (see Web Appendix A at **www.osborne.com**).

■ *Simplicity* is better.

■ Use the Remote Access Policies and IPSec Policies to their fullest extent.

■ Use a sniffer to ensure that the traffic you think is encrypted really is.

▲ Don't use the *default* settings, unless they meet your requirements.

We have covered a lot of territory and information. The mere fact that it has taken us so many pages to just cover the basics should be an indication of the complexity of the issues. Take the time to architect a proper solution—it will be worth it in the long run.

NOTE: As with other chapters, there are entire books that are devoted to these subjects. To keep up to date, you should get one of those books. The basics will be the same, and the principles in this chapter will serve you well, but other books will go into more depth on specific topics.

CHAPTER 17

Client/Workstation
Security

One of the most overlooked security problems is that of client workstations. Server security is the primary focus while client security is a lesser priority. But just like one shaky card in a house of cards, a weak client machine can have a dramatic effect on your overall security. Once a client workstation has been broken into, the keys to the users' server passwords are usually available. This produces a cumulative effect where one unsecured machine can lead to an overall security breach. In this chapter we are going to take a look at client and workstation security in an effort to protect your overall enterprise.

SECURITY RECOMMENDATIONS

So now that we know that clients are a security issue, let's look at what needs to be done to prevent these attacks on client machines.

One of the first steps a company should take is to create a strong security policy (usually written) that describes the requirements for protecting computer-related resources and information stored in these resources. This would include how a secure machine is configured, who has access to the data on the machine, the level of access users are allowed, the extent to which user actions will be monitored, and any legal notices that need to be presented to users prior to logging into the machine. See Chapter 4 for more details.

The next step is to take a proactive approach to security. Any new security patches should be applied to clients and workstations on a regular basis based upon the severity of the security flaw. There are many e-mail lists that can be subscribed to, including one from Microsoft (**http://www.microsoft.com/technet/security/notify.asp**), that send notices of new security patches. A quick Internet search should provide enough to get you started.

After the basics are done, a security template should be created to configure the security database for all client machines. This includes the base audit policy, Group Policy, and the account lockout policy.

You should limit privilege levels according to the principle of least privilege. This way, when users need higher access rights, they will have to be added—no more users surprising you that they were able to access files you thought were protected.

For Win2K client machines that are heavily utilized for network traffic, IPSec should be used when possible and sensitive data on the hard drive should be encrypted using the Encrypting File System (EFS).

Virus protection software and personal firewalls should be used to block questionable activity. This will limit what an intruder can do as well as protect internal users from potential Trojan Horses that are Web-based. Most virus-checking software will check the contents of e-mail as well as the attachments before the e-mail is opened. It is a good idea to have this set up and configured properly.

Finally, the e-mail that is sent and received should be encrypted using secure mail. This will help to verify that an e-mail was sent from a specific person as well as protect the transmission of the data while it traverses the Internet.

Establishing an Audit Policy

Once you have set up a security infrastructure, you need to be able to ensure that it's working properly. That's why establishing an audit trail is an important aspect of security. Monitoring the creation or modification of objects gives you a way to track potential security problems, helps assure user accountability, and provides evidence in the event of a security breach.

To help you do this, you need to enable auditing on the client. As discussed in Chapter 13, the default audit policy for Win2K clients and servers is No Audit. Thus, you should enable auditing on clients as well as on the server. The best method to accomplish this is via Group Policy.

Smartcards

Companies are increasingly looking for ways to increase the security of their networked resources. One of the methods gaining popularity is the use of smartcards. Smartcards are a relatively simple way to make it much harder for an unauthorized person to gain access to a network.

Smartcards, which are discussed in Chapter 11, are a very secure option for client login. Instead of entering a password, the user inserts a card into a reader attached to the PC, and enters the card's pass phrase. Win2K uses the private key and certificate that is stored on the card to authenticate the user to the Key Distribution Center (or KDC, see the Kerberos section in Chapter 11) on a Win2K domain controller. After authenticating the user, the KDC returns a ticket-granting ticket. From this point on, additional connections the user makes during the session use Kerberos authentication as just described.

File System Protection

Whenever possible we would like to prevent unauthorized alteration or deletion of data on our systems. We can do so via software controls. This is accessed via the Security tab on the directory properties dialog box, as shown in Figure 17-1.

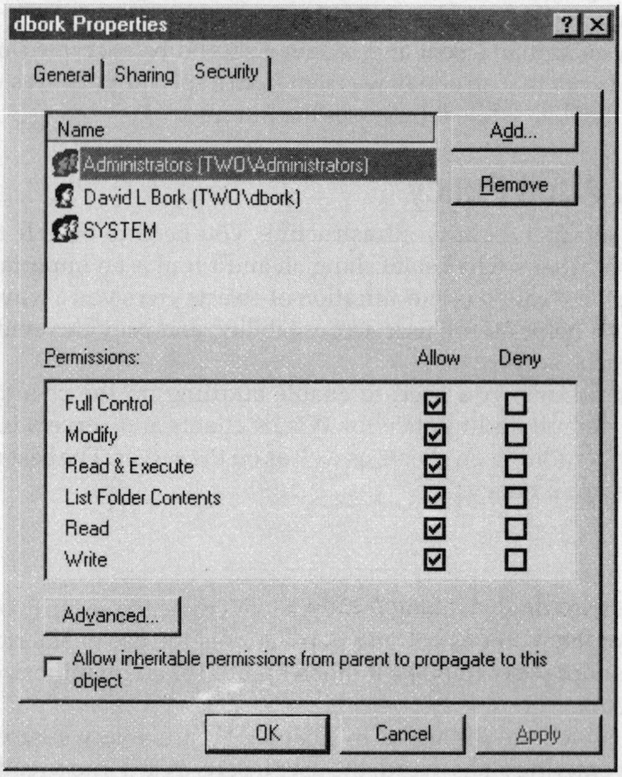

dbork Properties ? X

General | Sharing | Security

Name	
Administrators (TWO\Administrators)	Add...
David L Bork (TWO\dbork)	Remove
SYSTEM	

Permissions:	Allow	Deny
Full Control	☑	☐
Modify	☑	☐
Read & Execute	☑	☐
List Folder Contents	☑	☐
Read	☑	☐
Write	☑	☐

Advanced...

☐ Allow inheritable permissions from parent to propagate to this object

OK | Cancel | Apply

Figure 17-1. File system security properties

Because sensitive data is normally stored on a system for day-to-day use, it is important to protect your files. There are several ways of protecting data on your system.

File and Printer Sharing

File sharing is a major cause of security problems. There have been many utilities created to get information such as usernames and file share availability, including hidden share names, from the file-sharing system. File-sharing or peer-to-peer networking should be turned off in hostile networks. Even if you are connected to an internal network there are usually files that need protection such as employee reviews or pay increase information. So before turning this feature on, remember that file-sharing and workgroup collaboration is much more secure when placing files on a shared server instead of using any peer-to-peer functions.

If sharing has been turned on, it can be removed by opening the Network and Dialup Connection dialog box in the Control Panel. Right-click the network profile that you are using and remove the File and Printer Sharing for Microsoft Networks option.

Encrypting a File System

We have described techniques for protecting resources stored on a centralized network. But data stored on a desktop or laptop computer needs to be protected beyond simple password protection.

Windows 2000 Encrypting File System (EFS) allows for this protection. For added protection of data stored locally, EFS lets you encrypt designated files or folders on a local computer so unauthorized people can't read those files. The EFS is particularly useful for protecting data on a computer that might be physically stolen, such as a laptop. It is recommended that all laptops be configured to use EFS to ensure that all business information is encrypted in the user's My Documents folder as well as any e-mail files, such as *.pst.

Configuring a Password-Protected Screensaver

A password-protected screensaver protects the computer when the user walks away from the computer. It is common in marty offices that people abuse colleagues' computers that are left unattended with the account holder still logged in. People can play pranks like leaving rude mail to co-workers, hiding files, and reconfiguring the computer to use strange color schemes. One co-worker even placed a bitmap of the WinNT Stop message as the screen saver so that the user kept rebooting his system instead of checking to see if it was still working.

Configuring Clients with Group Policy

As discussed in Chapter 9, Win2K includes the security templates that can be distributed via Group Policy. Group Policies give the flexibility of having any level of control for managing the desktop while giving you the power of centrally managing a wide variety of settings. Multiple Group Policies can create policy conflicts and increase computer startup time. Minimize the number of Group Policy objects that apply to users and computers.

Setting Up Security Zones

Security zones can be used to provide the appropriate level of security for the various types of Web content that users will encounter in your organization. For example, because your company's intranet is protected, you can fully trust Web sites and allow users to be able to run all types of active content from those locations. To provide this capability, the Local intranet zone should be set to a low level of security. You might not feel as confident about sites on the Internet, so you can assign a higher level of security to the Internet zone. This higher level of security prevents users from running active content and downloading code to their computer. However, if there are particular sites that you trust, you can place individual URLs in the Trusted Sites zone. For known Web sites that potentially have harmful content, you can select the highest restrictions.

CAUTION: Outlook Express shares zone settings with Internet Explorer. Any changes made in one application will change the other.

Transport Security: IPSec

One of the often forgotten pieces of client security is the transport on the local LAN. It is important to protect the data as it is traveling over the network. To address this concern, you should use IPSec (see Chapter 16 for details).

The use of IPSec is extremely important when data travels outside a protected network. Telecommuters who are taking advantage of higher speed broadband connections like cable modem or DSL should use IPSec to send or receive data on corporate servers.

Personal Firewall

In the past, intruders presented a very small threat to Internet-connected users. Intruders spent most of their time attacking corporate networks where there was valuable information. Most personal computers were used to remotely dial into computers where the information was stored. Also, Internet connections were slow and extremely difficult to locate.

Today, a home client computer or a small office computer looks as appealing to an intruder as a network. Many clients are used to procure products on company credit cards and they store customer account information or even sensitive company information.

All users should install a personal firewall on their system. Cable modem users and DSL users are the most susceptible for network-born attacks. These users should be actively monitoring their firewall logs for any suspicious activity. Personal firewalls start by protecting your system from the outside. There are people actively probing systems on the Internet on a daily basis. It is not uncommon for home users running personal firewalls to get at least five alerts per day on their systems.

Personal firewalls will block an intrusion attempt as well as log the information to provide to the intruder's Internet service provider. This type of protection is called *packet filtering,* and it keeps intruders from getting to services that are blocked.

An additional benefit of having a firewall on the local system is the ability to prevent personal data from falling into the wrong hands. When you install a Web browser you provide personal information that can help identify you as well as the software you are using.

Some personal firewalls also come with software to verify and delete cookies held on the system's hard disk. (Cookies are used to keep the state of your preferences when returning to a Web site.)

Secure E-mail

In Win2K, secure mail is based on the Secure/Multipurpose Internet Mail Extensions (S/MIME) protocol, which is an extension of the original Multipurpose Internet Mail Extensions (MIME) standard. The S/MIME standard enables the digital signing and encryption of e-mail. Secure e-mail can be exchanged regardless of the e-mail software, operating system, or hardware platform that it is run on. All that needs to be implemented is e-mail software that supports the S/MIME standard. This allows S/MIME messages to be sent over the Internet without regard to the mail server that is going to forward or receive your e-mail message, because all cryptographic functions are performed on the clients and not on the servers. Mail servers accept messages as standard MIME.

Secure mail with S/MIME uses the industry standard X.509 version 3 digital certificates and public key technology. To provide message authentication, data integrity, and non-repudiation, secure mail clients can sign messages with the sender's private key before sending the mail. The receiver then uses the sender's public key to verify the message by checking the digital signature. Clients require a valid secure mail certificate before they can send signed mail. Also, receivers must have a copy of the client's secure mail certificate (the public key) before they can verify the originator's signature.

For protecting the contents of e-mail during transmission, secure mail clients can send and receive mail that is encrypted. Clients generate random symmetric keys and use the secret key to encrypt messages for confidentiality. Then they encrypt the symmetric key by encrypting it with the public key of each receiver and sending the encrypted key along with the encrypted message to each receiver. Clients must have a copy of the receiver's secure mail certificate before sending secure e-mail. Receivers use their private keys to decrypt the symmetric key; then they use the secret key to decrypt the message.

By using secure mail, senders are assured that the integrity of their messages is preserved and that only the intended receivers are able to read the mail messages. Receivers are assured that the message is genuine and originated from the sender.

Windows 9x

We need to address the lack of security mechanisms in the Win9x and ME (herein referred to as just Windows) operating system. One fundamental security weakness in Windows is that you can always boot to a DOS prompt (the command prompt) and access the hard drive directly. You can make breaking into a Windows computer more difficult by establishing system policies that limit what can be done from the Windows interface and by setting a BIOS password and disabling floppy disk booting.

Windows cannot provide any real protection for files stored on the local hard drive from an intruder. One way of protecting the system in Windows is by placing all the files remotely on the server, including the Windows operating system files for the client computer. This method creates significant loads on the file server as well as the network. Another alternative to this is to copy a safe image of the client computer's hard drive, including the operating system files, from the file server to the client computer when the client starts up. This increases the startup time of the client computer but then uses the local drive to relieve the load on the file server as well as the network.

Always require that the Windows machine uses the network logon. This means that users must be authenticated to the domain controller before they are allowed to run programs.

This also will help to enforce security for any network resources. Also, require user-level access control to shared resources in Windows. This will tie Windows share security into the domain security managed by the domain controller.

Cached passwords put other computers on the network at risk. If a client computer is compromised, the cached password list can be read easily. Never use password caching on a Windows machine. Also, never have Internet Explorer remember fields that are passwords or contain sensitive information.

For dedicated machines such as data entry terminals, disable the RUN command, the Desktop Explorer, the My Computer icon, and the My Network icon. Also, remember to disable the MS-DOS prompt and disallow the running of single-mode in the reboot to DOS shutdown screen. This makes it difficult to run other programs since booting from a floppy is disabled.

Restrict the Control Panel from all users except administrative accounts. Only administrators should be able to change any of the system settings. Also, disable any of the Registry editing tools such as regedit.exe. This protects configuration settings and user account names.

Restrict the running of all but the necessary programs on the computer. An even better solution would be to look for all executable files and then remove any of them that are not needed to use the system. This method takes a little trial and error so make sure this is done on a test machine before implementing it in a production environment.

RECOMMENDED SECURITY SETUP

To secure a Win2K client, follow these steps:

1. Rename the Administrator account to an obscure value to disguise its function.

2. Disable all unused and unnecessary services (see Chapter 21 for more details).

3. Use Group Policy to set security settings.

4. Enable strong password functionality (via Group Policy).

5. Set up proper ACLs on files and directories, Registry keys, shares, and so on (some of this can be done via Group Policy).

6. Enable auditing in a way that makes sense for the box (see Chapter 13 for more details).

7. Do not choose automatic logon after a clean install.

8. Only give accounts the level of access they need.

9. Disable and set a random, complex password on the disabled Guest account.

10. Do not connect to telephone lines unless detached from local networks.

RECAP

As you can see, a weak client install can create security risks for your entire organization. By following the recommendations in this chapter, you can prevent most security exposures. It is important to have both a strong security policy as well as a proactive approach to security. By taking an active security role with your users, you can secure the largest set of systems in your network.

Here are the best practices to help in deploying your client workstations:

▼ Establish a consistent audit policy.

■ Check for events on a regular basis.

■ Encrypt sensitive data on the system.

■ Make sure the system locks out users when they are away from their systems.

■ Use IPSec if data traverses over public networks.

■ Install personal firewalls.

▲ Encrypt sensitive e-mail using SMIME.

CHAPTER 18

Enterprise-Wide Security

"The bigger the business, the bigger the target."

—*Ken Sandlin*

Comprehensive coverage of enterprise-wide security could be a book (or several books) unto itself. With the many operating system, database, router, and firewall options that we find in the enterprise environment, no single set of audit or scanning tools is capable of discovering, reporting, and aiding in the patching of all network operating systems and appliances. Additionally, with Win2K's myriad of connection options to the Unix, NetWare, SNA, AppleTalk, and thin-client network worlds, just knowing how to discover your corporation's risk exposures, let alone solve them, can be a challenging adventure in self-protection and preservation.

Let's assume for a moment that you've read the rest of this book, and that after reading it, you've secured your Win2K servers and workstations, along with your Internet, Wide Area Network (WAN), and dial-in perimeters. What would your next task be? Your next task would be to secure your multi-operating system environments today, and then, with an eye to the future, manage your entire enterprise network as simplistically, but securely as possible. Effective management of the enterprise network is critical, because *if a network cannot be managed, it cannot be secured.*

For most enterprise networks, because of the far-flung geographic office locations, remote field users, and sheer lack of network security staff, it is impossible for the network security group to personally visit and check every desktop, laptop, print server, database server, Web server, routing device, firewall, and PDA on a regular basis to ensure the security of each of those systems. Therefore, you must consider automating much of your enterprise-wide network security monitoring and scanning. For large enterprise networks, remotely managed security tools are the key. There are many tools to choose from to help you in this task. While we make no specific vendor recommendations, we'll need to discuss the basics of these tools and how they differ in their approach, methodology, and examples of their actual use. But first, let's talk about what you're protecting yourselves from.

A BLUEPRINT FOR COMPROMISING THE ENTIRE ENTERPRISE, ONE VULNERABILITY AT A TIME

If you have a hundred Windows servers, each with the same five vulnerabilities, you have a total of five known methods of entrance into your enterprise. On the other hand, if you have a fully networked system with one Win2K server, one NetWare 5.*x* server, one Apple G4 Cube, one Red Hat Linux Web server, and one AS/400 Minicomputer, each with five known vulnerabilities, you have a total of 25 known methods of attack into your network. And all it takes is one of those 25 vulnerabilities to be discovered for an enterprise network exploit to begin. The idea is this: Once a single system has been compromised, the entire network is at risk. Especially where matching IDs and passwords are used across multiple systems.

Known Compromises in the Enterprise Environment

Although the following numbers will continue to change, SANS bulletins list the following approximate and generally agreed upon number of known security exploits for the various operating systems:

▼ Approximately 250 Unix exploits (in its various flavors)

■ Approximately 150 WinNT and Win2K exploits

■ Approximately 150 Linux exploits (in its various flavors)

■ Approximately 90 Windows 9.*x* and Millennium (ME) exploits

■ Approximately 5 NetWare exploits

▲ Approximately 5 Apple exploits

Known mainframe and minicomputer exploits are harder to track, but would fall towards the low end of the exploit list.

Unix's high number can be partially attributed to the long history of the operating system's use, allowing for more exploits to be discovered, and partially attributed to the lack of security inherently placed in the kernel of the OS itself. Win2K, WinNT, NetWare, and Macintosh all were built from the ground up with security in mind. In Unix, while some administrators would disagree, security is essentially an agreed-upon add-in to the various kernels themselves.

DOCUMENTING THE ENTERPRISE

Having a documented inventory of your enterprise computers and services contributes directly to both good security practices and a reduction of the enterprise's total cost of ownership (something senior-level management always appreciates!). An enterprise's initial design and ongoing network management dramatically affect its total cost of ownership. And day-to-day network management greatly affects network security.

A well-secured network is still at risk with each additional workstation or server installation, and with each software patch that is loaded. With the addition of each new operating system or service added to the enterprise, one can expect both the complexity of the network and the difficulty of network security management to increase. Unix, Linux, NetWare, SNA, and AppleTalk are just a few of the additional operating systems that are present in the enterprise environment. The better documented the network, the better managed the network, and the more secure that network becomes.

An enterprise network that cannot be easily managed is wide open to a security attack. Up-to-date diagrams, current configuration databases, a corporate security policy, and regular system scanning of the network all add up to a cohesive set of Enterprise Security Controls (ESCs), and the necessary ability to easily audit your systems for their compliance to your enterprise's security policies.

Countermeasures, Part II: Intrusion Detection Systems

Originally discussed in Chapter 3, countermeasures take on a whole new importance in the enterprise environment. Intrusion Detection Systems (IDS) monitor the enterprise networks in real time, watching for preset security-related, trip-wire events to occur. When a preset event such as a DoS attack occurs, the IDS notifies the security administrators through a variety of means that such an attack is occurring. Some of the products available today not only monitor for and send alerts regarding such attacks, but can also take defensive measures, such as shutting down the inbound TCP or UDP port, and in some rarer instances, initiate offensive measures such as launching its own retaliatory strike back at the source of the initial attack.

CAUTION: Offensive measures are *not* recommended. Whether you end up retaliating against the true source of the attack, or just striking back at an unfortunate pawn computer that was taken over by others to initiate the attack, any offensive measures taken by your IDS could very well land you in court as the defendant in a lawsuit. For more information on Intrusion Detection Systems, see Chapter 3 and Appendix C. That said...

Scan First and Ask Questions Later: Internet Security Systems Scanners

Unlike Intrusion Detection Systems that discover a system break-in as it is occurring, security scanner products are updated often and should be run regularly to discover new system vulnerabilities *before* a hacker can take advantage of your system weaknesses and gain entrance to your enterprise. Microsoft included a copy of the Internet Security Systems (ISS) scanner product on the Win2K CDs, and because we are certified and experienced with their products, we'll make particular note of the ISS scanner products. ISS makes the Internet Scanner, System Scanner, and Database Scanner products.

The Internet Scanner product is installed on a WinNT 4 workstation, and then remotely scans networked computers. The System Scanner console product is installed on WinNT 4 as well, but also requires that an agent be installed on the system(s) that is to be scanned. The agent then reports back to the System Scanner console via an encrypted connection the vulnerabilities that were discovered on the remote system.

Because the System Scanner product requires that an agent be installed on the machine to be scanned while the Internet Scanner does all its work remotely, the System Scanner reports tend to locate more potential vulnerabilities on the tested systems. However, Internet Scanner will scan the entire network, while System Scanner can only scan those machines that ISS has written an agent for. In a single enterprise environment, it is quite common to see both Internet Scanner and System Scanner used in tandem for system vulnerability testing. Internet Scanner can be used for many node network scans, where it would be impractical to visit each system and install an agent on every workstation and server, with the System Scanner product then used for securing critical information machines and those directly exposed to the Internet.

The latest version of the ISS Database Scanner product (version 4.0) installs on WinNT 4 Workstation and Win2K Professional and will remotely scan Microsoft SQL Server, Oracle Server, and Sybase SQL Server databases. Database Scanner searches for external attack vulnerabilities and internal database vulnerabilities, such as altered system stored procedures, stale login IDs, and database users with excessive permissions.

Two of the items that make any good scanner product stand out are regularly updated vulnerability checks and effective reporting tools, including a technician-level report that details each discovered vulnerability along with step-by-step instructions for fixing the vulnerabilities. When looking for scanning products, these are some of the features to be aware of and to shop for. In both of those respects, ISS' scanner products far exceed most other scanning products on the market today.

CAUTION: Remote scanning products, especially products that scan for denial-of-service (DoS) attacks, can on occasion actually cause the machine they are scanning against or routing devices (firewalls, routers, and hubs) that they are scanning through to either become unavailable or completely crash. After all, a DoS scan is checking for vulnerabilities that would take the system offline, and sometimes, the only way to test for a DoS vulnerability is to actually overload the computer or routing device.

TIP: It is a best practice to have all devices that are being scanned through or scanned against backed up and all configurations saved first (that is, have the router configurations saved and have your Emergency Repair Disks up to date for your WinNT and Win2K machines). Additionally, having someone available to reset those devices in case they do go offline is a great practice to use as well.

After-Hours Enterprise Scanning

Scheduled scans allow the network security administrator to check for vulnerabilities in the enterprise environment when most of the network is not in use. Thus, the scan itself runs less of a chance of interfering with the normal use of the network.

Since a scheduled scan may very well be run after hours, the chance of finding networked machines, in particular desktop machines, that are powered down is greater than during the regular work day. Automatically awaking network interface cards (NICs) will power on the machine when traffic is sent directly to their address.

If a company utilizes automatically awaking NICs, then the scan will successfully bring online all machines that are sleeping, test them for vulnerabilities, and then produce its report. However, a hacker could also use auto-awaking NICs to their benefit. After all, the best time for a hacker to attempt a system break-in is when no one is expected to be watching the network and when most of the workers are away. However, auto-awaking NICs pose a security risk themselves.

CAUTION: Consider disabling the "auto-awake" feature on your PCs' NICs (if they have it and most new NICs do). This causes the NIC to "awake" when traffic is sent directly to them, powering up a sleeping PC. A network intruder could use the auto-awake NICs to power up your company's computers and take control of them over a long holiday weekend.

Protecting the Scan Reports

After you have finished scanning your network, secure the reports, which contain detailed information on your company's known computer vulnerabilities and how to fix them. In the wrong hands, the scan reports could be used for the opposite of what they are intended to do: They could provide a step-by-step guide for exploiting your enterprise's computer system, one vulnerability at a time.

Additional IDS and Scanning Vendors

In addition to ISS' products, a variety of other vendor and freeware programs are also available for scanning and intrusion detection. CyberCop, the Intrusion Detection Scanner by Network Associates, Inc. (**www.nai.com**) offers IDS capabilities similar to ISS' RealSecure. Nessus Security Scanner is a freeware program (available at **www.nessus.org**). Nessus discovers operating system and installed software vulnerabilities across the network and is similar to ISS' Internet Scanner product. Bindview has an extensive suite of scanning products under the new bv-Control product line (formerly Hackershield) that can be found at **www.bindview.com**. Internet Security Systems, maker of RealSecure, SafeSuite, Internet Scanner, System Scanner, and Database Scanner, and whose product is included with the Win2K CD, can be found at **www.iss.net**.

Final Thoughts on Scanning

Use scanning tools to initially harden and then, as an ongoing activity, audit your systems regularly. A variety of scanner tools are available and, used together, they can discover the most comprehensive range of system vulnerabilities possible. Additionally, they can be used to validate each other's results.

In the past, when working with only one set of scanning or audit tools, we've seen results that would indicate all is well in the enterprise environment, only to find out that our false sense of security was indeed a house of cards built on sand—because sometimes scanning tools report false positives or worse, fail to report known vulnerabilities. Only by confirming one set of audits or scans with a second set of tools can security professionals be reasonably certain they are really detecting and patching their security vulnerabilities.

Single Enterprise ID, Single Enterprise Password, or Not?

Statistically speaking, the more IDs and passwords that the users of an enterprise network are required to use, the more often these very same IDs and passwords will be written down and stored in nonsecure locations. We've all seen supposedly secure locations with IDs and passwords posted on the monitors in plain sight for all to see. Why? Because users had more IDs than they could readily remember.

Enforcing computer security by limiting each ID's access to a small portion of the enterprise network means that any single ID has limited value. However, users can then completely obviate this compartmentalized security mechanism by writing all of their IDs down. The most convenient and available location for the security-conscientious user to write their logons down is usually under their keyboards on a yellow Post-It note!

Another way to secure the enterprise network is to use the exact opposite method of the compartmentalized, multiple-ID policy. Assign a single ID and password to all of the users for all of the systems. Statistically, with a single logon to remember, fewer users will allow their logons to be compromised by storing them in non-secure locations. However, if any one multisystem logon is compromised and exploited, the results could be disastrous. So we must carefully consider the ramifications of a successful attack into our computer network if we assign to our users only one enterprise account ID with access to all the systems in the enterprise environment.

Because of the various gateway services and logon synchronization methods, Win2K, Unix, NetWare, SNA, and AppleTalk all enjoy some form of either single sign-on IDs or pass-through authentication services where the same account ID with the same password can exist on both networks. If compromised, a single administrator-level ID could then walk through the entire enterprise network, gaining access to areas of that network that were previously well protected. Any illicit user of that administrator-level ID would then have the ability to reconfigure network access, backdoor access, and foment the removal or deletion of the network's files and records.

So which security logon philosophy is best? That depends on the functional requirements of the network and the needs of those accessing it. For starters, not all systems allow the same logon for all systems. Some computer systems are limited by ID and password length—meaning long IDs and strong passwords may not be a possibility for all systems.

A final thought: If a single logon ID is used, employ, where possible, time restrictions on network access, logging of users' access to systems, guest account disabling, and multifactor authentication.

Better Logons, Better Logging—PKI and Multifactor Authentication

In addition to scanning for vulnerabilities, and then correcting those discovered deficiencies in corporate information systems, non-repudiation of account access and multifactor authentication can be an important aspect of enterprise-wide security as well. They will keep the password guessers out and accurately track the actions of our users.

Strong passwords are not always enough (see Chapter 9 for more information regarding password policies). Utilizing multifactor authentication products like RSA's SecurID (which requires a user to enter both an account ID and a password based on a non-repeating, changing token number and pin code before they are allowed network access) can help to ensure a computer account is really being accessed by an authorized user, and not just someone who guessed their ID and password.

Once the user is authenticated and logged onto the network, Public Key Infrastructure (PKI) enables non-repudiation of user access through trusted certificates within the enterprise network. Simply stated, PKI enables the security administrator to absolutely track users' movements within the network. The security administrator can be certain of the documents that a user ID opened, the database items that they accessed, and the transactions they took part in on the enterprise-wide computer network. For more information on PKI see Web Chapter 1 at **www.osborne.com**.

ENTERPRISE NETWORK INTEROPERABILITY

In this section, we'll examine security as we look at five different methods to connect Win2K to the rest of the world. We'll first explore Win2K and Unix connectivity—version 2.0 of Windows Services for Unix offers extensive cross-platform management and logon authentication options, including two-way Kerberos authentication. Next we'll look at the brand new version of the old Microsoft SNA Gateway product called Microsoft Host Integration Server 2000. In addition to its new name, the Host Integration Server has some great new Win2K and SNA protocol functionality. Then we'll take a look at NetWare and Win2K connectivity options, including Gateway Services for NetWare and Services for NetWare version 5, which includes File and Print Services for NetWare. Next we'll discuss the latest security issues involving Win2K and Apple Macintosh interoperability with Services for Macintosh (SFM) and the optional security component, Microsoft User Authentication Module (MSUAM), which really isn't optional at all if we want a secure computing environment. We wrap up with a section on thin client security with Win2K Terminal Services and Citrix MetaFrame.

Win2K and UNIX Connectivity

Securely administrating a joint Win2K and Unix network was made tremendously easier by Windows Services for Unix (SFU) version 2.0. Because of its substantial feature set and its eye towards security administration, SFU is the preferred method to manage Win2K and Unix connected networks. An upgrade to the original product, SFU 1.0, which was released in 1999, SFU version 2.0 incorporates many security and interoperability enhancements:

▼ Server for NIS enables a Win2K domain control to become the primary server for NIS, allowing both the Unix NIS domain and the Win2K domain to be managed using Active Directory.

■ Server for PCNFS allows Win2K servers and WinNT servers to authenticate clients' access to NFS servers. In effect, the Windows servers emulate PCNFSD servers.

■ Server for NFS allows Win2K servers and WinNT servers to share their resources to NFS clients.

■ Client for NFS is loaded locally on a Windows client and permits access to NFS servers.

■ Gateway for NFS is a server application that allows Windows-based clients to access NFS resources without loading Client for NFS locally. Gateway for NFS is not managed from the Microsoft Management Console (MMC) like the other SFU applications. It is managed separately using the Gateway for NFS Shares application (gwconfig.exe).

■ Two-way password synchronization can be set up from Unix to Windows or from Windows to Unix. Included with SFU are precompiled Single Sign On Daemons (SSOD) for HP-UX 10.3+, Sun Solaris 2.6+, IBM AIX 4.3+, Digital True64 Unix, and Red Hat Linux 5.2 and 6.0. The SSOD source code and make files are included with SFU so that other Unix platform daemons can be custom-compiled at the work site. The password daemon runs on the Unix server to accept password changes from the Windows environment. A Password Authentication Mapper (PAM) is also installed on the Unix server to submit password changes back to the Win2K and WinNT servers.

- Win2K and Unix can now cross-authenticate using Kerberos, a very secure form of authentication. See Chapter 11 for more information.

- The User Name Mapping Server connects Windows and Unix accounts and allows users to access multiple NFS servers while only logging on to one Unix machine. In effect, the User Name Mapping Server becomes an authenticating domain controller for Unix.

- The NIS Active Directory Migration Wizard moves the Unix Network Information Service (NIS) database into the Win2K Active Directory for a single point of administration.

- ▲ SFU Telnet Server supports transparent, trusted Windows NT LAN Manager (NTLM) authentication. Normally, Telnet passwords are sent via cleartext. Unix machines, which lack an NTLM client capability, are unable to utilize the trusted authentication mechanism for Telnet Server. Unix machines still have to log in to Telnet the old-fashioned way.

Additional Notes on Password Synchronization

Unix to Win2K domain synchronization requires that the Password Synchronization service be installed on all domain controllers. Uninstalling the Password service from even one domain controller can result in password functionality failure issues.

Win2K standalones and workgroups can synchronize against Unix computers as well, but only when all Win2K computers in the workgroup have the Password Synchronization service installed. Since workgroups do not share an authentication database, as domain controllers do, the password service independently synchronizes each Win2K computer's local accounts database with the Unix machine. This raises the probability of passwords not matching in all instances.

One final item: Unix IDs are case-sensitive; Windows IDs are not. User accounts on Windows and Unix need to match identically. The User Name Mapping mechanism included with SFU can map names whose cases do not match up. User Name Mapping also supports one-to-many mappings, allowing one Win2K administrator ID to map to many Unix root IDs. In any event, make sure your account IDs either map up or match up.

Management of SFU

Services for Unix is managed through a Microsoft Management Console (MMC) snap-in. Within the MMC console, client machines can be grouped together for easier management, auditing can be enabled with the location and size of the log file determined, and the events to be audited can be configured. SFU can be managed from both the WinNT 4 Workstation and Server and the Win2K Professional and Server platforms.

For more information on Win2K and Unix connectivity, see Steve Burnett's excellent book, *The Windows 2000 and Unix Integration Guide* (Osborne/McGraw-Hill, 2000)

Microsoft Host Integration Server 2000 (Previously Named SNA Server)

Systems Network Architecture (SNA) was originally introduced in 1974 as a connection method for tying together IBM's 3270 product line. As a suite of protocols, SNA has stood the test of time by enabling mainframe hosts, minicomputers, terminals, and PC desktop computers to communicate in either a host-based architecture or peer-to-peer configuration.

Microsoft Host Integration Server 2000 contains all the functionality of the product it replaces, Microsoft SNA Server, with improvements in many areas, including security, scalability, and integration. Microsoft SNA Server and Microsoft Host Integration Server are gateway products that allow desktop computers to access SNA-based data systems. Host Integration Server supports automatic load balancing and automatic fail-over in case of either a host connection or Host Integration Server failure. In addition to TCP/IP, other supported network protocols include IPX, NetBEUI, and the Banyan VINES protocol, SPP.

The following operating system platforms are supported:

▼ Microsoft SNA Server 4.0 with Service Pack 3 will install on Win2K, without supporting the Active Directory tie-ins.

▲ Microsoft Host Integration Server 2000 will install and run on WinNT Server 4.0, minus support for COM+ Object Pooling and Active Directory.

Table 18-1 details the connectivity options in Microsoft Host Integration Server 2000.

AS/36 to Win2K Host Integration Server	802.2 over token ring
	Synchronous Data Link Control (SDLC) over leased or switched telephone circuits
AS/400 to Win2K Host Integration Server	802.2 over Ethernet, token ring, frame relay, or asynchronous transfer mode (ATM)
	SDLC over leased or switched telephone circuits
	X.25/QLLC over private or packet-switched networks

Table 18-1. Connectivity Options in Microsoft Host Integration Server 2000

Mainframe to Win2K Host Integration Server	802.2 over Ethernet, token ring, frame relay, or ATM SDLC over leased or switched telephone circuits X.25/QLLC over private or packet-switched networks ESCON channel over fiber-optic cabling Bus&Tag channel over copper cabling

Table 18-1. Connectivity Options in Microsoft Host Integration Server 2000 *(continued)*

Windows and Mainframe Password Synchronization

Improved in Host Integration Server, one-way Windows-to-mainframe password synchronization no longer requires a third-party host component. Mainframes with RACF, ACF/2, and Top Secret are supported with this new functionality. The Password Expiration Management (PEM) host component makes the changes locally on the mainframe. Two-way password synchronization is still possible with third-party products from either Proginet or NEON Systems. Additionally, the proprietary flat-file ID and password database used by SNA Server 4.0 was replaced in Host Integration Server with a flexible Microsoft Data Engine (MSDE) database that is based on Microsoft's high-end database product, SQL Server.

Host Integration Server General Security

With Host Integration Server, Microsoft provides some excellent general security options that further protect the enterprise environment:

▼ Host Integration Server requires that a Windows domain controller securely authenticate a user before that user is allowed to connect to a host through the Integration Server.

■ Users and groups can be assigned to specific logical units (LUs) or pools of LUs.

■ Workstations can be assigned to specific LUs by either workstation name or IP address.

■ Optionally, all data traffic between the desktop and the Host Integration Server can be encrypted. Host passwords, which are normally sent in cleartext, are protected along with all other desktop-to-Host Integration Server traffic.

▲ Single sign-on (SSO) to host applications is allowed via an automatic logon feature. SSO requires utilization of password synchronization between the mainframe and Host Integration Server.

NetWare and Win2K Connectivity

Over the last dozen years, Novell NetWare has been through numerous revisions of its networking software, with the latest version being 5.*x*. Many options exist for connectivity between Win2K and NetWare. The more commonly employed of those connectivity options are described here, along with specific security recommendations for each.

Client Services for NetWare

CSNW allows Win2K Professional clients to connect directly to NetWare version 2.*x*, 3.*x*, and 4.*x* servers. It allows the Win2K Professional clients to access file and printer resources on NetWare servers utilizing either Novell Directory Services (NDS) or bindery emulation security. Win2K Professional (including Service Pack 1 for Win2K) with CSNW does not currently allow for connectivity to NetWare 5.*x* servers due to CSNW's lack of support for the native IP used by NetWare 5.*x*. Either an IP/IPX gateway or a NetWare Core Protocol (NCP) compatible redirector that supports native IP could be used instead.

Type **net view /network:nw** from a Win2K Professional command prompt to test CSNW. Available NetWare servers will then be listed. Care should be taken in assigning permissions on the NetWare servers for the CSNW clients, and only those users with a need to access the NetWare servers should load CSNW on their Win2K Professional computers. Every additional service running on a computer potentially opens yet another entrance into the enterprise network for the industrious hacker.

Internetwork Packet Exchange/Sequenced Packet Exchange/NetBIOS-Compatible Transport Protocol (NWLink IPX/SPX)

The NWLink IPX/SPX protocol is Microsoft's version of NetWare's IPX/SPX protocols that were popular with earlier implementations of Novell's 2.*x*, 3.*x*, and 4.*x* networks, used before TCP/IP became popular in networking. Since TCP/IP is required for Win2K servers to utilize Active Directory, NWLink IPX/SPX is primarily included with both Win2K Professional and Server as a means of connecting to older NetWare and NetWare-compatible network implementations. Keep in mind that the more protocols loaded up on your network servers and clients, the more potential vulnerabilities will be created on your enterprise network. In short, don't install NWLink IPX/SPX, and any other superfluous protocols, unless required.

Gateway Service for NetWare (GSNW)

A Win2K Server service, GSNW allows both Win2K servers and Microsoft Windows clients access to NetWare 3.*x* and 4.*x* servers. An overloaded gateway can make access speed an issue. Given the choice between GSNW and CSNW, CSNW will deliver better performance. As with CSNW, care should be taken in granting access to the NetWare environment. Only those users with a need for NetWare server access should be granted connectivity through the gateway service. Limiting user connections through GSNW will also help performance for those users actively connecting through it.

Password Resets in NetWare Environments

Rotating passwords regularly is good policy regardless of your operating system. It is worth noting the method to reset NetWare's passwords, as it changed from versions 2.*x* and 3.*x*, where we used the command prompt SYSCON utility, to NetWare 4.*x* and 5.*x*, where the interface went GUI.

To change account passwords in NetWare 3.*x* environments, it will be necessary to run either the SETPASS command or use SYSCON and to change the NetWare account password on each individual NetWare 3.*x* server that the account exists on.

For NetWare 4.*x* and 5.*x* servers, use NWADMN32 to change the account password. The account password will only need to be changed once in a NetWare 4.*x* and 5.*x* environment because the accounts database exists in NDS.

Services for NetWare Version 5.0

Services for NetWare version 5.0 (also known as SFN5), provides a suite of Win2K server and NetWare server integration tools. Included in SFN5 is a directory synchronization tool for NDS and NetWare 3.*x* bindery servers; file and print server tie-ins (see the next section); and migration tools to migrate NetWare directories to the Win2K servers.

FILE AND PRINT SERVICES FOR NETWARE VERSION 5 (FPNW5)   File and Print Services for NetWare (also known as FPNW5) is included with Services for NetWare version 5. With FPNW5, a Win2K server appears as a NetWare file and print server to NetWare servers and clients. An added feature of FPNW5 is that the NetWare servers and clients are not required to alter their software configurations for connectivity back to the Win2K servers.

Win2K and Apple Macintosh Connectivity

Microsoft Win2K Server enables Macintosh connectivity via the Services for Macintosh (SFM). SFM allows a Win2K server to share files and printers, act as a remote access server to the Macintosh clients, and function as an AppleTalk router.

No additional software is required for Macintosh clients to utilize SFM. However, the optional security component, Microsoft User Authentication Module (MSUAM), should be installed. MSUAM provides better encryption for Macintosh client passwords as they log into a Windows Server. The standard Apple User Authentication Module employs weak encryption, and in some cases no encryption, as Macintosh's log into the Win2K domain. Potential password length is increased from 8 to 14 characters.

Additional features of MSUAM include:

▼ Strong encryption when changing a password from the Macintosh client

■ Expiration notices when passwords are within 14 days from expiration

▲ Improved interface for changing account passwords from the Macintosh client

Another component of SFM is File Server for Macintosh, also known as MacFile. MacFile allows a Win2K server directory to act as a Macintosh client-accessible volume. Here are some of the MacFile features:

▼ Valid filenames are enforced. MacFile guarantees that Macintosh files are created with valid Windows NTFS names on the Macintosh-accessible volume.

■ Win2K Server through the MacFile component controls file permissions in the Macintosh volume.

■ AppleTalk is not required as a network protocol. The Macintosh clients can connect to Win2K by using AFP over TCP/IP. TCP/IP is also faster.

■ True size volume reporting is enabled. AppleShare Client 3.8 or newer is required for this feature.

■ Print Server for Macintosh, also known as MacPrint, allows the spooling of print jobs to the Win2K server instead of monopolizing the local client's resources waiting for printing to stop. Windows users can view the print jobs in Print Manager.

■ Dial-in Macintosh clients can simultaneously access both AppleTalk and TCP/IP networks provided that the AppleTalk Control Protocol (ATCP) is installed. ATCP is available in Macintosh Remote Access client 3.0 or newer.

■ Encrypted File System (EFS) support through File System Filters allows encrypting and decrypting of data as it is written to and read from the disk. For more information on EFS, see Chapter 12.

▲ Disk Quota is supported for Macintosh clients. Clients can now be limited to a preset amount of disk space on the Win2K server.

Win2K Terminal Services and Citrix MetaFrame

Terminal Services for Win2K installs as a service on the Win2K server. Citrix MetaFrame installs on top of a Terminal Services installation. Both servers only receive the client keyboard entries and mouse movements, while sending back to the client the screen updates. The Terminal Services server or MetaFrame server performs all the application processing for the client. Terminal Services allows for remote offices with slow WAN links to manage remote Win2K servers, as well as access applications over WAN links that might not support a full client/server processing environment with a Windows-based client. MetaFrame allows both Windows and non-Windows clients to access the server applications. MetaFrame offers additional enhancements beyond Terminal Services offerings to the overall thin client architecture.

Terminal Services Client Support

Terminal Services supports the following client operating systems:

▼ Windows 2000

■ Windows 95/98/Millennium

- Windows NT 3.51 and 4.0
- Windows for Workgroups 3.11
- ▲ Windows CE-based terminals and handheld device clients

MetaFrame Client Support

MetaFrame supports a much broader range of enterprise connectivity options, far exceeding just the Windows-based clients of Terminal Server. MetaFrame supported clients are regularly updated and currently include

- ▼ Windows 2000
- Windows 95/98/Millennium
- 3.51 and 4.0
- Windows for Workgroups 3.11
- Windows CE
- DOS
- Macintosh
- Linux (Red Hat, Slackware, Caldera, SuSE)
- Unix (Solaris, SunOS, SCO, SGI, HP/UX, Compaq Tru64)
- Java (JDK 1.0, 1.1)
- ▲ Browsers (Internet Explorer, Netscape)

TIP: Citrix is continually expanding the supported operating systems for its MetaFrame product. Check the Citrix Systems Web site (**www.citrix.com**) for recent operating system client updates.

Both Terminal Services and MetaFrame allow the majority of the security management to occur at the Server location, with either the Remote Desktop Protocol (RDP) for Terminal Services or the Independent Computing Architecture (ICA) protocol installed for MetaFrame clients. An obvious benefit of either Terminal Services or MetaFrame is the ability to store a database securely in one location, yet allow users worldwide access to that database's information, all the while ensuring the physical security of the database server at a centrally located and controlled facility. Additional benefits such as backups and maintenance of the database server can be more effectively managed from that single location as well.

The client connectivity between either the Terminal server or the MetaFrame server and their clients is encrypted. Terminal Services' RDP ships with full encryption. For MetaFrame, it is strongly recommended that the SecureICA option pack be loaded, allowing 128-bit logon authentication and 40-, 56-, or 128-bit session encryption as well. Check with the Bureau of Export Administration in the U.S. Department of Commerce as to what levels of encryption are exportable. Some countries (France among others) completely prohibit the importation of encryption products.

For more information on Terminal Services and remote administration, see Appendix A. For more information on MetaFrame, contact Citrix Systems, Inc. at **www.citrix.com**.

RECAP

Enterprise-wide networks are higher-risk environments and require more special protection techniques than their smaller network cousins for the following reasons:

▼   The high profile of enterprise-wide networks practically guarantees attempted break-ins due to their organization's size, success, or notoriety.

■   Enterprise-wide networks are widely dispersed and not always well guarded at remote locations.

■   Their perimeters have numerous potential points of entrance.

■   Enterprise-wide networks are heavily inter-connected—a break-in at a poorly guarded remote location almost always allows connectivity to the network segment that headquarters or important divisions use.

■   They contain numerous systems types, each uniquely vulnerable, each adding to their organization's total number of vulnerabilities.

■   The total number of vulnerabilities will far exceed a smaller network's number.

■   Human engineering security exploits are easier in larger environments where every individual is not personally known.

■   Systems can be connected to their customers, partners, and vendors.

■   Single logons for multiple systems are usually present in some form, allowing for cross-system exploitations. Once a single system is breached, the entire network is potentially at risk.

▲   Enterprise-wide networks are a bigger target because the overall dollar value of the information stored in their computer systems is typically many times greater than what is stored in a smaller network.

Given these reasons, enterprise systems necessarily lend themselves to unique security requirements and specialized defenses. And among these defenses, initial network design, well-researched system configurations, current documentation, automated monitoring, and proactive scanning should be the first line of defense for the enterprise administrator in the highly connected world of enterprise networks.

PART V

Other Issues

PART V

Other Issues

CHAPTER 19

Securing the
Microsoft Internet
Information Server

The World Wide Web is built on top of the Internet and uses the TCP/IP protocols to transport information between Web clients and Web servers. As everyone has become aware, Web servers are not just for the Internet. Web servers also provide a very versatile way to make information available to internal network (*intranet*) users. Windows 2000 (Win2K) includes the Microsoft Internet Information Server, so your startup costs for implementing Web-based intranet or Internet servers are minimal.

Web browsers are used to access information from Web servers on any network; it doesn't matter whether it is an intranet or the Internet. They remove the mystery of the Internet and eliminate the need for users to understand arcane commands. Most browsers are free and most people begin accessing resources the first time they use a browser with little or no training. Because of this, it is worth your while to consider building your own internal networks using Web technologies.

Perhaps more importantly from a historical perspective, using a Web browser as the client front end for an application means that the client doesn't have to know what type of computer and what operating system is being used for the Web server or back-end application.

This chapter discusses security issues for the Microsoft Internet Information Server (IIS) version 5.0. If you plan to set up a Web server for internal or external access, this chapter will help you set up and maintain security for the server.

NOTE: This chapter touches on security issues for Microsoft Web clients and servers only. It does not discuss other vendors' Web products, nor does it explore the incredibly vast issue of security on the Web. For more information on Web security issues in general, check **www.gocsi.com** and **www.w3.org**.

INTRODUCTION TO IIS

The Microsoft Internet Information Server is primarily a Web server, but also an FTP, SMTP, NNTP, and potentially a proxy server. IIS was originally released with Windows NT version 3.5.1 and has been an optional component of Windows NT 4.0 since its initial delivery. Some of the more notable features are

- ▼ HTTP 1.1 compliance
- ■ Integrated management console administration
- ■ Delegation of administration tasks
- ■ Command-line and scriptable administration
- ■ Configuration backup and restore
- ■ Virtual servers

- ■ SNMP support
- ■ Logging
- ■ Application and component process isolation
- ■ Support for any ActiveX scripting language
- ■ Support for DCOM
- ■ Win2K Server security integration
- ■ Domain blocking by IP address and host name
- ▲ Link to AD for client certificate mapping

IIS as an Interface to Other Windows 2000 Systems and Services

You can view IIS as an interface to certain services running on the system. This is true for any Web server on any operating system that serves more than static HTML pages. The Win2K IIS server (IIS 5.0) provides a limited, but very functional, set of methods for accessing the following system resources:

- ▼ File system (through directory browsing and HTTP 1.1 GET and PUT commands)
- ■ User accounts (through server-side programs)
- ■ SQL Server (through Active Server Pages and other back-end CGI-type applications)
- ■ Certificate server (through executables)
- ■ Event logs
- ▲ Active Directory

HTTP VS. HTML

The underlying protocol for Web servers is Hypertext Transfer Protocol (HTTP). HTTP supports hyperlinks in documents. When a client running a Web browser types a server name (or IP address) in the Address field of a browser, the browser locates the address on the network and a connection is made to the designated Web server.

Web pages contain hyperlinks, which reference other information. When you click a hyperlink, you jump to another part of the same page, a new page at the same Web site, or to another Web site. You might also execute a program, display a picture, or download a file.

All of this hyperlinking is the work of the Hypertext Markup Language (HTML), which works in concert with HTTP. HTTP is the command and control protocol that sets up communication between a client and a server and passes commands between the two systems. HTML, on the other hand, is the document formatting language. Note that while HTML is the current format of most documents on the Web, the Extensible Markup Language (XML) is up and coming and will be used extensively in the future.

Who Is Steering the Ship?

The *Internet Engineering Task Force* (IETF) is an international community of network designers, operators, vendors, and researchers concerned with the evolution of Internet architecture and the operation of the Internet. The IETF accomplishes its function by using working groups, which are organized by topic into several areas (e.g., routing, transport, security, etc.). The IETF is open to anyone who would like to participate (**www.ietf.org**).

The *World Wide Web Consortium* is an organization dedicated to leading "the World Wide Web to its full potential by developing common protocols that promote its evolution and ensure its interoperability." W3C is a membership-based organization. See **www.w3c.org** for more information.

The W3C and IETF are ultimately in control of the process of adding to and refining the Web-related protocols that are used on the Internet. If you want to see what is the next greatest thing in the world of the Internet, the IETF is the place to start. When dealing specifically with Web-related protocols, start by checking with the W3C. In most cases, the IETF defers to the W3C when it comes to Web-related issues. However, you should be aware that some Web-related issues are delegated to the IETF. For example, the IETF has done the work on digitally signing XML documents, which is expected to be adopted by the W3C.

The Web Client-Server Model

As shown in Figure 19-1, the client makes a request to the Web server and the Web server sends HTML information back to the client. The client's Web browser properly formats and displays the HTML information from the server.

The HTTP protocol sets up the connection between the client and the server and in many cases that connection must be secure. For example, assume your company sets up an Internet Web server to provide sensitive documents to its mobile work force. These documents should not be accessible to anyone else (since the site is connected to the Internet, anyone could attempt to access them). To prevent unauthorized access, you set up private directories and require logon authentication. You can also do the following:

▼ Secure the TCP/IP channel between the client and the server by encrypting all the data that is transmitted.

■ Use certificates (digital IDs) to prove the authenticity of the Web client.

■ Use Win2K logon authentication to verify a user's access to his or her account.

▲ Use access controls (NTFS permissions) to restrict access to folders on the server.

Channel encryption and certificates are optional features that are handled by the security protocol layer as pictured in Figure 19-1 (in IIS 5.0 this is implemented as an ISAPI filter into the Security Support Provider Interface (SSPI). The SSPI is discussed in detail in

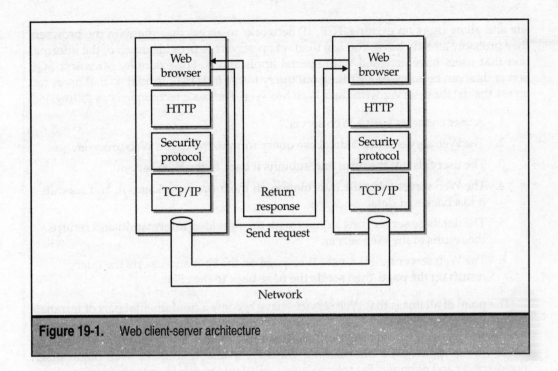

Figure 19-1.   Web client-server architecture

Chapter 11). To prove authenticity over the Internet, you need a *personal certificate* that is issued by a Certification Authority (CA), such as Verisign (**www.verisign.com**). To get this certificate, you go through a process of establishing your credentials with the CA and, if everything checks out, you are issued a certificate. This process is similar to applying for a credit card, where the bank is analogous to the CA. Servers also need certificates to prove their authenticity.

The certificate is used automatically when you connect with Web sites that require you to prove your identity. If necessary, the Web server can contact the CA to check your credentials in the same way that a retailer checks your credit card when you make a purchase.

These same techniques can be implemented on internal networks by installing certificate services on Win2K Server computers. Microsoft Certificate Services allow you to use an in-house server to issue certificates to your own clients based on your own requirements.

Keep in mind that Web Services provide a somewhat platform independent way to provide information to people on your internal network as well as on the Internet (note that vendors will always add their own "features" which will "differentiate" their product from others). With the secure channel and authentication features of Microsoft's Internet Explorer (and other browsers), you can establish secure connections between clients and servers on your network with little trouble.

Many organizations have made the transition to the Web client-server model because of its heterogeneous way of providing information to users. You can quickly set up a Web site and allow users on existing TCP/IP networks to access that site with the browsers they probably already have. You can then set up servers to provide much of the information that users have accessed with special applications. For example, Microsoft SQL Server data can be accessed by filling out query forms in HTML format so that users can access the database server with their Web browser. The basic technique is as follows:

1. A user connects with a Web server.

2. The Web server sends a database query form to the user's Web browser.

3. The user fills out the form and submits it back to the Web server.

4. The Web server takes the information off the form, repackages it, and submits it to a back-end database server.

5. The database server runs a query with the provided information and returns the results to the Web server.

6. The Web server builds a new Web page on the spot and inserts the query results on the page, then sends the page back to the client.

The point of all this is that Web services have become a fundamental part of intranets and have for the most part defined the Internet. The graphic nature of Web pages makes them attractive and the hypertext capabilities make them a much more interesting and useful way to disseminate information. Tools are available to make Web pages much more exciting and dynamic. For internal users, all of this translates into an interface that is easy to use and learn and that is consistent across many platforms. When you access systems with a Web browser, you rarely know or care about the type of server you are accessing. In this sense, Web browsers have become universal clients.

NOTE: The concept of a universal client is far from arrived. The fact that companies are still "enhancing" basic functionality almost guarantees that 100 percent functional compatibility will never happen.

The mere fact that even your old grade school probably has a Web site indicates that this technology is everywhere. In fact, with the Active Desktop that came in IE 4.0, the Web browser technology became the standard interface. Users access information on their own computer or anywhere on internal networks or the Internet in the same way.

BASIC IIS CONCEPTS

The following sections describe some of the basic concepts that are used in Web servers in general and IIS in particular.

Directory Structures

A typical Web server uses directories to store information and operates like any file server, except that the HTTP protocol is used to make requests for files. In most cases, those files are HTML documents, but, as you'll see, Web users can use HTTP to request just about any type of information on a Web server.

The Microsoft Internet Information Server sets up two directories when it is first installed. One branches from your `%systemroot%\System32` directory called `inetsrv`. This directory holds files and information related to the running and administration of the IIS server. The second branches from `%systemdrive%\Inetpub` by default, but you have the option to change it in the install. It has several directories that contain some sample HTML files and the `wwwroot` directory. When users connect to your Web server, they are automatically placed in the home directory for that server, which by default is the `wwwroot` directory, and the default file for that directory is automatically sent to and displayed on the user's Web browser.

This strategy of displaying a default document is the standard operating model for most Web servers, although you can alter the operation. The default document in the `wwwroot` directory is basically the *home page* for the Web site. From it, users navigate to other pages on the site. To create a home page for your site, use the HTML coding language and save the file in the `wwwroot` directory with the name `default.htm`.

By placing hyperlink buttons on your home page, you can let users link to any other directory and display the default document that exists in those directories. So the directory structure reflects the hyperlink structure of your Web pages in many cases. Alternatively, though, you can put all your hyperlink documents in a single directory. Refer to *Web Design: The Complete Reference* by Thomas Powell (Osborne/McGraw-Hill, May 2000) and to Microsoft TechNet for more information on this topic.

Two things can happen when users browse directories on the Internet Information Server (assuming the feature is set that allows directory browsing). If a directory has a file called `default.htm`, that document is displayed on the client's Web browser. If the file doesn't exist, a list of files in the directory appears, as shown in Figure 19-2. Each filename in the list appears as a hyperlink. If you click one of these hyperlink filenames, the file opens. You can also right-click a file to see the context menu, then choose one of the options listed. For example, you can choose Save Target As to save the file on your own system. In this respect, Web servers act like file servers, dishing up documents to Web clients.

NOTE: Directory browsing is disabled by default, and enabling it on Internet-connected servers could be dangerous because it would allow Internet users to see what files reside in your Web directories, as opposed to getting just the Web pages that you desire them to access.

After the server is installed, it is immediately ready to receive connections. There is one trick to this though; you will get an "Under Construction" page if you try to access it from a browser that is not on the server. This is because you have not defined a default page for this server. To get rid of the "Under Construction" page, just define a default page for that site. The Web page that is displayed when you run the local browser will describe the overall functions of IIS, and help you set up your own Web site. IIS comes with some sample optional pages as well. The sample pages are used to illustrate some of the more advanced features that IIS supports.

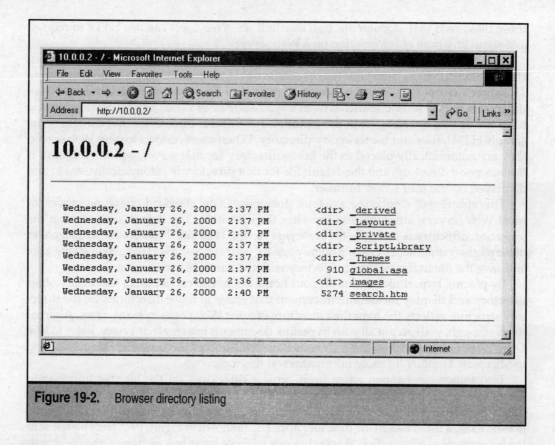

Figure 19-2.   Browser directory listing

CAUTION: It is highly recommended that you do *not* install the sample pages on a production server. Install them on a test platform to get familiar with the look and feel, but the security issues inherent in sample pages are not worth the risk. If you did install the optional sample pages, delete them before moving the server into production to prevent possible security problems. The sample pages are located in the `Default Web Site` directory.

Virtual Servers

Although Web servers are traditionally linked to a single domain name, the Microsoft Internet Information Server lets you configure several domain names on the same computer. For example, a single server could support domains such as **marketing.example.com**, **sales.example.com**, and **support.example.com**. This is possible because the Win2K Server will support multiple network interface cards and/or multiple IP addresses per card for the same computer.

When users attach to one of the domains, they may think that they are attaching to an individual server when in fact they are attaching to "virtual servers" running on a single computer. The thing about virtual servers is that they have to have a unique IP address and port number pair (IP/Port). So if you want a single server to listen on port 80, then each virtual server must have a different IP address. If you want them all associated with the same IP address, then they must have different port numbers.

When creating virtual servers, the virtual IP address will listen on all ports (except tcp139) bound to the real IP address. Take care to implement port-filtering ACLs on routers and firewalls to protect not only the real IP address, but also the virtual IP addresses.

> **NOTE:**   Virtual servers are also referred to as *virtual sites* or just *sites*.

Virtual Directories

As with virtual servers, you can have directories within a site that are not part of the main document tree. These are called *virtual directories*. These directories can be on the local machine, a network share, or a redirect to another server.

> **TIP:**   You should carefully weigh *any* decision to use network shares for virtual directories. All access is made in the context of the user you configure for that directory. This configuration has many potential security pitfalls, and should not be used if security is an issue. Also do *not* use network shares for Internet-based machines.

> **TIP:**   Make sure *all* file systems are NTFS!

Used in conjunction with the virtual servers, virtual directories allow you to host multiple sites, each with its own separate directory space and/or some shared file location.

Server Programs

Server programs, also known as *applications*, are used to add functionality to your Web site. When the Web first began, everyone was elated with static content and plain old HTML pages. Times have changed and now we are used to dynamic content. To provide this functionality, you need applications. You can write server applications using many different interfaces. IIS supports the following methods:

▼   Common Gateway Interface (CGI)

■   Extensible Markup Language (XML)

- Active Server Pages (ASP)
- Windows Scripting Components (via ASP)
- Active Directory Service Interface (ADSI)
- ▲ Internet Server API (ISAPI)

It is beyond the scope of this book to discuss all the aspects of the various content programming languages, but ASPs are probably the most widely used method to date on IIS. You can expect this to be replaced with XML over the next few years. One advantage of ISAPI is that the compiled programs (DLLs) can get loaded into the Internet server's memory and stay there, thus improving performance. Another advantage of ISAPI is achieved by pluggable filters, which allow preprocessing of requests and post-processing of responses. This feature permits site-specific handling of HTTP requests and responses.

Once you've written programs and scripts, you place them in the appropriate directory on the server. Internet Information Server creates a virtual directory called \SCRIPTS for this purpose. This directory has *Execute* permission (discussed later), so users can run programs. If the program interacts with other files, the Internet anonymous user account (or whatever account people will use to access your server) must have the right permissions to use those files.

Keep in mind that you are allowing remote users to run programs on the Internet Information Server. These programs might have a bug or hole that some hacker could exploit to break into your system. To prevent someone from uploading a virus or other destructive program and running it, never grant Write and Execute permissions on any directory that is accessible by Web users. The only exception to this rule should be in rare cases, such as with trusted users who have been fully authenticated.

TIP: It is also a security necessity to conduct code reviews for any application that is placed on the IIS server. The IIS server is one of the major focal points for hackers and thus you need to take extra steps to ensure the applications on the IIS server are coded with security as a primary attribute, not an afterthought.

Some Points on ISAPI Filters

▼ You can install ISAPI filters both in a server's master properties (global filters) and/or an individual Web site's (virtual servers) properties (site filters).

■ Global and site filters are merged when accessing the site, and the filters are run in order of priority. The global filters run first, and filters with the same priority from the same level (global or site) are run in the order specified in the properties.

▲ ISAPI filters are always run in the server process.

Database Integration

The Microsoft Internet Information Server integrates with Microsoft's SQL Server database system as well as other database systems. This enables content providers and businesses to provide information that is located in structured storage or use the input of users to update and/or access information in databases.

The Internet Server provides access to databases through a component called the Internet Database Connector (IDC), which is part of the Internet Server API (ISAPI). The Internet Connector uses ODBC (Open Database Connectivity) to gain access to databases. Because ODBC provides a layer of connectivity between back-end databases and front-end clients, it is used to provide connections to a variety of back-end database systems.

TIP: ODBC uses many different transports, protocols, and port numbers. These are referred to as *connectors*. It is very important that you install only the ODBC connectors you are *currently* using, and remove all the rest. The Jet and Text ODBC connectors are two connectors that have frequently been used to breach security and should not be run when security matters.

AUTHENTICATION

When a user connects to the Internet Information Server, all access to resources on the server is handled by whatever Internet services are running on that computer, either World Wide Web (WWW), Network News Transfer Protocol (NNTP), Simple Mail Transport Service (SMTP), or File Transfer Protocol (FTP). More specifically, the server "impersonates" the client so that users never access objects directly. This is true for all Web access to a Win2K system. For example, a Web user makes a request to the HTTP service, which presents the credentials of the user (username/password) to the security system for comparison to the access list of the resource being accessed.

Most Web servers on the Internet allow anyone to access information without prior logon. However, some sites (the *Wall Street Journal* site, for instance) require subscription accounts; you must register to get a password before you can access certain information. Note the following:

▼ Servers that let you log on without typing a password provide what is called *anonymous logon*. All anonymous users access the server under the same account (similar to the Guest account), which makes it difficult for administrators to know who is accessing the server.

▲ Logon access requires users to supply a username and password to gain access to restricted resources. Typically, a Web site will have some anonymous access but require logon when users attempt to access restricted areas. Some servers require logon right at the "front door." Logon access requires some type of authentication. This is typically a username and password, but Microsoft supports client side certificates for authentication.

Anonymous

When you install the Microsoft Internet Information Server, a special account is created with the name IUSR_*computername* (we refer to this account as the *anonymous user account*). This account is given the right to log on locally, so when someone accesses the Web server without providing any sort of logon credentials, they are granted access to the server under this user account as if they are logging on locally (at the console). The account is a member of the Everyone, Authenticated Users, Interactive, Guests Local, and Domain Users groups. When this option is enabled (the default), users can access directories in which the Everyone, Authenticated Users, Guests group, and/or the IUSR_*computername* accounts have access.

The anonymous user account does not require users to enter a username or password, which makes it easy for users to access your server—but you won't know who is accessing the server. Note the following:

▼ All requests from Web clients use this account if you allow only anonymous logons.

■ The account cannot delete or change files on NTFS file systems by default because it has only Read rights in Web server directories or Execute rights in script and program directories.

■ Because the account has limited rights, users cannot download files to the server or execute files except in designated directories.

■ On domain controllers, this account is added to the Active Directory.

▲ Other Web servers at your site will have similar anonymous accounts, but you can create a single anonymous account for the domain if necessary, then update the Anonymous User account information (as described in "Directory Security Controls") so that the Anonymous Logon Username field has the new name.

How Anonymous Users Access Directories

An important concept to keep in mind is that any user accessing Web services can access only files and directories, which are already defined in the default Web site tree or referenced by a virtual directory.

After a Web directory is created, there are three conditions when anonymous users can access a designated directory:

▼ If the Everyone group has at least Read or Execute rights in the directory.

■ If the IUSR_*computername* account has been specifically granted at least Read or Execute rights in the directory.

▲ If the Guests group (which IUSR_*computername* is a member of) has been specifically granted at least Read or Execute rights in the directory.

If you create a directory and you only want anonymous users to access the directory, remove the Everyone and Guests groups from the permissions list and add only the IUSR_*computername* account.

If the IUSR_computer account or one of the groups that user is in do not have permissions to access a directory, then anonymous users cannot access the directory. Removing the everyone group and this account is how you restrict a directory to prevent anonymous Web users and require logon access. Logon access is preferred using Basic, Digest, Integrated, or Certificates, as described next.

Basic (Clear Text)

The Basic option requires users to enter a username and password to access a secure folder. This is useful if you want to set up a subscription service that requires users to log on with a password once they have been registered with the service, as discussed earlier. This option sends passwords in scrambled clear text, a code that's easy for any hacker to break. The password could be compromised, and if it is the same password that users use to log in to more secure accounts, a hacker who captures the password could gain unauthorized access to those accounts. Use this option with care. However, if you require logon for users who access non-sensitive information, then perhaps you require passwords only as a "formality" and encryption is not essential.

TIP: If you use this type of authentication and password security is an issue, be sure to use a secure communications link with it. This is discussed more later in "Enabling Secure Communications."

Digest Authentication

This is a new feature in IIS 5.0. It provides the same basic functionality of Basic authentication, but it does not transmit the password in clear text over the network. The password (a.k.a. *authentication credentials*) are passed through a one-way function, to produce a hash (a.k.a. *message digest*). A *hash* is a cryptographic function that is not easily reversed (that is, it is very computationally expensive to reverse the hash to get the original text). The one downside to this type of authentication is that it can only be used with Win2K clients. If it is selected in mixed-mode domains, non-Win2K clients will resort to Basic authentication, thus dropping the total security level to Basic.

TIP: Use this instead of Basic if you have browsers that support Internet Exporer. That means that it is probably not a realistic option for Internet-based sites.

Digest authentication is a feature of HTTP 1.1, and may not be supported in older browsers. If this option is selected, and the browser does not support it, the server will reject the request and send the client an error message. You must have a Windows 2000 domain to use this feature.

Integrated Windows Authentication

This form of authentication uses the Kerberos v5 authentication protocol and/or the NTLM authentication protocol. Both are used by default, but if the browser does not support Kerberos, then only the NTLM challenge/response is used. These protocols use encryption techniques that prevent passwords from being transmitted across the network in the clear. However, at the time of this writing, only Microsoft Internet Explorer browsers support this type of authentication.

When the Web server receives a client request that contains credentials, the anonymous logon user account is bypassed and the credentials are used by the service to log the user on.

When this option is set, the header information in the user's HTTP requests, which contains the user's credentials (username and password), is used to log the user in to the restricted directory. This option is mostly used if the Web server is connected to an intranet and users on the network have already been logged in, although it can also be used over the Internet.

TIP: Integrated Windows authentication does not work over HTTP Proxy connections, so it is really only suited for intranet-based use, when the user and the Web server are in the same Active Directory forest.

Client Certificates

When using Secure Sockets Layer (see the "Enabling Secure Communications" section later in the chapter) you can set a site or directory to require a valid client certificate to access it. This differs from "authenticating users" (which is covered next in "Client Certificate Mapping"). You have the option to Ignore, Accept, or Require client-side certificates.

NOTE: If you require client-side certificates, you must require SSL connections.

Client Certificate Mapping

If you want those client certificates to map to actual user accounts for access permissions, then this is the option you should use. This option allows you to actually authenticate users if they present a valid client-side certificate. A certificate will contain pertinent information that is used to map that certificate (1 to 1) or a number of certificates (many to 1) to a given user account.

The options using client certificates are becoming increasingly popular but require a significant investment in a Public Key Infrastructure (PKI) to be scalable (see Web

Chapter 1 at **www.osborne.com**). If you have an existing PKI, then these options can provide a very secure method of server access and client authentication.

CheckCertRevocation Registry Entry

This key specifies whether client certificates are checked for revocation by IIS. This can be a performance issue, but should be set in a high-security environment, or if the revocation process is local. The following IIS Registry key setting is where you enable this functionality. Keep in mind this line was broken for readability and is actually one line. It is disabled by default and should be set to 1 to be enabled.

```
HKEY_LOCAL_MACHINE\SYSTEM\CurrentControlSet\Services\InetInfo\
Parameters\CheckCertRevocation
```

General Comments About the Maturity of PKI

While the whole concept of client-side certificates and using them for authentication is cutting edge (at this time), there is a problem with the immaturity of PKI. Because you need to have a method of administering the public-private key pairs, unless you have a very robust PKI deployed, you will find that using certificates in general requires much more administrative overhead than other methods of authentication. Please see Web Chapter 1 for more on Win2K Certificate Services.

Using Impersonation

All document (not necessarily scripts) access is done with *impersonation* (that is, a program or process such as IIS is run on behalf of a user, or more specifically it is run under the security context of that user). The purpose of a security context is to give the process running on behalf of users no more access to files and resources than they would have if they were running it themselves. As was described earlier, the IUSR_*computername* is the typical account that is used for impersonation, but if a user has authenticated, their credentials will be used. That means after a user is authenticated to the IIS server, any operation (such as accessing an HTML file) the Web server performs for the authenticated user will be in the security context of that user rather than the security context of the anonymous user (IUSR_*computername*).

Host-Based Authentication: IP Address Filtering

Another security option is the ability to restrict which hosts can and cannot access your Web site. You can specify who can access your Web server based on IP addresses or DNS domain name. For example, you might want to block the IP address or DNS domain name of a competitor to prevent people in that company from accessing your server or block the connections of someone who is overrunning your server with requests in a denial-of-service attack.

There are two models for specifying IP addresses:

▼ **Granted access**   Allows all hosts access to the Web server, except for the IP addresses that are listed.

▲ **Denied access**   Denies all hosts access to the Web server except for the IP addresses that are listed.

Restricting access by IP address is not a foolproof security measure. A hacker or someone else who you want to keep out of your system can simply move to a computer with a different IP address or change his or her IP address. It is, however, an effective way to block known users on your own internal network or users who are flooding your network with unnecessary or intrusive requests.

AUTHORIZATION

You use the Win2K Server security features in combination with the directory access controls in the Microsoft Internet Information Server to authorize Web users to access your server. Techniques for implementing these features are discussed in this section.

Directory security is fundamental to the security of your IIS server (no matter what service it is running). It allows you to set appropriate NTFS and Web directory access control settings that will ensure that any new file or directory created will inherit the proper permissions.

If you do not take the time to plan and set this up right, you can be almost assured that at some point your server will become an intrusion statistic.

Directory Security Controls

Web directories have two main protections: Directory Access Permissions and Filesystem Access Permissions. Both of these will need to be set for both "virtual" and normal directories that you define on your server. Note that if you add a subdirectory to a physical directory that is already listed in the site, you don't need to do anything to the new subdirectory, as it will inherit from its parent. Once you have added a new Web directory to the Web site, you will need to configure the Web-based controls on it.

Directory Access Permissions

There are four types of access control that you can specify for the Web directory permissions: Script source access, Read, Write, and directory browsing. These can be applied to regular and virtual directories.

SCRIPT SOURCE ACCESS   This kind of access control allows users to access the source of script files. Read or Write must be selected or this option is not available. This is primarily used for WebDAV publishing (discussed later in this chapter in the "Dealing with Web

Distributed Authoring and Versioning (WebDAV)" section). If your publishing directory has script files, you can deny access to the publishing functionality by making sure Script source access is not granted. If you are not using WebDAV (discussed later), then do not use it.

NOTE: This feature is not the same as the ASP Encoded Script feature, which supports a new script encoding that makes the programmatic logic unreadable.

READ   With the Read setting, users can view the files in the directory but cannot change the files or add files of their own. This is the most secure option and should be the default for all directories. You enable the Read option on publishing directories and disable it on directories that contain programs and scripts so clients can't download your programs or read source scripts.

People forget this and allow hackers the ability to download the source files for server-based applications. This allows for the perusal of source code in hopes of finding coding problems for future exploitation.

WRITE   With the Write setting, users can change file and directory contents as well as properties. This option supports the HTTP 1.1 PUT feature and allows users to upload files as well as change the contents of any file in the directory. This is the most insecure option as it gives remote users the ability to alter Web site contents. Use this with caution! It is not wise to enable this for directories that hold scripts or executables.

DIRECTORY BROWSING   This option allows users to view the files in a directory if no default page is configured. This is very similar to viewing local directory resources in Windows Explorer or FTP sites in browsers. Virtual directories will *not* appear in this listing; users must know the path to the virtual directory to access it. This option should *not* be set on Web directories. It gives too much information to people who are just perusing.

Controlling Access with NTFS

Don't forget that NTFS permissions are *always* applicable. So when setting up any Web server, you should be sure to utilize NTFS as your file system type and set permissions appropriately. Refer to Chapter 12 for more information.

Directory security and file security may not meet all of your needs. Sites desiring to create highly secure sites have resorted to using read-only media, such as CD-ROMs, for their Web pages and scripts. Often these sites have found that this has been insufficient. Attackers have been able to redirect the site to a different server through a variety of mechanisms. Remember that securing the file and directory permissions are only one aspect of securing an IIS server, although a very important aspect that is too frequently overlooked.

TIP: The default NTFS permissions for the physical paths that correspond to Web directories should grant Read Only access to the Everyone group, then grant higher permissions to groups who need it.

Application Protection

We already talked about the type of applications that we can run on the server. Now we will look at one means of securing them. IIS offers you the ability to separate applications into different processes. This is called *application protection*. There are three application protection modes under which the application is authorized and will run:

▼ **Low**   Same process as Web services (in-process).

■ **Medium**   A pooled process, separate from the Web services (out-of-process).

▲ **High**   Individual processes, separate from Web services (out-of-process).

These different options provide a means of protecting applications from stomping all over each other or causing the IIS server to crash. Medium is the default protection level.

When IIS is installed, two accounts are created: IUSR_*computername* and IWAM_*computername*, where *computername* is the name of the computer where IIS is installed. With the Low security setting, IIS uses the IUSR_*computername* account to service anonymous requests. Typically, IIS runs Web applications in the same process space as the IIS server; this is called an *in-process extension*. This means that a poorly behaving program may cause the IIS server or Web Service to crash (I differentiate, because IIS can run more than just the Web Service). This would result in a denial of service to all users of the IIS server. A successful buffer overflow attack on an in-process extension could also accomplish this.

IIS also provides support for out-of-process extensions in the Medium and High levels. These run under the context of the IWAM_*computername* account. An out-of-process extension runs in a process created by the Microsoft Transaction Server (MTS). A poorly behaving out-of-process extension cannot crash the IIS server or the Web Service. It can only crash the MTX.EXE process.

The tradeoff is that an out-of-process service should not result in a denial-of-service attack that affects all users, subject to specific application implementation details. It is important to understand though, that successful buffer overflow attacks of both types of extensions have the same potential security risks. This is because both the IIS server process and the MTX process are run as the LocalSystem account and do "impersonation" to get the permissions associated with either the IUSR_*computername* or the IWAM_*computername*, respectively.

Application Mappings

Another authorization-related feature is the ability to associate file extensions in a given virtual directory with an ISAPI or CGI program. IIS comes with a set of pre-configured "mappings" to support the most common applications. You may want to remove the mapping that you are not using to prevent inadvertent use of a default program or file that was not removed.

UNMAP UNUSED MAPPINGS   By default, IIS has a number of mappings that are not normally used in the day-to-day operations of the Web server, but are used by attackers. For example, the Microsoft Index Server uses `.idq` files, so if you don't use the Index Server, then you don't need the mapping.

The `.idq` example used is a common attack on IIS servers to determine the physical path of the Web directory. You should remove all unused file mappings; you can always add it later if you need it. By removing these mappings, you are taking just another step to make your server more secure. The mappings can be changed in the Internet Service Manager (ISM) | Home Directory | Application Settings for the Web server you are administering.

You can figure out what mappings you can delete by looking through your site and determining the extensions that you are using. A programmatic way of doing it is by using a site analysis tool such as Site Server Express or FrontPage.

TIP: Remember to record mapping settings prior to removing them, so you can redefine them later.

Application Permissions

Along with directory permissions, IIS provides the ability to limit what permissions the applications have in the directory. These are known as Execute Permissions and can have one of three values:

▼   **None**   This prevents any programs or scripts from running.

■   **Scripts Only**   This enables applications, such as ASP scripts, Perl scripts, or JavaScripts (see the previous "Application Mappings" section) in this Web directory and all of its subdirectories, to run. These applications must be mapped to a script engine.

▲   **Scripts and Executables**   This allows *any* application to run in this directory.

Scripts Only is safer than Scripts and Executables because it is more limiting. You should only use Scripts and Executables when you *have* to.

AUDITING

This section discusses the logging functionality of the IIS server.

Setting Up Logging

Logs are an essential part of security, as well as useful in troubleshooting. The IIS server has very good logging capability, but you have to enable it and use it wisely. You can collect information and store it in ASCII files or an ODBC-compliant database for later analysis. IIS logging is not integrated into the native Windows 2000 Event Logging System, while ASP error logging is optionally integrated. It should be noted that object access, which may be triggered by IIS, may appear in the native Event Logs. Please refer to Chapter 13 for more detailed information on native event logging. The logs in IIS can contain information such as:

▼ Who has visited your site

■ What pages and resources the visitor accessed

▲ When a particular piece of information was last viewed

TIP: Along with regular security auditing, you can use the logs to determine popular content and possible needs for future resource allocation.

To enable logging, you use the ISM and select the site you want to administer. Select Enable Logging, and determine the format of the log files. The options you have for IIS are

▼ Microsoft IIS Log File Format

■ NCSA Common Log File Format

■ ODBC Logging

▲ W3C Extended Log File Format

Your selection should be consistent with other Web and IIS servers on your network. This ensures that investment in log analysis tools will be effective for this IIS server as well. The most commonly used Web server log file format is W3C Extended Log File Format, which is a good default. You should be very careful in selecting an ODBC-based log file, as it probably logs to a database on a central logging computer. This could cause performance problems as well as missing logs, if there is a network problem.

Once you have selected the log file format, you can configure the properties for that specific format. The General Properties tab is the same for all the non-ODBC log file formats, and only the W3C log format has extended properties, which we will look at.

The General Properties are used for the maintenance of the log files. These settings should be based on your organization's standard practices, as well as disk resources on the IIS server. Nonetheless, it should be consistent throughout your organization. Figure 19-3 shows the Extended Properties tab of the Properties page for the log entry. There is an extensive list of attributes that you can log and it is beyond the scope of this book to describe them all. The Help button on that page gives a detailed explanation of all the options. You should, at a minimum, log the following: Date, Time, Client IP Address, User Name, Method, URI Stem, URI Query, and Referrer.

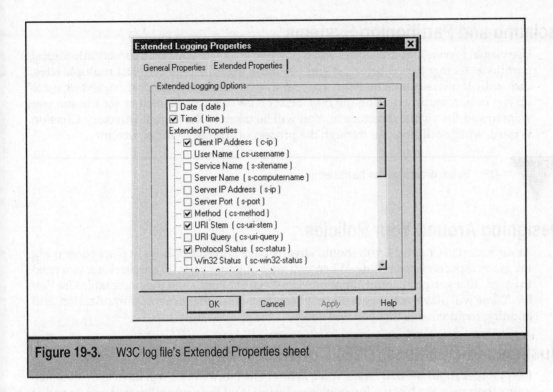

Figure 19-3. W3C log file's Extended Properties sheet

Setting Up Active Server Page (ASP) Logging

You can have ASP errors sent to the Windows Application EventLog. To do this, you must enable the Write Unsuccessful Client Requests to EventLog option in the Process Options properties. Another ASP logging option, AspErrorsToNTLog, has to deal with which ASP errors are sent to the EventLog. AspErrorsToNTLog is a metabase option and must be set programmatically. If it has a value of FALSE, then only a certain subset of ASP errors are sent to the EventLog. If it is set to TRUE, then all ASP errors are sent. For more information on the metabase and programmatic administration of IIS, see the online Help section entitled "Administering IIS Programmatically."

TIP: Use appropriate logging functions when internally developing applications.

A COUPLE MORE DESIGN ISSUES

Before we step into setting up the IIS server, we need to talk a bit more about architecture, and some things that we need to take into consideration when we design our site. Here are a few more items to consider when you are in the design phase.

Isolating and Partitioning Systems

Use virtual servers and directories when possible to isolate your Web servers into logical partitions. As mentioned before, if you use these together, you can host multiple sites, each with its own separate directory space and/or some shared file location. Setting these up can be accomplished using the ISM. Select New | Virtual Directory for the site you want to add the virtual directory to. You will be taken to the Virtual Directory Creation Wizard, which will step you through the process of adding a virtual directory.

TIP: Virtual directories can be nested.

Designing Around Your Policies

As discussed in Chapter 4, you should already have multiple policies in place concerning the many aspects of computing. When you are designing your IIS architecture, you need to ensure that you pay careful attention to the Security Policy and the Acceptable Use Policy. These will play a major part in understanding the authentication, authorization, and auditing requirements that you will need.

Business-to-Business (B2B) Considerations

Don't forget about the B2B issues you *will* face. The fact that you will have to do business with others over the Net is a foregone conclusion. And the probability that some or all of that will be Web-based interactions is very high. Some of the B2B issues that you will need to consider are

▼ **Guest accounts vs. trust relationships**   You will need to consider if you will trust the other business in terms of accepting their authentication for use on your systems. Or whether you will allow them to use guest accounts on your own systems. This issue should not be considered lightly; remember that security is only as strong as the weakest link.

■ **Firewalls and extranets**   How will you connect to each other? Will it be complete connectivity, with full access to one another's systems? Will you require a firewall between the two? Will you just allow access to servers (Web, FTP, and so on) that are on an extranet that you share?

NOTE: An *extranet* is a semi-private network that is used to securely share part of a company's private information with suppliers, vendors, partners, customers, or other businesses. It is used to limit access to your private (i.e. internal) network. An extranet can be viewed as part of a company's intranet that is extended to users outside the company.

▲ **The maturity of PKI**   If you will be using any type of certificate in the establishment of credentials, you will have to consider managing multiple types of certificates, the load imposed by checking for revocations, and how far you will follow the verification chain for the certificates you are using. These are not very big issues if there are just a few users, but for large corporations, · this may be a formidable task, and at this time the immaturity of PKI makes these big issues.

ADMINISTRATION

This section steps you through the tools used to administer the IIS server, as well as IIS installation and configuration.

Tools

We need to introduce the tools used for administration before we describe more of the features and uses. These tools will be referenced throughout this chapter, so knowing about them in advance is a must.

The Internet Services Manager

The Internet Services Manager (ISM) is an MMC snap-in that allows you to manage and configure the server and its security options. You use it to manage Web services, FTP services, NNTP services, and SMTP services. It is installed automatically on the Web server itself, and can be used to manage any other IIS 5.0 server. To start the utility, choose Start | Programs | Administrative Tools | Internet Service Manager. You then double-click the server you want to manage to open the Properties dialog box (shown in Figure 12-4). Then you can access the individual option sheets.

TIP: There are also collections of command-line scripts that can be used to administer the IIS server as well. Although these are nice in a pinch, we recommend that you use the ISM for all administrative tasks.

NOTE: There are two sets of properties for an IIS server: master and individual. All sites (a.k.a. virtual servers) inherit master properties, and individual properties are specific to a site. While master properties are "inherited" by individual sites, individual properties take precedence.

With the Properties sheets, you manage the following tasks:

▼ Establishing logon requirements

■ Configuring access permissions

■ Specifying home directories and other virtual directories

■ Creating multiple virtual servers on a single computer

■ Setting encryption options

■ Configuring event logging options

■ Viewing current sessions

▲ Enabling or disabling server access for specific IP addresses

REMOTE ADMINISTRATION   One of the issues you will have to face is how to administer the IIS server. The fundamental choice is whether you will allow remote administration at all. There may be some installations that might not want to enable any remote administration because of security reasons. For those that do, there are two default options for remote administration of IIS:

▼ HTTP/HTTPS Internet Services Manager (Web ISM)

▲ MMC Snap-in Internet Services Manager (ISM)

The host from which you will be doing the managing may determine your selection for this. If the machine is not on a Win2K host, then you will have to use the HTTP/HTTPS-based ISM. If you are running Win2K on your administration host, then our recommendation is that you use the MMC Snap-in exclusively. This tool seems to be better integrated and allows you to remove the administrative files from the accessible Web directories. Table 19-1 lists the pros and cons of the different IIS administration tools.

NOTE: There are other administration methods, such as using Terminal Services or writing your own programs to use the COM interfaces that affect IIS.

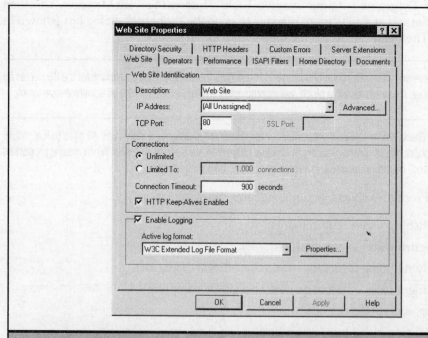

Figure 19-4.   Web Site properties sheet

Tool	Pros	Cons	Security Rating
Web ISM with HTTP	Not Microsoft-specific. Any current browser on any OS will work. Easily firewalled.	All administration ID done in clear text, including authentication.	Low
ISM MMC Snap-In	Microsoft-specific. Faster and more robust. Can use Win2K authentication.	Must run a Microsoft-specific OS. Uses MSRPC. Uses port numbers 139/TCP. Very hard to firewall.	Medium This is recommended for functionality.
Web ISM with HTTPS	Same as above, plus all traffic is encrypted.	Some functions do not work as well as with the MMC. Have to worry about maintaining SSL certificates.	High This is the recommended method if administering through a firewall.

Table 19-1.   Default Administration Tools Pros and Cons

Delegating Administrative Control

If you want other users and/or groups to be able to perform administration on the Web site itself, then you can add them as Operators on that site or Web directory. The Directory Properties sheet has a tab for Web Site Operators. The users and groups listed there have limited administrative privileges on individual Web sites. The Operators assigned to a site can only perform administration tasks that affect that Web site (normal or virtual). They cannot change properties that affect the IIS server, the underlying Win2K OS, or the network.

This functionality provides the ability for a company, say an ISP, to host multiple sites on a single IIS server and have Operators for each individual company's Web site. The following are some of the tasks an Operator can and cannot perform:

▼ **Operators can**   Set site access permissions, set directory security, enable logging, change the default document or footer, set content expiration, and enable content ratings features.

▲ **Operators cannot**   Change the identity of a site, configure the anonymous user, change bandwidth settings, create or modify virtual directories paths, or change application protection.

> **TIP:** You may not want the ability to administer your IIS server via the Web. If you want to, you can remove the physical directory `\%Systemroot%\System32\Inetsrv\iisadmin,` and the Administration Web Site (via the ISM).

Setup and Management

Microsoft Internet Information Server can be set up in a matter of minutes. It can be installed at the time you set up the Win2K server after the fact through the Windows Component in the Add & Remove control panel. It loads as a service and runs in the background once installed. In fact, after running the setup procedure, you can start a browser on your own network and access the Web server immediately (you will get an "under construction" page, but it is up).

Setting Up the Physical and Logical Configurations

There are three typical cases in which you will configure your Web server(s):

▼ A standalone system connected to the Internet

■ A member of a group of Web machines on the Internet (sometimes called a *farm* or *pool*)

▲ A member of an internal domain running on an intranet

Your primary security concern is ensuring that users do not get unauthorized access to resources. For example, on an Internet-based server, preventing hackers from getting access to the server so they can modify the actual Web pages is a high priority.

One of the first things to do is disable the bindings for Server, Workstation, and NetBIOS (if installed) on the network interface card that is connected to the Internet, as described in Chapter 21. Once these bindings are removed, Internet users won't be able to access your system by using standard Windows file services. You can also disable all ports except HTTP port 80 in the TCP/IP Properties | Advanced | Options | TCP/IP Filtering menu.

It is recommended that you ensure the Guest account is disabled on any Internet connected systems (use only the IUSR_*<computername>* account for anonymous logon) and make sure that the Everyone and Authenticated Users groups do not have excess permissions in sensitive directories. It is *important* to remember to set up your NTFS permissions and inheritance correctly. If you do not, there is a high likelihood that the Everyone and/or Authenticated Users groups could get access to any new directories you create. You should check permissions after creating new directories.

Refer to Chapter 21 for more information on hardening hosts.

Directory Security Controls

After you add a new physical NTFS directory to your server for Web users to access, you will need to add it as a virtual directory (or a Web directory), as discussed earlier. Once you have added a Web directory to the Web site, you can configure the properties for it with the ISM. From the ISM, you open the Properties dialog box for the Web directory you want to administer. The dialog box in Figure 19-5 appears. Not all the features of the Directory Properties dialog box are described here, only those concerned with security. For a full description, refer to the Help feature.

For the directory, you will need to set the permissions—Script Source Access, Read, Write, and Directory Browsing (described earlier)—as well as two other properties: Log Visits and Index This Resource. These are shown in the Virtual Directory tab of the Directory Properties dialog box.

DIRECTORY PERMISSIONS   These were described in the "Authorization" section earlier. Following are the recommended settings:

▼ **Script Source Access**   If you are not using WebDAV, then leave it clear.

■ **Read**   Enable for document directories; disable for script and executable directories.

■ **Write**   Disable (unless you *know* you need it).

▲ **Directory Browsing**   Disable.

LOG VISITS   This will cause each hit to this site to be logged. Logging (discussed earlier) for this site must be enabled for this to work.

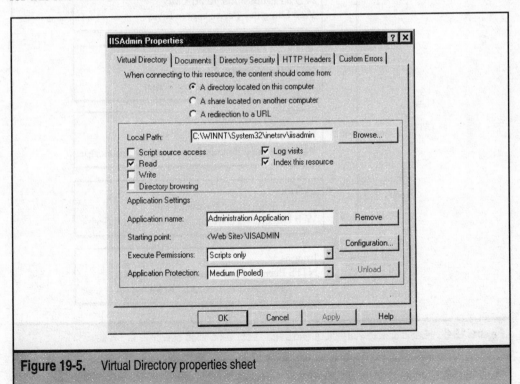

Figure 19-5.   Virtual Directory properties sheet

INDEX THIS RESOURCE   This option allows the Microsoft Index Server to do a full text index of this directory and its children. This allows full text searches to be performed on the directory tree. This is enabled by default and should be disabled unless specifically desired. Indexing of files that may be sensitive is the worst possible, and very likely, outcome of this service.

Recommended Directory Structure

We have talked about the fundamentals of directory structure, what resides in them, and some of the default settings. Now we offer some suggestions on a good basic setup. Figure 19-6 shows the basic directory structure and permissions for a Web server.

Here are the basic uses of each of the directories:

▼ **Documents**   Static pages.

■ **Scripts**   All files mapped to a script engine.

■ **Executables**   Any application that is not a script.

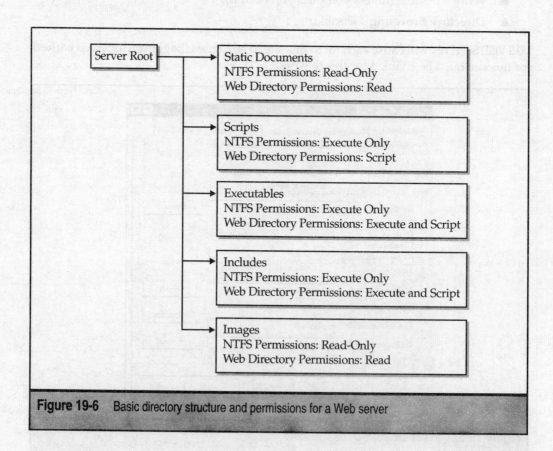

Figure 19-6   Basic directory structure and permissions for a Web server

■ **Includes**   Any server-side includes.

▲ **Images**   Any image files.

By using a proper directory structure, you can set appropriate NTFS and Web directory access control settings. This will ensure that any new file or directory created will inherit the proper permissions. If you do not take the time to plan and set this up right, you can almost be assured that at some point your server will become an intrusion statistic.

Enabling Authentication

If you want to require authentication, then you have to enable the server to use it. This is done in the Anonymous Access and Authentication Control section of the Directory Security tab of the Directory Properties dialog box, as shown in Figures 19-7 and 19-8.

Requiring User Account Logon

If you want to restrict access to a directory to only users who have accounts on the server and require those users to log on when they access the Web server, follow the steps outlined here.

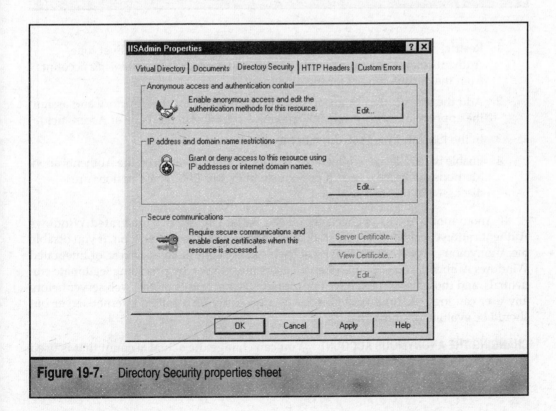

Figure 19-7.   Directory Security properties sheet

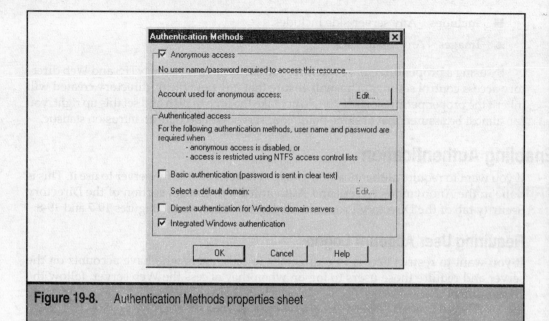

Figure 19-8.   Authentication Methods properties sheet

1. Restrict anonymous user access to directories by removing the Everyone, Authenticated Users, and Guests groups and the IUSR_*computername* accounts from the permission list for the directory.

2. Add the specific user or group that you want to access the directory and assign the appropriate access rights by making a selection in the Type of Access field.

3. In the ISM, add the Web directory to the site you want.

4. Enable Basic, Digest, or Integrated Windows Authentication on the Authentication Methods dialog box, shown previously in Figure 19-8. These options are discussed in the next section.

If Anonymous Access is checked and the Basic, Digest, and Integrated Windows Authentication checkboxes are cleared, only anonymous users can log on. If you disable the Anonymous Access option, you must enable at least one of Basic, Digest, or Integrated Windows Authentication options (then all users must log on by providing legitimate credentials, and those users must have appropriate user accounts on the Web server before any user can log on). Anonymous access is a necessity on a public Internet server but should be evaluated for internal use.

CHANGING THE ANONYMOUS ACCOUNT   You can change the actual account that is used for anonymous access with the Account Used for Anonymous Access option shown previously in Figure 19-8.

Enabling IP Address Filtering

The Directory Security tab in the Directory Properties dialog box, shown previously in Figure 19-7, is where you specify who can access your Web server based on IP addresses or DNS domain name. It also allows you to specify if the listed sites are allowed or denied.

▼   **Granted Access**   When enabled, allows all hosts access to the Web server, except for the IP addresses that are added to the exception list.

▲   **Denied Access**   When enabled, denies all hosts access to the Web server except for the IP addresses that are added to the exception list.

Enabling Secure Communications

If you want to ensure that the data flowing over the wire is not viewed by prying eyes, then secure communications is your answer. Win2K and IIS give you two built-in mechanisms to get the secure communications: Virtual Private Networks (IPSec, L2TP, PPTP) and Transport Layer Security (TLS, previously known as SSL). This section will focus on TLS/SSL because it is widely supported. See Chapter 16 for details on VPNs.

Microsoft Web clients and servers support the Secure Sockets Layer (SSL) and the Transport Layer Security (TLS) protocols for securing a communication channel. SSL is an older standard, while TLS is a more efficient and secure upgrade to the SSL protocol. TLS supports both certificates and password-based authentication.

You can require users to use an encrypted channel (HTTPS) with your Web server before they can access a certain Web site, directory, or file. In order to use this encrypted channel, you must set up your server to support encryption. For IIS, this means setting up a certificate for the server and configuring the specific Web site or directory to require SSL.

Only the Microsoft Internet Explorer 3.0 and later supports all of the protocols discussed here. Earlier versions of the Internet Explorer support only SSL.

NOTE: When you set the master configuration for the site, the rest of the directories and files belonging to that site inherit those properties, unless you explicitly set them otherwise.

Getting and Installing a Certificate

The first step is to get a certificate. You can either generate one for your own intranet use with the Certificate Services (see Web Chapter 1 at **www.osborne.com**) or you can get one from a publicly known certification authority.

TIP: Don't get too caught up in this process—the wizard associated with this operation will guide you through it. Also note that it will take days, not hours to get a certificate from an external certifying authority.

Once you have the certificate, then you can install it. Again, the wizard will take you through this step.

Configuring a Web Site or Directory to Use a Certificate

Now that you have the certificate and it's installed, you can configure a Web site or directory to use it. Use the ISM to select a Web site or Web directory and open its property sheets. Go to the Directory Security tab, then under Secure Communications click Edit. You will see the screen shown in Figure 19-9.

REQUIRE SECURE CHANNEL (SSL)   When Secure Sockets Layer is installed, the Require Secure SSL Channel option is available and allows for the private transmission of information in the directory to the client. When this option is enabled, an SSL channel with encryption is always used between the client and the server. Even if this option is not set, users can still establish a secure channel by indicating **HTTPS** instead of **HTTP** in the URL. This box is only needed if you want to require the user to use SSL.

TIP: SSL may cause a performance hit so ensure that you have adequate CPU resources to support it.

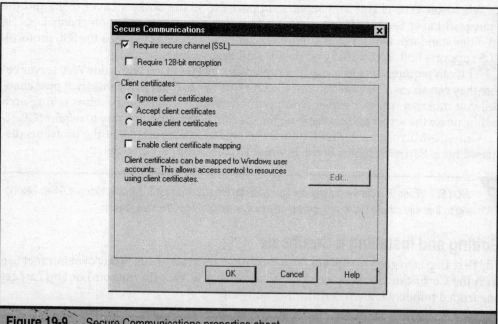

Figure 19-9.   Secure Communications properties sheet

A suboption is to require 128-bit encryption. This option should be selected if at all possible. There is a large likelihood that if you cannot mandate what level of browser your users will be using (that is, they are coming in from the Internet), then this option will probably cause client connections to fail due to insufficient security level. Due to export restrictions, 128-bit key strength is available only in the United States and Canada.

NOTE: Server-Gated Cryptography (SGC) is a feature that offers financial institutions solutions for worldwide secure financial transactions using 128-bit and 40-bit encryption. SGC is an extension of Secure Sockets Layer (SSL) that allows a server to facilitate 128-bit encryption sessions for restricted purposes (primarily protecting banking information). Thus U.S. export law allows SGC to use strong cryptography throughout most of the world. IIS version 3.5 supports SGC.

Client Certificates and Certificate Mapping

Remember that we discussed earlier that when you are using SSL you can set a site or directory to require a valid client certificate to access it. Also that you can use those client certificates to map to actual user accounts. Please see Web Chapter 1 at **www.osborne.com** for details on certificates and Certificate Services in Win2K.

RELATED TECHNOLOGIES AND SERVICES

Now that we have covered the setup of the most common Web site features, we will take some time to discuss securing some of the newer features in IIS.

FrontPage Server Extensions

IIS in Win2K now comes with FrontPage Server Extensions (FPSE) as a default feature. The extensions allow for such things as collaborative authoring and editing a Web site directly on the server. Once the FPSEs have been installed, they are enabled by default on all sites that are set up for the IIS server. In order to disable them, you must do it in the individual Web site properties.

What Are FPSEs?

First, let me say that there are numerous books devoted to this subject, so we will just be skimming the wave tops here with our discussion on how to secure their use. With that said, FPSEs are a way to extend the ability of a user to publish and administer a Web server remotely. If everyone has interactive administrative access to the server machine then FPSE would most likely not be needed, as other tools could be used to perform the same functions. FPSEs do the following:

▼ Add cutting edge technology to your Web server

■ Allow authors to collaborate on documents that exist on the server

■ Allow site designers to add functionality to their sites with little or no programming

■ Support many "add-on" functions, such as full-text searches and e-mail form-handling

■ Are available on non-Windows based operating systems, such as Unix

▲ Integrate well with other Microsoft products such as Microsoft Office, Visual SourceSafe, and Index Server

All in all, a very useful set of functions, but as with everything, there is a cost. That cost for the most part is an increased risk level. Like all things, FPSEs have an enormous amount of functionality, but with that can come serious security vulnerabilities. Most of the problems with FPSE can be eliminated with proper configuration and that is what the rest of this section will address.

Securing FPSE

This section discusses how to secure the FPSE *if* you decide to use it.

THE TOOL   You guessed it—the ISM is used to administer the FPSE (you can also use the FrontPage Server Extensions Resource Kit, available form Microsoft). There is an FPSE MMC Snap-in that is installed when you install the FPSE, and it is used to administer all the FPSE options. There are many options that can be configured with the ISM, but we will only be discussing the security-related options. Refer to the Server Extensions tab in the Web Site Properties screen shown in Figure 19-10.

The following items are defined in two locations: The Server Extensions for the IIS server and the Server Extensions for the individual Web sites on that server. The global settings are set on the IIS server and propagate down.

TIP: No security options are selected by default so you must go in and explicitly set them.

ENABLE AUTHORING (ROOT WEB ONLY)   This option enables FPSE on the selected Web site. If you clear this option, the FPSEs are disabled for this Web site. Normally, this option should be cleared and only enabled after careful consideration. It is highly recommended that you do not enable access to FPSE from Internet-based machines. There have been a number of vulnerabilities found in previous versions of this product, so it should be considered carefully. To disable FPSE, make sure that the Enable Authoring checkbox is not checked.

DON'T INHERIT SECURITY SETTINGS When you set the global security settings for the Web site, all the directories under it inherit the security permissions. If you want to override this, you can select this box and then set any of the following four options. By default, this box is cleared, and you should keep it that way unless there is a business need to do otherwise.

▼   **Log Authoring Actions** This causes the system to record the time, username, Web name, remote host, and data into a local file. By default, the file is in `_vti_log/Author.log`, in the root Web. This option should be selected and appropriate NTFS permissions should be set on this file.

   This is the only logging option available for FrontPage. This sets the Logging parameter in `frontpg.ini` to a value of **1**.

■   **Manage Permissions Manually** This removes the ability to administer file and directory security settings with FPSE admin tools. By selecting this option, the security setting functions of the FPSE admin tools are not useable on the server or site (wherever you set the option). It is recommended that you select this option and use local Win2K-based tools to administer security settings.

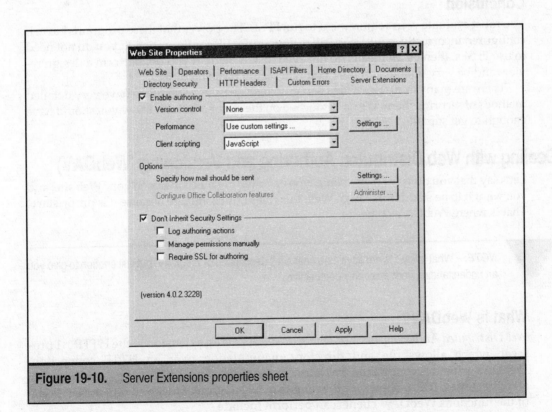

Figure 19-10.   Server Extensions properties sheet

Another reason you might want to manage permission manually is that FPSE will reset any custom settings you have placed on a file or directory. FPSE will reset the ACL, not just append or modify it. This option should be selected if you want to make sure that someone does not accidentally overwrite custom permissions set by someone else.

■ **Require Secure Sockets Layer (SSL) for Authoring**   This will require all FPSE operations to take place over an SSL link. If you are going to use FPSE, then this option should be required.

▲ **Allow Authors to Upload Executables**   This allows users to upload scripts or ASP to the selected IIS server. This option is disabled by default and should stay that way unless a clear business case can be shown. By keeping this option disabled, you prevent executables that could be buggy or malicious from being uploaded to your Web site.

NOTE: This option is only on the IIS server properties, not the individual site properties.

Conclusion

You must evaluate your requirement to run FPSE. The power that these programs have, if configured incorrectly, could jeopardize your entire IIS configuration. If you do not need to use FPSEs, then by all means do not even install them. If you do, perform a design review and be very detailed on how you will secure these features.

There are many more FrontPage Server Extension options and they have very detailed methods of securing them. We have touched on the major points and now you should have enough to get started.

Dealing with Web Distributed Authoring and Versioning (WebDAV)

Let's say that you do want to use some type of authoring mechanism on your Web site, and you want it to be standards-based. Well, this rules out FrontPage because it is proprietary. That is where WebDAV comes in.

NOTE: What follows is not anywhere near a full description of WebDAV, but just enough to give you an understanding from a security perspective.

What Is WebDAV?

Web Distributed Authoring and Versioning (WebDAV) is an extension to the HTTP 1.1 protocol, which allows file and directory manipulation over an HTTP connection. WebDAV provides commands that allow properties to be added to and read from files and directories. It also allows for the remote manipulation of files and directories. Some of the functions WebDAV clients can perform include

▼ **Manipulate Resources**   Copy and move files in a WebDAV directory

■ **Modify Properties**   Write to and read a file's properties

■ **Lock and Unlock Resources**   Allows for concurrent use of files

▲ **Search**   Allows searching of content and properties of files in a WebDAV directory

What Is the Difference Between FrontPage and WebDAV?

WebDAV is an authoring and version control environment; its primary function is to provide a collaboration environment. FrontPage, on the other hand, is designed to be a site builder and has many "hooks" into the Web server to perform various tasks, some of which provide the same functionality as WebDAV. It is hard to compare the two, and they both have their niches. You will have to decide which one, if either, fits your needs.

Setting Up and Securing WebDAV

You set up WebDAV the same way you do a virtual directory—using the ISM. You first create the NTFS directory, then create a virtual directory called WebDAV that references the NTFS directory. Once you have set up your WebDAV publishing directory, users can connect and start using the resource.

WebDAV uses the security features of both Win2K and IIS. That means that all of the previously described IIS permissions are used, as well as the DACLs in the NTFS file system.

TIP: Because this functionality allows manipulation of files, and access to these files is made in the context of the user authenticated to the server, you should ensure that the anonymous user is explicitly denied NTFS permissions to this directory.

WebDAV Clients

Currently any WebDAV-compliant client can access this directory. At the time of this writing there are only three Microsoft clients that can be used to access a WebDAV publishing directory:

▼ Windows 2000 through the Add Network Place Wizard

■ Internet Explorer 5

▲ Office 2000

Conclusion

As with all the services discussed to this point, you really need to evaluate if you need this. This is very new technology and the security issues have not been fully discovered. Like FrontPage Server Extensions, an improperly configured WebDAV directory could potentially affect your entire IIS setup. The basic rule of "if you don't need it, don't install it" applies here.

MORE SECURITY-RELATED CONSIDERATIONS

The following sections discuss other security-related considerations not covered so far.

Resilience

Win2K provides the ability to perform an action if a service crashes. You have the following options:

▼ Take no action

■ Restart the service

■ Run a file

▲ Reboot

For the IIS service, the default action is to run `%systemroot%\system32\iisreset.exe` with a `/fail=failreason` option. This will cause an event to be written to the system EventLog. This may be very important to sites that need maximum availability.

Socket Pooling

This will cause IIS 5.0 to listen to all IP addresses, which could cause a security risk in some configurations. To disable this option, issue the following at the command prompt:

```
c:\inetpub\adminscripts\cscript adsutil.vbs set w3svc/disablesocketpooling true
```

SECURING NON-WWW IIS SERVICES

The IIS Server provides many additional services in addition to its Web services, such as FTP, SMTP, and NNTP. The focus of this chapter is securing IIS, so we will address these services briefly, touching on the important security issues with each service.

FTP Server

The FTP server is an optional component, but is installed by default. It is very likely that you will want an FTP service and chances are you will use this one. If you do select the IIS FTP server, keep in mind that it is set up insecurely a significant portion of the time, so you need to understand how to secure it.

The purpose of the FTP server is simple—it allows you to remotely get and put files between the two machines (client and server). The protocol is well known, as are its security problems. The main security problem is that all the data (usernames, passwords, and files) pass over the network in the clear. This is cause for significant concern, especially if the traffic is leaving your trusted network. The decision to use FTP should not be made lightly and a more secure service should be sought if confidentiality of data is a concern. Another area of security concern is the tight integration between the FTP and WWW services on an IIS server. This tight integration can lead to a compromise of one service from the other. If you decide to run this service, and you probably will, you must be cautious as to the configuration.

Some of the key features of the IIS FTP server are

▼ Support of multiple domains with virtual servers

■ Support of passive mode FTP command (PASV)

■ Support of the Microsoft Management Console for administration

▲ Integration with Win2K features, such as SNMP, event logs, and transaction logs

The two most important decisions in securing the FTP server are the selection of authentication mechanisms and the assignment of directory permissions·(both FTP and NTFS). Given that thought, we will go over the FTP server security-related features and some recommendations on how to secure them.

Configuring Security Settings

Using the ISM, you can set the properties on the FTP server as seen in Figure 19-11.

THE FTP SITE TAB   You can set the following options on the FTP Site tab:

▼ **Identification**   The FTP Site tab allows you to set alternative ports for the FTP server to listen on, as well as specify the address that the server will listen on for incoming connections. This can be a very effective tool in securing your server.

Many sites will use a host with two interface cards. They will have the IIS server listening on the card facing the Internet and have the FTP server listening only on the card facing the internal firewall. This allows them to place files on the host with FTP and yet prevents users on the Internet from attempting to connect the FTP server.

▲ **Enable Logging**   The options and settings are exactly the same as with IIS. If you decide to run the IIS FTP server, then you need to set up logging. You set these permissions on the General tab.

THE SECURITY ACCOUNTS TAB   This tab is used to control who can use the resources of your server. It is used to specify if anonymous connections are allowed, and if they are, which account is used for anonymous requests. It also sets who can administer the site in the FTP Site Operators section. You will notice a tremendous similarity with the IIS Web setting for the similar functionality.

If you plan on placing files for general Internet access via Web browsers, you will need to have the Allow Anonymous Connections option enabled. This allows clients to anonymously access your server. Otherwise, a majority of your clients will not be able to connect to your server.

Once you have enabled that option, then you must select an account that will be used for those anonymous accesses. By default, IUSR_*computername* is used and it should be changed unless one or more of the following is true:

▼ The Web server and the FTP server will be accessing the same file system tree.

▲ The security exposure to the system is low.

The reason you should change the user used for anonymous access is that if it shares the same account as the Web server, then there is a high likelihood that a misconfigured FTP server would allow a user to place files in a Web directory that could, in effect, compromise the Web server. If the accounts are separate and the proper NTFS permissions are

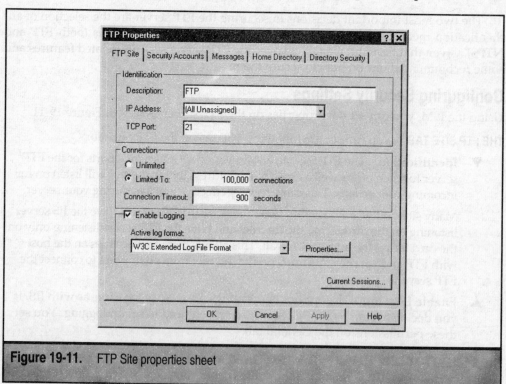

Figure 19-11.   FTP Site properties sheet

placed on the directories, then if the FTP server is misconfigured, it will only affect the FTP tree and not any other.

> **TIP:**   Restrict NTFS ACLs for the anonymous account to Explicit "No Access" ACL on all file systems, then remove No Access and replace with appropriate permissions on WINNT, WINNT\System32, and specific FTP directories.

It's a good idea to select the Allow IIS to Control Password option. It ensures that any changes to the account will get synchronized with the accounts database. It is selected by default and should be left on.

The Allow Only Anonymous Connections option ensures that users will not be able to attempt to connect as regular users with real usernames and passwords. This next section will guide you in making the right option based on your scenario.

TYPICAL FTP SERVER AUTHENTICATION SCENARIOS   There are really three authentication scenarios with FTP:

▼ *All users will be coming from the Internet.*   In this scenario, if you are not using a strong authentication method, you should only allow anonymous connections. This is to ensure that reusable clear text passwords and usernames, which are the default, are not sent across the Internet. Some examples of strong authentication are one-time passwords, Kerberos, or SecureID.

■ *Users are coming in from the local network only.*   In this scenario, you would not allow anonymous connections. You would want everyone to log in to their own account and use the underlying Win2K security features to provide security (that is, NTFS).

This has its own security problems, again dealing with clear text usernames and passwords. The only reason this *may* be acceptable is that the network is assumed to be trusted. This may or may not be a good assumption (for large networks, it is *not* a good assumption, in which case you fall back to the first scenario). Again, if you are using a strong authentication mechanism and the content of the data is acceptable if passed in the clear, then this is a legitimate way to provide access.

▲ *Users are coming in from the Internet and the local network.*   In this scenario, you would "allow" but not "allow only" anonymous connections. You would set a paper "policy" that did not permit users to FTP into the server from the Internet. You must understand that this policy is only enforceable to the extent that you monitor the logs and take action against those who break the rules.

This is the weakest form of authentication, because prevention of the security exposure (primarily clear text usernames and passwords) is technically unenforceable.

TIP: Require strong authentication if you need to use anything but anonymous access.

FTP SITE OPERATORS   This option on the Security Accounts tab provides the same function as the other Operators groups for the WWW, NNTP, and SMTP services. They are just Win2K groups that have limited administrative privileges on individual FTP sites.

THE HOME DIRECTORY TAB   Figure 19-12 shows the configuration settings for the main FTP directory. The options allow you to specify whether the home directory is a physical directory located on the server or a share off another server.

VIP: As we stated earlier, you should carefully weigh *any* decision to use network shares for virtual directories. All access is made in the context of the user you configure for that directory. This configuration has many potential security pitfalls and should not be used if security is an issue. Also, do *not* use network shares for Internet-based machines.

TIP: Make sure *all* file systems are NTFS!

The other critical Home Directory options are

▼   **Read**   Allows users to read, list, and download any file in the FTP site.

■   **Write**   Allows users to upload files to the FTP site.

▲   **Log Visits**   Will log users' connections. Logging must be enabled for this to work.

VIP: It is crucial that you set these correctly!

There is one very likely situation in which an FTP server can be incorrectly configured: setting up an incoming "drop" site.

This mostly deals with anonymous drop sites, say for users dropping a memory dump for tech support usage. You would set up an anonymous site where the user would place the file. The support people would then be able to access that directory and retrieve the files. The problem arises when the anonymous user can both write and read from the same directory. This will quickly become what is known as a *warez* site. Hackers will find it, and quickly! Then they will use your drop as a location to place pirated software. They will then point their friends to the site, and since they have the ability to Read (that is, download), they will pull the pirated software down. You can imagine the legal consequences of this.

If you did not allow Read and Write together, then the chances of this happening are significantly reduced (you never say "never" in security). Do not set up a configuration

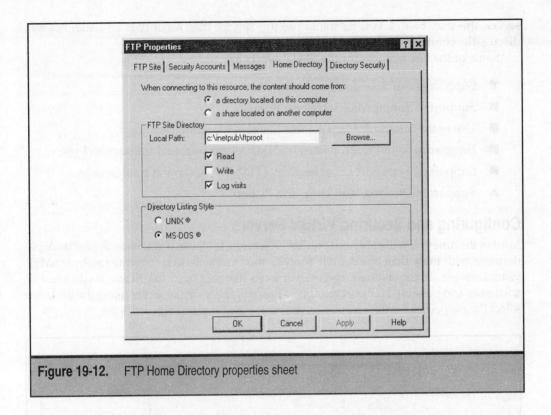

Figure 19-12.   FTP Home Directory properties sheet

where Read and Write permissions are enabled on the same directory (or portion of a directory) that is accessible by anonymous users.

The Directory Security tab provides the IP address filtering that was described earlier in the "Enabling IP Address Filtering" section.

VIRTUAL SITES AND DIRECTORIES   The IIS FTP server has the same concept of virtual sites and directories as the Web server (as described earlier in the "Basic IIS Concepts" section). Both are created the same way they are in the Web server and they have the same function. FTP virtual sites have all the same property settings as the main FTP site and were described earlier in this chapter. The FTP virtual directory properties are a subset of the FTP site properties. You can use them to set the directory location and permissions (Read, Write, and Log), as well as the IP restrictions.

SMTP (Mail) Server

IIS comes with a Simple Mail Transport Service (SMTP)–based mail server to send and receive messages. The server uses the SMTP (RFC 821 and 822) and has enhanced some of the delivery capabilities for this service.

This service is a nice addition, but should not be considered as a substitute for a full-featured mail system, such as Exchange. If you need a simple SMTP-based mail server, this may be it. If you decide to use this service then security is an issue. We will discuss the configuration and security considerations.

Some of the key features for the SMTP server are

▼ Support of multiple domains with virtual servers

■ Support of Simple Mail Transport Protocol

■ Use of the Microsoft Management Console for administration

■ Integration with Win2K features: SNMP, event logs, and transaction logs

■ Support of Transport Layer Security (TLS) for encrypting transmissions

▲ Support of Directed Mail Drop and Pickup

Configuring and Securing Virtual Servers

Most of the time you will only need one SMTP server. However, if you want to host multiple domains with more than one default domain, then you will need to create multiple SMTP virtual servers. To the end user, each server looks like a separate machine with different IP addresses and possibly TCP port numbers. To configure a virtual server using the ISM, you select the properties for the virtual server you are configuring (Figure 19-13).

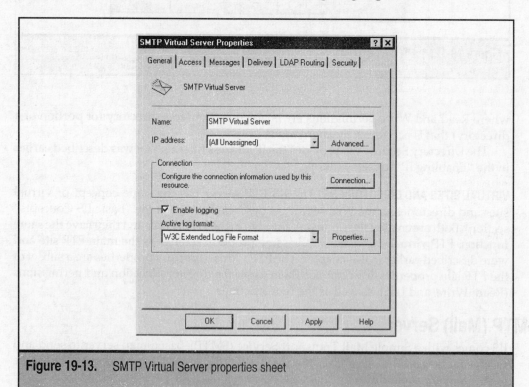

Figure 19-13. SMTP Virtual Server properties sheet

Many of the options on this screen and the corresponding tabs are for configuring different mail server characteristics, delivery and recipient options, and other non-security- related stuff. We are focusing on the security-related options you can set.

SECURITY: OPERATORS   This is the same functionality as the Operators option in all IIS services. It gives any user or group listed operator permissions for the SMTP virtual server. You set these permissions on the Security tab.

ACCESS: ACCESS CONTROL   There are three options for authenticating any incoming connections. You set these option by pressing the Authentication button and then you are presented with the following options:

▼ **Anonymous Access**   No username or password is required.

   This is the default that all Internet clients use. It will be required for any Internet-based server that you want to have as a general mail server.

■ **Basic Authentication**   This requires the client send a valid username and password.

   The username and password will be authenticated against the domain value you have entered in the Default Domain field. This username and password is in clear text, but you have the option to require TLS encryption. TLS requires a valid server certificate, just as the SSL server does in IIS (as discussed earlier).

▲ **Windows Security Package**   This requires that the client send valid credentials.

   This option uses the Win2K Security Support Provider Interface (SSPI) to perform native Win2K authentication of the passed credentials. This could use any of the supported mechanisms, such as Kerberos or NTLM.

ACCESS: OUTBOUND SECURITY   This option, which is set on the Delivery tab, allows you to select the credentials, if any, that will be used for outbound connections. You must enter a valid username and password for the remote machine for the authentication type you have selected. Unlike the inbound selection, which was made in the Access Control section, you can only choose one type of outbound authentication to use. By default, it uses anonymous access, as this is the way the rest of the Internet does SMTP mail.

There may be special circumstances where you want all the traffic between mail servers to be encrypted. If that is the case, then you can require TLS to encrypt the link. Currently, this is only supported when you are talking Microsoft to Microsoft. These options are set in the Delivery tab, and all the setting information is stored in the Registry for later use.

ACCESS: SECURE COMMUNICATIONS   This is the same functionality as the Secure channel (SSL) option in IIS. Like IIS, you must have a valid certificate to use this option. Then once you have a valid certificate, you can require the use of TLS, and even set the strength to 128-bit. You set these options in the Access tab.

This option is not practical to use at this time because most clients do not support it. If you can mandate what client your users use, and privacy of e-mail is an issue, then this may be a valid option. The decision to use or not use this option should be made in your security policy, not at the time of setup. As with outbound security, unless you are talking Microsoft server to Microsoft server, then I would leave it disabled.

ACCESS: CONNECTION CONTROL   This is the same functionality as the IP address restrictions in IIS and uses the same interface. It is not practical to use this on an Internet-based server, but does deserve consideration on an intranet or extranet. You set these options in the Access tab.

ACCESS: RELAY RESTRICTIONS   Some may not consider this a security-related setting, but the ability to relay through mail servers is a primary means of SPAM generation. This may be the most important and useful of settings. By default, the SMTP Service blocks relaying and you should leave it this way! There are ways to allow limited relaying, but you should limit this as much as possible. You set these options in the Access tab, and the screen in Figure 19-14 shows the related options.

- ▼ **Only the List Below**   Only the computers listed in the box can relay messages through the server. This is set by default.
- ◼ **All Except the List Below**   Just the opposite of the above.
- ▲ **Allow All Computers Which Successfully Authenticate to Relay, Regardless of the List Above**   If someone has successfully authenticated, then they can relay, regardless of the domains. This is set by default.

If your server is on the Internet, you shouldn't allow relaying at all! Keep the defaults.

LOGGING   The options and settings are exactly the same as with IIS. If you decide to run the IIS SMTP server, then you need to set up logging, if for nothing other than troubleshooting. You set these permissions in the General tab.

Conclusion

In summary, there are some very interesting features in this service, but they are not very practical since the architecture is not in place to utilize most of the functionality. Most people are looking for either end of the spectrum: a full-featured environment, or a simple, security-hardened store-n-forward. This server is neither. This IIS SMTP server can make a good, simple Internet mail host, as it is functional and easy to set up. If you do decide to use this service, make sure that you take the time to set it up correctly.

NNTP (News) Servers

IIS provides a Network News Transfer Protocol (NNTP) server as part of the standard distribution. The system is designed to facilitate what are sometimes called *discussion groups* or *newsgroups*. These groups are designed to spur discussions on various topics with each other and with external users.

Relay Restrictions ☒

Select which computer may relay through this virtual server:

⦿ Only the list below

○ All except the list below

Computers:

Access	IP Address (Mask) / Domain Name

[Add...] [Remove]

☑ Allow all computers which successfully authenticate to relay, regardless of the list above.

[OK] [Cancel] [Help]

Figure 19-14. SMTP Mailer Relay Restrictions properties sheet

Many of the security features are similar to those already discussed; however, this section will call out the security-related options, explain the ones specific to the NNTP Service, and provide some recommendations.

A few quick tidbits before starting:

▼ The NNTP Service also includes support for Simple Network Management Protocol (SNMP) monitors.

■ NNTP Service uses ACLs to manage access to newsgroups.

■ NNTP Service supports full-text and property indexing of newsgroup content using Microsoft Indexing Services.

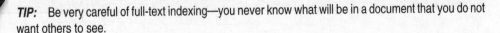

TIP: Be very careful of full-text indexing—you never know what will be in a document that you do not want others to see.

▲ Microsoft Content Replication System can be used to update the ACLs automatically across multiple Microsoft NNTP servers.

Configuring and Securing the Server

The NNTP Service properties are shown in Figure 19-15.

Many of the options on this screen and the corresponding tabs are for configuring different news server characteristics and other non-security related stuff. The following are the security-related options you can set.

GENERAL: OPERATORS, LOGGING, AND CONNECTION CONTROL   These are exactly the same as WWW, FTP, and SMTP servers under IIS and are set on the General tab.

ACCESS: ACCESS CONTROL   You set these options in the Authentication section of the NNTP properties Access tab by clicking the Authentication button (Figure 19-16).

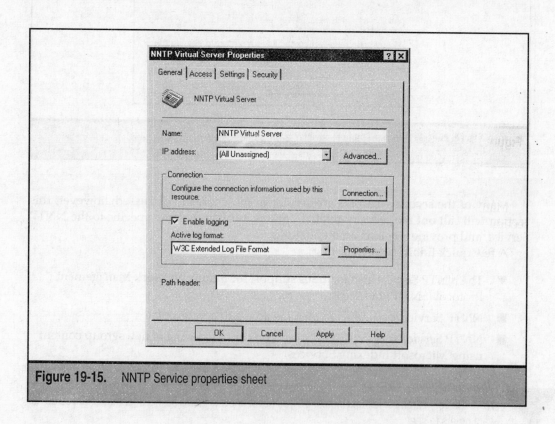

Figure 19-15.   NNTP Service properties sheet

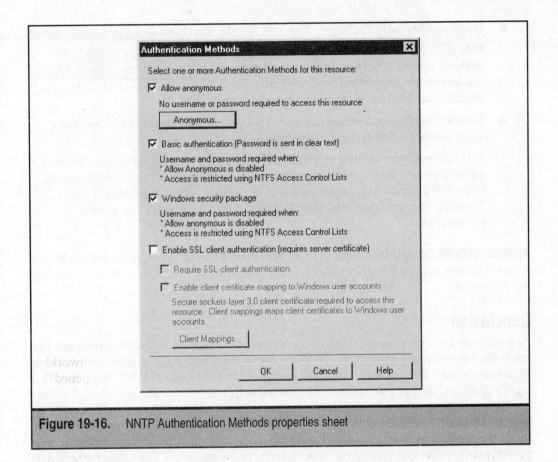

Figure 19-16.   NNTP Authentication Methods properties sheet

It provides four options for authenticating any incoming connections. The options include the following:

▼ **Allow Anonymous**   No username or password is required.

   This is the default that all clients support.

■ **Basic Authentication**   This will require the client send a valid username and password.

   The Standard NNTP security extension (AUTHINFO USER/PASS) is used to pass the username and password to the server. This username and password is in clear text so you will need to require SSL (see "Enabling Secure Communications," earlier in this chapter).

■ **Windows Security Package**   This will require the client sent valid credentials.

This option uses the Win2K Security Support Provider Interface (SSPI) to perform native Win2K authentication of the passed credentials. This could use any of the supported mechanisms such as Kerberos or NTLM. This requires the Microsoft Internet Mail and News client.

▲ **Enable SSL Client Authentication**   This will require the client to possess a valid certificate for authentication.

This option is very similar to the client-side certificates that can be used for user authentication (described in Web Chapter 1). Like many of the security options in the NNTP and SMTP services, this is probably overkill, especially if you "require" client-side certificates, but may have a very specific use in your environment.

ACCESS: SECURE COMMUNICATIONS   This allows you to set up a certificate for use by the server and then require the clients to access the server using SSL. You set these options in the Access tab.

Conclusion

Newsgroups are a very useful way to disseminate information and solve problems. For years the Usenet News system has been the intellectual backbone of major networking successes (where do you think the collaboration for HTTP and HTML happened?). I highly recommend that you utilize this functionality.

There are three primary uses for news servers: Private internal groups, external private groups, and external public groups. The configuration and security of these groups differ tremendously. The first would probably require some type of authentication and possibly encryption (depending on the sensitivity of the material). The second would definitely require authentication as well as encryption. The third would probably require neither, since it is public.

You must evaluate what requirements you have for security, given your architecture, and configure the system accordingly. The Microsoft NNTP server has many security features, and you should use them to the fullest.

MICROSOFT INTERNET EXPLORER

Microsoft Internet Explorer (IE) 5.0 is Microsoft's latest Web browser. IE provides many security features, such as

- ▼ Security zones
- ■ Authenticode
- ■ Digital certificates
- ■ TLA and SSL support
- ▲ Content advisor

IE supports SSL versions 2.0 and 3.0, as well as the PCT standard. It also allows servers to identify and authenticate clients using public key certificates (see Web Chapter 1 at **www.osborne.com** for more on public keys). IIS 5.0 (which is the IIS server included with Win2K) supports this public key authentication strategy. These security protocols and standards allow users to set up private communications with others that prevent electronic eavesdropping and to connect with sites on the Internet and be assured that the site is legitimate and not a masquerade. With this type of secure communications, Internet users can safely purchase items with their credit cards without worrying that someone might intercept private information.

Another advantage of these security protocols is user authentication. By implementing secure authentication capabilities and certificate-based authentication in its Web browsers and servers, Microsoft is extending the single-server logon concept available on Win2K internal networks to clients who connect with servers over the Internet.

IE version 3.0 and later can use 128-bit encryption, which provides a much higher level of security than previous versions of the Web browser. Microsoft claims that "it is virtually impossible for users to listen in on Internet traffic encrypted with 128-bit security." This is probably going too far, but it is sufficient to say that 40-bit encryption is totally inadequate for information that must be protected for more than a couple of hours.

Internet Explorer's personal certificate feature will automatically verify a user's identity when visiting sites that require user logon. Microsoft calls it the equivalent of "flashing your badge." Credentials are exchanged in the background so you don't need to get directly involved with the security validations every time you connect with a secure Web site. Web users can also store the certificates obtained at Web sites for future use.

You can obtain personal certificates to use with the Internet Explorer or any other Web browser from Verisign and other certification authorities. The company has a free "class 1" digital ID that provides e-mail authentication. It also has a "class 2" digital ID for personal identity authentication.

TIP: To get more detailed information in Internet Explorer, go to the Microsoft Web site at **http://www.microsoft.com/ie**.

SOME TIPS FOR A HIGH-SECURITY IIS SERVER

Here is a mini-checklist for a high-security IIS server starting point:

1. Remove system executables. Place the following command line utilities in a directory other than the `%Systemroot%` tree, and restrict to administrator-only access:

cmd.exe	ftp.exe	Regedit.exe
net.exe	ipconfig.exe	regedt32.exe
arp.exe	nbtstat.exe	rexec.exe
at.exe	netstat.exe	route.exe
atsvc.exe	nslookup.exe	rsh.exe
cacls.exe	ping.exe	secfixup.exe
debug.exe	posix.exe	syskey.exe
edit.com	qbasic.exe	telnet.exe
edlin.exe	rcp.exe	tracerout.exe
finger.exe	rdisk.exe	xcopy.exe

2. Restrict the number of user accounts on the machine.
3. Use Dual Network cards for internal and external network connections.

NOTE: In a highly secure environment, "sneaker-net" is still the best answer.

4. Use the Advanced Filtering option in the TCP/IP Network properties to block ports not used on internal and external interfaces.
5. Remove all default install directories for WWW and FTP.
6. Do *not* place Web files on the boot or system partitions.

7. Do not place executable content, such as scripts and applications, with non-executable pages.

8. Restrict NTFS ACLs for IUSR_*computername* and IWAM_*computername*: Explicit No Access ACL on all file systems, then remove No Access and replace with appropriate permissions on WINNT, WINNT\System32, and specific Web directories.

9. Use internal and external firewalls to provide port filtering

TIP: Please see **http://www.microsoft.com/security** and search for the IIS checklist for a more complete list.

NON-SECURITY RELATED FEATURES

There are a number of new features in IIS for Win2K that are not security-related. These features should be understood, but it is beyond the scope of this book to detail them. Table 19-2 lists the features with brief descriptions.

RECAP

This chapter discussed the many facets of the Microsoft IIS server and how it can function as a Web, SMTP, NNTP, and FTP server. There are whole books that are devoted to IIS, and if you are going to be setting up a site with any complexity or size at all, you should get one of those books. The security issues will be the same, and the principles in this chapter will serve you well, but other books will go into more depth on performance and scalability.

From a security standpoint, there are four things that you need to do religiously if you want to keep your server off the incident statistic list:

▼ Remove default directories and sites immediately after installation.

■ Apply Hotfixes and service packs in a very timely manner (within two weeks).

■ Code review any application or scripts that will be served by the machine.

▲ Monitoring your logs is the single most important factor in keeping you current on what people are trying on your site.

If you do these four things, the chances that your server will be compromised is significantly reduced.

Feature	Description
ASP Self-Tuning	A new ASP feature will allow ASP server to limit the number of threads if the CPU is overloaded.
Backup and Restore	Administrators can back up the metabase settings for easy restoration.
Browser CapabilitiesComponent	A new ASP feature that allows an ASP server to request exact capabilities of a browser.
DFS	You can use DFS as the underlying file system for IIS.
FTP Restart	An interrupted data transfer can now be resumed without having to download the whole file again.
HTTP Compression	Compression between the server and compression-enabled clients.
Internet Standards	IIS 5.0 complies with the HTTP 1.1 standard.
Performance-enhanced Objects	You can now get "performance-enhanced" versions of some installable ASP components.
PICS Ratings	Administrators can apply Platform for Internet Content Selection (PICS) ratings to sites.
Process Throttling	Allows the administrators to limit the amount of CPU time a Web application or site can use.
Bandwidth Throttling	Allows the administrators to limit the bandwidth each site uses.
Process Accounting	Allows administrators to monitor sites that use CPU resources.
Custom Error Messages	Allows administrators to send more informative messages to clients when errors occur.

Table 19-2.   Non-Security Related Features in IIS 5.0

CHAPTER 20

Fault Tolerance
and Data Protection

Your job as a system and network administrator is to make sure that information is both available to users and protected from corruption or loss. Attacks on your system by hackers, unauthorized users, or viruses can destroy your well-laid plans. Just as harmful is a system failure due to natural causes or overburdened systems. A downed system costs you more than frustration: It may cost your business hundreds or thousands of dollars in lost revenue and create a lot of customer dissatisfaction. It may also cost you your job.

This chapter covers five topics that directly or indirectly deal with protecting the data on your servers:

▼ Protecting operating system files

■ Providing fault tolerance with disk mirroring and disk striping

■ Providing fault tolerance and data availability by replicating data to other systems

■ Backing up data to tapes with the Win2K Backup utility

▲ Addressing and solving power problems

PROTECTING THE OPERATING SYSTEM

A server may crash because of a hardware problem or because a malicious user or hacker has managed to corrupt or destroy files. A virus or Trojan Horse program may also have attacked the system. The information presented here can help you quickly recover a system from such a disaster.

Safe Mode Boot

If a computer will not start, say after you installed a new piece of software or a new driver, you can now boot into Safe Mode. This will boot the system into a mode that has a minimum number of services running (that is, mouse, monitor, keyboard, mass storage, base video, default system services, and no network). This is very similar to the Safe Mode boot that users are familiar with in Win 9x. This mode allows you to change settings or remove the software or driver that caused the problem.

You can select the Safe Mode options that you desire by pressing F8 when the Starting Windows 2000 dialog appears (that is, the initial boot loader). This will bring you to the boot mode selection screen, which has the following options:

▼ **Safe Mode**   Will boot Win2K using only non-serial mouse, monitor, keyboard, mass storage, base video, default system services, and no network connections. If the system does not start in Safe Mode, you may need to use one of the repair modes discussed in a moment.

■ **Safe Mode with Networking**   This is Safe Mode with network connections enabled.

■ **Safe Mode with Command Prompt**   This is Safe Mode, but instead of the Explorer desktop, you have a command prompt.

■ **Enable Boot Logging**   Will boot Win2K normally, but will log all the drivers and services that were loaded (or not loaded) to the `%windir%\ntbtlog.txt` file. By default, the three previous Safe Mode boots will log to this file as well. This is useful in troubleshooting system boot problems.

■ **Enable VGA Mode**   Will boot Win2K normally, except the basic VGA driver is used. This is useful when you have video driver problems. By default, the basic VGA driver is used in any of the Safe Mode boots.

■ **Last Known Good Configuration**   Will boot Win2K using the Registry information that was saved at the last clean shutdown. This is known as the *last known good configuration* and is useful in correcting any problems that arise from the changes made since the last successful startup. Note that the Registry information that is used for the last known good configuration is overwritten once the user logon screen (that is, CTRL-ALT-DEL) appears.

■ **Directory Services Restore Mode**   Will boot a Win2K domain controller into a mode that allows the SYSVOL directory and the Active Directory directory service to be restored. This is used in conjunction with the Win2K Backup utility to restore previously backed up files. This is not applicable for Win2K Pro, member servers, or standalone servers.

▲ **Debugging Mode**   Will boot Win2K normally, but during the boot, it will send debug information through a serial cable to another computer.

VIP: There may be more options if you used the Remote Install Services to install Win2K on your system.

Recovery Console

The Recovery Console can be used if the Safe Mode options are not successful. It is a command-line console to an existing system on the system that you are running it on. It allows you to repair a system that won't start or load Win2K. You can use the Recovery Console to perform numerous command-line administrative tasks, such as starting and stopping services, formatting drives, and reading and writing data on a local drive. You will find it very useful if you need to reconfigure a service or copy correct files from a CD or floppy.

There are two ways to start the Recovery Console:

▼ Boot the system from the distribution media, and enter the Repair mode. Then select the Recovery Console option.

▲ You can be proactive and install the Recovery Console on your computer *before* you need it. To do this just insert the distribution media, then invoke \i386\winnt32.exe/cmdcons from your media, and follow the prompts. After it is installed, you can then select the Recovery Console option from the list of available operating systems.

VIP: You must know the local administrator password to use the Recovery Console.

Using the Recovery Console

To use the Recovery Console, boot into it using one of the options just described. Then enter the *local* (that is, not *domain*) administrator password. You will be at a command prompt in the \WINNT directory. From there, you can use the commands shown in Table 20-1 to perform actions.

TIP: You should try this before you need it, so you can be familiar with its operation.

The Emergency Repair Process

There may be a time in which the Safe Mode and the Recovery Console options will not fix your problems. There is one more step in between them and a total system re-install: the *emergency repair process*. This process requires the use of the Emergency Repair Disk (ERD) to restore your system. This assumes that you have a relatively recent copy of the ERD from the system when it was functioning well.

Here is what the Emergency Repair Disk can do:

▼ Repair bad Registry data

■ Restore corrupted or missing files on the system partition

■ Replace a corrupt *kernel*, the core of the Win2K operating system

▲ Replace a bad boot sector for a FAT partition

However, the repair disk is not a complete solution for protecting your system. It cannot repair any unmountable partitions except for the system partition, which is usually the C drive on *x*86-based computers. It also does not replace a damaged NTFS boot sector or fully restore the Registry. You must use the Backup utility to create fully recoverable backup sets for your systems.

Creating an ERD

The process for creating an ERD in Win2K is different than in WinNT. There is no RDISK command; you must use the Win2K Backup utility (NTBackup.exe) to create the ERD.

Command	Description
ATTRIB	Changes attributes on file or directory.
BATCH	Executes commands from a text file.
CD	Changes directory or displays name of current directory.
CHKDSK	Displays current status of disk.
CLS	Clears screen.
COPY	Copies file(s) to another location or name.
DEL	Deletes file(s).
DIR	Displays list of file(s) or directories.
DISABLE	Disables server or driver.
DISKPART	Manages partitions on drive(s).
ENABLE	Enables and starts a service or driver.
EXIT	Exits console and restarts computer.
EXPAND	Extracts file from compressed version.
FIXBOOT	Writes new boot sector.
FIXMBR	Repairs Master Boot Record.
FORMAT	Formats drive.
HELP	Displays lists of commands.
LISTSVC	Lists services/drivers on this system.
LOGON	Logs on to this system.
MAP	Displays mapped drive letters.
MD	Creates directory.
MORE	Pauses display of text file when screen is full.
REN	Renames a file.
RD	Deletes directory.
SET	Shows and sets environment variables.
SYSTEMROOT	Sets the current directory you are in to the %systemroot% directory.
TYPE	Prints file to screen.

Table 20-1.   Recovery Console Commands

You can start the Backup program by selecting Start | Run and entering **ntbackup**. Then create the ERD by selecting Tools | Create Emergency Repair Disk. You will see the following screen. You want to ensure that you select the Also Back Up the Registry to the Repair Directory option. This makes a backup of the current Registry files in the `%systemroot%/repair` directory. These will be necessary if you need to recover Registry information.

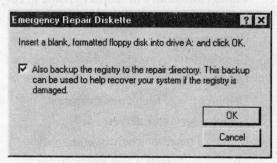

> **NOTE:** If you haven't created an ERD, you can still attempt to use the emergency repair process to fix your computer, but it may not be able to fix your problems.

The Process

The following steps provide a general overview of the emergency repair process when booting from distribution media:

1. Boot the system from the CD using either the Win2K Setup disks or CD.

2. Choose the Repair (R) option during the process.

3. Choose to repair via the emergency repair process.

4. You can then choose the type of repair: Fast or Manual. The *fast* repair option will try to fix problems associated with the Registry, system files, the partition boot sector, and startup environment. It will use a backup copy of the Registry in the `%systemroot%\Repair` directory and the information contained on the ERD. The *manual* option lets you choose to repair system files, partition boot sector problems, or startup environment problems. Note that you can't fix Registry problems in manual mode.

5. Insert the ERD and start the repair process. Note that even if you don't have an ERD, Win2K will attempt the repair anyway. Chances are that it will fail though.

6. Restart your computer.

Fatal Errors and System Shutdowns

The System option on the Control Panel displays options for controlling how Win2K starts and for managing its behavior in the event of a fatal system error. Fatal system errors can occur due to virus infections or because a Trojan Horse halts the system. You may see the dreaded "blue screen of death" in this event. For example, a Trojan Horse program might either cause some damage or ship information to an unknown e-mail address, and then crash the system to hide its tracks. You might incorrectly assume that the system has crashed due to a hardware problem or because a cosmic particle crashed into a critical memory location.

When a fatal system error occurs, the system does the following:

▼ Writes an event to the system log

■ Sends an administrative alert

■ Writes debug information to the file `%systemroot%\MEMORY.DMP` (a.k.a. full crash dump)

▲ Reboots the system automatically

You can enable or disable any of these options from within the System Control Panel | Advanced tab | Startup and Recovery, as shown in the following screen.

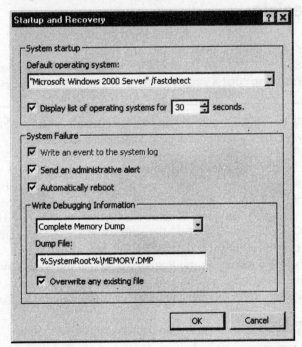

Win2K now supports limited crash dumps, in the form of Small Memory (64K) and Kernel Memory crash dumps. They are set in the Write Debugging Information section of the Advanced tab. You can use these to limit the amount of information that the dump contains. The Small Memory Dump (64K) option will only dump the first 64K of memory whereas the Kernel Memory Dump will ensure that the dump contains mostly kernel memory space. Both of these options make the dumps much smaller (by more then 50 percent), and helps the system to boot faster (by more than 50 percent) after a crash.

Because the MEMORY.DMP file is overwritten by default, you should copy it to another location after restarting your system. The file contains information that helps you determine the cause of the problem, but it requires evaluation by a qualified technical representative. Contact Microsoft or a certified representative for such an evaluation.

If the system fails to boot after a fatal error, use the Safe Mode Last Known Good Configuration during startup. This option will help you recover after you've installed defective drivers or set options that lock up the operating system.

When the Machine Blue Screens

When you see the blue screen of death (BSOD), record the first few lines of the screen and all the associated information, as this will help in troubleshooting the problem. The information can be input to Microsoft Technet (either online or from the CD) and solutions may be identified. This information can also be very helpful if you make a support call to Microsoft.

Protecting the Registry

The Win2K Server operating system stores critical operating information in the Registry. Security databases and system information are stored in files that are located in the %systemroot%\System32\CONFIG directory. This information is also automatically backed up to the %systemroot%\Repair directory as described previously.

VIP: Even with the Active Directory, the Registry still plays a vital role in Win2K and must be protected from network users who could change its contents in malicious ways.

By default, the Registry is backed up when you back up a system using NTBackup. Because parts of the Registry are always in use, a completely accurate backup of the Registry is hard to obtain. Two programs that do a good job of backing up are Registry Backup (REGBACK.EXE) and Registry Restore (REGREST.EXE). They are available in the Win2K Resource Kit (sold separately by Microsoft). REGBACK, for example, will back up parts of the Registry even if they are opened by the operating system.

Another method for backing up the Registry is to use the Save Key command in the Registry Editor. This is essentially a manual backup method that must be performed for each key in the Registry. Refer to Registry Help for more information on this method.

Using a Recovery Drive

Your operating system may become damaged because of a disk failure or malicious activity by a hacker or virus. To recover a damaged system, you can either reinstall the operating system or use a recovery process that includes restoring system configuration information from an Emergency Repair Disk. The second option requires some advance preparation to get your system back up and running as soon as possible. Options that will help you prepare for a system failure include the following:

▼ Use two separate drives in your server, one for the operating system and one for data. Then if the operating system is corrupted, you can quickly get it back online without needing to restore all the data as well.

■ Use the Backup utility to keep separate backup sets for the operating system and the data. In the event of a system failure, you might need to restore only the operating system information.

■ Any time you make a change to the system configuration, make an ERD both before and after making the changes. You might want to keep two disks with "before" and "after" information. Lock up the ERDs after you are done with them—particularly if they contain security information.

▲ In the event that you need to recover a failed system, restart it and use the emergency repair process to recover part of the operating system. Then reboot and use Backup to restore system partition information.

Keep in mind that the ERD does not contain a full backup of the Registry, nor can it fully restore the system partition information. Use the ERD to get the system back to a point where you can reboot it and restore the remainder of your operating system from backups. The backups include hardware-specific driver information.

One thing you can do in advance to ensure a speedy recovery from a system failure is to set up a "recovery drive," an extra disk that has the Win2K operating system installed on it. It can be attached to the server, but should be powered off during normal operations to prevent accidental or intentional modification by hackers. You can also use drives with removable disks as portable drives that you move from one server to the next.

On the recovery drive, install Win2K Server and configure a local paging file and tape driver. Create an Emergency Repair Disk for this configuration and make sure the BOOT.INI file contains a pointer to the recovery disk drive. In the event of a system failure, connect and/or start up the drive, and restart the computer using the Emergency Repair Disk you created for it. Then restore the latest system configuration and Registry information to this disk from your backup sets.

Procedures exist for repairing individual components of the operating system that may be corrupt. These procedures should be used with caution but, in some cases, may provide quick-fix solutions to specific problems. These procedures are available from Microsoft or certified Microsoft representatives. You can also search Microsoft's Knowledge Base, a collection of information about problems and solutions. Knowledge Base is available online at **www.microsoft.com/KB/**.

Other OS-Related Fault Tolerance Features

There are a number of other fault tolerance-related features provided by the Win2K OS, such as System File Protection, Network Load Balancing, Driver Verification, and Driver Signing. This section will discuss them briefly.

System File Protection (SFP)

SFP (a.k.a. Windows File Protection) protects essential system files, such as .sys, .dll, .ocx, .ttf, .fon, and .exe by preventing their replacement. If a file is replaced with a version that is not consistent with what is defined in the catalog file that is used to track correct versions, SFP will restore the correct version, according to the information in the catalog file.

SFP is a background thread that runs in the context of the Winlogon process and protects all files installed by the Win2K Setup program. SFP will check the file's digital signature and compare it to the signature in the catalog. If they do not match, then SFP will replace the file from the backup stored in the Dllcache folder (%systemroot%\ system32\dllcache) or the Win2K CD, or it will prompt you if the correct file is in neither location. SFP also writes an event to the event log, noting the file-replacement attempt.

By default, SFP is always enabled and only allows protected system files to be replaced when installing software via Windows Update tool, using Update.exe, Hotfix.exe, or Winnt32.exe.

USER TOOLS The System File Checker (sfc.exe) is a command-line utility that allows you to run a verification scan after you restart your computer. It is a command-line way of manually starting an SFP run. The program's command-line options are listed in Table 20-2.

The File Signature Verification (sigverif.exe) is a graphical utility that will report any files that are not digitally signed. The Advanced option brings up the Advanced File Signature Verification Settings dialog (shown here), which allows you to specify what will be scanned. It will only report files that are not digitally signed; it will not replace them as the System File Checker will.

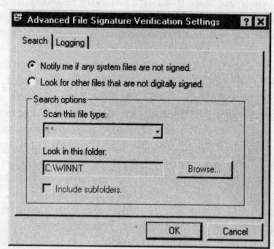

By default, it only looks for system files, but it can be configured to check for digital signatures on any file in any directory you choose. Realize that performing this on a directory with general files will yield a large list of files. The best option is to keep the defaults.

Command-Line Option	Description
/scannow	Scans all protected system files immediately.
/scanonce	Scans all protected system files once at the next boot.
/scanboot	Scans all protected system files at every boot.
/cancel	Cancels all pending scans of protected system files.
/quiet	Replaces all incorrect file versions without prompting the user.
/enable	Enables Windows File Protection for normal operation.
/purgecache	Purges the file cache and scans all protected system files immediately.
/cachesize=x	Sets the file cache size.

Table 20-2. System File Checker Options

DRIVER SIGNING   Part of the SFP mechanism is the fact that all Microsoft-developed drivers are signed and placed in the catalog file. If you develop your own driver, it can be submitted to the Microsoft Windows Hardware Quality Labs (WHQL) for testing. If it passes the tests, Microsoft can digitally sign it to certify that the driver being installed on a system is identical to the one Microsoft tested. There is no change made to the binary file that was sent for testing; instead a catalog file is created for each driver package, and then Microsoft signs that catalog file.

Driver Verifier

The Driver Verifier is a tool that can be used to "verify" that kernel-mode device drivers are operating correctly. Driver Verifier can test for the problems of memory corruption, writing to pageable data, and handling memory allocation errors. It looks for things like illegal function calls or using memory at an improper IRQL. The GUI can be launched from the command line by using the Verifier.exe command.

It should be used with caution, as it does have a performance penalty when it is run. You should use it when troubleshooting.

FAULT TOLERANCE IN WIN2K SERVER

Fault tolerance refers to the protection of systems against potential hardware failures, disasters, virus infections, hacker attacks, and other risks. You protect data by creating redundant copies, usually in real time, as well as backing up the data to magnetic tape and/or optical disk systems.

You can use the following methods to protect your data.

MIRRORED DISKS   In this configuration, two hard disks (or sets of hard disks) are used, and data is simultaneously written to and read from each disk, as pictured on the left in Figure 20-1. If one of the disks fails, the other can provide data to users until the mirrored set is restored. Notice on the right in Figure 20-1 that the disk controller can be duplicated to guard against failure of this component as well. Disk duplexing is just disk mirroring with the mirrored disks on separate controllers.

STRIPE SETS WITH PARITY   In this scheme, as pictured in Figure 20-2, data is written evenly over an array of disks rather than to one disk. Parity information is also written to the disks. The parity information is used to rebuild the data should one of the disks in the set fail. Striping spreads data evenly across multiple drives to improve performance and reliability. This is also known as a RAID-5 configuration.

A typical disk configuration for a data striping set is pictured in Figure 20-3.

TAPE BACKUP WITH OFF-SITE ARCHIVING   Here data is copied to multiple sets of tapes (or optical disks) and carried to safe remote sites for archiving. Backup methods are covered later in this chapter.

BACKUP POWER   Win2K also supports uninterruptible power supplies and includes a program that can detect power failures and provide advance warning before the UPS

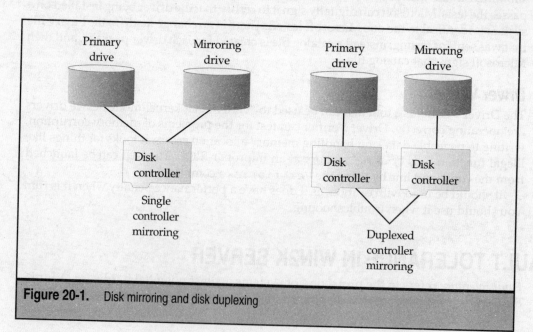

Figure 20-1.   Disk mirroring and disk duplexing

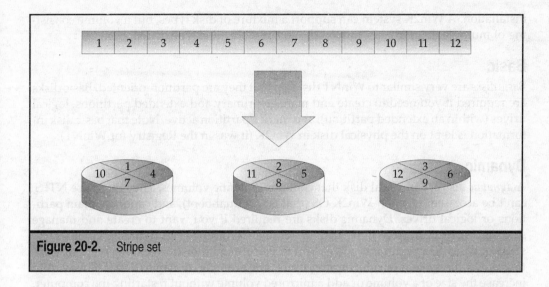

Figure 20-2. Stripe set

runs out of backup power. Power issues are covered under "Power Problems and Solutions" at the end of this chapter.

TIP: After creating or changing any disk configuration, choose the Configuration/Save command from the Partition menu to save the disk configuration information to a floppy disk.

Disk Types

Win2K supports two types of disks: basic and dynamic. By default all disks on Win2K are the basic type, but you can use the Upgrade Wizard to convert them to dynamic. New disks that were not configured at installation can be initialized as basic or dynamic after

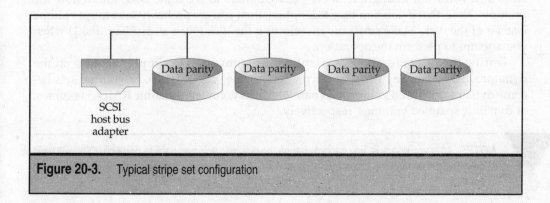

Figure 20-3. Typical stripe set configuration

installation. A Win2K system can support a mixture of disk types, but a volume consisting of multiple disks (that is, mirrored) must use only one type of disk.

Basic

Basic disks are very similar to WinNT disks, in that they are partition-oriented. Basic disks are required if you need to create and manage primary and extended partitions, logical drives (within an extended partition), and mark a partition active. Note that basic disk information is kept on the physical disk in Win2K (it was in the Registry for WinNT).

Dynamic

A *dynamic disk* is a physical disk that contains dynamic volumes. They must use NTFS, can't be accessed by a non-Win2K OS (that is, via dual-boot), and cannot contain partitions or logical drives. Dynamic disks are required if you want to create and manage spanned, striped, mirrored, or RAID-5 volumes. Working with dynamic volumes, instead of basic disk partitions, allows you to perform administrative tasks without shutting down the system or interrupting users. For example, dynamic disks allow you to increase the size of a volume or add a mirrored volume without restarting the computer. Just remember that if you want multiple-disk storage systems on Win2K, you need to use dynamic disks.

You may also come across the term *disk group*. A disk group is a collection of dynamic disks, which are managed as a single collection. Each disk in the group stores replicas of the same configuration data on the physical disk (as opposed to the Registry in WinNT). This enables you to move them to another computer or install another disk without losing the configuration information. All dynamic disks in a computer form a single disk group.

NOTE: New disks are always dynamic disks, and dynamic disks are not supported on mobile computers or removable media.

Converting Disks

To convert a basic disk to a dynamic disk, open the Disk Manager, and right-click the basic disk you want to upgrade, then select Upgrade to Dynamic Disk, and follow the prompts. Note, that if you don't see this option, then you are probably selecting a volume instead of the disk. Make sure you are selecting the disk (such as disk0 or disk1) when you attempt to perform the operation.

During the upgrade, all basic partitions are converted to simple volumes on the dynamic disk. Also, any existing mirror sets, stripe sets, RAID-5, or volume sets become dynamic mirrored volumes, dynamic striped volumes, dynamic RAID-5 volumes, or dynamic spanned volumes, respectively.

NOTE: After you upgrade, you cannot change the dynamic volumes back to partitions. You will have to delete all the dynamic volumes (and lose all data), then use the Action | Revert to Basic Disk option in the MMC.

Disk Mirroring

Disk mirroring, as shown previously in Figure 20-1, is a continuous backup method. Data is written to two disks at the same time. Because either disk in the set can continue providing data to users if the other fails, you can avoid the downtime and expense of recovering data from backup sets. *Disk duplexing* is a disk-mirroring technique that also duplicates the hardware channel to avoid downtime caused by the need to replace a disk controller.

Keep in mind that disk mirroring is a hardware backup technique that you use to recover from disk failures. You still need to back up data to protect information from corruption. If information is corrupted, it is stored in that corrupted state on both disks, and you'll need to restore from backup sets.

TIP: A mirrored set improves disk read performance because data can be read from either disk in the set.

Setting Up Disk Mirroring

You use the Disk Management tool (select Control Panels | Computer Management) to perform disk management tasks, such as setting up disk mirroring. To set up mirroring, you must first have at least two disks that are roughly the same size and are dynamic (remember, you can't set up any fault tolerance in Win2K on basic disks). Excess space on one of the disks is not used. You can mirror any existing volume, including the system and boot volumes, onto an available volume of another disk. The disks can use the same or different controllers. Follow these steps to build the mirrored volumes:

1. Install any new disks in your system that are required to create the mirrored volumes.

2. In the Disk Management tool, select the unallocated space on one of the dynamic disks where you will create the mirrored volume; then right-click and select Create Volume.

3. In the Create Volume Wizard, click Next and then Mirrored Volume, and follow the prompts.

A mirrored volume is created from the free space on each volume. If one disk is larger than another, its extra free space will go unused. Once the set is created, a single drive letter is assigned to all of the volumes and they are viewed as one drive by the operating system.

If an error occurs on one of the disks in the mirrored set, you need to first break the mirror, then replace the defective disk. While you are replacing the disk, the other disk can handle requests from users.

To break a mirrored set, first select one of the disks in the set, then right-click and select Break Mirror. Confirm that you want to break the set. The remaining volume becomes a separate volume with its own drive letter. You then replace the defective disk and follow the preceding numbered steps to create a new mirrored volume. The disk with existing data is automatically copied to the new disk to synchronize the new mirrored volume.

Disk Striping with Parity (RAID-5)

Disk striping in Win2K lets you spread data over an array of up to 32 disks. The disks appear as a single volume to users. Striping divides the data at the byte level and interleaves the bytes over each disk. Parity information is also written to each disk partition in the volume to give a level of data protection that is equivalent to disk mirroring but requires less disk space and provides faster read performance.

Disk striping provides high performance, especially when users read data more than they write it. Writing to striped sets is slower than writing to mirrored sets, but if high-performance servers and drives are used, you won't notice.

Disk striping with parity for Win2K Server requires a minimum of three disks to accommodate the way that parity information is striped across the disk set. Disks should be roughly the same size. Any extra space on partitions is not used.

Creating Stripe Sets

You use the Disk Management tool (select Control Panels | Computer Management) to perform disk management tasks, such as creating stripe sets. To create a stripe set with parity (that is, RAID-5), you must have three or more disks in the server, and they must all be dynamic. Follow these steps to create the stripe sets:

1. Install disks in your system for the stripe set. SCSI host adapters and drives are preferable.

2. In the Disk Management tool, select the unallocated space on one of the dynamic disks where you will create the RAID-5 volume, then right-click and select Create Volume.

3. In the Create Volume Wizard, click Next, then RAID-5 volume, and follow the prompts.

The size you select is divided by the number of disks to create equal-sized unformatted partitions. The entire set is assigned a single drive letter, and you can then format the stripe set as a single disk. If you want to remove a stripe set, select it in the Disk Management tool, and then right-click and select Delete. Confirm that you want to delete the volume. All the data is lost, and the volumes that are left will need to be reconfigured.

If a portion of a physical disk fails, you can install a new disk, and re-create the data that was on the failed portion from the remaining data and parity. Using the Disk Management tool, select free space that is the same size or larger than the other members of the RAID-5 volume, and then regenerate the data (right-click and select Regenerate). The system automatically reconstructs the data of the missing member and writes it to the new member.

DATA REDUNDANCY WITH Dfs

The Microsoft Distributed file system (Dfs) provides a method of data replication between its members. This replication can be used to replicate data in real time for means of availability and redundancy. You should have Dfs up and running before you decide what to replicate. This section will cover the replication portion of Dfs; please see Chapter 12 for details on setting up Dfs.

File Replication Service (FRS)

The File Replication Service (FRS) performs Dfs replication. In Chapter 8, we described how the FRS was used to replicate Active Directory information also; the processes are very similar. FRS replaces the replication mechanism of WinNT (LMRepl) and provides a much more robust mechanism for replicating files. It is multithreaded, which allows it to simultaneously replicate different files between different computers. When the file is replicated, all attributes including ACLs are maintained. It is multimaster, so files will be replicated by all servers that have them to all other servers (just like the AD), which increases the speed at which a total replication occurs. You can also schedule replications between sites (remember sites in the AD?).

Like LMRepl though, FRS will replicate an entire file even if you only change a couple of bytes. FRS knows a file has changed because it uses the NTFS change journal as a method of indicating a change to a file. The change journal will indicate when a file has been modified and closed, and FRS will only replicate a file after that cycle has completed. This also ensures that FRS does not lose track of a changed file even during system shutdowns.

The FRS will automatically start on Win2K DCs (to replicate the AD and Sysvol), but you have to manually start it on member servers. FRS is not available on Win2K Pro. FRS uses Kerberos for authentication between members for replication.

Dfs and Replication

You can enable automatic replication of files and folders between Win2K systems running Dfs. To configure replication on a Dfs root or Dfs link, you must first set up replica sets. By default Dfs replica sets do not replicate content between each other. This is probably not a good idea, unless the content is very static, so automatic replication is a good idea. We will look at setting up replication on the Dfs root \\nt.systemexperts.com\ Data. To do this, you use the Dfs snap-in to select the Dfs root, and then select Action | New Root Replica. You will be prompted through a few screens, where, in this example, you specify the replication partner to be Kadima and the share point to be replicated between \\Kadima\Data2. After this is complete, you would see the screen shown here. You would repeat this process for all the systems you want to set up replication between.

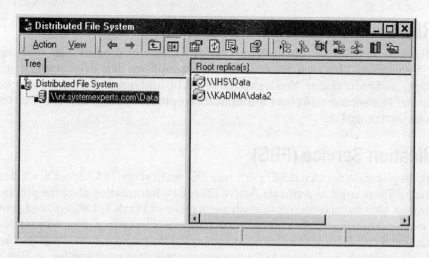

Now you can select the Dfs root (\\nt.systemexperts.com\Data), and then select Action | Replication Policy. This will allow you to configure two or more of the Dfs replicas to replicate their data between them using FRS. In our example, we have configured both of the systems to replicate between each other (see the following screen). If there were more than two systems, you could just choose to replicate between some of them, but that could potentially mean the files available on different Dfs replicas would not be consistent.

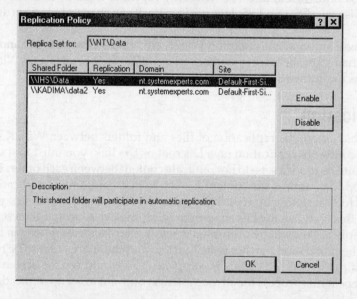

When you set the replication policy, you can also define the initial master from which the replication will start. This is important, because all of the other systems will end up looking like this one!

NOTE: The replication policy can be different for each Dfs root and link.

It is important to remember that as you are replicating files, changing the permissions on one replica will change them on each member of the replica set. If you don't use FRS to replicate, then you must set the permissions and manually propagate any changes.

Scheduling Replication

You cannot force Dfs replication in the same way you can with the AD. If you want replication to occur, you must manipulate the schedule. You can change the FRS schedule for an individual replica or replica set using the Advanced Features view on the Active Directory Users and Computers tool. Select System | File Replication Service | Dfs Volumes, and expand the Dfs root or link that has the replica set you want to change the schedule for (shown here).

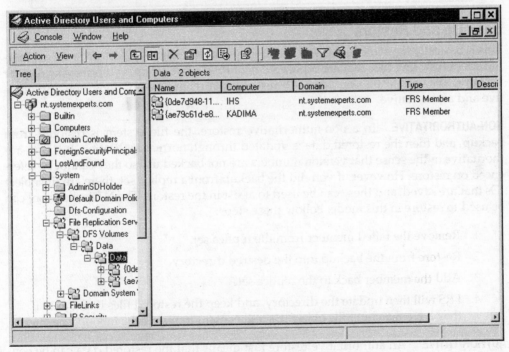

Select the Replica set, and then right-click and select Properties | Schedule. You will then see the schedule window shown here, and you can specify when replication is or is not available.

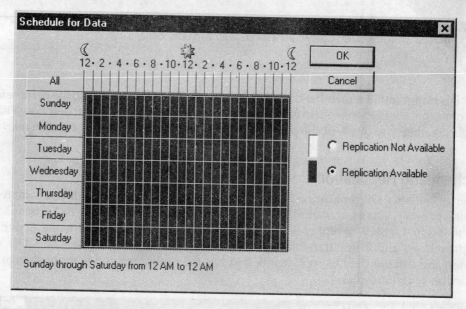

Back Up and Restore

This is basically the same process as backing up and restoring the AD, since we are talking about restoring files that are replicated via FRS. To back it up, you just make regular backups, say with `NTBackup.exe`. To restore it, you have two options: non-authoritative and authoritative.

NON-AUTHORITATIVE   In a non-authoritative restore, the file system is restored from backup, and then the restored data is updated through normal replication. It is non-authoritative in the sense that version numbers are not backed up, so they cannot be referenced on restore. However, if you did the backup from a replica set, there are file object IDs that are saved, and these can be used to assist in the restore. The NTBackup tool can be used to restore in this mode. Follow these steps:

1. Remove the failed member from the replica set.
2. Restore from the backup into the desired directory.
3. Add the member back to the replica set.
4. FRS will then update the directory, and keep the restored files if and only if they have matching file object IDs and content to that of the inbound partner.

AUTHORITATIVE   An authoritative restore just means that the restored data can be considered authoritative for replication matters (that is, its data *is* designated to take precedence over any other instances of those objects on other replicas). So when replication occurs, the restored data will be propagated out. This type of restore is usually used to restore from a known good state, for example before objects were deleted. If you are restoring in this mode, there is an assumption that all of the replicas have bad data. To restore in this mode, you need to perform the following steps:

1. Remove the failed member from the replica set.

2. Restore from the backup into the desired directory on one of the servers, using the option, When Restoring Replicated Data Sets, Make the Restored Data as the Primary for All Replicas to enable an authoritative restore.

3. Add the member back to the replica set.

4. FRS will then update the other members of the replica set, because the restored data is now considered authoritative.

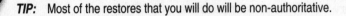

TIP: Most of the restores that you will do will be non-authoritative.

What's Not Replicated?

By default, encrypted (EFS) files and folders that are computer-specific, files with names starting with ~, files with .bak or .tmp extensions, NTFS mount points, and all reparse points are *not* replicated.

You can change the file or folder filter using the Advanced Features view on the Active Directory Users and Computers tool. Select System | File Replication Service | Dfs Volumes, and expand the Dfs root and link that you want to change the filters on. Select the Replica set, and right-click to open the Properties window (shown here). Then enter your changes in the File Filter box.

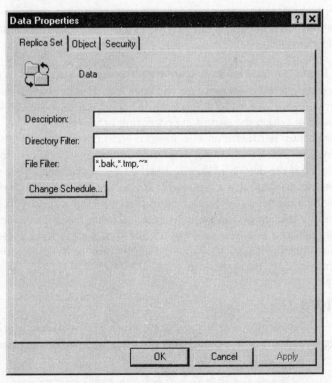

BACKING UP DATA

It's essential to back up the data on your server's hard drives. There are a number of ways you can perform backups, including copying data to magnetic tape or optical disks, or by copying or replicating information to other systems.

The traditional medium for backing up data is tape backup. Tapes are relatively inexpensive, which makes it economical to devise an archiving scheme where you store tapes permanently at safe locations, rather than reusing the tapes. Here are some points to keep in mind:

▼ Back up the entire system regularly or whenever you make major changes to its software, directory structure, or configuration.

■ Perform incremental backups to the files that have changed since you last made a major backup. If the information on your server changes constantly, you'll need to back up constantly.

■ Store a duplicate backup set at an off-site location to protect the backups from local disasters such as fires, earthquakes, and floods.

■ Schedule all of your backups during hours when fewer files are likely to be opened by users.

▲ Before you put your server into service, back it up, and then try restoring the information to make sure everything works and that you are familiar with the process.

NOTE: Before you can use the Backup utility included with Win2K, you must install a tape drive and tape driver in your system.

If possible, locate the tape backup system on the server you need to back up, rather than on a device connected elsewhere on the network. This will keep backup traffic off the network. However, you should still schedule backups after hours to keep them from affecting the speed at which the server is processing other tasks.

Choose your backup hardware wisely. Speed is an important consideration. If you need to restore your system, you'll want to get it up and running as soon as possible. The best performance is obtained if the device is directly attached to the apparatus you want to back up and restore. The primary tape-drive types used for server backup include quarter-inch cartridge (QIC), digital audiotape (DAT), and 8mm cassette. High-capacity, high-performance tape drives generally use Small Computer System Interface (SCSI) controllers.

To make backups and restores easier, put your Win2K operating system and data on separate partitions or physical disks. Then if one partition or disk gets corrupted or fails, you'll need to restore only that partition.

Backup Operators

By default, the Administrator and Backup Operators groups have the right to back up files, even though members of the group may not own the files they are backing up. Other users can back up any files that they own or that they are authorized to read. However, they cannot restore a file to a directory if they lack access to the directory or Write access to the file.

Since the Backup Operators group needs access to files that must be backed up and restored, members of this group have both Backup and Restore rights to read, change, and write any file. A hacker or intruder who gains access to the account could take advantage of these rights to steal files or gain further access into a system. Designate only trusted people as backup operators, and make sure their rights are limited to only those files and directories they need to back up. As an added precaution, you can log all backup operator activities in the Audit log.

Tape Security Issues

When you back up files on NTFS drives with the NTBackup utility, all the permissions, ownership rights, and audit flags associated with files can be written with files to tape. Files restored in an existing directory inherit the permissions of the directory, but if the directory has no special permissions, the file retains its previous permissions.

When a new tape backup set is created using the Win2K Backup utility, the user making the backup can restrict access to the tape by choosing the Allow Only the Owner and the Administrator Access to the Backup Data option. This designates the tape as *secure* and allows only the system administrator, the tape creator, and a person with the Back Up Files And Directories right to access the tape. If you are the tape creator, you must be logged on to the computer where the tape was originally created.

However, you should keep in mind that this security method is a relatively low level of access restriction. Anyone who gets hold of the tapes and really wants to look at the information on them can use various utilities that are designed for that purpose.

When the tape is restored, the permissions are copied back with the files. The permissions do not restrict access to files on the tape, but keep in mind that the username and computer name are stored in the headers of the tape. A person who has either a different username from the person who created the tapes or a different computer name from the computer that the tapes were created on cannot read a tape.

Keep the following points in mind with regard to "securing" backup tapes:

▼   System administrators, tape creators, and users with the Back Up Files And Directories right are allowed to read, write, and erase the tape. Other users cannot modify or delete the tapes using the NTBackup utility; this restriction provides a level of security that prevents accidental deletion.

■   If you need to transfer files between computers, do not set the Allow Only the Owner and the Administrator Access to the Backup Data option. However, anyone can read, write, or erase such tapes.

▲   Tapes made with the NTBackup utility are not encrypted, do not provide a high level of security, and should be locked up to prevent theft by someone who would attempt to read tape data using non-Win2K utilities.

Types of Backup

There are five types of backup: *normal, incremental, differential, copy,* and *daily*. The type of backup you choose depends on how many tapes you use, how often you want to back up, whether you are archiving tapes at a permanent storage location, and whether you rotate copies of your tapes off-site.

Normal Backup

A normal backup copies all the files selected for backup to a backup device and marks the files with a flag to indicate that they have been backed up. This method is the easiest to use and understand, because the most recent tape has the most recent backup. However, you'll need more tapes and more time for backup since all the selected files are backed up.

Incremental Backup

Incremental backup backs up only files that have been created or changed since the last normal or incremental backup. Files are marked with an archive flag so that they don't get backed up in the next backup unless they have been changed. This method requires that you create a normal backup set on a regular basis. If you need to restore from backup, you first restore the normal backup, then restore each incremental backup in order.

Differential Backup

With differential backup, you back up only files that were created or changed since the last normal (or incremental) backup. This method does not mark files with an archive flag to indicate that they have been backed up; consequently, they are included in a normal backup. If you implement this method, you should still create a normal backup on a regular basis. If you need to restore, first restore the normal backup, then restore the last differential backup tape.

Copy Backup

With copy backup, you copy all selected files to the destination, but do not mark each file as having been backed up. This method does not mark files with an archive flag to indicate that they have been backed up; consequently, they are included in normal and incremental backups. As with differential backups, you should still create a normal backup on a regular basis.

Daily Backup

A daily backup is just a copy backup on files that were modified that day.

Tape Rotation Methods

The number of backups you perform depends on the number of copies you want to keep, whether you want to keep on-site and off-site copies, and the age of the last backup (hours, days, weeks). You should consider a backup rotation method, which keeps incremental copies of backup data available.

The backup rotation method discussed here stores current and older data on a set of media that you can store in other locations, thus reducing the risk of losing your only backup set. If you have a five-day workweek, you need 20 tapes. Increase the number of tapes if you have six- or seven-day workweeks. Here are the key points of this rotation method:

▼ Four tapes are labeled Monday, Tuesday, Wednesday, and Thursday. Use these tapes for incremental or differential backup.

■ Four tapes are labeled Week 1, Week 2, Week 3, and Week 4. Create a complete backup to these tapes every Friday.

■ Twelve tapes are labeled for each month of the year; back up to these tapes at the end of each month. These tapes are stored off-site.

▲ To create a duplicate backup set that you can carry to an off-site location, double the number of tapes.

NOTE: This is only one example of a rotation method. You may need to alter this technique to fit your own needs.

With any backup system, you need to run a restoration test to ensure that your backup and restore procedures work. You might want to set aside spare servers and then run restoration tests using these servers on a regular basis. Before dismissing the concept of spare servers as an unjustifiable expense, consider how much a downed server could cost you in dollars and in customer dissatisfaction.

The Win2K Backup Utility

The Win2K Backup utility (NTBackup.exe) can use SMB/CIFS to back up servers attached to the network from the central location where the tape drive is installed. You can use the utility to back up and recover files on NTFS, HPFS, or FAT volumes, place multiple backup sets on a tape, span multiple tapes for a backup set or file, and automate the backup process. You can also use it to back up the System State files for the AD directory service data.

NOTE: You can run the Backup program only on the system where the tape drive is installed, but you can back up almost any other type of computer on the network once you get the program running.

If Backup encounters an open file, it normally backs up the last saved version of the file. During a restore, if a file on disk is newer than the file on tape, Backup asks for a confirmation to replace it.

To help you manage tapes in a backup set, each tape has the following information associated with it.

▼ A user-specified tape name

■ An original tape-creation date plus the date and time that each backup set was created

■ The computer name and the username of the user who created the tape

▲ A tape sequence number in the case of tape sets

The basic steps for using the Backup utility are described in the following sections. For detailed steps, refer to Backup's Help menus. To start the Backup utility, choose Start | Run and enter **ntbackup**. A Backup dialog box similar to this one appears:

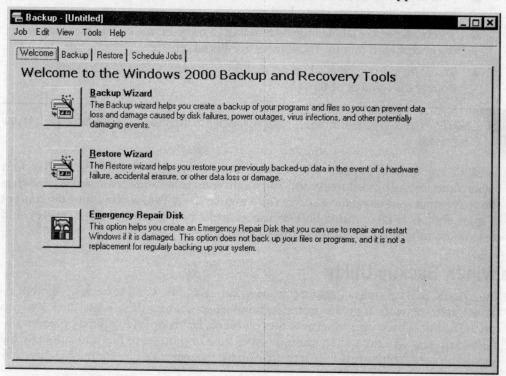

You can use the wizards, or select the appropriate tab to commence the backup.

Backup and Restore Modes

There are two basic modes of operation: Backup and Restore. In Backup mode, you can select the local drives, System State, and local or remote files and directories you want to back up. In Restore mode, you can choose a previously created backup set to restore to your system. Remember the following:

▼ You can use either the Backup Wizard or the Backup tab to perform a backup, or the similar options with the Restore Wizard to restore previously backed up files.

■ The Drive window shows a tree view of your hard drives and network shares. You can double-click on any drive to expand its view.

■ Checkboxes appear in front of each drive, directory, or folder in the expanded view. When you check a box next to a drive, directory, or file, that entity is included in the backup or restore.

■ If you click the checkbox for a drive, all the folders and files on the drive are included in the backup. However, you can open the drive and exclude any folders and files by deselecting the corresponding checkbox.

■ The Tools | Media Tools menu has the tools that are used to prepare physical tapes for use, such as Erase Tape, Re-tension Tape, and Format Tape.

▲ The Tree, View, and Window menus provide commands for manipulating windows and options, such as the status bar and toolbar in the Backup utility.

Once you've selected files to back up, you can click the Start Backup button. The following dialog box will appear:

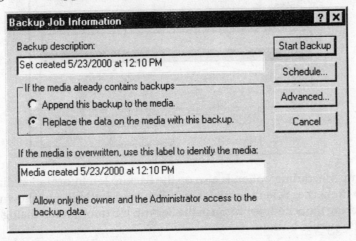

From the Backup Job Information dialog box, you can do the following:

▼ Set the description.

■ Choose to append to existing backups or replace an older set with a new one.

■ Secure the tape to limit access by checking the Allow Only the Owner and the Administrator Access to the Backup Data option (not available if appending to a set).

▲ Set the label on a new backup set.

You can also select advanced options (shown in the following screen), which allow you to do the following:

▼ Select the backup type.

■ Back up data in remote storage.

■ Confirm backup accuracy by selecting the Verify Data After Backup checkbox.

■ Compress the data on the tape media by selecting the If Possible, Compress the Backup Data to Save Space checkbox.

▲ If you are backing up System State, you can back up the protected system files also by selecting the Automatically Backup System Protected Files with the System State checkbox.

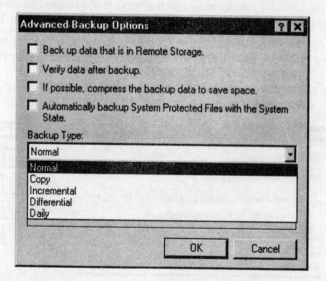

The backup scheduling option is also on the Backup Job Information dialog box. The Schedule Job Properties Schedule tab (shown first) and Settings tab (shown next) are accessed by clicking the Schedule button in the Backup Job Information dialog box and then clicking the Properties button.

▼ **Schedule Tab** Allows you to set the schedule: once, daily, weekly, monthly, at system startup, at logon, or when idle. For each selection, the appropriate other settings are displayed to be set (for example, if once, at what time?).

▲ **Settings Tab** Allows you to set completion rules, idle time parameters, and power management dependencies.

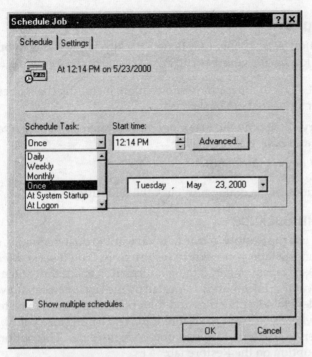

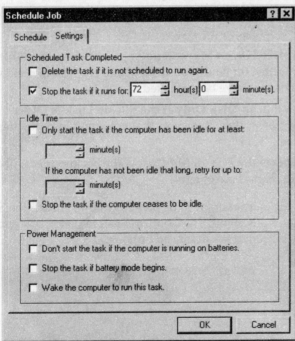

Logging Options

The log information (select Tools | Options | Backup Log) is where you specify that you want to create a log file for your backup. You set one of the following options:

▼ **Detailed**   Log all operations information, including the names of all the files and directories that are backed up.

■ **Summary**   Log only the major operations, such as loading a tape, starting the backup, and failing to open a file.

▲ **None**   Log no information.

After setting options in the dialog box, click the OK button.

Restoring from Backups

To restore tapes, use the Restore Wizard. If you want to do it manually, select the Restore tab, and then find the tape you want to restore from. You'll see a selection of previous backup sets. Backup tapes contain catalog information about the contents of the tape. For sets of tapes, the catalog information is located on the last tape. Step down the tree view of the files and folders to select the files and folders that you want to restore.

Then select where you want to restore it to. You can restore your backed-up data to the original folder, to an alternate folder, or to a single folder. This option is selected in the Restore Files To option on the Restore tab.

Then set the restore options by selecting Tools | Options | Restore. You must select one of three options:

▼ **Do Not Replace File on My Computer**   This will prevent files that exist from being overwritten on your hard disk. This is the best method when you are restoring files that have been deleted.

■ **Replace the File on Disk Only If the File on Disk Is Older**   This will restore only newer files. It ensures that you don't lose the changes you have made to files.

▲ **Always Replace the File on My Disk**   The backup files will overwrite the existing files, regardless of age.

After selecting tapes, backup sets, or files to restore, choose the Start Restore command from the Operations menu. The Confirm Restore dialog box appears, and you can click the Advanced button to set advanced options:

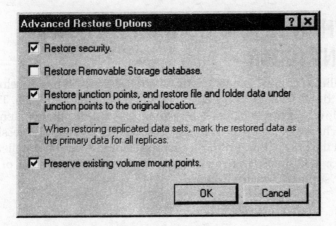

You can set the following options in this dialog box:

▼ **Restore Security**   Restores permission information along with the file. If this box is left disabled, files inherit the permissions of the directory into which they are restored.

■ **Restore Removable Storage Database**   Restores the removable storage database if it was corrupted.

■ **Restore Junction Points, and Restore Files and Folder Data Under Junction Points to the Original Location**   Restores data that is associated with junction points (that is, links).

■ **When Restoring Replicated Data Sets, Mark the Restored Data as the Primary for All Replicas**   Enables an authoritative restore.

▲ **Preserve Existing Volume Mount Points**   Keeps the mount points that currently exist.

Restore permissions only if you are restoring files to computers in the same domain as the original owner's account. Do not restore file permission if you are restoring to another computer outside the domain or to a computer that has not been completely restored following corruption of the operating system.

When you have set all the options for restoring files, click the OK button. The Restore will commence.

WINDOWS CHANGE AND CONFIGURATION MANAGEMENT (CCM)

Using the Intellimirror and Remote OS Installation, Microsoft has developed a technology called Windows Change and Configuration Management (CCM). The Remote OS Installation allows a sysadmin to use Pre-Boot eXecution Environment (PXE)-based remote-boot technology to perform remote installations of Win2K Professional (Server is not available at the time of this writing). After the Win2K system is installed and running, the Intellimirror takes over and provides policy-based management of users' Win2K desktops, data, settings, and applications.

Intellimirror

Intellimirror is not a specific service or program; rather it is a set of three technologies: Software Installation and Maintenance, User Settings Management, and User Data Management.

▼ **Software Installation and Maintenance**   Through the use of Group Policy, an administrator can specify a set of applications that will always be available to a user or group of users. It can be configured to automatically be installed, if it does not already exist. If it needs to be repaired (for any reason), updated, or removed, this can also be automated.

■ **User Settings Management**   Using the Active Directory, Roaming User Profiles, Offline Files, and Group Policy, you can manage all aspects of a user environment.

▲ **User Data Management**   Using the Active Directory, Synchronization Manager, Folder Redirection, Disk Quotas, and Group Policy, you can allow users to have access to the data they need at any system they log onto. It will also resynchronize Offline Files when the user reconnects to the network.

Offline Files

Offline Files allows you to work with network files and programs even when you are not connected to the network. Win2K uses the file system caching mechanism to implement this functionality and Group Policy to control its use. To make these resources available "offline," Offline Files stores a version of them in a reserved portion of the local disk, which allows them to be accessed regardless of whether the system is connected to the network or not. Each system that shares files can specify the caching (that is, offline) settings for that share. The caching properties (shown here) are configured on the individual share properties (select Share, and then right-click and select Properties).

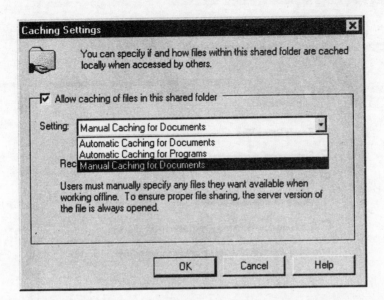

There are three caching options to choose from when sharing files:

▼ **Manual Caching for Documents**   This provides remote users the ability to specify which shared folder they want to cache. This is the default option when you set up a shared folder to be used offline.

■ **Automatic Caching for Documents**   This automatically makes every file that a remote user opens (and only those they open) from the shared folder available to them offline. If the user did not open the file, it is not available offline.

▲ **Automatic Caching for Programs**   This provides automatic access to every file in a shared folder. The caveat is that there is an assumption that the folder contains read-only files (that is, they will not change as documents do). The importance is that once the user has "cached" the folder, further access to the files in it are always local, without using the versions on the network in any way.

CONFIGURING YOUR COMPUTER TO USE OFFLINE FILES   To use Offline Files, you must configure your computer to use it. To do this, the preferred method is to use Group Policy (see Chapter 9). You can also set it up individually via Explorer by selecting Tools | Folder Options and clicking the Offline Files tab (shown here). Then select Enable Offline Files, and configure the desired options. Ensure that the Synchronize All Offline Files Before Logging Off option is set.

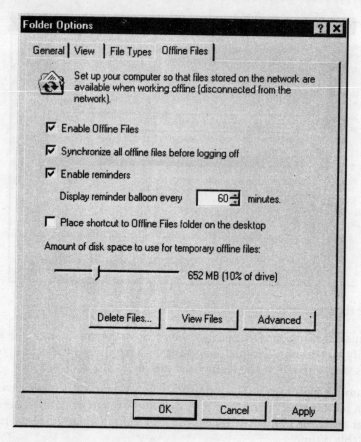

To make a file or folder available offline, you can select a shared folder (in Explorer), and then choose File | Make Available Offline. You should note that this option is only available if you have configured your system for Offline Files.

Synchronization Manager

The Synchronization Manager (`mobsync.exe`) helps to maintain proper data synchronization between the local system (that is, cache) and the server where the data is stored. It provides a single location that can be used to synchronize all Offline Files. You can use it to set up when synchronization will occur (as shown in the next illustration): at logon/logoff, at idle time, or on a specific schedule. You can also use Group Policy to control when user data is synchronized.

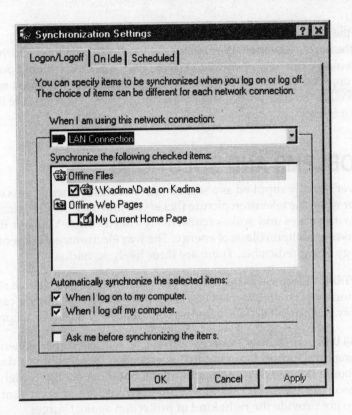

Folder Redirection

Folder redirection allows you to redirect what are normally local folders (such as My Documents) to a network share. Using Group Policy, you can configure a setting that allows you to redirect certain folders to other locations on the network. Using this in concert with Remote OS Installation and Software Installation and Maintenance allows for very simple workstation replacement.

A CCM Example

Let's say you had a workstation fail hard (that is, it could not be recovered as described earlier). The process to get it back is pretty straightforward: rebuild it, and then restore the data and settings. The real issue is the length of time it takes to get this done. There are a number of options that many people use:

▼ Rebuild from media, and then restore from backup or re-install apps from CD.

■ Use a disk image to rebuild (such as Symantec Ghost), and then restore the differences between the image and latest running version.

▲ Use CCM.

We'll look at the last option here.

Let's say the hard disk failed. We replace the hard disk, and then use the Remote OS Installation to install the base operating system. Then after the system boots, and when the user logs on, Intellimirror will ensure that any applications assigned to the user are available, as well as the user profile and data. Group Policy will configure the computer, and the system is back!

POWER PROBLEMS AND SOLUTIONS

Electrical power is rarely supplied as a smooth wave of steady energy, as is evident when lights flicker or when the television picture flickers off and back on. Electrical connections are polluted with surges and spikes (collectively called *noise*). You can think of these surges and spikes as shotgun blasts of energy. The way electronic equipment handles this transient energy is unpredictable. There are three likely scenarios.

DATA CORRUPTION   Electrical disturbances can cause memory to change states and can disrupt the information in data packets traversing a wire. These glitches can alter a program in memory and cause it to fail. Such errors are frequently mistaken for program bugs.

EQUIPMENT FAILURE   If transient energy is high, it will cause permanent damage to equipment. Small microprocessor circuitry is especially susceptible to damage. Surge suppressors should be used to protect equipment, but if the energy is high enough, the surge suppressor can burn out. You'll see a bit later in this chapter that some surge suppressors do not provide the right kind of protection against surges.

SLOW DEATH   Equipment that is repeatedly subjected to low-energy surges will fail over time. The delicate circuits in a chip break down, and the equipment eventually fails for no apparent reason. *Transients* that cause this type of problem "sneak" through surge suppressors that are not designed to protect against them. After a period of abuse, the chips themselves weaken and energy is released in unknown patterns that ultimately destroy the chip.

Power Solutions

If your server is connected to a network, you can protect systems from some power problems by connecting the entire network to one central power source and ground. However, this is usually impractical and defeats the purpose of a network, which is to spread computing resources to users at outlying locations. Two solutions are outlined next.

Using a Power Conditioner and a UPS

Place a power conditioner (to smooth out surges) and an uninterruptible power supply at the server. The power conditioner provides a clean source of power and a solid reference ground. Ground any network cables to the power conditioner ground. Surge suppression equipment should be placed at the feed (outside) to electrical panels. If the surge suppressors are placed on the branch circuits (inside), they will divert surges to the ground and back into the circuits of other systems through the ground connection.

Using a Nonconductive Fiber-Optic Cable

If you need to interconnect networks that are using different power supplies, use a nonconductive fiber-optic cable between the systems to eliminate ground loops. The primary reason for ensuring the separation of the power sources is that they will most likely have different ground potentials, which can cause problems in sensitive electrical equipment if they are linked together.

Ensure that a single LAN segment is connected to circuits that branch from a single power source, and that no point in the segment shares a ground with other power sources. An electrical contractor can perform this service.

Using Uninterruptible Power Supplies

Your basic power and grounding system can be augmented by an uninterruptible power supply (UPS). A UPS provides electrical power to computers or other devices during a power outage. A UPS can be any of the following:

▼ A battery system

■ A rotary device that uses the inertia of a large flywheel to carry the computer system through brief outages

▲ Internal combustion motors that run AC generators

UPS devices come in two forms: online and standby. A *standby device* kicks in only when the power goes down. Therefore, it must contain special circuitry that can switch to backup power in less than five milliseconds. An *online device* constantly provides the source of power to the computer. Because of this, it doesn't need to kick in. If the outside source of power dies, the batteries within the unit continue to supply the computer with power. Although online units are the better choice, they are more expensive than standby units. But because online units supply all the power to a computer, that power is always clean and smooth.

RECAP

We have covered a number of features that can be used to enhance the fault tolerance of your Win2K systems and networks. The most important part of it all is knowing how they work and if they work (when was the last time you did a restore?). There are a number of best practices that you should follow:

▼ Back up volumes as opposed to individual files and folders; they are more efficient to restore.

■ Always back up the System State.

- Implement a software mirror of two separate hardware-controlled RAID arrays on highly critical systems.

- Have hot spares for critical systems, or at least a base system onto which you could place data disks.

- Use CCM to rebuild Win2K Pro systems.

- Use the Hardware Compatibility List (HCL) as much as possible.

- Implement a robust backup and restore process, and document it!

- Avoid single points of failure.

- Use multiple network interfaces for server machines.

- Use DFS to replicate files and folders.

▲ Watch your systems and networks. Continually monitor for and analyze the cause of failures. It is a good idea to keep a log book on individual systems for trend tracking.

Most of all, be prudent and consistent. Remember: The turtle beat the hare, not because he was faster, but because he kept at it.

CHAPTER 21

Hardening Windows 2000

O ne of the most frustrating things that system administrators have to do is to determine what steps they need to take to secure a system. This chapter will look at a methodic way of securing a Win2K system. The focus will be on the Win2K Server.

AN OVERVIEW

This chapter is a step-by-step look at setting up a hardened Win2K system. Since there are a large number of variations on configurations, depending on what services you install where, we will take it to a secure baseline. From that baseline, you can work forward with any and all of the services that we have covered in this book. *Use this chapter in concert with the other chapters, not in a vacuum!*

When you get done with this chapter, you should be able to set up a hardened Win2K box and have a good understanding of the tools you can use to check things out. You should also be able to take concepts out of this chapter and apply them to almost any hardening situation. They are all helpful in their own right. They are just layers on the security onion.

As with any security-related services, you must ensure that the underlying operating system is as secure as possible. To do this, we will go about hardening the Win2K Server.

THE REQUIREMENTS

Like anything, you have to start with architecture, especially when hardening systems. There are a few fundamental questions that you need an answer to in order to ensure that the systems you configure are not too "hard" or too "soft" when all is said and done. Here are the questions to ask:

▼ *Can the system be self-contained (that is, a workgroup), or does it need to be part of a group (that is, a domain)?*

■ *If in a domain, can you have native-mode, or will you require mixed-mode?* If there will be WinNT or Win 9*x* boxes, then you must use mixed mode.

■ *How many interfaces does the machine require?* This is usually more applicable to firewall machines, which require at least two network interface cards (NICs). A third card would be used for an extranet.

■ *What services will it be providing?*

▲ *What protocols will you be using?*

Once you have the answers, then you can press on to configuring the system. If you don't have the answers, then get them *before* you start.

THE HARDWARE

Win2K security, as with its predecessor WinNT, relies strongly on physical security and proper hardware setup. If I can get to the disk, or boon another copy of Win2K or some other OS, then there is a high likelihood that I can get at resources that I shouldn't be able to. To minimize this, we need to perform the following tasks and configure the system appropriately:

▼ Install case locks on all publicly accessible systems.

■ Put critical or highly sensitive systems in cages.

■ If removable media (that is, floppies, CDs, ZIP drives) are allowed, then you should set the hardware to boot from the hard drive first.

▲ Set the EEPROM boot password.

INSTALLING THE OPERATING SYSTEM

In this section, we will go through the process of the initial installation of Win2K Server. When you are installing for security, you should start from scratch (that is, not upgrade from a previous OS like WinNT), as there are potential unknowns about the software and state of applications on that system. You will save yourself a lot of time and potential frustration if you do a clean install.

VIP: One important item of note is that if you do install from scratch, the default NTFS and registry permissions are adequately secure. This was not the case in WinNT and should be enough of a motivator in and of itself to get you to start clean.

Here are the steps in the install process that have security implications:

1. The install starts with a number of screens about licensing and so on; they are pretty standard and self-explanatory.

2. You will come to the disk configuration screen (shown here). You will want to ensure that the disk is partitioned into at least two separate partitions. One for

the system and OS files, and the other for data files. In our example, we have made 850MB and 148MB partitions.

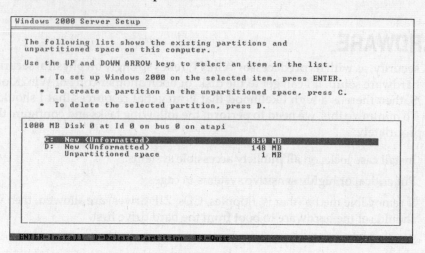

3. The next screen will ask you for the format of the disks; you should choose NTFS (which is the default selection).

4. You will then be prompted to configure proper regional settings (this is especially important for timestamps on logs), name and organization, and license modes.

5. Following that, you will enter the computer name and the administrator password as shown in the following illustration. It is *very* important to select a strong password for the administrator. This will be the password that is stored in the local SAM database. See Chapter 10 for more on the Administrative user.

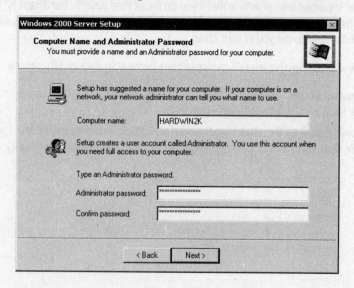

6. The next screen, shown here, will allow you to specify which Win2K components
   are installed. You should uncheck all the options. We want a minimum install
   and will go back later to add anything that we actually need. Remember that
   we are going for a minimalist system, then build it up to what we want later.

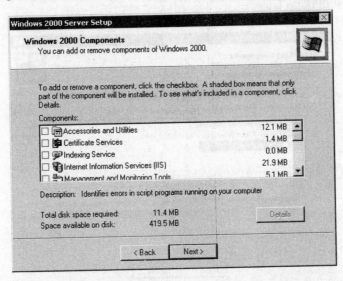

7. The next option is Networking Settings, as shown in the following illustration.
   We will be using the Custom Settings to enter the specific networking setup
   configurations that we want. Typical Settings would configure the TCP/IP
   protocol, Microsoft Networking support for both client and server, and IP
   address assignment via DHCP.

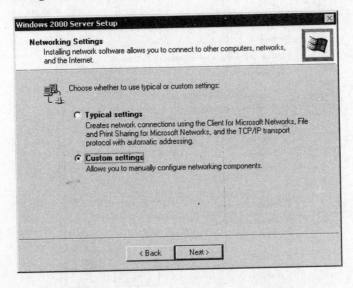

8. Because we choose the Custom Settings option, we will have the opportunity to configure each and every network interface card that is in the system. For each interface, you should ensure that the only thing that is selected is Internet Protocol (TCP/IP) as shown here. If you need more services or protocols, you can install them later.

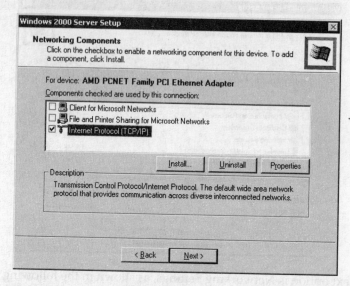

9. The general screen on the NIC, shown in the following illustration, allows us to set the IP addresses. We want to make sure that we use static IP addresses for highly secure systems. You may choose to use DHCP (that is, assign automatically), but that is a call you must make.

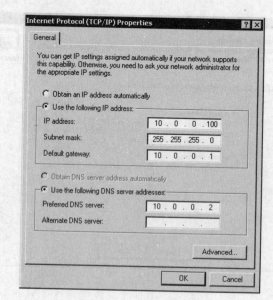

10. Click the Advanced button to configure the DNS and WINS configuration on the NIC. The DNS configuration, shown here, is set up to have the system attempt to perform dynamic updates to the DNS server. If you do not support this, then you are encouraged to disable the Register This Connection's Address in DNS option. Since this is information that we are sending out, and not accepting, it is of minimal risk from this system's perspective.

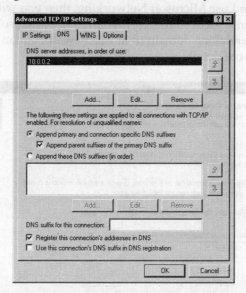

You will also want to disable the Enable LMHOSTS lookup and select the Disable NetBIOS Over TCP/IP option on the WINS tab, shown here. This effectively disables a large portion of the NetBIOS that is in Win2K.

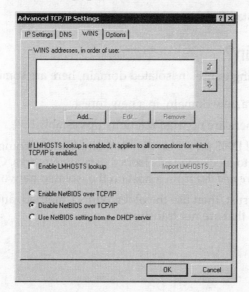

11. Next you will determine if the system is to be part of a domain or workgroup (shown in the next illustration). The setting of this is determined by the answers to the questions that you were asked at the beginning of the chapter. The best bet is to specify that the machine is part of a workgroup, and *not a* domain. If it is self-contained, this means that there is no need for any Microsoft Networking communications between it and any other host. If you put it in a Workgroup and use Microsoft Networking, then you will be using NTLM authentication instead of Kerberos. If you require Microsoft communications, then set up a standalone domain (that is, a new domain in a new forest). See Chapter 8 for more details.

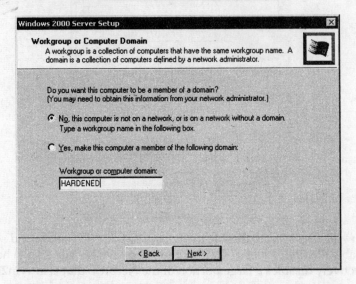

12. Then let the install finish.

What About a Domain?

Note that if you are going to use an isolated domain, here are some guidelines:

▼ Make sure it is a new domain, in a new forest.

■ Validate that there are no trust relationships established.

■ Run an internal DNS server on that domain. Use screening routers and DNS configurations to block requests from external networks. Configure DNS to *only accept secure updates* from a host on the isolated network.

▲ If you require trust, then use the older WinNT method, and establish specific one-way trusts that are not transitive.

What If You Can't Start Anew?

There may be times when there is no option but to go with what you have. In that case, all is not lost, but you have your work cut out for you. In order to go this route, you should configure the system using the Local Security Policy tool. In this tool, use the security policy templates (`setup security.inf` for all systems; then in addition to that, use `DC security.inf` for domain controllers) located in `%systemroot%\winnt\security\templates`, to reconfigure the local system to the level of a freshly installed system. (Note that this has a high probability of causing stuff to break, and that is where the work comes in.) Also, ensure that all of these system requirements are set (that is, with strong passwords and NTFS).

TIGHTENING THE SYSTEM

Once the system reboots and starts up, you need to go to the second phase of "hardening," which consists primarily of disabling services that you did not have a choice to install (and there are a number of them), and setting local security policy. Policy deals with things such as SMB signing, authentication accepted, legal notices, auditing, and more.

Hardening Services

For each service that exists on a Win2K system, you have a number of controlling options. You can also disable the startup of options so they don't run at all. The basic strategy is to run as few services as possible so hackers can't exploit any bugs those services might have. Another strategy is to run services under less-privileged accounts. All default services runs under the context of the Local System account, which has privileges to the entire system. If you install a defective program that runs under this account, it could damage your system. Worse, a hacker might take advantage of a hole in the program to attack your system with the full privileges of the System account. Many attacks in the Unix environment took place under similar conditions.

Disabling Services

The biggest layer on the security onion is disabling unused and unneeded services. This is probably the hardest thing to get right, mostly because of the horrid lack of documentation from Microsoft as to each service's complete function and dependencies. As a matter of principle, it is easier to define what should be enabled (that is, what's required for basic functionality) for a basic TCP/IP system, and turn off the rest, rather than trying to turn off what is bad.

VIP: It is important to know what each service is used for. Appendix A details each of the services available on Win2K to help assist in this evaluation.

For a medium- to high-security system, ensure the services listed next are the only ones running. The asterisks (*) indicate the minimal services required to operate the box—all others are optional and represent potential risk.

▼ DNS Client*
■ EventLog*
■ IPSec Policy Agent
■ Logical Disk Manager*
■ Network Connections Manager
■ Plug and Play*
■ Protected Storage*
■ Remote Procedure Call
■ Remote Registry Service
■ RunAs Service
■ Security Accounts Manager*
■ Server
▲ Workstation

For a domain controller you will need

▼ DNS Server
■ File Replication Service
■ Kerberos Key Distribution Center
■ Net Logon
■ NT LM Service Provider
■ RPC Locator
▲ Windows Time

To disable the services that are running but are not needed at this time, we will use the Services control panel. To start it up, select Start | Settings | Control Panel | Administrative Tools | Services. Then open (double-click) the appropriate service. This will bring up the service's Properties sheet (the Alerter Properties sheet is shown in the following illustration). From there, you change the Startup Type field to Disabled. Since this will prevent it from starting at the next boot, we will need to stop the service now. To do this, click the Stop button in the Service Status section.

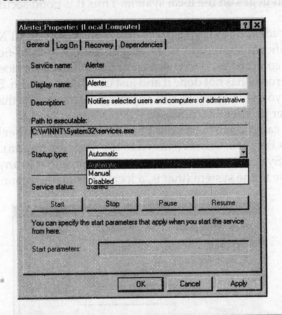

TIP: When you're not dealing with highly secure hosts, but just want to generally secure systems, this still applies. The general premise of not installing services unless you need them, and then disabling the ones you cannot uninstall is still valid. You will have to take some time and effort to understand the exact setup for any architecture you need, but this should give you a good feel for how to go about it.

DISABLING OR DELETING?   There is always a question as to whether it is best to *disable* or *delete* a service. The basic premise is that a disabled account can be restarted by enabling, then starting it. This is a simple and easy process *if* you have the right permissions on the system. A deleted service, on the other hand, cannot be started until it is re-installed, thus it is significantly harder to have this happen maliciously, especially for Win2K core services. The answer seems simple, but it's not. The problem is that it is very hard (impossible perhaps) to actually remove some of the services. The best bet for time and efficiency is to disable services that have no easy installation method (that is, are installed at this point in the setup), and delete/uninstall others that you may add later in the process.

Changing Service Logon Account

Services are started up under the context of some user, most of the time the Local System account. As you know from many other sections in this book, that account has almost unlimited privileges on the local system. Thus it is good security practice to use it as little as possible.

That is a great idea, but very impractical for most, if not all Microsoft services. It would take a significant amount of work and documentation to figure out the account configuration that could be used to run each of the different services, which is probably the reason that Microsoft has not done it and just uses Local System. Even though it seems to be a lost cause, you should try to run anything that you can (that is, third-party services) under a lesser privilege account.

To do this, you can change the account that a service runs under by using the Log On tab on the service's Properties sheet (shown in the next illustration). By default, they are all using the Local System account, but you could change that to any account that can be used to authenticate to the system (that is, a local or domain account).

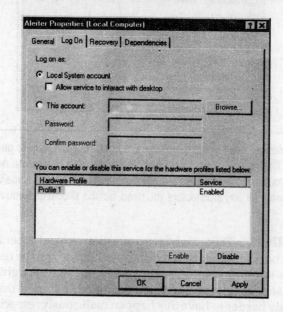

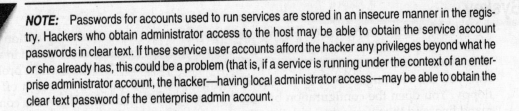

NOTE: Passwords for accounts used to run services are stored in an insecure manner in the registry. Hackers who obtain administrator access to the host may be able to obtain the service account passwords in clear text. If these service user accounts afford the hacker any privileges beyond what he or she already has, this could be a problem (that is, if a service is running under the context of an enterprise administrator account, the hacker—having local administrator access—may be able to obtain the clear text password of the enterprise admin account.

Finding Dependencies

One of the major problems with Microsoft services has been the (in)ability to easily determine which services relied on other services. In the Dependencies tab on the service's Properties sheet, you can view this information. The Alerter service's dependencies are shown here.

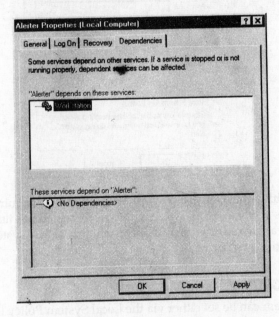

Syskey

By default, Win2K strongly encrypts the local Sam database. This is the Syskey option in WinNT. The potential problem is that the key used to decrypt the database is stored in an obfuscated form in the registry. This could be a potential problem. To eliminate the problem, you can reconfigure Syskey to require manual password entry or to read it off a floppy. You open the configuration by running the SYSKEY command from the command line, and then using the Update option to get to the screen shown next:

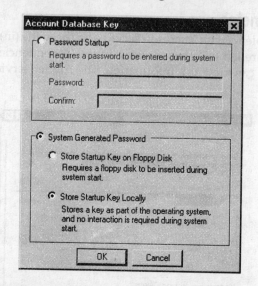

The problem with either of these two options, is that they require some level of user intervention (unless you leave the floppy in the drive, which has its own security problems). So you will want to reconfigure this only for highly secure systems that will require manual intervention to start up.

Setting System Policy

The policy of a system can be set either via the Local System Policy tool or Group Policy (see Chapter 9). For our purposes, we have chosen a self-contained (that is, no domain) type system, so we will be using the Local System Policy tool to set our policy.

Password Policies

Make sure that the following options have been configured in the Password Policy section of the local policy. Set the values in accordance with your company's policy.

Enforce Password History	Enabled (recommended value is 5)
Maximum Password Age	Enabled (recommended value is 60)
Minimum Password Age	Enabled (recommended value is 5)
Passwords Must Meet Complexity Requirements	Enabled
Store Password Using Reversible Encryption	Disabled

Account Lockout Policies

Make sure that the following options have been configured in the Account Lockout Policy section of the local policy. Set the values in accordance with your company's policy.

Account Lockout Threshold	Enabled (recommended value is 5)
Account Lockout Duration	Enabled (recommended value is 30)
Reset Account Lockout Threshold After	Disabled (recommended manual reset of accounts)

Audit Policy

Make sure that the following options have been configured (at a minimum) in the Audit Policy section of the local policy. Set the values in accordance with your company's policy, but at a minimum, you should audit success and failure for the following audit categories:

▼ Audit Account Logon Events
■ Audit Account Management
■ Audit Logon Events
■ Audit Policy Change
▲ Audit System Events

AUDIT LOG SETTINGS   You need to ensure that there is adequate space in the audit logs for the audits that will be generated. This is especially important if you will halt the system on audit failure (see "Security Options"). You should configure the systems to handle your log capacity (you will have to test to see what that is) plus another 50 percent. Remember to set your rotation policy as well. This should be consistent with whatever policy you have.

User Rights

Make sure that the following options have been configured in the User Rights section of the local policy. Ensure that they have the users and groups you want in them. A good rule of thumb is that the Administrator has most of them. You should be validating the entries that are done during the setup, as they are pretty good. If anything, you should be removing accounts and groups, or adding specific groups that you require. See Chapter 10 for more details on users and groups.

▼ Access This Computer From the Network

■ Act as Part of the Operating System

■ Back Up Files and Directories

■ Change the System Time

■ Create a Token Object

■ Debug Programs

■ Force Shutdown From a Remote System

■ Increase Scheduling Priority

■ Load and Unload Device Drivers

■ Log On as a Service

■ Log On Locally

■ Manage Auditing and Security Log .

■ Modify Firmware Environment Values

■ Profile Single Process

■ Profile System Performance

■ Replace a Process Level Token

■ Restore Files and Directories

■ Shut Down the System

▲ Take Ownership of Files or Other Objects

Additionally, if your systems are part of a domain, you should validate the users and groups that have the following rights:

▼   Add Workstations to Domain

■   Deny Access to this Computer from the Network

■   Deny Logon Locally

■   Enable Computer and User Accounts to Be Trusted for Delegation

▲   Synchronize Directory Service Data

Security Options

Make sure that the following options have been configured in the Security Options section of the local policy. You should be validating the entries that are done during the setup, as they are pretty good, but should be specific to your installation. The settings dealing with signing and encrypting of SMB and the Secure Channel are of critical importance if you are using Microsoft Networking.

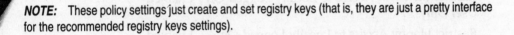

NOTE: These policy settings just create and set registry keys (that is, they are just a pretty interface for the recommended registry keys settings).

Additional Restrictions for Anonymous Connections	No access without explicit anonymous permissions
Allow System to Be Shut Down Without Having to Log On	Disabled
Audit Use of Backup and Restore Privilege	Enabled
Clear Virtual Memory Pagefile When System Shuts Down	Enabled
Digitally Sign Client Communication (Always)	Enabled (for high security) (See Chapter 12 for issues with digital signing.)
Digitally Sign Client Communication (When Possible)	Enabled (for medium security)
Digitally Sign Server Communication (Always)	Enabled (for high security)
Digitally Sign Server Communication (When Possible)	Enabled (for medium security)
Disable CTRL-ALT-DEL Requirement for Logon	Disabled
Do Not Display Last User Name in Logon Screen	Enabled (for multiuser systems)

LAN Manager Authentication Level	Send NTLMv2 responses only/refuse LM & NTLM (See Chapter 11 for compatibility issues.)
Message Text for Users Attempting to Log On	Get from your legal department
Message Title for Users Attempting to Log On	Get from your legal department, something along the lines of "Authorized Users Only"
Number of Previous Logons to Cache (In Case Domain Controller Is Not Available)	0
Prevent Users From Installing Printer Drivers	Enabled
Recovery Console: Allow Automatic Administrative Logon	Disabled
Rename Administrator Account	Rename this to something other than "admin" or "administrator"
Restrict CD-ROM Access to Locally Logged-On User Only	Enabled
Restrict Floppy Access to Locally Logged-On User Only	Enabled
Secure Channel: Digitally Encrypt or Sign Secure Channel Data (Always)	Enabled (for high security) (See Chapter 11 for issues with digital signing or encrypting.)
Secure Channel: Digitally Encrypt Secure Channel Data (When Possible)	Enabled (for medium-high security)
Secure Channel: Digitally Sign Secure Channel Data (When Possible)	Enabled (for medium security)
Secure Channel: Require Strong (Windows 2000 or Later) Session Key	Enabled (for ultra-high security)
Send Unencrypted Password to Connect to Third-Party SMB Servers	Disabled
Shut Down System Immediately If Unable to Log Security Audits	This should be consistent with your policy. It is very drastic and can be used as a DoS attack
Strengthen Default Permissions of Global System Objects (e.g. Symbolic Links)	Enabled
Unsigned Driver Installation Behavior	Do not allow
Unsigned Non-Driver Installation Behavior	Do not allow

Unbinding Services

The best way to secure a system is to use it for one purpose and secure it around that specific purpose. This should be your goal: one service, one system. The reality, though, is that many people will not heed this advice and will run systems that support multiple functions, because either they do not see the problem with it, or they have financial constraints that prohibit them from doing it the right way.

The best way to understand this is with a scenario. Let's say you want to be able to administer all aspects of the Win2K box from your internal network, as well as provide Web and FTP services to Internet users. This model poses a potential problem, in that external users may be able to access the administration services that were meant for internal users only. To set this up securely, you will not only "disable" services, but also you will "unbind" specific services from specific network interfaces.

Networking Services

Consider that there are two basic categories of networking services available on a Win2K computer system:

▼ Microsoft's File and Print services (a.k.a. Microsoft Networking), that is SMB or CIFS. This is the native method for almost all Microsoft-related API transports. These services are installed by default.

▲ General TCP/IP and Internet services such as Web servers and FTP servers. They are installed as optional services.

The major problem with Microsoft Networking is that it is more than likely set up for backward compatibility, and not set up to enforce any of its security features. This is not to say that the general TCP/IP services are any more secure, but individually they usually are limited in the scope of what they do. This tends not to be the case with Microsoft Networking. Suffice to say that we need to ensure that "default" Microsoft Networking never reaches any untrusted network (that is, the Internet).

The best way to ensure this is to not install it, or just disable it. This may be easier said than done though; completely disabling Microsoft Networking may not be practical. Assume you set up the Web server to publish information about your company on the Internet. Now suppose the marketing people in your company need to frequently update information on that Web server. If the Web server is isolated and locked up in some closet, they are going to have a tough time making those updates. If the content is complex, transferring it to the Web server via floppy disk, tape, or other media will be difficult and they will probably rely on you, the system administrator, to handle those updates. Here are two possible solutions to this problem:

▼ Use another method of updating the Web server, such as FrontPage extensions.

▲ Install Microsoft Networking and "disable" it on all non-internal interfaces.

You decide on the second option because it is something you can control and watch very closely.

NOTE: It would be trivial to set up an IDS system to detect any "anomalous" activity coming from this service on this machine.

Disabling or Unbinding

To unbind Microsoft Networking, select Start | Settings | Network and Dial-Up Connections. Then highlight NIC, go to the menu bar, and select Advanced | Advanced Settings to bring up the Advanced Settings dialog box, as shown in the following illustration. For this scenario, we will say that LAN2 is our external network card.

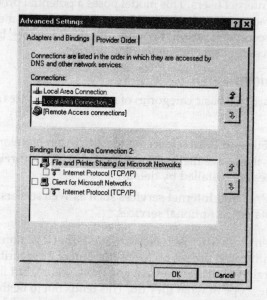

To disable the Microsoft Networking service protocol on the LAN2 adapter, you would select the LAN2 adapter in the Connections panel, and clear the checkboxes associated with the Microsoft Networking services (as shown previously).

NOTE: A reboot is *not* required to set this feature. Unbinding the File and Printer Sharing for Microsoft Networks option will prevent remote machines from connecting to CIFS/SMB services on this machine and will close port 445 tcp and idp. Tcp 139 will still be listening on this NIC, but will not return any information to the remote machine. If the Client for Microsoft Networks option is still enabled, the host itself will still be able to perform SMB connections to remote hosts even though it won't accept any incoming requests (if the file and printer sharing option is disabled).

Once you have completed this, now you will be able to access Microsoft Networking and the Web server on this machine from your internal network, while only allowing Web access from the Internet.

VIP: This setup should not be used on DMZ or firewall systems. Anyone concerned with security should not use any Microsoft Networking on firewall or DMZ systems.

For security reasons, consider requiring that all server administration take place at the console of the server itself, thus eliminating the need for Microsoft Networking connectivity (unless you use a domain architecture). To do this, set the Deny Access to This Computer from the Network local policy for the Administrators group, thus revoking network logon privileges for the Administrators.

Digging Deep

Sometimes you have to dig deep to get the desired results. For example in WinNT, just because you unbound NetBIOS from the interfaces, didn't mean it quit listening; you had to disable the WINS driver to get it to stop listening completely. The question is, what do you have to do to get your desired effects? That all depends on your security needs. Just keep in mind, that you may have to "dig deep" to get what you want.

Filtering TCP/IP Connections

Another option in the hardening process is to set up the TCP/IP filters on a system to help secure it. This should be used on systems that are directly connected to untrusted networks (that is, the Internet) or on systems that you want a higher level of assurance in the security of the system.

There are two methods to accomplish this task: IPSec filters and TCP/IP filtering. The latter is the same method that WinNT provided. It is not as granular as IPSec filters, but it is a bit easier to set up, so we will cover that first. IPSec filters are a great way to provide detailed filters but are more complex to configure. You should use IPSec filters, as they can be implemented in Group Policy, where TCP/IP filtering is only locally configurable.

TCP/IP Filtering

To continue with the Web and FTP server example, we can set up filtering using the Network and Dial-Up Connections control panel. Select the interface you want to set up the filter on, and select Properties | General | Internet Protocol (TCP/IP) | Properties | Advanced | Options | TCP/IP Filtering | Properties (shown in the next illustration). As shown, we have set up the filter to allow inbound TCP connections to ports 21 (ftp), 80 (http), and 443 (https). Also, we have allowed no UDP (that is, by permitting no ports), and set it to only allow IP protocol 6 (TCP). Rebooting is required to enable this feature.

> **NOTE:** Even though we have not chosen to allow IP protocol 1 (ICMP), ICMP traffic will still be allowed to and from this host. ICMP can be blocked via the Local Security Policy for IPSec.

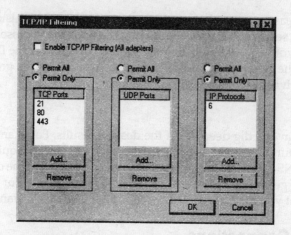

You do not want to deploy this on every system for two very good reasons: administration and Denial of Service (DoS). Since the TCP/IP filters must be administered on the local system, you have a major administration issue. But the more pressing issue is that if you don't get the ports right, then you will create a DoS yourself. When you set up filtering, it is important to understand every port that will be open, and when you have RPC-based services, which many of the Microsoft services are, you can't be sure what is running where. A good rule of thumb is to use this on systems that are offering services with well-known ports (that is, Web and Mail).

IMPORTANT "FEATURES"   TCP/IP filtering has some very important "features" that you should be aware of:

▼ It does *not* affect any outbound packets or inbound packets for already established connections. Thus a system with everything blocked in the filter rules can still communicate as normal, as long as the local system in question initiates the packets.

▲ It does not really understand the IP portion of the stack, in that even if you say to only permit IP protocol 6 (TCP), it will still allow ICMP in. Thus, there can be no assurance that it will block any other IP-based protocol that is apparently not allowed. It is really only useful for filtering TCP and UDP protocols.

IPSec Filtering

The setting up of IPSec filters is covered in detail in Chapter 16, so we will just summarize what needs to be done to filter our "Web and FTP" server. As you may recall, IPSec policies are managed from either the Local Security Policy, Group Security Policy, or the individual IPSec Policy snap-in, and are activated via the Local or Group Policy. The three key configurations that we will need to set are

- ▼ IPSec filter lists
- ■ IPSec filter actions
- ▲ IPSec policy rules

First you will create an IPSec policy; in our example, we will call it **Web & FTP**. Then, within the new Web & FTP policy, we will add an IPSec filter list that will be used to hold the IPSec filter actions we want applied. In other words, we are creating a filtering *policy* that will contain a *list* of filter *actions* that will be applied to network traffic entering and leaving the system.

Figure 21-1 shows the IPSec filter actions associated with the IPSec filter list we are creating. As you can see, the filter allows traffic from any IP address with a destination of the Web server with a destination port of HTTP (port 80), HTTPS (443), FTP (port 21), and FTP-DATA (port 20). It also has a rule to allow PASV FTP in terms of the FTP server actually initiating the FTP-DATA connection from port 20 to any IP address. By default, all filters are *mirrored*, which means that packets with source and destination addresses reversed will also match the filter.

After you save all the information in the different configuration panels, the filter actions are stored in the filter list, which is then stored as part of a filter policy. Once you have the filter policy, you can use the IP Security Policies on Local Machine (or Group Policy) to then assign the policy. To do this, right-click the policy you want to assign (to activate), and select Assign. Once the policy is assigned, it will immediately start filtering packets; no reboot is required.

NOTE: Interestingly enough, the filtering capabilities that we are using here have nothing to do with IPSec; they just happen to be configured using the IPSec interface. That is to say you can use the filters without using full IPSec.

ightening TCP/IP

There are a number of TCP/IP settings that can be applied that will increase the robustness of the stack, as well as increase the security level. As with everything we have covered in this chapter, this is not the "total" fix, but another layer on the security onion.

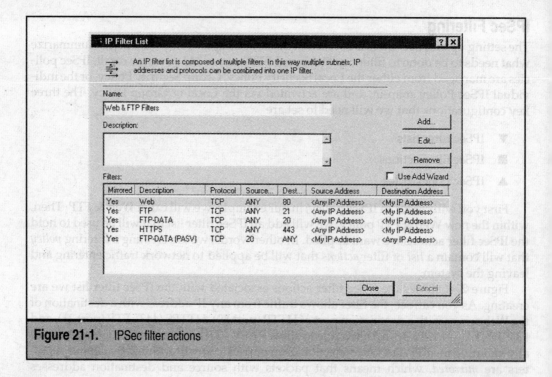

Figure 21-1. IPSec filter actions

VIP: When you change the registry, you have the potential to make the system unusable. Use a test system to validate your settings before you place them on a production system.

The following parameters are located under `HKEY_LOCAL_MACHINE\System\CurrentControlSet\Services\Tcpip\Parameters`:

▼ **SynAttackProtect** SynAttackProtect is a semi-dynamic way to reduce the time the system will wait for SYN-ACKs, thus protecting itself from a SYN attack. It is a REG_DWORD, with a range of 0–2, (default is 0, recommended is 2). Value of 0 gives no protection; 1 reduces retransmission retries and delays route cache entry; and 2 is just 1 plus a delay indication to WinSock.

■ **TcpMaxHalfOpen** This determines the number of connections in the SYN-RCVD state allowed before SYN-ATTACK protection begins to operate. It is a REG_DWORD, with a range of 100–0xFFFF (default is 100 for Win2K Pro and Server and 500 for Advanced Server). You will need to test this in your environment to get a proper value.

- **TcpMaxHalfOpenRetried**   This determines the number of connections in the SYN-RCVD state for which there has been at least one retransmission of the SYN sent before SYN-ATTACK protection begins to operate. It is a REG_DWORD, with a range of 80–0xFFFF (default is 80 for Win2K Pro and Server and 400 for Advanced Server). You will need to test this in your environment to get a proper value.

▲ **PerformRouterDiscovery**   This controls whether Win2K will try to perform router discovery (RFC 1256). This is on a per-interface basis. It is located in `Interfaces\<interface>` and is a REG_DWORD, with a range of 0–2, (default is 2 and recommended is 0). Value of 0 is disabled; 1 is enabled; and 2 DHCP controls the setting.

TIDYING UP

Now that the majority of work is done, there is still some tidying up to do. This section addresses those issues.

Installing Service Packs and Hotfixes

Once you have installed the OS and installed the applications and services that you will be using on the system, you need to take the time to install any service packs and hotfixes. You should ensure that you install not only the OS-specific service packs and hotfixes, but also those applicable to the applications and services that you have running on the system. But do not install hotfixes for services that you do not have installed! The old adage "If it ain't broke, don't fix it!" is applicable here.

Removing Unneeded Subsystems

You should remove the OS2 and Posix subsystems from the computer. To do this, you can remove the OS2 and Posix registry values from the `HKLM\System\CurrentControlSet\Control\Session Manager\SubSystems` registry key. Then delete the associated files (`os2*`, `posix*`, and `psx*`) in `%systemroot%\System32`.

Protecting Binaries

Many exploits leverage the fact that the LocalSystem account and Local Administrators group have access to basic system utilities. To help reduce the likelihood of a successful exploit, you should create a separate admin group, say ToolsAdmin. Then place the users that you want to use the tools in that group. Change the ACLs on the following tools to "remove" LocalSystem and the Administrators group, and give ToolsAdmin ownership and the ability to Read and Execute.

arp.exe	ipconfig.exe	Nbtstat.exe
at.exe	net.exe	Netstat.exe
atsvc.exe	nslookup.exe	ping.exe
cacls.exe	posix.exe	qbasic.exe
Cmd.exe	rcp.exe	rdisk.exe
debug.exe	regedit.exe	regedt32.exe
edit.com	rexec.exe	route.exe
edlin.exe	rsh.exe	Runonce.exe
finger.exe	secfixup.exe	syskey.exe
ftp.exe	telnet.exe	Tracert.exe
xcopy.exe		

Cleaning Up Anonymous Registry Access

By default, the majority of the registry is secured, but the Allowed Paths | Machine key (see Web Appendix B at **www.osborne.com**) has a number of entries that allow the anonymous user too much access. The only real option that you should allow in there by default is the System\ CurrentControlSet\Control\ProductOptions; all the others should be evaluated and removed unless you *know* that you need them.

Other Stuff

Once you have gotten to this point, the system should be fairly secure. However, there are some other settings and precautions that you may want to take:

▼ Use the Encrypting File System (EFS) to encrypt sensitive files.

■ Validate permissions on application directories.

■ Configure the system to boot immediately into the OS. Select My Computer | Properties | Advanced | Startup and Recovery | System Startup and set the boot time to 0.

■ Configure system dumps (on the same screen as previous item).

▲ Run an integrity-checking software (such as Tripwire) over the final system to get a baseline for later Trojan Horse or file corruption detection.

SECURING APPLICATIONS

Now that every path and hotfix that you need is installed, you can tighten down the applications/service the best you can. You should look at the individual chapters for securing the application/service, and if they are not covered in this book, find a book that covers the specific application. A good starting point is the software manufacturer documentation. Other places are things like Usenet news groups and information on the Web.

TESTING SECURITY SETTINGS

Once you have the system(s) configured, you will want to test them to see what you can get at from the outside. To do this, you will need some testing tools:

▼ **Port Scanner**   You will need some type of UDP and TCP port scanner. The freeware tool for Win2K and WinNT called Superscan () will work great for tcp port scanning. If you have a Unix system with a compiler close, use NMAP (**http://www.insecure.org**).

■ **RPCDump**   You will use this tool to help you determine which RPC services have which ports open. This is available from the Microsoft Windows 2000 Resource Kit.

▲ **Netstat**   You will use this tool on the local host to identify its open ports. This comes with Win2K and WinNT.

Once you have the tools, then scan the system to see what is open. Hopefully, it is what you think. If not, then use RPCDump and Netstat (on the host) to determine what is running on the ports. As you figure things out, then start turning them off.

Win2K May Still Fall Short

Unless you are hardening a single host, there is a high likelihood that you will be using some type of service that will be relying in some manner on Microsoft Networking (either NetBIOS, SMB/CIFS, or RPC). If this turns out to be the case, then you cannot rely only on Win2K to protect itself; you will have to use other security measures to isolate those systems from people that you do not intend to access those Microsoft services. In reality, a simple screening router will accomplish the task just fine, but you may choose to have a more full-featured firewall.

RECAP

There is really no cookbook answer to the question of how to harden a Win2K system, especially with the vast number of services that can potentially be run on it. This chapter hopefully gave you good insight into the issues surrounding that hardening and made it possible for you to go about hardening your own systems.

There are a few critical things that you should remember:

▼ Use good user and group security administration practices (that is, no role accounts, administrators have individual admin accounts, and so on).

■ Run only minimal services.

■ Use a self-contained system if possible.

■ Run specific service-related servers, not general multi-service servers.

■ Disable Microsoft Networking access from untrusted networks.

▲ Use strong passwords.

If you follow these steps, you will be a long way down the road to security.

PART VI

Appendixes

PART VI

Appendixes

APPENDIX A

Management, Monitoring, and Auditing

In general, Microsoft has had a long practice of providing the plumbing for major features and services, without providing expansive, feature-rich applets in the Windows product line that use or implement that plumbing. They have left the enhancements and feature-rich application domain to the third-party vendors—and, frankly, that has been good for everyone.

In that regard, this section covers both the native Win2K tools that you should consider, as well as the ever-increasing third-party solutions that you may need to augment your requirements. Note, I say "may," because each of these products requires more time, effort, and expertise on your part. Many a network and security manager's bookcase is filled with products that seemed like a good idea, but time demands never allowed for actual implementation and use. Pick these products with a clear understanding that if you're using them, there should be some payback; because while you are using them, there are other things that you aren't doing. Microsoft asks you, "Where do you want to go today?" You should ask yourself, "How do I want to get there?"

WBEM SUPPORT AND WMI

One of the most interesting management and monitoring capabilities of Win2K is the *Web-Based Enterprise Management (WBEM)* support, which is provided through Microsoft's WBEM-compliant Windows Management Instrumentation (WMI).

WBEM got its start in the mid-1990s when Microsoft, Compaq, BMC, and various other companies formed an alliance to improve enterprise management, with the goal of reducing cost of ownership.

The WBEM standards are overseen by the Distributed Management Task Force (**www.dmtf.org**), and incorporates the following:

▼ **DEN**   The Directory Enabled Network specification is designed to provide the building blocks for more intelligent networks by mapping users to network services, and mapping business criteria to the delivery or network services. This will enable applications and services to transparently leverage network infrastructures on behalf of the user, empower end-to-end services, and support distributed network-wide service creation, provisioning, and management. DEN specifies a common data model with LDAP mappings from CIM to X.500.

■ **CIM**   The Common Information Model is a conceptual way of describing management that is not bound to a particular implementation. It provides for a common format that supports collection, storage, and analysis of network objects using a meta schema.

▲ **DMI** The Desktop Management Interface provides a standard framework for managing and tracking components in a desktop PC, notebook, or server. DMI is currently the only desktop standard in adoption by the leading PC manufacturers. DMI also has SNMP mapping support, so an SNMP MIB can communicate DMI-specific information.

Additionally, WBEM is directly related to other standards such as SNMP. It is based on XML and uses HTTP as a primary transport mechanism. It's in your immediate future, and your product specifications should start to include WBEM as a requirement.

One of the first things that you have to determine is if the cost of implementing WBEM products, learning curve and all, will actually be more or less than the reduction in costs, or create enough value to justify the investment. Here is a brief listing of WBEM/WMI enabled products for Win2K:

▼ BMC Software's Patrol Agent with WBEM Support

■ Computer Associate's Real World Interface for Windows 2000

■ Compuware EcoTOOLS

■ HP OpenView ManageX

■ NetIQ AppManager WMI Agent

▲ Tivoli Management Agent

If you start using these types of management solutions, you have to be careful about the Web-based risk factors. Throughout this book, we've pointed out various security considerations about Web technologies. Most of the vulnerabilities published for Microsoft products in the past year have been related to Web technologies. If you are going to use WBEM, you have to implement, track, and manage your WBEM solutions with security in mind. That said, the tools provided through the WMI architecture offer you some compelling opportunities.

MANAGEMENT AND WIN2K

You might ask why you should be concerned with enterprise management products anyway—after all, you're reading this book to identify security issues. Well, again, security is measured by confidentiality, integrity, and availability (CIA) as minimum criteria. To achieve that and monitor it, we use management, monitoring, and auditing products that keep us properly informed about such issues. We want to know if the system is up, and more importantly, if something is happening with the system that will impact availability if it goes uncorrected. We want to know if we have unauthorized attempts to access the system, and we want to be able to identify who is making changes to the system.

Remember, security has costs associated with it. Make sure you are implementing the solutions discussed in this section because you can make a business case for it, not just because you can implement some new piece of cool technology. Some of the solutions listed have serious learning curves, which add complexity, and can stretch a network and security staff beyond prudent limits.

ACCOUNT MANAGEMENT

The Win2K account management capabilities are really pretty good for what they are intended to do. Unfortunately, there are things that you may want to do that aren't supported by Win2K and that's where some of the third-party products come into play. While there are certainly other vendors, reviewing the following three vendors' products should help identify features that Win2K cannot address natively, and give you pause to consider whether you need to have the enhanced functionality for your network.

NetIQ

Directory and Resource Manager, from NetIQ (**www.netiq.com**), allows you to do many things with Active Directory that are not available "out of box." Policies can be created, propagated, and enforced across both Win2K and WinNT systems. You can manage users, groups, and resources across operating systems, domains, and organizational unit (OU) boundaries by grouping these items into virtual custom domains. NetIQ also brings automated policy enforcement, comprehensive auditing, and extensive security reports to Win2K.

BINDVIEW

bv-Admin for Windows 2000 (**www.bindview.com**) is also a product that provides for central management of users, groups, and systems across different operating systems, domains, and OUs. Its strengths are role-based delegation of authority, and central auditing and logging of all administrative actions. It provides 11 predefined roles that are customizable and allow complete control over 85 discrete administrative tasks.

FULLARMOR

Perhaps not well known (yet), FAZAM 2000 (**www.fullarmor.com**) is one of the best third-party Group Policy solutions in the marketplace. The product provides you with detailed information on your Resultant Set of Policies (RSoP), excellent policy maintenance, reporting, searching, scripting, and delegation of administration features.

For instance, the product supports selective backup and recovery of GPOs, and documents the configuration. So, if you need to know what the configuration of a GPO looked like before it became corrupted, you have it. FAZAM 2000 also gives you GPO search features that Win2K doesn't provide. If you want to know which GPOs afford access to a certain resource, now you have a tool that will tell you. The product works as an MMC snap-in, as it should.

AUTOMATING MANAGEMENT TASKS

There are a number of cases where you may want to automate a process and this is supported in Windows. For instance, you can automate controls and tasks when users log on to systems, a process to stop and start services while you run diagnostics, and a process to tape backup activities. Regardless of your requirements, you'll find the facilities in Win2K can be adapted to meet your needs.

Task Scheduler

Most folks have heard about the Windows AT command, but many have never used it. It's not like it was especially intuitive, but on the other hand, it really wasn't that hard to use. Now, in Win2K, it's really easy to use with the wizard providing a graphic interface and the ability to run tasks in different security contexts. You'll find it in the Control Panel as Scheduled Tasks. Just click Add Scheduled Task and you're off to see the wizard. You'll find several choices, depending on what software you have loaded. For instance, Figure A-1 shows that you can set a Task Scheduler wizard to clean up your hard drive every week, on Saturday, at 3:13 A.M. Just make sure that you are not scheduling conflicting tasks with other activities, like a remote backup running from the servers.

This is a language-independent scripting tool with both a GUI version (`wscript.exe`) and a command console (`cscript.exe`) mode. The Windows Scripting Host supports Windows 98, Internet Information Server 4.0, and the Win2K product family.

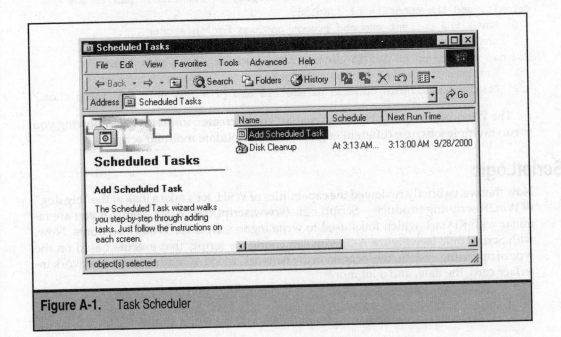

Figure A-1.   Task Scheduler

One of the major advantages over the original DOS version is the language independence, supporting VBScript, JScript, and Perl. This gives the WSH environment amazing extensibility, but you need to add some know-how to get things done. For instance, here are the command options available in `cscript.exe` for your consideration.

Type the following at the command prompt:

```
csript [script name] [host parameters] [script parameters]
//B  Specifies batch mode, which will not display alerts, scripting errors,
 and input prompts.
//D  Turns on the debugger.
//E:engine  Specifies the scripting language used to run the script.
//H:cscript
```

or

```
//H:wscript  Registers cscript.exe or wscript.exe as the default application
for running scripts. If neither is specified, wscript.exe is assumed as the
default.
```

```
//I  Specifies interactive mode, which displays alerts, scripting errors,
and input prompts. This is the default, and the opposite of //B.
//J: xxxx  Runs the specified job.
//Logo  Specifies that the banner will display at run time. This is the
default, and the opposite of //Nologo.
//S  Saves the current command prompt options for this user.
//T:nnnn  Specifies the maximum time the script can run in seconds.
You can specify up to 32,767 seconds. The default is no time limit.
//X  Launches the script in the debugger
//?  Displays available command parameters and provides help for using them.
```

The Windows Scripting Host also enables you to create `.ws` script files, allowing you to run multiple jobs, use different engines, and consolidate modular scripts.

ScriptLogic

Now that we've briefly reviewed the capabilities of WSH, let's take a look at the "big dog" of Win2K scripting products—ScriptLogic (**www.scriptlogic.com**). Many of you are familiar with KiXtart, which folks used to write logon scripts for WinNT accounts. Now, with ScriptLogic (see Figure A-2), you can configure scripts that execute based on the type of operating system, the location in the network, the MAC address of the network interface card, the date, and a lot more.

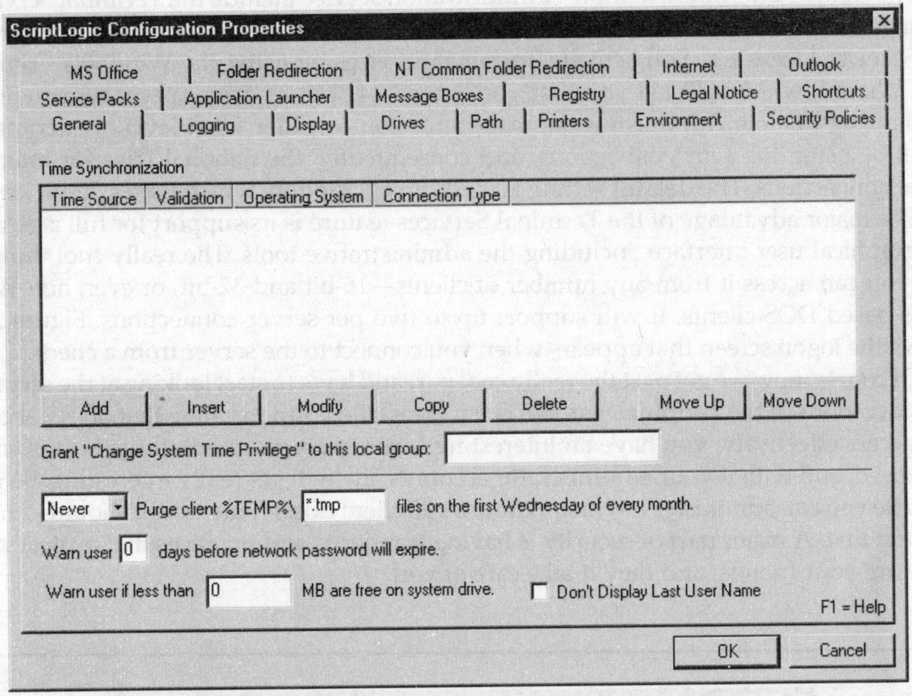

Figure A-2.   ScriptLogic screen

Let's take the last example and cover something fairly creative. Let's say you have a security education and awareness program, and currently you have to e-mail a daily security training message to everyone. The users—crafty devils that they are—see the e-mail come into their inboxes and delete it unread. So much for security education. Well, with ScriptLogic you can create a logon process that puts the Daily Security Message on their screens and requires them to acknowledge it before they can advance. The process can be scripted so that it changes based on a parameter you define. If you need to use scripting to achieve your security objectives, this is the product for you.

WIN2K TERMINAL SERVICES

Terminal Services provides services through one of two modes, Application Server and Remote Administration. We'll be covering the Remote Administration mode in this section. Any Win2K Server can be managed using this feature, which runs as a service—so you can set it to run automatically or manually, or you can disable it.

The components of the Remote Administration service include the Terminal Services Manager, Terminal Services Configuration, Terminal Services Client Creator, and Terminal Services Licensing. You activate Terminal Services by using the Windows Component Wizard, which will tell you that you'll need 14.3MB of drive space. When you're configuring Remote Administration, make sure you consider what level of encryption you'll be using for your connections, and consequently, the national laws for international connections. The default setting is medium encryption, which uses a 56-bit key.

The major advantage of the Terminal Services feature is its support for full access to the graphical user interface, including the administrative tools. The really cool thing is that you can access it from any number of clients—16-bit and 32-bit, or even non-Windows-based DOS clients. It will support up to two per-server connections. Figure A-3 shows the logon screen that appears when you connect to the server from a client.

Of course, now we get past the really cool part and have to start looking at the security considerations. If the Terminal Services client is installed on a machine that does not control access effectively, you have an interesting security predicament. If the host is compromised, and with it your administrator accounts, life will get really interesting. So just because you can administer it with a Windows 95 client doesn't mean you should—think about it first. A major part of security is having standards and practices that protect you. They are your friends, and they'll take care of you.

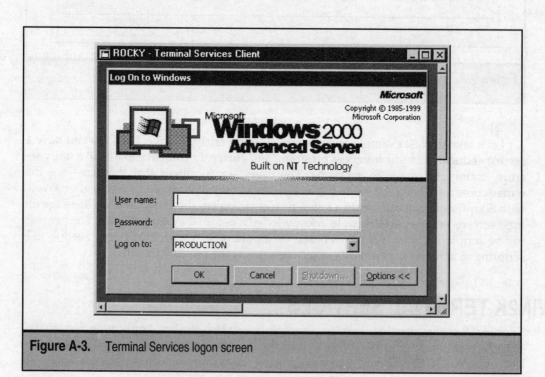

Figure A-3. Terminal Services logon screen

> **NOTE:**   One of the special considerations, as pointed out in Chapter 11 is the restriction for using smartcards with Terminal Services or Citrix MetaFrame. It doesn't work, because your smartcard reader is not connected to the machine where the authentication is occurring.

MONITORING AND WIN2K

Again, the architecture for monitoring is really a product of the Windows Management Instrumentation, Microsoft's implementation of WBEM discussed earlier.

NetIQ

The NetIQ (**www.netiq.com**) AppManager Suite allows you to proactively monitor the performance of WinNT/2000 systems and applications. Through the use of a central console you can monitor all of the systems and applications of a highly distributed network. AppManager also allows you to integrate legacy network systems management products (Tivoli Enterprise, CA Unicenter TNG, HP OpenView and Cabletron Spectrum) by using "connectors."

BMC

Patrol by BMC Software (**www.bmc.com**) is a product that provides a comprehensive enterprise-wide view of your network environment. It provides monitoring for systems, applications, and communications. These monitors can inform selected personnel through Web, pager, or telephone notification.

AUDITING AND WIN2K

Several of the other sections of the book have covered auditing from different angles. Here we'll concentrate on auditing alternatives other than Event Viewer and how auditing is set in Win2K. Auditing considerations should also include methods for determining whether the system configuration is representative of what you expect it to be. For most security managers, especially where there is a separation of the administration and security functions, auditing revolves around determining if system control objectives are being achieved, and validating the integrity of the system. This includes any automated and manual review of system configurations versus security policy and configuration management controls.

The solutions reviewed in this section are not meant to be exhaustive; there are too many excellent solutions out there to cover. However, there are third-party solutions that can help you meet challenges that Win2K does not address. One of the security-specific resources that you can use to identify other products is **www.securityfocus.com**.

Ecora

This product allows you to take snapshots of your network domain controllers and verify that the configuration conforms to what it should be. It will very quickly generate a comprehensive report for you that identifies things like the service pack level; your Windows license number; number of accounts; password management details; whether automatic logon is disabled; which services are configured and running; how the event log parameters are configured; trust relationships; enabled shares; and DHCP, WINS, and DNS settings. These are just a few examples of the numerous settings and configuration values that Ecora reports will generate.

All of these things may have a bearing on your security configuration, and you can run periodic reports to ensure that the network configuration conforms to any policy, standards, or guidelines you have in effect. Validation is an important part of security management, and this is an excellent tool to help you in this area (**www.ecora.com**).

Tripwire

This is an excellent integrity assessment tool (**www.tripwire.com**) that monitors and reports on the configuration of systems and whether the configuration has been changed. It does this by comparing detailed information—up to 28 attributes on each file—including file size, write-times, create-times, number of alternate file streams, and up to four cryptographic checksums of the file contents. The checksums are used to provide validation and make sure that the comparison is accurate and unmodified. If you have high assurance requirements or need to monitor the integrity of your Web servers, this is a product you should be looking at.

Tripwire is available for Win2K, NT, Solaris, Linux, HP-UX, IBM AIX, and other platforms supporting a heterogeneous environment. The company also offers a consolidated management station product that allows the various platforms to report current state information back to a central monitoring site, supporting enterprise-level management.

ISS SAFEsuite

If you hang around the information security marketplace, you're going to run into the ISS (Internet Security Systems) SAFEsuite line of products (**www.iss.net**), which includes Internet Scanner, Database Scanner, and System Scanner. ISS and its competitors offer you the ability to scan your own network as part of an audit and assessment program. The products identify configuration issues that create risk, and quantify the risk into categories so you can identify how they should be prioritized for corrective action. More importantly, the product signature files can be updated, so as you re-scan your network on a scheduled basis, you can identify if you have a new vulnerability or exploit exposure.

If you are a security manager in a large network, you are going to want to strongly consider a solution that provides this type of ongoing monitoring. It provides reporting for three types of audiences—Executive, Line Management, and Technician. The Technician reports also identify where to find corrective action information. As is the case with all security reporting tools, be careful about how you store and secure these types of reports. In the wrong hands, they can be used against you.

SPQuery

One of the problems with trying to keep a network security profile up to date is just trying to keep the service packs and hotfixes current. Especially if you don't want to visit every machine every time you have a new update to apply. SPQuery (**www.spquery.com**) allows you to take inventory of your systems, and identify and update the current service pack and hotfix level across your network—all from the comfort of your chair.

Remember, however, not all hotfixes are regression tested and they may not be supported by Microsoft if something goes wrong. Make sure you can roll a system backwards using uninstall, tape backups, or whatever it takes. Hotfixes should not be blindly installed. If you do not have a need for the hotfix correction, do not apply it.

NTObjectives

This isn't so much a product, but more of a Web resource (**www.ntobjectives.com**) of excellent auditing tools for Windows that is being constantly updated and added to. On this site you'll find NTLast, an enhanced security log analyzer; VisualLast, the GUI version of NTLast; and NTO Scanner, a fast TCP/IP port scanner that provides more information than just active ports, such as what product it sees using that port. The site also has some free tools. There are other Internet sites, but you'll find this one helpful.

Federal IAM Standards

As a number of administrators currently support a government network, or may work on a government network in the future, this section reviews the 18 critical areas that the government is using to conduct INFOSEC Assessment Methodology (IAM) evaluations of networks. Reviewing this will help you to identify where you can improve your security posture.

The IAM format was developed jointly by the National Security Agency (NSA) and the National Institute of Standards and Technology (NIST), both U.S. government entities, to establish a baseline methodology for evaluating networks. The program is managed under the identity of the National Infrastructure Assurance Partnership (NIAP). While I don't agree with the exact format, it provides a reasonable starting point. If you're subject to this standard, get ready—an assessment is coming your way.

▼　**Security Documentation**　Includes a review of policy, guidelines and requirements, System Security Plans, Standard Operating Procedures (SOP), Concept of Operations (CONOPS), user system security manuals, or equivalent guidance.

■　**Security Roles and Responsibilities**　Reviews the relationship, guidance, and leadership provided by upper management; impact on systems operation; and the level of appropriate understanding by the user community. Training is addressed in a separate section; however, the users should understand where they have responsibilities for security, the degree of coordination required, and with whom coordination should be conducted, as it pertains to security. *It must provide the proper balance.*

This section should address information ownership, and the commitment, support, and oversight of upper-level management, which sets the security culture for the organization. This section also reviews the appointment and support of the security department within the organization.

- **Identification & Authentication (I&A)**   Reviews the implementation and management of proper identification and authentication (I&A) practices and standards within the information system(s). *Identification* is the manner in which users present their identity, and *authentication* is the manner in which the system validates the credentials of users. A third part, *authorization*, is covered in another section. Authorization is the level of access the system will provide to users once they have completed the I&A process.

  The fundamentals of I&A are "something you are," "something you have," and "something you know." If only one of these is used, it is called *single-factor authentication*. Combining more than one of the three attributes creates *two-factor* or *three-factor authentication*. As part of I&A implementation, an appropriate review and determination process must occur for each information system component where I&A is conducted to protect the system, how the process addresses the business requirements, and identification of the appropriate practices and standards.

- **Account Management**   Reviews the documented account management policy and procedures. For instance, password and user group characteristics and administration are covered in this section. Other considerations include the manner in which a user account is coordinated, approved, implemented, and the associated permissions assigned. It also includes the lifecycle management of a user account, such as periodic reviews, the change process as a user changes responsibilities within the organization, and finally the manner in which an account is terminated or suspended. Of particular note, this section reviews the management of privileged accounts, assignment, and protection. It also reviews requirements to have the user acknowledge, in writing, organizational expectations about *due care* of the account assigned.

- **Session Controls**   Provides the guidelines and standards for protected access to the system, warning banners, account history banner, user acknowledgement, appropriate use statements, system lock-outs after unsuccessful login attempts, session time-outs during inactivity, and adherence to the concepts of *least privileged access*.

- **External Connectivity**   Provides a broad review of external connectivity to the organization. It includes modems, dedicated circuits, and Internet gateway entry points. Areas of concentrated review include trusted versus untrusted networks, the manner in which they are separated, and the policies and technical restrictions on these access points. A review of enforcement and control objectives is also reviewed.

■ **Internet Connectivity**   Conducts a detailed review of Internet policy, default permissions management, firewall controls, access limitations in the rule base, authentication from the Internet, and the firewall audit practices. This also encompasses reviewing the network boundaries protected by the firewall, which is associated with the External Connectivity section. A review of internal firewalls, with more restricted polices is reviewed, if appropriate.

■ **Modems**   Associated with External Connectivity, and may be associated with Internet Connectivity, depending on the network architecture. It covers policies controlling modem use, such as restrictions, formal justification reviews, controls, dial-in/dial-out capabilities, and use of security features such as termination and disconnects after a period of inactivity. Of particular interest, you should review the oversight of the modems through usage monitoring and reviews of continued requirements.

■ **Dedicated Connectivity**   Focuses on formal agreements and levels of connectivity and services for dedicated connections. This may include interconnects within the trusted network, where administrative oversight may be decentralized, or where some business objective requires dedicated connectivity within the trusted network segments.

■ **Telecommunications**   Related to the four previous areas, this section concentrates on documented requirements and procedures for transmitting data, encryption issues, alternate routes for increased availability, topology, and routing protocol usage.

■ **Auditing**   Provides a review of the protection of audit logs, retention policy and practices, coordination, and usage for detecting network intrusion activity. Auditing also reviews external independent audits, and the practice of incorporating audit information into any "continuous improvement" program(s) the organization may have.

■ **Virus Protection**   Reviews the policy; personal use; restrictions to loading and downloading software; scans of incoming data; update and management of the engine and signature patterns; and the employee education, awareness, and requirements for training.

■ **Contingency Planning**   Reviews the requirements, documentation, methodology, and identification of critical systems, and protection from environmental risks such as power. Also reviews roles and responsibilities to include authority for determining activation and implementation of contingency plans. Relocation planning and periodic scheduled testing are also reviewed, as appropriate.

- **Maintenance** The policies and procedures, personnel roles, responsibilities and clearance level, control of diagnostic software, and remote maintenance access procedures are reviewed in this section. Preventative maintenance practices and the recording of information in maintenance records are also reviewed.

- **Configuration Management** Reviews the documented configuration control plan as well as the practices and oversight of a Configuration Control Board (CCB), existence of current system diagrams (logical, functional, and physical), listing of system resources, and controls over relocation of services or systems. This section is related, and has interdependencies with both Contingency Planning and Maintenance.

- **Back-Ups** Related to Contingency Planning and Maintenance, this section reviews the documented standards and practices, including adherence. It reviews the schedule and technical implementation, proper storage, and periodic testing and determines if it is appropriate given the information criticality.

- **Labeling** Reviews the policies and requirements, including the documentation, of standard practices required for the organization. Special emphasis is given to labeling of sensitive information to ensure proper handling. Proper training of employees, including standardized instructions, is identified. Labeling standards for systems, information, and media are all covered in this section.

- **Media Sanitization/Disposal** Reviews documented policy and determination of requirements for media sanitization and disposal. This includes identification of information subject to standardized requirements, methods, established responsibilities, and user and administrator awareness. If contracted, a review of any third-party agreement is considered.

- **Physical Environment** Identifies the ramifications of the physical environment on the overall security posture. This includes a review of physical security controls, access requirements, and the system location within the building. It includes a review of fire and other environmental systems that address disaster and disruption of service scenarios.

- **Personnel Security** Reviews requirements for background checks, any requirements for security clearances, signed user agreements, and employee awareness of social engineering techniques.

- **Training and Awareness** Reviews documentation of requirements as well as formal and informal training and awareness programs. This area is central to proper information security management and can mitigate more system risks than just about any of the other evaluation criteria. Users are generally the weakest link in security. This section has a direct correlation to the Roles and Responsibilities and the Auditing sections of the report.

More information can be found at **niap.nist.gov**.

COBIT

If you're really serious about the auditing process, and you need a thorough reference, look at the COBIT standard. Published by the Information Systems Audit and Control Foundation (**www.isaca.org**), this ISO 9000-based standard is used in over 100 countries and by some of the leading information security firms. COBIT focuses on business objectives, and how they are supported by IT criteria, IT processes, and IT resources. There are four domains: Planning and Organization, Acquisition and Implementation, Delivery and Support, and Monitoring. Planning and Organization has 11 separate evaluation areas, Acquisition and Implementation is comprised of 6 areas, Delivery and Support has 13 areas, and Monitoring has 4 areas. This isn't a trivial exercise—you really need to understand the methodology—but it's an excellent reference. It is also the basis for the Certified Information Systems Auditor exam, which is given only once a year and is very difficult to pass.

RECAP

If you are spending time looking around in the marketplace, you'll quickly determine that there are a significant number of products that can enhance your capabilities to manage, monitor, and audit your systems. In fact, more products than you have time and money to utilize.

The most important thing for you to remember along the way is to be requirements driven. If you have a requirement and Win2K can't address it out of the box, you should be looking at the third party solutions. You'll probably find what you are looking for. Also, try to focus on identifying problems before they become serious—whether you're trying to identify an unauthorized attempt to access the system or your RAID controller is reporting errors, you need to see this information in a timely manner. It doesn't help to find out after the damage is done, and there are few things that you can't get Win2K to tell you if you don't have the right tools.

APPENDIX B

Internet Security and Acceleration (ISA) Server

A s we were finishing writing this book, Microsoft introduced the Internet Security and Acceleration (ISA) Server. ISA Server is code-named Comet, and it is the replacement for the Proxy Server described in Chapter 15. This appendix will briefly discuss the major "enhancements" that Microsoft has made to the Proxy Server.

INTRODUCTION

The ISA Server, much like the Proxy Server, provides security functionality in terms of blocking packets, acting as a Proxy Server or a NAT box (as described in Chapters 15 and 16). It also provides enhanced functionality in the caching and publishing functionality of MS Proxy. There are a number of other improvements such as using the Network Load Balancing aspects of Win2K as well as the Quality of Service (with built-in bandwidth controls) features to enhance reliability. The major security-related improvements are in the areas of configuration granularity and integration with Win2K (that is, the AD).

The ISA Server offers a much-needed improvement in certain security areas for the Proxy Server, such as granular packet filtering, a certain degree of stateful packet filtering, and integration with the AD for policy deployment (both security and Web publishing). The ISA is extensible, as it allows developers to add functionality to both the security and performance of the ISA Server.

FEATURES

There are a number of new security-related features that ISA brings into the picture. This section discusses those new features.

Gatekeeper Service (H323 Gateway)

The ISA Server supports the gatewaying of the H323 standard with the Gatekeeper service. The H323 protocol is used for streaming audio, video, and data communications over IP. Its primary purpose in ISA is to support the NetMeeting service, but it can be used to gateway any other application that uses the protocol. This is supported with a future looking toward wide deployment of streaming multimedia, such as IP telephony (Voice over IP or VoIP), and wizard support for some of the new Exchange 2000 services that take advantage of this—specifically, the new Conference Server features.

IP Packet Filters

The ISA incorporates the same packet filtering ability as Proxy 2.0 (circuit and packet level), with some notable additions: the filtering on IP fragments and IP options. By setting the Packet filter options, the ISA Server can be configured to drop all IP fragments and/or any IP packet that has any of the options flags set. This is a great improvement over Proxy 2.0, and may in itself be motivation to migrate from Proxy to ISA.

Unlike the Proxy Server, the ISA Server has integrated the routing portion of RRAS; thus, you can use the ISA Server to perform routing. In this configuration, the ISA Server just routes all traffic to and from the connected networks. This is basically a filtering rule that says "allow all."

The ISA Server also supports *stateful packet inspection,* in that the server allows you to evaluate packets in terms of the state of the connection and the protocol that is being used. Also dynamic filters are used to open ports on behalf of internal user requests and only for the life of a session.

If you enable packet filtering, all packets on the external interface(s) are dropped unless explicitly allowed. They can be allowed statically with packet filters, or dynamically with access policy or publishing rules.

NOTE: The ISA Server never routes between the internal and external network; all TCP/UDP traffic is either "NATted" or "proxied." However the ISA Server can be configured to route between networks in the LAT (VPN, Dial-In, or LAN).

Secure Network Address Translation (SecureNAT)

SecureNAT provides address transparency for networked clients (much like the NAT described in Chapter 16). The terminology gets a bit muddy, but when Microsoft refers to a NAT client, they are referring to a client using the NAT features of the RRAS or another NAT box. When they refer to SecureNAT, they are talking about client computers that use the ISA Server as their firewall, but do not have the Firewall client software installed. The main difference between Microsoft's regular NAT and SecureNAT is that the SecureNAT client can be controlled by such ISA Server features as access control (IP address and/or protocol type) and application filters. Here's a description from the ISA online help:

"ISA Server extends the Windows 2000 NAT functionality by enforcing ISA Server policy for SecureNAT clients. … all ISA Server rules can be applied to SecureNAT clients, despite the fact that Windows 2000 NAT does not have an inherent authentication mechanism—policies regarding protocol usage, destination, and content type are also applied…."

User-level authentication is not possible because

▼ The NAT box should be transparent to the client.

■ It is designed for non-Windows clients to be able to make use of the firewall. Those clients cannot handle NTLM challenges or other challenges, as they are not aware of the firewall.

▲ NAT cannot handle secondary connections without NAT editors. ISA allows application filters, which serve a similar function and allow more flexibility and better control. ISA can allow application filters (described later) to be plugged in at any time providing practically limitless protocol support for NAT.

SecureNAT applies outbound firewall policies without requiring client side software or configuring browser settings. The main drawback is that these clients cannot utilize the high-level protocol support and user-level authentication provided by the ISA Server.

NOTE: The security advantage of SecureNAT over regular NAT is that of access control. There is nothing inherently more secure about the NAT portion. The fact that packet filters are dynamically opened for outgoing traffic and only corresponding incoming traffic is allowed adds to the "Secure" in SecureNAT.

VIP: You cannot have the RRAS NAT (or Internet Connection Sharing) and ISA SecureNAT enabled on the same system; they are mutually exclusive.

Application Filters

The ISA supports extensions called *application filters*. These filters are special in that they have access to the datastream (TCP) or datagrams (UDP) associated with a session. They are registered with the Firewall service and work basically as an application proxy. They can be used to validate protocol-related information such as packet format or content, as well as perform system-related tasks like virus checking. One of the more advanced uses of these filters is to define protocols and enable protocol definitions. This would allow a semi-dynamic opening of protocols and ports given a specific triggering event in an application filter.

NOTE: Developers can use the ISA Software Developer's Kit (SDK) to create additional application filters. See the ISA SDK for more details.

Intrusion Detection

Along with the packet filtering updates, Microsoft added the ability to detect potential Denial-of-Service (DoS) attacks to the packet-filtering portion of the ISA Server. The ISA Server can be configured to compare network traffic and log entries to well-known attack signatures and methods. If there is a match, the ISA Server can also be configured to perform actions such as starting or stopping a service, logging to the event log, or running a program. By default, the ISA Server can detect the following DoS attacks:

- ▼ All-ports scan attack
- ■ Enumerated-port scan attack
- ■ IP-half scan attack
- ■ Land attack
- ■ Ping of death attack
- ■ UDP bomb attack
- ▲ Windows out of band attack

> **NOTE:** The ID modules are not user customizable and are based on technology from Internet Security Systems, Inc. (**www.iss.net**).

Report Data Consolidation

The ISA Server reporting system enables you to collect data from the packet filter, Firewall service, and Web Proxy logs in a single report. The main benefit of this is that there are canned reports, so you do not have to write your own SQL queries or custom scripts. The reporting can be logged to either a text file or an ODBC-compliant database.

Generating Reports

If you are running in an array architecture, the reporting mechanism will collect and collate logs from all of the ISA Servers in the array into a database on each ISA Server. When you generate a report, the data, as defined in the report period, from all the databases is combined into a single database on a single ISA Server. The server that is selected should be consistent as the reports can only be viewed on that server, and once the data has been combined, it is flushed off the other systems.

Predefined Reports

The ISA Server has a number of predefined reports.

▼ **Summary Reports**   Data from the Web Proxy service and Firewall service logs. Used to view network traffic usage by application.

■ **Web Usage Reports**   Data from Web Proxy service logs. Used to view top Web users, common responses, and browsers.

■ **Application Usage Reports**   Data from Firewall service logs. Used to view application usage, top traffic users, applications, and destinations.

■ **Traffic and Utilization Reports**   Data from Web Proxy and Firewall service logs. Used to view total traffic usage, average traffic, peak simultaneous connections, cache hit ratio, and errors.

▲ **Security Reports**   Data from Web Proxy service, Firewall service, and Packet Filter logs. Used to view data that would reveal potential security problems.

All of these reports can be scheduled to be run at daily, weekly, or monthly intervals. Each report can also contain data based on daily, weekly, monthly, or yearly information.

Policy Rules (Policy-Based Administration)

The ISA Server uses rules to authorize actions. There are two main policies that the ISA Server uses: array policy and enterprise policy.

▼ **Array Policy** This includes site and content rules, protocol rules, Web publishing rules, and packet filters that apply to all ISA Servers in an array. It is primarily used to refine the enterprise policies.

▲ **Enterprise Policy** This includes site and content rules and protocol rules. It can be applied to any/all array(s) in an Active Directory, and may optionally be fine-tuned with the array policy.

Active Directory Integration

When an array of ISA Servers is set up in a Win2K domain, the resulting configuration data can be stored in the AD. To accomplish this, you must *first* add the ISA schema extensions to the AD schema that you are now a part of. The instructions and actual utility to perform this are on the ISA CD. This will allow the storage and retrieval of array configuration information from the AD. After this is accomplished the AD will also hold the array policy and the enterprise policy.

Being a part of the domain/AD also provides you the ability to use the users and groups in the AD in the access controls section of the ISA configurations.

Policy Configuration with COM

The ISA Server is COM-scriptable in that you can write scripts (that is, VBScript, Jscript, or Perl) that use COM objects from the ISA Server to administer and configure it. You can use some of the sample scripts that are part of the distribution as a starting point. The ISA SDK has more information on this topic.

System Hardening

The ISA Server comes with a System Security Wizard, which can be used to apply security templates to the underlying Win2K OS. There are three security options:

▼ **Secure** Least secure setting. Appropriate for a system that will be hosting other services such as IIS, or will be used on a corporate intranet.

■ **Limited Services** A moderate security setting. Appropriate when the system is acting in "integrated" mode, that is, a combined firewall and cache server.

▲ **Dedicated** Most secure setting. Appropriate when the ISA Server is performing firewall-only functions.

Similar Proxy 2 Features

As stated at the beginning of the appendix, there are a number of similarities between the MS Proxy and ISA Server, such as

▼ Basic packet filtering (both static and dynamic)

■ Application proxies (that is, Web service and WinSock proxy)

■   Authentication mechanisms

▲   Report locations (text file or in an ODBC-compliant database) and creation (daily, weekly, or monthly)

THE ISA SECTIONS

One of the best ways to understand what the ISA Server does is to look at the ISA Manager (that is, the management GUI) and the sections it contains. The ISA manager has eleven sections (see Figure B-1) : Monitoring, Server (configuration), Access Policy, Publishing, Bandwidth Rules, Policy Elements, Cache Configuration, Monitoring Configuration, Extensions, Network Configuration, and Client Configuration. The following sections will give a description of each.

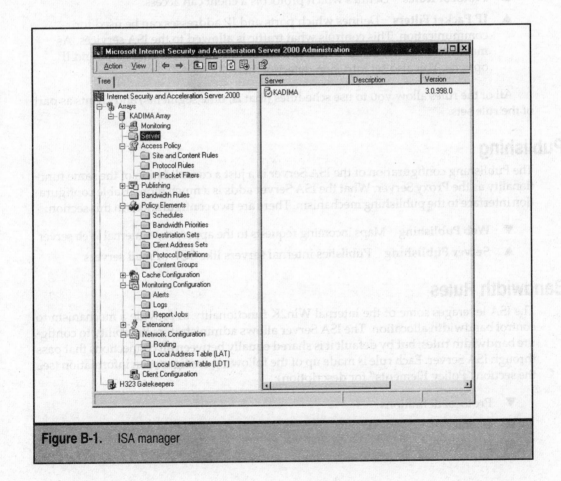

Figure B-1.   ISA manager

> **VIP:** For the remainder of the appendix, each client is defined as User, Group, or IP address behind the ISA Server.

Access Policy Rules

The Access Policy rules are a set of configurations and restrictions that determine which external sites can be accessed by which internal clients and at what times. They also allow you to control inbound and outbound access and traffic. This is a portion of the array policy described earlier, and it is used to configure the site and content rules, protocol rules, and IP packet filters.

▼ **Site and Content Rules**   Defines the sites (by domain names or IP addresses) that can be accessed by the clients.

■ **Protocol Rules**   Defines which protocols a client can access.

▲ **IP Packet Filters**   Defines which ports and IP addresses can be used for communication. This controls what traffic is allowed to the ISA services. As mentioned earlier, this is where you enable filtering on IP fragments and IP options. You also set intrusion detection here.

All of the rules allow you to use schedules (that is, time segments) and clients as part of the rule sets.

Publishing

The Publishing configuration of the ISA Server is a just a consolidation of the same functionality as the Proxy Server. What the ISA Server adds is a much more usable configuration interface to the publishing mechanism. There are two configurations in this section:

▼ **Web Publishing**   Maps incoming requests to the appropriate internal Web server.

▲ **Server Publishing**   Publishes internal servers like SQL or mail servers.

Bandwidth Rules

The ISA leverages some of the internal Win2K functionality to provide a mechanism to control bandwidth allocation. The ISA Server allows administrators the ability to configure bandwidth rules, but by default it is shared equally between all connections that pass through ISA Server. Each rule is made up of the following configuration information (see the section "Policy Elements" for description):

▼ Protocol definitions

■ Clients

■ Destination sets

■ Schedule

▲ Content types

Policy Elements

This section allows you to predefine many of the items that will be used in other configurations of the ISA. The following elements can be defined here:

▼ **Schedules**   Defines time windows in which the policies are either in effect or not.

■ **Bandwidth Priorities**   Usage priorities that can be used in bandwidth rules (see previous section) to prioritize traffic.

■ **Destination Sets**   A group of external hosts (IP address or host name) that can be used in rule sets.

■ **Client Address Sets**   A group of internal hosts (IP address only) that can be used in rule sets.

■ **Protocol Definitions**   Definitions of protocol types that rules will allow or deny. Include port number, IP protocol type, direction of the connection, and any secondary connections.

▲ **Content Groups**   Groups of MIME types to be used in rules that control access to those types.

Cache Configuration

Much like the publishing section, the Cache Configuration is the same as the Proxy Server, but the management is consolidated. This section allows you to configure all cache-related parameters.

Monitoring Configuration

This section is where the ISA really adds some significant functionality and manageability. This section is used to configure not only the monitoring, but also the reporting functions of the ISA Server.

▼ **Alerts**   The ISA supports the sending of *alerts* on the occurrence of a specific event. It can also be configured to trigger a series of actions, not just an alert, when an event occurs. The ISA Server supports its own "alert service" that performs all the alert management and event filtering for the alerts. Its main purpose is to catch events, then check whether certain conditions are met, and execute corresponding actions. The ISA Server allows you to configure "alert conditions," which are things such as the number of times per second the event should occur before issuing an alert, or the number of events that should occur before the alert is issued. Then, based on an alert condition, you can have an "alert action" like sending e-mail, logging an event, or running a program.

■ **Logs**   This allows you to configure the log options for the packet filters, Firewall service, and the Web Proxy service, specifying the location, type, and fields to be logged. You also have the option to set the log rotation period: daily, weekly, or monthly.

▲ **Report Jobs**   This allows you to schedule the reports based on the data collected from the log files. You can run them daily, weekly, or monthly.

Extensions

This section is used to enable the ISA extensions. You can enable/disable the application filters, which were described earlier, and the Web filters, which are extensions used to monitor, evaluate, and intercept the Web traffic going through the Web Proxy service. They can be used in much the same way as the application filters. There are no Web filters installed by default, but there are eight default application filters installed and enabled with the ISA Server:

▼ **SMTP Filter**   Used to intercept all SMTP traffic that arrives on ISA Server's port 25.

■ **Streaming Media Filter**   Allows the server to "proxy" Streaming Media and split live Windows Media streams (i.e. to save bandwidth).

■ **HTTP Filter**   Redirects all Firewall client and SecureNAT client connections at port 80 to the ISA Server's Web Proxy service.

■ **FTP Access Filter**   Monitors Microsoft FTP access and looks for anomalies.

■ **DNS Intrusion Detection Filter**   Attempts to detect DNS attacks.

■ **POP Intrusion Detection Filter**   Attempts to detect POP buffer overflow attack.

■ **RPC Filter**   Allows you to filter Microsoft RPC. Allows you to select the RPC interfaces to expose.

▲ **H.323 Filter**   WinSock proxy filter for the H.323 protocol.

As noted in the first section, these are not user-customizable. They can only be enabled or disabled. If you want to add functionality, you will have to use the ISA SDK to write an extension.

Network Configuration

The Network Configuration section is used to configure the routing rules, the Local Address Table, and the Local Domain Table. This is a convenient location to configure the same information that is available in the MS Proxy.

▼   **Routing (Array Not IP)**   Allows you to make routing rules that will decide where to send Web Proxy client requests—either directly to the Internet, to an upstream Proxy Server, or somewhere else.

■   **Local Address Table (LAT)**   Defines which IP addresses are considered to be local (or inside/trusted). This is the same as the LAT for Proxy.

▲   **Local Directory Table (LDT)**   Same as LAT, but uses domain names instead of IP addresses.

Client Configuration

This allows you to configure the client information for use with the ISA Server. This is essentially the same as the Web Proxy and WinSock Proxy client configurations described in Chapter 15.

▼   **Web Browser**   Allows you to configure which ISA Server to connect to, which destinations can be accessed directly, and a backup route in case the default ISA Server fails.

▲   **Firewall Client**   Allows you to configure which ISA Server to connect to.

OTHER THOUGHTS

While the ISA Server has its share of impressive features, there are a couple things that you should think about:

▼   There is no "single" point of view to the full configuration, especially the equivalent of the Firewall policy. You have to go through several parts of the ISA administration tool to get this information.

■   Default settings block everything inbound, and allow everything outbound. This policy is risky, as it allows an improperly configured (or compromised) internal system to "leak" internal information out of the firewall by default. A better stance would be to deny everything inbound and outbound by default.

■   The ISA Server is heavily wizard-driven, but there are few details about what is actually changing in the security configuration.

▲   There is currently an issue establishing an IPSec tunnel with an ISA Server. The tunnel can be established, but the data will not flow. *We expect Microsoft to have fixed this problem by the time this book is published.*

RECAP

This was a very quick and dirty look that has just skimmed over the functions of the ISA Server. If you are really looking at using the ISA Server, then we highly recommend that you step through the online tutorial (even experienced Proxy Server administrators will learn something about the ISA Server).

The main benefit of ISA over proxy is the extremely fast caching performance using RAM caching, which provides real firewall class protection to the LAN and SecureNAT connectivity to non-Windows platforms without the use of any client software; the reporting mechanism enhancements; integration with the AD; tighter integration with RRAS; and added filtering functionality of IP fragments and IP options. It is worth the time and effort it takes to upgrade from MS Proxy.

VIP: If you are upgrading from Proxy Server, read the upgrade documents on the ISA CD-ROM, as it addresses some migration concerns.

APPENDIX C

Intrusion Detection Systems

As defined in Chapter 3, Intrusion Detection (ID) is the art of detecting inappropriate, incorrect, or anomalous activity. There are many reasons why we need ID, such as more sophisticated opponents, more complex systems, more protocols, and connected business partners. ID provides compensating controls, offsetting some of the risk of modern-day Internet connectivity. It provides a method to find the bad guys, provides a legal record for lawsuits, and helps you meet the "due care" principle. This appendix describes the basics of ID systems (IDS), and some of the things to look for in a system.

TIP: Although this is a book on Win2K, your IDS should be heterogeneous. Any and all systems are potential intrusion points.

MODELS OF DETECTION

Models of detection describe how the ID systems will recognize an intrusion when it happens. Currently, there are two primary models for how this is accomplished: *anomaly* detection and *misuse* detection. These models have different methods of intrusion detection, but the end result is the same: attack identification. There are also hybrid systems that attempt to combine features of both.

Anomaly (Behavior-Based)

Anomaly detection performs ID by means of detecting deviations from normal usage patterns. This is based on the assumption that there are "normal" traffic patterns for your company and that they can be identified. This "normal" traffic would be called the *baseline*. Then, when there is a deviation from that baseline, the ID system would evaluate it and make a determination as to what to do. The basic assumption is that computer attacks can be detected from abnormal system activity.

This may or may not be a good assumption based on your system usage. If you have a system that is relatively stable and provides a limited number of services, then you may be able to get a baseline that can be used for this type of detection. But there is a high probability that if you have a fairly complex system, the "normal" traffic pattern will be so varied that it will be practically impossible to distinguish "abnormal" from "normal."

Misuse (Knowledge-Based)

Misuse detection spots intrusions by pattern recognition (a.k.a. *attack signature recognition*). This is based on the fact that known attack signatures can describe exploitation of vulnerabilities. This is how current virus detectors work.

The positive aspect of this type of ID is that it is very reliable: It will alarm on what you tell it to. If you want to know when anyone attempts to Telnet into a system with a blank password, you can set this as a "signature" and it will alarm on it. From that standpoint, it can tell you only what you want to know, that is, the anomaly will tell you what it thinks you want to know. There are problems with signature-based ID, though:

▼ **Reactive in nature**   You have to know the signature for the attack, so that means it must have happened already.

■ **False positives**   Many attack "signatures" also match regular legitimate traffic, but since the ID system only knows signatures, it will alarm on legitimate traffic that matches as well. For example, a mail message that has a string describing an attack would set off an alarm just as the attack would.

▲ **Signatures need to be updated**   Because the only attacks that will be identified are the ones with signatures that are in your IDS, the signature database needs to be updated every time a new vulnerability is released.

DATA SOURCE

Like models of detection, there are different data sources that ID systems use. The two sources of data are the host or the network. These are described next. Note that both of the previously described ID methods can be used with either of the data sources. For example, you can have a host-based anomaly detector, a host-based signature detector, or a host-based hybrid.

Host

Host-based ID uses events generated on the host itself for input into the ID system to generate the alerts. The sources of the host-based information can vary greatly, but the three most likely data sources are system audit logs, special "instrumentation" tools (a.k.a. agents), and application logs (such as Web servers or database servers).

With these three sources, you can

▼ Monitor authentication events.

■ Watch for unusual events such as reboots, processes consuming too much CPU time, or network level RAW sockets.

▲ Look for application-specific errors that may indicate an exploit attempt.

Network

Network-based ID monitors network packets as input into the ID system to generate the alerts. Unlike the host-based systems, which have multiple sources, this has only one— the network. It has one purpose: to look at network traffic to determine if an intrusion has occurred. Network-based systems can really be classified as "smart sniffers." Most of the network-based ID systems, as well as the host-based systems, are misuse detectors and not anomaly detectors.

METHODS OF DETECTION

There are two primary ways that ID systems detect intrusions or intrusion attempts: by post-event analysis or real-time analysis. Many of the ID systems today record events, such as the network traffic or host logins for subsequent analysis, and a few will actually analyze the events in real time (this is becoming more the norm).

▼ **Real-time analysis** ˙ The real-time systems do exactly the same thing as the post-event analysis, they just need to do it faster. There are some limitations to this in that correlation of data is not really possible in current real-time systems. That is not to say that as we get technological gains it won't be, but for now real-time systems can only detect what they can see.

▲ **Post-event analysis**   On the other hand, post-event analysis systems are designed to be global in their scope (or at least should be). They usually consist of a central logging or data collection machine that performs analysis of the data it receives to determine intrusions. It usually receives input from many different key systems on the enterprise using things like syslog, EventLog, SNMP traps, or other proprietary protocols.

There are other problems to deal with when correlating events. You must synchronize the clock of the machines. If the clocks do not synchronize, then it is impossible to correlate events. This should not be as big of an issue with Win2K because of the use of Kerberos. Kerberos is time-dependent, so it requires synchronized clocks; if your clocks are not synchronized, you will have much more serious problems than correlating logs. You should try to normalize the event information. In order to correlate events, times, addresses, and ports need to be represented in uniform manner.

Things to Look For

Some of the more pertinent things that you should be looking for are

▼ **Login events**   Such as top ten logins, logins on accounts idle more than three weeks, source of successful authentication

■ **Privileged events**   All events that elevate privileges of users, or administrative actions (such as adding a user or group)

▲ **Unusual events**   Reboots, router reconfigurations, or files being added or deleted in administrative directories

WHERE TO DEPLOY

There is always the discussion as to where to deploy IDS systems. Here are a few recommendations on the systems and potential location characteristics that make up a good IDS:

▼ Deploy in areas where traffic is concentrated, such as Internet entry points, choke points, adjacent to access routers, or adjacent to firewalls.

■ Deploy in areas where traffic is particularly sensitive, such as inside protected networks, in front of credit card–processing systems, next to the HR database or the finance system, or in a business partner's DMZ.

■ Deploy an IDS for all machines exposed to untrusted networks.

■ Deploy host-based IDS on all critical infrastructure machines.

■ Deploy the IDS that works with your hardware constraints: today's higher bandwidth networks make our work harder; switches and VLANs make it next to impossible; SPAN ports on switches help; some routers have ID agents built in.

■ Deploy network IDS where you will get the traffic you need. You don't usually need to see all the traffic to match on a signature.

▲ Deploy your systems in the locations you have designed for them. You need to design your networks to be monitored.

You should also consider that some ID systems will dynamically reconfigure a firewall or filtering router to block an "attack," so you should factor that into the design. Also, one of the major drawbacks of the network ID systems is that if the packet data is encrypted, you won't be able to see the contents, and thus an attack can get by unnoticed. One of the advantages of host-based ID systems is that the host is the *only* place to detect encrypted attacks.

HOW TO DEPLOY

Once you have selected what to deploy, you will have to determine how to deploy it. Remember that deploying any complex system must be done in an incremental manner, like eating an elephant—one bite at a time. You should expect to spend at least a month fixing misconfigured systems and getting the deployment to a "stable" state. But take to heart that even the most humble beginnings will pay a dividend. A little bit done correctly is better than a lot done incorrectly. Ultimately, your IDS deployment is a process, not a project.

The following is a recommended IDS deployment process, which should give you a fairly robust ID system in the end.

1. **Policy first** This is management's way to communicate its will to those who carry out the organization's mission. It should cover things such as

   - How to protect the company in terms of evaluating and responding to attacks

   - Who will assume the risk for decisions (for example, who can decide to take down the site)

   - What is being protected (to help you focus your efforts)

   - What privacy issues need to be considered with respect to network monitoring or content analysis

2. **Architect next** You need to ensure that the data you will be getting is the data that you will need to identify intrusions. If your data is not relevant, then it will be ignored after just a short bit of time.

3. **Host-based on firewall systems** Since these are the most important systems from a protection standpoint, you need to ensure that they are not compromised.

4. **Network-based on firewall network** This is the most likely spot for external intrusions. Since we have the firewall hosts monitored, the next place to look is at traffic coming in from the untrusted networks.

5. **Host-based on critical hosts** Next line of defense is the critical hosts. If the firewall or the network ID does not catch an attacker, then this should. This will also catch internal attackers (the first two probably won't).

6. **Network-based on internal network** Now you would start watching all internal network traffic.

7. **Host-based on internal hosts** The last location would be host-based on noncritical hosts. This would be an early warning indicator for a potential attack on the critical systems.

Spot-Check Strategies: Another Approach

Some companies like to take the "spot-check" approach to IDS. In this approach, they will check things on a semi-regular basis, just to see what they can see. This is not an effective way to do ID, because ID is *not* like spot-checking a manufactured product. In manufacturing, if one is good, then there is reason to believe that others may be good as well. This cannot be said for attacks. Attacks are semi-random and have no set cause and event. Attacks are more like finding needles in a haystack. Finding one may or may not mean you have found the last.

Significant technical expertise is required to be able to do this type of ID correctly. This type of skill is expensive and hard to find. The "expert" has to know what she is looking for; chances are tracks have been hidden. It is also only reactive and not proactive in nature.

If and when you find an intrusion, then you will have to determine what you will do. You will need an escalation procedure (which should be in your polices and procedures, as described in Chapter 4). You will also need to determine how far in the attacker has gone.

Spot-checking ID is not a great solution, *but it is better than nothing*. Anything is better than nothing. The question you have to ask is, how much better?

How Are Others Deploying IDS?

At the writing of this book, summer and fall 2000, most organizations were using misuse-type detectors on both the network and host. For the networks, they are deploying them at Internet entry points and partner network entry points. For the host-based ID, they are concentrating on key systems.

RECAP

A stated in Chapter 2, an IDS is not a silver bullet by a long shot. It provides you with some type of indicator that something is wrong, and then you must take action. This appendix has discussed some of the more important issues with ID systems and hopefully has given you a better understanding of what they are and where and how to use them.

You need to design your networks to be monitored; make sure you look for the following characteristics in any ID solution:

▼ Report generation capabilities: good built-in reports, ability to generate custom reports

■ Ability to add signatures

■ A distributed model, with central reporting and management

■ Ability to aggregate data

▲ Security between the agents, data storage, and reporting/management stations

Also remember that there are some hurdles to overcome. To keep yourself from being overly optimistic, here are some points for you to ponder as a reality check:

▼ ID systems are non-trivial to set up and non-trivial to support.

■   You get what you pay for, whether the currency is cash, sweat, or both.

▲   Windows 2000/NT is where most new commercial development is taking place.

Last but not least, here is a list, although by no means exhaustive, of some of the more popular ID systems on the market today:

Cisco Secure IDS	www.cisco.com
ISS RealSecure	www.iss.net
NAI CyberCop	www.nai.com
Network Flight Recorder	www.nfr.com
Axent Intruder Alert and NetProwler	www.axent.com
Tripwire	ww.tripwiresecurity.com
Kane Secure Enterprise	www.intrusion.com
Black ICE	www.networkice.com
Dragon	www.network-defense.com
ARMOR	www.hivermute.com
Centrax	www.cybersafe.com

INDEX

D

H

I

R

S

T

U